Communications in Computer and Information Science 1535

More information about this series at https://link.springer.com/bookseries/7899

Miguel Botto-Tobar · Sergio Montes León ·
Pablo Torres-Carrión ·
Marcelo Zambrano Vizuete ·
Benjamin Durakovic (Eds.)

Applied Technologies

Third International Conference, ICAT 2021
Quito, Ecuador, October 27–29, 2021
Proceedings

Springer

Editors
Miguel Botto-Tobar ⓘ
Eindhoven University of Technology
Eindhoven, The Netherlands

Sergio Montes León ⓘ
Universidad de las Fuerzas Armadas (ESPE)
Sangolquí, Ecuador

Pablo Torres-Carrión ⓘ
Universidad Técnica Particular de Loja
Loja, Ecuador

Marcelo Zambrano Vizuete ⓘ
Universidad Técnica del Norte
Ibarra, Ecuador

Benjamin Durakovic ⓘ
International University of Sarajevo
Sarajevo, Bosnia and Herzegovina

ISSN 1865-0929   ISSN 1865-0937 (electronic)
Communications in Computer and Information Science
ISBN 978-3-031-03883-9   ISBN 978-3-031-03884-6 (eBook)
https://doi.org/10.1007/978-3-031-03884-6

This Springer imprint is published by the registered company Springer Nature Switzerland AG
The registered company address is: Gewerbestrasse 11, 6330 Cham, Switzerland

Preface

The 3rd International Conference on Applied Technologies (ICAT) was held on the main campus of the Universidad de las Fuerzas Armadas ESPE, in Santo Domingo, Ecuador, during October 27–29, 2021, and it was organized jointly by Universidad de las Fuerzas Armadas ESPE and GDEON. The ICAT series aims to bring together top researchers and practitioners working in different domains in the field of computer science to exchange their expertise and to discuss the perspectives of development and collaboration. The content of this volume is related to the following subjects:

- Communication
- Computing
- e-Government and e-Participation
- e-Learning
- Electronics
- Intelligent Systems
- Machine Vision
- Security
- Technology Trends

ICAT 2021 received 201 submissions written in English by 435 authors from 12 different countries. All these papers were peer-reviewed by the ICAT 2021 Program Committee consisting of 185 experienced researchers. To assure a high-quality and thoughtful review process, we assigned each paper to at least three reviewers. Based on the peer reviews, 40 full papers were accepted, resulting in an 19% acceptance rate, which was within our goal of less than 40%.

We would like to express our sincere gratitude to the invited speakers for their inspirational talks, to the authors for submitting their work to this conference, and the reviewers for sharing their experience during the selection process.

October 2021

Miguel Botto-Tobar
Sergio Montes León
Pablo Torres-Carrión
Marcelo Zambrano Vizuete
Benjamin Durakovic

Organization

General Chair

Miguel Botto-Tobar   Eindhoven University of Technology,
The Netherlands

Program Committee Chairs

Miguel Botto-Tobar   Eindhoven University of Technology,
The Netherlands

Sergio Montes León   Universidad de las Fuerzas Armadas (ESPE),
Latacunga, Ecuador/Universidad Rey Juan
Carlos, Spain

Pablo Torres-Carrión   Universidad Técnica Particular de Loja, Ecuador

Marcelo Zambrano Vizuete   Universidad Técnica del Norte, Ecuador

Benjamin Durakovic   International University of Sarajevo, Bosnia and
Herzegovina

Organizing Chairs

Miguel Botto-Tobar   Eindhoven University of Technology,
The Netherlands

Henry Cruz   Universidad de las Fuerzas Armadas (ESPE),
Ecuador

Sergio Montes León   Universidad de las Fuerzas Armadas (ESPE),
Latacunga, Ecuador/Universidad Rey Juan
Carlos, Spain

Armando Reyna Bello   Universidad de las Fuerzas Armadas (ESPE),
Santo Domingo, Ecuador

Steering Committee

Miguel Botto-Tobar   Eindhoven University of Technology,
The Netherlands

Angela Díaz Cadena   Universitat de Valencia, Spain

Program Committee

A. Bonci	Marche Polytechnic University, Italy
Ahmed Lateef Khalaf	Al-Mamoun University College, Iraq
Aiko Yamashita	Oslo Metropolitan University, Norway
Alejandro Donaire	Queensland University of Technology, Australia
Alejandro Ramos Nolazco	Instituto Tecnólogico y de Estudios Superiores Monterrey, Mexico
Alex Cazañas	University of Queensland, Australia
Alex Santamaria Philco	Universitat Politècnica de València, Spain
Alfonso Guijarro Rodriguez	University of Guayaquil, Ecuador
Allan Avendaño Sudario	Escuela Superior Politécnica del Litoral (ESPOL), Ecuador
Alexandra González Eras	Universidad Politécnica de Madrid, Spain
Ana Núñez Ávila	Universitat Politècnica de València, Spain
Ana Zambrano	Escuela Politécnica Nacional (EPN), Ecuador
Andres Carrera Rivera	University of Melbourne, Australia
Andres Cueva Costales	University of Melbourne, Australia
Andrés Robles Durazno	Edinburgh Napier University, UK
Andrés Vargas Gonzalez	Syracuse University, USA
Angel Cuenca Ortega	Universitat Politècnica de València, Spain
Ángela Díaz Cadena	Universitat de València, Spain
Angelo Trotta	University of Bologna, Italy
Antonio Gómez Exposito	University of Seville, Spain
Aras Can Onal	Tobb University Economics and Technology, Turkey
Arian Bahrami	University of Tehran, Iran
Benoît Macq	Université Catholique de Louvain, Belgium
Benjamin Durakovic	International University of Sarajevo, Bosnia and Herzegovina
Bernhard Hitpass	Universidad Federico Santa María, Chile
Bin Lin	Università della Svizzera italiana (USI), Switzerland
Carlos Saavedra	Escuela Superior Politécnica del Litoral (ESPOL), Ecuador
Catriona Kennedy	University of Manchester, UK
César Ayabaca Sarria	Escuela Politécnica Nacional (EPN), Ecuador
Cesar Azurdia Meza	University of Chile, Chile
Christian León Paliz	Université de Neuchâtel, Switzerland
Chrysovalantou Ziogou	Chemical Process and Energy Resources Institute, Greece
Cristian Zambrano Vega	Universidad de Málaga, Spain/Universidad Técnica Estatal de Quevedo, Ecuador

Cristiano Premebida	Loughborough University, UK
Daniel Magües Martinez	Universidad Autónoma de Madrid, Spain
Danilo Jaramillo Hurtado	Universidad Politécnica de Madrid, Spain
Darío Piccirilli	Universidad Nacional de La Plata, Argentina
Darsana Josyula	Bowie State University, USA
David Benavides Cuevas	Universidad de Sevilla, Spain
David Blanes	Universitat Politècnica de València, Spain
David Ojeda	Universidad Técnica del Norte, Ecuador
David Rivera Espín	University of Melbourne, Australia
Denis Efimov	Inria, France
Diego Barragán Guerrero	Universidad Técnica Particular de Loja (UTPL), Ecuador
Diego Peluffo-Ordoñez	Yachay Tech, Ecuador
Dimitris Chrysostomou	Aalborg University, Denmark
Domingo Biel	Universitat Politècnica de Catalunya, Spain
Doris Macías Mendoza	Universitat Politècnica de València, Spain
Edison Espinoza	Universidad de las Fuerzas Armadas (ESPE), Ecuador
Edwin Rivas	Universidad Distrital de Colombia, Colombia
Ehsan Arabi	University of Michigan, USA
Emanuele Frontoni	Università Politecnica delle Marche, Italy
Emil Pricop	Petroleum-Gas University of Ploiesti, Romania
Erick Cuenca	Université Catholique de Louvain, Belgium
Fabian Calero	University of Waterloo, Canada
Fan Yang	Tsinghua University, China
Fariza Nasaruddin	University of Malaya, Malaysia
Felipe Ebert	Universidade Federal de Pernambuco (UFPE), Brazil
Fernanda Molina Miranda	Universidad Politécnica de Madrid, Spain
Fernando Almeida	University of Campinas, Brazil
Fernando Flores Pulgar	Université de Lyon, France
Firas Raheem	University of Technology, Iraq
Francisco Calvente	Universitat Rovira i Virgili, Spain
Francisco Obando	Universidad del Cauca, Colombia
Franklin Parrales	University of Guayaquil, Ecuador
Freddy Flores Bahamonde	Universidad Técnica Federico Santa María, Chile
Gabriel Barros Gavilanes	INP Toulouse, France
Gabriel López Fonseca	Sheffield Hallam University, UK
Gema Rodriguez-Perez	LibreSoft/Universidad Rey Juan Carlos, Spain
Ginger Saltos Bernal	Escuela Superior Politécnica del Litoral (ESPOL), Ecuador
Giovanni Pau	Kore University of Enna, Italy

Guilherme Avelino	Universidade Federal do Piauí (UFP), Brazil
Guilherme Pereira	Universidade Federal de Minas Gerais (UFMG), Brazil
Guillermo Pizarro Vásquez	Universidad Politécnica de Madrid, Spain
Gustavo Andrade Miranda	Universidad Politécnica de Madrid, Spain
Hernán Montes León	Universidad Rey Juan Carlos, Spain
Ibraheem Kasim	University of Baghdad, Iraq
Ilya Afanasyev	Innopolis University, Russia
Israel Pineda Arias	Chonbuk National University, South Korea
Jaime Meza	Universiteit van Fribourg, Switzerland
Janneth Chicaiza Espinosa	Universidad Técnica Particular de Loja (UTPL), Ecuador
Javier Gonzalez-Huerta	Blekinge Institute of Technology, Sweden
Javier Monroy	University of Malaga, Spain
Javier Sebastian	University of Oviedo, Spain
Jawad K. Ali	University of Technology, Iraq
Jefferson Ribadeneira Ramírez	Escuela Superior Politécnica de Chimborazo, Ecuador
Jerwin Prabu	Bharati Robotic Systems, India
Jong Hyuk Park	Korea Institute of Science and Technology, South Korea
Jorge Charco Aguirre	Universitat Politècnica de València, Spain
Jorge Eterovic	Universidad Nacional de La Matanza, Argentina
José A. Tenreiro Machado	Polytechnic Institute of Porto, Portugal
Jorge Gómez Gómez	Universidad de Córdoba, Colombia
Juan Corrales	Universidade de Santiago de Compostela, France
Juan Romero Arguello	University of Manchester, UK
Julián Andrés Galindo	Université Grenoble Alpes, France
Julian Galindo	Inria, France
Julio Albuja Sánchez	James Cook University, Australia
Kelly Garces	Universidad de Los Andes, Colombia
Kester Quist-Aphetsi	Center for Research, Information, Technology and Advanced Computing, Ghana
Korkut Bekiroglu	SUNY Polytechnic Institute, USA
Kunde Yang	Northwestern Polytechnic University, China
Lina Ochoa	CWI, The Netherlands
Lohana Lema Moreira	Universidad de Especialidades Espíritu Santo (UEES), Ecuador
Lorena Guachi Guachi	Yachay Tech, Ecuador
Lorena Montoya Freire	Aalto University, Finland
Lorenzo Cevallos Torres	Universidad de Guayaquil, Ecuador
Luis Galárraga	Inria, France

Pablo Lupera	Escuela Politécnica Nacional, Ecuador
Pablo Ordoñez Ordoñez	Universidad Politécnica de Madrid, Spain
Pablo Palacios	Universidad de Chile, Chile
Pablo Torres-Carrión	Universidad Técnica Particular de Loja (UTPL), Ecuador
Patricia Ludeña González	Universidad Técnica Particular de Loja (UTPL), Ecuador
Paulo Batista	University of Évora, Portugal
Paulo Chiliguano	Queen Mary University of London, UK
Pedro Neto	University of Coimbra, Portugal
Praveen Damacharla	Purdue University Northwest, USA
Priscila Cedillo	Universidad de Cuenca, Ecuador
Radu-Emil Precup	Politehnica University of Timisoara, Romania
Ramin Yousefi	Islamic Azad University, Iran
René Guamán-Quinche	Universidad Nacional de Loja, Ecuador
Ricardo Martins	University of Coimbra, Portugal
Richard Ramirez Anormaliza	Universitat Politècnica de Catalunya, Spain
Richard Rivera	IMDEA Software Institute, Spain
Richard Stern	Carnegie Mellon University, USA
Rijo Jackson Tom	SRM University, India
Roberto Murphy	University of Colorado Denver, USA
Roberto Sabatini	RMIT University, Australia
Rodolfo Alfredo Bertone	Universidad Nacional de La Plata, Argentina
Rodrigo Barba	Universidad Técnica Particular de Loja (UTPL), Ecuador
Rodrigo Saraguro Bravo	Universitat Politècnica de València, Spain
Ronald Barriga Díaz	Universidad de Guayaquil, Ecuador
Ronnie Guerra	Pontificia Universidad Católica del Perú, Perú
Ruben Rumipamba-Zambrano	Universitat Politecnica de Catalanya, Spain
Saeed Rafee Nekoo	Universidad de Sevilla, Spain
Saleh Mobayen	University of Zanjan, Iran
Samiha Fadloun	Université de Montpellier, France
Sergio Montes León	Universidad de las Fuerzas Armadas (ESPE), Ecuador
Stefanos Gritzalis	University of the Aegean, Greece
Syed Manzoor Qasim	King Abdulaziz City for Science and Technology, Saudi Arabia
Tatiana Mayorga	Universidad de las Fuerzas Armadas (ESPE), Ecuador
Thomas Sjögren	Swedish Defence Research Agency (FOI), Sweeden
Tiago Curi	Federal University of Santa Catarina, Brazil
Tony T. Luo	A*STAR, Singapore

Trung Duong	Queen's University Belfast, UK
Vanessa Jurado Vite	Universidad Politécnica Salesiana, Ecuador
Waldo Orellana	Universitat de València, Spain
Washington Velasquez Vargas	Universidad Politécnica de Madrid, Spain
Wayne Staats	Sandia National Labs, USA
Willian Zamora	Universidad Laíca Eloy Alfaro de Manabí, Ecuador
Yessenia Cabrera Maldonado	University of Cuenca, Ecuador
Yerferson Torres Berru	Universidad de Salamanca, Spain/Instituto Tecnológico Loja, Ecuador
Zhanyu Ma	Beijing University of Posts and Telecommunications, China

Organizing Institutions

Sponsoring Institutions

Collaborators

Trang Duong
Vanessa Jiundo Vite
Walile Orellana
Washington Velasquez Vargas
Wayne Staats
William Zamora

Yesenia Cabrera Maldonado
Yerisson Torres Bravo

Zhaoyu Ma

Queen's University, Belfast, UK
Universidad Politécnica Salesiana, Ecuador
Universitat de Valencia, Spain
Universidad Politécnica de Madrid, Spain
Sandia National Labs, USA
Universidad Laica Eloy Alfaro de Manabí, Ecuador
University of Cuenca, Ecuador
Universidad de Salamanca, Spain/Instituto
Tecnológico Loja, Ecuador
Beijing University of Posts and Telecommunications, China

Organizing Institutions

Sponsoring Institutions

Collaborators

Contents

Intelligent Systems

Machine Vision

Security

Technology Trends

Communication

Communication

Rating Meter for Digital Terrestrial Television with ISDB-T Standard Through Transport Stream Analysis

Gonzalo Olmedo[1]([✉]), Erick Malusin[2], and Nancy Paredes[1]

[1] WiCOM-Energy Research Group, Department of Electrical, Electronics and
Telecommunications, Universidad de Las Fuerzas Armadas ESPE, Sangolquí, Ecuador
{gfolmedo,niparedes}@espe.edu.ec

[2] Engineering in Electronics and Telecommunications, Universidad de Las Fuerzas Armadas
ESPE, Sangolquí, Ecuador
exmalusin@espe.edu.ec

Abstract. The television programming rating represents, as a percentage, the number of households or viewers who find the television turned on a given channel, program, day, and time. In this project, a rating meter was implemented for the international ISDB-T system based on the analysis of the Program Specific Information tables and Service Information tables of the Transport Stream that carries the information of the television channels and the content of the Electronic Programming Guide, whose data is recorded in a database implemented for this purpose, where the viewer does not need to interact or answer questions about the programming. The implemented prototype uses a full-seg ISDB-T receiver to capture the signal from the air and obtain the transport flow. For the information processing, an interface was designed in Java that evaluates the flow based on the service tables, event information, time offset, and the descriptors that describe information about each event. The data with the name of the channel, name of the program, type of service, start and end time are recorded in the database and automatically generate the rating report. The tests were carried out with the reception of open television channels in the city of Quito in Ecuador.

Keywords: Rating meter · TDT · ISDB-T · EPG · EIT · TOT · SDT

1 Introduction

The word Rating has multiple definitions. The most used meaning in our environment is the one that refers to the index or calculation that people who are watching a specific television program, channel, or tuning in to the radio. Taking the term Rating in reference, we can say that it is essential within the study of the media. It is the one that establishes the value of each channel in front of advertisers or people who are looking for a medium that is in high demand so that the ads they are going to publish have the desired impact, and this will determine whether to invest in advertising a product or campaign and will decide the means of communication through which it is transmitted.

© Springer Nature Switzerland AG 2022
M. Botto-Tobar et al. (Eds.): ICAT 2021, CCIS 1535, pp. 3–17, 2022.
https://doi.org/10.1007/978-3-031-03884-6_1

Within its main business axis, the open television industry highlights the generation of advertisements, in this case, audiovisual advertising, campaigns, and even highly important public information that wants to reach the audience optimally and efficiently. When determining the programming of a channel, some considerations and variables must be taken, such as defining to which audience the programming is directed, the schedule, impact, and importance that said programming would cause on the audience.

In Ecuador, the electronic audience measurement service is quantified through equipment called People Meters, which have the ability to calculate all cable television systems to more than open channels without neglecting those peripheral devices at the same time, television such as VHS, DVD, and Videogames. Through this technology, Ibope Time in our country provides household and public audience estimates for various broadcast television channels and contiguously for cable television channels and UHF channels. The People Meter determines the audience, minute by minute, person to person, inventorying each of these details, and that is in accordance with the market requirement [1].

The rating measurement within Ecuador is carried out only in two cities, Quito and Guayaquil. To carry out the operational sample, about 275 households are needed in each area to be measured, while to make comparisons with international levels, 250 households must be transmitting information daily.

According to Ibope standards, a People Meters is installed in each home for each television with a maximum number of 5 per home. Within the entire Ecuadorian territory, there are around 1000 People Meters installed and in the entire operation.

In [2], a remote census and a survey that works for Digital Terrestrial Television (DTT) was carried out on the international ISDB-T standard, on GINGA NCL, in an Android TV operating system, where a multiple-choice survey is presented to the which the viewer must respond with the help of his television remote control.

In this project, unlike the Rating meters that are based on surveys that the viewer responds to, a rating meter was implemented for the international ISDB-T system based on the analysis of the Program Specific Information tables (PSI) and Service Information tables (SI) of the Transport Stream (TS) that carries the information of the television channels and the content of the Electronic Programming Guide (EPG), whose data is recorded in a database implemented for this purpose. A low-cost USB full-seg receiver captures the TS, and the captured data is processed on a computer with a Linux operating system (Ubuntu). The tests were carried out with the reception of open television channels in the city of Quito in Ecuador. In the second section, the Transport Stream and the PSI / SI tables used are mentioned; In the third section, the receiver implementation methodology is explained, and the results of each stage are shown. The fourth section presents a discussion and the conclusions of the project.

2 Transport Stream

The Transport Stream (TS MPEG-2) is a digital format used to transfer and collect video data, audio, and program and system information protocols. All this transfer of files or data is carried out employing packets of fixed size, the same that have a determined size of 188 bytes, of which 4 bytes belong to the header and 184 to the payload. Each TS packet is identified by a packet identifier number (PID) found inside the header, and carries specific information, be it audio, video, data, and the PSI/SI configuration tables [3–5].

The Program Specific Information (PSI) tables are used for the automatic configuration of the receiver, to demultiplex and decode the elementary packet streams (PES). These tables are mandatory in the transmission process of a television station. Within the ISDB-T system standard, each table has its identifier and PID identifier in the generation and multiplexing stage. Table 1 describes the PSI tables [3, 4].

The System Information tables (SI) carry information available on services and events. They are private tables and, in some cases, optional. Table 2 shows the main tables that belong to this set.

Table 1. PSI table

Table_id	Table	PID	Description
0 × 00	Program Association Table (PAT)	0 × 00	It informs about the general content of the TS and contains the list of programs
0 × 01	Conditional Access Table (CAT)	0 × 01	This table is not mandatory except when the transmission includes conditional access
0 × 02	Program Map Table (PMT)	Value assigned by the PAT	It contains the specific information of each program carried by the TS

Table 2. SI table

Table_id	Table	PID	Description
0 × 40 0 × 41	Network Information Table (NIT)	0 × 10	Contains information about the physical organization of a specific network
0 × 42 0 × 46	Service Description Table (SDT)	0 × 11	The programs carried by the TS are described in detail
0 × 4E 0 × 4F 0 × 50–0 × 5F 0 × 60–0 × 6F	Event Information Table (EIT)	0 × 12 0 × 26 0 × 27	Contains the information on the Electronic Programming Grid (EPG)
0 × 70	Time Date Table (TDT)	0 × 14	It is used as a reference to report the current date and time
0 × 73	Time Offset Table (TOT)	0 × 14	It informs about the date, time, time zone, and daylight-saving time
0 × 4A	Bouquet Association Table (BAT)	0 × 11	Contains information about the grouping of programs

The SDT, EIT, and TOT tables are mainly analyzed to develop the rating meter, which will be detailed below.

Service Description Table (SDT)

This table has the structure presented in Fig. 1 and describes the programs carried by a specific TS stream, is descriptive, and has information on the names of the services transmitted. The SDT table has a PID of 0×11 or 17 in decimal and is identified by Table_id 0×42 or 0×46. The SDT table reports on the existence of the EIT table and uses several descriptors presented in Table 3 [3–6].

Number of bits	Syntax
	service_description_section(){
8 (0x42,0x46)	table_id
1	section_syntax_indicator
1	reserved_future_use
2	reserved
12	section_length
16	transport_stream_id
4	reserved
5	version_number
1	current_next_indicator
8	section_number
8	last_section_number
16	original_network_id
8	reserved_future_use
	for (i=0;i<N;i++){
16	service_id
6	reserved_future_use
1	EIT_schedule_flag
1	EIT_present_following_flag
3	running_status
1	free_CA_mode
12	descriptors_loop_length
	for (j=0;j<N;j++){
	descriptor()
32	}
	}
	CRC_32
	}

Fig. 1. SDT data structure.

Table 3. SDT descriptors.

Tag value	Descriptor
0 × 42	Stuffing descriptor
0 × 48	Service descriptor
0 × 49	Country availability descriptor
0 × 4A	Linkage descriptor
0 × 4B	NVOD reference descriptor

Event Information Table (EIT)

The EIT Table is shown in Fig. 2, and it contains the information of the electronic programming grid, precisely the start time, end time, and duration of each program transmitted in each service, called events, under a chronological list format. TS packets

Number of bits	Syntax
	event_information_section(){
8 (0x4E)	table_id
1	section_syntax_indicator
1	reserved_future_use
2	reserved
12	section_length
16	service_id
4	reserved
5	version_number
1	current_next_indicator
8	section_number
8	last_section_number
16	transport_stream_id
16	original_network_id
8	segment_last_section_number
8	last_table_id
	for(i=0;i<N;i++){
16	event_id
40	start_time
24	duration
3	running_status
1	free_CA_mode
12	descriptors_loop_length
	for(i=0;i<N;i++){
	descriptor()
	}
	}
32	CRC_32

Fig. 2. EIT data structure.

carrying the EIT table must be transmitted with PID 0×012 or 18 in decimal and are associated with some of the table identifiers described in Table 4. The EIT Table can include one or more of the descriptors detailed in Table 5 [3, 4, 6].

Table 4. Transmission levels and Table_id values allocation for EIT Table.

Table_id	Description	Transmission
$0 \times 4E$	Present and following program of the actual stream	Required
$0 \times 4F$	Present and following program of the actual stream	Optional
$0 \times 50 - 0 \times 5F$	Program within 8 days of the actual stream Program after 8 days of the actual stream	Optional
$0 \times 60 - 0 \times 6F$	Program within 8 days of the other stream Program after 8 days of the other stream	Optional

Table 5. EIT descriptors.

Tag value	Descriptor
0×42	Stuffing descriptor
$0 \times 4A$	Linkage descriptor
$0 \times 4D$	Short event descriptor
$0 \times 4E$	Extended event descriptor
$0 \times 4F$	Time shifted service descriptor
0×50	Component descriptor
0×53	CA Identifier descriptor
0×54	Content descriptor
0×55	Parental rating descriptor
0×57	Telephone descriptor
$0 \times 5E$	Multilingual component descriptor
$0 \times 5F$	Private data specifier descriptor
0×61	Short smoothing buffer descriptor
0×64	Data broadcast descriptor
0×69	PDC descriptor
0×76	Content identifier descriptor
$0 \times 7F$	Extension Descriptor

Time Offset Table (TOT)

The TOT Table informs about the time, date, time zone, and daylight-saving time. It transmits the date and the UTC (Universal Time Coordinated) and indicates UTC's local time differential. This TOT section shall be transmitted in TS packets with a PID value of 0×0014, and the Table_id shall take the value 0×73. The TOT Table structure is shown in Fig. 3 [3, 4, 6].

Number of bits	Syntax
	time_offset_section(){
8 (0x73)	table_id
1	section_syntax_indicator
1	reserved_future_use
2	reserved
12	section_length
40	UTC_time
4	reserved
12	descriptors_loop_length
	for(i=0;i<N;i++){
	descriptor()
	}
32	CRC_32
	}

Fig. 3. TOT data structure.

3 Methodology and Results

Rating Meter Structure

This project was developed on the NetBeans platform, using the open-source Java programming language. A database was created on a MySQL server, a relational data storage system that works with the SQL language, and several users can access the same information and manage it simultaneously.

To obtain the Transport Stream file samples, a television tuner from the PixelView brand was used, shown in Fig. 4, which consists of a USB digital television receiver, whose main characteristics are to receive signals in high definition (Full-seg, HD), standard definition (Full-seg, SD) and low definition (One-seg, LD). It has a DibCom tuner, which is native to Ubuntu systems [7].

Fig. 4. USB Digital TV Tuner (ISDB-T/SBTVD Full-SEG.

Through the PixelView tuner and the VLC media player software [8], the signals of the television channels broadcast in Quito were captured in TS format. Figure 5 shows the 'Ecuavisa' channel tuned from a computer with Ubuntu operating system.

Fig. 5. Capture of the channel 8 signal in Quito (Ecuavisa).

A graphical interface was developed for the rating meter. The main screen is shown in Fig. 6, which contains the Open_TS option, allowing choosing the captured TS format file that will be analyzed. The Base_Connect option allows connecting the base data created on the MySQL server. Then, the Excel_Load option allows any television channel's programming to be recorded in an Excel file. Finally, the Start_Meter option starts the analysis of the TS file.

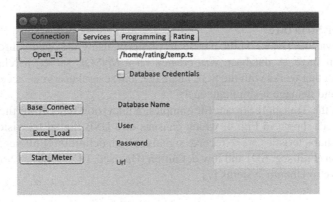

Fig. 6. Rating Meter software main screen.

Database
The database was created on the MySQL server. It consists of 3 tables: services, programming guide, and rating. As shown in Fig. 7, the service table contains the following columns:

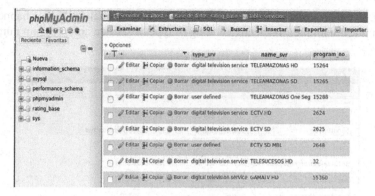

Fig. 7. Database structure

- type_srv.- Column where the type of service is recorded. For ISDB-T, the TS in the SDT table defines it as a digital television service.
- name_srv.- Column where the service's name is stored, is the name of the television channel that the TS of the SDT table captured.
- program_no.- It allows the storage of the program number, which is a unique number for each tuned channel.

It was necessary to analyze the SDT table presented in Fig. 1 that includes the services that the TS contains within the loop, where the service identifier "service_id" indicates the value corresponding to the Program Number (program_no). In the service descriptor, the structure of which is presented in Fig. 8 [6], the type of service (type_svr) is an 8-bit field, where 0x01 represents a digital terrestrial television service. In the *char* option, we find in bytes in a hexadecimal-ASCII format the name of the service provider, and in *Char*, the name of the service (name_svr) that corresponds to the television channel. For example, in the first row of Fig. 7, the name of the service is recorded "TELEAMAZONAS HD".

Number of bits	Syntax
	service_descriptor(){
8 (0x48)	descriptor_tag
8	descriptor_length
8	service_type
8	service_provider_name_length
	for (i=0;i<N;I++){
8	char
	}
8	service_name_length
	for (i=0;i<N;I++){
8	Char
	}
	}

Fig. 8. Service descriptor.

In Fig. 9, the program screen is presented with the information of the channels that have been tuned with their respective coding of type of service and program number.

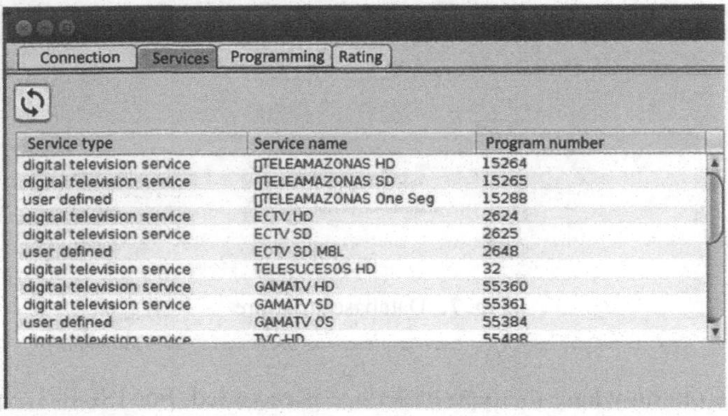

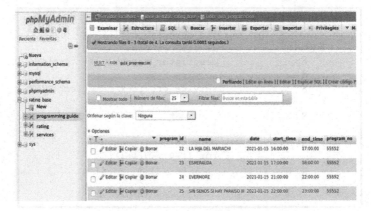

Fig. 9. Services screen.

The following columns structure the programming guide table: program_id, name, date, start_time, end_time, and program_no, as can be seen in Fig. 9.

- name.- It allows storing the name of the event that is being transmitted at that moment..
- date.- Records the date the file being analyzed was recorded.
- start_time.- Records the time when the broadcasting program started in the TS file.
- end_time.- Records the end time of the program being broadcast in the TS file samples.

In the programming tab, once the file has been analyzed, we proceed to find the programming guide. For this, the short event descriptor in the EIT table was used, which, based on Table 5, is found in the Tag_value 0x4D that in decimal is equivalent to the number 77. The structure of this descriptor is presented in Fig. 10, where the fields

Fig. 10. Structure the programming guide table

required for the analysis are the following: event_name_length that indicates the size in bytes for the name of the event that is being displayed, event_name_char (name), which indicates in characters the name of the event in hexadecimal-ASCII format and text_char that indicates in a text a brief description of the current event [3, 4, 6].

In Fig. 11, ISO_639_language_code represents a 24-bit field contains the ISO 639 [9] three-character language code of the language of the following text fields. Each character is coded into 8 bits according to ISO/IEC 8859–15 shown in Fig. 12 [10] and inserted in order into the 24-bit field. For example, the codes for Spanish and Portuguese are showed in Table 6.

Number of bits	Syntax
	short_event_descriptor(){
8 (0x4D)	descriptor_tag
8	descriptor_length
24	ISO_639_language_code
8	event_name_length
	for (i=0;i<event_name_length;i++){
8	event_name_char
	}
8	text_length
	for (i=0;i<text_length;i++){
8	text_char
	}
	}

Fig. 11. Short event descriptor.

SP 0020	! 0021	" 0022	# 0023	$ 0024	% 0025	& 0026	' 0027	(0028	) 0029	* 002A	+ 002B	, 002C	- 002D	. 002E	/ 002F
0 0030	1 0031	2 0032	3 0033	4 0034	5 0035	6 0036	7 0037	8 0038	9 0039	: 003A	; 003B	< 003C	= 003D	> 003E	? 003F
@ 0040	A 0041	B 0042	C 0043	D 0044	E 0045	F 0046	G 0047	H 0048	I 0049	J 004A	K 004B	L 004C	M 004D	N 004E	O 004F
P 0050	Q 0051	R 0052	S 0053	T 0054	U 0055	V 0056	W 0057	X 0058	Y 0059	Z 005A	[005B	\ 005C	] 005D	^ 005E	_ 005F
` 0060	a 0061	b 0062	c 0063	d 0064	e 0065	f 0066	g 0067	h 0068	i 0069	j 006A	k 006B	l 006C	m 006D	n 006E	o 006F
p 0070	q 0071	r 0072	s 0073	t 0074	u 0075	v 0076	w 0077	x 0078	y 0079	z 007A	{ 007B	| 007C	} 007D	~ 007E	

Fig. 12. 8-bit encoded characters according to ISO / IEC 8859–15.

In the EIT of Fig. 2, the date and times of the event are obtained through the "start_time" and "duration" sections to determine the start and end time of the programming. The TOT table in Fig. 3 is used to determine the recorded universal coordinate time. The "start_time" is a 40-bit field that contains the start time of the event in Universal Time Coordinated (UTC) and Modified Julian Date (MJD). This field is coded as 16

Table 6. Code of the language - ISO / IEC 8859–15.

(HEX)	24-bit	Caracter ISO/IEC 8859–15	Language
73 70 61	0111 0011 0111 0000 0110 0001	spa	Spanish
70 6F 72	0111 0000 0101 1111 0111 0010	por	Portuguese

Table 7. Examples of Universal Time Coordinated (UTC) and Modified Julian Date (MJD).

Table_id	m_{JD}	Date	Time (BCD)
0 × C079124500	0 × C079 = 49273	13–10–1993	12:45:00
0 × D764032454	0 × D764 = 55140	05–11–2009	03:24:54
0 × DF28165204	0 × DF28 = 57128	16–04–2015	16:52:04
0 × E823082554	0 × E823 = 59427	01–08–2021	08:25:54

bits giving the 16 LSBs of MJD followed by 24 bits coded as six digits in 4-bit Binary Coded Decimal (BCD) [6].

Table 7 shows examples of the star_time encoding, where the time is obtained in BCD through the conversion of the last 6 bytes, and the date is obtained with the value of the MJD code, m_{JD}, using the decimal value of the first 4 bytes in the following that are detailed below, considering the constants $a = 15078.2$, $b = 365.25$, $c = 14956$ and $d = 30.6001$.

$$y = \frac{m_{JD} - a}{b}; m = \frac{m_{JD} - (c + 0.1) - \lfloor yb \rfloor}{d} ; \ If \begin{cases} m = 14 \text{ or } m = 15 \ K = 1 \\ \text{other} \quad\quad\quad K = 0 \end{cases}$$

$$Day = m - c - \lfloor yb \rfloor - \lfloor md \rfloor \tag{1}$$

$$Month = m - 12K - 1 \tag{2}$$

$$Year = 1900 + y + K \tag{3}$$

In Fig. 13, the screen where the programming is detailed is presented, which includes the program's name, the start and end time, and the coding of the program number.

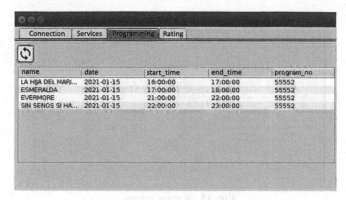

Fig. 13. Programming screen.

The rating table is structured with the following columns: program_id, srv_name, name, start_time, end_time, and counter, as can be seen in Fig. 14. The only new parameter added within the rating table is the counter column, whose functionality indicates how many times a specific program has been analyzed. Finally, the rating screen is presented in Fig. 15.

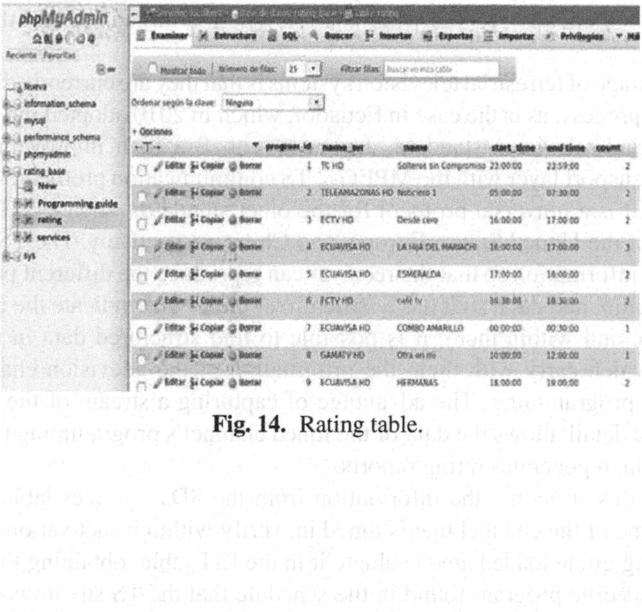

Fig. 14. Rating table.

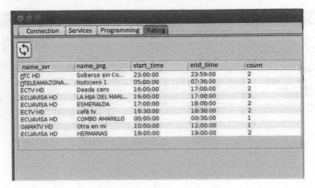

Fig. 15. Rating screen.

4 Discussion and Conclusions

The rating is the measure of TV or radio consumption and indicates the average number of people who watch a program or channel during a given time. That is, it relates the population and the amount of time seen over the total population and possible minutes. The use of people-meters is the main way to measure national television audiences around the world. A people-meter is an electronic device that is installed in selected homes and automatically records when the television is turned on, and the channel is tuned.

The advantage of terrestrial television systems is that they are currently digitized, or in a digitization process, as is the case in Ecuador, which in 2010 adopted the international ISDTB-T digital television standard, Japanese with Brazilian improvements., which works in its transport layer with the MPEG-2 TS communication protocol, which should be noted that it is a universal protocol for the other standards, such as ATSC, DVB-T, and DTMB, of the United States, Europe, and China, respectively. The TS flow carries the necessary information so that the receiver can reproduce the different programming, both video, audio, and data, so it has a structure of tables that indicate the configuration of the system, and within them, it is possible to find structured data in the so-called descriptors, which carry with them the information of the television channel and the details of the programming. The advantage of capturing a stream of the TS type and analyzing it in detail allows the data of the tuned channel's programming to be saved in a database, which generates rating reports.

Based on this structure, the information from the SDT services table was used to obtain the name of the channel that is tuned in, verify within its activation bit if there is a programming guide loaded, and evaluate it in the EIT table, obtaining the data on the name of the specific program found in the schedule that the TS stream is captured and the start and end times of the schedule, based on the current schedule that is recorded in the TOT table.

In the first instance, this information was obtained from most digital channels on the air in the city of Quito since some channels, when they are in transmission test mode, do not have the programming guide active. However, at least It is possible to register the name of the television channel at the time the signal was captured, since the SDT table is mandatory in the transmission process, in addition to the NIT table that provides channel data.

On the other hand, important information can also be captured to improve the relevant data of a rating measurement system, such as the information on the type of programming about its content and age, which is also transmitted in the event descriptors. Moreover, parental control allows a blocking process to be carried out on the receiver with a password if this option has been configured.

The designed prototype meets the proposed objective and provides processes for receiving and capturing the TS flow, which allows other types of information to be recorded, such as capturing messages and emergency codes from the EWBS system or decompressing applications. Interactive programs that arrive in the air, among other types of data that can be transmitted.

References

1. IBOPE Homepage, http://www.ibope.com.ec/ibopetime/views/faq.php
2. Pabón, D., Acosta, F., Olmedo, G.: Digital real-time audience polling system for digital terrestrial television with ISDB-Tb standard, ACI, **11**(2) (2019) https://doi.org/10.18272/aci.v11i2.747
3. ABNT, ABNT NBR 15603–2, Digital terrestrial television - Multiplexing and information services (IS) Part 1: SI of the broadcasting system, ISDB-T Brazil Standard (2007)
4. Digital Video Broadcasting (DVB), Specification for Service Information (SI) in DVB systems. Niza: European Broadcasting Union (2019)
5. Uehara, M.: Application of MPEG-2 systems to terrestrial ISDB (ISDB-T). Proc. IEEE **94**(1), 261–268 (2006). https://doi.org/10.1109/JPROC.2005.859695
6. ABNT, ABNT NBR 15603, Digital terrestrial television - Multiplexing and information services (IS) Part 2: Data structure and definitions of the basic information of SI, ISDB-T Brazil Standard (2009)
7. Perón, J.: How do ISDB-T digital TV tuners work on Ubuntu 18.04LTS 64-bit? (2018). https://ubuntuperonista.blogspot.com/2018/06/como-hago-funcionar-la-sintonizadora-de.html
8. VIDEOLAN Homepage, https://www.videolan.org/vlc/index.es.html
9. ISO 639–2, https://www.loc.gov/standards/iso639-2/php/code_list.php
10. ISO IEC 8895–15, https://www.iso.org/standard/29505.html

Wide Band Antennas for Energy Harvesting

Felix Reinoso[1] , Carlos Gordón[1](✉) , Myriam Cumbajín[2] ,
and Carlos Peñafiel[3]

[1] GITED Research Group, Facultad de Ingeniería en Sistemas, Electrónica e
Industrial, Universidad Técnica de Ambato, UTA, 180150 Ambato, Ecuador
{freinoso6500,cd.gordon}@uta.edu.ec
[2] SISAu Research Center, Facultad de Ingenieria y Tecnologias de la Información y la
Comunicación, Universidad Tecnologica Indoamerica, UTI, 180103 Ambato, Ecuador
myriamcumbajin@indoamerica.edu.ec
[3] Facultad de Ingeniería. Universidad Nacional de Chimborazo, UNACH,
060108 Riobamba, Ecuador
carlospenafiel@unach.edu.ec

Abstract. This work shows the design and manufacture of two compact,
low-cost, frequency-independent antennas in microstrip technology that
operate within a very wide frequency range for electromagnetic energy
harvesting applications, which were optimized with the help of the CST
software and manufactured on FR4, the operating frequencies are established mainly within the range of the spectrum, where the different cellular operators have been concessioned for 2G, 3G, 4G LTE technology
in Ecuador, and even WIFI which is currently the band of greater use,
with very wide bandwidths, which allows the effective collection of electromagnetic energy for frequencies of greater presence and more used in
the Ecuadorian territory.

Keywords: Energy harvesting · Antenna · Microstrip · Multiband ·
Electromagnetics

1 Introduction

Currently there are a number of scientific studies that indicate the great importance of obtaining alternative and sustainable energy to power the different
electronic devices, in order that they acquire autonomy; In addition, the energy
used is the most friendly to the environment and does not generate a greater
impact on environmental pollution. One of the most popular and whose study
is growing is the so-called "Energy Harvesting", which consists of the process
by which energy present in the environment is extracted to produce electrical
energy that will later be stored or used by low-consumption devices [1]. The Electromagnetic energy generated by Radio Frequency (RF) systems, which consists
mainly of collecting the energy emitted by the different antennas installed at

© Springer Nature Switzerland AG 2022
M. Botto-Tobar et al. (Eds.): ICAT 2021, CCIS 1535, pp. 18–33, 2022.
https://doi.org/10.1007/978-3-031-03884-6_2

throughout a geographical area. Electromagnetic Energy collection systems are developed in stages, the first stage is the Antenna, which is responsible for capturing the electromagnetic energy from the environment, the second stage is the collection system that converts the captured energy into voltage to store it and later It may be used by an electronic device. The best known systems in relation to the "harvest" of electromagnetic energy are the so-called "Rectenas", they take that name from the combination of Antenna + Rectifier, we find several works related to this topic as in [2] that despite not obtaining good results in the implementation, it serves as a reference on the progress of research in this field with different models and designs corresponding to the capture stage of energy through the antennas, as well as the collection system.

In the research work carried out by [3], It shows us in detail several research articles published over the years, comparing them and establishing conclusions based on the most significant parameters that allow us to have a global vision of the progress of research in the scope of this topic where it is observed that the operating frequency of WIFI networks (2.4–2.45 GHz) is the frequency with which most work is done. For the stage itself of the antenna we have reviewed several articles of interest regarding the designs and manufacture of the antennas considering those that work in multi-frequencies. An important contribution is found in [4] where a patch type antenna is designed that works at the frequencies of 2.4 GHz and 4.9 GHz, the results of which suggest that they can be used to harvest RF energy. It is of great help in this way. To define the techniques that will be used in the design and manufacture of the antennas for the present research work, on the other hand in [5] a multiband antenna in Microstrip technology is designed, which covers band frequencies from 900 MHz to 6 GHz for electromagnetic energy harvesting applications, exhibits good radiation characteristics and reflection at 900 MHz (GSM), 2.4 GHz (Bluetooth/WLAN), 3.2 GHz (Radiolocation, 3G), 3.8 GHz (for LTE, 4G) and additional band of 5 GHz (new signals of WIFI) and its overall dimension is very small (41 mm (width) × 4 mm (length) × 1,778 mm (thickness)). A very similar and current study is [6] which shows the development of the design of a patch antenna with some variants that allows it to resonate at various frequencies such as 0.924 GHz, 1.88 GHz, 2.112 GHz, 3.4 GHz, and 3.844 GHz, considered a multiband antenna, which consists of a rectangular patch that as a novelty includes pentagonal and symmetrical slots in order to operate at the frequencies detailed above with a minimum bandwidth requirement of 50 MHz and directional radiation pattern. A complete study of antennas used for the application of Energy Harvesting in RF is presented in [7] where it first focuses on a spectral study of the entire city taking as reference points the London Underground stations, with this it determines the frequency bands at which it is going to design the antennas and the energy harvesting devices. On the other hand, the research work carried out by [8] performs an interesting design of antenna arrays and establishes the main advantages of using the type of flat spiral antennas such as: A good Q factor, Greater inductance per unit area and Compact capacity. In this work, the so-called frequency-independent antennas were considered for the design. Also, This type of antennas, has been verified in the bibliography and are presented in various ways and their designs are very varied [9].

It attracted a lot of attention and it is very common for the collection of electromagnetic energy to use Archimedean Spiral Antennas, in relation to which, we have reviewed the work done by [10] which is a graduate work where the design of an Archimedean spiral antenna to operate at a central frequency of 2.4 GHz establishes optimal operating parameters such as the VSWR factor and the S11 parameter with which it determines the operation of the antenna, which it optimizes through software simulations specialized such as the CST MICROWAVE STUDIO. Continuing with this theme in the article [11] as indicated by the same author, the procedure for designing the printed Archimedean spiral is explored. The results are analyzed taking into account the criterion of maintaining a SWR (standing wave ratio) value lower than 3 in the band of interest, they are obtained through simulation and optimization using the CST software (Microwave Studio). The design does it for a frequency band from 600 MHz to 3200 MHz with the same antenna. A more recent work such as that of [12] shows us the design of an Archimedean spiral antenna that works in the range of frequencies from 1.2 GHz to 5 GHz, which is a wide range of frequencies that are associated with various communication systems, the results obtained make it possible to determine that the antenna works efficiently within the design band.

This work shows the design and manufacture with their respective simulation tests and practical operation of two frequency-independent and multi-frequency antennas for energy harvesting applications focused on RF energy and that can be used to keep low-consumption equipment active such as those used in IoT. The antennas designed, Arquimides Spiral Antenna (AEAR) with its respective Balum and a Log-Periodic Antenna with dipole arrangements (ALOG) work within the most widely used bands in Ecuadorian territory, such as those assigned to cell phone operators for 2G, 3G and 4G LTE technology, as well as in the WIFI operating frequency and provides a contribution to the study of multi-frequency antennas and electromagnetic energy capture in Ecuador. Another of the types of frequency-independent antennas that caught our attention, are the so-called Log-Periodic, on this subject we find the one developed by [13] that allows us in an easy way to identify the manufacturing process of different types and models of Antennas within this classification that with the help of specialized software optimizes the designs until obtaining results according to what is expected and then put them into practice, proving to obtain compact designs with good results with respect to the bandwidth of each elaborated antenna. For a better design of the Log-Periodic Antennas we are based on articles such as [14] considered the pioneer in its time on the study of this type of antennas and establishes the fundamental bases for the development of research in this field that likewise that in [15] and [16] give us the bases for the design of periodic log antennas and with which the main parameters to be considered are established. This work is distributed as follows: section two describes the methodology that includes the design, the calculations and the material used to make the antennas. Section 3 presents the result of the simulation, the analysis and finally the conclusions.

2 Methodology

The process used has been the design, simulation, manufacture and characterization of the proposed antennas, then we will deal with each of the processes:

2.1 Design

The AEAR has been designed to work at frequencies from 1GHz to 3GHz, while the ALOG has been designed to work at frequencies between 1.5 GHZ and 2.5 GHz, for the calculation of the parameters, both have variables which are of great importance to determine the dimensions of the antennas, in the AEAR the most important factor is the inner radius of the arms and for the ALOG it is the scale factor, once with the calculations of the parameters we proceed to enter the values in the CST STUDIO software that helps us to Simulate the operation of the designs and in the same way to optimize to obtain the required results or the closest to what was planned.

Archimedean Spiral Antenna Design (AEAR). Knowing the frequencies at which the proposed antenna will operate, we proceed to perform the calculations and find the most important parameters with which it is designed in the CST software, which are shown in Fig. 1.

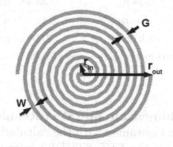

Fig. 1. Parameters to be calculated for the design of the Archimedean Spiral Antenna (AEAR) [17]

Inside Radius:

$$r_{in} = \frac{c_0}{2\pi f_h \sqrt{\epsilon_{eff}}} \qquad (1)$$

Where r_{in} corresponds to the inner radius, c_0 is the speed of light, f_h is the highest design frequency and finally ϵ_{eff} corresponds to the effective permittivity of the dielectric corresponding to the material used to make the antenna.

Outside Radius:

$$r_{out} = \frac{c_0}{2\pi f_l \sqrt{\epsilon_{eff}}} \qquad (2)$$

Where r_{out} corresponds to the outer radius, c_0 is the speed of light, f_l is the lowest design frequency and finally ϵ_{eff} corresponds to the effective permittivity of the dielectric corresponding to the material used to make the antenna.

Spiral Arms Width:

$$L = N2\pi R_m \tag{3}$$

Where L is the length of the spiral arm, N is the number of turns of the arm, and R_m is the mean radius.

Mean Radius:

$$R_m = \frac{r_{in} + r_{out}}{2} \tag{4}$$

Where R_m is the mean radius, r_{in} corresponds to the inner radius and r_{out} corresponds to the outer radius. Replacing the values in each of the variables, we obtain the results as shown in Table 1.

Table 1. Calculated parameters for Archimedean Spiral Antenna (AEAR) design

Parameter	Value	Unit
Maximum frequency f_h	3	GHz
Minimum frequency f_h	3	GHz
Inner radius r_{in}	8.014	mm
Outer radius r_{out}	23.44	mm
Number of turns N	4	u
Arms width w	0.964	mm
Separation between arms g	0.964	mm

Geometry of the Archimedean Spiral Antenna (AEAR): With the design parameters of Table 1 obtained with the calculations carried out, we proceed to build the antenna in the CST STUDIO software, where, after several optimizations, which consist of varying the width of the arms and the number of turns of the spiral, we were able to obtain the results closest to what was projected in the simulation, leaving the design as shown in Fig. 2.

Log-Periodic Antenna Design (ALOG): For the design of the Log-Periodic Antenna, the steps proposed in [13] are followed, where we first calculate the length and width of the first dipole as a reference value, the width will take the same value as the transmission line which is calculated considering the substrate used for the design in our case FR4, $w = 3.051$ and thus also the lowest operating frequency and the input impedance, which for our case are 1.5 GHz and 50 Ω respectively, to determine the Throughout the first dipole we use the CST STUDIO software and we simulate between $\frac{\lambda}{2}$ and $\frac{\lambda}{4}$ of the lowest frequency, until we determine the final value at which the dipole resonates at that frequency.

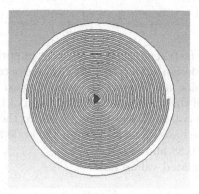

Fig. 2. Archimedean Spiral Antenna Geometry in CST STUDIO

Wavelength at Lowest Frequency:

$$\lambda_l = \frac{c_o}{f_l} \tag{5}$$

Where c_o is the speed of light and f_l corresponds to the lowest frequency of the design, in our case 1.5 GHz.

Length of the First Dipole: As we mentioned earlier, this value is obtained when simulating in the CST software from $\frac{\lambda_l}{2}$ and $\frac{\lambda_l}{4}$, after the simulation carried out it was found that the length of the first dipole that resonates at the lowest frequency proposed for the design is:

$$L = 76 \, \text{mm}$$

With the dimension of the first dipole we establish the number of elements or dipoles necessary, with the following formula:

$$N = 1 + \frac{\ln B_s}{\ln \frac{1}{\tau}} \tag{6}$$

Where B_s corresponds to the design bandwidth and is given by the equation:

$$B_s = B * B_{ar} \tag{7}$$

Where B is the desired bandwidth and B_{ar} is the bandwidth of the active region, and they are given by the following equations:

$$B = \frac{f_h}{f_l} \tag{8}$$

$$B_{ar} = 1.1 + 7.7(1 - \tau)^2 \cot \alpha \tag{9}$$

$$\alpha = \tan^{-1}\left[\frac{1-\tau}{4\sigma}\right] \tag{10}$$

Where τ is the scale factor, considered the most important value to be determined in the antenna design and σ is the relative space, both determine the directivity of the grouping and are related according to [18]. As mentioned in [13] the typical values of the scale factor in the design of traditional log periodic antennas are in the interval between 0.7 and 0.95. In the design of the printed log periodic antennas we have taken a value for the scale factor $\tau = 0.88$, widely used, in this sense: $\tau = 0.88$ and $\sigma = 0.161$

In this way the calculated values have:

$$N = 8$$
$$B = 1.67$$
$$\alpha = 0,184$$
$$B_{ar} = 1,696$$
$$B_s = 2,83$$

We proceed to calculate the other elements from the values found and from the first dipole that we have already found its width and length, firstly, we find the separation of the first dipole with the second and from there the following equations are used to find the other elements.

$$S_N = \frac{1}{2}[L_N - L_{N-1}]\cot\alpha \tag{11}$$

$$\tau = \frac{L_{N+1}}{L_N} = \frac{S_{N+1}}{S_N} = \frac{W_{N+1}}{W_N} \tag{12}$$

Where L_N is the length of the dipole N, S_N is the value of the separation between contiguous dipoles and W_N corresponds to the width of the dipole, which we can better appreciate in Fig. 3.

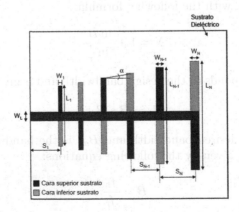

Fig. 3. Sample design for fabrication and calculations of an ALOG [13]

Once the calculations have been made with the equations presented above, the results are as shown in Table 2, the results obtained are measured in mm.

Table 2. Calculated values for ALOG design

Dipolus	Length	Separation	Widths
1	76	24.50	3.50
2	66.88	21.56	3.08
3	58.85	18.97	2.71
4	51.79	16.70	2.39
5	45.58	14.69	2.10
6	40.11	12.93	1.85
7	35.29	11.38	1.63
8	31.06	36.60	1.43

Log-Periodic Antenna Geometry: With the values obtained and presented in Table 2. We proceed to design our antenna in the CST STUDIO software, as shown in Fig. 4 below.

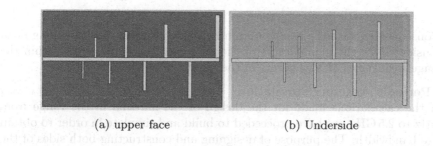

(a) upper face   (b) Underside

Fig. 4. ALOG geometry in CST STUDIO

2.2   Simulation

Each of the antennas have been designed and simulated in the CST STU-DIO software, where the results corresponding to the parameter S11 called the antenna reflection parameter are mainly analyzed to determine the operating frequencies, as well as the VSWR parameter. The results are discussed below.

Simulation of the Antennas in the CST STUDIO Software

Archimedean Spiral Antenna Simulation

Next, we show the results of the simulations regarding the parameters S11 in Fig. 5 and VSWR in Fig. 6 which show that the antenna is Multifrequency and that for each resonance frequency it has a considerable bandwidth taking as reference a −10 dB value as the resonance "threshold" and the VSWR value below 2.

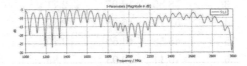

Fig. 5. S11 AEAR parameter simulation result

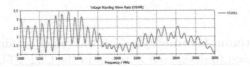

Fig. 6. VSWR AEAR parameter simulation result

Consequently, with the results obtained, we determined that this design can be considered for the manufacture of the antenna since it resonates within the coverage frequencies of 3G and 4G in the mobile network and WIFI.

Log-Periodic Antenna Simulation

With the calculations made for the design of the antenna in the range from 1.5 GHz to 2.5 GHz, we have proceeded to build and simulate in order to obtain a large bandwidth. The purpose of designing and constructing both sides of the substrate as shown in Fig. 4 is to simulate the conventional feed on the dipole arrays in this way, better antenna resonance results are obtained.

Next, we observe in Figs. 7 and 8 the result of the simulation in terms of the parameters S11 and VSWR of the ALOG respectively, with which we determine that the designed antenna obtains excellent results with an enormous bandwidth that goes from 1.5 GHz to 2.5 GHz with a resonance peak of −45 dB at 2 GHz

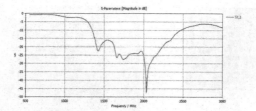

Fig. 7. S11 ALOG parameter simulation result

With the results of the simulation it is determined that the geometry of the antenna is optimal for the manufacture of the antenna for use within the range of 1.5 to 2.5 GHz with a wide bandwidth.

2.3 Manufacturing

Construction Antennas

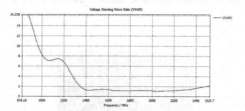

Fig. 8. VSWR ALOG parameter simulation result

For the manufacture it has been done on the FR4 substrate, the printing of the antennas on said substrate was sent to the APM Micro company in the city of Quito who used the artisanal ironing technique to print the design of the antennas.

Archimedean Spiral Antenna (AEAR)

The AEAR is manufactured on an FR4 substrate in the upper part the design of the antenna itself is reflected, in the lower part the ground or reference as we can see in Fig. 9, in addition an impedance adapter was manufactured by line widening transmission over FR4 for coupling the antenna to a 50 Ω input that is placed on one side to the SMA and on the other side directly to the beginnings of the arms of the AEAR.

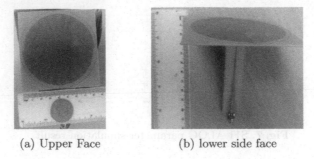

(a) Upper Face   (b) lower side face

Fig. 9. AEAR manufacturing

Antenna Log-Periodic (ALOG)

This antenna like the AEAR is designed on FR4 substrate but this time both sides of the component are used to print the antenna simulating the conventional feeding of the dipole array as can be seen more deeply in [9] and in practice in [13] and as shown in Fig. 10 below, in the part where the antenna is fed there is an SMA connector whose characteristic impedance is 50 Ω determined according to the design.

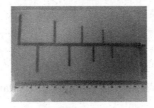

Fig. 10. ALOG manufacturing

2.4   Characterization

To carry out the measurement of results in practice, it has been done with the help of MiniVNA-TINY, which is a compact antenna analyzer which is connected to a USB port of any computer.

Archimedean Spiral Antenna (AEAR)

Next, Fig. 11 shows the measurement result of the S11 parameter of the Archimedean spiral antenna obtained with the MiniVNA-TINY equipment.

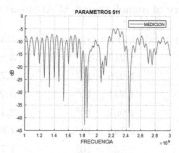

Fig. 11. AEAR measurement result S11 parameter obtained with the MiniVNA-TINY equipment

Antenna Log-Periodic (ALOG)

Next, Fig. 12 shows the measurement result of the S11 parameter of the Archimedean spiral antenna obtained with the MiniVNA-TINY equipment.

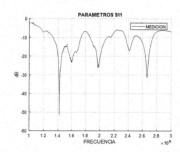

Fig. 12. ALOG measurement result S11 parameter obtained with the MiniVNA-TINY equipment

3   Analysis of Results

It consists of the comparison between the simulation in specialized software and the value measured in practice.

AEAR Analysis

In the practical result it is determined that the antenna designed and manufactured is a multi-frequency antenna that can be used for the collection of electromagnetic energy in the range from 1 GHz to 3 GHz, the resonance frequencies of the antenna are summarized in Table 3 with their respective bandwidths, analyzing the S11 parameters according to the measurements in practice.

Table 3. Summary of manufactured AEAR measurements results

Initial frequency (Hz)	Final frequency (Hz)	Band width (Hz)
1.174×10^9	1.213×10^9	3.9×10^7
1.239×10^9	1.276×10^9	3.7×10^7
1.709×10^9	1.741×10^9	3.2×10^7
1.756×10^9	1.967×10^9	2.11×10^8
1.984×10^9	2.146×10^9	1.62×10^8
2.364×10^9	2.538×10^9	1.74×10^8
2.570×10^9	2.591×10^9	2.1×10^7
2.633×10^9	2.833×10^9	2×10^8

Figure 13 shows us the comparison of the values obtained in the simulation with the values measured in practice considering the parameter S11.

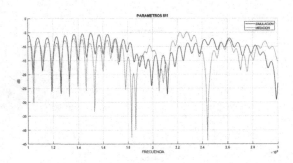

Fig. 13. Comparative results of Archimedean spiral antenna with coupling Balum, parameter S11

We use the following Eq. 13 to determine the margin of error between the simulation and the value measured in practice

$$\%error = \frac{|V_{aprox} - V_{real}|}{V_{real}} * 100\% \tag{13}$$

We consider finding this value for frequencies of interest such as 1.7 GHz, 1.9 GHz, 2.1 GHz and 2.4 GHz corresponding to the operating frequencies for cellular operators in Ecuador for 2G, 3G and 4G LTE technology in addition to the WIFI frequency.

Frequency 1700 MHz %error = 0.41%, Frequency 1900 MHz %error = 1.83%, Frequency 2100 MHz %error = 0.38%, Frequency 2400 MHz %error = 0.2%

In all the analyzed frequencies, it is verified that the percentage of error is minimal between the practical measurement and the simulated thing, varying the resonance level to a greater extent.

ALOG Analysis

In the practical result, it is determined that the designed and manufactured antenna is a multi-frequency antenna that can be used for the collection of electromagnetic energy in the range from 1.3 GHz to 2.7 GHz, despite the fact that the design was established from 1.5 GHz up to 2.5 GHz, the resonance frequencies of the antenna are summarized in Table 4. With their respective bandwidths, analyzing the $S11$ parameters according to the results obtained in practice.

Table 4. Summary of manufactured ALOG measurements results

Initial frequency (Hz)	Final frequency (Hz)	Band width (Hz)
1.331×10^9	1.731×10^9	4×10^8
1.866×10^9	2.091×10^9	2.25×10^8
2.364×10^9	2.474×10^9	1.1×10^8

Figure 14 shows us the comparison of the values obtained in the simulation with the values measured in practice considering the parameter $S11$.

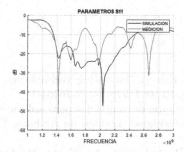

Fig. 14. Comparative result simulation vs. practical measurements antenna log-periodic of parameter $S11$

In the same way as was done with the AEAR, we consider finding the value of Eq. 13 to find the percentage of error in this case of the frequencies with the highest resonance, in this sense the following frequencies are taken into consideration:

Frequency 1400 MHz %error = 0.42%, Frequency 2000 MHz %error = 2.78%

The percentage of error for the first frequency is quite low, in the case of the second resonance there is a lag between what is simulated and what is obtained in practice, with these results we can determine that this manufactured antenna, like the Spiral Antenna of Arquímedes manufactured in the present research work, it can be used for the coverage frequencies of 3G and 4G LTE assigned to the cellular operators of Ecuador, as well as in the WIFI frequency range that is the most used.

4   Conclusions

This article presents two antennas designed and manufactured for multi-frequencies that can be used for the capture of electromagnetic energy in the frequency range from 1 GHz to 3 GHz with considerable bandwidths, in the case of the Archimedean Spiral Antenna it reaches up to 2.11×10^8 Hz bandwidth in the frequencies between 1.7 GHz and 1.9 GHz as in the frequencies between 2.6 GHz and 2.8 GHz with a return loss of up to -43.79 dB for the frequency of 2.44 GHz; In the case of the Log-Periodic Antenna, it achieves a bandwidth of up to 4×10^8 Hz at frequencies from 1.3 GHz to 1.7 GHz, with a return loss of up to -51.32 dB at the frequency of 1.4 GHz, both antennas can operate in communication systems in 2G, 3G, 4G LTE and WIFI technology.

Acknowledgements. The authors thank the invaluable contribution of the Technological University Indoamérica, for his support in carrying out the project "ESTUDIO DE ALGORITMOS DE MACHINE LEARNING PARA LA INTEGRACIÓN INTELIGENTE DE ENERGÍAS RENOVABLES", Project Code: 219.168.2021. Also, the authors thank the Technical University of Ambato and the "Dirección de Investigación y Desarrollo" (DIDE) for their support in carrying out the project "Sistema de Captación de Energía Electromagnética para Abastecimiento de Energía en Terminales de Internet de las Cosas (IoT) en entornos de Quinta Generación (5G).", project code: SFFISEI 04.

References

1. Priya, S., Inman, D.J.: Energy Harvesting Technologies, vol. 21. Springer, Boston (2009). https://doi.org/10.1007/978-0-387-76464-1
2. Mezquita, J.: Diseño de antenas compactas para aplicaciones de energy harvesting. Ph.D. dissertation, Universidad Técnica de Ambato. Facultad de Ingeniería en Sistemas (2015)
3. Dana, R., Sardhara, P., Sanghani, A., Mehta, P.: Una encuesta detallada de rectenna para la recolección de energía: en un amplio rango de frecuencias. In: Tecnologías ópticas e inalámbricas. Springer, Heidelberg (2020)
4. Jain, J., Sharma, A.: Diseño de antena de parche de microbanda rectangular de doble banda para la recolección de energía de rf. In: Tecnologías ópticas e inalámbricas. Springer, Heidelberg (2018)
5. Taghadosi, M., Albasha, L., Qaddoumi, N., Ali, M.: Miniaturised printed elliptical nested fractal multiband antenna for energy harvesting applications. IET Microwaves Antennas Propag. 9(10), 1045–1053 (2015)
6. Venkata Suriyan, S., Jegadish Kumar, K.J.: Design of slotted pentagonal structure patch antenna for RF energy harvesting in mobile communication band. In: Smys, S., Bestak, R., Chen, J.I.-Z., Kotuliak, I. (eds.) ICCNCT 2018. LNDECT, vol. 15, pp. 527–535. Springer, Singapore (2019). https://doi.org/10.1007/978-981-10-8681-6_47
7. Piñuela, M., Mitcheson, P.D., Lucyszyn, S.: Recolección de energía de rf ambiental en entornos urbanos y semiurbanos. Transacciones IEEE sobre teoría y técnicas de microondas (2013)

8. C.C., Olokede, S.S., Mahyuddin, N.M., Ain, M.F.: Recolección de energía de radiofrecuencia utilizando una antena inductora en espiral circular. In: WAMI-CON 2014 (2014)
9. Aznar, Á.C., Robert, J.R., Casals, J.M.R., Roca, L.J., Boris, S.B., Bataller, M.F.: Antenas. Univ. Politèc. de Catalunya (2004)
10. Morales, J.: Diseño de una antena espiral de arquímedes para la frecuencia de 2.4 ghz. Ph.D. dissertation, Universidad Central "Marta Abreu" de Las Villas (2013)
11. Barros, O.P.: Antena independiente de la frecuencia, espiral de arquímides impresa. Revista Telemática **16**(3), 41–52 (2018)
12. Mansour, M., Le Polozec, X., Kanaya, H.: Enhanced broadband RF differential rectifier integrated with Archimedean spiral antenna for wireless energy harvesting applications. Sensors **19**(3), 655 (2019)
13. Navarro, E.Á.: Diseño, modelado, fabricación y medida de antenas impresas para comunicaciones inalámbricas. Doctoral, Departamento de Ingeniería de Sistemas Industriales, Universidad Miguel Hernández de Elche, España (2008)
14. Isbell, D.: Log periodic dipole arrays. IRE Trans. Antennas Propag. **8**(3), 260–267 (1960)
15. DuHamel, R., Ore, F.: Logarithmically periodic antenna designs. In: 1958 IRE International Convention Record, vol. 6, pp. 139–151. IEEE (1966)
16. DuHamel, R., Isbell, D.: Broadband logarithmically periodic antenna structures. In: 1958 IRE International Convention Record, vol. 5, pp. 119–128. IEEE (1966)
17. Hinostroza, I.: Design of wideband arrays of spiral antennas. Ph.D. dissertation, Supélec (2013)
18. Balanis, C.A.: Antenna Theory: Analysis and Design. Wiley, New York (2016)

Computing

Human–Machine Interfaces to NX100 Controller for Motoman HP3L Robot in Educational Environment

João P. Ferreira[1]([⊠]) [iD], Inês Simões[1], A. Paulo Coimbra[2] [iD], and M. Crisóstomo[2] [iD]

[1] Department of Electrical Engineering, Superior Institute of Engineering of Coimbra, Coimbra, Portugal
ferreira@isec.pt

[2] ISR - Department of Electrical and Computer Engineering, University of Coimbra, Coimbra, Portugal

Abstract. With the increasing use of robots, industrial environments have changed. Industrial robots can perform heavy and repetitive tasks at high speed and precision. They are usually programmed to perform one or more specific tasks. Errors, alerts messages, restarts, indefinite stops with the need for someone to reset to the initial settings are some of the problems encountered when using robots. Because man and robot coexist in the same space, it is relevant to improve how they do relate, how they do communicate, and how they interact each other.

The present educational project is devoted to the human–robot interaction with the development and evaluation of interfaces to an industrial robot. It was developed in the context of a Master Electrical Engineering Dissertation. The robot used was a Motoman HP3L with an NX100 controller through RS232 communication. The developed interfaces consist in different combination of hardware and software like buttons, wired communication, use of a mobile phone and Bluetooth communication. One of the developed interfaces applies to both the real and a virtual robot. These interfaces were evaluated through the application of Usability Tests in order to compare and draw conclusions about the different interfaces and robot programming systems under study.

Keywords: Human–robot interface · Industrial robot · Usability tests · Engineering education · Virtual and real robot

1 Introduction

With the fast development of industries and the constant pursuit of technological advances, the human–robot interaction is gaining more and more importance [1]. The integration of the robot's operator in the automatic world increases the interface importance [2]. Even in industries where robots perform the majority of the tasks, they need to be supervised and maintained by humans. It is recognized that human capabilities, combined with robots, bring advantages in industrial production, such as work optimization, quality improvement and better cost effectiveness [3].

M. Botto-Tobar et al. (Eds.): ICAT 2021, CCIS 1535, pp. 37–52, 2022.
https://doi.org/10.1007/978-3-031-03884-6_3

ISO 9241–110 defines interface as "all parts of an interactive system (software or hardware) that provide information and controls necessary for the user to perform a particular task with the interactive system" [4]. Examples of such hardware are: buttons, keywords, joysticks, touchscreens, Inertial Measurement Units (IMU), and vision systems. Software can be produced using Labview, Matlab, C, Java, Python, etc.

The simplicity of use, application or learning, as well as satisfaction and level of operator safety, are prerequisites for successful interfaces. Knowing the level of user satisfaction and his opinion on interaction with different technologies, allows finding the better hardware and software for improving Human–Robot Interface (HRI) [5–7].

The goal of this educational project is to develop and study different devices with different hardware and software to manipulate the HP3L robot of Motoman with an NX100 controller, and evaluate them through Usability Tests. These Usability Tests were applied to different Engineering undergraduate students of several levels in order to guaranty an intuitive study of robot programming to engineering students. The interaction between students of different levels has the advantage of higher motivation for the area of robotics programming and better learning outcome.

The interface devices used are: a new developed cube device, a mobile phone and a gamepad. All of these devices allow to input the same variables as the standard interface: the teach pendant of the robot controller. They all allow to make the rotation of the robot joints or the translation and rotation of the end-effector, to open or close the gripper, to save their positions to create trajectories, reproduce them and choose the velocity of the movements. Figure 1 presents the overview of the project with all interfaces to control the Motoman HP3L Robot.

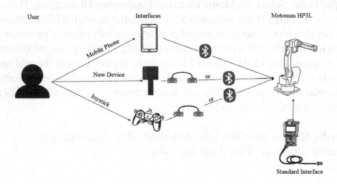

Fig. 1. Overview of the robot interface devices and communications.

2   Material and Method

2.1   Motoman HP3L Robot

The Motoman HP3L is an industrial robot with six degrees of freedom, which is ideal for assembly, picking and placing, packaging and material handling [8]. It uses an NX100 controller with a color and tactile teach pendant that is able to control up to four robots [9].

2.1.1 Direct Kinematics

The direct kinematics allows obtaining the trajectory of the different links of the robot in relation to its base link. It is represented by a group of matrices, the matrices of Denavit-Hartenberg, $^{i-1}T_i$, which transform coordinates from coordinate system of link i into the coordinate system of link i-1. To determine these matrices it is necessary to obtain the Denavit-Hartenberg parameters ai, αi, θi and di. The ai and the αi parameters correspond to X axis translation and rotation, respectively, and the θi and the di parameters correspond to Z axis rotation and translation, respectively. Figure 2 represents the configuration of the axes along the robot joints to obtain the parameters of Denavit-Hartenberg. They are indicated in Table 1.

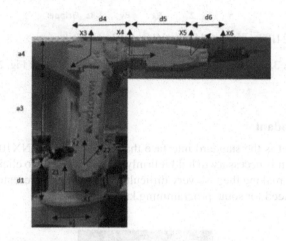

Fig. 2. The configuration of the axes along the robot HP3L joints.

Table 1. Parameters of Denavit-Hartenberg of robot HP3L.

Axis system $i-1 \rightarrow i$	Joint number	ai	αi(°)	θi(°)	di
$0 \rightarrow 1$	1	0	0	$\theta 1$	d2
$1 \rightarrow 2$	2	a2	-90	$\theta 2$-90	0
$2 \rightarrow 3$	3	a3	180	$\theta 3$	0
$3 \rightarrow 4$	4	a4	90	$\theta 4$	d4 + d5
$4 \rightarrow 5$	5	0	90	$\theta 5$	0
$5 \rightarrow 6$	6	0	-90	$\theta 6$	d6

2.1.2 Work File for RS232 Communication

The work file, designated job, is the file that has the instructions, in Inform language, to execute actions or tasks in the Motoman robot. In this project a job was implemented to do the communication between the HP3L Motoman and the interfaces, via RS232. In this job, the message received from the interfaces has the format shown in Fig. 3, where the first three values are the Cartesian coordinates (thousandths of a millimeter) of the tip of the last link and the next three values are the orientation angles (hundredths of a degree) of the gripper, and the last value represents the state of the gripper, open (1) or close (0). The character "," means that the message is incomplete and there are more information in the work file. The character ":" means the end of message and the letter "f" means the end of program. Serial communication is configured at a transmission rate of 9600 bps, 8 bits and 1 stop bit. The job sends back the six joint angles of the robot, and the state of three external buttons.

X	Y	Z	Rx	Ry	Rz	Gripper
724189	-75536	165660	-1607	-8102	-17009	0 :

Fig. 3. Message format (coordinates of the robot pose of Fig. 2).

2.1.3   Teach Pendant

The teach pendant is the standard interface that comes with the NX100 controller. To use this interface it is necessary to hold it firmly and, sometimes, to click in four buttons at the same time, making the task very difficult for the user, as presented in Fig. 4, and also there is the need for some programming knowledge.

Fig. 4. User holding and using the teach pendant.

2.2   Interfaces Developed

2.2.1   New Cube Device

The developed cube interface consists of a cube and a handle with push buttons in each face, which allows an intuitive representation of the three-dimensional world coordinate system to assist the user in the orientation of the coordinate axes. The handle allows the holding by the user's hand and possess other control push buttons. An embedded Arduino processes all data and the RS232 serial port adapter and the Bluethooth-RS232 adapter communications. Figure 5 shows the use of this interface.

Fig. 5. User holding and using the new cube device.

Hardware

The main components of the new cube device are presented in Fig. 6.

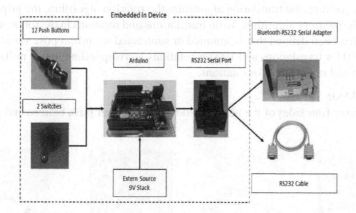

Fig. 6. Main components of the new cube device.

Each push button on the device's face allows the rotation about or the translation along one of the coordinate axis. For the user to have a good interaction it is necessary to know the orientation of the axes in the device, as shown in Fig. 7.

The user should orientate the device according to the base coordinate system of the robot. The push buttons are connected to the Arduino's digital and analog inputs. Each button is assigned an input/output pin, and its function is defined in the software. Figure 8 presents the function of each digital and analog input.

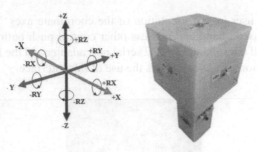

Fig. 7. Configuration axes in the new cube device.

Fig. 8. Correspondence of each button to their digital or analog input/output of Arduino.

Software

The software was developed in the Arduino IDE, being implemented a set of algorithms: the speed algorithm, the translation algorithm, the rotation algorithm, the gripper algorithm and the memory algorithm. To do translations and rotations in the robot, a constant step value has been defined that is summed or subtracted to current pose variables. This value is 1000 for translations and 100 for rotations, corresponding to one millimeter for translations and one degree for rotations.

Operating Mode

Figure 9 shows four sides of the new cube device, with their push buttons and switches.

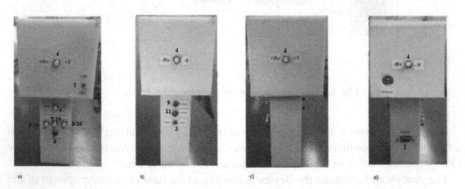

Fig. 9. New cube device. a) Front Side, b) Back Side, c) Left Side, d) Right Side.

The user selects the RS232 or the Bluetooth communication and must turn on the switch in the device (number 2 in Fig. 9) to initiate the interaction. In the handle there is another switch (3) to select between the teach and the playback modes. The teaching mode allows the user to teach the robot by moving the Motoman links by pressing the different buttons (4).

To perform a rotation, the rotation button (5) must be pressed continuously, otherwise a translation is performed. In the handle there is also the speed button (6) that allows doubling, tripling or quadrupling the speed, the gripper open (7) and close (8) buttons, the save way point button (9), the trajectories buttons (10) and delete button (11). Saving way points is only possible in teach mode. In playback mode the user must choose trajectory 1, 2, or 3 by pressing one of the buttons (10).

2.2.2 Mobile Phone

The mobile phone interface was developed to explore the use of a device available to almost everybody and because wireless communication is very interesting to the industry. This interface consists of an Android application that uses the phone's accelerometer to change the position of the robot. The graphical interface contains several buttons to select axes, to change speed, and to save and playback the trajectories. The application was developed using the online open source App Inventor for Android. Figure 10 shows a user interacting with a Motoman robot using the mobile phone interface.

Fig. 10. User interacting with a Motoman robot using a mobile phone.

Hardware
The hardware consists on a standard Android mobile phone having a 3-D accelerometer and a Bluetooth-RS232 serial adaptor connected to the robot controller (Fig. 11).

Fig. 11. Hardware used in the mobile phone interface: left) Android mobile phone having a 3-D accelerometer; right) Bluetooth to RS232 serial adaptor.

Figure 12 presents the local axes system of the mobile phone application, which the user should align with the robot global axes for a proper use.

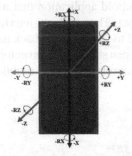

Fig. 12. Axes definition in the phone application.

Software
The software was developed in App Inventor 2 for Android, as mentioned previously [10]. It consists of the App Inventor Designer, Fig. 13, and App Inventor Blocks Editor, Fig. 14.

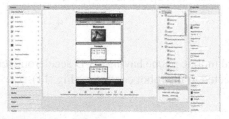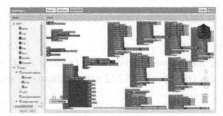

Fig. 13. Layout of App Inventor Designer.   **Fig. 14.** Layout of App Inventor Block Editor.

The App Inventor Designer aims to design the application's graphical interface: to choose the configuration and position of icons, buttons, images, drop lists, checkboxes, text, etc. The App Inventor Blocks Editor is where the icons, buttons, sliders, checkboxes, etc., placed in the App Inventor Designer are defined and programmed. The software is constituted by blocks with different functions, which interconnect through conditions, states or variables to form algorithms.

Operating Mode

The first step to use the application is to establish communication with the robot via Bluetooth, clicking in the "Conectar/Connect" icon. Selecting this icon provides a list of wireless networks. The user must select the network of the Bluetooth serial adapter and enter his password. Then should select the "Iniciar/Start" icon to place the robot in its initial position. The "Sair/Exit" icon ends the interaction at any time. There are a series of icons that correspond to the individual translation or rotation of the end effector. To select an axis the mobile phone must be shaken in that axis direction. Only one axis can be selected at once. To modify the speed of the end effector, the "Velocidade/Speed" slide can be shifted to the right to double, triple or quadruple the speed, relatively to the predefined robot's minimum speed. To close the Motoman gripper, the "Fechar Garra/Close Gripper" icon should be selected.

The "Guardar Coordenada/Save Coordinate" icon allows to save robot positions. All positions of the taught trajectory are saved in a text document (.txt) and to playback the saved trajectory a simple click on the "Selecionar Trajetória/Select Trajectory" icon is needed. The interface has no limit on stored positions. Figure 15 presents the application mentioned.

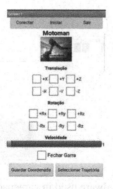

Fig. 15. Android application layout for the Motoman robot.

2.2.3 Gamepad

The gamepad is a small and light device and is easy to handle. It is widely used in video games and in machine control, being a very common device. This interface consists in using gamepad device to control the Motoman HP3L physically and in a virtual mode, using Matlab software. In virtual mode, the user interacts with a virtual Motoman HP3L robot through a Matlab GUI (Graphical User Interface). It is like an offline programming, where the robot is manipulated virtually. In physical mode, the real robot control is done in the GUI and using RS232 communication with the robot controller NX100. In other words, it is possible to graphically visualize the virtual robot movements that are occurring in real time. The RS232 communication can be done through the RS232 serial port or through the Bluethooth-RS232 adapter. Figure 16 shows the user using the gamepad interface.

Hardware

The hardware consists of a gamepad, in a PC with Matlab software and in the RS232 converters, shown in Fig. 17.

Fig. 16. User using a gamepad to interact with Motoman.

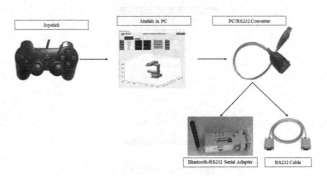

Fig. 17. Hardware used in gamepad interface.

To provide the interaction it was necessary to assign the needed functions to several buttons and sticks as shown in Fig. 18. Figure 19 shows the axes orientation in the gamepad.

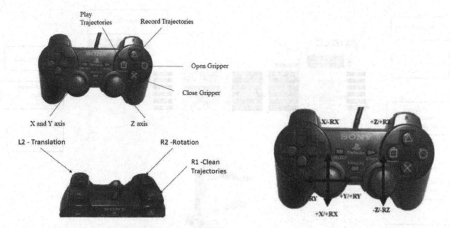

Fig. 18. Function of each stick and buttons of the gamepad.

Fig. 19. Axes orientation in the gamepad.

Software

The GUI created in Matlab features a Motoman HP3L and a set of blocks and buttons with different functions. It has the "Start Position" button to move the Motoman to its home position, the "Close Gripper" button to close or open the gripper, the "Program Terminate" button to end the interaction, and the option to turn on the gamepad, that allows the switching between the physical mode and the virtual mode. Near the left upper corner the sliders of each axis, X, Y, Z, Rx, Ry, Rz, and their values are shown. The sliders can be operated to move Motoman. The rotation and translation step values are the same as in the other interfaces.

Near the right upper corner are indicated the value of the angles returned by the robot, the angles theta1, theta2, theta3, theta4, theta5, theta6 corresponding to the conversion, through the internal inverse kinematics of the robot, to the coordinates X, Y, Z, Rx, Ry, Rz. Figure 20 shows the GUI and the description of this interface.

Operating Mode

Translations are performed with the constant pressure of the L2 button, and at a same time selecting the axis by manipulating the left or right analog sticks according to Fig. 19. For rotations it is necessary to constantly press button R2, and at a same time select the axis as before.

The user can open and close the gripper by pressing the respective buttons. The user can also record way points, playback a trajectory and delete it. The interface is capable of recording a trajectory with unlimited number of way points.

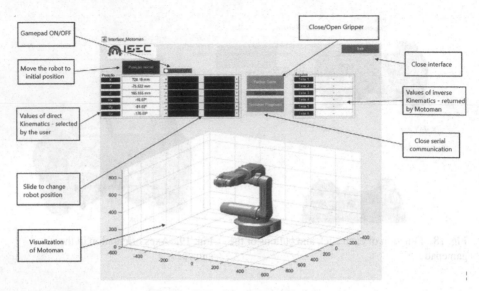

Fig. 20. GUI of the gamepad interface.

3 Results and Discussions

Usability tests are tests that aim to quantify and qualify the interaction between a user and a certain product or service. It is mostly applied in the evaluation of software, hardware and websites. They make a major contribution to product development as they allow usability issues to be detected at the development stage so that they can be fixed and improved until final release and mass production. Thus, usability test are often applied to prototypes with different details and finishes, to arrive at a better product. A typical test consists of asking several users to experiment the product and then answer a questionnaire about the product usability. The analysis of the survey results allow to highlight user issues and opinions, weaknesses and strengths of the product [11].

The model adopted to perform the usability testing is the Usefulness, Satisfaction and Ease of use (USE) model. This model is based on the evaluation of four parameters: usability, ease of use, ease of learning and satisfaction. These parameters are evaluated by 30 questions, each rated in a scale from 1 to 7, where 1 represents the lower scale, "completely disagree", and 7 represents the higher scale, "completely agree" [12].

The procedure for the application of the tests consists of 5 stages:

1. Presentation of the different interfaces and explanation of the mode of operation to each participant;
2. Explanation of the usability tests;
3. Execution of the task by the participant: use the interface to manipulate the robot, and move an object from location A to location B, record and reproduce trajectories and adjust the speed.
4. Answering the questionnaire by the participant;

5. General evaluation of each interface, clarification of doubts, suggestions and improvements.

The usability tests were applied to 18 students and each evaluated the four interfaces. The results of the usability tests are presented in Fig. 21. The questions are divided in Usability (1), Ease of Use (2), Ease of learning (3) and Satisfaction (4).

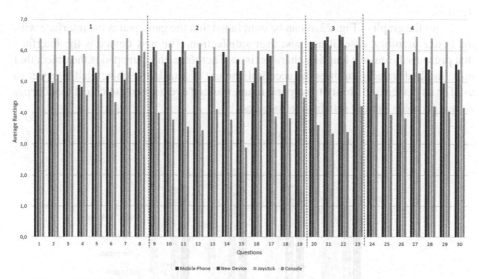

Fig. 21. Results of the application of the usability tests – Average by question, grouped in four parameters: Usability (1), Ease of Use (2), Ease of learning (3) and Satisfaction (4).

When analyzing the graph the first evidence of the results is the low teach pendant (console) interface rating on all questions. The questions with lower scores are questions 15 "I can use it without written instructions", 21 "I easily remember how to use it", 22 "It is easy to learn to use it", 20 "I learned to use it quickly", 11 "It is user friendly", 14 "Using it is effortlessly", with the scores of 2.9, 3.3, 3.4, 3.6, 3.6, 3.8, respectively. This confirms the usability problems previously mentioned about the teach pendant. It has many icons and keys to monitor the robot, requires knowledge of the Inform programming language, it is complex and unintuitive, and several keys have to be pressed simultaneously.

The new cube device has better results in questions 9, 10, 11, 20, 21 and 22. The results show that in the cubic shape, the buttons and how they are distributed helps the user to have intuitive and easy-to-learn interaction. The lowest result is found in question 6 "It saves me time when I use it", averaging 4.7. Nevertheless it is better scored in this question than the teach pendant. Question 13 "It is flexible" is not as well scored as the gamepad because of the shape of the extension of new device that is a parallelepiped, which can make it difficult to handle.

The mobile phone interface scored the lowest on question 18 "I can recover from mistakes quickly and easily" and on question 4 "It gives me more control over activities in my life". Both were scored under 4.9 because the device's method of selecting the moving axis with accelerometer readings has been found to be very sensitive, leading to unwanted movements of the robot. The highest rating was found in question 22 "It is easy to learn to use it", maybe because the mobile phone is an everyday object.

The gamepad interface turned out to be the highest scored interaction device. The highest values were found in question 3 "Is it useful", question 14 "Using it is effortless" and question 25 "I would recommend it to a friend" averaging about 6.7. Even in its lowest scored questions it was assessed with similar or better score of the other interface devices.

From the graph of Fig. 22, it can be concluded that the gamepad is the interface with the better usability, ease of use, and user satisfaction. The new device is the interface that presents the easiest learning characteristic. Therefore, the gamepad is the object that most facilitates and simplifies the accomplishment of a task, the object that is easier to use for its design and ability to respond to unexpected events, and the object that during its use provides greater satisfaction to users.

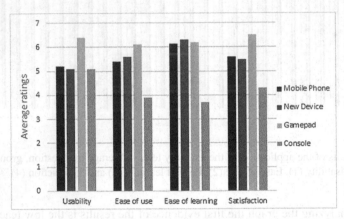

Fig. 22. Results of the application of the usability tests – Average by parameter.

4   Conclusions

An easy and simple interaction between humans and robots is perceived as crucial in the industry and in education in robotics, today. Growing relevance is given to parameters of usability, ease of use, ease of learning and satisfaction, which are often overlooked by manufacturers, lecturers and managers.

The present educational project was developed in the context of a Master Electrical Engineering Dissertation using students of different levels to evaluate the usability of four interfaces to a Motoman HP3L robot. The interaction between students of different levels has the advantage of higher motivation for the area of robotics programming and better learning outcome.

It was concluded that some of the described interfaces allow to simplify the interaction between the user and the robot. However, through the results of usability tests, some new improvements to the interfaces were demonstrated. In the developed new cube device the software should be modified so that while the user is pushing a button the robot movement remains constant, and the robot is stopped only when the button is released. This change will save time in task execution. The extension of new cube device, which is shaped like a parallelepiped, should be replaced by a cylinder shaped extension and an insertable stand, which will provide greater comfort for the user's handling.

The mobile phone interface can be improved by placing an icon to stop the readings of the accelerometer of the phone at any time, freezing the moving axis selection, as it was very sensitive to the user movements on the phone. Another solution to be tested would be to use the gyroscope together with the phone accelerometer.

The gamepad interface is the interface that satisfies the larger number of questionnaire parameters in the interaction with the robot, partly because it mainly consists of two joystick handlers that allows a quick exchange of the selected axis to be moved and also because it is ergonomic and pleasant to use. The virtual mode operation allows the testing of the robot programming using a virtual robot before actuating on the real one.

With this work, the lab was equipped with new real and virtual interface tools, increasing the training options of students.

As future work, it is proposed to improve the interfaces as described, and apply the usability tests again to evaluate their influence. It is also proposed to integrate the best interface characteristics in the new cube device, substituting the movement buttons with a X–Y gamepad handler (joystick) on one of the new device's main face and a Z-movement joystick in the extension. This Z-movement joystick should be usable with the hand that is holding the new interface device. A GUI should also be added to the new device's main face.

Acknowledgements. The authors acknowledge Fundação para a Ciência e a Tecnologia (FCT) for the financial support to the project UIDB/00048/2020.

Compliance with ethical standards.

Conflict of Interest. All authors declare that they have no conflict of interest.

References

1. Villani, V., Pini, F., Leali, F., Secchi, C.: Survey on human–robot collaboration in industrial settings: safety, intuitive interfaces and applications. Mechatronics **55**, 248–266 (2018)
2. Scholtz, J.: Theory and evaluation of human robot interactions. In: 36th Annual Hawaii International Conference on System Sciences, USA (2003)
3. Esmaeilian, B., Behdad, S., Wang, B.: The evolution and future of manufacturing: a review. J. Manuf. Syst. **39**, 79–100 (2016)
4. Ergonomics of human-system interaction — Part 110: Interaction principles. ISO 9241–110:2020(en).
5. Berg, J., Lu, S.: Review of interfaces for industrial human-robot interaction. Curr. Robot Rep. **1**, 27–34 (2020)

6. Maurtua, I., Fernández, I., Tellaeche, A., Kildal, J., Susperregi, L., Ibarguren, A., et al.: Natural multimodal communication for human–robot collaboration. Int. J. Adv. Robot Syst. (2017)
7. Ivaldi, S., Lefort, S., Peters, J., Chetouani, M., Provasi, J., Zibetti, E.: Towards engagement models that consider individual factors in HRI: on the relation of extroversion and negative attitude towards robots to gaze and speech during a human–robot assembly task. Int. J. Soc. Robot. (2017)
8. RobotWorx. https://www.robots.com/robots/motoman-hp3
9. Motoman NX100 Controler - HP3 Manipulator Manual, Motoman Incorporated (2007)
10. MIT App Inventor: http://appinventor.mit.edu/explore/designer-blocks
11. What is usability testing? https://www.experienceux.co.uk/faqs/what-is-usability-testing/
12. Lund, A.M.: Measuring usability with the USE questionnaire. Usability Interface **8**(2), 3–6 (2001)

Analysis of Physical Fitness Indicators and Metabolic Risk in University Students During the Covid-19 Pandemic with the Support of a Technological Platform

E. Loaiza-Dávila[1]([⊠]) [iD], J. Mocha-Bonilla[1] [iD], J. Hernández Valdebenito[2] [iD],
and L. Ruíz Jiménez[1] [iD]

[1] Universidad Técnica de Ambato, Facultad de Ciencias Humanas y de la Educación, Unidad de Investigación y Desarrollo FCHE, Carrera PAFD, Ambato, Ecuador
{e.loaiza,ja.mocha,la.jimenez}@uta.edu.ec
[2] Director de Ciencias e Investigación de la Sociedad Chilena para la Educación Física, Recreación y la Salud, SCHEFRES, Santiago_de_Chile, Chile
jhernandez@educacionfisicachile.cl

Abstract. With the arrival of the pandemic, we proposed to analyze indicators of physical condition and metabolic risk in university students in Ecuador to establish prevention strategies. A cross-sectional study was applied in a sample of 400 university students in Ecuador (77.3% male and 22.7% female). Physical fitness and metabolic risk indicators were assessed using the R-Fit physical fitness and metabolic risk assessment platform. The body composition parameters calculated were waist circumference, fat percentage, muscle mass, residual mass and visceral fat, allowing categorization of metabolic risk levels. The results between the groups by sex determined statistically significant differences at a level of $P \leq 0.05$, in all body composition parameters, with higher percentages in risk levels in the male sex. In relation to the level of metabolic risk, no significant differences were observed at a level of $P \geq 0.05$, showing that in the risk levels the female group was found and in the elite levels mostly the male group. It is concluded that the R-Fit platform determines several parameters for the study of body composition and metabolic risk, analyzes very large samples and in a simple manner, allows categorization and application of statistics in relation to metabolic risk.

Keywords: Physical condition · Metabolic risk · Pandemic · Technological platform · Physiological indicators

1 Introduction

With the arrival of the pandemic at the end of 2019, which worsened worldwide for the year 2020, in Ecuador health and biosecurity standards were established to try to mitigate the effects of covid-19 [1], however, on several occasions the confinement of the population was established due to the high levels of contagion, This type of mandatory quarantine to which the population was not accustomed has produced levels

© Springer Nature Switzerland AG 2022
M. Botto-Tobar et al. (Eds.): ICAT 2021, CCIS 1535, pp. 53–64, 2022.
https://doi.org/10.1007/978-3-031-03884-6_4

of sedentary lifestyle due to lack of regular physical activity, so that throughout the year 2020 the Ecuadorian population led a sedentary lifestyle because of sarcov-2 [2]. These types of sedentary behaviors in addition to physical inactivity and inadequate nutrition produce a state of vulnerability in people, especially the so-called disorders of metabolic order product of confinement, since individuals spend between 6 and 8 h sitting [3] in front of their computers attending intellectual activities, work, educational and academic activities that are currently developed virtually.

Metabolic syndrome is one of the main public health problems worldwide, a consequence of the consumption of hypercalorific diets and low energy expenditure [4], i.e., a set of obesity risk factors associated with cardiovascular diseases CVD, presenting high concentrations in triglycerides, cholesterol and glucose, which are considered predictors of morbidity and mortality [5]. According to WHO, CVD is the leading cause of death worldwide, it has been estimated that during 2015 17.7 million people died from this cause, in turn each year 6.7 million died due to cerebral vascular accidents or stroke. To control these effects, all WHO member countries agreed on the "Global Action Plan for the Prevention and Control of Nocommunicable Diseases 2013–2020", which aims to reduce NCDs by 2025. Therefore, it is essential to assess the nutritional status of the individual, as obesity is a metabolic and nutritional disorder that leads to several health consequences [6].

The nutritional status of an individual can be assessed using simple and inexpensive techniques, where anthropometry is fundamental to analyze body composition [7], the simplest method is the assessment by means of the Body Mass Index BMI, another method used is the measurement of body fat GC, also to evaluate comorbidities the waist and hip index CC is used, being that the waist circumference is a predictive indicator of one or more metabolic risk factors [8], as well as the waist height index ICE which allows to evaluate abdominal fat, being a predictor of metabolic cardiovascular risk [9]; being that this was the highest cause of mortality in the pandemic stage, since 75% of deaths were associated with underlying cardiovascular, cardiac and diabetes diseases [10].

Based on the above, it has been proposed to integrate the parameters of metabolic risk assessment that is performed in person using the ISAK anthropometry method [11], however, for the health confinement stage, an intelligent platform was developed with the requirements based on anthropometry formulas to perform the assessment of physical fitness and metabolic risk online (R-fit platform); What makes the use and management of the platform useful in times of pandemic is the fact that it provides immediate answers related to the individual's physical and metabolic condition. The platform provides a benchmark, i.e., a significant amount of data in qualitative form, i.e., information related to the metabolic risk presented by a person being evaluated; The entry and collection of data, as well as the final reading "Scoring" R-Fit (indicator of the level of physical condition and metabolic risk), allows the evaluation to have a personalized report which is sent by email, that is, to create a metabolic report of the person who enters their personal data, so the research group set out to analyze indicators of physical condition and metabolic risk in university students in Ecuador to establish prevention strategies through the use of the R-FIT technology platform.

2 State of the Art

Body mass index plays an important role in a person's physical activity, hence physical fitness; the purpose of the study was to determine the relationship between BMI and VO2max in a population of physical therapy students, a six-minute walk test including heart rate, blood pressure Spo2 and dyspnea using the Borg scale was used. Some results show that performing more hours of weekly physical activity results in higher VO2max and lower BMI values [12].

On the other hand, technological applications have been used to analyze BMI; one study shows the creation of a mobile application called "eHealth-UTA", an automated system that allows obtaining data to perform a Body Mass Index analysis, determining body composition and basal metabolism of individuals; the study takes the BMI table established by the World Health Organization, while for basal metabolism it applies the Harris-Benedict formula to suggest the daily caloric intake. It is concluded that technology is fundamental when applying comprehensive health programs and analyzing the metabolism of individuals [13].

While analyzing body fat equations based on BMI: Womersley (BMIWOMERSLEY), Jackson (BMIJACKSON), Deurenberg (BMIDEURENBERG) and Gallagher (BMIGALLAGHER) it is stated that it presents a large error in white Hispanics and non-Hispanic whites, which is due to the inability of BMI in accounting for the differences between fat mass and fat-free mass, therefore, variations in muscle strength should be accounted for through relative grip strength (RHG), which may help improve the accuracy of a BMI-based body fat equation. Practitioners who can use the BMINICKERSON to assess adiposity in individuals are encouraged [14].

There is now varied supporting literature related to metabolic risk or syndrome [15], defining it as a highly dangerous disease, since it affects the person in a multisystemic way, being obesity and insulin resistance, the ones considered highly dangerous; from here arises the need to strengthen the recommendations of weight control, decrease of sugar intake and increase of physical activity as a prevention in the mortality of cardiovascular and cerebrovascular diseases. There are scientific works related to anthropometric parameters, including a study that refers to the diagnostic accuracy of the triponderal mass index to identify the phenotype of metabolic risk in obese children and adolescents, which presents a cross-sectional study with the measurement of anthropometric parameters, for which the ROC curves, the z-score value of the zsIMC, the ICT waist index and several FOMS components were used; it is concluded that the diagnostic accuracy of the IMT is very similar to the BMI and the ICT, and it is also simpler to identify the metabolic risk of children and adolescents who present obesity in both sexes [16].

In turn, the waist-height index (WHI) has been studied and is widely used to assess abdominal fat at all ages. However, abdominal fat (visceral fat) is associated with high risk and metabolic complications associated with blood levels of glucose, cholesterol and triglycerides. It is concluded that the ICE method is a more efficient indicator versus BMI to identify metabolic risk in school-aged children [17]. Another study related to abdominal circumference presents cut-off points in an adult population in Cuenca, Ecuador. The study presents a random sampling in both sexes, performed by anthropometric measurements and laboratory studies. ROC curve groupings were performed to determine the abdominal circumference cut-off points according to metabolic syndrome criteria. It is concluded that the cut-off points in the study sample differ from those proposed for the Latin American population [18].

When talking about metabolic risks, the metabolically healthy obese phenotype FOMS can be appreciated, this phenotype is associated with a lower risk of cardio-vascular disease and type 2 diabetes in adulthood. The study establishes the predictive capacity of the so-called triponderal mass index IMT, the ROC curve was used to find the cut-off point of the body mass index, the z-score value, the waist-to-height ratio and the FOMS components plasma glycemia and triglycerides, HDL cholesterol and blood pressure. It is concluded that there is accuracy of IMT to identify metabolic risk similar to BMI and ICT [19]; finally a study reveals that the intake of extra virgin olive oil EVOO whose phenolic compound oleocanthal OC, presents great antioxidant and anti-inflammatory properties, it is concluded that EVOO supplementation with a high concentration of OC is associated with the reduction of body weight and body mass index; therefore, benefits were obtained in the parameters to reduce the metabolic risk of the study subjects [20].

The benefits of physical activity and exercise are fundamental for individuals. We can find scientific evidence in the medical conditions of the person, this includes cardio-vascular disease and premature mortality, physical activity provides multiplex benefits in the system: Immune, hemostatic, autonomic, hormonal and metabolic, therefore, are multiplex in the benefits that bring the practice of physical exercise; however, it is nec-essary before prescribing exercise to make an analysis of cardiovascular, osteoarticular and metabolic risks, for self-care. This is how integral health becomes a challenge to address the problems and establish public policies [21].

3   Methodology

The present study was conducted under a quantitative approach and a cross-sectional descriptive research design based on the analytical-deductive method because of its theoretical foundation towards the problem statement and the generation of results that have contributed to self-care in the Covid-19 pandemic stage.

Subjects. We worked with a study sample corresponding to 400 university students of the Pedagogy of Physical Activity and Sport career of the Technical University of Ambato in Ecuador, ages between 18 and 37 years old respectively.

Instrument. To know the body composition and calculate the physical condition and metabolic risk, the R-Fit Physical Evaluation and Metabolic Risk Platform was applied as an instrument, created, validated and patented by the Chilean Society of Physical Education, Recreation and Health –SCHEFRES. The platform provides measurements such as bioimpedanciometry, the 4-fold method and measurement with tape measure, along with basic and physiological input data of the person, it was tested through an in-person metabolic census conducted during the years 2008 to 2012 with 7. 575 people evaluated in central Chile [22], however, due to the pandemic stage, adjustments were made to the system to operate in an online way; passwords were established to enter and register data for each of the participants, in order to contribute to personal health care. The evaluation was carried out by applying the online evaluation instructions developed for non-face-to-face evaluations for the COVID-19 emergency.

The parameters of the anthropometric equations proposed make it possible to assertively adapt 99.5% to the entire world population since they have standard deviation derivation for all ethnic groups and age groups over 15 years of age. Although the special population study done in Chile has the somatic nuance of that country, the standards used are internationally validated by the ISAK and taking into account that the different ways of evaluating the human form are concentrated in the anthropometric model of Heat-Carter, considered a quantified description of the physical form, which is expressed through a numerical and graphical scale, with the objective of universally conciliating these protocols.

A virtual training process was developed on the ISAK level 1 anthropometric method, specifically the measurement of body weight, height, hip, relaxed right arm, right medial leg and waist circumference, using SECA home scales, measuring rod and anthropometric tapes, as well as the correct measurement of systolic and diastolic blood pressure with home blood pressure monitors.

As complementary data, data related to chronological age, sex, physical practice or inactivity, frequency of training, as well as tobacco and alcohol consumption were requested on the platform and validated by experts in nutrition, physical activity and training, representatives of the Chilean Society of Physical Education, Recreation and Health.

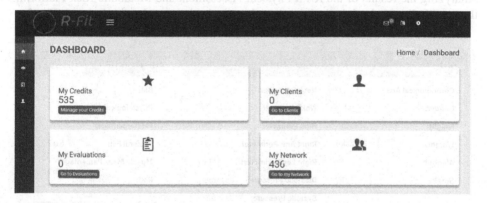

Fig. 1. R-Fit platform.

Technical Characteristics of the R-Fit Platform
The special characteristics of Big Data mean that its data quality faces multiple challenges. These are known as the 5 Vs: Volume, Velocity, Variety, Veracity and Value, which define the creation of the platform.

It is an anthropometric analysis software, remote and/or face-to-face anamnesis was developed as follows:

Frontend. The frontend (or visualization of the panel on the web) is developed in JavaScript, using the Angular framework. This frontend communicates with the API (backend) through HTTP requests (by Ajax), where all the logic of the system is worked.

Backend. The backend (or server side) is developed in PHP 7 using the Laravel 6.x framework with connection to MySQL databases (MariaDB). The backend of R-Fit is a closed API, to which you can connect the frontend necessary for the operation of the system (currently it is designed only for web but is working to be implemented via App).

Currently the server where the system is located has an uptime of 99.9% and supports multiple evaluations simultaneously. This allows 3,200 simultaneous operations while maintaining the maximum efficiency capacity of the R-Fit platform.

The information generated by the platform can be used to identify user behaviors through data mining techniques since the qualitative value selection of its "Big Data" (mostly landed data is part of the anthropometric assessment, metabolic risk habit conditions used by the WHO), and the interaction of its "Data Science" data, allows to designate ranges of metabolic risk classification and fitness levels since it has a unique scoring range. The interaction of its "Data Science" data allows the designation of metabolic risk classification ranges and physical condition levels, since it has an exclusive scoring range.

4 Results

Analyzing the results of the R-Fit Physical Assessment and Metabolic Risk Platform, the calculation of physiological data based on the basic input data is observed (Fig. 2).

BASIC INFORMATION				PHYSIOLOGICAL DATA	
Chronological Age:	18	Neck Perimeter:	34 Cm.	BMI:	16.67
Gender:	Male	Waist Perimeter:	69.00 Cm.	Physiological Age:	5
Height:	180 Cm.	Hips Perimeter:	90 Cm.	Fat Percentage:	5.14%
Weight:	54.00 Kg.	Right Arm Perimeter:	26.00 Crn.	Visceral Fat:	5 a 7
Alcohol:	No	Right Leg Perimeter:	47 Cm.	Muscle Mass Percentage:	58.86%
Smoke:	No	Diastolic Pressure:	65 mmHg.	IMB:	1296 calories
		Systolic Pressure:	102 mmHg.		

Fig. 2. Calculation of physiological data based on the basic input data in the R.Fit platform.

The physiological data calculated are BMI, physiological age, percentage of fat (%), visceral fat in stages, percentage of muscle mass (%) and IMB in total calories.

Similarly, the platform performs the calculation of data that characterize body composition, such as the percentage of residual mass, fat weight, muscle weight, residual mass, as well as visceral fat determined in points, specified and categorized in different stages (Fig. 3).

The R-fit platform performs the calculation of fat weight, muscle weight, residual mass; in addition to the percentages of fat, muscle mass, residual mass, which are represented in two types of graph.

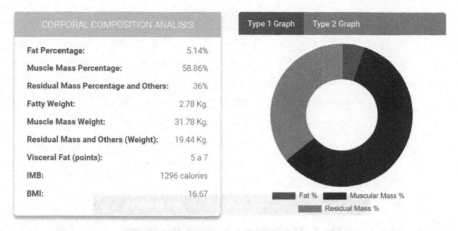

Fig. 3. Body composition analysis and percentage distribution graphs of the study variables.

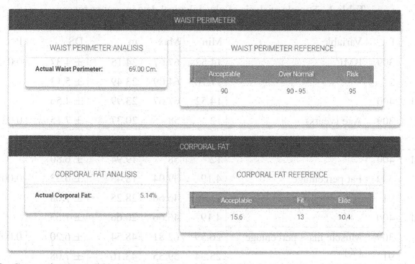

Fig. 4. Categorization analysis according to risk of waist circumference, body fat, muscle mass and visceral fat values.

Based on the waist circumference analysis, 3 levels are established (acceptable - above normal - risk), body fat (acceptable - fit - elite), muscle mass (acceptable - normal - fit - elite) and visceral fat (good - bad - very bad).

In relation to the level of metabolic risk, the R-Fit platform determines the individual level of each person evaluated, based on the entry level calculated by the body composition profile, the scoring calculated on the basis of physical activity or inactivity, the frequency of practice or the seasonality of physical inactivity (Fig. 5).

In the figure the entry level, scoring and class level of the evaluated are determined.

The minimum (Min), maximum (Max), mean (m) values and their standard deviations (SD), BMI, physiological age, percentage of fat (%), percentage of muscle mass

Entry Level	Scoring	Class Level
High Risk	3.6 - 7	Basic Level
Risk	2.6 - 3.5	Basic Level
Sedentary	1.1 - 2.5	Basic Level
Normal Sedentary	0.3 - 1	Intermediate Level
Normal	-0.5 - 0.2	Intermediate Level
Fit	-1.5 - -0.6	Intermediate Level
Sports	-2.9 - -1.6	Advanced Level
Atletic	-3.9 - -3	Advanced Level
Elite	-5 - -4	Advanced Level

Fig. 5. Metabolic risk level of R-Fit platform.

Table 1. Sample analysis of physiological data in groups by sex.

Sex	f	Variable	Min	Max	m	DS	P
M	309	BMI	14.52	67.67	24.15	± 4.37	0.032*
F	21		17.78	64.09	23.49	± 5.13	
Total	400		14.52	67.67	23.99	± 4.56	
M	309	Age (years)	12	58	20.37	± 7.15	0.039*
F	91		13	33	18.48	± 5.25	
Total	400		12	58	19.94	± 6.80	
M	309	Fat percentage	4.19	39.04	18.43	± 6.23	0.00*
F	91	(%)	11.30	46.66	28.25	± 7.08	
Total	400		4.19	46.66	20.66	± 7.63	
M	309	Muscle mass percentage	26.59	62.81	48.54	± 6.20	0.00*
F	91	(%)	25.34	59.55	43.16	± 7.08	
Total	400		25.34	62.81	47.32	± 6.79	
M	309	Percent residual mass (%)	27	36	33.04	± 1.34	0.00*
F	91		27.01	33.01	28.59	± 1.63	
Total	400		27	36	32.03	± 2.34	
M	309	BMR	960	4368	1661.59	± 314.45	0.00*
F	91	(calories)	864	3456	1246.59	± 285.27	
Total	400		864	4368	1567.18	± 353.60	

(%), percentage of residual mass (%) and BMI were analyzed, determining their significant differences at levels of (*) P ≤ 0.05, between the variables under analysis by sex groups. The specific data based on the study sample allowed us to observe both descriptive and statistical differences by sex groups (Table 1).

The analysis of the 400 students evaluated allowed us to establish a percentage distribution of the different categories based on the established parameters (Table 2).

Table 2. Percentage distribution analysis of body composition variables in groups by sex.

Variable	Level	Sex					
		Male		Female		Total	
		f	%	f	%	f	%
Waist circumference	Acceptable	220	71.2	86	94.5	306	76.5
	Above normal	43	13.9	4	4.4	47	11.8
	Risk	46	14.9	1	1.1	47	11.8
Total		309	100	91	100	400	100
P		0.000*					
Body fat	Risk	31	10.0	0	0	31	7.8
	Acceptable	35	11.3	2	2.2	37	9.3
	Fit and in shape	43	13.9	3	3.3	46	11.5
	Elite	200	64.7	86	94.5	286	71.5
Total		309	100	91	100	400	100
P		0.000*					
Muscle mass	Acceptable	32	10.4	30	33.0	62	15.5
	Normal	35	11.3	21	23.1	56	14.0
	Fit and in shape	58	18.8	13	14.3	71	17.8
	Elite	184	59.5	27	29.7	211	52.8
Total		309	100	91	100	400	100
P		0.000*					
Visceral fat	Good	144	46.6	29	31.9	173	43.3
	Bad	68	22.0	36	39.6	104	26.0
	Very Bad	97	31.4	26	28.6	123	30.8
Total		309	100	91	100	400	100
P		0.003*					

The frequencies (f) and percentages (%) of the variables waist circumference, body fat, muscle mass and visceral fat in their different levels were analyzed by sex groups, determining significant differences between them at a level of (*) $P \leq 0.05$.

In relation to the waist circumference variable, most of the members of the study sample presented an acceptable level, especially in the female group, where only one person was found to be at risk. In relation to the body fat variable, the male group presented a percentage of those evaluated at risk, with the exception of the female group in which no risk was found. In relation to the variable of muscle mass, a little more than 50% of those evaluated were at an elite level, unlike the female group in which only about 1/3 of those evaluated were at this level. In relation to the variable of visceral fat, the male group presented the highest percentage in the good level, in contrast to the female group in which the majority were in the bad level.

After evaluating the 400 students, the percentage distribution of each level of metabolic risk was analyzed by sex group and in general for the study sample (Table 3).

Table 3. Analysis of percentage distribution of metabolic risk levels in groups by sex.

Metabolic risk level	Sex					
	Male		Female		Total	
	f	%	f	%	f	%
High Risk/Basic Level	4	1.3	3	3.3	7	1.8
Basic Risk/Level	12	3.9	6	6.6	18	4.5
Sedentary/Basic Level	29	9.4	9	9.9	38	9.5
Normal Sedentary/Intermediate Level	21	6.8	10	11	31	7.8
Normal/Intermediate Level	32	10.4	8	8.8	40	10
Fit/Intermediate Level	44	14.2	14	15.4	58	14.5
Sporty/Advanced Level	76	24.6	17	18.7	93	23.3
Athletic/Advanced Level	42	13.6	9	9.9	51	12.8
Elite/Advanced Level	49	15.9	15	16.5	64	16
Total	309	100	91	100	400	100
P	0.598**					

The frequencies (f) and percentages (%) of the metabolic risk levels were analyzed by sex groups, determining significant differences between them at the level of (**) $P \geq 0.05$. The sample analysis determined that the male sex group showed that 14.6% of those evaluated between the high risk, risk and sedentary levels belonged to a basic level of physical activity practices, in contrast to the female sex group where 19.8% were at these levels. Among the normal sedentary, normal and fit levels, with an intermediate level of physical activity practice, 31.6% of the male group and 35.2% of the female group were found. Finally, among the sports, athletic and elite levels, with an advanced level of physical activity practice, 54.1% of those evaluated were found in the male group and 45.1% in the female group. Despite showing that there are descriptive differences between the groups by sex, at the statistical level no significant differences were found with a value of $P \geq 0.05$, showing the equality in levels of metabolic risk between the study groups.

5 Conclusions

The application of technological platforms for the evaluation of body composition profile and metabolic risk levels allows the evaluation of any number of samples to be evaluated in face-to-face and virtual conditions, thanks to its diversity of data calculation, speed of analysis, ease and specificity of collection and entry of input data.

The evaluation of the study sample of university students of physical activity and sport pedagogy allowed to describe a general profile of body composition and a categorization in the different levels of metabolic risk, scientifically constructed and validated by the R-Fit tool.

The body composition profile, taking into account specific variables of fat percentage, muscle mass and residual mass, allowed us to show statistically significant differences between the groups by sex. In relation to the levels of metabolic risk, despite showing descriptive differences, there were no statistically significant differences between these groups.

Acknowledgement. The authors would like to thank the Technical University of Ambato (UTA) and the Directorate of Research and Development (DIDE) for their support for the successful execution of this work through the research project entitled "GENETIC PROFILE AS A DETERMINANT OF HEALTH AND METABOLIC RISK IN UNIVERSITY STUDENTS AFTER HOME ISOLATION", code PFCHE17.

References

1. Ruiz, G.P.: Evolución de la enfermedad por coronavirus (COVID-19) en Ecuador. La Ciencia al Servicio de la Salud, **11**(1), 5–15 (2020). https://doi.org/10.47244/cssn.Vol11.Iss1.441
2. Seong, J.Y.: Association between aerobic exercise and handgrip strength in adults: a cross-sectional study based on data from the Korean National Health and Nutrition Examination Survey (2014–2017). J. Nutr. Health Aging **24**(6), 619–626 (2020)
3. Ricci, F.I.: Recommendations for physical inactivity and sedentary behavior during the coronavirus disease (COVID-19) pandemic. Front. Public Health, **8**, 199 (2020). https://doi.org/10.3389/fpubh.2020.00199
4. Fernández-Travieso, J.C.: Síndrome metabólico y riesgo cardiovascular. Revista CENIC. Ciencias Biológicas **47**(2), 106–119 (2016)
5. Veloza, L., et al.: Variabilidad de la frecuencia cardíaca como factor predictor de las enfermedades cardiovasculares. Revista Colombiana de Cardiología **26**(4), 205–210 (2019). https://doi.org/10.1016/j.rccar.2019.01.006
6. La Daza, C.H.: obesidad: un desorden metabólico de alto riesgo para la salud. Colomb. Med. **33**(2), 72–80 (2020)
7. Geraldo, A.P.: Métodos Y Técnica Antropométrica Para El Cálculo De La Composición Corporal. Revista Ingeniería, Matemáticas y Ciencias de la Información, **5**(10), 61–70 (2018). https://doi.org/10.21017/rimci.2018.v5.n10.a49
8. Domínguez-Reyes, T., et al.: Anthropometric measurements as predictive indicators of metabolic risk in a Mexican population. Nutricion hospitalaria, **34**(1), 96–101 (2017). https://doi.org/10.20960/nh.983

9. Asensi, G.D.: Critical overview of current anthropometric methods in comparison with a new index to make early detection of overweight in Spanish university students: the normalized weight-adjusted index. Nutrición hospitalaria: Órgano oficial de la Sociedad española de nutrición parenteral y enteral **35**(2), 359–367 (2018)

10. Isaifan, R.J.: The dramatic impact of Coronavirus outbreak on air quality: has it saved as much as it has killed so far? Global J. Environ. Sci. Manage. **6**(3), 275–288 (2020). https://doi.org/10.22034/gjesm.2020.03.01

11. Alcívar, J.E.: Anthropometric cardiovascular risk of university students. Rev. Cuba. Cardiol. Cir. Cardiovasc. **26**(1), 1–9 (2020)

12. Torrandell, M.X.B., Conti, J.V.: Influencia de padres, amistades y profesorado en la actividad física y la capacidad aeróbica de los jóvenes (Influence of parents, friends and teachers on physical activity and aerobic capacity on young people). Retos **42**, 714–723 (2021)

13. Mocha-Bonilla, J.A., Guerrero, J.S., Jiménez, L.A., Poveda, M.P., Barona-Oñate, R.V., Guerrero, A.G.S.: Analysis of the body composition index and basal metabolic rate through the mobile application eHealth-UTA. In: 2018 International Conference on eDemocracy & eGovernment (ICEDEG), pp. 386–391. IEEE (2018)

14. Nickerson, B.S., Esco, M.R., Fedewa, M.V., Park, K.S.: Development of a body mass index-based body fat equation: effect of handgrip strength. Med. Sci. Sports Exerc. **52**(11), 2459–2465 (2020)

15. Pereira-Rodríguez, J.E., Melo-Ascanio, J., Caballero-Chavarro, M., Rincón-Gonzales, G., Jaimes-Martin, T., Niño-Serrato, R.: Síndrome metabólico. Apuntes de interés. Revista cubana de cardiología y cirugía cardiovascular, **22**(2), 109–116 (2016)

16. Ávila-Alpirez, H., Gutiérrez-Sánchez, G., Guerra-Ordoñez, J., Ruíz-Cerino, J., Martínez-Aguilar, M.: Obesidad en adolescentes y criterios para el desarrollo de síndrome metabólico. Enfermería universitaria **15**(4), 352–360 (2018)

17. Valle-Leal, J., Abundis-Castro, L., Hernández-Escareño, J., Flores-Rubio, S.: Índice cintura-estatura como indicador de riesgo metabólico en niños. Rev. Chil. Pediatr. **87**(3), 180–185 (2016)

18. Torres-Valdez, M., et al.: Punto de corte de circunferencia abdominal para el agrupamiento de factores de riesgo metabólico: una propuesta para la población adulta de Cuenca, Ecuador. Revista argentina de endocrinología y metabolismo **53**(2), 59–66 (2016)

19. Yeste, D., et al.: Diagnostic accuracy of the tri-ponderal mass index in identifying the unhealthy metabolic obese phenotype in obese patients. Anales de Pediatría (English Edition) **94**(2), 68–74 (2021)

20. Patti, A.M., et al.: Daily use of extra virgin olive oil with high oleocanthal concentration reduced body weight, waist circumference, alanine transaminase, inflammatory cytokines and hepatic steatosis in subjects with the metabolic syndrome: a 2-month intervention study. Metabolites **10**(10), 392 (2020)

21. González, N.F., Rivas, A.D.: Actividad física y ejercicio en la mujer. Revista Colombiana de Cardiología **25**, 125–131 (2018)

22. Contreras-Órdenes, M., Hernández-Valdebenito, J., Zuleta-Alfaro, R.: Plataforma de Evaluación Física y Riesgo Metabólico RFit: un Aporte de SCHEFRES a los profesionales de la salud física, la prescripción de ejercicio físico y el entrenamiento. Revista Con-Ciencias del Deporte **2**(2), 62–88 (2020)

e-Government and e-Participation

Technologies Applied to Solve Facility Layout Problems with Resilience – A Systematic Review

Jorge Vázquez[1](✉) (iD), Juan Carlos Llivisaca[2] (iD), Daysi Ortiz[3], Israel Naranjo[3], and Lorena Siguenza-Guzman[1,4] (iD)

[1] Department of Computer Sciences, Faculty of Engineering, University of Cuenca, Cuenca, Ecuador
{jorge.vazquez,lorena.siguenza}@ucuenca.edu.ec

[2] Department of Applied Chemistry and Production Systems, Faculty of Chemical Sciences, University of Cuenca, Cuenca, Ecuador
juan.llivisaca@ucuenca.edu.ec

[3] Faculty of Systems, Electronics and Industrial Engineering, Technical University of Ambato, Ambato, Ecuador
{dm.ortiz,ie.naranjo}@uta.edu.ec

[4] Research Centre Accountancy, Faculty of Economics and Business, KU Leuven, Leuven, Belgium

Abstract. In the industry, the need to optimize daily tasks became mainly a requirement to stay competitive. The Facility Layout Problem (FLP) arises from this need and is the most used technique to improved manufacturing processes. Over the years, the distribution of the different facilities became more complex and more susceptible to interventions in their usual workflow. Hence, FLPs emerged to solve these interventions. This capacity to solve various problems is known as resilience. By searching the literature for information on technologies used to solve FLP, many software solutions can be obtained. Still, none of them manage resilience as a factor in the solution. They have also not been compiled in an analysis to determine the most modern options for existing solutions. The current study reviews the most widely used software tools that solve FLP and how these studies view resilience. A systematic literature review was applied to select relevant studies from 2015–2021. This work allowed analyzing a final sample of 133 articles obtained in two different search strings. As a result, this study identified two manners to solve FLP with software tools: using already developed tools and developing an own tool. In the former, three proprietary software were identified: MATLAB, CPLEX, and LINGO. When developing their software tool, the technology used varies significantly between studies. They use very different language programming, depending on the researcher's domain. Furthermore, the results do not find any case in which some resilience factor was part of the solution obtained.

Keywords: Facility layout problem · Resilience · Technology · Software · Solution · Systematic review

The original version of this chapter was revised: The author's name has been corrected as "Daysi Ortiz". The correction to this chapter is available at
https://doi.org/10.1007/978-3-031-03884-6_41

1 Introduction

The Facility Layout Problem (FLP) is a concept that wants to find the optimal distribution of facilities based on criteria and objectives to be met, commonly limiting the result in a set of restrictions imposed by the facility's physical space [1]. This concept is used in many areas, like industrial engineering, architecture, and optimization. FLP is a concept first developed in 1957 by Koopmans and Beckmann. Since then, many researchers have tried to solve these problems optimally. However, all the cases had something in common, the complex mathematical process required to obtain a result [2]. Moreover, these mathematical models become more complicated to solve when the number of facilities increases. It is in these cases that computers play a fundamental role in the FLP resolution. Commonly, these computer solutions use heuristic techniques and, although they do not guarantee an optimal solution, they do ensure an efficient solution [3].

The first software tool to solve these problems appeared only six years after the FLP concept was conceived. In 1963, CRAFT (Computerized Relative Allocation of Facilities Technique) was born, developed by Armor and Buffa. This is the first FLP software registered in the literature [4]. It provided a quantitative approach to solving FLP, working with an algorithm with the same name (CRAFT) [5]. From there, a diverse group of software tools appeared over the years [3]. For instance, CORELAP (Computerized Relationship Layout Planning) was developed by Lee and Moore in 1967, using an algorithm with the same name. It situated the facilities with a total closeness classification represented in a rectilinear path [6]. In 1973, Khalil presented FRAT (Facilities Relative Allocation Technique), a heuristic procedure developed in FORTRAN IV that combines several techniques suggested by other authors in previous models [7]. In 1982, Robert Johnson presented SPACECRAFT, a computerized method for allocation facilities based on the original CRAFT of 1963. But, with the difference, that SPACECRAFT is adapted to the construction of several floors [8]. CLASS (Computerized Layout solutions using Simulated annealing) is an algorithm presented in 1992 by Jajodia. As the previous tools, CLASS also had its own software to execute the algorithm. This algorithm specializes in solving layout problems in a cellular manufacturing environment [9]. Apart from these examples, there are more that demonstrate the tendency to develop a new computational solution for each new algorithm presented.

Resilience engineering is a discipline responsible for preserving the functional efficiency of a system or organization and for providing the ability of a system or organization to respond efficiently to emerging disruptions [10]. Resilience engineering has five fundamental principles: preparedness, prevention, protection, response, and recovery [10]. Over the years, the usefulness of these software tools has been overshadowed by the more powerful processing capabilities of newer computers. As a result, the most recent analysis of the existing FLP software is from 2005. In this analysis, Singh et al. [11] identify 35 different software tools. Still, the constant evolution of technology requires analysis with more contemporary studies, especially if there are no records of whether current and previous FLP software tools consider resilience principles in their operations.

This study aims to analyze the most used software tools to solve FLP and determine the most common FLP types solved with these tools. Additionally, it is examined whether current studies consider any principle of resilience engineering in their approach to solving the problem. For this, a systematic literature review is developed through the following sections. First, in Sect. 2, the methodology is described. Next, results and discussion are detailed in Sect. 3. Finally, in Sect. 4, the most relevant conclusions obtained are explained.

2   Methodology

This systematic review applies an adapted version of Barbara Kitchenham's methodology [12]. This methodology has been used for systematic literature reviews, mainly in the area of software engineering. This methodology consists of three stages: 1) Planning. 2) Carrying out the review. And, finally, 3) Reporting the review.

2.1   Planning

The planning stage was made up of five steps: 1) research questions; 2) search strategy; 3) selection criteria for primary studies; 4) selection of primary studies; and 5) quality evaluation.

Research Questions. This systematic literature review aims to identify the software tools used to solve FLP, considering the principles of resilience engineering. To meet this objective, the following research question was posed: What software tools are used to solve facility layout problems that have considered principles of resilience engineering? From this primary question, the following specific research questions were de-fined.

- RQ1. What kind of software tools are used or developed to solve facility layout problems?
- RQ2. What principles of resilience engineering are considered in facility layout problems?
- RQ3. How do studies applying resilience engineering principles solve facility layout problems?
- RQ4. How have the studies based on software tools been carried out to solve facility layout problems considering resilience engineering principles?

Search Strategy. The search strategy was performed with automatic searches. This strategy required a combination of keywords based on the research questions. For this systematic literature review, the following scientific databases were selected, Taylor & Francis, Springer Link, Scopus, Web of Science, and IEEE. The first four databases are multidisciplinary and with a comprehensive catalog of articles. IEEE was included because the literature review has a technical approach focused on software tools.

This study defined two search strings, the first considering resilience terms and the second without resilience. Both search strings were used because, in the primary studies selected with the first string, only 19 studies were accepted. The first search string defined was: *("Facility Layout Problem" OR "Facility Planning" OR "Facility Allocation Problem" OR "Resilient Facility Location" OR "RFL" OR "FLP" OR "FP" OR "FAP") AND ("Resilience engineering" OR "Resilience") AND (Software OR Comput*) AND (technolog* OR tool* OR solution*).* The second search string defined was:

(*"Facility Layout Problem" OR "Facility Planning" OR "Facility Allocation Problem"*)
AND (*Software OR Comput**) *AND (technolog* OR tool* OR solution**).

Selection Criteria for Primary Studies. The extraction criteria (EC) were used to
answer the defined research questions. The strategy was used to guarantee compliance

Table 1. Extraction Criteria (EC) utilized for primary studies

Criteria	Name	Options
RQ1. What kind of software tools are used or developed to solve facility layout problems?		
EC01	Name	
EC02	Method of obtaining the software tool	Use, Developing
EC03	Software tool license	Free, Pay
EC04	Available software tool	Available, No Available
EC05	Source code availability	Available, No Available
EC06	Tool category	Optimization, Monitoring, Modeling
RQ2. What principles of resilience engineering are considered in facility layout problems?		
EC07	Resilience Engineering Principle	Preparation, Prevention, Protection, Answer, Recovery does not apply resilience
RQ3. How do studies applying resilience engineering principles solve facility layout problems?		
EC08	Facility layout problem type	Aperiodic FLP, Capacitated FLP, Directed Circular FLP, Double-row FLP, Dynamic FLP, Fixed-Shape FLP, Location Routing Models, Loop FLP, Multi-floor FLP, Multi-objective FLP, Multiperiod FLP, Multi-row FLP, Open-field FLP, Parallel row FLP, Other
EC09	Mathematical model applied to the facility layout problem	
EC10	Algorithm used to solve the plant distribution problem	
RQ4. How have the studies based on software tools been carried out to solve facility layout problems considering resilience engineering principles?		
EC11	Phase	Analysis, Design, Implementation, Test-Ing
EC12	Type of validation	Proof of concepts, Survey, Study Case, Quasi experiment, Experiment, Prototype, Others
EC13	Approach scope	Industry, Academy
EC14	Methodology	New, Extension
EC15	Year	
EC16	Country	

with the extraction criteria and helped classify the studies. Table 1 shows the specified extraction criteria.

Selection of Primary Studies. The articles resulting from the searches in the scientific databases went through a selection process. This selection consisted of three steps: 1) evaluation of inclusion and exclusion criteria; 2) selection of articles by title; 3) selection of articles through in-depth reading.

For the first search string, the inclusion criteria included articles from the 2000s, and for the second search string, papers were considered from 2015. However, the range of years was reduced in the second search string because the results were focused on the software technology used, ignoring the resilience of the problem analyzed. Therefore, the inclusion and exclusion criteria were:

- Inclusion criteria

  – Studies using software tools to solve FLP.
  – Studies developing software tools to solve FLP.
  – Studies analyzing FLP from an approach related to resilience engineering.
  – Studies using techniques or methods related to resilience engineering in FLP.

- Exclusion criteria

  – Introductory articles or special editions for magazines, books, and conferences.
  – Duplicate studies in different sources.
  – Articles of less than five pages.
  – Articles written in other languages except for English.
  – Articles not specifying the software tool used to solve the problem.

The search results with the two search strings are listed in the following tables. Table 2 reports the individual results of the first search string, and Table 3, the individual results of the second.

Table 2. Summary of the first search string

Database	Search string result	Selected (Step 1 and 2)	Accepted (Step 3)	Percentage of the total accepted
Taylor & Francis	220	19	8	42,11%
Springer Link	137	11	2	10,53%
Scopus	22	7	3	15,79%
Web of Science	36	7	2	10,53%
IEEE	20	6	4	21,05%
TOTAL	435	50	19	

Table 3. Summary of the second search string

Database	Search string result	Selected (Step 1 and 2)	Accepted (Step 3)	Percentage of the total accepted
Taylor & Francis	149	29	18	15,59%
Springer Link	546	23	17	14,91%
Scopus	121	31	21	18,42%
Web of Science	109	66	45	39,47%
IEEE	740	27	13	11,40%
TOTAL	1665	176	114	

The total of articles selected in Steps 1 and 2 was 50, of which the total accepted papers were 19. This number was minimal for the literature review; therefore, it was necessary to expand the search results with a second search string. The parameters related to resilience were removed to focus the search on the software technology used to solve FLP. After the second round, the total of articles selected in Steps 1 and 2 was 176, of which the total of papers accepted was 114. Thus, with the results of both search strings, the sample of articles for this systematic review was 133 articles. The complete list of sources used in the literature review can be found in Appendix A.

Quality Assessment. In this study, the aspect that was considered to assess the quality of the studies was the number of citations per article. Therefore, according to Google Scholar's academic citation counter, the ranking was done in three categories: High, Medium, and Low (Table 4).

Table 4. Categories of the citations counter

Category/Score	Criteria	# Papers
High	Articles with more than five citations	81
Medium	Articles with one to five citations	33
Low	Articles without citations	19

3   Results and Discussion

This section presents the results obtained in the systematic literature review, using the Atlasti 9 software to analyze and label the content of the retrieved studies. The results are divided into two categories: 1) Metadata analysis and 2) Content analysis.

3.1 Metadata Analysis

As presented in Table 1, EC15 and EC16 contain demographic information. For EC15, the distribution of studies by country reveals the geographic area in which researchers are primarily focused on using software tools to solve the FLP. Figure 1 shows that countries such as China, India, and Iran contribute more to the scientific community in this type of study. The Asian continent is a major provider of data and analysis for solving different FLPs using software tools. The European continent contributes to a lesser extent to this area, but with the participation of more countries in this territory. In Latin America (LA), only Brazil and Mexico appear in this analysis with two studies each. Needless to say, there are more studies from LA countries that focus on the FLP. However, these studies do not specify the software tool used.

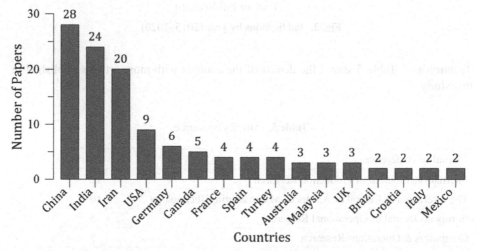

Fig. 1. Distribution of the primary studies that solve FLP with software tools by country

In EC16, the year of publication, for both search strings, the studies were considered from 2015. But, in the second case, some older results appeared in the initial results that were discarded. Considering the accepted results of both search strings, Fig. 2 shows that, from 2015 to the present day, the number of studies detailing which software tool was used to solve the problem has increased. This means that the community studying FLP began to give more importance to technology to solve these problems. In addition, the scientific community is trying to provide more efficient ways to solve these problems. This is most evident when the results of the studies explain the execution times of the software tools they used and compare these times with other studies that used similar data. For this analysis, the articles from 2021 were not included since this year has not yet finished.

Finally, in this study, 76 sources were identified between journals and congresses. Of these 76, 56 were the source of a single study, six were the source of two studies, and eight were the source of three studies. Most articles were published at the "International Journal of Production Research" and "The International Journal of Advanced Manufacturing

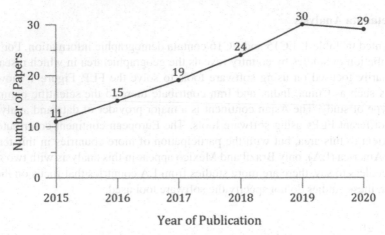

Fig. 2. Publications by year (2015–2020)

Technology". Table 5 shows the details of the sources with more articles published in this study.

Table 5. Articles by source

Journal or conference	# Articles
International Journal of Production Research	12
The International Journal of Advanced Manufacturing Technology	10
European Journal of Operational Research	5
Computers & Operations Research	5
INFOR: Information Systems and Operational Research	5
International Journal of Industrial Engineering Computations	4

3.2 Content Analysis

First, the research question: What software tools are used or developed to solve facility layout problems? The studies describe two manners to use software tools to solve FLP. The first is when researchers use an already developed tool, and the second is when they create a new tool based on the requirements of the study. In this sense, 70% of the studies preferred to use a tool already developed. In this case, the most used tools were MATLAB, CPLEX, and Lingo software. All of these have a paid license. In these tools, Lingo and CPLEX are classified as optimizing tools [13, 14], and MATLAB is a mathematics and computation software package with an extensive catalog function such as simulation and data analysis [15]. In one of the most relevant studies, Tofighi et al. [16], with 219 citations, used the second most used software tool of the sample, CPLEX. In the third most cited study, Manopiniwes et al. [17] used a completely different software tool, Gurobi, which is a commercial optimization software released in 2008 with the last stable version released in 2019. This software can solve various optimization problems, like Linear Programming, Quadratic Programming, and others [18]. In the sample of this study, only four articles used Gurobi, the already mentioned study of Manopiniwes, and the works of Becker et al. [19] using a hybrid solution with Gurobi and C+ +, Yang et al. [20] and Hungerlander et al. [21].

In the studies that prefer to develop their software tool, seven programming languages were identified, but 70% of these studies prefer to use an object-oriented language such as Java or C++ [22, 23]. In addition, only 16% of the studies used a mathematical optimization language, such as AMPL (A Mathematical Programming Language) [24], or a scientific programming language, such as Python [25]. Figure 3 shows how the programming languages were used in the studies. As can be seen, languages do not offer a definite behavior pattern. Therefore, the researchers used the most convenient programming language based on their domain. Furthermore, the studies that reported the availability of source codes within their studies represent only 3% of the articles. Therefore, 97% do not share the solution implemented in the study, but only the results obtained.

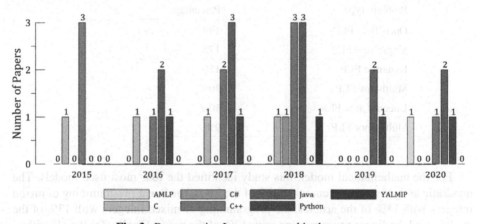

Fig. 3. Programming Languages used in the years.

The latest trend in FLP is to use an already developed software tool. In effect, researchers select a robust, high-performance tool for their studies. Tools like MATLAB or CPLEX have a complete catalog of plugins or extensions to solve a wide variety of FLPs. These add-ons make more accessible the work of researchers wanting to find optimal and faster solutions for their studies. When researchers prefer to develop their tool, the reason may be the ease of customization of the solution process. With this facility, researchers can test different algorithms and create their algorithms without restricting an already developed tool.

For the second research question: What principles of resilience engineering are considered in facility layout problems? The results showed that 81% of the studies do not consider any resilience engineering principle. This is because two different search strings were used, and, in the second, where the most studies were accepted, the resilience engineering keywords were discarded. In the case of the studies using one or more principles of resilience engineering, the most considered was the prevention with 16% of the studies and recovery and preparation with 8% of the studies each. Those principles were taken from the article by Thoma et al. [10]. In the studies considering any resilient principle, this principle is not part of the solution obtained with the software tool. Instead, resilience is considered before or after the definition of the problem as a concept that the solution must meet or consider.

In the third research question, how do studies applying resilience engineering principles solve facility layout problems? The extraction criteria focused on three characteristics of the different FLPs: 1) Type of plant distribution problem, 2) Mathematical model and 3) Algorithm used. Initially, 14 different types of FLP were identified, of which six of them are the most used, the open field FLP was solved in 19% of the studies, the single row FLP was used in 17% of the cases. Table 6 shows the percentage of studies for the most commonly used types of FLP.

Table 6. Most used FLP types

Problem type	Percentage
Open-field FLP	19%
Single-row FLP	17%
Dynamic FLP	11%
Multi-row FLP	10%
Unequal area FLP	10%
Multi-floor FLP	9%

For the mathematical model, this study identified the four most used models. The quadratic assignment problem with 16% of the cases, the linear programming of mixed integers with 14% of the articles, the programming of mixed integers with 13% of the studies, and the linear programming with 12% of the cases. Finally, for the algorithm, two of the most used were the genetic algorithm and the simulated annealing with 19% and 10%, respectively.

For the fourth and final research question: How have the studies based on software tools been carried out to solve facility layout problems considering resilience engineering principles? Many of the studies used data from another source or earlier studies developed by other researchers, 66% reuse data from another source, and only 27% get their data from a specific case study. The articles mainly focused on analysis, with 45% of the studies focusing on this research phase. Testing is the second most widely used phase of research by 26% of studies, and implementation and design were the last with 17% and 12%, respectively.

4   Conclusions

In this study, a systematic literature review was developed to define the software tools most used in the scientific community to efficiently solve a facility layout problem. The results show that 70% of the researchers prefer to use an already developed software tool, such as CPLEX or MATLAB. These software tools provide a robust environment to solve the different FLP cases using existing techniques. However, 30% of the case studies prefer to develop their software tool. Still, this analysis does not find any relationship between the programming language used and the resolved FLP type. Therefore, the analyzed data present an unpredictable behavior when the researchers use different programming languages to solve their FLPs. Consequently, it can be concluded that researchers use the most comfortable tool according to their abilities and software developing knowledge.

Unlike the latest compilation study of software tools to solve FLP, the trend is changing. In the early 21st century, i.e., in the early days of software tools to the FLP, the researchers attempted to develop a custom tool for each algorithm or technique developed. But, with today's high throughput, new studies have the ease of using more powerful existing tools that only need small setups to meet the researchers' goal. Nevertheless, they still exist to a lesser extent, the researchers who prefer to develop their tools. Therefore, they have instruments adapted to their specific needs. Unfortunately, these developments tools are not published for the other researchers to use in their studies.

This work aimed to define basic metrics in the research and report articles where the FLP was solved to help develop a new software tool with resilience engineering. The absence of a defined behavior in the studies in which a software tool was developed allows future projects the freedom to choose the most appropriate implementation technology according to their capabilities and knowledge. Future work plans may include creating detailed comparative studies of the identified tools, advantages, and disadvantages in different FLPs and comparing recognized programming languages to determine the most optimal solutions to these problems and the computational complexity of the various software tools.

Acknowledgments. The authors would like to thank to Corporación Ecuatoriana para el Desarrollo de la Investigación y Academia - CEDIA for the financial support given to the present re-search, development, and innovation work through its CEPRA program, especially for the CEPRA XV-2021–01-Resil-TEX. In addition, this research was partially funded by the University of Cuenca, Technical University of Ambato and University of Azuay.

Appendix A – Full List of References Read in the Systematic Literature Review

The list of sources used in the literature review can be found online at https://imaginere search.org/wp-content/uploads/2021/07/FLP_Rev_Appendix_A.pdf.

References

1. Hosseini-Nasab, H., Fereidouni, S., Fatemi Ghomi, S.M.T., Fakhrzad, M.B.: Classification of facility layout problems: a review study. Int. J. Adv. Manuf. Technol. **94**(1–4), 957–977 (2017). https://doi.org/10.1007/s00170-017-0895-8
2. Drira, A., Pierreval, H., Hajri-Gabouj, S.: Facility layout problems: a survey. Annu. Rev. Control **31**(2), 255–267 (2007)
3. Canen, A.G., Williamson, G.H.: Facility layout overview: towards competitive advantage. Facilities (1996)
4. Armour, G.C., Buffa, E.S.: A heuristic algorithm and simulation approach to relative location of facilities. Manag. Sci. **9**(2), 294–309 (1963)
5. Mohamadghasemi, A., Hadi-Vencheh, A.: An integrated synthetic value of fuzzy judgments and nonlinear programming methodology for ranking the facility layout patterns. Comput. Ind. Eng. **62**(1), 342–348 (2012)
6. Mejia, H., Wilches, M.J., Galofre, M., Montenegro, Y.: Aplicación de metodologías de distribución de plantas para la configuración de un centro de distribución. Sci. Tech. **3**(49), 63–68 (2011)
7. Khalil, T.M.: Facilities relative allocation technique (FRAT). Int. J. Prod. Res. **11**(2), 183–194 (1973)
8. Johnson, R.V.: SPACECRAFT for multi-floor layout planning. Manag. Sci. **28**(4), 407–417 (1982)
9. Jajodia, S., Minis, I., Harhalakis, G., Proth, J.-M.: CLASS: computerized layout solutions using simulated annealing. Int. J. Prod. Res. **30**(1), 95–108 (1992)
10. Thoma, K., Scharte, B., Hiller, D., Leismann, T.: Resilience engineering as part of security research: definitions, concepts and science approaches. Eur. J. Secur. Res. **1**(1), 3–19 (2016)
11. Singh, S.P., Sharma, R.R.: A review of different approaches to the facility lay-out problems. Int. J. Adv. Manuf. Technol. **30**(5–6), 425–433 (2006)
12. Kitchenham, B.: Procedures for performing systematic reviews. Keele UK Keele Univ. **2004**(33), 1–26 (2004)
13. Manual, C.U.: Ibm ilog cplex optimization studio. Version. **12**, 1987–2018 (1987)
14. Tan, R.R., Aviso, K.B., Promentilla, M.A.B., Yu, K.D.S., Santos, J.R.: Programming in LINGO. In: Input-Output Models for Sustainable Industrial Systems. Springer, Cham, pp. 29–46 (2019). https://doi.org/10.1007/978-981-13-1873-3_3
15. Knight, A.: Basics of MATLAB and Beyond. CRC Press (2019)
16. Tofighi, S., Torabi, S.A., Mansouri, S.A.: Humanitarian logistics network design under mixed uncertainty. Eur. J. Oper. Res. abril de **250**(1), 239–250 (2016)
17. Manopiniwes, W., Irohara, T.: Stochastic optimisation model for integrated decisions on relief supply chains: preparedness for disaster response. Int. J. Prod. Res. 16 de febrero de, **55**(4), 979–96 (2017)
18. Optimization, I.G., et al.: Gurobi optimizer reference manual, 2018. URL Httpwww Gurobi Com. (2018)
19. Becker, T., Zajac, S., Steenweg, P.M., Imhoff, L., Block, J.S.: Multi-level departments-to-offices assignment with different room types. Comput. Oper. Res. octubre de **110**, 60–76 (2019)
20. Yang, X., Cheng, W., Smith, A.E.: Amaral ARS. An improved model for the parallel row ordering problem. J. Oper. Res. Soc. 3 de marzo de, **71**(3), 475–490 (2020)
21. Hungerlander, P., Maier, K., Pocher, J., Truden, C.: On a new modelling approach for circular layouts and its practical advantages. In: 2017 IEEE International Conference on Industrial Engineering and Engineering Management (IEEM) [Internet]. IEEE, Singapore, [citado 14 de abril de 2021], pp. 1581–1585 (2017). http://ieeexplore.ieee.org/document/8290159/

22. O'Regan, G.: Java programming language. In: The Innovation in Computing Companion. Springer, Cham, pp. 171–174 (2018). https://doi.org/10.1007/978-3-030-02619-6_35
23. O'Regan, G.: C and C++ programming languages. In: The Innovation in Computing Companion. Springer, Cham, pp. 63–68 (2018). https://doi.org/10.1007/978-3-030-02619-6_14
24. Gay, D.M.: The AMPL modeling language: an aid to formulating and solving optimization problems. In: Numerical Analysis and Optimization. Springer, Cham, pp. 95–116 (2015)
25. Muller, E., Bednar, J.A., Diesmann, M., Gewaltig, M.-O., Hines, M., Davison, A.P.: Python in neuroscience. Front. Neuroinform. 9, 11 (2015)

Decision-Making of the University Libraries' Digital Collection Through the Publication and Citation Patterns Analysis.
A Literature Review

Tania Landivar[1], Ronaldo Rendon[1], and Lorena Siguenza-Guzman[1,2(✉)] (iD)

[1] Department of Computer Sciences, Faculty of Engineering, Universidad de Cuenca, Cuenca, Ecuador
lorena.siguenza@ucuenca.edu.ec
[2] Research Centre Accountancy, Faculty of Economics and Business, KU Leuven, Leuven, Belgium

Abstract. In recent years, different bibliometric methods and indicators, data mining techniques, and collection and visualization tools have been presented to analyze publication patterns and citations of scientific production. Moreover, some criteria and strategies for acquiring bibliographic databases allow forming a knowledge base for decision-making. Unfortunately, these data, methods, and tools are scattered in the literature. In this context, the objective of this article is to determine if the discovery of publication and citation patterns is being used to analyze scientific production in university libraries that helps decision-making on the subscription/acquisition of bibliographic databases. Fink's methodology was applied in conjunction with the PICO structure for the literature review. This systematic review made it possible to compile relevant information from 167 articles published during the 2016–2020 period into a findings matrix and perform a metadata and content analysis. Among the study's primary results, it stands out that the analysis of citations, the number of citations, and the VOSviewer collection and visualization tool have been the most outstanding for the study of scientific production. However, it has not had a significant impact as an aid to the acquisition/subscription of bibliographic databases.

Keywords: Publication patterns · Citation patterns · Acquisition criteria · Subscription criteria · Bibliometric · Indicators · Data mining tools · Techniques · Library

1 Introduction

Bibliometric studies have increased significantly in the last five years, evaluating scientific production through statistical and mathematical methods [1]. As a result of these studies, publication and citation patterns are obtained, which can be used in decision-making. Around the world, these bibliometric studies have been used for decades to

© Springer Nature Switzerland AG 2022
M. Botto-Tobar et al. (Eds.): ICAT 2021, CCIS 1535, pp. 80–94, 2022.
https://doi.org/10.1007/978-3-031-03884-6_6

measure scientific activity and its impact, and Latin America is not the exception [2–5]. For example, in Mexico, Guerrero-Sosa et al. presented a system to measure the productivity and impact of publications using bibliometric indicators, metadata, and semantic textual similarity [6]. In Ecuador, Zhimnay et al. analyzed the importance of measuring science to evaluate the academic excellence of universities [7]. Bibliometrics has also been used to improve collection management. For example, Gureev and Mazov built a bibliographic collection in Russia according to user needs [8]. In Belgium, Siguenza-Guzman et al. evaluated the importance of the library collection by combining four types of pattern analysis: *publications*, the journals where the institution's professors/researchers publish and their collaborations; *citations*, the references cited in those publications; *downloads*, statistics of journals consulted and downloaded provided by database providers; and, *impact factor*, the importance of a journal when establishing rankings by specialty [9]. Additionally, to increase the value of bibliometric studies, data mining techniques have been introduced through tools that allow the collection, analysis, and visualization of scientific production. They are based on bibliographic mapping and clustering techniques to develop network maps, such as citation-based author networks, co-citations, and bibliographic coupling [10].

Therefore, the use of publication and citation patterns for decision-making has become a fundamental element. Some journals carry out this type of study to find publication trends by studying authorship and citation patterns, analyzing links and connections between institutions, countries/territories, and research areas [11–13]. This is to know how the journal develops and where it should go. Furthermore, there are many studies to determine the productivity of research in a particular field, finding open or restricted access journals, years, journals and institutions published the most, collaboration networks between authors, etc. Finally, the use of publication patterns and citations for collection management aims to determine which resources (e.g., journals, bibliographic databases, and repositories) are the most used by researchers, thus providing information for collection maintenance.

The objective of this study was to investigate and establish which methods, bibliometric indicators, data mining techniques, and collection and visualization tools have been the most used for the discovery of publication and citation patterns in the analysis of scientific production. And if they are being used to support the decision-making process about the subscription/acquisition of bibliographic databases in university libraries. This article is structured as follows. First, the second section, the methodology used for the systematic literature review is presented. Then, the third section presents the results obtained and their respective discussion, in which the metadata analysis and descriptive analysis are detailed. Finally, the last section presents the conclusions and findings that will contribute to science and future research related to the subject.

2 Methodology

In this literature review, the methodology proposed by Arlene Fink [14] was applied. This procedure allowed for a structured and focused systematic review for research purposes. Finks' method consists of seven steps: (1) selection of research questions, (2) selection of bibliographic databases, (3) selection of search terms, (4) application of practical detection criteria, (5) application of methodological detection criteria, (6) development of the review, and (7) summary of the results.

The initial step was the selection of research questions for which the PICO structure was used to design the questions and develop search strategies that allow delimiting the study's objective [15, 16]. The term PICO stands for *Population* where the problem is identified. For the present study, this element analyzed whether deciding to acquire bibliographic databases in university libraries was based on a methodological analysis by discovering publication and citation patterns. *Intervention* where the intervention criteria were established in which the methods/strategies/criteria of acquisition and subscription, bibliometric methods and indicators, data mining techniques, and tools for collecting and visualizing scientific production were defined. *Comparison* between the terms mentioned above and *Outcomes* the analysis hopes to obtain the most relevant criteria for acquiring bibliographic databases, bibliometric methods, and indicators, data mining techniques, tools most used for the study of scientific production with the discovery of publication and citation patterns. It also analyzes whether these patterns have been used as a source for decision-making to acquire and subscribe. Consequently, the following questions were posed: (a) What are the criteria, methods, or strategies for acquiring bibliographic databases in university libraries? (b) What bibliometric methods are used for the discovery of publication patterns and citations? (c) What are the most used bibliometric indicators for the analysis of publication patterns and citations? (d) What are the most commonly used data mining techniques for analyzing publication and citation patterns? (e) What tools for the collection and visualization of scientific production are used to analyze publication patterns and citations?

The second step corresponded to the selection of bibliographic databases to consult. This step was carried out through a bibliographic search, and resources such as books, scientific journals, websites, and bibliographic databases were considered. This study focused on two digital databases: Scopus, of great international relevance [17], and Scielo, which stands out in the Hispanic region [18], allowing a complete investigation. Subsequently, as a third step, it was necessary to determine the keywords, which, for this research, were derived mainly from the following basic terms: "Acquisition and Subscription", "Bibliometric Methods and Indicators", "Data Mining Techniques and Visualization Tools". The detail of the bibliographic databases, search terms, and the number of results obtained is shown in Table 1.

Table 1. Search terms utilized for the literature review

Query	Scopus	Scielo
("Acquisition" OR "Subscription") AND "e-journals" AND "University Libraries"	9	0
"Bibliometric Methods" AND ("Publication Patterns" OR "Citation Patterns")	22	1
"Bibliometric Indicators" AND ("Publication Patterns" OR "Citation Patterns")	36	25

(*continued*)

Table 1. (*continued*)

Query	Scopus	Scielo
"Analysis" AND "Scientific Publications" AND "Data Mining" AND "Techniques"	11	0
("Collection Tool" OR "Visualization Tool") AND ("Publication Patterns" OR "Citation Patterns"	47	16
Total	125	42

The fourth step was applying practical screening criteria since many articles were obtained in the preliminary searches. Articles published between 2016–2020, in English and Spanish, were selected. The Spanish language made it possible to find principles, guidelines, and indicators applied in local institutions. English is the universal scientific language [19]; therefore, it is essential in all investigations. Using the practical criteria, it was defined that only item-type documents would be reviewed. The main reason for this decision was that journal articles currently represent the highest level of research with current and high-quality information, unlike congresses that are working in progress and have not concluded; moreover, the information is more mature in the books. Therefore, the places where practical applications can be found are journal articles [20].

The result was 167 documents, 5.4% (9 out of 167) corresponded to the search criteria of subscription to bibliographic databases, 6.6% (11 out of 167) to data mining techniques, 13.8% (23 out of 167) to bibliometric methods, 36.5% (61 out of 167) to bibliometric indicators, and 37.7% (63 out of 167) to tools for collecting and visualizing scientific production.

Once the information has been selected, the fifth step was the application of the methodological selection criteria. This step established the review of the article's methodology, results, and conclusion sections to find criteria for acquisition or subscription to bibliographic databases, methods used for bibliometric analysis and bibliometric indicators, data mining techniques, and software tools used for the extraction and visualization of scientific production. To compile the results, a "Findings Matrix" was required, which has the function of listing essential data after implementing the practical and methodological filter. This matrix contains strategic information such as the publication year, the author's name, the document's title, the content information, research area, abstract, and conclusions. It was used to perform a quick content analysis that helped determine if the articles contained relevant information to the research.

The sixth step corresponded to the study of the selected literature. For this, each document was reviewed to identify the information that allowed answering the questions posed in the first step.

And finally, the results were formulated in the seventh step. The data was exported to a spreadsheet for content and metadata analysis. Metadata analysis is an approach to improve the accuracy of resource discovery, and it allows information to be organized in a structured manner [21]. A variety of criteria and procedures may be required for different types of metadata. In addition, it supports content analysis that contributes to developing a dialogue about the evaluation of the quality of metadata [22] and whether it fulfills the purpose and objectives of the selected study.

For the content analysis, several sections were established within the matrix according to the intervention criteria in the PICO methodology and those already set above to find criteria and strategies for the acquisition of bibliographic bases, methods, and bibliometric indicators with their respective description and main characteristics. Also, a descriptive statistical study was carried out for the latter for the metadata analysis through the information frequencies, such as year of publication, productivity by country, research area, bibliometric methods and bibliometric indicators, and collection and visualization tools.

3   Results and Discussion

In this section, the main findings obtained from the systematic literature review are specified, whose results allowed to know the better state of the art on the use of methods, indicators, and tools to discover publication and citation patterns.

3.1   Metadata Analysis

The metadata of the reviewed articles provided statistics such as productivity per year, by country, and research area. The results are detailed below.

Concerning the first metadata analysis, this began with the criteria of *purchase or subscription to bibliographic databases*, where it is observed that few studies have been carried out. There is a productivity of 44.4% (4 out of 9) in 2020, 33.3% (3 out of 9) in 2019, 11.1% (1 out of 9) in 2018 and 2017, respectively. The country with the most publications is India with 33.3% (3 out of 9), followed by Nigeria and the United States with 22.2% (2 out of 9), Taiwan and Canada with 11.1% (1 out of 9). Figure 1 shows the productivity by country mentioned above.

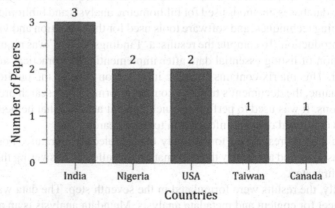

Fig. 1. Amount of information retrieved on productivity per country.

Studies have focused on evaluating the availability and use of information resources in university libraries [23], the prospects for the formation of consortia [24], inventories of electronic journal subscriptions to improve internal documentation, in addition to analyzing the degree of user satisfaction with library resources and facilities [25].

Regarding *bibliometric methods and indicators*, the publications in Scopus and Scielo are distributed as follows. With 23.9% (20 out of 84) of the year 2020, 22.6% (19 out of 84) of the year 2019, 20.2% (17 out of 84) in 2018, 15.4% (13 out of 84) in 2017 and 17.9% (15 out of 84) in 2016. These results reflect an increase in the number of studies published year after year. Figure 2 shows the most prolific countries according to Scopus, China 13.8% (8 out of 58) and India 10.3% (6 out of 58). In Scielo, Cuba stands out with 26.9% (7 out of 26).

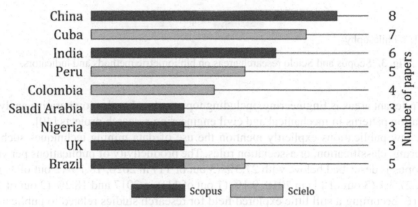

Fig. 2. Number of publications about bibliometric methods and indicators by country

Bibliometric methods and indicators have allowed finding years of higher production, prominent authors, the origin of the authors, specific field of study [26, 27], visibility and impact of research [28], the growth rate of publications, characteristics of research activities, citation bursts and chronological map [29], to name a few examples. This makes possible a reliable mapping of scientific development [30].

The research areas to which the studies of bibliometric methods and indicators have been directed both in Scopus and Scielo can be seen in Fig. 3. In Scopus, the area of Health Sciences stands out with 25.9% (15 out of 58), followed by Scientometrics with 22.4% (13 out of 58) and Engineering with 17.2% (10 out of 58). Regarding Scielo, the results confirm Health Sciences and Scientometrics as the most relevant with 34.6% (9 out of 26) and 19.2% (5 out of 26), respectively.

Within the Health Sciences, topics such as Oncology [26], Complementary Medicine [31], and Orthopedics [32] are treated. Bibliometric studies are carried out on these topics seeking to obtain years of greater production, outstanding authors, the origin of authors, among others [33]. It is followed by Scientometrics, which develops activities such as publication trends [11] and analysis of the kinetics of self-citations of a journal [34], the international scientific collaboration of researchers [35], mapping of scholarly communication in publications [35], preprints such as accelerator of scholarly communication [36], text analysis [37], measurement and visualization of collaboration and research productivity [38], research impact and country productivity [39]. Finally, one of the

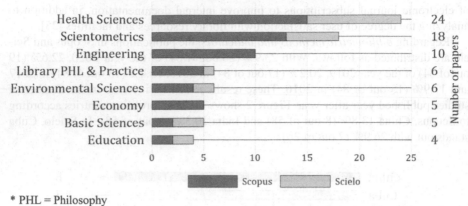

* PHL = Philosophy

Fig. 3. Scopus and Scielo research areas on bibliometric methods and indicators.

three relevant areas is Engineering, including topics related to the comparative analysis of citation patterns in mechanical and civil engineering research projects [40].

A few publications explicitly mention the use of data mining techniques such as clustering, classification, or association rules. The productivity of publications per year in Scopus is described below, with 27.3% (3 out of 11) in 2020, 18.1% (2 out of 11) in 2019, 27.3% (3 out of 11) in 2018, 9.1% (1 out of 11)) in 2017 and 18.2% (2 out of 11) in 2016, becoming a still little explored field for research studies related to publication and citation patterns. Scielo's results are null. Regarding productivity by country, Spain stands out with 18.2% (2 out of 11).

Finally, the use of tools to compile and visualize scientific production in bibliometric studies has been remarkable. Scopus reflects in 2020 a productivity of 31.9% (15 out of 47), 23.4% (11 out of 47) in 2019, 19.1% (9 out of 47) in 2018, 17% (8 out of 47) in 2017 and 8.5% (4 out of 47). 47) in 2016. These results are closely related to those presented at the beginning of this section since they use at least one collection and visualization tool to carry out these studies. Figure 4 presents the most prolific Scopus and Scielo countries. In Scopus, the United States stands out with 25.5% (12 out of 47), China with 12.8% (6 out of 47), and India with 10.6% (5 out of 47). The results related to Scielo have a productivity of 6.3% (1 out of 16) in 2020, 31.3% (5 out of 16) in 2019, 25% (4 out of 16) in 2018, 31.3% (5 out of 16) in 2017 and 6.3% (1 out of 16) in 2016. Likewise, as shown in Fig. 4, the country with the most publications is Brazil with 81.2% (13 of 16), high above Argentina, Mexico, and Singapore with a productivity of 6.3% (1 of 16), respectively. Scielo is a more local bibliographic library in Latin America; therefore, there is a considerable difference concerning productivity with Scopus, a global database. This allows concluding that there is still a gap in research with other countries despite the work done in Latin America.

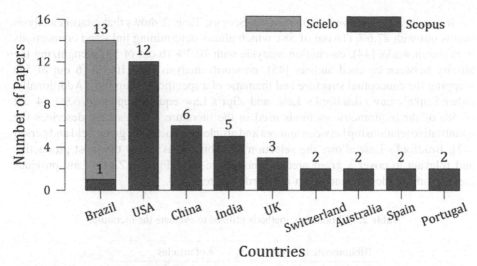

Fig. 4. Amount of information about collection and visualization tools (Scopus and Scielo).

3.2 Content Analysis

In this part of the paper, research questions established in Sect. 2 were answered. Regarding the question: *1) What are the criteria, methods, or strategies for acquiring bibliographic databases in university libraries?* The articles describing the entities or institutions that subscribe or acquire a digital repository were identified. The articles focus on the assessment of the availability of digital resources and library services [41], mention knowledge management for the development of collections [42], and emphasize providing and maintaining access to electronic journals [24].

The most relevant strategies for acquiring or subscribing to bibliographic databases are formalizing and strengthening the links between undergraduate students and library staff to improve access to information [41], networking, cataloging, classification, and exchanging information materials [43]. Another strategy consists in hiring selectors, i.e., library personnel who possess a great deal of tactical knowledge and subject areas, in addition to knowing which books or journals are of interest and which formats are preferred [42]. Likewise, an additional strategy is the formation of consortia between libraries where each has a representative participating in decision-making for the consortium's collection [24]. Finally, it is important to mention that all this can be a challenge for those who have not been directly involved if they do not know about purchasing, licensing, negotiations with suppliers, budget planning, and policy creation [42].

Regarding the research questions, *2) What bibliometric methods are used to discover publication and citation patterns, and 3) What are the most used bibliometric indicators for analyzing publication and citation patterns?* For their evaluation, the frequency of the different bibliometric methods and indicators was analyzed. Regarding bibliometric studies, Web of Science was the primary data source used with 51.7% (30 out of 58), followed by Scopus with 29.3% (17 out of 58), PubMed, and Medline with 5.2% (3 out of 58), respectively.

Regarding the *bibliometric methods* in Scopus, Table 2 shows that citation analysis stands out with 27.6% (16 out of 58), which allows determining links and connections in research works [44], co-citation analysis with 10.3% (6 out of 58) recognizing the affinity between co-cited authors [45], co-words analysis with 10.3% (6 out of 58) mapping the conceptual structure and thematic of a specific domain [46]. Additionally, either Lotka's Law, Bradford's Law, and Zipf's Law equally represent 6.9% (4 out of 58) of the bibliometric methods used in the literature. Lotka's Law describes the quantitative relationship between authors and articles produced in a given field and period [47]. Bradford's Law allows the selection of publications and is the most productive and relevant to cover a given area of knowledge [48]. Finally, Zipf's Law provides mechanisms to identify and select keywords in a text [49].

Table 2. Bibliometric methods utilized to evaluate the literature.

Bibliometric method	# of articles
Citation analysis	16
Co-citation analysis	6
Co-words analysis	6
co-authorship analysis	5
Lotka's Law	4
Bradford's Law	4
Zipf's Law	4

As it can be seen in the Scopus results in Table 3, the number of citations stands out with 37.9% (22 out of 58) as the most used *bibliometric indicator*, followed by the number of articles with 25.9% (15 out of 58), the number of authors with 20.7% (12 out of 58), the h-index with 18.9% (11 out of 58), the impact factor with 13.7% (8 out of 58) and the citation score with 5.2% (3 out of 58). Likewise, the publications metadata are extracted for the bibliometric analysis, such as author, subject, country, institution, journal, year of publication, category, language, affiliation, and title. Finally, the results corresponding to Scielo are also presented, in which the number of articles with 80.8% (21 out of 26) stood out, followed by the number of citations with 65.4% (17 out of 26) and the number of authors with 53.9% (14 out of 26). These results ratify those presented in Scopus, which determines the number of articles and citations as the most relevant.

Regarding question *4) What are the most used data mining techniques for analyzing publication patterns and citations?* Data mining techniques are commonly used to find hidden information in large amounts of data [50]. It can be applied to different areas. For example, Torres Berrú et al. present a study whose purpose is to find algorithms that identify specific characteristics of fraud or corruption [51]. On the other hand, Marcos-Pablos et al. describe a methodology to help adapt, filter, and synchronize the search and selection of articles for bibliographic reviews [52].

A list of data mining techniques is obtained between the second, third, and fourth search terms for Scopus since no results on this topic were found in Scielo. The findings

Table 3. Bibliometric indicators Scielo y Scopus

Bibliometric indicator	Scopus	Scielo
Number of articles	15	21
Number of citations	22	17
Number of authors	12	14
h-index	11	7
Impac factor	8	5
CiteScore	3	3

show that clustering stands out with 11.6% (8 out of 69), classification with 10.1% (7 out of 69), and multiple regressions with 5.8% (4 out of 69), these percentages being relatively low. However, the next question shows tools dedicated exclusively to bibliometric studies that include data mining functionalities.

Finally, on the research question, *5) What tools for collecting and visualizing scientific production are used to analyze publication and citation patterns?* To identify the collection and visualization tools, the total number of documents obtained from Scopus was taken from the search terms of bibliometric methods and indicators, together with the collection and visualization tools, giving 105 papers. The tools that stand out in data collection are HistCite with 4.8% (5 of 105), CiteSpace with 2.9% (3 of 105), ScientoPy with 1.9% (2 of 105), and Endnote with 1.9%. For the visualization tools, Spreadsheet was found with 20.9% (22 of 105), Tableau, DAVID, SPSS, Sci2, Ucinet, and Pajek, all with a percentage of 1.9% (2 of 105), respectively. Finally, the most used tool for collecting and visualizing with 28% (29 out of 105) is VOSviewer since it is a software tool to build and visualize bibliometric networks. These networks can include, for example, individual journals, researchers, or publications and can be created from citations, bibliographic links, co-citations, or co-authorship relationships [53, 54]. In addition, VOSviewer also offers data mining functionality to build and visualize co-occurrence networks of important terms drawn from a body of scientific literature [55].

Table 4. Collection and visualization tools reported in Scopus.

Tool	Number of articles
VOSviewer	29
Spreadsheet	22
HistCite	5
CiteSpace	3
Pajek	2
ScientoPy	2
EndNote	2

Table 4 shows the collection and visualization tools found in Scopus that stood out the most. Regarding Scielo, the tools that stand out in data collection and visualization are Spreadsheet with 45.2% (19 of 42), VOSviewer with 14.3% (6 of 42), EndNote with 9.5% (4 of 42), and Cochrane with 7.1% (3 of 42), shown in Table 5.

Table 5. Collection and visualization tools reported in Scielo.

Tool	Number of articles
Spreadsheet	19
VOSviewer	6
EndNote	4
Cochrane	3
SPSS	3
Ucinet	3
NetDraw	2

4   Conclusions

This article describes a systematic review to establish the most widely used bibliometric methods and indicators, data mining techniques, and collection and visualization tools to discover publication patterns and citations. In addition, they determine if they are being used in the decision-making process in university libraries regarding the subscription/acquisition of bibliographic databases. In this work, the PICO structure and Fink's model of the research literature review were applied based on a definition of research questions that allowed identifying resources related to the research topic [7]. In the first part of the literature review, two bibliographic databases (Scopus and Scielo) developed a search for information. Later, practical and methodological selection criteria were applied, establishing a sample of 167 articles with scientific content for their analysis.

The development of this review determined that the ability to use publication and citation patterns for collection management has not been exploited, specifically to decide which journal, database, or repository to acquire or subscribe, a decision that university libraries must constantly occupy. As can be seen, these decisions are made by staff with a high degree of knowledge in licensing, budget planning, etc. However, if there were another manner to support such decisions, it would make the analysis more objective and thus improve the maintenance of the collections.

The next point corresponds to the bibliometric methods, which stand out, the citation analysis allowing to determine links and connections in the research work; the co-citation analysis that recognizes the affinity between cited co-authors; and, finally, the study of common words mapping the conceptual and thematic structure of a specific domain. These methods are valuable because, after a certain process, they result in co-authorship maps, cross-country comparisons, connections between research topics, i.e., a lot of information to analyze. However, to apply these methods, the unit of measurement called "bibliometric indicator" is necessary. Also, the most important aspect in this study is the number of citations, number of articles, and H-index, which allow evaluating different characteristics of science activity linked to both the production and the consumption of information.

Bibliometric studies have increased considerably; thus, there are a series of tools that facilitate this activity. VOSviewer is the most used not only for the collection and visualization of information but also for data mining capabilities. In addition, a Spreadsheet should be considered a key tool that can be regarded as unique because depending on the topic this works with, it adapts to the needs of users, ranging from data management, calculations with information to visualization of summary of results by graphs.

This article reviews a topic of interest in any field for academics and professionals because research is a worldwide effort applicable to the diverse scientific community and society in general. Furthermore, the work can be seen as an initial conceptual framework for developing research projects and constructing new tools for the analysis of scientific production. Therefore, for future work, it is recommended to create a software or tool that allows uniting these methods, indicators, and tool functionalities whose objective is to provide information for decision-making in university libraries for collection maintenance.

Acknowledgements. This research was funded by the Vice-Rector's Office for Research of the University of Cuenca.

Appendix A – Full List of References Retrieved in the Literature Review from Scopus and Scielo

The list of sources used in the literature review can be found online at https://n9.cl/ctdhg.

References

1. Solis, B.P., Argüello, J.C.C., Barba, L.G., Gurrola, M.P., Zarhri, Z., TrejoArroyo, D.L.: Bibliometric analysis of the mass transport in a gas diffusion layer in PEM fuel cells. Sustainability **11**, 1–18 (2019)
2. Glänzel, W.: Bibliometrics as a Research Field: A Course on Theory and Application of Bibliometric Indicators. Course Handouts (2003)
3. González Alcaide, G., Gorraiz, J.I.: Assessment of researchers through bibliometric indicators: the area of information and library science in Spain as a case study (2001–2015). Front. Res. Metr. Anal. **3** (2018). https://doi.org/10.3389/frma.2018.00015
4. Abramo, G.: Bibliometric evaluation of research performance: where do we stand? VO 112–127 (2017). https://doi.org/10.17323/1814-9545-2017-1-112-127
5. Beaudry, C., Larivière, V.: Which gender gap? Factors affecting researchers' scientific impact in science and medicine. Res. Policy **45**, 1790–1817 (2016). https://doi.org/10.1016/j.respol.2016.05.009
6. Guerrero-Sosas, J.D.T., Chicharro, F.P.R., Serrano-Guerrero, J., Menendez-Dominguez, V., Castellanos-Bolaños, M.E.: A proposal for a recommender system of scientific relevance. Procedia Comput. Sci. **162**, 199–206 (2019). https://doi.org/10.1016/j.procs.2019.11.276

7. Zhimnay, C., Fernández Landivar, J., Albarracín, J., Sadaba, I., Sucozhanay, D.: Mapping of scientific production in social sciences in Ecuador, 1 March 2019
8. Gureyev, V., Mazov, N.: Assessment of the relevance of journals in research libraries using bibliometrics (a review). Sci. Tech. Inf. Process. **42**, 30–40 (2015). https://doi.org/10.3103/S0147688215010050
9. Siguenza-Guzman, L., Holans, L., Abbeele, A.V.D., Vandewalle, J., Verhaaren, H., Cattrysse, D.: Towards a holistic analysis tool to support decision-making in libraries. Undefined (2013)
10. Tuppal, C.P., Gallardo-Ninobla, M.M., Arquiza, G.S., Vega, P.D.: A bibliometric analysis of the Philippine J. Nurs. (1966–2017). https://www.herdin.ph/index.php/herdin-home?view=research&cid=71335
11. Ullah, S.: Publication trends of Pakistan heart journal: a bibliometric study. Libr. Philos. Pract. (e-Journal) (2019)
12. Wang, W., Laengle Scarlazetta, S., Merigó Lindahl, J., Yu, D., Herrera Viedma, E., Cobo, M.J., Bouchon Meunier, B.: A bibliometric analysis of the first twenty-five years of the international journal of uncertainty, fuzziness and knowledge-based systems. Int. J. Uncertain. Fuzziness Knowl.-Based Syst. (2018). https://doi.org/10.1142/S0218488518500095
13. Peter, M., Samuel, S.A., Idhris, M., Subbarayalu, A.: Saudi Arabian top four medical journals bibliometric study. Libr. Philos. Pract. (e-Journal) (2020)
14. Fink, A.: Evaluation Fundamentals: Insights into Program Effectiveness, Quality, and Value. SAGE Publications, Thousand Oaks (2014)
15. BA, K., Charters, S.: Guidelines for performing systematic literature reviews in software engineering, **2** (2007)
16. Shokraneh, F.: PICO framework: two decades of variation and application (2016)
17. Zhu, J., Liu, W.: A tale of two databases: the use of web of science and Scopus in academic papers. arXiv:2002.02608 [Cs]. http://arxiv.org/abs/2002.02608 (2020)
18. Bojo Canales, C., Sanz-Valero, J.: Indicadores de impacto y de prestigio de las revistas de ciencias de la salud indizadas en la red SciELO: Estudio comparativo (2020). https://repisalud.isciii.es/handle/20.500.12105/10992
19. Ramírez, M.G., Falcón, I.A.L.: Importancia del lenguaje en el contexto de la aldea global. Horizontes Educacionales. **15**, 95–107 (2010)
20. Siguenza-Guzman, L., Saquicela, V., Avila-Ordóñez, E., Vandewalle, J., Cattrysse, D.: Literature review of data mining applications in academic libraries. J. Acad. Librariansh. **41**, 499–510 (2015). https://doi.org/10.1016/j.acalib.2015.06.007
21. Chen, Y., et al.: A metadata lifecycle for content analysis in digital libraries (2001)
22. Moen, W.E., Stewart, E.L., McClure, C.R.: The role of content analysis in evaluating metadata for the U.S. Government information locator service (GILS) (1997)
23. Tukur, L., Kannan, S.: An appraisal of availability and utilization of information resources and library services by undergraduate students in three agriculture university libraries in Northern Nigeria (ABU, FUAM, FUTM). Libr. Philos. Pract. (e-Journal) (2020)
24. Zhao, W., Zhao, S., MacGillivray, K.-S.: Providing and maintaining access to electronic serials: consortium and member university library's perspectives. Ser. Libr. **72**, 144–151 (2017). https://doi.org/10.1080/0361526X.2017.1309831
25. Urban, S.G.: Using e-journal subscription inventories to improve internal documentation and patron access. Tech. Serv. Q. **36**, 269–280 (2019). https://doi.org/10.1080/07317131.2019.1621568
26. Danell, J.-A.B.: Integrative oncology from a bibliometric point of view. Complement. Ther. Med. **52**, 102477 (2020). https://doi.org/10.1016/j.ctim.2020.102477
27. Simao, L.B., Carvalho, L.C., Madeira, M.J.: Intellectual structure of management innovation: bibliometric analysis. Manag. Rev. Q. **71**, 651–677 (2021). https://doi.org/10.1007/s11301-020-00196-4

28. Sahoo, S., Pandey, S.: Bibliometric analysis and visualization of global ocean acidification research. Sci. Technol. Libr. **39**, 414–431 (2020). https://doi.org/10.1080/0194262X.2020. 1776194

29. Guo, Y., Hao, Z., Zhao, S., Gong, J., Yang, F.: Artificial intelligence in health care: bibliometric analysis. J. Med. Internet Res. **22**, e18228 (2020). https://doi.org/10.2196/18228

30. Ellegaard, O.: The application of bibliometric analysis: disciplinary and user aspects. Scientometrics **116**, 181–202 (2018). https://doi.org/10.1007/s11192-018-2765-z

31. Danell, J.-A.B., Danell, R., Vuolanto, P.: Scandinavian research on complementary and alternative medicine: a bibliometric study. Scand. J. Publ. Health **48**, 609–616 (2020). https://doi.org/10.1177/1403494819834099

32. Shon, W.Y., et al.: Assessment of Korea's orthopedic research activities in the top 15 orthopedic journals, 2008–2017. Clin. Orthop. Surg. **11**, 237–243 (2019). https://doi.org/10.4055/cios.2019.11.2.237

33. Shi, X., Cai, L., Jia, J.: The evolution of international scientific collaboration in fuel cells during 1998–2017: a social network perspective. Sustainability **10**, 4790 (2018). https://doi.org/10.3390/su10124790

34. Heneberg, P.: From excessive journal self-cites to citation stacking: analysis of journal self-citation kinetics in search for journals, which boost their scientometric indicators. PLoS ONE **11**, e0153730 (2016). https://doi.org/10.1371/journal.pone.0153730

35. Mohan, B.S., Rajgoli, I.: Mapping of scholarly communication in publications of the astronomical society of Australia, publications of the astronomical society of Japan, and publications of the astronomical society of the Pacific: a bibliometric approach. Sci. Technol. Libr. **36**, 351 (2017). https://doi.org/10.1080/0194262X.2017.1368427

36. Wang, Z., Chen, Y., Glänzel, W.: Preprints as accelerator of scholarly communication: an empirical analysis in mathematics. J. Inform. **14**, 101097 (2020). https://doi.org/10.1016/j.joi.2020.101097

37. Ranaei, S., Suominen, A., Porter, A., Carley, S.: Evaluating technological emergence using text analytics: two case technologies and three approaches. Scientometrics **122**, 215–247 (2020). https://doi.org/10.1007/s11192-019-03275-w

38. Leidolf, A., Baker, M., Porter, A., Garner, J.: Measuring and visualizing research collaboration and productivity. J. Data Inf. Sci. **3**, 54–81 (2018). https://doi.org/10.2478/jdis-2018-0004

39. Barrot, J.: Research impact and productivity of Southeast Asian countries in language and linguistics. Scientometrics **110** (2016). https://doi.org/10.1007/s11192-016-2163-3

40. Osueke, C.O., Idiegbeyan-ose, J., Botu, T., Aregbesola, A., Emmanuel, O.: Analysis of mechanical engineering research activities using bibliometric method: a case study of undergraduate projects. Int. J. Mech. Eng. Technol. **9**, 1014–1021 (2018)

41. Tukur, L.M., Kannan, S.: An appraisal of availability and utilization of information re-sources and library services by undergraduate students in three agriculture university libraries in Northern Nigeria (ABU, FUAM, FUTM). **27** (2017)

42. Proctor, J.: Knowledge management for collection development: transforming institutio-nal knowledge into tools for selectors. Ser. Librar. **76**(1–4), 118–122 (2019). https://doi.org/10.1080/0361526X.2019.1551668

43. Babatunde, T., Alhassan, J., B.: Effective resource sharing services in university libraries in North Central Nigeria (2020)

44. Andalia, R.: Los análisis de citas en la evaluación de los trabajos científicos y las publicaciones seriadas. **7** (1999)

45. Miguel, S., Moya-Anegón, F., Herrero-Solana, V.: El análisis de co-citas como método de investigación en Bibliotecología y Ciencia de la Información. Investigación bibliotecológica. **21**, 139–155 (2007)

46. Galvez, C.: Análisis de co-palabras aplicado a los artículos muy citados en Biblioteconomía y Ciencias de la Información (2007–2017). Transinformação. **30**, 277–286 (2018). https://doi.org/10.1590/2318-08892018000300001
47. Alvarado, R.U.: La ley de Lotka y la literatura de bibliometría. Investigación bibliotecológica. **13**, 125–141 (1999)
48. Urbizagástegui Alvarado, R., Urbizagástegui Alvarado, R.: El crecimiento de la literatura sobre la ley de Bradford. Investigación bibliotecológica. **30**, 51–72 (2016). https://doi.org/10.1016/j.ibbai.2016.02.003
49. Urbizagastegui, R., Restrepo Arango, C.: Zipf's law and Goffman's transition point in the automatic indexing. Investigacion Bibliotecologica. **25**, 71–92 (2011)
50. Alvarez-Jareño, J., Badal-Valero, E., Pavia, J.: Aplicación de métodos estadísticos, económicos y de aprendizaje automático para la detección de la corrupción. **9** (2019)
51. Torres Berrú, Y., Batista, V., Torres-Carrion, P.: Data mining to detect and prevent corruption in contracts: systematic mapping review. RISTI - Revista Iberica de Sistemas e Tecnologias de Informacao, 13–25 (2020)
52. Marcos-Pablos, S., García-Peñalvo, F.J.: Information retrieval methodology for aiding scientific database search. Soft Comput. **24**, 5551–5560 (2020). https://doi.org/10.1007/s00500-018-3568-0
53. Pandey, S., Sahoo, S.: Research collaboration and authorship pattern in the field of semantic digital libraries. DESIDOC J. Libr. Inf. Technol. **40**, 375 (2020)
54. Sahoo, S., Pandey, S.: Evaluating research performance of Coronavirus and Covid-19 pandemic using scientometric indicators. Online Inf. Rev. **44**, 1443–1461 (2020). https://doi.org/10.1108/OIR-06-2020-0252
55. Yi, W., Wang, Y., Tang, J., Xiong, X., Zhang, Y., Yan, S.: Visualization analysis on treatment of coronavirus based on knowledge graph. Zhonghua Wei Zhong Bing Ji Jiu Yi Xue. **32**, 279–286 (2020). https://doi.org/10.3760/cma.j.cn121430-20200225-00200

e-Learning

Inferential Statistical Analysis in E-Learning University Education in Latin America in Times of COVID-19

Rodrigo Bastidas-Chalán[1]([✉]) [ID], Gisella Mantilla-Morales[1] [ID],
Omar Samaniego-Salcán[2], Christian Coronel-Guerrero[3] [ID],
Milton Andrade-Salazar[3] [ID], Daniel Nuñez-Agurto[3] [ID],
and Eduardo Benavides-Astudillo[3] [ID]

[1] Departamento de Ciencias Exactas, Universidad de las Fuerzas Armadas ESPE.
Sede Santo Domingo, Vía Santo Domingo-Quevedo km 24,
Santo Domingo de los Tsáchilas, Ecuador
{rvbastidas,gbmantilla}@espe.edu.ec
[2] Instituto Superior Tecnológico Japón, Av. Galápagos y Cuenca,
Santo Domingo de los Tsáchilas, Ecuador
hsamaniego@itsjapon.edu.ec
[3] Departamento de Ciencias de la Computación, Universidad de las Fuerzas Armadas
ESPE. Sede Santo Domingo, Vía Santo Domingo-Quevedo km 24,
Santo Domingo de los Tsáchilas, Ecuador
{cacoronel,mtandrade,adnunez1,debenavides}@espe.edu.ec

Abstract. Since the appearance of COVID-19, the teaching-learning processes in higher education have changed. This article shows a focus on university education and e-learning, performing a statistical analysis on university students in Ecuador, obtaining significant evidence that the use of ICTs improves academic performance in the subject of statistics. In the first case, two third semester courses are taken, the experimental group is made up of 23 students, to which e-learning is applied and an application developed in Scilab that shows the resolution process for descriptive and inferential statistics; while the control group is made up of 14 students, in which only e-learning and traditional teaching are used. In the second case, 2 courses are taken, the first is formed by 14 students and the second by 22 students, using e-learning and traditional teaching. First, the Shapiro Test is used to determine if the population has a normal distribution, then the Student's T test is applied in the hypothesis test of difference of means to determine if academic performance is improved with the use of ICTs. Finally, for $\alpha = 0.05$, it is verified that the developed application improves academic performance. Another important finding is that only using traditional teaching with e-learning does not significantly change academic performance.

Keywords: E-learning · Scilab · Inferential statistical analysis

© Springer Nature Switzerland AG 2022
M. Botto-Tobar et al. (Eds.): ICAT 2021, CCIS 1535, pp. 97–107, 2022.
https://doi.org/10.1007/978-3-031-03884-6_7

1   Introduction

1.1   A Subsection Sample

Face-to-face education worldwide has had valuable representation due to the access to collaborative practices, experimental environments and the ease of interaction in real time between the teacher and students; But, this form of learning changed completely due to the Covid-19 pandemic, and despite the fact that virtuality has been an attractive form of study, it has strengthened in recent years.

Most of the University Education institutions have platforms for students to carry out autonomous work activities in synchronous and asynchronous time that undoubtedly helps the teaching-learning process, and the use of Information and Communication Technologies have become essential academic support tools. Research related to the use of E-learning platforms affirms that the application of e-learning education in universities allows the enrichment of teaching [1]. Currently, these institutions seek to technify their educational model to offer virtual services that facilitate the obtaining of information in a dynamic way with the support of quality teaching and with accessible programs that adapt to the needs of society.

E-learning as an educational environment originated with the appearance of internet networks and by the 70s it proliferated thanks to email, turning it into a communicational tool of a governmental and business type, and teleconferencing was the most common training mechanism. Used for staff training. In the 90s, virtual platforms for teaching emerged with basic contents that were not difficult to manipulate, since great knowledge was not required for their mastery. The new millennium accelerates the evolution of learning because technological innovation, a product of globalization, has made it possible to be at the forefront of the generation of content and new forms of instruction in developed countries.

At the Latin American level is where the need for pedagogical structures that ensure educational quality is most observed, therefore, the demand of the market for virtual education is to have instruments that allow them to learn in a meaningful way. Argentina, one of the pioneers in the creation of content through the use of internet networks in South America, analyzes the problem of the universalization of higher education and, through the Latin American Institute and the Quality Criterion in Distance Higher Education, defines that the evaluation and accreditation of education is key in virtual education, likewise it worries that traditional teaching based on empirical and theoretical compression does not allow objective evaluation, obstructing the generation of new learning paradigms [2].

The pandemic restricted face-to-face activities, affecting almost all social sectors and education in general was no exception. The measures to control the growth of contagions forced the University Education Institutions to opt for virtuality. At present, access to information is abundant since the internet has digital repositories and selective search engines to obtain quality content, however, that does not mean that education is better since other components are required for the process of teaching-learning be successful. In a study carried out, the term engagement is used to express the integration of some factors such as the availability of ICTs, technological autonomy, behavior, competence and the interest of the learner [3]. E-learning is an educational alternative that is permanently contributing to the training of professionals committed to society and always renewing their way of teaching to meet market expectations.

It is essential that in post-pandemic education collaborative work is promoted through e-learning programs with the active participation of the teacher so that students feel supported and advised in a personalized way through the use of Information Technologies and Communication. It must be clarified that e-learning is not the same as distance education, its difference establishes that the first requires the guidance of a professional in the teaching area and the use of computational means, and the second may or may not use technology.

Contemporary educational technology uses illustrative applications to facilitate learning, favoring the development and organization of the virtual environment. Due to its flexibility to create interaction environments in synchronous time, the exchange of criteria makes the construction of knowledge more dynamic and entertaining, leading to obtaining more effective results. Another research contribution is expressed that the use of electrical means for the learning process is on the increase, in addition the use of computers for assisted teaching creates skills according to the needs of the market [4]. Undoubtedly, there is a favorable trend to use applications in teaching-learning processes since their dynamism, participation, collaboration and interaction are key elements of education in the 21st century.

Although it is true that technology has facilitated the creation of educational environments and a simpler access to knowledge, we continue to observe transitions that increasingly make the university education process more technical; This is where the pedagogical model must be clear, explicit and strengthened through the implementation of technological resources, teacher training and student adaptability. A publication on Education in Times of Pandemic (2020) states that E-learning, M-Learning and B-learning are increasingly used in the educational field [5].

Research is part of the activities carried out in university education, achieving representative results for society during the last decade. The development of digital technologies according to the World Conference on Higher Education in the XXI century encourages knowledge with the accompaniment of ICTs [6]. Currently, it is known that there is a favorable response capacity towards university initiatives to improve higher education, this thanks to the fact that through the use of innovative methods they are getting students to obtain meaningful and quality learning, counteracting the adversities of the environment that they affect not only the infrastructure and tools for the academy, but also the procedure used in teaching.

In an investigation carried out in Mexico and Costa Rica [7], using a Likert scale to measure the integration of ICTs in university students, it was determined that the use of ICTs is valued but they are exclusive with people who do not have mastery in these fields. In Ecuador there are initial studies that try to measure the perception of ICTs in a quantitative and descriptive way [8], it is imperative to ask the question Do e-learning education and ICTs tools improve university education?

2   Materials and Methods

To perform the inferential statistical analysis, both confidence intervals and hypothesis tests can be used [9], with confidence intervals being more used. However, in the present study it is used as average data of grades in a subject, for which a test of the hypothesis of difference of means was used, such as the study carried out in Guadalajara [10].

In the present investigation has been realized the following stages:

2.1   Application Developed in Scilab

The use of ICTs improves knowledge management [11], which is why an application was developed using the free software Scilab, which added to e-learning, created a virtual learning environment, to ensure that education adapts to the needs of the non-contact work of the students [12]. This tool allows you to visualize the process of developing problems, both for inferential statistics and descriptive statistics, because most programs such as Matlab, SPSS, R, Python, etc., only show the result. There are online programs that also solve statistical exercises, such as Symbolab or Wolfram, but that require a paid subscription to view the resolution of exercises.

To achieve the exercise resolution visualization effect, the data entered by the user in numerical variables are acquired, then they are processed according to the required statistical operation, and then the value obtained is stored in variables as a character string. Finally, the results obtained with both the mathematical signs and the grouping signs involving the operation are concatenated and they are shown as if they were a single character string.

In Fig. 1 you can see the descriptive statistics part allows the calculation and development of the process for calculating measures of dispersion, central tendency and frequency tables.

Also in Fig. 2, specifying the number of classes can be obtained polygon graphs of frequency or pie diagram. In Fig. 3 you can see the inferential statistics part allows to solve hypothesis tests when the variance is known (Standard Normal Distribution Z) as well as when it is unknown (T Student). When it comes to tabulated data in Excel it can be imported.

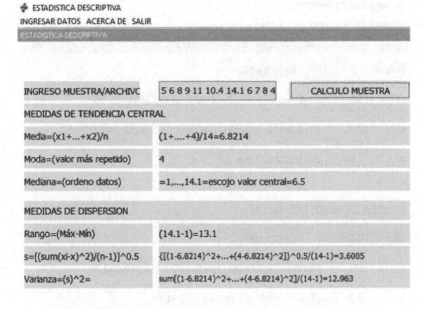

Fig. 1. Functioning of the application in descriptive statistics.

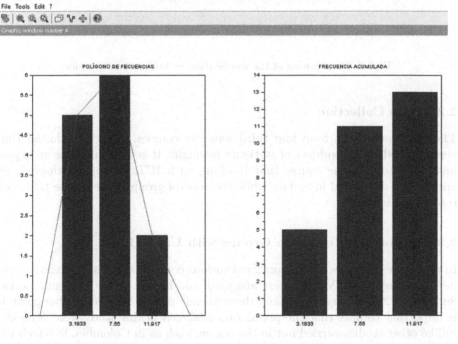

Fig. 2. Functioning of the application for graphics.

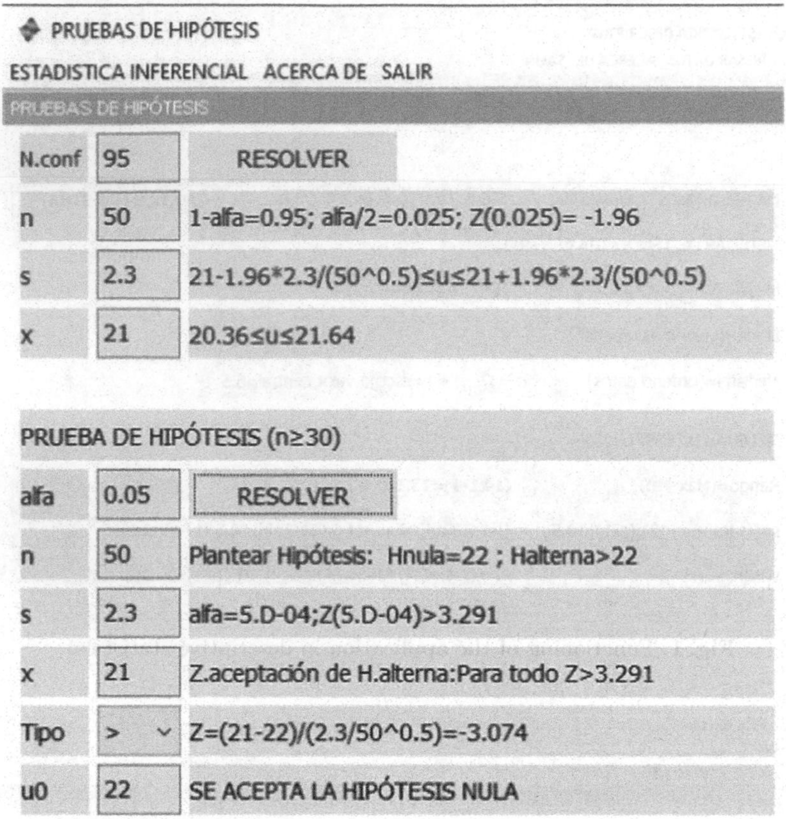

✦ PRUEBAS DE HIPÓTESIS

ESTADISTICA INFERENCIAL   ACERCA DE   SALIR

PRUEBAS DE HIPÓTESIS

N.conf	95	RESOLVER
n	50	1-alfa=0.95; alfa/2=0.025; Z(0.025)= -1.96
s	2.3	21-1.96*2.3/(50^0.5)≤u≤21+1.96*2.3/(50^0.5)
x	21	20.36≤u≤21.64

PRUEBA DE HIPÓTESIS (n≥30)

alfa	0.05	RESOLVER
n	50	Plantear Hipótesis: Hnula=22 ; Halterna>22
s	2.3	alfa=5.D-04;Z(5.D-04)>3.291
x	21	Z.aceptación de H.alterna:Para todo Z>3.291
Tipo	> ˅	Z=(21-22)/(2.3/50^0.5)=-3.074
u0	22	SE ACEPTA LA HIPÓTESIS NULA

Fig. 3. Functioning of the application in inferential statistics.

2.2   Data Collection

The data were taken from four third semester courses, in an Ecuadorian University, in which the subject of statistics is taught. It is determined as an experimental group, to the course that teaching with ICTs is applied through an application developed in Scilab; while the control group is the course that uses traditional teaching.

2.3   Hypothesis Testing in Groups with Use of ICTs

In this stage, averages of students from various courses before and after the pandemic caused by COVID-19 were analyzed, specifically in the academic period September 2019-January 2020 and the academic period May-September 2020. It is important to note that the population analyzed in this study were students, unlike other studies carried out in the region, such as in Colombia, in which the study population was teachers [13].

The samples belong to two independent populations, that is, the averages of two different courses are handled, the first of 14 students and the second of 23 students, likewise, the first corresponds to the course before the pandemic and the other after the pandemic, but that they received classes with the same teacher, in the matter of statistics. To avoid atypical data, data belonging to students who withdrew from the subject are eliminated. The first group is the control group because traditional teaching is used, without the use of Tics, while the second group is the experimental group, with which, apart from using an e-learning teaching, the developed application was also used.

As the first part of the statistical analysis, it is verified that the data used belong to a population with a normal distribution. Then, a mean difference hypothesis test was carried out to verify if the use of e-learning and the application developed improved the performance of students, before and after the pandemic caused by COVID-19. This analysis was carried out with the R software. The result is shown in Table 1:

Table 1. Comparison of the average in the experimental and control groups with ICTs.

	Control group	Experimental group
Epoch	Before the pandemic	After the pandemic
Shapiro test	$p - value = 0.1509$	$p - value = 0.2937$
T test	$p - value = 0.0006508$	

As can be seen in Table 1, when applying the Shapiro Test to the control group, the value obtained is $p - value = 0.1509$, with which it is verified that it has a normal distribution, while in the experimental group a $p - value = 0.2937$, that is, it also has a normal distribution.

In the T student test, the value obtained is $p - value = 0.0006508$ for an $\alpha = 0.05$, so it can be concluded that the use of virtual environments, that is, use of the application developed in Scilab and online education, improved the average in the subject of statistics.

2.4   Hypothesis Testing in Groups Without Use of ICTs

The samples belong to two independent populations, that is, the averages of two different courses are handled, the first of 14 students and the second of 22 students, likewise, the first corresponds to the course before the pandemic and the other after the pandemic, but that they received classes with the same teacher, but different from the previous groups, in the matter of statistics. To avoid atypical data, data belonging to students who withdrew from the subject are eliminated. Traditional teaching is used in both groups, but e-learning was necessary for the second group due to the pandemic.

As the first part of the statistical analysis, it is verified that the data used belong to a population with a normal distribution. Then, a mean difference hypothesis test was carried out to verify if only with online education there are significant changes in student performance, before and after the pandemic caused by COVID-19. This analysis was carried out with the R software. The result is shown in Table 2:

Table 2. Comparison of the average in the groups without ICTs.

	First group	Second group
Epoch	Before the pandemic	After the pandemic
Shapiro test	$p - value = 0.4772$	$p - value = 0.2963$
T test	$p - value = 0.5939$	

As can be seen in Table 2, when applying the Shapiro Test to the group before the pandemic, the value obtained is $p - value = 0.4772$, with which it is verified that it has a normal distribution, while in the group after the pandemic pandemic, a $p - value = 0.2963$ was obtained, that is, it also has a normal distribution.

In the student T test, the value obtained is the $p - value = 0.5939$ for an $\alpha = 0.05$, so it can be concluded that only with online education and using traditional education, that is, without the use of the application developed in Scilab, there is no evidence that the statistical averages are different before and after the pandemic.

3   Results and Discussions

The first statistical inference shows that the average of the course (after the pandemic) that received statistics classes improved compared to the course (before the pandemic) that received classes in a traditional way, obtaining a $p - value = 0.0006508$.

For the second statistical inference, technological tools that help to improve the teaching-learning process of the subject of statistics were not used, but rather the same traditional teaching, but online. The result obtained, $p - value = 0.5939$, indicates that there is no significant difference in the averages of the courses.

In the study carried out in Portugal on a virtual platform [14] to improve the subject of statistics, it is mentioned positively in a qualitative way how students show interest in said platform, however, it lacks content and only shows previously developed exercises.

In Spain, at the University of Zaragoza [15], to improve the teaching of statistics, e-learning is used through a platform with videos, mind maps, videoconferences, tutorials and gaming. To measure the degree of effectiveness of the teaching-learning process, student satisfaction surveys are used. This platform only allows interaction between teacher and students.

In Ecuador, specifically in the province of Azuay, both active methodology and ICTs [16] were used to improve mathematics learning. To determine if this methodological proposal was useful, surveys were conducted with students, obtaining positive comments from the students. No app was developed in this study, nor is there significant evidence of improvement in education.

Other investigations carried out, for example, the one carried out in Colombia [17], focus qualitatively on analyzing teachers who teach mathematics subjects and the use of ICTs in the teaching-learning process. Like the previous research, a specific tool is not developed that contributes to education.

In Peru, a mixture of techniques is used, among them Blended-Learning, Tics and Constructivism [18] to contribute to the teaching of statistics. Basically what is done is a teaching that motivates the use of tics so that students have more resources available in their university education. However, it must be emphasized that a specific tool is not used, but rather a set of options that allow finding the answer to a certain statistical problem.

Other studies try to determine the use of ICTs tools, for example a study carried out on university students in Mexico [19], the use of these tools was analyzed while for university students in Peru [20] it was tried to measure the degree of relationship of use of ICTs.

4   Conclusions

E-learning allows teaching in university education, however it does not mean that academic performance improves, in the case of study, the average of two courses was practically the same.

The incorporation of ICTs tools such as the application developed in Scilab, allows not only to develop exercises but also to improve academic performance, which was demonstrated with a hypothesis test.

It is important to mention that it has been statistically shown that the use of Tics improves average learning in university students, in addition, in the present study it was also shown that the use of Tics with traditional education does not improve academic performance.

The incorporation of new technologies and the applications that can be developed improved the teaching-learning process in higher education, thereby achieving the proposed objective of this research.

Data Availability: R code and data used in this study is available in: https://drive.google.com/drive/folders/1YqE4qSVqEzT0VjAaYfYVxOF3qzuy3b3h?usp=sharing

.

References

1. Bermúdez, F., Fueyo, A.: Transformando la docencia: usos de las plataformas de e-learning en la educación superior presencial. Revista Mediterránea de Comunicación **9**(2), 259–274 (2018)
2. Pontoriero, F.: E-learning en la educación superior argentina-Modelo de evaluación de calidad a partir del aporte de referentes clave. Virtualidad, Educación y Ciencia **12**(22), 22–45 (2021)
3. Estrada, O., Fuentes, D., García, A.: El engagement en la educación virtual: experiencias durante la pandemia COVID-19. Texto Livre: Linguagem e Tecnologia **14**(2), e33936 (2021)
4. Mascaró, E.A., Moretta, J.: Las tic y el e-learning en el proceso de enseñanza aprendizaje de los estudiantes universitarios. Revista Científica Especialidades Odontológicas UG **4**(2) (2021)
5. Cóndor, O.: Educar en tiempos de COVID-19. CienciAmérica **9**(2), 31–37 (2020)
6. Paredes, A., González, Inciarte, A., Walles, D.: Educación superior e investigación en Latinoamérica: Transición al uso de tecnologías digitales por Covid-19. Revista de Ciencias Sociales **26**(3), 98–117 (2020)
7. Astudillo, M., Chévez, F., Oviedo, Y.: La exclusión social y las Tecnologías de la Información y la Comunicación: una visión estadística de su relación en la educación superior. LiminaR **18**(1), 177–193 (2020)
8. Pacheco, D., Martínez, M.: Percepciones de la incursión de las TIC en la enseñanza superior en Ecuador. Estudios pedagógicos (Valdivia) **47**(2), 99–116 (2020)
9. Flores, P.: Comparación de la eficiencia de las pruebas de hipótesis e intervalos de confianza en el proceso de inferencia. Estudio sobre medias. Revista de Ciencias **22**(2), 65–85 (2018)
10. López, M.: Impacto de las tecnologías de la información y la comunicación (TIC) en el docente universitario: el caso de la Universidad de Guadalajara. Perspectiva educacional **52**(2), 4–34 (2013)
11. Ocaña, Y., Valenzuela, A., Gálvez, E., Aguinaga, D., Nieto, J., López, T.: Gestión del conocimiento y tecnologías de la información y comunicación (TICs) en estudiantes de ingeniería mecánica. Apuntes Universitarios. Revista de Investigación **10**(1), 77–88 (2020)
12. Rué, J.: Definir un entorno virtual para la enseñanza y aprendizaje (EPA), criterios y enseñanzas. Cuaderno de Pedagogía Universitaria **17**(34), 5–18 (2020)
13. Mendoza, H., Burbano, V., Valdivieso, M.: El rol del docente de matemáticas en educación virtual universitaria. Un estudio en la Universidad Pedagógica y Tecnológica de Colombia. Formación universitaria **12**(5), 51–60 (2019)
14. Cabanillas, J., Catarreira, S., Luengo, R.: Diferencias entre alumnado y profesorado en la valoración del uso de una plataforma virtual para la enseñanza y aprendizaje de las matemáticas. New Trends Qual. Res. **2**(5), 378–389 (2020)
15. Muerza, V.: Metodología de enseñanza-aprendizaje de Estadística: caso de adaptación durante la covid-19. In: 4th International Virtual Conference on Educational Research and Innovation, Spain, pp. 253–254 (2020)
16. Valencia, F., Guevara, C.: Uso de las TIC en procesos de aprendizaje de matemática, en estudiantes de básica superior. Dominio de las Ciencias **6**(3), 157–176 (2020)
17. Hernández, C.: Teaching perspectives in teachers who integrate a mathematics network: perceptions about the integration of ICT and the ways of teaching. Revista Virtual Universidad Católica del Norte **1**(61), 19–41 (2020)

18. Limache, E., Choque, C., Piaggio, M.: La gestión de la información en el aprendizaje de la estadística. Conrado **16**(72), 222–233 (2020)
19. Mejía, G.: La aplicación de las TIC en los procesos de enseñanza-aprendizaje en estudiantes de nivel medio superior en Tepic, Nayarit. Revista Iberoamericana para la Investigación y el Desarrollo Educativo **11**(21) (2020)
20. Molina, C., Salazar, I.: Uso de herramientas TIC en investigación científica de los estudiantes de administración en la UNAS-Tingo María. Investigación y Amazonía **8**(5), 40–47 (2021)

Virtual Learning Environments: A Case of Study

Fredy Gavilanes-Sagnay[1,2]([✉]) [iD], Edison Loza-Aguirre[1] [iD],
Cristian Echeverria-Carrillo[1], and Hugo Jacome-Viera[1] [iD]

[1] Departamento en Informática y Ciencias de la Computación, Escuela Politécnica Nacional,
Ladrón de Guevara, 11-253 Quito, Ecuador
{fredy.gavilanes,edison.loza,cristian.echeverria,
hugo.jacome}@epn.edu.ec
[2] Universidad de las Fuerzas Armadas ESPE sede Santo Domingo de los Tsáchilas, Parroquia
Luz de América, km 24 vía a Quevedo, Santo Domingo, Ecuador
fmgavilanes1@espe.edu.ec

Abstract. Virtual Learning Environments are innovative platforms that gain
strength and relevance as an alternative to traditional education. In this case study,
we have implemented an Open Simulator platform in three dimensions, where
it is intended that students can achieve a certain degree of skill through training between 2 levels; the first level can be freely deployed through the designed
laboratories and implemented within the infrastructure, on the other hand, at the
second level, users will be able to solve the challenges that arise within the field of
structured cabling. To validate this Virtual Learning Environment, the methodology named: Technologies Acceptance Model methodology has been used, which
is based on two factors of influence of the user: the user's perception of usefulness
and the degree to which a person believes that using a particular system would
enhance his or her job performance. At the end of this work, the results are exposed
to obtain the results.

Keywords: Virtual Learning Environments · Virtual worlds · OpenSim
platform · Educational platform

1 Introduction

The absence of suitable environments to run simulations on practical subjects such as
Structured Cabling in both 2D and 3D, has led to a problem because it is not possible to
make a link between the theoretical part with the real practical part that students face in
the world of work and its problems.

That is why in the present work, we propose the first approach in the adaptation of
a Virtual Learning Environment in 3D developed under the OpenSimulator platform,
where students can have a virtual visualization of the faculty, as a proposal so that both
teachers and students can adapt to a simulation environment that fundamentally requires
the predisposition of the participants [1] in its use.

OpenSimulator is a development platform for virtual environments in 3D, especially
associated with the conception of virtual worlds such as Second Life [2] and distributed

M. Botto-Tobar et al. (Eds.): ICAT 2021, CCIS 1535, pp. 108–120, 2022.
https://doi.org/10.1007/978-3-031-03884-6_8

by Linden Labs, Inc. To use it from various perspectives [3], in this case, the perspectives of the instructor and of students who are going to use it as a useful tool in developing their skills. By using it as an educational potential for its ability to stimulate logical ability, the development of different strategies aimed at achieving problem-solving [4]. Among the advantages of OpenSimulator, you can determine its ease to install the server, it contains an interface, which is very intuitive for users from beginner to intermediate level, it also has the advantage that it is a portable platform and that it has a moderate consumption of computational resources.

In this case study, it is intended to determine the usefulness in training in the subject of structured cabling, to take advantage of the advantages inherent to the use of 3D EVA, through this platform it is intended to solve well-defined types [5], where according to the author, the main characters in this type of problem is that there are one or more solutions that are known and correct, unlike the so-called ill-defined problems, where the solutions may be different, all this It will depend on the conditions, assumptions, evidence and even opinions that are determined.

Although in this sense, it has been determined that 3D EVAs also have their drawbacks that can be evaluated to make corrections in time, these can be the followings: problems related to knowing what is happening within the virtual world to identify conflictive user behaviors [6–8] or tracking the students' interactions with elements of the virtual world [9, 10], lack of indicators to follow up the progress of the students in the courses [11], lack of implementation of well-defined evaluation parameters [11], difficulties for evaluating the collective and individual contributions while the students handle tasks [12], difficulties for keeping students engaged and motivated [13], a very time-consuming teachers' supervision in the search for signs of doubt, frustration, stress or fatigue from students [14], pedagogical issues that are inherent to conventional learning [15, 16], absence of tutors with experience to guide the learning process [16, 17]. These problems raise the need to pursue the quest of mechanisms to improve the use of Virtual Worlds in education and guarantee the effective fulfillment of learning objectives [18, 19].

2 Related Works

TAM [20], Technology Acceptance Model is an information systems theory in where help us to understand how users come to accept and use technology; in our case this virtual learning environment, TAM suggests that after analyzing the external type variables called Perceived usefulness (PU) and Perceived ease of use (PEOU), where the qualitative evaluation, it can be deduced that the comments are mostly positive in relation to the comments negative or neutral, it can be determined that the system subjected to evaluation by TAM, this system will be adopted and used by potential users.

In addition, the evaluation through these external variables also leads to the change of a negative attitude to a positive attitude in relation to the acceptance of the use of a system or technology, in this case, the acceptance for the use of a developed 3D Virtual Learning Environment platform in OpenSIM.

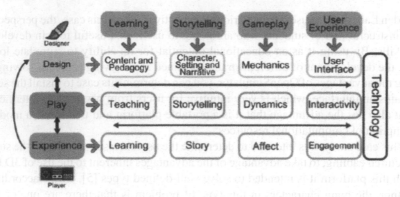

Fig. 1. Framework design play experience

3   Methods

TAM [20], Technology Acceptance Model is an information systems theory in where help us to understand how users come to accept and use technology; in our case this virtual learning environment, TAM suggests that the users when using new technology, several factors influence their decision about how and when they will use according to two factors: (1) Perceived usefulness (PU) that the author defined as "the degree to which a person believes that using a particular system would enhance his or her job performance," in other words, whether or not someone perceives that technology to be useful for what they want to do, and (2) Perceived ease of use (PEOU), that is defined as "the degree to which a person believes that using a particular system would be free from effort," this concept tries to explain if technology is the ease of use, then the barriers conquered, if it is not easy to use and the interface is complicated, no one has a positive attitude towards it. Also, this model is helpful to apply when the number of users is limited, how in our virtual learning environment.

The framework named Design Play Experience (DPE) [21] is mainly useful for designing and developing in serious games such as our virtual learning environment; this framework in Fig. 1, presents an organizational structure a formal process as a methodology to design and develop virtual environments such as serious games for this we need to adapt our product in four layers: learning, storytelling, gameplay and user experience layer.

3.1   Learning Layer

This layer is where the content and pedagogy are designed, that is, what you want to obtain as a result of learning or, in other words, the content you wish to transmit for players who enter the 3D Virtual learning Environment. The first thing that is done is to identify the skills the player wants to achieve through the game using techniques and instructions described later in the Storytelling layer.

That is, it is considered as the virtualization of the design, and the methodology must be carried out as if it were carried out by an instructor in the development of their curriculum, where the learning results are defined by the instructional design techniques to be used.

3.2 Storytelling

The Storytelling layer has two clearly defined perspectives: the designer's story and the more player's story.

About the designer's story, it refers to the narration that is designed for the game where the main purpose must be designed to be achieved through the interaction of the game through the transmission of content; it also focuses on the design of both the characters as well as the objects with which the player will interact, on the other hand, the narrative becomes an ideal setting where the player, will follow the instructions exactly, will understand and understand the content to be transmitted.

The other perspective is that of the player's story, where it is the reality of the player's interaction with the objects designed from the perspective of the designer's story, where the player, depending on their expertise and ability to follow the correct instructions, can be determined to a certain degree of certainty the transmission of the desired message through the use and interaction of the 3D Virtual Learning Environment. Gameplay Layer.

The possible paths in which the player will navigate in the serious game are defined, which will depend on the factors that converge in relation to the actions, decisions, routes, and functions to observe, navigate and interact with the virtual world to achieve this, is subdivided into 3 sublayers.

3.3 Gameplay

This layer defines what the player does in the game. It is a description of what decisions the player makes within the interaction of the game, and when adding the decisions that ramifications are generated based on the paths decided by the player in the rest of the game. Three types of sublayers must be determined within this layer: mechanical, dynamic, and effects, which are described below.

Mechanics

Here the future actions within the 3DVLE are defined, that is, the actions that the user can execute, the challenges that will be imposed and the objectives that they will have to achieve.

Dynamics

These are the results that are obtained once the mechanics are executed while the player's interaction with the 3DVLE lasts.

Effects

Basically, it is the perception of the user while observing, navigating, and interacting with the 3DVLE.

3.4 User Experience Layer

It is considered as the surface layer, that is, what the player actually visualizes; This is where the game design is tested, where the main challenge for the designer is that the game is trained and with an interface that gives access to the game. Where the main objective of the designer is to design that the game or the content to be transmitted is entertaining for the player in such a way that it does not exceed the limits from the lower point of view where it is considered an easy game to become dull or exceeding the upper limit that becomes unattainable for the player and that in the same way as in the previous case is frustrating for the player, this should be applied in serious games, where the purpose of the user interface is also to create a link to achieve the desired content.

4   Case of Study

In this case study, the environment based on two levels of the infrastructure of the Faculty of Systems Engineering of the Escuela Politécnica Nacional is presented.

Before entering the Virtual Learning Environment, you must register for the user generation through the University intranet. In Fig. 2, you can see the site for managing the user account. From Fig. 3, 4, 5 and Fig. 6 the virtual learning environment is depicted from the user's perspective.

Fig. 2. Website for the generation and creation of user accounts for the OpenSim platform.

From this scenario, the student will be able to meet several learning objectives directly related to structured cabling, from which it can be determined:

- Virtual navigation in 2 levels present in the simulation, each of these levels is in different coordinates and can be exchanged through the teleportation option through a portal.
- The use of components through an inventory of objects for structured cabling.

- At level 1, users will be able to: (1) Scroll through the seven laboratories distributed in the virtual building of the faculty. (2) The teacher can share the concepts and real experiences through the platform. (3) Browse freely to place the different structured cabling components such as ducts, network points, racks. (4) Enter the data center of the building to place the different necessary components. (5) Manipulate the communications rack present in the data center.

Fig. 3. Virtual Learning Environment based on platform OpenSim about the Escuela Politécnica Nacional.

- At level 2, it contains the structure of the FIS faculty building, with the exception of the structured cabling components displayed at level 1. (1) In a level 2 environment, the student will be able to move through the 3-story building with 8 rooms on each floor. (2) Solve for each student the challenges that arise. (3) On the first floor, the creation of 6 work areas for each workroom is requested. (4) On the second floor, the student will have to create the building's data center. (5) The creation of 7 laboratories with 15 work areas for each laboratory is also requested. (6) On floor 3, the creation of 8 classrooms with 8 communication boxes, two on each wall of the classroom, is expected.

5 Artifact Description

In the description of this artifact, we are going to take into account the design and the playing of our proposal, for that we are going to break it down according to the structure of the MDA framework [23], in its respective layers:

Fig. 4. Workspace for skill development within structured cabling based on platform OpenSim.

5.1 Learning

To develop this layer we start from the central theme, which is structured wiring, for the design is considered the building where the Faculty of Systems of the National Polytechnic School in Quito-Ecuador works, it is this building modeled in 3D, it is a player You will be able to access an experience of a functional structured cabling model, both in relation to horizontal cabling and vertical cabling, as well as trying to represent aspects that the player could find in the real world, applying certain restrictions such as:

1. The player cannot extend any connection for a distance greater than 100 m,
2. the player must establish a minimum distance of 35 cm between the structured wiring tray and the electrical wiring of the building, and
3. straight curves must be avoided that force to force the cable.

Fig. 5. View of the building instance where the student learns and the instance where the student applies the knowledge.

The player will also contain a virtual-type inventory system, where he is limited to using only the components stored there. We decided to limit the necessary objects within this system so that the student can meet the required learning objectives; it should be emphasized that among the limitations, verification will not be carried out on the way of wiring installation in real life because it would be necessary special certification machines, but it has an analysis of the results that the student obtains when making their wiring model, taking into account certain points of the standard.

Fig. 6. Inventory of trays and accessories, for the user to use Structured Cabling in the user's inventory.

5.2 Storytelling

Two levels are determined where the player can interact; each one offers different options, the first level is designed so that the player grasps and understands the notions of structured wiring at the same time that the instructor can guide the basic notions, the player can move around the building having access to options such as opening doors, sitting down, turning on the lights, moving objects and making certain objects invisible to meet certain learning objectives such as visualizing the wiring layout, in this specific case, where it is The gutters, access points, the communications room are installed.

The next level contemplates that the player can design his proposal of the structured wiring model; for this, he will have to take into account the conditions of the building, its disposition, location of beams, walls, ducts of the building, for this, the player must have the inventory system that will contain the accessories and elements such as gutters, racks, ports, and equipment that will allow you to assemble a wiring system within the building, among the tasks that the student will have to perform are:

1. They must assemble a communications room based on the rules and requirements defined by the instructor,
2. You will have to build a gutter system that allows you to reach all points of the building based on the needs that arise, and
3. You will need to add cabinets communication if you consider it necessary

5.3 Gameplay

The player, having two levels of interaction, will have to differentiate the dynamics of each one; in the first level, he is limited to a visual interaction because he can only perform actions such as turning lights on or off, hiding or appearing objects, and open or close doors. On the other hand, in the second level of interaction, the player will be able to expand actions because the player has an inventory of objects where they can find objects such as racks, gutters, and the necessary equipment so that they can interact and create in this level of the environment with actions such as: placing ports, tables, equipment, communication cabinets and designing a communication room.

5.4 User Experience

Our 3DVLE platform is oriented for user-environment interaction; depending on the level of the game, the player can interact visually with limited interactions at the initial level or can increase interaction through the inventory system created for a higher level of player interaction with the platform. It is through this interaction that the development of competencies oriented to the knowledge, abilities, and skills of the simulation of the real world through the environment is intended, it is justifiable to simulate these real environments, which are complex to live because of the cost or the space necessary for this, that is why the simulation must become the link between the theoretical part of structured cabling with reality.

6 Results

After the present solution that we propose is implemented, the two different levels of player interaction can be determined, where the first level is focused on the facilitator or guide to share the knowledge, concepts, and experience with the player through interaction with the platform, in our platform, is located in the datacenter with the servers, I am a direct link with the internet service provider, from where the structured cabling connection is centralized to the rest of the building.

Table 1. TAM model comparison table.

Ease of use		Usefulness	
Positive	Negative	Positive	Negative
18	7	15	1

While the next level, the player's avatar will have to move to the building where he will find a 3-story building with 8 rooms on each floor; on the first floor, you have to create 6 work areas for each room, on the second floor is requested to create the communications room or called datacenter of the building, in addition, the design of the 7 laboratories is requested, where each one must have 15 workstations and finally on the third floor of the building the creation of 8 classrooms with 8 boxes is requested communication, 2 boxes on each wall of the classroom, for this the player will have the inventory with the objects that are needed to meet each of the objectives.

The present environment has been tested with guides from the structured cabling subject of the National Polytechnic School, and the students of these subjects have used the present environment, the results have been obtained through interviews with the guides instead of the students, have entered their opinions through surveys. To evaluate the acceptance of our environment, the qualitative evaluation methodology of user acceptance based on the TAM [20] (Technology Acceptance Model) technology acceptance model has been used. In this case, evaluating this environment is valid Due to the reduced number of users who have managed to use and validate the present virtual environment, for this TAM provides us with the model of how users accept and use technology, establishing the criteria that allow us to understand the intention of the user behavior, which basically Two determinants will be taken into account: perceived ease of use and perceived utility, factors that influence the individual attitude of the user.

For the player, it focuses on three questions that are: (1) How easy do you find using the environment? (2) Does this tool seem useful to you to learn the Structured Cabling subject? and (3) What recommendations could you give regarding the environment? The results of the survey are shown in Table 1.

In addition, the qualitative results mentioned by the players after playing the 3D Virtual Learning Environment, the most relevant comments can be cited:

- "I think it is very easy since it has all the necessary tools to just add, move or delete something that you do not want."
- "I found it to be very easy to use, the interaction is very good, and its speed is excellent, the tools are useful."

In relation to the usefulness, the most relevant comments can be determined as follows:

- "I think it is very easy since it has all the necessary tools to just add, move or delete something that you do not want."
- "I found it very easy to use, the interaction is very good, and its speed is excellent, the tools are useful."

Finally, the relevant comments based on the suggestions to improve the virtual learning environment are:

- "Allow an object created to be editable by other users or not"
- "Add a tutorial on how to use each tool a description of each tool."
- "Improve the names of the objects, maybe implement a preview before to know which object is to be used."

7 Conclusions

- Based on the results that can be seen in Table 1. it can be determined that, in relation to the perception of ease by users, a number of 18 positive comments have been obtained compared to a number of 7 negative comments, which allows us to obtain the relationship of 18: 7, for which the virtual environment presented would have a positive result complying with this determinant of the model.
- Regarding the perception of usefulness by player users, a total of 15 comments of a positive type have been determined out of a total of 16 comments, which can determine a ratio of 15: 1, so it can be admitted that the virtual environment would fulfill this determinant in a positive way.

8 Future Works

As part of future contributions, we will expand the range of students that interact with VLE, students from more than one university in Ecuador.

Another work that is planned is the development of an intelligent virtual tutor so that in real-time, it evaluates and makes predictions about the possible future movements of the player and guides him to make the correct decisions when carrying out the proposed activities.

Finally, the implementation of genetic algorithms to optimize the VLE routes to obtain the best paths, distances, and costs in relation to the implementation of structured cabling. In addition, the evaluation through these external variables also leads to the change of a negative attitude to a positive attitude in relation to the acceptance of the use of a system or technology, in this case, the acceptance for the use of a developed 3D Virtual Learning Environment platform in OpenSIM.

References

1. Galindo-Domínguez, H.: Videogames in the multidisciplinary development of primary education curriculum: the minecraft case. Pixel-Bit Rev. Medios y Educ. 57–73 (2019). https://doi.org/10.12795/pixelbit.2019.i55.04
2. Weber, A., Rufer-Bach, K., Platel, R.: Creating Your World: The Official Guide to Advanced Content Creation for Second Life. Wiley (2007)
3. Rodríguez Malebrán, M.E., Manzanilla Castellanos, M.A., Peña Angulo, E.A., Occelli, M., Ramírez Rivera, C.: Evaluación del videojuego educativo "Aphids Attack" a través de modelos log-lineales para la enseñanza de las interacciones ecológicas en el nivel primario. Pixel-Bit Rev. Medios y Educ. 59, 201–224 (2020). https://doi.org/10.12795/pixelbit.77888
4. del Mar Badia Martin, M., Muntada, M.C., Pros, R.C., Sáez, T.D., Busquets, C.G.: Alumnos De Primaria. Video games, television and academic performance. Rev. Medios y Educ. 1, 25–38 (2015)
5. Kitchner, K.S.: Cognition, metacognition, and epistemic cognition. Hum. Dev. 26, 222–232 (1983). https://doi.org/10.1159/000272885
6. Cruz-Benito, J., et al.: Monitoring and feedback of learning processes in virtual worlds through analytics architectures: a real case. In: Iberian Conference on Information Systems and Technologies, CISTI. IEEE Computer Society (2014). https://doi.org/10.1109/CISTI.2014.6877097

7. Virvou, M., Katsionis, G., Manos, K.: Combining Software Games with Education: Evaluation of its Educational Effectiveness (2005). http://www.jstor.org/stable/pdf/jeductechsoci.8.2.54. pdf#page_scan_tab_contents. https://doi.org/10.2307/jeductechsoci.8.2.54

8. Bremer, P.T., Weber, G., Tierny, J., Pascucci, V., Day, M., Bell, J.: Interactive exploration and analysis of large-scale simulations using topology-based data segmentation. IEEE Trans. Vis. Comput. Graph. **17**, 1307–1324 (2011). https://doi.org/10.1109/TVCG.2010.253

9. Wojciechowski, R., Cellary, W.: Evaluation of learners' attitude toward learning in ARIES augmented reality environments. Comput. Educ. **68**, 570–585 (2013). https://doi.org/10.1016/j.compedu.2013.02.014

10. Williams, D.: The mapping principle, and a research framework for virtual worlds. Commun. Theory. **20**, 451–470 (2010). https://doi.org/10.1111/j.1468-2885.2010.01371.x

11. de Oliveira, F.S., Santos, S.: PBLMaestro: a virtual learning environment for the implementation of problem-based learning approach in computer education. In: 2016 IEEE Frontiers in Education Conference (FIE), pp. 1–9. IEEE (2016). https://doi.org/10.1109/FIE.2016.7757388

12. Bandura, A.: Perceived self-efficacy in cognitive development and functioning. Educ. Psychol. **28**, 117–148 (1993). https://doi.org/10.1207/s15326985ep2802_3

13. Hmelo-Silver, C.E.: Problem-based learning: what and how do students learn? Educ. Psychol. Rev. **15**, 22–30 (2004)

14. Goncalves, S., Carneiro, D., Alfonso, J., Fdez-Riverola, F., Novais, P.: Analysis of student's context in e-Learning. In: 2014 International Symposium on Computers in Education (SIIE), pp. 179–182. IEEE (2014). https://doi.org/10.1109/SIIE.2014.7017726

15. Panchoo, S.: Learning space: assessment of prescribed activities of online learners. In: 2017 International Conference on Platform Technology and Service (PlatCon), pp. 1–4. IEEE (2017). https://doi.org/10.1109/PlatCon.2017.7883715

16. Boojihawon, D., Gatsha, G.: Using ODL and ICT to develop the skills of the unreached: a contribution to the ADEA triennial of the Working Group on Distance Education and Open Learning, pp. 12–17 (2012)

17. Abrami, P., et al.: A review of e-learning in Canada: a rough sketch of the evidence, gaps and promising directions. learntechlib.org (2006)

18. Carmody, K., Berge, Z.: Existential elements of the online learning experience. Int. J. Educ. Dev. ICT **1**(3), 108–119 (2005)

19. Panayides, P.M.: The impact of organizational learning on relationship orientation, logistics service effectiveness and performance. Ind. Mark. Manag. **36**, 68–80 (2007). https://doi.org/10.1016/J.INDMARMAN.2005.07.001

20. Davis, F.D.: Perceived usefulness, perceived ease of use, and user acceptance of information technology. MIS Q. Manag. Inf. Syst. **13**, 319–339 (1989). https://doi.org/10.2307/249008

21. Winn, B.M.: The design, play, and experience framework. In: Handbook of Research on Effective Electronic Gaming in Education, pp. 1010–1024. IGI Global (2009). https://doi.org/10.4018/978-1-59904-808-6.ch058

22. Ibadango-Galeano, E., Vargas-Chagna, L., Gallegos Varela, M., Vélez-Meza, M., Placencia-Enriquez, E.: Storytelling digital: experience and technology in designs of tele-collaborative projects in higher education. In: Botto-Tobar, M., Montes León, S., Camacho, O., Chávez, D., Torres-Carrión, P., Zambrano Vizuete, M. (eds.) ICAT 2020. CCIS, vol. 1388, pp. 151–163. Springer, Cham (2021). https://doi.org/10.1007/978-3-030-71503-8_12

23. Hunicke, R., LeBlanc, M., Zubek, R.: MDA: a formal approach to game design and game research, vol. 4, p. 1722. aaai.org (2004)

Therapy Using Serious Games to Improve Phonological Awareness in Children with Functional Dyslexia

Shirley-Mishell Pérez-Quichimbo(✉), Milton-Patricio Navas-Moya,
Sergio-Raúl Montes-León, Patricia-Aracely Sambachi-Chilig,
and Erick-David Barrera-Quimbita

Universidad de las Fuerzas Armadas ESPE, Sangolquí, Ecuador

{smperez7,mpnavas,srmontes,pasambachi,edbarrera}@espe.edu.ec

Abstract. Nowadays, there are many pedagogical methods for the treatment of children with dyslexia. However, the results are not always as expected, due to heavy and repetitive methods. Therefore, to contribute to the problem, this research aims to develop a video game based on a methodological guide for the application of strategies to support the teaching-learning process, which is characterized by being interactive. The MeISE software development methodology facilitated the creation of the educational software since it analyzed the most common learning problems of reading and writing in children with dyslexia. In order to evaluate the acceptance and incidence in relation to the traditional method, the proposal has been applied in a psychological center for children with special difficulties. Among which, the indicators used for the evaluation of the interactive software resulted in the majority acceptance of the children and an improvement of 44%. The case studies suggest that the video game awakens in children a greater interest in the treatment and improves their visual and reading skills.

Keywords: Dyslexia · Learning · Literacy · School stress · Treatment · Psychological center · Serious games · Video game · MeISE methodology

1 Introduction

The difficulties with accurate and fluent word recognition, incorrect spelling and decoding are dominant factors in children with special educational needs. Although there is a deficit in the phonological component of language, people with special disabilities such as dyslexia do not have a low intellectual level.

Smart children are generalized to high IQ populations on the basis that literacy and intelligence are moderately related. However, the International Dyslexia Association (IDA) states that dyslexia is a specific learning disability of neurobiological origin. And that it often involves increased effort in cognitive and tentative skills within a classroom [1].

© Springer Nature Switzerland AG 2022
M. Botto-Tobar et al. (Eds.): ICAT 2021, CCIS 1535, pp. 121–134, 2022.
https://doi.org/10.1007/978-3-031-03884-6_9

Developmental dyslexia are associated with social and emotional consequences that are not considered core features of the disorder. Therefore, in the early years of life in particular, children with dyslexia must take constant learning and reading resolution therapies. However, many of these therapies are physically and emotionally exhausting, causing discomfort to the child with this learning disorder. Therefore, there was a need to captivate the child's interest through the use of the computer.

Currently, computer games generate a great impact at the educational level, even improving the learning factor [2]. This positive impact gave rise to the creation of a new computer game.

This positive impact gave rise to the creation of an iterative video game for children with dyslexia, aimed at improving written and spoken language skills.

The game tries to improve the phonological awareness of girls and boys with dyslexia, for the design of an educational software engineering methodology called MeISE was followed, an exploration of several works referring to the development of software tools for the treatment and diagnosis of dyslexia is performed, consecutively different principles are considered for the design of the game [15].

The video game consists of several activities, each one focused on different levels and with a specific characteristic, i.e., it evaluates word, syllabic memory ability, verbal work, auditory memory, syllable and word reading ability [3].

These activities help to propose the differences between letters. The main objective of the video game is for dyslexic children to recognize and distinguish the letters p, q, b, d, m, and w [4]. The development of the application is focused on improving visual, auditory, and cognitive disabilities [5].

2 State of the Art

Dyslexia is a language disorder that primarily affects the ability to read and write [6]. Children with dyslexia have problems in the rate and speed of learning written language, as well as in acquiring an adequate level of performance [7]. In studies, a high number of children with the disorder tend to have problems in written and spoken language, but this does not imply that they are able to learn [13].

Researchers from the University of Padua have pointed out that ten children with dyslexia who played a video game for nine sessions each on of 80 min increased their reading speed, without errors, thus reaching the result that video games improve visual attention and reading ability, two of the deficits suffered by people with dyslexia, [14].

Previously many video games applications have been developed for dyslexic children improving their cognitive learning with 2D and 3D graphics some of them are described below [8].

2.1 ILearnRW

The game provides a tool for children to work on their literacy skills. It aims to maintain active participation for an unlimited number of play sessions, with this they hope to improve learning outcomes and motivate children to play at home as well [9].

The game consists of an adaptive mechanism based on two modules. The first, the student module is directly linked to the information displayed on the social network. The second, the lesson planner plots the upcoming character encounters in the game world and prepares the content to be used in the game activities [9].

2.2 Madrigal

It is an educational action game that aims to boost the phonological formation and visuospatial attention of children with dyslexia who are between 7 and 9 years old. This game consists of two phases, one in which the child must correctly order the word as quickly as possible and another in which the application highlights the letters while pronouncing them [10].

2.3 Dyslexia Baca

The application "Dyslexia Baca" is specifically developed to help dyslexic children to recognize the alphabet, which motivates them to learn and remember the information in a fun and didactic way. "Dyslexia Baca" is developed in Malay language using a multi-sensory approach and incorporating a learning ecosystem suitable for children with dyslexia [4].

2.4 MeISE Methodology

For the development of the serious game, the methodology used was Educational Software Engineering (MeISE), [11] proposed by Abud in 2009, who exposes a life cycle divided into two stages: definition and development, as shown in the Fig. 1.
In the first stage, the requirements, analysis and initial design are defined, i.e., it is determined what is intended to be achieved with the software. The objectives or what the software is intended to achieve are specified in a general way, and it is finished with a plan of iterations, taking care that the product that is released in each plan is didactically complete [12].

The second stage proceeds to develop the software, so that the development team takes each iteration, designs, builds, tests and implements it, making an evaluation at the end considering that it has a feedback process to proactively detect and improve the difficulties that arise in the teaching-learning process with a literacy character.

3   Implementation

Educational software plays a great role in the learning of children with special difficulties. Therefore, for its implementation, requirements were used in order of priority reinforcement with the methodology of Educational Software Engineering (MeISE), which consists of two stages of definition and development that facilitates the implementation of activities in a structured manner.

MeISE Methodology

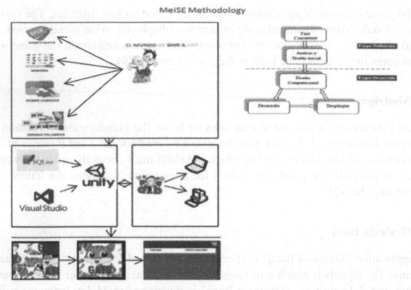

Fig. 1. Scheme of the MeISE methodology

This methodology is considered a support tool for the reading and writing process, since it allows the child to develop logical abilities, classification, recognition, retention, selection and classification skills.

The iterative didactic video game is entitled "The world of Shir&Path", and its purpose is to improve the child's spatial orientation, memory capacity, visual, lexical and orthographic development (Fig. 2).

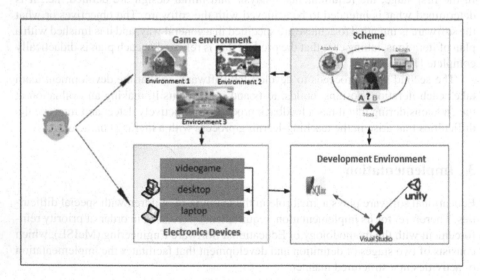

Fig. 2. Scheme of the implementation

According to the defined context, using the MeISE methodology, different schemes were designed that propose an iterative approach and include computational, pedagogical and communication aspects. This methodology proposes a cycle divided into two stages, the main one is to define a list of requirements and preliminary design in order to address the teaching conditions identified in the study of learning disabilities.

The MeISE methodology allows the video game to obtain a quality product from technical and didactic points of view, since aspects of pedagogical design and human-computer interface are included. Therefore, auditory and visual stimuli are included where motivational messages such as "very good", "go ahead", "try again" are found, so that the child realizes the success or failure.

Once these main guidelines are established, the second stage begins, where the software is proposed to be developed. The video game is focused on activities or exercises that automate the development of literacy learning, such as the perception and selection of a figure, the ability to correctly divide words, perceive the position of an object in relation to its position in space, and the ability to accurately distinguish the differences and similarities between letters and words.

The main benefit of MeISE is to focus on the design of the video game and peripheral devices, as these contribute to the improvement of literacy skills in children with dyslexia. In this way, the Unity tool was used for the video game functions, since it contributes aspects of didactic pedagogical design. This tool is complemented with the use of the C # language in which the game functionalities are defined based on object-oriented programming units. Then, all the player's information is stored in the SQLite database.

3.1 Main Screens

Fig. 3. Main screen

These screens allow us to interact with the video game, where we must create a user, who will help us to enter and participate, all the information entered here is used to measure the progress of the treatment (Fig. 3).

The interface is friendly to the user's eye with colors and content that were approved by a specialist in the area of psychology. This avoids the possible initial distractions of an application.

3.2 Puzzle

Fig. 4. Puzzle game screens.

To work on visual dyslexia, the Puzzle game has been implemented. The objective of this activity is that the child learns to distinguish between right, left, up and down. The user is presented with a set of pieces that make up the image (Fig. 4).

With this activity, the child develops the ability to recompose the image by correctly combining flat pieces. This treatment serves to develop cognitive skills such as observation, attention, visual memory, organization and logic. The importance of this game is to stimulate their spatial intelligence. These activities are based on visual-motor coordination to develop the ability to retain images.

At the beginning of the game the instructions will be presented in a clear and summarized way, the person in charge of the child will have to introduce the number of rows in which the image will be divided and then using the button load image select the image that the child wants to assemble, previously the tutor must have a folder with downloaded images with the theme that the child wants to present, once this is done, the child will begin to move the pieces with the mouse and fit each one in its place to form the image, it is necessary that the tutor shows the child before the image that will be used to fulfill the puzzle. Within the video game a statistic will be kept of the number of attempts the child has made to form the image.

3.3 Memory

Fig. 5. Memory game screens

In the memory activity, the user is presented with several images in succession. For each image, the child must find its respective pair. This matching exercise helps the child to develop the classification skill, which involves the patient perceiving the object and picture, joining the matching images to form the pair. The game will count the number of attempts to form pairs and the time it takes to complete each level (Fig. 5).

3.4 Labeling Objects

The Label Object mini-game was implemented to help the child develop visual and auditory skills. At the beginning of the game, the instructions are presented in a clear and summarized way, and the person in charge of the child must explain the meaning of each image. At the top of this activity there are four words, two correct and two distracting words. The child must associate in each box the word of the visualized images, understanding its meaning. The game will count the number of attempts and the time the child has spent to solve the activity (Fig. 6).

3.5 Order Syllables

The syllable matching mini-game is oriented to work on visual and auditory skills. The child is presented with a set of syllables, with which he/she can build the word of

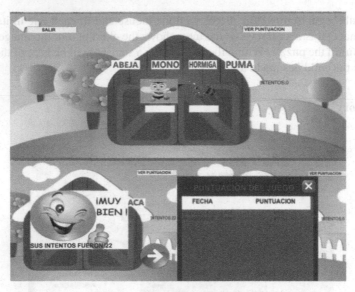

Fig. 6. Label object game screens.

Fig. 7. Memory game screens

the given image in the company of an educational sound devoid of distractors. At the beginning of the game the instructions are presented in a clear and summarized way, the person in charge of the child must explain the meaning of each image and the type of word according to the number of syllables, once this is done the child will begin to place the order of syllables to form the word of the image. The game will count the number of attempts and the time the child has spent to solve the activity (Fig. 7).

4 Evaluation of Results

In order to evaluate the incidence of the interactive video game in the treatment of children with dyslexia, a study was carried out in a psychological center. With the help of a specialist, a sample of 20 children was selected by non-probabilistic sampling of typical subjects who met the specific characteristics of having dyslexia disorder and being between 5 and 9 years old. The children and their tutors were given an induction on the functioning and objectives of the video game. To carry out the study, a test was applied to the children before and after using the video game, which evaluated each of the reading and writing skills that the video game was intended to reinforce in the children, using a 10-point scale (0–2 = very low, 3–4 = low, 5–6 = regular, 7–8 = high, 9–10 = very high).

At the end of the study, a comparison was made of the results of the tests applied in its different stages, as well as those obtained with the traditional method commonly used in the treatment. Where an evident difference could be observed.

The table above shows the averages of the tests performed in the initial, intermediate and final stages of the study for both the traditional and the game method, through which it can be concluded that during the 6-week period of time proposed for the research, 73.17% had better performance in learning to read and write using the video game, while 29.14% obtained better results with the traditional method.

Most children with dyslexia react differently to the learning process, being digital natives, most of them tend to quickly become familiar with technology.

Based on the previous results, the playful method shows great acceptance and progress in relation to the traditional method, although as could be observed in some patients, a better performance is maintained with the traditional method.

Figure 8 represents graphically the results of the study carried out on children with dyslexia in the different stages of the study, it can be seen that by applying the playful method in the treatment of dyslexia, children improve in their learning of reading and writing with the use of educational video games, these create an interesting environment where the child interacts with each of the functionalities of the application, increasing their interest in the treatment and achieving an improvement of 44% in relation to the traditional methods commonly used.

Table 1. Results of the studied evaluation

Method	Traditional				Playful			
Children	Test 1	Test 2	Test 3	%	Test 1	Test 2	Test 3	%
1	1,083	2,202	2,756	20,13	7,105	8,212	8,816	80,44
2	1,921	2,512	3,012	24,81	5,909	6,622	7,096	65,42
3	2,794	3,75	4,583	41,66	6,702	7,691	8,503	80,97
4	2,156	2,601	3,124	26,27	6,003	6,591	7,983	68,59
5	1,356	2,478	3,136	23,23	6,356	7,869	8,194	74,73
6	1,201	2,369	3,156	22,42	5,201	6,369	7,156	62,42
7	1,815	2,697	3,206	25,72	6,005	7,699	8,234	73,12
8	2,105	2,743	3,497	27,81	6,115	7,841	8,596	75,17
9	1,996	3,593	4,417	40,05	5,869	7,501	8,456	79,78
10	1,625	2,894	3,503	26,74	5,536	6,881	7,561	66,59
11	1,195	2,917	3,597	25,69	5,205	6,901	7,795	66,33
12	1,469	2,981	3,713	27,21	6,963	7,589	8,619	77,23
13	1,994	2,667	3,851	28,37	5,989	6,769	7,959	69,05
14	1,315	2,203	3,294	22,70	6,315	7,593	8,494	74,67
15	2,667	3,833	4,667	37,22	5,756	7,938	8,714	74,69
16	2,369	3,569	4,417	39,93	6,592	7,698	8,687	81,92
17	1,623	2,252	2,951	22,75	5,623	6,382	6,915	63,06
18	3,694	4,015	4,369	40,26	7,694	8,251	8,395	81,13
19	2,632	3,5	4,167	38,33	6,823	7,609	8,378	79,93
20	1,698	1,902	2,841	21,47	5,536	6,952	7,961	68,16
%-total				29,14				73,17

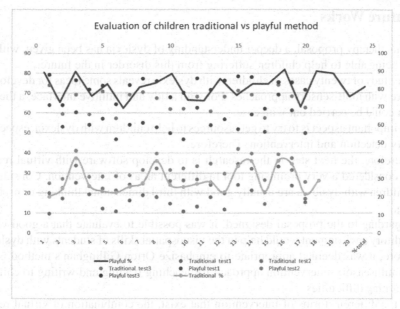

Fig. 8. Graphic representation of the playful treatment.

5 Discussion

In recent years, the advance of information and communication technologies has had a great influence on the transmission of knowledge. Based on twenty case studies, it was found that the MeISE methodology favors the understanding of the content by the child with dyslexia, since it is supported by psycho-pedagogical bases on learning, as well as the basic principles of software engineering that allow the software to be successfully implemented.

The inclusion of technological tools with therapeutic and educational objectives in children with dyslexia at an early age, is a tool to support their social-emotional and educational development that promises positive results. The video game had a great acceptance by the children awakening their interest in the treatment, children develop their cognitive skills better through games, so they are improving day by day, which requires scalability of the software through the development of new levels in order to increase its complexity as the treatment progresses, since the 3 games proposed by the consultant psychologist, are those that enhance the method of the teaching-learning process.

6 Future Works

With this therapy proposal, a deeper understanding of dyslexia has been given, with the aim of being able to help children suffering from this disorder in the future.

The study of twenty cases of children with dyslexia reveals some ideas for developing software with multisensory approaches. For with a tidy and intuitive interface, a therapy session could be carried out with ease.

An important aspect is to try to get resources to help children with dyslexia, especially for early detection and intervention. Therefore,

Therefore, the next step in the research is to develop software with virtual reality, as it is considered a very promising tool in different areas of intervention. Considering that children with dyslexia are usually good with third dimensional thinking or problem solving.

Regarding to the proposal designed, it was possible to evaluate that a good visual and auditory environment would help in the visuospatial skills of students with dyslexia. Therefore, it was deemed appropriate to emphasize Orton Gillinghan's method, since it is a multisensory intervention approach for teaching reading and writing to children with learning difficulties.

Of the different forms of intervention that exist, the combination of virtual reality with the Orton Gillinghan method provides a more effective training of phonological awareness at the level of visual and semantic skills.

7 Conclusions

A child with dyslexia may have normal intelligence, however, within society, he or she feels undervalued. Therefore, it is necessary to start treatment from an early age.

With technological advancement, children today no longer show interest in traditional games resulting in video games being considered as a tool to help in skill development and learning.

The video game has shown a positive effect on the improvement of phonological, visual and literacy skills. Therefore, the design of the video game responds to the needs of children with dyslexia, becoming a fundamental tool for the therapeutic processes related to the teaching and learning process.

On the other hand, the MeISE Software Engineering methodology used for the development of the video game, determines the characteristics of the expected software product, based on the pedagogical requirements of communication and technological architecture.

References

1. International Dyslexia Association: International DYSLEXIA Association (2021)
2. Cardona, J.P., Velazquez, C., Dominguez, G., Munoz, J., Alvarez, F.: Remedial training with learning objects to reduce dyslexia in children. In: 2019 International Conference on Inclusive Technologies and Education (CONTIE), San Jose del Cabo, Mexico, October 2019, pp. 68–683 (2019). https://doi.org/10.1109/CONTIE49246.2019.00022
3. Haridas, M., Vasudevan, N., Iyer, A., Menon, R., Nedungadi, P.: Analyzing the responses of primary school children in dyslexia screening tests. In: 2017 5th IEEE International Conference on MOOCs, Innovation and Technology in Education (MITE), Bangalore, November 2017, pp. 89–94 (2017). https://doi.org/10.1109/MITE.2017.00022
4. Daud, S.M., Abas, H.: "Dyslexia Baca" mobile app – the learning ecosystem for dyslexic children. In: 2013 International Conference on Advanced Computer Science Applications and Technologies, Kuching, Malaysia, December 2013, pp. 412–416 (2013). https://doi.org/10.1109/ACSAT.2013.87
5. Arteaga, J.M., Pinedo Rivera, D.I.: A process model to develop educational applications for children with dyslexia. In: 2018 6th International Conference in Software Engineering Research and Innovation (CONISOFT), San Luis Potosí, Mexico, October 2018, pp. 79–87 (2018). https://doi.org/10.1109/CONISOFT.2018.8645896
6. Mahmoodin, Z., Mansor, W., Lee, K.Y., Mohamad, N.B.: An analysis of EEG signal power spectrum density generated during writing in children with dyslexia. In: 2015 IEEE 11th International Colloquium on Signal Processing & Its Applications (CSPA), Kuala Lumpur, Malaysia, March 2015, pp. 156–160 (2015). https://doi.org/10.1109/CSPA.2015.7225637
7. Tunmer, W., Greaney, K.: Defining dyslexia. J. Learn. Disabil. 43(3), 229–243 (2010). https://doi.org/10.1177/0022219409345009
8. Bhatti, Z., Bibi, M., Shabbir, N.: Augmented reality based multimedia learning for dyslexic children. In: 2020 3rd International Conference on Computing, Mathematics and Engineering Technologies (iCoMET), Sukkur, Pakistan, pp. 1–7 (2020). https://doi.org/10.1109/iCoMET48670.2020.9073879
9. Cuschieri, T., Khaled, R., Farrugia, V.E., Martinez, H.P., Yannakakis, G.N.: The iLearnRW game: support for students with dyslexia in class and at home. In: 2014 6th International Conference on Games and Virtual Worlds for Serious Applications (VS-GAMES), Valletta, Malta, September 2014, pp. 1–2 (2014). https://doi.org/10.1109/VS-Games.2014.7012167
10. Di Tore, P.A., Di Tore, S., Ludovico, L.A., Mangione, G.R.: MADRIGALE: a multimedia application for dyslexia and reading improvement gamifying learning experience. In: 2014 International Conference on Intelligent Networking and Collaborative Systems, Salerno, September 2014, pp. 486–491 (2014). https://doi.org/10.1109/INCoS.2014.48
11. Abud, F.: MeISE: Metodología de Ingeniería de Software Educativo. en Revista Internacional de Educación en Ingeniería 2(1), 1–9 (2009)
12. Laura, P., Giovanni, S.: CONSTRUCCIÓN DE MATE-MOVIL A TRAVÉS DE LA METODOLOGÍA MEISE, pp. 2–3. Publisher, México (2017)
13. Madeira, J., Silva, C., Marcelino, L., Ferreira, P., García Zapirain, B.: Assistive mobile applications for dyslexia. Procedia Comput. Sci. 64, 417–424 (2015)

14. Ouherrou, N., Elhammoumi, O., Benmarrakchi, F., El Kafi, J.: A heuristic evaluation of an educational game for children with dyslexia. In: 2018 IEEE 5th International Congress on Information Science and Technology (CiSt), Marrakech, Morocco, pp. 1–5 (2018). https://doi.org/10.1109/CIST.2018.8596393
15. Eutsler, L., Mitchell, C., Stamm, B., Kogut, A.: The influence of mobile technologies on preschool and elementary children's literacy achievement: a systematic review spanning 2007–2019. Educ. Technol. Res. Dev. **68**(4), 1739–1768 (2020). https://doi.org/10.1007/s11423-020-09786-1

Electronics

Smart IoT Monitoring System
for Pico-Hydropower Station Based
on Permanent Magnet Generator
with Radial Flux

Myriam Cumbajín[1] , Patricio Sánchez[1] , Estefanía Flores[2] ,
and Carlos Gordón[2](✉)

[1] SISAu Research Center, Facultad de Ingeniería y Tecnologías de la Información y la
Comunicación, Universidad Tecnológica Indoamérica, UTI, Ambato 180103, Ecuador
{myriamcumbajin,patriciosanchez}@indoamerica.edu.ec
[2] GITED Research Group, Facultad de Ingeniería en Sistemas, Electrónica e
Industrial, Universidad Técnica de Ambato, UTA, Ambato 180150, Ecuador
{eflores8220,cd.gordon}@uta.edu.ec

Abstract. We present the development of an Intelligent Internet of
Things Monitoring System for a Pico-Hydropower Station based on a
radial flux permanent magnet generator. The system mainly acquires the
physical and electrical variables of the Pico-Hydropower Station located
in the Ambato - Huachi - Pelileo irrigation channel, in the province of
Tungurahua in Ecuador and then provides the information in real time
on a Web page and stores it in a database. The IoT Monitoring System
mainly provides information for the efficient management of the Pico-
Hydropower Station. The IoT Monitoring system uses voltage, current,
and Hall effect sensors that feed the information to an Arduino Uno
development board. The data is then sent to a Raspberry PI development board, where it is displayed on a monitor screen at via VNC, they
are published on the website and stored for further processing. The IoT
Monitoring System is a convenient system to provide information on electricity production at any time and allows monitoring the appearance of
any problems which is a valuable information to make the right decision
when is required. So the system is a good contribution to maintenance
management and smart cities of the future.

Keywords: Monitoring platform · Radial flux · Electrical power

1 Introduction

Internet of Things (IoT) is the network of physical objects integrated with software, hardware that collects and exchanges data with each other. IoT plays an
important role in different domains, for example, transport, education, health
and banking [1,2]. IoT is a promising example that combines heterogeneous
and versatile objects with different communication and computational power to

© Springer Nature Switzerland AG 2022
M. Botto-Tobar et al. (Eds.): ICAT 2021, CCIS 1535, pp. 137–149, 2022.
https://doi.org/10.1007/978-3-031-03884-6_10

obtain information about the physical world of a network. With the advent of IoT, devices can interact with each other remotely using portable devices such as smartphones, tablets, or computers that have a wired or wireless Internet connection. Integrated IoT devices with restricted resources are used to monitor and control the intelligent environment [3]. Network bandwidth and power consumption should not be ignored. IoT devices are introduced with limited resources and different protocols that consume less power and low network bandwidth, respectively.

Today, developers are creating applications to integrate software with physical devices on a large scale, known as an IoT network [4]. These applications include smart grids and transportation systems. These applications require real-time controls, large-scale data centers, and powerful processing capabilities. These requirements can be met by using the Cloud of Things (CoT). CoT provides the platform to integrate IoT devices with CoT [5,6].

Pico-Hydroelectric power plants are typically an autonomous hydroelectric system built to provide electricity to rural communities and are adopted as renewable energy due to their advantages over large hydroelectric plants [7]. With the above, it is said that these systems are the most economical option to supply energy in isolated rural areas.

In this power generation system, it depends a lot on the variation of the water, and this is where generators are used to maintain its level. There are two types of permanent magnet machines for generators [8–10].

The presented IoT system consists of current and voltage sensors which store the value of the physical variable and send to an Arduino Uno which processes the data in an appropriate way and then through a serial connection send them to a Nodemcu that performs the Information is sent through a Wi-Fi connection and the RaspBerry PI receives it in a database which displays the values in a user-friendly graphical environment. This platform monitors in real time the voltage in a range from 0 to 50 [V], the current from 0 to 20 [A] and the generator power is calculated. Allow the generator of the pico hydroelectric plant to be constantly monitored with Internet access. Then, it is important to mention that the previously studied articles do not have any kind of monitoring system in the Pico-Hydropower Stations.

2   Related Works

The number of IoT application deployments has grown in industries such as automotive, utilities, healthcare, logistics, and home automation at an unprecedented rate in recent years [11]. Due to the increasing number of devices, there is a need to develop middleware in the cloud to manage a large number of sensors and actuators. There are IoT frameworks based on open-source components for disseminating and processing data [12].

Much research has been done on the interaction of IoT and cloud computing [13]. The main focus of the research is to gain a comprehensive understanding of the integration of cloud computing and IoT models to fill the gap identified during analysis in existing approaches. Due to the heterogeneity of different objects, IoT and cloud computing emerged to solve the problems [14]. CoT is capable of solving challenging problems such as management, aggregation, and storage for large-scale IoT platforms [15,16].

The Internet of Things research is exploring ways to connect these networks and strengthen intelligence [17]. To facilitate these connections, many low-power network protocols have been developed in the fields of research and industry in recent years [8–15,17,18]. However, with more and more connections, it is a difficult task to integrate smart things into composite applications. To solve this problem, many platforms have emerged in recent years that suggest an integrated architecture. Some of them are implemented on some devices and are largely incompatible with each other. Furthermore, due to their complexity and lack of known tools, they are accessible to relatively small expert developer communities, so their use in applications is very limited [19]. The authors proposed an event-driven framework that supports the collaboration of heterogeneous distributed production resources, in accordance with the principles of the Industry 4.0 paradigm by combining various technologies such as industrial IoT, semantic web, and multi-agent-based systems. The proposed system allows the resources to be updated on the changes that have occurred in their context [20].

3   Formulation of the Problem and Methodology

The IoT system for the pico hydroelectric plant located in an irrigation channel takes advantage of the data collected by the devices for remote monitoring with the help of IoT. The physical variables to be monitored are voltage and current. This central peak continuously generates electricity to illuminate the channel itself and, if possible, provide electricity to neighboring communities. The sensing will allow to know what is the consumption of this plant, in what hours its consumption becomes maximum.

3.1   Component Selection

From the generator it has been decided to obtain the value of some of the variables involved in the power generation process, which are its voltage and current. To carry out the monitoring of the data obtained from the generator to later be compared with those obtained by simulation, it is necessary to use a device that allows it to be done, there is a good amount of technological tools available in the local market that have the necessary requirements to carry it finished.

To develop the monitoring of the data obtained from the generator and to be compared later with those obtained by simulation, it is necessary to use devices that allow this to be done, of which there is a considerable amount of technological tools available in the local market that have the necessary requirements to develop.

To obtain and process data through the sensors, an Arduino Uno will be used, which is a microcontroller board based on the ATmega 328 and it is depicted in

Fig. 1. It consists of 14 digital IN/OUT pins, 6 analog inputs, 4 UARTs, speed of 16 MHz, USB connection, a power connector [21].

Fig. 1. Arduino Uno board

Likewise, for the convenience in capacity, accessibility and price, the Raspberry pi 3 model B will be used, since it has the functionalities to fulfill the desired possibilities, such as data visualization [22]. The Raspberry PI 3 model B is shown in Fig. 2.

For the visualization of the variables, a monitor connected to the HDMI port of the Raspberry PI 3 was initially used, to configure it and then it can be connected to it without the need for an additional monitor or screen and the connection to the Raspberry is made PI 3 through VNC (Virtual Network Computing), which is a free software program based on a client-server structure that allows observing the actions of the server computer remotely through a client computer. VNC does not impose restrictions on the operating system of the server computer compared to that of the client: it is possible to share the screen of a machine with any operating system that supports VNC by connecting from another computer or device that has a ported VNC client [23]. The screen of the Raspberry connected by VNC is sketched in Fig. 3.

Table 1. Characteristics of current sensors.

Features	ACS712	TA12-200	SCT-O 13-030
Sensor type	Inductive	Non invasive	Non invasive
Current type Work	AC-DC	AC	AC
Temperature	40 a 85 C	−55 a 85 C	−40 a 70 C
Consumption	2.5 [mA]	2.5 [mA]	3.2 [mA]
Operating voltage	5 [V]	3 [V]	5 a 10 [V]
Current range	−5 a 5 [A],−20 a 20 [A], −30 a 30 [A]	0 a 5 [A]	0 a 30 [A]
Resolution	66 mV/A, 100 mV/A, 185 mV/A	2000 V AC/1 min 5 mA	1000 V AC/1 min 5 mA

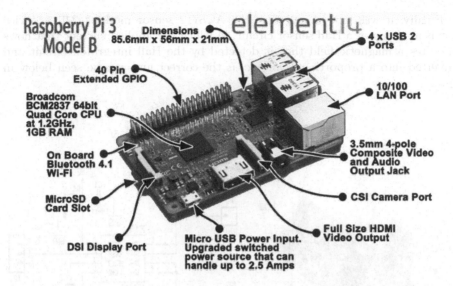

Fig. 2. Raspberry PI 3 model B

Fig. 3. Raspberry PI screen connected by VNC

Likewise, for the voltage measurement, the arduino direct signal was used and for the current measurement, several sensors that can be easily found on the market were taken into account, as shown in Table 1.

Finally, it was determined that the ACS712 sensor module [24], a device that is made up of a Hall sensor circuit, in which the applied current that flows generates a magnetic field that is detected by the Hall integrated circuit and converted into a proportional voltage, is the correct and can be seen below in Fig. 4.

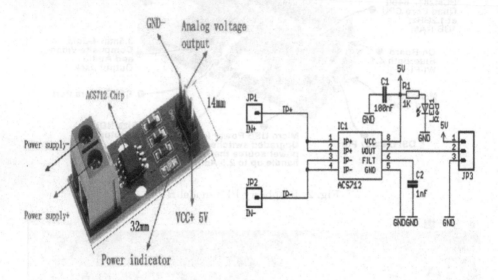

Fig. 4. ACS712 current sensor

For the voltage measurement, the ZMPT101B AC Voltage Sensor was used [25], which sends the direct signal to the Arduino Uno board and it is depicted in Fig. 5. This is a voltage transformer module, it has an active single-phase output. In addition, it contains an op amp circuit to compensate for the analog output offset. It can measure low voltage and the analog output is adjustable with the potentiometer on the board. It is an ideal module for energy monitoring applications, very common in home automation applications. Due to the nature of transformers it can only measure AC voltage.

4   Design

Monitoring platform connection diagram. For the realization of the monitoring circuit, the following components were used, which are detailed below:

Fig. 5. ZMPT101B AC voltage sensor

- Raspberry PI 3 model B
- Arduino Uno board
- Nodemcu
- Fan
- ACS712 Current sensor
- ZMPT101B AC Voltage Sensor

Figure 6 shows how all the components used for IoT monitoring have been connected.

4.1   Storage in the Database

This process consists of two parts, Data acquisition and Database Storage, as shown in Fig. 7.

The data is obtained on the Arduino Uno board. Besides, the connection of the Voltage and Current sensors is depicted in Fig. 8, the measurement has been carried out on a single phase, with the data obtained the power can be obtained.

4.2   Send to the Database

The Raspberry PI OS operating system has been installed on the Raspberry PI on the microSD card, for the database storage we proceed to install a manager of these which is phpMyadmin which will allow us to manage the database graphically. Figure 9 depicts the data obtained in the Database.

Fig. 6. Components for IoT monitoring

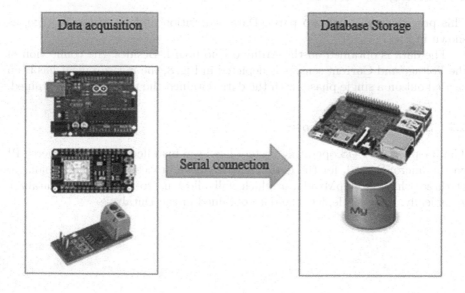

Fig. 7. Data acquisition scheme

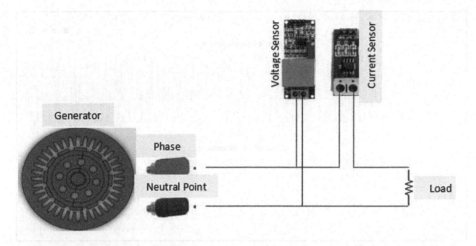

Fig. 8. Connection of voltage and current sensors

Fig. 9. Data obtained in the database

Then, you can see the monitoring screen of the Voltage and Current measurements in Fig. 10. Next, the same information and the calculated power is provided in the web page, which is shown in Fig. 11.

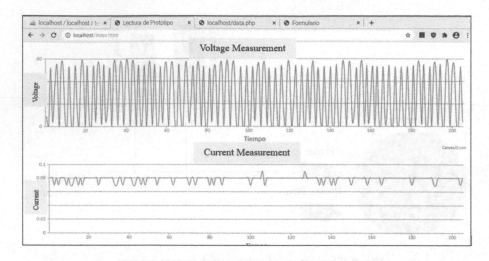

Fig. 10. Voltage and current measurements

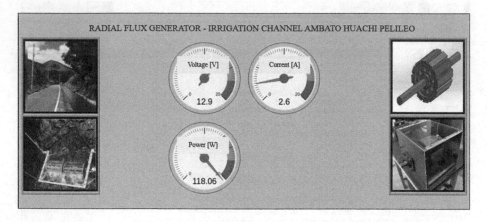

Fig. 11. Viewing the data on the web page

Complete Structure of the Hydroelectric Power Station. In order to have a better visualization of the connection to be made in the Pico-Hydropower Station, the connection block diagram is shown below in Fig. 12.

Then you can see in Fig. 13 the physical connection that the Pico-Hydroelectric power station must have.

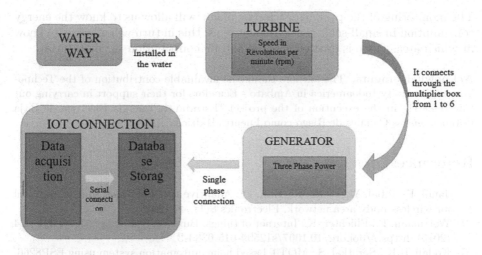

Fig. 12. Block diagram of the pico-hydropower station

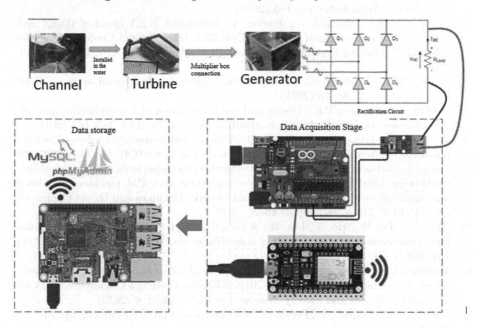

Fig. 13. Physical connection of the pico-hydropower station

5   Conclusions

The document presents the implementation of an IoT application, created using Raspberry Pi 3 model B, ACS712 current sensor. The cloud application displays the data collected from the Raspberry Pi and the current and voltage sensors. The collected data can be stored in a database created on some database server.

The monitoring of the peak hydroelectric plants will allow us to know the energy consumption in small-scale generation systems, this in turn will allow us to know in which areas there is greater demand and its contribution to smart cities.

Acknowledgements. The authors thank the invaluable contribution of the Technological University Indoamerica in Ambato - Ecuador, for their support in carrying out this research, in the execution of the project "Estudio de Energía Eléctrica de Baja Potencia en los Canales de Riego como Fuentes Hídricas".

References

1. Jamil, F., Iqbal, M., Amin, R., Kim, D.: Adaptive thermal-aware routing protocol for wireless body area network. Electronics **8**(1), 47 (2019)
2. Wortmann, F., Flüchter, K.: Internet of things. Bus. Inf. Syst. Eng. **57**(3), 221–224 (2015). https://doi.org/10.1007/s12599-015-0383-3
3. Kodali, R.K., Soratkal, S.: MQTT based home automation system using ESP8266. In: Proceedings of the 2016 IEEE Region 10 Humanitarian Technology Conference (R10-HTC), Agra, India, pp. 1–5 (2016)
4. Al-Jaroodi, J., Mohamed, N., Jawhar, I., Mahmoud, S.: A cloud of things middleware. In: Proceedings of the 2017 IEEE 37th International Conference on Distributed Computing Systems Workshops(ICDCSW), Atlanta, GA, USA, pp. 214–219 (2017)
5. Truong, H.L., Dustdar, S.: Principles for engineering IoT cloud systems. IEEE Cloud Comput. **2**, 68–76 (2015)
6. Dehury, C.K., Sahoo, P.K.: Design and implementation of a novel service management framework for IoT devices in cloud. J. Syst. Softw. **119**, 149–161 (2016)
7. Mhlambi, B., Kusakana, K., Raath, J.: Voltage and frequency control of isolated pico-hydro system. In: 2018 Open Innovations Conference (OI), pp. 246–250 (2018)
8. Chen, A., Nilssen, R., Nysveen, A.: Performance comparisons among radial flux, multi-stage axial flux and three-phase transverse flux PM machines for downhole applications. In: IEEE International Electric Machines and Drives Conference (2017). IEEE Trans. Ind. Appl. **46**(2), 1017
9. Chen, Y., Fu, W., Ho, S., Liu, H.: A quantitative comparison analysis of radial-flux, transverse-flux, and axial-flux magnetic gears. IEEE Trans. Magn. **50**(11), 1–4 (2014)
10. Madhavan, R., Fernandes, B.: Comparative analysis of axial flux SRM topologies for electric vehicle application. In: 2012 IEEE International Conference on Power Electronics, Drives and Energy Systems (PEDES), pp. 1–6 (2012)
11. Vandikas, K., Tsiatsis, V.: Performance evaluation of an IoT platform, pp. 141–146 (2014)
12. Ahmad, S., Mehmood, F., Kim, D.: A DIY approach for the design of mission-planning architecture using autonomous task-object mapping and the deployment model in mission-critical IoT systems. Sustainability **11**(13), 3647 (2019)
13. Cavalcante, E., et al.: On the interplay of internet of things and cloud computing. Comput. Commun. **89**, 17–33 (2016). Elsevier Science Publishers B
14. Mehmood, F., Ullah, I., Ahmad, S., Kim, D.H.: Object detection mechanism based on deep learning algorithm using embedded IoT devices for smart home appliances control in CoT. J. Ambient Intell. Human. Comput. (3), 1–17 (2019). https://doi.org/10.1007/s12652-019-01272-8

15. Farahzadi, A., Shams, P., Rezazadeh, J., Farahbakhsh, R.: Middleware technologies for cloud of things: a survey. Digit. Commun. **4**(3), 176–188 (2018)
16. Khudoyberdiev, A., Jin, W., Kim, D.: A novel approach towards resource auto-registration and discovery of embedded systems based on DNS. Electronics **8**(4), 442 (2019)
17. Borgia, E.: The internet of things vision: key features. Comput. Commun. **54**, 1–31 (2014)
18. Prabaharan, J., Swamy, A., Sharma, A., Bharath, K., Mundra, P., Mohammed, K.: Wireless home automation and security system using MQTT protocol. In: Proceedings of the 2017 2nd IEEE International Conference on Recent Trends in Electronics, Information and Communication Technology (RTEICT), vol. 19, no. 2, pp. 2043–2045 (2017)
19. Stastny, S.: UbiBazaar: app store for the internet of things. Master's thesis, NTNU, Trondheim, Norway (2015)
20. Modoni, G.E., Trombetta, A., Veniero, M., Sacco, M., Mourtzis, D.: An event-driven integrative framework enabling information notification among manufacturing resources. Int. J. Comput. Integr. Manuf. **32**, 241–252 (2019)
21. PlusElectric. https://pluselectric.wordpress.com/2014/09/21/arduino-uno-especificaciones-y-caracteristicas/. Accessed 28 July 2021
22. Raspberry Shop. https://www.raspberryshop.es/raspberry-pi-3.php. Accessed 28 July 2021
23. Redes Zone. https://www.redeszone.net/2019/08/18/controla-ordenador-forma-remota-vnc/. Accessed 28 July 2021
24. Embtronik. https://www.embtronik.com/producto/sensor-de-corriente-acs712/. Accessed 28 July 2021
25. Electropeak. https://electropeak.com/learn/interfacing-zmpt101b-voltage-sensor-with-arduino/. Accessed 28 July 2021

General Track

Estimation of the Dynamic Elastic Properties and Energy Dissipation Capacity of Wood from Ochroma Pyramidale (Balsa)

Christian Narváez-Muñoz[1], Luis Javier Segura[1,2]([✉]), Andrea López López[1], Andrés García[1], Oswaldo Mauricio González[1], and Edison E. Haro[1]

[1] Universidad de las Fuerzas Armadas ESPE, Av. Gral. Rumiñahui s/n, Sangolquí, Ecuador
ljsegura@espe.edu.ec
[2] Industrial and Systems Engineering, University at Buffalo,
SUNY Buffalo, Buffalo, NY 14260, USA

Abstract. The research of this paper aims at understanding, from an engineering perspective, the optimized mechanical efficiency of senile balsawood stem-tissues as concept generators for potential applications. Particularly, the objectives of this study are to determine, evaluate, and analyze the dynamic elastic properties and energy dissipation capacity of senile lightweight balsawood. To achieve these objectives, in accordance with the current American Society for Testing and Materials (ASTM) standards, a total of 40 specimens (i.e., 20 low-density and 20 high-density samples) were tested under static bending mechanical mode and technics of transversal vibration to determine static and dynamic Modulus of Elasticity (MOE), respectively. On the other hand, 8 samples (i.e., 4 low-density and 4 high-density samples) were subjected to Scanning Electron Microscope (SEM) process to compare the internal tissue of high and low density samples and their relationship with the dynamic and static MOEs. The dynamic MOE data were validated throughout 10 Finite Element Analyses (FEA) in LS-Dyna. The results show a high correlation between static and dynamic MOEs ($R2 = 96.47\%$), which are directly proportional to density. Furthermore, SEM analysis reflects that the increase of double wall thickness affects the material energy dissipation capacity which consequently derives that low density balsa wood is the most suitable for energy dissipation applications.

Keywords: Balsa · Energy dissipation · Dynamic properties · Density

1 Introduction

The potential of using wood species has not been addressed in Ecuador in order to propose innovative and feasible engineering alternatives. It is indeed not possible to take advantage of the great potential offered by nature when it is mostly unknown from some viewpoints. Considering this, some properties of the balsa wood species have been studied up to now, yet such studies still fall short of completely determining the whole range of potentials of this biomaterial. The balsa species is a woody plant (i.e., trees

M. Botto-Tobar et al. (Eds.): ICAT 2021, CCIS 1535, pp. 153–164, 2022.
https://doi.org/10.1007/978-3-031-03884-6_11

that enclose wood within their main stems' tissue-structure; generally comprising large branches and roots covered by a layer of bark [1]). Additionally, according to the plant taxonomy, the Ochroma pyramidale is a woody plant classified as hardwood (i.e., wood from dicotyle-donous trees) that belongs to the Malvaceae family [1]. This dicot species is a fast-growing tree with a tapered and regular cylindrical stem shape that can grow up to 30 m high [2]. From the microscopic level of hierarchical structure (e.g., scaling from 0.1 mm to 1 μm [3, 4]), balsa wood has a spongy texture (i.e., foam-like structure) due to large cells filled with water. Therefore, balsa wood is a lightweight biomaterial with a basic density (i.e., a ratio of oven-dry weight to green volume) which depends on the tree's age and geographical location of growth [2]. Among its mechanical properties can be highlighted [1] an average MOE parallel to the fibers equals 3400 MPa, [2] an average Modulus of Rupture (MOR) parallel to the fibers equals to 14.9 MPa, and [3] an average MOR perpendicular to the fibers equals to 21.6 MPa. All previous values are given for an average basic density of 180 kg/m^3 at 12% of moisture content [2]. The characteristic balsa wood mechanical properties reflect a biomaterial with the highest flexibility among all other wood species versus moderate bending and compressive strengths. Despite its very low density, balsa wood has an enhanced mechanical efficiency (i.e., mechanical performance per unit mass of the material [5–7]) that makes it suitable for several engineering applications such as balsa lightweight core material in bio-composite sandwich wall panels, wind turbine blades, and aircraft cockpits, etc. Balsa is an Ecuadorian native wood species that is widely grown in plantations all around the country due to a high demand of the international market. In fact, Ecuador is currently producing over 90% of the world's balsa supply, which is predominantly exported as oriented strand boards and laminated veneer lumbers [8]. Yet, there are still massive plantations of Ochroma pyramidale along the coastal region of Ecuador that are totally disregarded for engineering applications and potential developments. These observations were the driving forces behind the work of this investigation. In hardwoods, fibers (referred to as grain for woody plants) are axially elongated cellulosic elements of small diameter that, in high proportion, form the wood groundmass. Additionally, the fiber walls are commonly multi-layered and their primary function is to support the tree. Thus, the density, mechanical strength, and stiffness are mostly governed by the number of fibers within the hardwood tissue-structure [1]. As abovementioned, form-structure-function relationships for several wood species and especially for balsa wood, have been investigated at different levels of hierarchical structure [9–13]. However, for Ochroma pyramidale specifically, the dynamic elastic properties and energy dissipation capacity have not been analyzed from the structural mechanic's point of view; this is essential to determine the influence of fiber distribution on the biomaterial mechanical performance. Hence, the study performed herein is relevant since the acquired results may be relevant as concept generators for innovative energy dissipation applications.

2   Materials and Methods

The samples of Balsa wood (Ochroma Pyramidale) were obtained from El Vergel, province of Los Ríos. Five and four years old trees were selected randomly according to their good phytosanitary status (i.e., absence of phytophthora in the base and heart of water in the xylem), good straightness, and scarce presence of knots. Once the tree was cut, paraffin emulsion was applied to the ends exposed to the air. Subsequently, drying the harvested wood took two weeks for each tree. In the first week, the wood was dried at room temperature and in the remaining seven days the wood was dried in the oven. Finally, at the end of the drying process, the moisture content was approximately 12%. All mechanical tests were performed in specimens free of defects. To develop the experiments, the specimens were cut into three-dimensional sections of 750 × 50 × 50 mm.

2.1 Microstructure Analysis

The SEM, Tescan, MIRA3 LMU, from the Nanoscience and Nanotechnology Center of the Universidad de las Fuerzas Armadas ESPE was used. The collected information includes morphology, the structure of the channels, and the orientation of the fibers that constitute the specimens. For this analysis, four low-density specimens and four high-density specimens with dimensions of 10 × 3 × 3 mm were used, as well as a parallel cut to the fibers of the tangential and longitudinal plane for visualization of the tracheids.

2.2 Static Bending

The analysis of the static Elastic Modulus (EM) was based on the ASTM D-143-14 standard. The tests were carried out in a MTS TK/T5002 universal testing machine, using load cell type S Quantrol A ± 1N. A continuous load was applied at a speed of 1.3 mm. With the static bending test data, the MOE and the MOR were obtained using Eq. (1) and Eq. (2), respectively.

$$MOE = \frac{PL^3}{48\delta_{max}I} \tag{1}$$

$$MOR - \frac{My}{I} \tag{2}$$

where P is the load value in the elastic zone, L the length between supports, δmax the deflection in the center of the beam, I the inertia of the cross section, M is the maximum bending moment, and y is the distance from the neutral axis to the extreme fiber.

2.3 Dynamic Analysis

Several non-destructive methods exist to determine the modulus of elasticity. The most commonly used are based on ultrasound [14, 15], transverse vibrations [16, 17], near-infrared spectroscopy [18], and among others. The transverse vibrations, which are also called resonance, are the most inexpensive and effective method. Many studies have reported a strong linear correlation between static modulus of elasticity and dynamic modulus of elasticity in various wood species [14, 17, 19–23]; these studies determined the resonance frequencies from induced vibrations by impacting a small steel hammer at the end of the specimen. In like manner, equipment was designed in such a way that vibration is induced to perform the resonance analysis. Figure 1 shows the scheme of the equipment.

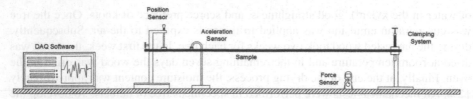

Fig. 1. Scheme of the experimental device to measure dynamic regime

The vibration is produced by gently hitting a hammer on top of the free end of the specimen. The tapping originates a vibratory wave that is taken by an accelerometer placed 50 mm from the left edge of the specimen. The accelerometer will acquire the signal of the vibration, and the natural frequency can be known by applying the fast Fourier transformation. Furthermore, LS-DYNA®, a commercial FEA software, is used to validate the results. In the software, the Von Mises theory was selected since it uses a criterion of elastic failure and, above all, its results showed great uniformity. Thus, the influence of torsion is neglected. The Finite Element Method (FEM) used in the program is accurate enough without losing the physical details of the problem and is modeled mathematically with no loss of accuracy. The theoretical model used to describe the behavior of free vibration of a damped beam is given by Eq. (3) [24].

$$\frac{\partial^2}{\partial x^2}\left[MOE(x)\frac{\partial^2 w(x,t)}{\partial x^2}\right] + \rho A(x)\frac{\partial^2 w(x,t)}{\partial t^2} \tag{3}$$

The Eq. 3 can be rewritten as Eq. 4. Then, the dynamic MOE of the beam can be determined by solving the Eq. 5

$$\frac{d^4 w(x)}{\partial x^4} - \beta^4 w(x) = 0 \tag{4}$$

$$MOE_d = \frac{w^2 \rho A l^4}{(\beta l)^4 l} \tag{5}$$

In the above equations MOEI is the bending rigidity, ρ is the density, A is the cross-sectional area, ω is the natural frequency of vibration, and the constant βl is determined by the boundary conditions, which in our case is 1.875104.

3 Analysis of Results

For the analysis, twenty balsa samples of each low and high density were chosen. The wood microstructure was analyzed by utilizing SEM images. The remaining section is devoted to explaining the static MOE, the coefficient of elasticity, the dynamic MOE, and a comparison between static and dynamic MOEs.

3.1 Microstructure Analysis of Balsa Wood

The analysis of balsa wood microstructure was carried out as shown in Fig. 2, where the main cells are presented. Previous studies by Da Silva and Kyriakides [10] on the morphological composition of balsa wood, determined that the volume fraction of the sap channels/vessels is the smallest, meanwhile, rays and fibers constitute the fraction of 8–15% and 80–90%, respectively.

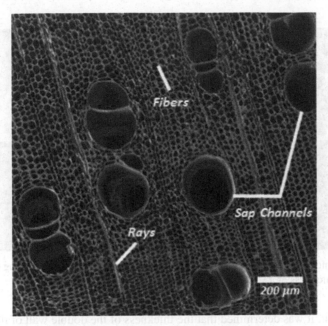

Fig. 2. Cross-section of high density balsa

Additionally, the measurements of tracheid and prismatic cell thickness and diameter have been taken. [25], this is observed in Fig. 3. In addition, a longitudinal section was extracted and the tracheids can be observed (Fig. 3(a)). Then, Fig. 3(c) shows that the cellular microstructure of balsa wood fibers has an irregular polygonal shape in the cross section, often similar to a hexagon; where h and t represent de cell side length and wall thickness, respectively. However, they were modeled as regular hexagons.

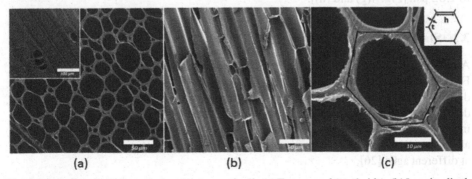

Fig. 3. Balsa wood micrograph showing types of cells (a) Transversal (tracheids), (b) Longitudinal and (c) Prismatic cell

The length of the side of the prismatic cell was determined. For samples of low density, the values are between 18.25–23.48 μm; while for the high density ones the values are between 14.91–15.46 μm. Therefore, the irregular polygon in low density wood is 1.3 times greater compared to a high density sample.

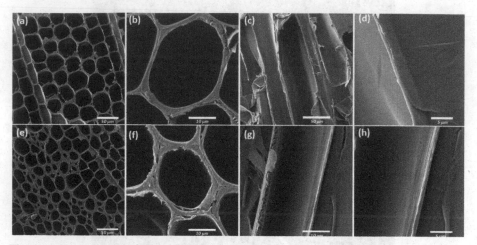

Fig. 4. SEM micrograph of the cross-section of low and high density balsa showing the geometry and cell wall thickness of a vessel element

In addition, it was determined that the thickness of the double wall of the prismatic cell has an increment of 1.67 times in high density wood (Fig. 4(a) and (e)). The double wall thickness in balsa wood fibers ranges from 1.53 to 1.93 μm, increasing with density to a range between 2.36–3.68 μm (Fig. 4(b) and (f)).

In the last section, the prismatic cell has been analyzed considering the radial-tangential plane. However, internally there are oval geometries shapes which are also known as tracheids (Fig. 4(c) and (d)). It was observed that while the density increases from 121.26 to 299.34 kg/m^3, the tracheids diameter decreases from 60.17 to 18.55 μm. Furthermore, the thickness of the tracheid walls increases in high density balsa wood in the range of 1.15 to 2.54 μm, and the range for low density wood decreases from 0.67 to 1.02 μm [Fig. 4(g) and (h)].

3.2 Static Modulus of Elasticity

As aforementioned, the specimens were classified into low and high density especimens. From the analysis, it was specified that the boundary between samples of low and high density is 192.93 kg/m^3. Figure 5 shows that the static MOE is proportional to the balsa density and there is a strong correlation (97.49%) between the Young's modulus and the tree's density. Flexural tests were performed to obtain the static MOE. The density is also related to the age of the trees and this was probed by obtaining the density of trees at different ages [26].

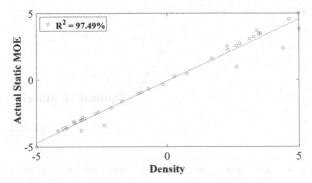

Fig. 5. Linear relationship between static MOE and density

3.3 Dynamic Modulus of Elasticity

To have a complete study of the dynamic MOE, the transverse vibration of beams theory was deployed by implementing numerical simulations. For the FEA, it was necessary to develop a convergence study of the model. The geometrical configuration, their dimensions, and fiber directions corresponding to each sample were tested. The optimal FEM was selected based on three parameters (1) aspect ratio (relationship between width and height) for each element greater than 10, (2) convergence of results of acceleration, and (3) data processing time.

3.4 Convergence Analysis

Table 1 shows the results of the convergence study when the model is gently hit by a hammer on top of the free end. Ten models with different numbers of elements of the mesh and different aspect ratios for each element were constructed Table 1.

Table 1. Convergence processing time vs number of elements.

N°	Elements	Mesh			Size (mm)			Aspect ratio			Aceleration (m/s²)	Processing time
		L	T	R	L	T	T	L/R	L/T	R/T		
1	40	10	2	2	120,00	25,00	25,00	4,80	4,80	1,00	2,63	40 min 51 s
2	320	20	4	4	60,00	12,50	12,50	4,80	4,80	1,00	3,14	43 min 25 s
3	875	35	5	5	34,29	10,00	10,00	3,43	3,43	1,00	3,39	1 h 0 min 37 s
4	2205	45	7	7	26,67	7,14	7,14	3,73	3,73	1,00	3,66	1 h 21 min 8 s
5**	4050	50	9	9	24,00	5,56	5,56	4,32	4,32	1,00	3,75	1 h 51 min 32 s
6	5500	55	10	10	21,82	5,00	5,00	4,36	4,36	1,00	3,73	2 h 26 min 52 s
7	7260	60	11	11	20,00	4,55	4,55	4,40	4,40	1,00	3,74	2 h 45 min 31 s
8	9000	90	10	10	13,33	5,00	5,00	2,67	2,67	1,00	3,75	3 h 36 min 56 s
9	12960	90	12	12	13,33	4,17	4,17	3,20	3,20	1,00		
10	14400	100	12	12	12,00	4,17	4,17	2,88	2,88	1,00		

*L,T, and R are the longitudinal, transversal and radial directions of the sample, respectively.
**Highlighted values corresponds to the optimal FEM in this investigation.

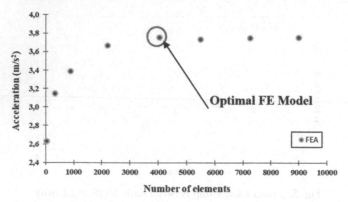

Fig. 6. Convergence study-acceleration vs number of elements

In reference to Table 1 and Fig. 6, the optimal FE Model (FEM No. 5 for this case) for the transversal vibration, consists of 4050 three-dimensional hexahedral elements, with a maximum aspect ratio of 4.32 whose data processing time was 1 h 51 min 32 s.

The dynamic MOE is a function of the density and the natural frequency, this information was extracted by running several tests in the experimental device. Furthermore, it was corroborated in the results of the numerical simulation.

A multi-regression analysis was performed and it was determined that the natural frequency and the density are the most influential factors as it is shown in Table 2 by reading the p-values which are zero. The Analysis of Variance (ANOVA) analysis is performed in the same fashion as in [27, 28].

Table 2. Analysis of variance of the regression model

Source	DF	SS	MS	F-value	p-value
Regression	2	63.6325	31.8162	2417.98	0
Density (kg/m³)	1	37.6213	37.613	2859.15	0
Frequency (Hz)	1	2.7467	2.7467	208.74	0
Error	37	0.4869	0.0132		
Total	39	64.1193			

Additionally, Fig. 7 shows that there is no interaction between frequency and density although the spectral amplitude reduces its value while the density increases. The coefficient of determination between frequency and density is 21.68%, which explains that the frequency and density are not correlated.

3.5 Relationship Between Dynamic and Static MOEs

The dynamic and static MOEs were analyzed and they showed a strong relationship as it is shown in the Fig. 8, where the static and dynamic MOEs were normalized between

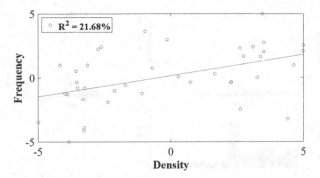

Fig. 7. Relationship between frequency and density

−5 to 5. The strong relationship can be drawn from the coefficient of determination, which is 96.47%. From the analysis, it can be seen that the dynamic MOE computation is very close to the static MOE, thus strengthening the validity and accuracy of the non-destructive approach to estimate the MOE without inducing any damage to the test specimens.

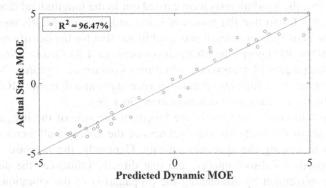

Fig. 8. Relationship between the dynamic and static MOEs

Additionally, the model assumptions (i.e., normality, independent and identically distributed condition, etc.) for the dynamic MOE estimation are validated by residual plots, see Fig. 9.

Figure 9(a) and (b) shows no concentrations of the cloud of points, hence showing that the residuals are independent and randomly distributed. The error standard deviation is not biased and the model performance is valid. The residuals' histogram, Fig. 9(c), is close to a normal distribution (i.e., Gaussian), and this is corroborated by Fig. 9(d). Figure 9(d) clearly shows a linear trend, which shows that a normal distribution is a food fit for the estimation model. Furthermore, no outliers can be seen and no data removal is necessary to assure the accuracy of the estimation.

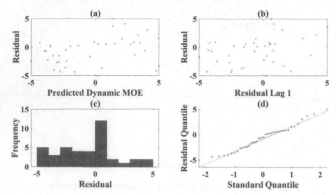

Fig. 9. Residual analysis: (a) Residual versus predicted, (b) Autocorrelation of residuals, (c) Histogram, and (d) QQ plot for residuals

4 Conclusion and Discussion

This work presents the experimental results of the relationship between the static MOE and the dynamic MOE; and the balsa's ability to dissipate energy under different regimes of densities. First, the bending tests were carried out in the longitudinal direction of the specimens. It was found that the values of static and dynamic MOEs were related to the value of the density. Moreover, it was established that for the density range varying from 120 kg/m^3 to 300 kg/m^3, the MOE ranges between 1.84 GPa to 5.96 GPa. While applying the techniques of transversal vibration to obtain the dynamic MOE, it was determined that there is a high correlation between static and dynamic MOEs, which is corroborated by the coefficient of determination (96.47%).

As the prismatic cells decrease in the length of the side of the irregular polygon and the diameter of the tracheids, the thickness of the double wall increases, and this contributes to increasing the specimen density. Generally, the increase of thickness affects the capacity to absorb energy, and that directly influences the dissipation of the transverse movement by attenuating the propagation of the vibrations. Thus, the spectral amplitude decreases when the thickness of the double wall of the prismatic cells increases, consequently low density balsa wood is the most suitable for energy dissipation applications.

References

1. Butterfield, B.G., Meylan, B.A., Peszlen, I.M.: Three Dimensional Structure of Wood, Hungarian edn. Chapman and Hall Ltd., London (1997). 9630488124
2. Bergman, R., et al.: Wood Handbook, Wood as an Engineering Material, Department of Agriculture, Forest Products Laboratory, United States (2010)
3. Knippers, J., Speck, T.: Design and construction principles in nature and architecture. Bioinspir. Biomim. 7(1), 1–10 (2012). 1748-3190. https://doi.org/10.1088/1748-3182/7/1/015002
4. Speck, T., Burgert, I.: Plant stems: functional design and mechanics. Annu. Rev. Mater. Res. 41(169–193), 1531–7331 (2011)

5. Gibson, L.J.: The hierarchical structure and mechanics of plant materials. J. R. Soc. Interface **9**(76), 2749–2766 (2012). 1742-5689
6. Wegst, U.G.K.: Bending efficiency through property gradients in bamboo, palm, and wood-based composites. J. Mech. Behav. Biomed. Mater. **4**(5), 744–755 (2011). 1751-6161
7. Gonzalez, O.M., Nguyen, K.A.: Influence of density distribution on the mechanical efficiency of coconut stem green tissues. In: World Conference on Timber Engineering, Austria, Vienna (2016). ISBN: 978-390303900-1
8. Osorio, B.G., Molina, X.C., Navarrete, E.T., Fonseca, C.S., Ochoa, L.S.: Caracterizacion del cultivo de balsa (Ochroma Pyramidale) en la Provincia de los Ríos-Ecuador. Revista Ciencia y Tecnología **3**(2), 7–11 (2010). 1390-4043
9. Gibson, L.J., Ashby, M.F.: Cellular Solids: Structure and Properties, 2nd edn. Cambridge University Press, Cambridge (1999). 0521499119
10. Da Silva, A., Kyriakides, S.: Compressive response and failure of balsa wood. Inter. J. Solids Struct. **44**(25–26), 8685–8717 (2007). 0020-7683
11. Khalifa, A., Barbero, E., Miranzo, P., Navarro Ugena, C.: Caracterización dinámica mediante barra Hopkinson de materiales cerámicos monolíticos y compuestos (2002)
12. Kotlarewski, N.J., Belleville, B., Gusamo, B.K., Ozarska, B.: Mechanical properties of Papua New Guinea balsa wood. Eur. J. Wood Wood Prod. **74**(1), 83–89 (2016). 0018-3768
13. Vural, M., Ravichandran, G.: Dynamic response and energy dissipation characteristics of balsa wood: experiment and analysis. Int. J. Solids Struct. **40**(9), 2147–2170 (2003). 0020-7683
14. Ballarin, A.W., Nogueira, M.: Determinação do módulo de elasticidade da madeira juvenil e adulta de Pinus taeda por ultra-som. Engenharia Agrícola, pp. 19–28 (2005)
15. Bucur, V.: The Acoustics of Wood (1995). CRC Press, Boca Raton (2017)
16. Murphy, J.F.: Transverse vibration of a simply supported beam with symmetric overhang of arbitrary length. J. Test. Eval. **25**(5), 522–524 (1997)
17. Leite, E.R.D.S., Hein, P.R.G., Souza, T.M.D., Rabelo, G.F.: Estimation of the dynamic elastic properties of wood from Copaifera langsdorffii Desf using resonance analysis. Cerne **18**(1), 41–47 (2012)
18. Schimleck, L.R., Evans, R., Ilic, J.: Estimation of Eucalyptus delegatensis wood properties by near infrared spectroscopy. Can. J. For. Res. **31**(10), 1671–1675 (2001)
19. Ilic, J.: Relationship among the dynamic and static elastic properties of air-dry Eucalyptus delegatensis R. Baker. Holz als Roh-und Werkstoff **59**(3), 169–175 (2001)
20. Ilic, J.: Dynamic MOE of 55 species using small wood beams. Holz als Roh-und Werkstoff **61**(3), 167–172 (2003)
21. Brancheriau, L., Bailléres, H.: Natural vibration analysis of clear wooden beams: a theoretical review. Wood Sci. Technol. **36**(4), 347–365 (2002)
22. Brancheriau, L., Bailléres, H., Détienne, P., Gril, J., Kronland, R.: Key signal and wood anatomy parameters related to the acoustic quality of wood for xylophone-type percussion instruments. J. Wood Sci. **52**(3), 270–273 (2006)
23. Wang, Z., Li, L., Gong, M.: Measurement of dynamic modulus of elasticity and damping ratio of wood-based composites using the cantilever beam vibration technique. Constr. Build. Mater. **28**(1), 831–834 (2012)
24. Mukhopadhyay, T., Adhikari, S., Alu, A.: Probing the frequency-dependent elastic moduli of lattice materials. Acta Mater. **165**, 654–665 (2019)
25. Borrega, M., Ahvenainen, P., Serimaa, R., Gibson, L.: Composition and structure of balsa (Ochroma pyramidale) wood. Wood Sci. Technol. **49**(2), 403–420 (2015)
26. Almeida Molina, F.X., Martínez Martínez, M.A.: Caracterización dinámica de la madera de balsa de Ecuador. Bachelor's thesis, Universidad de las Fuerzas Armadas ESPE. Carrera de Ingeniería Mecánica (2017)

27. Cano, J.S., Cordova, G.D., Narvaez, C., Segura, L., Carrion, L.: Experimental study of the incidence of changing a synthetic jet orifice in heat transfer using a Taguchi method approach. J. Thermal Sci. Eng. Appl. 11(3), 031011 (2019)
28. Castro, K., Segura, L.J., Castellanos, S.D., Alves, J.: Optimization of geometric quality in a 5 axis machining of curved surfaces in a EN-AW-7075 alloy by Taguchi method. In: da Silva, L.F.M. (ed.) Materials Design and Applications. ASM, vol. 65, pp. 347–360. Springer, Cham (2017). https://doi.org/10.1007/978-3-319-50784-2_26

Lean Startup as a Project Management Method in Science Organizations

Zornitsa Yordanova(✉) iD

University of National and World Economy, 8mi dekemvri, Sofia, Bulgaria
zornitsayordanova@unwe.bg

Abstract. The paper analyzes the Lean Startup method as a project management tool and its possible application in scientific organizations. The research is motivated by some unsatisfied results in the development of innovation in many scientific organizations that follow standard project management methodologies. No matter, the Lean Startup method is typically used to develop software, product, or startup management, most of the processes that the method facilitates are also valid for general project management. The research methodology goes through a review of the literature on the main objectives of the study: project management and Lean startup and outlines the main characteristics of transforming the traditional approach to project management in research organizations to a flexible model for developing more innovative scientific results. The contribution of the study is valuable for scientists who want to implement more flexible project management to achieve more sustainable innovative results (transfer of methodological knowledge from the startup and technology industry to scientific organizations and universities).

Keywords: Innovation in science · Lean startup · Project management · Technology management · Innovation management

1 Introduction

The current research was provoked by the increasing trend of unsuccessful science projects related to innovation development [1, 2], ready for commercialization and the extending gap between science and market needs [3]. Previous research has already revealed insufficient project management skills in science organizations [4], weak knowledge about the full cycle of innovation development [5], absence of practical approach for developing innovations which solve real problems [6] and lack of knowledge for developing innovations with fast product-to-market innovation management approaches [7].

The current paper aims at analyzing the application of Lean Startup method in science projects for strengthening both project and innovation management. Essential limitation in the study is its focus on practical science projects and not on fundamental ones. Lean Startup has already been proved as a successful method for innovation development, first in startup companies [8] and then, in corporates [9] and even in research [10]. There are also some researches about how it can be implemented as a vertical methodological

© Springer Nature Switzerland AG 2022
M. Botto-Tobar et al. (Eds.): ICAT 2021, CCIS 1535, pp. 165–175, 2022.
https://doi.org/10.1007/978-3-031-03884-6_12

approach in different sectors (industrial and governmental), but it has not been used as a holistic project and innovation management in science organizations yet. The research goes through a literature review so as to elucidate the essence of the analyzed method Lean Startup and its practical implications. Second focus of the research is the traditional project management approach in science organizations, influenced by common project management methodologies as those of Project Management Institute (PMI), Prince, etc., which are a common practice for both business and science projects. Bearing in mind both Lean Startup and the traditional way of managing projects, the paper presents a new design for a flexible model for developing more innovative science outcomes in applied science projects. The outcomes of the paper are relevant for both academic and business audience with focus on result-driven project management for innovation development.

2   Theoretical Background

2.1   Traditional Project Management in Science Organizations

Project management is that part of project knowledge that explores and studies the more successful management of these initiatives. Organizations are becoming more project-oriented [11], and projects are the preferred management instrument especially for implementation of new activities [12, 13]. However, because projects are constantly delayed, exceeding, and often technically unsuccessful, project management is often explored for opportunities for improvement. These threats increase with the complexity of the project. There is also research on how Lean Startup is used in a diverse variety of sectors and industries such as healthcare, transportation, even in governmental projects. However, it has not yet been used as a project management approach in scientific organizations and universities.

Science and educational institutions usually use a traditional approach for project management. The main knowledge sources of these kind of project management methodologies are the International Project Management Association (IPMA), the Project Management Institute (PMI) which publishes a book on the areas of knowledge in project management (A Guide to the Project Management Body of Knowledge, PMBOK Guide), European Project Management Organizations (EPMO), Association of project management (APM), etc. Most recognized methodology for project management in universities is reported to be PMBOK by PMI [14].

As a structure, the methodology has been developed in nine main areas of knowledge and an additional one for integrity. The main areas of knowledge are: Integrity management; Project scope management; Project time management; Cost management; Quality management; Human resources management; Project communication management; Risk management; Procurement management [15]. An additional area added in recent years is the Management of the Code of Ethics in the project, which each project manager undertakes to comply with. Very often projects are implemented through processes. They are implemented by the project participants and fall into two categories: (1) Project management processes - for planning, organizing, coordinating and managing the project work. They are universal and standardized in the contractor's project management system. (2) Product Oriented Processes - to specify and create the project product.

In the literature are also known some attempts for developing and evaluating a project management methodology for university-industry collaborative projects [16] but still they are based on traditional approaches.

2.2 Innovative Applied Projects in Science Organizations

The study is limited to science applied projects with innovative outcomes or innovation projects and fundamental research stays out of scope. The Project Management Institute (PMI) defines project as a temporary phenomenon that has a definite beginning and end in time and a certain scope as well as necessary resources to achieve the goal. The project is unique and not a routine operation, consisting of a specific set of operations designed to achieve a single goal. So the project team often includes people who don't usually work together - sometimes from different organizations and in different geographical areas [15]. Other definitions state that "a project is an operation limited in time and cost to achieve a set of specific results (scope to meet project objectives) to quality standards and requirements" [17]. The project can also be defined as a "unique process consisting of a set of coordinated and controlled activities with start and end dates undertaken to achieve a goal that meets specific requirements, including time, cost and resource constraints" [18]. By definition, a project has certain characteristics that distinguish it from operational management. The goal is to create something unique that has not been done before and to achieve a certain goal of the organization. The project has a novelty in terms of time, place and team performing the task, product, service or result provided.

According to Schumpter, innovation is expressed in several activities that are inherent in entrepreneurs [19]. These are the introduction of new products or services, including the improvement of existing ones; introduction of a new method in production; development of new markets; use of new sources of raw materials or their delivery and changes in the organization of the enterprise.

Innovative projects are considered to be those projects which meet the requirement of both project and innovation definitions. Based on the definition for innovation and its entrepreneurial element, innovative science projects are only the applied ones in the current research. There are plenty of views on the nature of innovative projects. The topic of innovation project management and their specifics is discussed by Joyce Wycoff and Richardson [20]. It concludes that although most organizations have a high level of competence in project management, the understanding of innovation project management is not clear and insufficiently defined. The reason for this is the misunderstanding in the categorization of innovative projects, which further complicates project managers in their management. For Besner and Hobbs [21] innovation project is a project that produces a new product or that involves a new concept or a new technology. Innovative projects are also seen as systematically managed ways that use materials to turn them into results with a certain scope and aim to achieve something new, in a new way or to improve something that exists [22]. Usually, innovative projects and innovation projects are used interchanging in the literature. In this research, an innovative applied project in science organization are reckon as:

Innovative applied project is a temporary effort in a science organization, made to create a unique product, service or result and meanwhile aimed at turning an idea or invention into a good or service that creates value and it is ready for market commercialization.

Since innovative applied projects are more complicated than simple projects are, the traditional projects management seems not always to be sufficient. Aiming at knowledge transferring best practices from industry (especially from high performing organizations as the startups are) and aiming at contributing for their management, the current research focuses on the possible transfer of expertise from Lean Startup method.

2.3 Lean Startup

The Lean Startup model for development and subsequent innovation management is based on four main pillars for optimal innovation management: (1) systematic and continuous innovation management, (2) developed and two-way communication between the company and its potential customers, (3) the efficient use of resources and (4) the achievement of a cost-effective and optimal price.

The term Lean Startup was first mentioned by startup entrepreneur and consultant Eric Rees in his personal blog Startup Lessons Learned in September 2008. The name is borrowed from the philosophy of lean production developed at Toyota by Taiichi. Ono and Shigeo Shingo [23]. Some of the main principles of "lean" production are to give employees a tool to share their knowledge of production procedures and to develop the concept of production just in time, which increases innovation and reduces the consumption of unnecessary resources. Since its inception in 2008, the Lean Startup method has become widespread and recognizable among innovators and entrepreneurs around the world. Initially, its popularity was expressed as "Good Practice in Systematic Innovation Management" among companies in Silicon Valley, San Francisco, USA. Subsequently, with the accumulation of empirical data, research and results, it is built as a method. Officially, the method was published in 2011. by Eric Rees, who describes it in his book, Lean Srat-Up: How Continuous Innovation is at the Heart of Successful Business [24]. Etymologically, the term is composed of two concepts - lean (tight) and startup. The category of startup, despite its wide distribution and usability, is not strictly defined and for the purposes of a comprehensive presentation of the Lean startup method, it should be clarified.

The Lean Startup method is based on five fundamental principles:

- Entrepreneurs are everywhere - by entrepreneurs, the author of the method means people or startups that create products or services in conditions of high uncertainty, regardless of the size or sector of the company. With this first principle, the Lean Startup method claims that it is applicable to any type of entrepreneurship.
- Entrepreneurship is management - and deserves a new type of management, focused on its specific challenges and opportunities.
- Validated learning - startups exist to learn how to build a sustainable business. Learning as a system, the author of the method accepts as a process of continuous testing and validation of ideas and vision of entrepreneurs to prove their rationality, the right direction and, if necessary, to be a signal for necessary correction.
- Action/build - Measure - Learn - the startup company must have predefined criteria and metrics that give an indication of the fulfillment of the set goals. Based on this

reporting from the created metrics and set goals, entrepreneurs can assess whether the direction followed is correct or it is necessary to make a change.

- Innovation accountancy - although they are the result of creativity, experimentation or vision, in order to be successful, innovation must be measurable. This is necessary for them to be managed systematically: to take into account the progress, the priorities, to set the next goals and direction.

The Lean Startup method introduces some terms that are the basis of its implementation as a management system for startups and innovative projects in established companies. With their presentation, the main points in the concept of the method are clarified.

- Customer feedback - part of the systematic model of innovation management, which the method adopts is the continuous customer feedback. It is proactive, applied at the earliest stage and not only reflects the needs and desires of customers, but also takes into account side effects such as product perception, unwarranted validation (which is not based on analysis but on customer emotion and sensitivity).
- Minimum viable product (MVP) - The aim of the minimum applicable product is to test the business hypothesis through a quickly produced, clean product model that can be quickly and cheaply placed on the market and validate the concept of the idea.
- Continuous deployment - this is a development technique that involves continuous updating of products that are already on the market, based on feedback and even several times a day. This characterizes the products and services that have adopted the technique of "continuous implementation" as highly adaptable and flexible.
- Decomposition of the elements of the product and marketing of several different versions of the product or service simultaneously (split testing, versioning) - through the method different combinations of the product and the discovery of the optimal and preferred combination by customers are possible.
- "Significant" metrics and "Meaningless" metrics (Actionable metrics and vanity metrics) - Metrics are important, but their meaning is important and reporting of real and significant results. The metrics that startups need should be such that they carry specific information related to their business goals. Meaningless metrics are those on the basis of which no specific decision or action can be taken and are not appropriate.
- Change of direction (Pivot) - the concept of change of direction is the ability and need of the startup company to change elements of the product, marketing strategy or other elements of its existence as a result of customer feedback or metrics that it collects and analyzes. The change of direction is intended to minimize the loss of resources when there is reason to believe that the current direction is not correct and does not reveal potential.

3 Research Design

The research design steps on the benefits of knowledge transfer for achieving better managerial results. The fast developing technology and science often produce blurring the boundaries between industries, economic sectors, businesses and this is especially relevant to science fields [25]. A tendency for eliminating borders between countries, overlapping of markets [26], merging of multinational companies [27] has been reported. In this collaborating and globalizing world, knowledge transfer is an essential process that aims at boosting effectiveness, productivity and innovativeness of industries, companies and countries [28]. Knowledge transfer between two economic fields is usual/ordinary and commonplace [29]. It aims at creating synergy and adding value by combining some strengths specific to each of the economic fields, which are included in that interaction [30]. Pursuing effectiveness and boosting productivity in project management in science organizations for the purposes of specific projects as innovative ones, a possibility of knowledge transfer is researched in this paper.

Following the knowledge transfer best practices, here in this research, we propose some knowledge transferring from lean startup to project and innovation management in science organizations. The research presents in its results' section a transition from lean startup elements and techniques to a new research management approach in science organizations. The results are driven from a deep analysis and presents a methodological design. It will be further empirically tested in science research projects which aim at delivering practical research and innovative results. The results are delivered as a transition from some well-known project and innovation management best practices to their lean startup equivalents with a respective analysis on how these will improve the results. The project management initial point for analyses in the research are taken from the best recognized source for project management in universities - PMBOK® and are selected based on their recognition amongst project managers (mini action research for elicit the main element of traditional project management was conducted to select the initial points for analyses. It was done with the support of a PMP certified project manager with 15 + years project management practice). The criteria of selection were those project elements which usually bring complexity and difficulties.

4   Results and Discussion

Analyzing Lean Startup for the purposes of project and innovation management in science organizations, several conclusions can be drawn about the benefits of its use. First, the Lean Startup method is a comprehensive concept for the management of innovative projects and innovative companies, which covers all aspects, phases and main management activities that are part and object of the management of innovative projects. The deduction is valid provided that the management of innovation projects differs from the general principle of project management, which covers a number of other management activities such as time management, scope, costs, communication, human resources, risk, integration, supply, quality and stakeholders. The "Continuous Implementation" tool implies, on the one hand, a systematic management of the continuous process of product innovation and, on the other hand, a system for extending the life cycle of the innovation. The "significant metrics" tool gives the Lean Startup method an advantage over similar methods for managing innovative projects with the preliminary creation of expected criteria for project success and their systematic measurement and reporting. In most cases, innovation projects are measured by standard metrics for investment projects such as payback period, cost-benefit analysis, discounting and compound interest on project cash flows, net present value, internal rate of return. Significant metrics differ from those listed in that they are individually implemented and are consistent with the type of project and its funding, cash flows and profit expectations. The method proclaims the need for specific management for entrepreneurs to structure and systematize the actions of entrepreneurs. The classical theory of entrepreneurship supports the thesis that entrepreneurs are highly adaptable, flexible and individually suited to the changing environment and market conditions, which is a competitive advantage for them. On the other hand, the Lean Startup method offers a systematic management that maximizes profits, optimizes costs, efficiency and surpluses, which according to the method are typical of entrepreneurship. The method offers tools and predefined processes for continuous communication and gathering feedback from customers and potential customers.

As a first research delivery, the next table presents the results from a discussion on possible knowledge transfer from Lean Startup to science projects for delivering ready-for-market innovations based on specific project management objectives, typical for innovative projects.

Table 1. Potential knowledge transfer from Lean Startup to managing scientific projects

Traditional project management in science projects	Lean startup response
Scope creep	Iteration development
Scope prioritization	Customer feedback
Project scope statement	Minimum viable product (MVP)
Product scope	Minimum viable product (MVP)
Project scope	Minimum viable product (MVP)
Verified deliverables	Validated learning
Data collection	Change of direction (Pivot)
Gathering requirements	Continuous deployment
Categorization of requirements	Action/build - Measure - Learn
Create WBS	Action/build - Measure - Learn
Control scope	Customer feedback
Time compression	Continuous deployment
Activity list	"Significant" metrics and "Meaningless" metrics
Dependencies	Continuous deployment
Critical path	"Significant" metrics and "Meaningless" metrics
Three point estimating	Entrepreneurship is management

(continued)

Table 1. (*continued*)

Traditional project management in science projects	Lean startup response
Monte Carlo analyses	Continuous deployment
Milestone charts	Entrepreneurship is management
Resource optimization	Continuous deployment
Analogous estimating	Build-measure-learn
Critical chain method	Change of direction (Pivot)
Re-estimating	Validated learning
Cost baseline	Validated learning
Value analysis	Validated learning
Bottom-up estimating	Entrepreneurship is management

In Table 1 are presented some answers of Lean Startup for possible reaction to the standard project management objectives which usually are subject of high complexity in innovative projects. During the analysis and possible knowledge transfer between both management methods, the following assumptions took place:

Scope creep is often a critical factor for the success of an ordinary project, but sometimes it might be an opportunity in innovative project. In innovative projects the outcome and its market/customer acceptance and adoption is difficult to be predicted and Lean Startup is the method which proposes many process steps in the innovation development for customer validation and customer feedback which essentially might provoke scope creep with positive results when it comes to market readiness of the project end-product. The critical path as a project management method aims at scheduling the fastest way to achieve all project tasks for minimum time. This project management element is again factor for project failure because scheduling, sequence and dependencies in projects are often changing. This is much more relevant for innovative projects. Lean Startup's answer in this regard is the tool "Significant" metrics and "Meaningless" metrics which aim at creating metrics for each tasks and thus it gives flexibility for their re-scheduling. Project scope is amongst the most difficult tasks to manage in projects. In innovative projects, scope is not well defined since scope are all tasks needed for achieving the goal of a project. However, in innovative projects the tasks are not so clear at the beginning as well as the time necessary for their realization and the resources needed. The concept of Minimum viable product (MVP) proposes an alternative for project and product statement and scope to achieve such a result which is ready for market and will get positive customer feedback. Milestone charts are often presented from product perspective and do not bring real value of the product development of an innovative project. In Lean Startup, the substitute is the main principle for Entrepreneurship as management approach, which transform the major phases and their outcomes of a project into some customer-translated deliverables. Controlling scope in traditional projects or in innovative projects using traditional project management is a process of comparison between agreed terms and achievements/work done during a project. Essentially, this approach is controversial to innovation management which aims at experimenting, searching for the customer feedback and implementing it.

Generally, all presented possible transfers of best practices from startup management and innovation management to traditional project management are reasonable and already happened. However, these all possible knowledge transfer is not yet tested and validated in science organizations. Since the project failure rate in science organizations is extremely high and does not respond fast enough to the market needs for changes and innovations, such a proposal should be taken seriously as an alternative to the traditional project management approaches. This assumption is even more close to innovative projects and applied project in science organizations which often struggles of lack of market values and fail exactly in the phase of commercialization.

5 Conclusion

In conclusion of the presented possible best practices from Startup Management and Lean Startup method as a successful approach for managing of innovative projects, the paper achieved the following tasks:

- The study presents an analysis of an approach for both project and innovation management by the possible use of Lean Startup;
- The study analyzes the specifics of the innovative applied projects in science organizations and proposes knowledge transferring of Lean Startup management practices for handling some common difficulties;
- The paper demonstrated an interpretation of some common difficulties in innovative project by the use of Lean Startup.
- The research presented in the paper gives a tool for both scientists and practitioners in science organizations to align their project work, research and experiments to some of the recommendations presented and provokes experimentation for achieving closer to market outcomes of innovative applied projects in science organizations.

The future work of the author will be focused on a real implementation of the principles of Lean Startup in innovative applied projects in science organizations so the analyzed LS principles to be measured and sized for their applicability in this specific object such universities are. This study also calls for further research on the application of other well proven methods in management and their experimentation in the field of managing science projects within the specific environment of the scientific organization and universities. Such a management tool is Six Sigma which is recognized as a working method that is adaptable to the specific needs and priorities of each partner and field [31]. LS principles might be applied as well in the facility management in scientific organizations and innovative projects, which has not been tried so far [32]. Conflictology as a specific horizontal area of governance, in terms of innovative projects and innovative development in universities, also seems to be a space where the principles of LS can be applied and studied for relevance [33] and have not yet been used.

Acknowledgments. The work on the study and publication was supported by BG NSF Grant No KP-06 OPR01/3–2018.

References

1. Etzkowitz, H., Zhou, C.: The Triple Helix: University–Industry–Government Innovation and Entrepreneurship. 2nd edition, ISBN 9781315620183 (2017)
2. Leahey, E.: From sole investigator to team scientist: trends in the practice and study of research collaboration. Ann. Rev. Soc. **42**:1, 81–100 (2016)
3. Turel, O., Kapoor, B.: A business analytics maturity perspective on the gap between business schools and presumed industry needs. Commun. Assoc. Inf. Syst. **39**(6) (2016). https://aisel.aisnet.org/cais/vol39/iss1/6/
4. Pinto, J., Winch, G.: The unsettling of "settled science:" the past and future of the management of projects. Int. J. Project Manage. **34**(2), 237–245 (2016)
5. Hauge, S., Pinheiro, M., Zyzak: Knowledge bases and regional development: collaborations between higher education and cultural creative industries. Int. J. Cult. Policy **24**:4, 485–503 (2018). https://doi.org/10.1080/10286632.2016.1218858
6. Pearce, J.: Teaching Science by Encouraging Innovation in Appropriate Technologies for Sustainable Development (2019)
7. Stock, G., Greis, N., Fischer, L.: Organisational slack and new product time to market performance. Int. J. Innov. Manage. **22**(04), 1850034
8. Fitzgerald, B., Conboy, K., Power, K., Valerdi, R., Morgan, L., Stol, K.-J. (eds.): LESS 2013. LNBIP, vol. 167. Springer, Heidelberg (2013). https://doi.org/10.1007/978-3-642-44930-7
9. Abrahamsson, P., Corral, L., Oivo, M., Russo, B. (eds.): PROFES 2015. LNCS, vol. 9459. Springer, Cham (2015). https://doi.org/10.1007/978-3-319-26844-6
10. Still, K.: Accelerating research innovation by adopting the lean startup paradigm. Technol. Innov. Manage. Rev. May 2017 **7**(5), 32–43 (2017)
11. Morris, P., Pinto, K.J.: The Wiley Guide to Project, Program, and Portfolio Management. Wiley (2007)
12. Filippov, S., Mooi, H.: Innovation project management: a research agenda. J. Innov. Sustain. **1**(1), 1–22 (2010). ISSN 2179–3565
13. Ghaben, R., Jaaron, A.: Assessing innovation practices in project management: the case of Palestinian construction projects. Int. J. Innov. Sci. Res. ISSN 2351–8014, August, Vol. 17, No. 2, pp.451–465 (2015)
14. Shinoda, M., Nishioka, K., Mishima, A.: Systematization of the method of project management for education in university. Educational Alternatives ISSN 1314–7277, vol. 15 (2017)
15. Project Management Institute, Project management body of knowledge, PMBOK (2017)
16. May, C.C.M., Hwa, Y.E., Spowage, A.: Developing and evaluating a project management methodology (PMM) for university-industry collaborative projects. Product: Manage. Dev. **9**, 121–135 (2011). https://doi.org/10.4322/pmd.2012.004
17. International Project Management Association: IPMA Competence Baseline Version 3.0. International Project Management Association, Nijkerk (2006)
18. ISO 10006:2017, Quality management — Guidelines for quality management in projects
19. Schiller, B.R.,Crewson, P.E.: Entrepreneurial origins: a longitudinal inquiry **35**(3), 523–531 (1997)
20. Wycoff, J., Richardson, T.: Transformation thinking: tools and techniques that open the door to powerful new thinking for every member of your organization, Berkley Trade (1995)

21. Besner, C., Hobbs, B.: Discriminating contexts and project management best practices on innovative and noninnovative projects. Project Manage. J. **39**(1_suppl), S123–S134 (2008)
22. Yordanova, Z.: Innovation project tool for outlining innovation projects. Int. J. Bus. Innov. Res. **16**(1), 63–78 (2018)
23. Ohno, T.: Toyota Production System: Beyond Large-Scale Production (1988)
24. Ries, E.: The lean startup: How today's entrepreneurs use continuous innovation to create radically successful businesses (2011)
25. Gilsing, et al.: Differences in technology transfer between science-based and development-based industries: transfer mechanisms and barriers. Technovation **31**(12), 638–647 (2011)
26. Kohonen, A.: On detection of volatility spillovers in simultaneously open stock markets. J. Empirical Finan. **22**, pp. 140–158 (2013)
27. Heidenreich, M.: The social embeddedness of multinational companies: a literature review. Soc. Econom. Rev. **10**(3), 549–579 (2012)
28. Argote, L., Ingram, P.: Knowledge transfer: a basis for competitive advantage in firms. Organ. Behav. Hum. Dec. Process. **82**(1), 150–169 (2000)
29. Cano-Kollmann, M., Cantwell, J., Hannigan, T., et al.: J. Int. Bus. Stud. **47**(3), 255–262 (2016). https://doi.org/10.1057/jibs.2016.8
30. Bagheri, S., Kusters, R., Trienekens, J., van der Zandt, H.: Classification framework of knowledge transfer issues across value networks. Prod. Serv. Syst. Across Life Cycle Proc. CIRP **47**, 382–387 (2016)
31. Boneva, S.: Financial Instruments for Funding the Cross Border Western Balkan Regions in the Period 2007–2013. Econom. Alternat. (1), 129–143 (2011)
32. Trifonova, S., Pramatarov, A.: SWOT analysis of the facility management of hospitals: the case of Bulgaria. Acad. Contemp. Res. J. **V**(I), 1–9 (2016)
33. Ivanov, I.: Public-private partnership for critical industrial infrastructure protection: basic issues and the case of Bulgaria. Econom. Alternat. (3), 71–82 (2014)

Influence of Ultrasonication on the Properties of Hybrid Electrospun Polyacrylonitrile and Silver Nanoparticles Fibers and Their Potential Use in Water Decontamination

Christian Narváez-Muñoz[1], Camilo Zamora-Ledezma[4],
Luis M. Carrión-Matamoros[1]([⊠]), Ivan E. Guerrero[1], Alexis Debut[3], Karla Vizuete[3],
Edison E. Haro[1], Andrea López López[1], and Ezequiel Zamora-Ledezma[2]

[1] Universidad de las Fuerzas Armadas ESPE, Av. Gral. Rumiñahui s/n, Sangolquí 171-5-231B,
Ecuador
lmcarrion1@espe.edu.ec

[2] Facultad de Ingeniería Agrícola, Universidad Técnica de Manabí (UTM), Avenida Urbina y
Che Guevara, Portoviejo 130105, Ecuador
ezequiel.zamora@utm.edu.ec

[3] Centro de Nanociencia y Nanotecnología, Universidad de las Fuerzas Armadas ESPE,
Sangolquí, Ecuador

[4] Tissue Regeneration and Repair: Orthobiology, Biomaterials Tissue Engineering Research
Group, UCAM - Universidad Católica de Murcia, Avda. Los Jerónimos 135, Guadalupe, 30107
Murcia, Spain

Abstract. The fabrication of hybrid polymer-based membranes with nanoparticles (NPs) has drawn great attention because they combine the intrinsic NPs properties with those from the polymer fibers to enhance the performance of the final membrane. Silver nanoparticles (AgNPs) are one of the most used. In this work, it is reported an approach to fabricate hybrid polyacrylonitrile (PAN) electrospun fibers decorated with silver nanoparticles (AgNPs). We evaluate the influence of ultrasonication on the structure and properties of the fibers. Nanoparticles and nanocomposites were characterized by Rheology, X-ray Diffraction (XRD), and Electron Microscopy. The nanoparticle diameters and distribution assessment were elucidated via electron microscopy analysis and demonstrate the efficiency of sonication during fibers processing. PAN/AgNPs composite fiber membranes were evaluated to filtrate microorganisms in natural hydric sources. The results show that PAN/AgNPs composite membranes inhibit Gram-negative and fungi microorganisms but showed less efficacy for Gram-positive bacteria.

Keywords: AgNPs · PAN · Membranes · Filtration · Antibacterial

1 Introduction

The design of custom-made hybrid polymer-based nanocomposite materials has experienced significant growth [1] due to their intrinsic characteristics of catalysis, adsorption,

© Springer Nature Switzerland AG 2022
M. Botto-Tobar et al. (Eds.): ICAT 2021, CCIS 1535, pp. 176–188, 2022.
https://doi.org/10.1007/978-3-031-03884-6_13

and high reactivity [2]. The control and improvement of the final performances of such materials are still challenging and depend on many physic-chemical parameters [3]. It is well known from the literature that nanoparticles dispersion, distribution, and orientation order are key parameters for processing novel and high-performance nanocomposites. Polymer nanocomposites are regularly used in several day-to-day life applications including coatings, packaging, electronic, structural, environmental, biomedical, automotive, aerospace among others [3–7, 46]. Most of these applications need a rational design by taking into account the functionality, costs, environmental aspects, processing, among others [8]. Typical approaches to achieve a homogeneous distribution of the nanofiller are often assisted by an external energy injection [9, 10].

Different fabrication approaches from double screw extrusion, spin coating, dip coating, drop casting and electrohydrodynamic processing also offer an effortless route to fabricate functional coatings, membranes, films, 2D or 3D nanocomposites structures or scaffolds [6, 9, 11–13]. Among these techniques, electrospinning had shown to be a simple and versatile method to fabricate tailor made nanostructures with diameters down to few nanometers for a vast range of applications [13–15, 44]. The electrospinning technique (Fig. 1) consists of atomizing a conductive solution into a spray of fine droplets by applying an electric field. The stabilization of the electrospray process occurs when the electrostatic forces overcome the surface tension of the liquid.

Concerning environmental applications, the electrospinning method had shown to be useful for innovative water treatment applications [16, 17]. It offers an excellent opportunity to fabricate next-generation and high performance wastewater systems [18]. Polyacrylonitrile (PAN) is one of the most widely used polymers to produce polymer-based nanocomposites, fiber, and membranes. It belongs to the family of acrylic resins. It exhibits also highly resistant to most solvents and has low permeability to gases [21]. In the last decades, the preparation of hybrid fibrous polymer-based membranes decorated with nanoparticles has drawn great attention because they combine the intrinsic characteristics of the NPs with those from the polymer precursor [22, 23]. Silver nanoparticles (AgNPs) are one of the most widely used nanomaterials mainly due to their antimicrobial potential, but it's also reported to be very promising against non-living organisms including emerging human immunodeficiency virus which can induce several viral diseases [24, 25].

This work reports an approach to fabricate hybrid PAN electrospun fibers decorated with AgNPs. The influence of ultrasonication on the structure and properties of the fibers is evaluated. On the other hand, both Nanoparticles and nanocomposites were characterized by Rheology, X-ray Diffraction (XRD), and Electron Microscopy. The nanoparticle diameters and distribution assessment were elucidated via electron microscopy analysis and demonstrate the efficiency of sonication during fibers processing. The antimicrobial properties of PAN/AgNPs composite membranes were evaluated by assessing the microbial growth i) Escherichia coli (Gram-negative bacteria), ii) Staphylococcus aureus (Gram-positive bacteria), and iii) Candida albicans (Fungi). According to our results, PAN/AgNPs composite fiber membranes were very performant to inhibit Gram-negative and fungi microorganisms but showed a mediocre inhibition for Gram-positive bacteria. These results suggest that similar hybrid nanocomposites fiber membranes would be excellent candidates for the selected water treatment processes and antimicrobial applications.

2   Materials and Methods

Polyacrylonitrile powder (PAN, Mw = 150000) CAS number 9003-05-8, was acquired from Minmet Refractories Corp-China and silver nanoparticles powder with 20–40 nm of average diameter (AgNPs, 99.99%) was acquired from Yurui Chemical Co., LTD-Shangai.

2.1   PAN/AgNPs Nanocomposite Suspensions and Fibers Fabrication

In a typical procedure, the polymer precursor (PAN) was firstly dissolved in DMF under magnetic stirring at room temperature for 24 h until a homogeneous yellow like solution was obtained at different polymer content: 8 wt.% ¡ PAN ¡ 14 wt.%. Then the desired amount of silver nanoparticles (AgNPs) powder was added to the former PAN solution and vigorously stirred for 24 h at room temperature. Samples were wept sealed to avoid undesired evaporation. We use AgNPs content in the range of 6 wt.% ¡ AgNPs ¡ 12 wt.%. To assess the sonication effect on the nanoparticle distribution, a set of four samples were prepared using a 10 wt.% PAN solution with 10 wt.% of AgNPs, but sonicated during different times at 0, 10, 20, and 30 min respectively. The electrospinning experimental set-up was provided by EHDTECH. It consists of a syringe pump and a high voltage source, connected to a spray head and a collector plate. The solution was inserted into a 10 mL Nipro plastic syringe. The experiments were carried out at room temperature 21 ± 2 °C and a relative humidity $48 \pm 5\%$. All solutions were pumped at a flow rate of 0.5 ml/h for 1 h, and the voltage of 8.1 kV. In the case, of the sonicated samples, all fibers were fabricated immediately after the sonication was stopped.

2.2   Nanomaterials Characterization

Rheological measurements were performed at 25 °C using a controlled stress rheometer TA Instruments DHR-2 model, which was adapted with the cone-plate (40 mm diameter, 2° cone angle, 100 m gap) accessory. The steady flow-sweep tests were performed in the 0.1–1000 s1 range. To this end, a 100 s1 pre-shear rate during 60 s was applied to the sample to relieve stresses and assure repeatability and reproducibility of the experimental data.

An X-ray diffractometer was used to verify the presence of AgNPs. X-ray diffraction (XRD) patterns were collected using an EMPYREAN diffractometer (PANalytical) in a Bragg-Brentano configuration at 45 kV and 40 mA and monochromatic X rays of Cu K- wavelength (=1.541 Å).

Morphological and structural characterization were carried out through a Field Emission Gun Scanning Electron Microscope (FEG-SEM), used in transmission mode (STEM). The STEM measurements were carried out by applying 30 kV in the bright field configuration. The elemental analysis was obtained by Energy Dispersive X-Ray Spectroscopy (EDX) which was performed on the FEG-SEM chamber using a Bruker

X-Flash 6/30 detector, with a 123 eV resolution at Mn K. The sample was fixed in a stub previously covered with two layers of double coated carbon conductive tape and covered by 20 nm of a conductive gold layer (99.99% purity) using a sputtering evaporator Quorum Q150R ES to avoid any interference from the stub.

2.3 Antimicrobial Properties

The antimicrobial effectiveness of our membranes was assessed using tree microorganisms well recognized as human pathogens: a) Escherichia coli (Gram-negative bacteria), b) Staphylococcus aureus (Gram-positive bacteria), and c) Candida albicans (Fungi). E. coli and S. aureus were cultured in Luria-Bertani broth liquid medium [33, 36, 37]; C. Albicans was grown on yeast extract-peptone-dextrose (YPD) liquid medium [38]. The microorganisms were harvested by centrifuge, washed with 1 phosphate-buffered saline (PBS), and then re-suspended in PBS. A serial 10-fold dilution of PBS was performed with ultrapure water. The density of microorganisms was determined by spectrophotometry and adjusted to standardize the inoculum (optical density at 600 nm). Then, 50 L of this suspension of bacterial cells was poured into a 24-multiwell plate and adding a 1 cm^2 piece of nanomembranes, which were incubated in an orbital shaker at 37 °C, 120 rpm for 24 h. A control well-sample was included with the same conditions but without membranes. The results are expressed as optical density at 600 nm.

3 Results and Discussion

The suspensions and fibers based on nanomaterials were prepared satisfactorily by applying standard protocols. To evaluate the performance of nanoparticles we prepared nanomaterials with different combinations of PAN and AgNPs, as was described in the materials and methods section. All nanomaterial prepared shown very good stability which evidence that the fabrication process was reliable.

3.1 Nanomaterial Characterizations

Figure 1 shows the typical flow and viscosity curves to illustrate the rheological behavior of the studied fluids in terms of shear stress (τ)/viscosity(μ) vs. shearrate(γ), respectively. In the present solutions in the 8wt.%¡PAN ¡14wt.% concentration range exhibit a Newtonian behavior, i.e. their viscosity is indep.

Besides, their intrinsic viscosity slightly increases from 0.3 to 1.7 Pa.s as the polymer content increases as expected for similar melted polymer solutions. While for all the PAN/AgNPs nanocomposites, rheological properties signatures change dramatically. As observed in the lower shear rate regime, the viscosity decreases from 277 to 0.5 Pa.s as the shear rate increases up to 10 s1, exhibiting a typical shear-thinning behavior. For larger shear rate values, the viscosity becomes fairly constant as in Newtonian fluids. Another important rheological feature of these nanocomposites is the presence of a yield stress module (τ_y). Defined as the applied stress at which irreversible plastic deformation is first observed on samples. The yield stress is a key parameter in complex fluids formulations allowing control particle stabilization, prevents phase separation, sedimentation, aggregation, but also allows to control of the flow under shipping vibrations and gravity among others. It is worth noting that this parameter will be very sensitive to the type and quantity of the filler, the shape and particle size, and the polymer/particle interaction/synergy. The present results are in total agreement with similar polymer/additives systems reported in the literature where increasing yield stress is achieved as the content of additives increases. Figure 1 shows the typical flow and viscosity curves to illustrate the rheological behavior of the studied fluids in terms of shear stress (τ)/*viscosity*(μ) *vs. shearrate*(γ), *respectively. In the present case, PAN solutions in the 8wt.%¡PAN ¡14wt.% concentration range exhibit a Newtonian behavior, i.e. their viscosity is indep.*

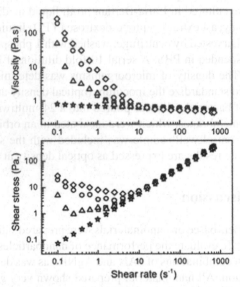

Fig. 1. Viscosity in Pa.s under shear rate scan (a) and shear stress in Pa under shear rate scan (b) for solutions of PAN and PAN/AgNPs nanocomposites at different AgNPs wt.% concentration: i. 0 (stars), ii. 6 (squares), iii. 8 (circles), iv. 10 (triangles) and v. 12 (diamonds).

X-Ray Diffraction (XRD). To study the crystalline nature of the nanoparticles and the hybrid fiber nanocomposites we have performed X-ray crystallography. The diffracted intensities were recorded from 5° to 80°. The XRD diffractograms of AgNPs, PAN, and the PAN/AgNPs composites fibers are shown in Fig. 2. As observed in Fig. 2a, the main Bragg reflections for the silver nanoparticles are observed as expected a 38.45°, 46.35°, 64.75° and 78.05° which corresponds to the planes of (1 1 1), (2 0 0), (2 2 0) and (3 1 1) respectively [39]. On the other hand, Fig. 2b exhibits a typical XRD pattern of PAN composites in which a single crystalline peak centered at 18° is attributed to the polymer phase [40]. Finally, as expected for PAN/AgNPs nanocomposites fiber XRD pattern (Fig. 2c), we observe the polymer pattern accompanied by the strongest Bragg reflection for AgNPs located at 38.45 °. These results are in agreement with the literature indicating that the structure of both PAN and AgNPs is preserved in the final composite [39, 40].

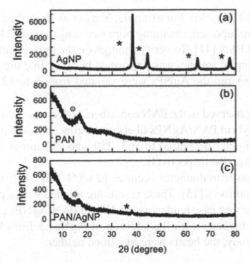

Fig. 2. Diffractogram of XRD typical patterns from a) Silver nanoparticles, ii) PAN fiber and iii) PAN/AgNPs nanocomposite fibers mats. Main Bragg reflections peaks for AgNPs (stars) and PAN (closed circles) are marked respectively.

Scanning Electron Microscopy (SEM). The microstructure of PAN fibers was analyzed varying their wt.% concentration from 8 to 14 (Figs. 3a–3d). It systematically found that pore size (average diameter) in nanofibers increases with concentration (wt.%) of the polymer. The average diameter ranged from 131 nm at PAN 8 wt.% to 240 nm at PAN 14 wt.%. Another interesting finding was the presence of beads only at the lower PAN

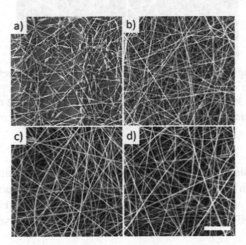

Fig. 3. SEM morphology of PAN fibers with diameter df. Each micrography shows the variation of PAN concentration (wt.%): a) 8 (df 131 ± 10 nm), b) 10 (df 139 ± 20 nm), c) 12 (df 202 ± 44 nm) and d) 14 (df 240 ± 50 nm). SEM images have the same magnification and the scale bar represents 5 μm.

concentration (8 wt.%) (Fig. 3a). For example, Yang et al. described the same pattern of diameter increase here reported, obtaining pore size ranged from 240 nm at 11 wt.% to 925 nm at 13 wt.% of PAN [41]. To verify changes on the hybrid nanofibers microstructure an additional setup of images was performed but this time the PAN concentration was fixed (at 10 wt.%) and the AgNPs were variated from 6 to 12 wt.%, respectively (Figs. 4a–4d).

Unlike what was observed in the PAN nanofibers, a decrease in the average diameter was observed in the hybrid PAN/AgNPs fibers as the concentration of AgNPs increased. Thus, the average diameter decreased to 563, 350, and 217 nm at the addition of 6, 8, and 10 and wt.% of AgNPs, respectively.

Then, slight increases in diameter occur at 12 wt.% (Fig. 4d). There was no found bead in the hybrid nanofibers [15]. These results are aligned with a previous study [41], which reported similar decrease tendencies on hybrid PAN/AgNPs fibers, reaching 450, 324, and 196 nm of diameter with the addition of AgNps 3 from 9, 10, and 11 wt.% respectively. In this study, the beads were identified neither.

Fig. 4. SEM morphology of hybrid PAN/AgNPs fibers with the respective average diameter (d_f). PAN concentration was fixed (10 wt.%) but AgNPs concentrations (wt.%) varies: a) 6 (d_f 563 ± 62 nm), b) 8 (d_f 350 ± 61 nm), c) 10 (d_f 217 ± 34 nm) and d) 12 (d_f 228 ± 39 nm). All SEM images have the same magnification and the scale bar represent 5 μm.

Scanning Transmission Electron Microscopy (STEM). The microanalysis of silver nanoparticles is shown in Fig. 5a. The hybrid PAN/AgNPs nanofibers with 10 wt.% PAN and AgNPs 10 wt.%, with 30 min of sonication is also shown in Fig. 5b. Both images demonstrate that AgNPs could not be visible by using SEM analyses but with STEM.

Figure 5b shows the AgNPs as white patches over the fibers. In order to check the spatial distribution of AgNPs on the PAN fibers as a function of sonication time, an additional assay was performed kept fix the PAN and AgNPs concentration (10 wt.%, respectively) but changing the sonication time as follow:

0, 10, 20 and 30 min (Figs. 6a–6d). This experiment reveals that AgNPs are located on the fibers as big clusters when no sonication or the low time of exposure to (Figs. 6a and 6b).

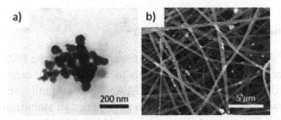

Fig. 5. STEM micrographs for silver nanoparticles (AgNPs) (a) and Secondary electron (SE) SEM image for hybrid PAN/AgNPs fibers nanocomposite (b) with 10 wt.% PAN and AgNPs respectively, by applying 30 min of sonication.

Then, after 20 min of sonication, the AgNPs begin to exhibit a better spatial distribution in the fibers, indicating a more uniform and homogeneous spatial pattern (Figs. 6c and 6d). This pattern of better spatial distribution with increases of sonication time has been reported with similar nanoparticles for the same or other uses [27, 42, 43]. The optimal concentration ratio (1:1) for 10 wt.% PAN/10 wt.% AgNPs was used to evaluate the effect of sonication in the dispersion of AgNPs on the fibers. A set of samples was

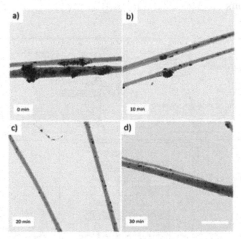

Fig. 6. Selected STEM images for hybrid PAN/AgNPs fibers nanocomposites subjected to different sonication time during mixing. a) 0 min, b) 10 min, c) 20 min and d) 30 min. PAN and AgNPs content were kept constant at 10 wt.%. All images have the same magnification and the scale bar represents 2 μm.

prepared using different times of sonication. Typical SEM images of PAN/AgNPs fibers are shown in Fig. 4. The STEM images show the dispersion of the AgNPs on the PAN fibers. There is a clear difference between the fibrous membranes with and without sonication treatment, however, no significant change is observed for those fibers sonicated during 10, 20, and 30 min. This could be attributed to the longtime collection of the fibers, in which the solution remains almost static on the syringe for the duration of the electrospinning process. During this time, the nanoparticles can agglomerate as reported in Pradhan et al. [27].

3.2 Filtration and Antibacterial Properties

In the first part of this study, the parameters used to fabricate the PAN sub micrometric fibers were researched. To fabricate a fibrous membrane many experiments were performed using the different concentrations of PAN solution until obtaining the optimal protocols. The flow rate was kept constant to get a better jet stabilization only the electric field was varied. The optimal concentration obtained for the polymer precursor was 10 wt.%. The morphology of the fibers was uniform without any beads as shown in Fig. 3(b–d). As observed, the morphologies can be tuned from fibrous + beads to single fibers as a function of the polymer precursor content (Fig. 3).

Cells Reduction By Nanofiltration and Antimicrobial Application. The results showed that PAN and hybrid PAN/AgNPs membranes exhibit different efficacy as microorganisms capturer (fecal coliforms) (Fig. 7a). These preliminary results evidence a reduction of fecal coliforms present in the water, from more than 1000 to 70 (PAN/AgNPs 8 wt.%) or 100 (PAN/AgNPs 10 wt.%) colonies per 100 mL, which represents 93 and 90% of reduction, respectively. This result is similar to previous studies that reported the coliforms capture efficiency of around 81% [34] using silver coated PAN membranes under similar conditions.

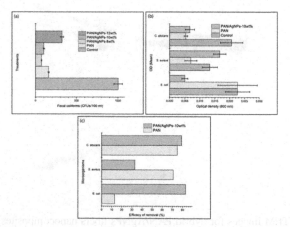

Fig. 7. Microbiological applications of hybrid nanofibers. a) Efficacy of fecal coliform capture from PAN and PAN/AgNPs nanomembranes. b) Optical density of microorganisms exposed to PAN and PAN/AgNPs nanomembranes (10 wt.%) after 24 h of incubation. c) Removal efficacy (%) of microorganisms exposed to PAN and PAN/AgNPs nanomembranes (10 wt.%) after 24 h of incubation

After observing the promising results with PAN and hybrid PAN/AgNPs membranes in the filtration process, the antimicrobial potentiality was also tested on three different microorganisms. This result evidences the antimicrobial effect of PAN membranes (10 wt.%) on the physiological pattern of E. coli (Gram -) and C. albicans (Fungi), obtaining an optical density of 0.004 and 0.005, respectively, after 24 h of incubation (Fig. 7b). The PAN membranes without AgNPs also shown an inhibitor effect on C. albicans and S. aureus (Gram+), obtaining an optical density of 0.006 and 0.007, respectively. The efficacy (%) of bacteria and fungi removal using PAN or hybrid PAN/AgNPs nanofibers, in comparison with the control sample (contaminated water without membranes), is shown in Fig. 7c. This result demonstrates that PAN/AgNPs membranes (10 wt.%) are very good tools to control or inhibit the growth of both E. coli (83%) and C. albicans (79%). Likewise, PAN membranes showed an interesting inhibitor effect on both C. albicans (75%) and S. aureus (71%). This removal efficacy is slightly lower than those reported previously, in which 99% of microorganisms reduction was reached using PAN/AgNPs membranes but no reduction was observed in the presence of PAN membranes without AgNPs [34].

4   Conclusion

The nanoparticle diameters and distribution assessment were elucidated via electron microscopy analysis and demonstrate the efficiency of sonication during fibers processing. Another important factor that should be mentioned is the key role played by the rheological properties of PAN/AgNPs nanocomposites solutions used for electrospraying. The antimicrobial properties by assessing the microbial growth inhibition of the hybrid PAN/AgNPs membranes with Escherichia coli, Staphylococcus aureus, and Candida albicans. According to the results, PAN/AgNPs composite fiber membranes were very performant to inhibit the Gram-negative bacteria and fungi but showed less inhibition efficacy for the Gram-positive bacteria.

These results suggest that such hybrid nanocomposites fiber membranes would be excellent candidates for antimicrobial or environmental applications, specifically on the biological water treatment process. These results are very promising and open a new potential research and application area in Ecuador.

Acknowledgment. This work was supported by a) the research project PIC-16-BENS-002, ENSAM- BLE scholarship program of the SENESCYT, b) the research project "Ecotoxicological evaluations of materials with potential agricultural and environmental use" financed by the Universidad Técnica de Manabí in the 2019 internal call, and c) the research project "Nanofertilizers in soil and nitrous oxide emissions" (ID475) financed by FONTAGRO in the 2020 call.

References

1. Hulla, J., Sahu, S., Hayes, A.: Nanotechnology: history and future. Hum. Exp. Toxicol. **34**(12), 1318–1321 (2015). https://doi.org/10.1177/0960327115603588

2. Müller, K., et al.: Review on the processing and properties of polymer nanocomposites and nanocoatings and their applications in the packaging, automotive and solar energy fields. Nanomaterials 7(4), 74 (2017). https://doi.org/10.3390/nano7040074

3. Kolahalam, L.A., Kasi Viswanath, I.V., Diwakar, B.S., Govindh, B., Reddy, V., Murthy, Y.L.N.: Review on nanomaterials: synthesis and applications. Mater. Today Proc. 18, 2182–2190 (2019). https://doi.org/10.1016/j.matpr.2019.07.371

4. Li, R., Zhang, L., Wang, P.: Rational design of nanomaterials for water treatment. Nanoscale 7(41), 17167–17194 (2015). https://doi.org/10.1039/C5NR04870B

5. Lu, H., Wang, J., Stoller, M., Wang, T., Bao, Y., Hao, H.: An overview of nanomaterials for water and wastewater treatment. Adv. Mater. Sci. Eng. 2016, 1 (2016). https://doi.org/10.1155/2016/4964828

6. Tlili, I., Alkanhal, T.A.: Nanotechnology for water purification: electrospun nanofibrous membrane in water and wastewater treatment. J. Water Reuse Desalin. 9(3), 232–248 (2019). https://doi.org/10.2166/wrd.2019.057

7. Hu, T.Y., Frieman, M., Wolfram, J.: Insights from nanomedicine into chloroquine efficacy against COVID-19. Nat. Nanotechnol. (2020). https://doi.org/10.1038/s41565-020-0674-9

8. Schummer, J.: Multidisciplinarity, interdisciplinarity, and patterns of research collaboration in nanoscience and nanotechnology. Scientometrics 59(3), 425–465 (2004). https://doi.org/10.1023/B:SCIE.0000018542.71314.38

9. Akpan, E.I., Shen, X., Wetzel, B., Friedrich, K.: Design and synthesis of polymer nanocomposites. In: Polymer Composites with Functionalized Nanoparticles, pp. 47–83. Elsevier (2019). https://doi.org/10.1016/B978-0-12-814064-2.00002-0

10. Torres-Canas, F.J., Blanc, C., Zamora-Ledezma, C., Silva, P., Anglaret, E.: Dispersion and individualization of SWNT in surfactant-free suspensions and composites of hydrosoluble polymers. J. Phys. Chem. C 119(1), 703–709 (2015). https://doi.org/10.1021/jp5092015

11. Huang, Z.-M., Zhang, Y.-Z., Kotaki, M., Ramakrishna, S.: A review on polymer nanofibers by electrospinning and their applications in nanocomposites. Compos. Sci. Technol. 63(15), 2223–2253 (2003). https://doi.org/10.1016/S0266-3538(03)00178-7

12. Teo, W.E., Ramakrishna, S.: A review on electrospinning design and nanofibre assemblies. Nanotechnology 17(14), R89–R106 (2006). https://doi.org/10.1088/0957-4484/17/14/R01

13. Xue, J., Xie, J., Liu, W., Xia, Y.: Electrospun nanofibers: new concepts, materials, and applications. Acc. Chem. Res. 50(8), 1976–1987 (2017). https://doi.org/10.1021/acs.accounts.7b00218

14. Han, J., Xiong, L., Jiang, X., Yuan, X., Zhao, Y., Yang, D.: BioFunctional electrospun nanomaterials: from topology design to biological applications. Prog. Polym. Sci. 91, 1–28 (2019). https://doi.org/10.1016/j.progpolymsci.2019.02.006

15. Narvaez-Muñoz, C.P., et al.: Tailoring organic poly(vinylpyrrolidone) microparticles and fibers with multiwalled carbon nanotubes for reinforced composites. ACS Appl. Nano Mater. 2(7), 4302–4312 (2019). https://doi.org/10.1021/acsanm.9b00758

16. Gehrke, I., Somborn-schulz, A.: Innovations in nanotechnology for water treatment. Nanotechnol. Sci. Appl. 8, 1–17 (2015)

17. Ray, S.S., Chen, S.-S., Li, C.-W., Nguyen, N.C., Nguyen, H.T.: A comprehensive review: electrospinning technique for fabrication and surface modification of membranes for water treatment application. RSC Adv. 6(88), 85495–85514 (2016). https://doi.org/10.1039/C6RA14952A

18. Qu, X., Alvarez, P.J.J., Li, Q.: Applications of nanotechnology in water and wastewater treatment. Water Res. 47(12), 3931–3946 (2013). https://doi.org/10.1016/j.watres.2012.09.058

19. Kenry, Lim, C.T.: Nanofiber technology: current status and emerging developments. Prog. Polymer Sci. 70, 1–17 (2017). https://doi.org/10.1016/j.progpolymsci.2017.03.002

20. WHO, UNICEF: Progress on Drinking Water, Sanitation and Hygiene (2017)
21. Jiang, H., Wu, C., Zhang, A., Yang, P.: Structural characteristics of polyacrylonitrile (PAN) fibers during oxidative stabilization. Compos. Sci. Technol. **29**(1), 33–44 (1987). https://doi. org/10.1016/0266-3538(87)90035-2
22. Wang, Y., et al.: Preparation of silver nanoparticles dispersed in polyacrylonitrile nanofiber film spun by electrospinning. Mater. Lett. **59**(24–25), 3046–3049 (2005). https://doi.org/10. 1016/j.matlet.2005.05.016
23. Yu, D.-G., Zhou, J., Chatterton, N.P., Li, Y., Huang, J., Wang, X.: Polyacrylonitrile nanofibers coated with silver nanoparticles using a modified coaxial electrospinning process. IJN 5725 (2012). https://doi.org/10.2147/IJN.S37455
24. Galdiero, S., Falanga, A., Vitiello, M., Cantisani, M., Marra, V., Galdiero, M.: Silver nanoparticles as potential antiviral agents. Molecules **16**(10), 8894–8918 (2011). https://doi.org/10. 3390/molecules16108894
25. Parekh, S., David, R., Bannuru, K., Krishnaswamy, L., Baji, A.: Electrospun silver coated polyacrylonitrile membranes for water filtration applications. Membranes **8**(3), 59 (2018). https://doi.org/10.3390/membranes8030059
26. Wang, Y., et al.: Preparation of silver nanoparticles dispersed in polyacrylonitrile nanofiber film spun by electrospinning. Mater. Lett. **59**(24(25)), 3046–3049 (2005). https://doi.org/10. 1016/j.matlet.2005.05.016
27. Pradhan, S., Hedberg, J., Blomberg, E., Wold, S., Odnevall Wallinder, I.: Effect of sonication on particle dispersion, administered dose and metal release of non-functionalized, non-inert metal nanoparticles. J. Nanopart. Res. **18**(9), 1–14 (2016). https://doi.org/10.1007/s11051-016-3597-5
28. Nguyen, V.S., Rouxel, D., Vincent, B.: Dispersion of nanoparticles: from organic solvents to polymer solutions. Ultrason. Sonochem. **21**(1), 149–153 (2014). https://doi.org/10.1016/j.ult sonch.2013.07.015
29. Henrist, C., Mathieu, J.-P., Vogels, C., Rulmont, A., Cloots, R.: Morphological study of magnesium hydroxide nanoparticles precipitated in dilute aqueous solution. J. Crystal Growth **249**(1(2)), 321–330 (2003). https://doi.org/10.1016/S0022-0248(02)02068-7
30. Lin, H.-W., Hwu, W.-H., Ger, M.-D.: The dispersion of silver nanoparticles with physical dispersal procedures. J. Mater. Process. Technol. **206**(1(3)), 56–61 (2008). https://doi.org/10. 1016/j.jmatprotec.2007.12.025
31. Bittmann, B., Haupert, F., Schlarb, A.K.: Ultrasonic dispersion of inorganic nanoparticles in epoxy resin. Ultrason. Sonochem. **16**(5), 622–628 (2009). https://doi.org/10.1016/j.ultsonch. 2009.01.006
32. Dickson, D., Liu, G., Li, C., Tachiev, G., Cai, Y.: Dispersion and stability of bare hematite nanoparticles: effect of dispersion tools, nanoparticle concentration, humic acid and ionic strength. Sci. Total Environ. **419**, 170–177 (2012). https://doi.org/10.1016/j.scitotenv.2012. 01.012
33. USEPA. Method 1604: Total Coliforms and Escherichia Coli in Water by Membrane Filtration Using a Simultaneous Detection Technique (MI Medium). Standard Methods, 18 September 2002. EPA-821-R-02-024
34. Parekh, S.A., David, R.N., Bannuru, K.K.R., Krishnaswamy, L., Baji, A.: Electro-spun silver coated polyacrylonitrile membranes for water filtration applications. Membranes **8**(3), 26–29 (2018). https://doi.org/10.3390/membranes8030059
35. APHA-AWWA-WEF. 9221 A-C Multiple-Tube Fermentation Technique for Members of the Coliform Group, 9221D Presence-Absence Coliform Test 9221 E FecaColiform Procedure. Standar Methods for the Examination of Water and Wastewater, 20th Edition, pp. 47–56 (2002)

36. Fricker, C.R., Bullock, S., Murrin, K., Niemela, S.I.: Use of the ISO 9308-1 procedure for the detection of E. Coli in water utilizing two incubation temperatures and two confirmation procedures and comparison with defined substrate technology. J. Water Health **6**(3), 389–397 (2008). https://doi.org/10.2166/wh.2008.049

37. Tortorello, M.L.: Indicator organisms for safety and quality-uses and methods for detection: minireview. J. AOAC Int. **86**(6), 1208–1217 (2003)

38. Creger, P.E., Blankenship, J.R.: Analysis of gene expression in filamentous cells of candida albicans grown on agar plates. J. Biol. Methods **5**(1), 84 (2018). https://doi.org/10.14440/jbm.2018.211

39. Jyoti, K., Baunthiyal, M., Singh, A.: Characterization of silver nanoparticles synthesized using Urtica dioica Linn. Leaves and their synergistic effects with antibiotics. J. Radiat. Res. Appl. Sci. **9**(3), 217–227 (2016). https://doi.org/10.1016/j.jrras.2015.10.002

40. Saud, P.S., et al.: Photocatalytic degradation and antibacterial investigation of nano synthesized Ag3VO4 particles @PAN nanofibers. Carbon Lett. **18**, 30–36 (2016). https://doi.org/10.5714/CL.2016.18.030

41. Yang, W., Li, L., Wang, S., Liu, J.: Preparation of multifunctional Ag-NPs/PAN nanofiber membrane for air filtration by one-step process. Pigment Resin Technology (2020)

42. Taurozzi, J.S., Hackley, V.A., Wiesner, M.R.: Ultrasonic dispersion of nanoparticles for environmental, health and safety assessment-issues and recommendations. Nanotoxicology **5**(4), 711–729 (2011)

43. Skandalis, N., et al.: The effect of silver nanoparticles size, produced using plant extract from Arbutus unedo, on their antibacterial efficacy. Nanomaterials **7**(7), 178 (2017)

44. Narvaez-Muñoz, C., Ryzhakov, P., Pons-Prats, J.: Determination of the operational parameters for the manufacturing of spherical PVP particles via electrospray. Polymers **13**(4), 529 (2021)

45. Zamora-Ledezma, C., Negrete-Bolagay, D., Figueroa, F., Zamora-Ledezma, E., Ni, M., Guerrero, F.A.V.H.: Heavy metal water pollution: a fresh look about hazards, novel and conventional remediation methods. Environ. Technol. Innov. **22**, 101504 (2021)

46. Castro, C.M.J., Puig, R., Zamora-Ledezma, C., Ledezma, E.Z.: Caracterización preliminar de la ceniza de cáscara de arroz de la provincia Manabí, Ecuador, para su empleo en hormigones. Revista Técnica de la Facultad de Ingeniería Universidad del Zulia **44**(1), 44–50

MySQL vs MongoDB: A Preliminary Performance Evaluation Using the YCSB Framework

Julio C. Mendoza-Tello[1]([✉]) and Jenny Villacís-Ramón[2]

[1] Faculty of Engineering and Applied Sciences, Central University of Ecuador, Quito, Ecuador
jcmendoza@uce.edu.ec
[2] IT Consultant, N35-49 Julio Moreno Street, Quito, Ecuador

Abstract. Information systems manage and process data for the fundamental tasks and specific requirements of each business. A database is thus an essential component of an information system. Database research involves two approaches, namely: relational and non-relational. A relational database is defined by rigid structures that provide consistency and referential integrity. However, this causes delays in response times and affects the availability of the schema. On the other hand, a non-relational database is schemaless and provides great flexibility for organizing and retrieving data; however, this characteristic does not guarantee strict consistency. An analysis of the performance of both database approaches is necessary to support the implementation of information systems. This research focuses on two datastores: MySQL (a relational database), and MongoDB (a non-relational database). Thus, the aim of this paper is to evaluate and compare the performance of both databases. For this, six evaluation scenarios were defined and executed using *Yahoo! Cloud Serving Benchmark*. This document highlights the best and worst performance scenarios for both databases based on three parameters: overall runtime, latency, and throughput. Finally, conclusions and future works are provided at the end of the paper.

Keywords: NoSQL · MongoDB · MySQL · YCSB

1 Introduction

Relational databases have shown great versatility for structuring definitions and rules based on processing logic and referential integrity that guarantee a high degree of consistency. Indexing, CRUD operations (create, read, update, and delete), and multi-user synchronization are also allowed.

Relational databases are designed using third normal form. The complexity of multi-table queries (JOINS) and clauses (such as ORDER BY, UNION) consumes computational resources and degrades system performance [1]. This situation is aggravated if the volume of data accessed occupies a greater amount of memory allocated to the database [2]. Thus, big data is a challenge for relational databases because it involves processing

© Springer Nature Switzerland AG 2022
M. Botto-Tobar et al. (Eds.): ICAT 2021, CCIS 1535, pp. 189–201, 2022.
https://doi.org/10.1007/978-3-031-03884-6_14

and memory costs to meet response times. Due to this inconvenience, non-relational databases are used to improve the availability of the system.

Non-relational databases (called NoSQL) are schemaless; that is, the data model is not essential. There are several types of NoSQL databases for solving a specific type of requirement or problem. Among these, the document-oriented database stands out due to its flexibility for organizing large volumes of structured and semi-structured data, which leads to improved performance. However, the use of this type of database does not guarantee strict consistency; that is, it eventually accepts inconsistencies [3]. Despite this disadvantage, performance is an important and decisive factor in the implementation of information systems. Data volume, access concurrency, latency, and throughput are important considerations for analyzing database performance. In this context, it is necessary to clarify which are the best use scenarios for both approaches. In particular, the document focuses on two databases (MySQL and MongoDB) to compare their runtimes and provide a performance benchmark.

This document is organized as follows: Sect. 2 explains the methodology, Sect. 3 provides a background and literature review, Sect. 4 defines the experimental setting, Sect. 5 interprets and discusses the results and finally, conclusions and future works are described at the end of the document.

2 Methodology

In this preliminary research, the following three open-source software were used: MongoDB (a non-relational database), MySQL (a relational database), and YCSB (Yahoo! Cloud Serving Benchmark). In this context, a brief review of the essential characteristics of both databases is provided (Table 1). Then, a summary of the test scenarios proposed by YCSB is explained. Data workloads are generated and evaluated to obtain measurements of overall runtime, latency, and throughput.

3 Background and Literature Review

Core theoretical concepts and works related to this research are presented in this section.

3.1 MongoDB Overview

MongoDB is an open-source document database written in C++ language. An overview is provided below using the model, data replication, CAP theorem, and BASE approach.

– Data model. Database, collection, and field are identified. Each database contains non-relational entities called collections. Each collection allows several records called documents to be stored. Each document is a set of key-value pairs and is identified by a 128-hash object called _id. The number of fields is not the same for all documents in the same collection. The model supports CRUD operations, that is, create, read, update, and delete documents. It does not require prior definition of field structures and data types to perform these operations; it thus has a schemaless property. Each document can be redefined during the execution of operations without altering the pattern of previous documents belonging to the same collection. For this, MongoDB uses JSON (Java Script Object Notation) as the format for data interchange, and BSON (binary-encoded serialization of JSON) for using additional data. Also, semi-structured data types like CSV, XML, and YALM are accepted. Multikey, compound, text, hashed, and 2dSphere indexes are supported. Each document has a maximum size of 16 MB. For larger sizes, GridFS is used as a specification to divide documents into smaller pieces of maximum 256 KB (called CHUNKS).

- Data replication. A replica is a set of mongod processes that maintain the data integrity of the entire schema. Two types of nodes are configured: master (called primary) and slave (called secondary). Primary nodes provide replicas to secondary nodes. Through a vote, the role of both can change; that is, a primary node can become secondary, and vice versa. This provides greater reading support because any query can be sent to different server machines. Replication modes are as follows: single master/single slave, single master/multiple slaves, multiple master/single slave, cascade, master/master, interleaved, pairs, and sets. Sharding techiques are used to fragment the data on various machines, and each machine is responsible for its data set [1]. Thus, replication becomes a technique that provides data redundancy and increases the availability and level of fault tolerance.
- CAP Theorem and BASE approach. CAP defines three principles (consistency, availability, and partition tolerance) and affirms that any distributed system can usually satisfy only two principles. MongoDB prefers consistency and partition tolerance over high availability. That is, it guarantees the operation of the scheme, even if there are system failures or data loss (tolerance partition); also, it carries out read operations from last write (consistency). Additionally, MongoDB is based on BASE approach, i.e., basic availability, soft state, and eventual consistency. Causal consistency is allowed inside a client session [4].

3.2 MySQL Overview

MySQL is an open-source relational database written in C and C++ languages. An overview is provided below with the model, data replication, and ACID requirements.

- Data model. Database, table, fields are identified. Each database is a set of related tables. Each table is a matrix of rows and columns. Columns define common characteristics of objects. The number of columns is fixed and equal for all rows of the table. Rows are records that store the values of those columns. As a relational database, it supports CRUD operations, that is, create, read, update, and delete rows. To carry out any operation, it is necessary to define an entity-relationship model-based fixed structure. For this, MySQL uses a Structured Query Language (SQL) to define, modify and control data, and support transactions. Data types such as date, time, numeric, spatial, string (character and byte), and JSON are accepted.
- Data replication. Replication copies data from one server (called master) to another (called slave). MySQL allow four replication methods: asynchronous, synchronous, semisynchronous, and delayed. By default, MySQL uses asynchronous replication;

that is, slaves are not permanently connected to receive information (unlike the synchronous method). Semisynchronous replication occurs on the master blocks and returns to the session that produced the transaction if at least one slave registers these transactional events. In contrast, a delayed replication allows a slave to be deliberately delayed with respect to the master for a certain time. MySQL allows three replication formats: statement, row, and mixed.

- ACID requirements. A relational database provides reliability if it meets the requirements of atomicity, consistency, isolation, and durability for its transactions. Currently, MySQL provides multi-version concurrency control and transactional capacity. Additionally, the database engine allows row-level locking to support transactions, foreign key constraints, concurrent reads, writes, rollback, and fault recovery [5].

Table 1. MongoDB versus MySQL: overview

Features	MongoDB	MySQL
Development Language	C++	C, C++
Data Model	Non-relational Database Collection Document Schemaless No referential integrity	Relational Database Table Row Fixed schema Referential integrity
Query language	JavaScript	SQL
Scalability	Horizontal	Vertical
Data storage	BSON	Since 8 version, InnoDB
Data replication	Single master/single slave, Single master/multiple slaves, Multiple Master/single slave, Cascade, Master/master, Interleaved	Master/single with four replication methods: asynchronous, synchronous, semisynchronous and delayed
Integrity model and Principles	Consistency and partition tolerance (CAP theorem), and BASE approach	Atomicity, consistency, isolation, and durability (ACID requirements),
Operating system	Solaris, Linux, Windows, Mac OS, and Linux	Solaris, Linux, Windows, Mac OS, and Linux

3.3 YCSB Overview

Yahoo! Cloud Serving Benchmark (YCSB) is an open-source framework for evaluating the performance of databases and cloud storage schemas; its modular and portable architecture extends connectivity to new databases by implementing CRUD interfaces. YCSB functionality is based on two components: workload generator, and scenarios.

Evaluation scenarios are called workloads. In each scenario, a workload generates and stores test data within a database. Each test data is represented by a random character set and organized within registers (or rows). Each record occupies 1KB (key and ten fields). Each Workload performs a combination of CRUD operations on the generated data. According to the scenario, it is possible to configure the runtime, number of operations, and threads [6]. YCSB defines six evaluation scenarios [3], as follows:

- Workload A (Update heavy workload). This scenario proposes a mix of 50% read, and 50% update.
- Workload B (Read mostly workload). This scenario proposes a mix of 95% read, and 5% update.
- Workload C (Read only). This scenario proposes 100% read.
- Workload D (Read latest workload). This scenario proposes a mix of 95% read (recently inserted record), and 5% insert.
- Workload E (Short ranges). In this scenario, short ranges of records are queried, rather than individual records. This scenario proposes a mix of 95% scan, and 5% insert.
- Workload F (Read-modify-write). In this scenario, a client will read and modify a record, and then rewrite the changes. This scenario proposes a mix of 50% read and 50% read–modify–write (rmw).

3.4   Related Work

Information Review. The review was conducted according to Kitchenham's recommendations [7]. For this, four activities were executed.

First, search strategy. Scopus is a bibliographic database to search documents from prestigious publishers, such as: Elsevier, Springer, Emerald, IEEE, and ACM digital. The search was refined using the following keywords: "MySQL", "MongoDB", and "performance". In the first stage, 159 documents were found. However, 121 documents did not correspond to the focus of this research, so only 38 documents remained.

Second, definition of exclusion and inclusion criteria. The language chosen for the bibliographic review was English. Only book chapters, conference papers, and journal articles were considered.

Third, quality evaluation. Documents with a formal structure were considered; that is, complete studies that included analysis, methodology, results, and conclusions. With these considerations, 24 documents were eliminated and 14 remained.

Fourth, data synthesis. MS Excel and Mendeley were used for the extraction and synthesis of bibliographic references. This review culminated on April 30, 2021.

Review Synthesis. Work on the performance of MongoDB was as follows. MongoDB and PostGis were compared for the spatial data management of clusters [8] based on Amazon web services [9]. In addition, MongoDB was compared with CouchBase to evaluate the storage and retrieval of images using the java web application and cloud computing services [10]. An application based on Node.js was used to evaluate the performance of two drivers for MongoDB, namely: MongoClient and Mongoose. CRUD operations were executed to measure execution time, CPU usage, and memory consumption [11]. This performance was improved through sharding techniques for load balancing [12], and indexing for scan operations [13]. However, performance was affected by the number of replicas in cloud clusters [14].

Work on the performance of MySQL was as follows. The performance of Apache Pig, Apache Hive, and MySQL Cluster was evaluated [15]. Load and response times were considered for query execution using CPU and GPU. The use of GPU dramatically reduced effort and accelerated queries [16]. Similarly, MySQL was compared with Cassandra and HBase to evaluate heavy write operations using a REST web application [17]. In addition, OLTP Workloads were used to measure performance in big data environments [18] using Hive Partition-Bucketing, Apache Pig [19], and Facebook [20].

4   Experimental Environment

In this research, the YCSB architecture client interacted with the database. This architecture had two components: a workload executor (which drove several client threads), and stats. Each thread interacted with the database and carried out two operations: data upload (called loading phase), and execution of workloads (called transaction phase). Each thread measured throughput and 99% percentile latencies. Then, these measurements were sent to the stats module.

To minimize variations in performance, tests were conducted three times, including a computer reset. The hardware resources and operating systems were identical for both databases. Hardware and software were as follows: Operating system: Windows 10, RAM: 16 GB RAM, CPU: Intel Core i7 10th generation, Benchmarking tool: YCSB version 0.15.0, MongoDB version 4.2.3 (database and collection), MySQL version 8.0 (database and table).

5   Results and Discussion

This section describes the results of two consecutive phases, namely: loading and transaction. The results of the loading phase are based on overall runtime. The results of the transaction phase are based on latency and throughput.

5.1   Loading Phase

Two databases were used: MySQL and MongoDB. The loading phase generated a 1 GB size for both databases; that is, 1 million records of 1 KB. In addition, 16 client threads were defined to obtain generation times. The overall runtime obtained for each workload (in minutes: seconds) was as follows.

– The best overall runtime for MongoDB was 01:53 with Workload C; that is, it was faster for 100% reading operations. However, the worst overall runtime for MongoDB was 02:31 with Workload B; that is, it was slower when there were 5% updating operations.

- The best overall runtime for MySQL was 21:13 with Workload D; that is, it was faster when 95% of reading operations were performed on newly inserted records. However, the worst overall runtime for MySQL was 28:57 with Workload E; that is, it was lower when there were 95% scanning operations on short records.
- In general, MongoDB was faster than MySQL on all workloads (between 8 and 14 times). MongoDB stood out in Workload C because it had a runtime of 01:53, 14 times faster than MySQL. Figure 1 shows the overall runtime obtained for each workload.

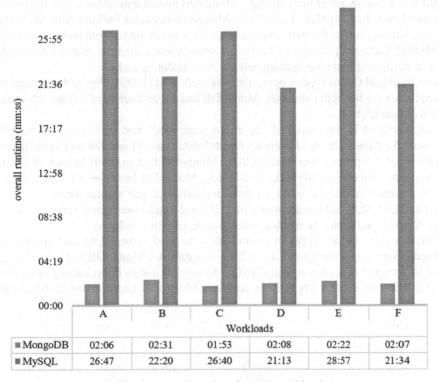

	A	B	C	D	E	F
■ MongoDB	02:06	02:31	01:53	02:08	02:22	02:07
■ MySQL	26:47	22:20	26:40	21:13	28:57	21:34

Fig. 1. Overall runtime for each workload

5.2 Transaction Phase

Two metrics were used in this phase: latency defined in milliseconds (ms), and throughput defined in operations per second (ops/sec). A total of 1 million operations with 16 threads were considered for both database tests.

Latency. The time taken by the database to answer a request. The latencies obtained for each workload are shown below.

- For Workload A, two types of operations were used: read (50%), and update (50%). Figure 2 compares the latencies for both databases. MongoDB had a read latency of 4.6 ms, 10 times lower than MySQL. MongoDB had an update latency of 4.7 ms, 24 times lower than MySQL. In addition, MongoDB latencies for both read and update were similar; that is, the performance behavior was similar for both tasks. In contrast, MySQL showed a read latency of 45.1 ms, 2.5 times lower than the update latency; that is, it performed better on reading tasks than on updating tasks.
- For Workload B, two types of operations were used: read (95%), and update (5%). Figure 3 compares the latencies for both databases. MongoDB had a read latency of 6.1 ms, 5.3 times lower than MySQL. MongoDB had an update latency of 6.3 ms, 9.9 times lower than MySQL. In addition, MongoDB latencies for both read and update were similar; that is, the performance behavior was similar for both tasks. In contrast, MySQL had a read latency of 32.9 ms, 1.9 times lower than the update latency; that is, it performed better on reading tasks than on updating tasks.
- For Workload C, one type of operation was used: read (100%). Figure 4 compares the read latencies for both databases. MongoDB had a read latency of 4.0 ms, 32.7 times lower than MySQL.
- For Workload D, two types of operations were used: read (95%) and insert (5%). Figure 5 compares the read latencies for both databases. MongoDB had a read latency of 4.3 ms, 5.6 times lower than MySQL. MongoDB had an insert latency of 4.4 ms, 11.1 times lower than MySQL. In addition, MongoDB latencies for both read and insert were similar; that is, the performance behavior was similar for both tasks. In contrast, MySQL had a read latency of 24.3 ms, 2 times lower than insert latency; that is, it performed better on reading tasks than on inserting tasks.
- For Workload E, two types of operations were used: scan (95%) and insert (5%). Figure 6 compares the read latencies for both databases. MongoDB had a scan latency of 16.7 ms, 6.5 times lower than MySQL. MongoDB had an insert latency of 16.0 ms, 11.1 times lower than MySQL. In addition, MongoDB latencies for both scan and

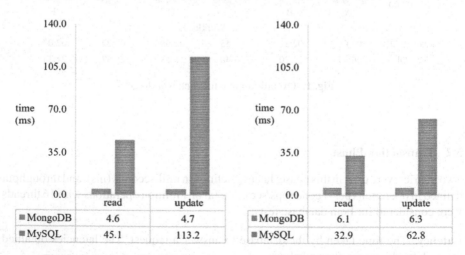

	read	update			read	update
■ MongoDB	4.6	4.7		■ MongoDB	6.1	6.3
■ MySQL	45.1	113.2		■ MySQL	32.9	62.8

Fig. 2. Latency for Workload A　　　　**Fig. 3.** Latency for Workload B

insert operations were similar; that is, the performance behavior was similar for both tasks. Similarly, it also occurred with MySQL latencies.
– For Workload F, three types of operations were used: read, modify, and write. Figure 7 compares the read latencies for both databases. MongoDB had a read latency of 4.9 ms, 7.1 times lower than MySQL. Additionally, MongoDB had a read-modify-write latency of 9 ms, 10.2 times lower than MySQL.

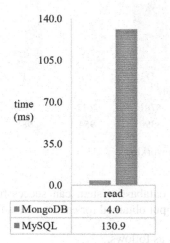

	read
■ MongoDB	4.0
■ MySQL	130.9

Fig. 4. Latency for Workload C

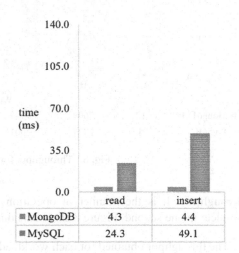

	read	insert
■ MongoDB	4.3	4.4
■ MySQL	24.3	49.1

Fig. 5. Latency for Workload D

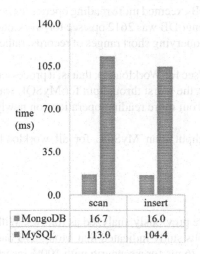

	scan	insert
■ MongoDB	16.7	16.0
■ MySQL	113.0	104.4

Fig. 6. Latency for Workload E

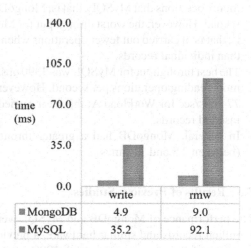

	write	rmw
■ MongoDB	4.9	9.0
■ MySQL	35.2	92.1

Fig. 7. Latency for Workload F

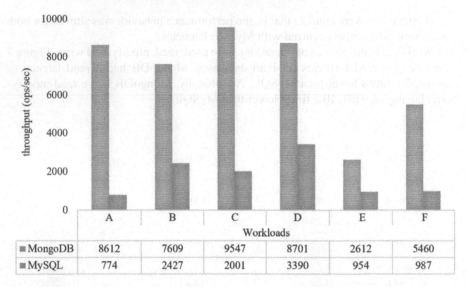

Fig. 8. Throughput for each workload

Throughput. It is the number of operations the database system can successfully complete in one second. Figure 8 shows the throughput obtained for each workload.

The throughput obtained for each workload was as follows.

- The best throughput for MongoDB was 9547 ops/sec for Workload C; 4.77 times more operations that MySQL; that is, MongoDB executed more reading operations per second. However, the worst throughput for MongoDB was 2612 ops/sec for Workload E; that is, it carried out fewer operations when querying short ranges of records, rather than individual records.
- The best throughput for MySQL was 3390 ops/sec for Workload D; that is, it processed more reading operations per second. However, the worst throughput for MySQL was 774 ops/sec for Workload A; that is, it carried out more reading operations on newly inserted records.
- In general, MongoDB had a greater throughput than MySQL for all workloads (between 2.5 and 11 times).

5.3 Results of Previous Studies

The performance of MongoDB and MySQL were previously analyzed as follows. With 1 million records and similar hardware, a previous study indicated that MongoDB had a latency of 1 ms for a scenario with 100% read; 76 ms for a scenario with 100% insert, and 195 ms for a scenario with 100% update [21]. These values differed from our results because our research used 16 threads instead of a single thread.

Similarly, previous research indicated that MongoDB had a latency of 50,000 ms for a scenario with 100% read; 86,500 ms for a scenario with 100% create, and 250 ms for a scenario with 100% update [11]. These values differed from our results because our research ran 1 million operations, 1 GB database, and 16 threads, instead of 200 thousand operations, 3 GB database, and 18 thousand threads. Finally, a previous study showed that MySQL had a throughput of 21 thousand operations per second with 100 threads for a scenario with 100% read. Our results showed 2,000 operations per second with 16 threads. This difference is because our research used less computational power.

Previous studies did not consider the combination of CRUD operations; that is, 100% for only one operation. In contrast, this research defined workloads that combined these operations for six different scenarios, namely: A (50% read, 50% update), B (95% reads, 5% update), C (100% read), D (95% read, 5% insert), E (95% scan, 5% insert), y F (50% read, 50% read–modify–write).

6 Conclusions

6.1 Contribution

This document compares the performance of two databases (MySQL and MongoDB). For this, six workload scenarios were executed. It provides guidelines for choosing the best option according to the use scenario. In each scenario, 1 million records (1GB) were used with 16 threads. In general, the performance of MongoDB was better than MySQL. Nevertheless, this experiment highlighted the best and worst performance scenarios for both databases based on three parameters:

– Overall runtime. For MongoDB, workload C was the best scenario and workload B was the worst. For MySQL, workload D was the best scenario, and workload E was the worst.
– Latency. For MongoDB, all scenarios obtained similar values, except for Workload E, where the latencies had a ratio of 4 to 1 compared to the other scenarios. For MySQL, workload D was the best scenario and workload E was the worst.
– Throughput. For MongoDB, workload C was the best scenario, and workload E was the worst. For MySQL, workload D was the best scenario, and workload A was the worst.

6.2 Limitations and Future Work

With respect to latency and throughput, the worst scenario for both databases was E. For future work, it is necessary to include multiple indexes within each database. This will help verify the proportion to which scenario E is improved. In addition, it is necessary to analyze the scalability between other NoSQL databases, namely: columnar, document, and graph. This will allow the behavior to be understood when the number of threads and the volume of data are increased. In short, these comparisons provide a guide for choosing the most appropriate database according to computing resources and current business requirements.

References

1. Membrey, P., Plugge, E., Hawkins, T.: The Definitive Guide to MongoDB - The NoSQL Database for Cloud and Desktop Computing. Apress, New York (2020)
2. Alapati, S.: Expert Apache Cassandra - Install, Configure, Optimize, and Secure Apache Cassandra Databases. Apress, Berkeley (2018)
3. Chandra, D.G.: BASE analysis of NoSQL database. Futur. Gener. Comput. Syst. **52**, 13–21 (2015). https://doi.org/10.1016/j.future.2015.05.003
4. Chellappan, S., Ganesan, D.: MongoDB features and installation. In: MongoDB Recipes, pp. 1–24. Apress, Berkeley (2020)
5. MySQL: MySQL 8.0 Reference Manual (2020)
6. Friedrich, S., Ritter, N.: YCSB. In: Sakr, S., Zomaya, A. (eds.) Encyclopedia of Big Data Technologies, pp. 1–4. Springer, Cham (2018). https://doi.org/10.1007/978-3-319-63962-8_1 31-1
7. Kitchenham, B.: Guidelines for performing systematic literature reviews in software engineering. Durham, UK (2007)
8. Agarwal, S., Rajan, K.S.: Performance analysis of MongoDB versus PostGIS/PostGreSQL databases for line intersection and point containment spatial queries. Spat. Inf. Res. **24**(6), 671–677 (2016). https://doi.org/10.1007/s41324-016-0059-1
9. Makris, A., Tserpes, K., Spiliopoulos, G., Zissis, D., Anagnostopoulos, D.: MongoDB Vs PostgreSQL: a comparative study on performance aspects. GeoInformatica **25**, 241–242 (2021). https://doi.org/10.1007/s10707-020-00424-9
10. Chopade, R.M., Dhavase, N.S.: MongoDB, CouchBase: performance comparison for image dataset. In: 2017 2nd International Conference for Convergence in Technology, I2CT 2017, pp. 255–259 (2017)
11. Cayres, L.U., de Lima, B.S., Garcia, R.E., Correia, R.C.M.: Analysis of Node.js application performance using MongoDB drivers. In: Rocha, Á., Ferrás, C., Montenegro Marin, C.E., Medina García, V.H. (eds.) ICITS 2020. AISC, vol. 1137, pp. 213–222. Springer, Cham (2020). https://doi.org/10.1007/978-3-030-40690-5_21
12. Kumar Pandey, S., Kumar Pandey, S.: An approach to improve load balancing in distributed storage systems for NoSQL databases: MongoDB. In: Pattnaik, P., Rautaray, S., Das, H., Nayak, J. (eds.) Progress in Computing, Analytics and Networking, Advances in Intelligent Systems and Computing, pp. 785–793. Springer, Singapore (2018)
13. Chopade, R., Pachghare, V.: MongoDB indexing for performance improvement. In: Tuba, M., Akashe, S., Joshi, A. (eds.) ICT Systems and Sustainability. AISC, vol. 1077, pp. 529–539. Springer, Singapore (2020). https://doi.org/10.1007/978-981-15-0936-0_56
14. Haughian, G., Osman, R., Knottenbelt, W.J.: Benchmarking replication in Cassandra and MongoDB NoSQL datastores. In: Hartmann, S., Ma, H. (eds.) DEXA 2016. LNCS, vol. 9828, pp. 152–166. Springer, Cham (2016). https://doi.org/10.1007/978-3-319-44406-2_12
15. Fuad, A., Erwin, A., Ipung, H.P.: Processing performance on Apache Pig, Apache Hive and MySQL cluster. In: Proceedings of 2014 International Conference on Information, Communication Technology and System, ICTS 2014, pp. 297–301 (2014)
16. Grandhi, B., Chickerur, S., Patil, M.S.: Performance analysis of MySQL, Apache Spark on CPU and GPU. In: 2018 3rd IEEE International Conference on Recent Trends in Electronics, Information and Communication Technology, RTEICT 2018 – Proceedings, pp. 1494–1499. IEEE (2018)
17. Jogi, V.D., Sinha, A.: Performance evaluation of MySQL, Cassandra and HBase for heavy write operation. In: 2016 3rd International Conference on Recent Advances in Information Technology, RAIT 2016, pp. 586–590. IEEE (2016)

18. Tongkaw, S., Tongkaw, A.: A comparison of database performance of MariaDB and MySQL with OLTP workload. In: ICOS 2016 - 2016 IEEE Conference on Open Systems (ICOS), pp. 117–119 (2017)

19. Kumar, A.S.: Performance analysis of MySQL partition, hive partition-bucketing and Apache Pig. In: 1st India International Conference on Information Processing (IICIP), pp. 1–6 (2017)

20. Dawodi, M., Hedayati, M.H., Baktash, J.A., Erfan, A.L.: Facebook MySQL performance vs MySQL performance. In: 2019 IEEE 10th Annual Information Technology, Electronics and Mobile Communication Conference, IEMCON 2019, pp. 103–109. IEEE (2019)

21. Aboutorabi, S.H., Rezapour, M., Moradi, M., Ghadiri, N.: Performance evaluation of SQL and MongoDB databases for big e-commerce data. CSSE 2015 - 20th International Symposium on Computer Science and Software Engineering (2015). https://doi.org/10.1109/CSICSSE. 2015.7369245

Optimization Models Used in the Textile Sector: A Systematic Review

María Belén Toledo[1] , Christian Torres Torres[1] , Juan Carlos Llivisaca[2,3] ,
Mario Peña[3,4] , Lorena Siguenza-Guzman[1,5] , and Jaime Veintimilla-Reyes[1(✉)]

[1] Department of Computer Sciences, Faculty of Engineering, Universidad de Cuenca, Cuenca,
Ecuador
{belen.toledo,marcelo.torres,lorena.siguenza,
jaime.veintimilla}@ucuenca.edu.ec
[2] Faculty of Chemical Sciences, University of Cuenca, Cuenca, Ecuador
juan.llivisaca@ucuenca.edu.ec
[3] Department of Applied Chemistry and Systems of Production, Faculty of Chemical Sciences,
Universidad de Cuenca, Cuenca, Ecuador
mario.penao@ucuenca.edu.ec
[4] Research Department (DIUC), Universidad de Cuenca, Cuenca, Ecuador
[5] Research Centre Accountancy, Faculty of Economics and Business, KU Leuven, Leuven,
Belgium

Abstract. In recent years, several works have been published dedicated to obtaining optimization models. Many of them have been applied in the textile sector because they are part of the economic development areas of a country. This article's main objective is to review the literature published on optimization models and understand what methods their authors used to solve the optimization problems in the textile sector. A systematic methodology was applied to select research questions, digital databases, and search terms to utilize practical and methodological filters later to carry out this systematic review. This procedure allowed performing a review and synthesis of the results obtained on the optimization models. It was found that the models resulting from the systematic review vary depending on the areas to be optimized. The most frequent applications were logistics and production, followed by cost minimization. They were optimized mainly with linear programming, integer programming, Markov chains, genetic algorithms, and multi-objective programming.

Keywords: Textile · Optimization · Logistics · Systematic review

1 Introduction

Micro, small and medium-sized enterprises (MSMEs) are part of the retail trade. This is one economic sector that includes organizations belonging to the mass consumption sectors and the marketing of products and services to the final consumer. Thus, they become the main generators of economic resources within a country [1]. According to the National Institute of Statistics and Censuses of Ecuador, retail is a fundamental

© Springer Nature Switzerland AG 2022
M. Botto-Tobar et al. (Eds.): ICAT 2021, CCIS 1535, pp. 202–213, 2022.
https://doi.org/10.1007/978-3-031-03884-6_15

part of the growth of the productive matrix since it generates sources of employment and contributes to improving the economic indexes of the population [2]. Within retail, textiles represent a significant sector due to the breadth of its processes, which are a series of related activities ranging from obtaining fibers to manufacturing and their subsequent acquisition by a user. In the end, this production process can be divided into the textile industry, which includes fiber manufacturing, spinning preparation, spinning and weaving, and the clothing industry, with phases as product design, pattern making, cutting, ironing, packaging, and transport. And, depending on the product manufactured, the embroidery or quilting phases can be added. In addition, the products offered by this sector are considered mass consumption products. This work focuses on conducting a bibliographic review of the optimization models used in the textile sector. This sector has been affected by changes in its internal logistics processes such as product demand, sales, customer service, transportation, inventory management, and processing orders. One way to solve the textile sector's changes has been using mathematical models, where a tool is generated. This tool allows strategic decision-making that offers an operational analysis of the efficiency of the activities carried out, being an instrument of research and forecasting [3]. While mathematical models help decide what to optimize for, it must be considered that intangible factors, such as human behavior, can be crucial in making a final decision. Furthermore, these factors can positively or negatively influence the sector in which the mathematical model is applied [4].

It is worth mentioning that various classical and metaheuristic methods have been developed within operational research by using mathematical models. These methods try to find an optimal solution in the search space, seeking to achieve a global optimum through flexibility in handling the problem. However, these models do not guarantee convergence since the quality of the solution obtained is unknown [5]. One of the classic methods developed is Linear programming that allows the optimization of an objective function by applying various restrictions to its decision variables [6]. In Integer Linear Programming, the decision variables can only take integer values, and the coefficients involved in the problem must also be integers [6]. Mixed Linear Programming addresses issues where the decision variables are continuous and can only take integer values [6]. Binary linear programming involves a binary variable that can only take 1 or 0; these variables are used to solve inclusion or exclusion problems [7]. Multi-objective programming allows solving models in several instances, revealing their robustness and showing how it can help find a balance between the main objectives related to supply chains [8]. Also, within the metaheuristics, Genetic algorithms work on a set of solutions or a population represented as a binary chain or chromosomes. These algorithms cross the individuals with the highest aptitude to renew the population and eliminate those with less aptitude, obtaining a chromosome with greater aptitude that will represent the solution to the problem posed [9]. Markov chains are a stochastic process. The states of a process are presented using transition probabilities that go from state x to y, allowing knowing the possibilities of each state in the long term [10]. Ant colonies are based on the real behavior of ants and it is a probabilistic technique that helps find the best routes or paths in graphs [11].

It is worth mentioning that the systematic review was carried out because a similar work focused on optimization models in the textile sector was not found. Even so, undergraduate and academic outcomes were found in which a literature review was carried out to justify the use in the study of the method used for their optimization models. The rest of the paper is organized as follows. Section 2 indicates the methodology used to review the optimization models used in the textile sector systematically. Section 3 presents the results and discussion. Finally, the conclusion of the paper is provided in Sect. 4.

2 Material and Methods

The systematic review design responded to the purpose of collecting, selecting, evaluating, and summarizing the evidence found regarding the optimization models used in the different areas of the textile sector. To carry out this systematic review, the Fink methodology was used, consisting of the following tasks: 1) Select Research Questions, 2) Select Bibliographic Databases and Web Sites, 3) Choose Search Terms, 4) Apply Practical Screen, 5) Apply Methodological Quality Screen, 6) Do the Review, and 7) Synthesize the Results [12].

The systematic review began with the selection of research questions. It was established that the main question to be answered was: Which optimization methods have been applied to the textile sector? Subsequently, the search sub-questions were defined, whose objective was to obtain information to delimit the field of research studied. These questions were: What areas of the textile sector are being optimized? Why is it necessary to find out the management of production processes within internal logistics? What tools or solvers are being used to solve optimization models? What parts are involved in the optimization process? How are the results of the optimization model being compared with the real data of a case study? What indicators are used to validate the results of the optimization model?

Once the research field was defined, it was necessary to select the bibliographic databases and websites. Therefore, ACM Digital Library, Google Scholar, Scopus, and Springer Link were selected. They are part of the most recognized digital databases and have topics related to what is being discussed in this study.

To search for scientific papers in the databases above, a set of terms were proposed that include "Model", "Optimization", "Logistics", "Production", "Sales" and "Textile Sector", with which Search strings were built. In addition, the search requirements used in each database were included. For example, in the case of Google Scholar, the following search strategies were considered for each search string: the exact phrase or at least one of the words, word placement, articles published between 2015–2021, and the language. For the search of the primary articles to reference this work, different search strings were used. In the case of Google Scholar, the following string was used "Model" and "Optimization" and ("Logistics" or "Production" or "Sales") and "Textile Sector". The string was made up of the relevant terms mentioned above and logical connectors, allowing combining different terms and establishing logical relationships between them. With these search strings being structured according to the requirements of each database, 658 articles were retrieved (see Table 1 and Table A1). Practical filters were applied to these articles, such as interval of years and language. In addition, methodological filters were utilized to review the title, keywords, and abstract to discard duplicates and unrelated documents to the topic.

Table 1. Number of documents per database

Database	Number of results
Digital Library ACM	105
Google Scholar	491
Scopus	22
Springer Link	40

With the results obtained after applying the first filters, the articles meeting the inclusion criteria were selected, such as 1) Studies presenting information about optimization methods and techniques in the textile sector. 2) Studies presenting information about optimization areas in the textile sector. In addition, the following exclusion criteria were also considered: 1) Studies duplicated in the different digital libraries. 2) Articles in languages other than English or Spanish.

Once all the filters had been applied, a manual review of the references of the papers was carried out to determine secondary sources. The 31 articles were read to know their reliability. Next, the articles that justified using an optimization method and showed how to use it, the objective functions, the restrictions, and the results obtained with their proposed model were selected. Through this selection, a total of 11 articles were obtained for the systematic review.

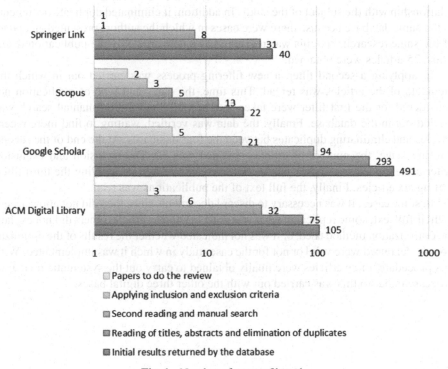

Fig. 1. Number of papers filtered

Figure 1 shows the number of articles found after applying the first filters, compared with the number of articles after using the inclusion and exclusion criteria with the number of papers accepted for this systematic literature review.

3 Results and Discussions

This section presents the main findings found in this systematic review and synthesizes the results obtained after filtering the papers.

Figure 1 presents the number of articles initially obtained in the digital databases. It shows that after applying filters, 11 articles were selected to reference this work. Thus, as mentioned in previous sections and seen in Fig. 1, the number of papers to be reviewed was significantly reduced. For instance, taking the ACM Digital Library as an example, the article selection process was started by entering the search string in the search bar of the digital database. Then, the search parameters were configured according to the database, and the initial results were obtained. For this database, there were 105 articles, of which the citations were exported in BibTeX format to generate a file used to process reference lists. Subsequently, this file was opened with a bibliographic reference manager, in this case, Zotero. The item type can be displayed in this tool, such as a journal article, a book, a thesis, or a conference article. In addition, the title of the publication, the author or authors, the abstract, the date of publication were indicated. And, depending on the type of publication, the volume, issue, pages, ISSN, and DOI were also considered. Finally, the first filter was applied to 105 exported articles, which consisted of reading the titles of the publications, the abstracts and determining their relationship with the subject of the study. In addition, it eliminated duplicate documents in the same database because there were cases in which the authors presented an update of the same research, and this was registered as a new article by the publication dates. Thus, 75 articles were obtained.

In applying a second filter, a new filtering process was carried out in which the metadata of the articles was reread. This time, the dates and type of publication not considered for the first filter were taken into account, and a brief manual search was carried out in the database. Finally, the data was verified, waiting to find more recent articles and eliminating duplicates between the four databases. At the end of the second filtering stage, the number of articles obtained was 32. The inclusion and exclusion criteria mentioned in the previous section were considered in applying the third filter, getting six articles. Finally, the full text of the publications was read.

In some cases, it was necessary to discard documents since they did not allow access to their full text, some replicated what was done in another article, others did not explain the optimization method used, or it was not indicated whether the results of the optimization model raised were valid or not for the case study in which it was implemented. With this procedure, three articles were finally obtained to carry out the systematic review. A process similar to this was carried out with the other three digital bases.

Considering the extraction criteria mentioned in the previous section, the articles helpful for this literature review were classified. Therefore, the criteria were grouped according to the sub-research questions and the possible answers to these questions.

3.1 Research Questions

In research sub-question 1: *What areas of the textile sector are being optimized?* Two criteria were established: 1) Optimized areas of the textile sector and 2) Optimized areas in the internal logistics of the textile sector. The possible answers are Labor Costs, Inventory Management, Production Costs, Production and Demand Control, Waste Reduction, Product Demand, Sales, Customer Service, Transportation, Inventory Management, and Order Processing. In research sub-question 2: *Why is it necessary to determine the management of production processes within internal logistics?* The criteria of internal logistics production processes were established. The possible answers are Forecast Demand, Purchasing, Production planning, Inventories, Warehouse, Pick & pack, Distribution plan, Transportation, and Customer service. In research sub-question 3: *What tools are being used to solve optimization models?* The criterion was established: tools for solving optimization models, and the possible answers are LINGO, GUROBI, Xpress_MP, WINQSB, GAMS, Large Scale Solver, and CPLEX Concert. In research sub-question 4: *What parts are involved in the optimization process?* Two criteria were established: calibration and validation of optimization models. The possible answers are: Adjustment could be used for calibration parameters, Inverse engineering, and Probabilistic models. In addition, it is possible to evaluate parameter settings, Distributions shown by the model, and Parametric tests to validate the models. In research sub-question 5: *How are the optimization model results being compared with the real data of a case study?* The criteria of Optimization model comparisons were established, and the possible answers are Procedures iterative, Value of convergence of the algorithms, Simulation scenarios, and Historical data of the company. In research sub-question 6: *What indicators are used to validate the results of the optimization model?* Two criteria were established: Manners to interpret the behavior of an optimization model and the importance of analyzing the behavior of the models. The possible answers are Sensitivity analysis and scenario analysis. And, to determine the significance of the behavior of the models, the most common solutions are making better decisions, ensuring quality control, and allocation of resources in an appropriate manner.

The results of the systematic review have allowed knowing the main characteristics of ten optimization methods, such as nonlinear programming of mixed integers, deterministic mathematical programming with multiple objective functions, Markov chains, integer programming, multi-objective programming, Algorithm dynamic genetic, Integer linear programming with Industry 4.0 techniques, Hub and Spoke with PDNDP (Parcel delivery Network Design Problem) and p-median, linear programming with the least cost method and linear programming. Therefore, they have been used in different areas of the textile sector, as can be seen in Table 2. Furthermore, it was noted that these methods could work by themselves or be combined with other optimization processes or statistical techniques to improve the model's performance.

Table 2. Optimization methods and area in which they are used

Method	Area
Mixed-integer nonlinear programming	Production and distribution
Linear programming with the minimum cost method	Transportation
Linear programming	Supply chains, Labor, Inventory Management
Whole linear programming with Industry 4.0 techniques	Production and recycling (Water and Energy)
Deterministic mathematical programming with multiple target functions	Production
Markov chains	Production times
Whole programming	Production and distribution
Multi-objective programming	Production and transportation
Dynamic genetic algorithm	Production of dyeing, recycling (water)
Hub and Spoke with PDNDP (Parcel Delivery Network Design Problem) and P-Medium	Distribution network and transportation

As shown in Table 2, the areas of the textile sector that have been optimized in the different studies are supply, production, and distribution chains. In addition to minimizing the costs of labor, transportation, and inventory management, it has also sought to optimize water and energy consumption in this sector. The areas that appear the most in the revised bibliography are production and sales since they are considered the most conflictive areas within a company. These areas present conflicts because, in many cases, the sales team wants to offer a greater quantity of products in the shortest possible time. Still, the production department must take the time to provide finished products [13].

One of the most optimized areas of the textile sector is the production chains, where several optimization models have already been carried out. For example, the model proposed by Zhang aims to optimize a dual-channel production and distribution network based on pre-sales and the construction of a tiered supply chain made up of manufacturers and distributors. The extra information needed is obtained through feedback from numerical simulations utilizing normal distribution channels. Using the model allowed increasing sales revenue, overall profit, and solving excess inventory problems [14]. Zhang used mixed integer nonlinear programming because many variables and constraints were complex to solve with traditional methods. Gómez et al. designed a mathematical model with linear programming applied to planning the production and distribution of products seeking to obtain operational efficiency throughout the production chain. They thus sped up organizational decision-making, getting positive results in its execution [15]. The study carried out by Trifan et al. seeks to create a model that optimizes a clothing assortment structure through deterministic mathematical programming with multiple objective functions [16]. The authors indicate that since there are numerous objective functions, the optimal solution for this function cannot always be optimal for the other functions. Thus, the authors resort to using a solution defined as "the best compromise", a non-dominant solution, and considered a Pareto optimal solution [16]. Within the production area, it is possible to optimize times as indicated by Badea et al. Since there are many steps to follow for the textile manufacturing process, stochastic processes can be used to design a Markov chain. One of its advantages is that a correct approximation of the manufacturing time can be obtained, taking into account that repeated and critical stages are observed in which products that need repair or waste may appear at any time [5].

In some companies in the textile sector, it was found that it is necessary to optimize distribution processes such as transportation since the costs of contracting this service are very high. Indeed, acquiring a fleet for companies can also mean an important investment since not only will the price of the vehicles be taken into account, but they require fuel and maintenance for their correct operation. Ferrer et al., in their study, have sought the creation of an optimization model through linear programming that allows reducing transport costs by developing strategies that consider the costs of the variables and the volumes of cargo to be transported [17]. Similarly, Moreno et al. developed a model that allows optimizing the distribution network of a transport company, considering that these companies can have a large number of clients with different facilities and a high number of vehicles to manage [18]. The generated model allows the allocation of goods to customers in each distribution network installation based on conditions such as vehicle load. Ahlaqqach et al. indicate that it is necessary to create economical and sustainable logistics solutions. The authors have worked on a multi-objective optimization model for hospital textile collection problems, seeking to optimize problems on vehicle routes. In addition to linear scheduling, they manage the heterogeneity of vehicle fleets and compliance with time windows [19]. The result obtained by combining these methods was a robust model for reverse logistics that allowed finding the equilibrium point between the main objectives.

Water is a fundamental resource within the textile sector since it is used in various parts of the production process, such as dyeing, where chemical products are applied that make it challenging to treat. Therefore, there will be a large amount of sewage that will cause environmental problems in the future. Motivated by this, researchers such as Zhou et al. have created studies on optimizing production to save water, using genetic algorithms to optimize the dyeing process based on color and depth of dyeing [20]. They also compared the results obtained with the optimization model versus the no model, where it was shown that the use of the optimization model did reduce water consumption. Tsai combined mathematical programming and Industry 4.0 techniques to plan and control organic production in the textile sector. Mathematical programming is used to determine product combinations, and Industry 4.0 techniques oversee the production process [21].

When creating a company, one of the objectives is always linked to obtaining a more significant profit; hence, it is necessary to minimize costs. Campo et al. recommend optimizing aggregate production costs, minimizing labor costs, inventory management, and outsourcing [22]. This model considers characteristics such as fabrics, product losses, employee efficiency, and time to train a new employee. In addition, the model allowed the identification of strategies such as increasing production capacity, storage by process, and variation in labor in each planning period.

The authors of the reviewed articles use various tools to solve their optimization models. Some include in their articles how the results obtained were verified. These verifications were mainly carried out by implementing the models in real companies or comparing their results with the historical data.

4 Conclusions

This document presents a systematic literature review of works using various optimization methods in different areas of the textile sector. The most frequent regions were production and logistics and minimization of costs to obtain a more significant benefit, considering that this does not affect the efficiency of the production processes and the quality of the final products. To answer the main research question on which optimization models have been applied in the textile sector, it has been found that each author decided to use the method that best suited their needs after conducting their bibliographic review. The authors obtained suitable solutions using linear programming methods, mixed-integer nonlinear programming, multi-objective programming, Markov chains, and genetic algorithms. They could verify their results by applying these models to real case studies, or these results could be compared with historical company data. Despite their excellent results, these methods can be improved by combining them with traditional optimization methods, metaheuristics, or other techniques such as Industry 4.0. It is also important to mention that some of these models can be used by other sectors related to logistics, supply chains, production, planning, and the organization of transport processes. Regardless of the model used, it seeks to represent real conditions or particular processes mentioned above, modifying only the parameters for the sector to be used. This systematic review aims to facilitate decision-making on the optimization models that can be used in areas of the textile sector, taking into account the effectiveness and efficiency that these had when applied in real scenarios. Based on this systematic review, if it is necessary to choose a model to test it in a real case study-oriented to the textile sector, the information that must be taken into account are the company's size and the need. The latter is the most relevant as it will allow deciding on an optimization method.

Acknowledgments. This research was carried out under the project "Incorporating Sustainability concepts to management models of textile Micro, Small and Medium Enterprises (SUMA)" funded by the Flemish Interuniversity Council (VLIR) and the Vice-Rector's Office for Research of the University of Cuenca.

Appendix A

Table A1. Complete list of references read in the systematic review.

Paper	Author
1	Badea, L., Constantinescu, A., Grigorescu, A., Visileanu, E.: Time optimization of the textile manufacturing process using the stochastic processes/Optimizarea timpilor procesului de fabricatie textila folosind procesele stochastice. Industria Textila, 67(3), 205 (2016)
2	Olivos, P., Carrasco, F., Flores, J., Moreno, Y., and Nava, G.: Modelo de gestión logística para pequeñas y medianas empresas en México. Contaduría y administración, 60(1), 181–203 (2015)
3	Zhang, L.: Dynamic Optimization Model For Garment Dual Channel Supply Chain Network: A Simulation Study. Int k simul model, 14, (2015)
4	Gómez, A., Armas, A., Toapanta, M., Sinchiguano, E.: Diseño de un modelo matemático aplicado a la planeación de la producción y distribución de productos de consumo masivo. Revista Publicando, 4(12 (2)), 348–364 (2017)
5	Trifan, A., Brătucu, G., Madar, A.: Optimization model for an assortment structure of textile confections. DE REDACTIE, 365, (2015)
6	Ferrer, M., Ariza, Y., Martínez, J., Garizao, J., Pulido-Rojano, A.: Modelo de optimización colaborativo para la minimización de los costos variables de transporte de carga por carretera en Colombia. Investigación y desarrollo en TIC, 10(1), 26–36 (2019)
7	Moreno, S., Serna, M., Uran, C., Zapata, J.: Modelo matemático para la optimización de la red de distribución de una empresa de transporte de paquetería y mensajería terrestre. Dyna, 87(214), 248–257 (2020)
8	AHLAQQACH, M., BENHRA, J., MOUATASSIM, S., LAMRANI, S.: Modeling and solving the multi objective Heterogeneous vehicles routing problem in the case of Healthcare Textile. In ITMC2017-International Conference on Intelligent Textiles and Mass Customisation 1(1), (2017)
9	Zhou, L., Xu, K., Cheng, X., Xu, Y., Jia, Q.: Study on optimizing production scheduling for water-saving in textile dyeing industry. Journal of cleaner production, 141, 721–727 (2017)
10	Tsai, W.: Green production planning and control for the textile industry by using mathematical programming and industry 4.0 techniques. Energies, 11(8), 2072 (2018)
11	Campo, E., Cano, J., Gómez-Montoya, R.: Optimización de costos de producción agregada en empresas del sector textil. Ingeniare. Revista chilena de ingeniería, 28(3), 461–475 (2020)
12	Wang, H., Memon, H., Shah, H., Shakhrukh, M.: Development of a quantitative model for the analysis of the functioning of integrated textile supply chains Mathematics, 7(10), 929 (2019)

References

1. Trombetta, M.: El sector Retail como motor de cambio. Found. Adv. Ser. Problem Driven Res. **1**(1), 7–9 (2012). https://www.ie.edu/fundacion_ie/Home/Documentos/El%20Sector%20Retail%20como%20Motor%20de%20Cambio.pdf
2. Visualizador de Estadísticas Empresariales I Tableau Public. https://public.tableau.com/app/profile/instituto.nacional.de.estad.stica.y.censos.inec./viz/VisualizadordeEstadisticasEmpresariales/Dportada. Accessed 10 Jul 2021
3. Correa, J., Rodríguez, L.: Modelo para la simulación de un ruteo logístico interno para una empresa que importa textil desde China Colombia (2014)
4. Stingl, E., Pohlhammer, J.: Modelo de optimización de la logística de distribución de una empresa de alimentación (Doctoral dissertation, Pontificia Universidad Católica de Chile). (2002). https://www.researchgate.net/profile/Jose_Maldifassi/publication/301542662_modelo_de_optimizacion_de_la_logistica_de_distribucion_de_una_empresa_de_alimentacion/links/5717dbf008aed8a339e5b045/modelo-de-optimizacion-de-la-logistica-de-distribucion-de-una-empresa-de-alimentacion
5. Badea, L., Constantinescu, A., Grigorescu, A., Visileanu, E.: Time optimization of the textile manufacturing process using the stochastic processes/optimizarea timpilor procesului de fabricatie textila folosind procesele stochastice. Industria Textila **67**(3), 205 (2016)
6. Winston, W.: Investigación de operaciones aplicaciones y algoritmos, 4th edn. Publisher, Mexico (2005)
7. Roger Rodríguez: Programacion Lineal Entera. https://es.slideshare.net/RogerRodrguez6/programacion-lineal-entera. Accessed 23 Jun 2021
8. Munier, N., Carignano, C., Alberto, C.: Un Método De Programación Multiobjetivo. Revista De La Escuela De Perfeccionamiento En Investigación Operativa **24**(39) (2017)
9. Vélez, M., Montoya, J.: Metaheurísticos: Una Alternativa Para La Solución De Problemas Combinatorios En Administración De Operaciones. Revista EIA **8**, 99–115 (2007)
10. Bouillon, A.: Optimización de procesos markovianos de decisión a través de un modelo de programación lineal: El caso de inversión en activos financieros riesgosos. Rev. Global Manage. **4**(1), 79–85 (2019)
11. Algarín, C.: Optimización por colonia de Hormigas: Aplicaciones y Tendencias. Ingeniería Solidaria **7** (2010)
12. Fink, A.: Conducting Research Literature Reviews: From the Internet to Paper. SAGE Publications, Thousand Oaks (2013)
13. Olivos, P., Carrasco, F., Flores, J., Moreno, Y., Nava, G.: Modelo de gestión logística para pequeñas y medianas empresas en México. Contaduría y administración **60**(1), 181–203 (2015)
14. Zhang, L.: Dynamic optimization model for garment dual channel supply chain network: a simulation study. Int k simul model 14 (2015)
15. Gómez, A., Armas, A., Toapanta, M., Sinchiguano, E.: Diseño de un modelo matemático aplicado a la planeación de la producción y distribución de productos de consumo masivo. Revista Publicando **4**(12(2)), 348–364 (2017)
16. Trifan, A., Brătucu, G., Madar, A.: Optimization model for an assortment structure of textile confections. De Redactie **365** (2015)
17. Ferrer, M., Ariza, Y., Martínez, J., Garizao, J., Pulido-Rojano, A.: Modelo de optimización colaborativo para la minimización de los costos variables de transporte de carga por carretera en Colombia. Investigación y desarrollo en TIC **10**(1), 26–36 (2019)
18. Moreno, S., Serna, M., Uran, C., Zapata, J.: Modelo matemático para la optimización de la red de distribución de una empresa de transporte de paquetería y mensajería terrestre. Dyna **87**(214), 248–257 (2020)

19. Ahlaqqach, M., Benhra, J., Mouatassim, S., Lamrani, S.: Modeling and solving the multi-objective Heterogeneous vehicles routing problem in the case of Healthcare Textile. In: ITMC2017-International Conference on Intelligent Textiles and Mass Customisation, vol. 1, no. 1 (2017)
20. Zhou, L., Xu, K., Cheng, X., Xu, Y., Jia, Q.: Study on optimizing production scheduling for water-saving in textile dyeing industry. J. Clean. Prod. **141**, 721–727 (2017)
21. Tsai, W.: Green production planning and control for the textile industry by using mathematical programming and industry 4.0 techniques. Energies **11**(8), 2072 (2018)
22. Campo, E., Cano, J., Gómez-Montoya, R.: Optimización de costos de producción agregada en empresas del sector textil Ingeniare. Revista chilena de ingeniería **28**(3), 461–475 (2020)

Internal Logistics Optimization Based on a Multi-objective Linear Model for Micro, Small, and Medium Textile Enterprises

Christian Torres Torres[1] , María Belén Toledo[1] , Juan Carlos Llivisaca[2,3] ,
Mario Peña[3,4] , Lorena Siguenza-Guzman[1,5] , and Jaime Veintimilla-Reyes[1(✉)]

[1] Department of Computer Sciences, Faculty of Engineering,
Universidad de Cuenca, Cuenca, Ecuador
{marcelo.torres,belen.toledo,lorena.siguenza,
jaime.veintimilla}@ucuenca.edu.ec
[2] Faculty of Chemical Sciences, University of Cuenca, Cuenca, Ecuador
juan.llivisaca@ucuenca.edu.ec
[3] Department of Applied Chemistry and Systems of Production, Faculty of Chemical Sciences,
Universidad de Cuenca, Cuenca, Ecuador
mario.penao@ucuenca.edu.ec
[4] Research Department (DIUC), Universidad de Cuenca, Cuenca, Ecuador
[5] Research Centre Accountancy, Faculty of Economics and Business,
KU Leuven, Leuven, Belgium

Abstract. Daily, textile companies seek to increase production levels through available resources and improve their profit projections over time. Therefore, it is essential to manage the products to be manufactured based on their raw materials resources and time availability. This work proposes improving decision-making in textile production planning by applying a multi-objective linear optimization model to internal logistics within micro, small, and medium-sized enterprises (MSMEs) of the Ecuadorian textile sector. The application of this optimization model results in a balanced production plan between the objectives related to profit maximization and the use of the time available for production. This article includes the description of the studied case, the definition of the optimization model executed by using the Gurobi solver, the results of the application of the optimization model with the data provided by a case study, and the discussion of the results through a sensitivity analysis.

Keywords: Multi-objective optimization · Internal logistics · Decision making · Textile sector

1 Introduction

Ecuador has many micro, small, and medium-sized enterprises (MSMEs) in the commercial, service, and industrial sectors that are the primary sources of job creation. Thus they play a crucial role in the economy since they participate in internal trade and

© Springer Nature Switzerland AG 2022
M. Botto-Tobar et al. (Eds.): ICAT 2021, CCIS 1535, pp. 214–228, 2022.
https://doi.org/10.1007/978-3-031-03884-6_16

labor markets [1]. However, the textile industry has faced disadvantages over the last decade. According to preliminary data from the Ecuadorian Textile Industry Association (AITE), 2020 was considered the most difficult within the Ecuadorian textile and fashion industry. Unfortunately, the COVID-19 pandemic aggravated this problematic situation. Indeed, the country registered the worst historical data in the industry, with a decrease of at least 5% [2]. As a result, manufacturers are faced with the challenge of improving or optimizing their manufacturing techniques [3].

According to the regulation on the structure and institutional framework for the productive development of investment and the mechanisms and instruments for effective promotion, established in the Organic Code of Production, Trade and Investments, the classification of companies is based on their workers and the value of their income. Thus, micro-enterprises obtain an income of less than $ 100,000, and their staff ranges from 1 to 9 people; for a small company, its values range from $ 100,001 to $ 1,000,000 with a total of 10 to 49 people; medium companies have incomes from $ 1,000,001 to $ 5,000,000 between 50 to 199 people; finally, large companies obtain revenues of more than $ 5,000,001 with more than 200 people [19].

The problem addressed in this project arises within the textile area of an MSME. This problem is based on helping to decide how much and what to produce in a given time. This research project included a case study of a textile company. This company has considered making the most of the available manufacturing time since its workers maintain a fixed salary of 160 h per month and not for the preparation time, which is less than these 160 h. Additionally, they seek to increase their profits in the process. In this manner, this study aims to solve two closely related problems: obtaining a maximum net profit and sequentially taking advantage of the working time in person-hours available to manufacture textile products. To solve the proposed problem, mention is made of the scientific approach to operations research and its use in decision-making, specifically in optimization models [4]. This approach uses mathematical models, i.e., mathematical representations of real situations, to make better decisions and solve the proposed problem [5]. Thus, this work aims to develop a multi-objective linear optimization model generating a production plan that solves the proposed problem. Considering the existing capacity constraints and the objective functions involved, guidance was provided to the manufacturer regarding efficient production and profit-maximizing strategies. Furthermore, a sensitivity analysis was considered to observe how the final result was modified by an increase or decrease of factors [6].

This work includes several sections. First, Sect. 2, materials and methods, describes the case study, the solution methodology, and the definition of the optimization model. Then, in Sect. 3 of results and discussions, the values obtained from applying the optimization model to the dataset provided by the case study and an analysis of the results are provided. Finally, Sect. 4 indicates whether the optimization model meets the objectives based on the results obtained.

2 Materials and Methods

This section is structured in three subsections described in the order presented or reviewed within the optimization model creation project. The first subsection mentions the solution and analysis of the optimization model methodology and the conditions in terms of hardware and software to obtain the results. The second subsection describes the case study based on the information received and gathered. Finally, the third subsection defines the conditions to which the optimization model to be used is subject and its mathematical formulation.

2.1 Solution Methodology

The process used for the development of this project, i.e., the optimization model, consists of five steps (see Fig. 1).

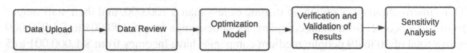

Fig. 1. Solution methodology for the multi-objective linear optimization model.

The data accessed to load and create the optimization model belongs to a set of documents. The MSMEs detailed their financial statements, purchases, sales, raw materials, and inventories between the years 2018–2020. In addition, they included values for the time of manufacture by using stopwatches according to the garment or category to be manufactured. All data is placed in predetermined templates for the creation of the multi-objective linear optimization model. These templates were generated based on the available information and the textile company's extra information.

The data delivered by the case study was sent directly by the textile company, precisely by its finance department; therefore, the values used in the optimization model are considered real and revised. For confidentiality reasons, data about products and/or inventories are not disclosed. It is important to mention that the sale to the final consumer is directly considered and not to wholesalers; in this manner, it seeks to generalize the results.

The multi-objective linear optimization model was created, the number of decision variables, restrictions were indicated, and the objective functions were defined based on the information provided by the case study, which is already in the format for the creation of the model.

To obtain the results of the optimization model, the Gurobi Optimizer solver was used in version 9.1.1. This software was used for its high capacity to process problems with many variables and restrictions [20]. The result of the optimization model was subjected to verification and validation processes. The first process verified that the data used was correct and that the Gurobi solver created the model correctly. The second process was carried out using a historical reference indicating the sales value in one month. Thus, it was sought to determine if the data provided by the optimization model were correct and close to reality [7].

The restrictions on the type of fabric available and the manufacturing time were examined to complement the analysis of the optimal solution for each proposed scenario [7]. In addition, the shadow prices, known as dual prices, were identified, which correspond to the value of the marginal rates of variation of the objective function value.

This case corresponds to the mixture before the unit variations of the right side of the restrictions and how these parameters can be modified; in this manner, the solution found remains optimal [20].

2.2   Case Study

The case study or textile company focuses its activities mainly on the production of lingerie for the home, earns less than $ 100,000, and its staff ranges from 1 to 9 people according to data provided by the financial department of the textile company; therefore is considered an MSMEs. This company seeks to implement sustainable management models to optimize its performance in manufacturing garments through production plans that involve increasing profits and maximizing garments to be manufactured in the available work time.

2.3   Definition of the Optimization Model

When looking at the literature on optimized models in the textile industry during the last five years, it can be seen the use of mathematical models to create management models for the optimization of various logistics processes such as inventory management, productivity, and supply chains [9].

Linear programming emphasizes optimizing profits and reducing labor costs [8]. It should be noted that optimization models with linear programming manage to represent the specific real conditions of the production process, which allows simple changes of parameters and strategic decisions in operational management [10].

On the contrary, nonlinear mixed-integer programming models have been used to optimize production and distribution networks because they can handle many variables and constraints [11]. In addition, multi-objective programming can be used to solve the model in some instances, demonstrate its robustness, and help find a balance between the objectives associated with the supply [22].

From the revised optimization models, it has been decided to implement a multi-objective or multi-criteria linear optimization model, whose primary purpose is to provide a solution that satisfies multiple objectives and does not focus on a single function to optimize. This approach handles the objective functions as restrictions and uses a system of goal variables to optimize the objective function [12]. Two methods were considered to specify the multiple functions [13].

The first approach is combined, as in Fig. 2, where the user defines the weights for each objective function. These weights are then used to connect the objectives into a single objective function [14].

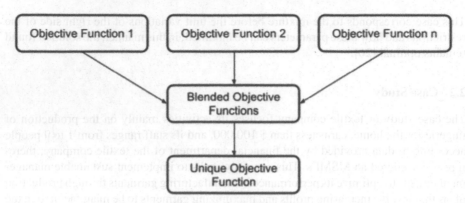

Fig. 2. Multi-objective blended optimization approach.

The second approach is hierarchical, as seen in Fig. 3, in which each objective function is assigned a priority and optimized in descending order of this priority [14].

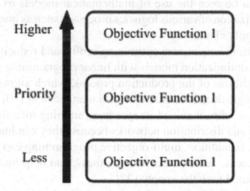

Fig. 3. Multi-objective hierarchical optimization approach.

A mixed approach with weights was used to solve the profit and production time problem occurring in the textile company. Thus, the weights of each objective function can be defined, giving higher priority to greater profit or maximizing the number of garments to be made in the available production time as desired.

2.4 Assumptions of the Optimization Model

A linear optimization model can make use of static values, as well as variables in time [23]. For constructing the multi-objective linear optimization model with a mixed approach with weights, the reader must remember that static values were used. Therefore, the following six conditions or assumptions were considered to create the optimization model. First, a garment can make use of a maximum of two different types of cloth types. Second, the production costs of textile products consider the direct costs of labor and raw materials. Third, to calculate available working hours, working days are multiplied by working hours per day, from Monday to Friday, for eight working hours per day for four weeks, giving a total of 160 h available. Fourth, all garments are processed through the same manufacturing machines. Fifth, the workers in charge of the garment area receive a fixed salary and are not based on the hours of the employed workers. Finally, sixth, all textile products resulting from the optimization model are sold or traded.

2.5 Definition of Variables and Optimization Parameters

Table 1 indicates the indices, parameters, and variables used to construct the multi-objective linear optimization model and their description.

Table 1. Definition of variables and parameters for the creation of the multi-objective linear optimization model.

Type	Name	Description
Indices	j	It belongs to the name of the products to be made
	i	It belongs to the type of fabric available for making the products
Parameters	person_hours	Indicates available working hours, pays attention to multiplying the working days by working hours per day
	num_workers	Number of workers focused on production
	assembly_time	Total sum of the assembly time of the product on the machine
	product_time	Time to make a product j
	num_meters j i	Number of meters of cloth type i used to make the product j
	existing_quantity i	Quantity of product j in inventory
	cost j	Cost of product j
	price j	Product price j
Variables	X j	Quantity of textile products j to be made

2.6 Definition of Objective Functions and Restrictions

The multi-objective linear optimization model developed determines a production plan where the objective function (1) referring to increasing profit obtains a higher priority concerning the second objective function (2). The priority values assigned to each objective function are according to the importance indicated by the textile company.

The first objective function (1) refers to maximizing net profit in a month. The value-added tax (VAT) is subtracted from the product price to create this objective function. The cost of production includes manufacturing values such as the cost of raw materials, basic services, and payment to employees. In this manner, the net benefit of a product is found.

$$max\left(\sum_j \left(price_j - \left(price_j * \frac{12}{100}\right) - cost_j\right) * X_j\right) \tag{1}$$

$$j \in Textile\ products$$

The second objective function (2) maximizes the products manufactured in the available monthly labor time. This objective function seeks to make the most of the time available to the garment staff. This is because workers are paid for a fixed time and not for hours worked or garments.

$$max\left(\sum_j \left(product\_time_j * X_j\right)\right) \tag{2}$$

$$j \in Textile\ products$$

A total of four conditions were handled to which the optimization model is subject.

1. A constraint was created based on the historical data from the case study. Thus, the optimization model was intended to be faithful to the reality of the case study (3)

$$\sum_j \left(price_j * X_j\right) \le monthy\_value \tag{3}$$

$$j \in Textile\ products$$

2. Hours of work available according to the number of workers (4).

$$\sum_j \left(\left(product\_time_j + assembly\_time\right)X_j\right) \le person\_hours * num\_workers \tag{4}$$

$$j \in Textile\ products$$

3. Number of cloth types available per product (5).

$$\sum_i \sum_j \left(num\_meters_{ij} * X_j \le existing\_quantity_i\right) \tag{5}$$

$$j \in Textile\ products$$

4. No negativity (6).

$$X_j \ge 0 \tag{6}$$

$$j \in Textile\ products$$

3 Results and Discussion

The textile company for this project, through its administrative department, has sent a total of 34 documents related to sales reports, suppliers, purchases, costs, and expenses. These data have been categorized into products, machine times, discounts, and types of cloth present in inventory.

The multi-objective linear optimization model with a mixture approach was tested with the data set proposed by the textile company. The resulting model has 81 products or variables, 14 restrictions, and two objective functions. The optimization time with the Gurobi solver was 0.06 s. To calculate this value, the model was executed within the solver 30 times to obtain the average.

Bertsiminas and Stellato [24] compared the execution times of the Gurobi solver with different numbers of constraints and decision variables. The time measured resulted in 1,633 s with 538 variables and 1,257 restrictions. This time it was the highest, for the shortest time recorded. There was a total of 88 variables and 207 restrictions where the time to solve was 0.009 s. These values were taken as a reference and stocked to the lowest value obtained by Bertsiminas and Stellato since the data are similar to the present study due to a difference of seven decision variables and 193 restrictions. As a result, it is observed that the time difference to solve the model was 0.051 s. Based on the highest value obtained by Bertsiminas and Stellato, which does not exceed 2 s, it can be concluded that the execution time obtained is within the expected times.

Based on the verification, the textile company provided the data set used for the optimization model. The records and their values were obtained from its accounting department, resulting in data verified by the textile company itself. The validation of the results was based on the historical values in terms of the money obtained in sales in a given month. For a better interpretation, the historical sales references were handled in three scenarios, optimal, appalling, and normal for 2019. The recorded sales registered for 2019 indicate that the maximum value is $ 40,611, corresponding to December. This value and month were considered as the optimal scenario. In September, the textile company recorded $ 4,188; this value is the smallest within the sales data set. Therefore, this month was considered an appalling scenario. Finally, it was assumed that the value of $ 9,472 for August is normal since the 3-month sales have a difference of less than $ 250, with August being the closest to the average made for the three months with a difference from $ 20.

Based on the results obtained when applying the optimization model (see Table 2), it is observed that the model adheres to the real values of the case study in two of the three scenarios, optimal and worst, giving a difference of less than $ 12 in their results. This difference results in the model adhering to the reality of the textile company in the case study. However, for the optimal scenario, the result differs from the historical value by a value of $ 28,511.08.

Based on the results obtained with the optimization model, it was found that the production program obtained for an optimal scenario (see Table 3) resulted in a value of $ 12,099.92. Assuming that the case study sells all products in December, labor and administrative costs and basic services were removed from the total sale. This results in a net profit of $ 1,355.98, with product 34 and product 79 being the products indicated for the production plan for the specified month.

Table 2. Comparison of the net profit value between the historical values and the linear optimization model.

Stage	Month	Sale (Historical)	Optimization model (Sale)
Optimum	December	$ 40611	$ 12099.92
Appalling	September	$ 4188	$ 4184.46
Normal	August	$ 9472	$ 9460.50

Table 3. Results of the optimization model in an optimal scenario.

Product name	Quantity	Price	Total sale	Net profit
Product 34	217	$ 17.68	$ 3,836.56	$ 429.31
Product 79	476	$ 17.36	$ 8,263.36	$ 926.67

The results presented in Table 3 indicate that a more significant profit is obtained by selling a greater quantity of product 79 at a lower price. This greater quantity of product 79 is recommended since the manufacturing time of 34.50 min is less compared to product 34 with a time of 43.48 min. This helps to make better use of the manufacturing time available to create the most products. In addition, it is linked under the assumption that all the articles produced are marketed in one month. Thus, the objective function of increasing your net profits and taking advantage of the available production time is fulfilled.

For the normal scenario (see Table 4), the result was that the case study obtained a total sale of $ 9,460.50, assuming that the textile company sold all the products in August. Of the total sale value, payments for labor, administrative costs, and basic services must be canceled, resulting in a value of $ 1,057.68 as net profit. The resulting production plan suggests that fewer products should be sold at a high price in this scenario.

Table 4. Results of the optimization model in a normal scenario.

Product name	Quantity	Price	Total sale	Net profit
Product 66	386	$ 11.16	$ 4307.76	$ 482.80
Product 80	314	$ 16.41	$ 5152.74	$ 574.87

The resulting production plan suggests that only one product should be put up for sale in the appalling scenario, i.e., product 53. According to the results, the quantity to be made is 574 units at an individual price of $ 7.29, giving a sale per month of $ 4,184.46 and a net profit of $ 467.92. Thus, the result of a single product responds that the production plan suggests making the product with the lowest costs.

3.1 Sensitivity Analysis

From the results obtained in the sensitivity analysis for the optimal scenario (Table 5), it is observed that cloth type 1 and cloth type 3 used to implement the production plan suggested by the optimization model had a residue of 4721.62, and 0 m(m) of cloth type, respectively. Of the two restrictions, it can be mentioned that for cloth type 1, its use can be reduced by up to 146 m. For cloth type 3, there should be maximum use of 1585.45 m of cloth type.

Table 5. Sensitivity analysis of the right side for the type of fabric available in an optimal scenario.

Restriction	Right side value	Upper range	Lower range	Slack	Dual
Cloth type 1	4,867.62 m	Infinite	146	4,721.62	0.0
Cloth type 2	1,461.63 m	Infinite	0.0	1,461.63	0.0
Cloth type 3	1,101.00 m	1,585.45	0.0	0.00	0.69
Cloth type 4	246.15 m	Infinite	0.0	246.15	0.0
Cloth type 5	142.10 m	Infinite	0.0	142.10	0.0
Cloth type 6	255.52 m	Infinite	0.0	255.52	0.0
Cloth type 7	1,253.55 m	Infinite	0.0	1,253.55	0.0
Cloth type 8	116.76 m	Infinite	0.0	116.76	0.0
Cloth type 9	207.24 m	Infinite	0.0	207.24	0.0
Cloth type 10	290.00 m	Infinite	0.0	290.00	0.0
Cloth type 11	89.27 m	Infinite	0.0	89.27	0.0
Cloth type 12	104.50 m	Infinite	0.0	104.50	0.0

For Table 5, cloth type 3 is completely consumed, i.e., all the products that could be made with cloth type 3 were manufactured, which leads to this type of cloth having a greater impact within the optimal scenario. In addition, 0.69 m of extra fabric must be added to increase the manufacture of a single product with this type of material. The rest of the fabric type resources are left with a dual value of 0. This is because they have not been taken into account for the manufacture of products since these products have not been considered.

From the results obtained for the normal and appalling scenarios, it was observed that, in both cases, the same type of fabric was used, with type 1 and type 3, in equal measure. This differs from the optimal scenario in which the same material was used but in other values. This indicates that the same type of fabric was still used; however, the resulting products were different, as seen in Table 3 and Table 4.

Table 6 and Table 7 indicate the same values because the difference in profit between them is less than $ 12. Therefore, the present values suggest that the available fabric has not been fully used, only the type 1 and 3 used. Table 5, Table 6, and Table 7 indicate that many of their garments have not been worn. Therefore, the model does not consider a minimum or maximum quantity of products and/or categories to be elaborated.

Table 6. Sensitivity analysis of the right side for the type of fabric available in an appalling scenario.

Restriction	Right side value	Upper range	Lower range	Slack	Dual
Cloth type 1	4867.62 m	Infinite	162.35	4705.27	0.0
Cloth type 2	1461.63 m	Infinite	0.0	1461.63	0.0
Cloth type 3	1101.00 m	Infinite	726.11	374.88	0.0
Cloth type 4	246.15 m	Infinite	0.0	246.15	0.0
Cloth type 5	142.10 m	Infinite	0.0	142.10	0.0
Cloth type 6	255.52 m	Infinite	0.0	255.52	0.0
Cloth type 7	1253.55 m	Infinite	0.0	1253.55	0.0
Cloth type 8	116.76 m	Infinite	0.0	116.76	0.0
Cloth type 9	207.24 m	Infinite	0.0	207.24	0.0
Cloth type 10	290.00 m	Infinite	0.0	290.00	0.0
Cloth type 11	89.27 m	Infinite	0.0	89.27	0.0
Cloth type 12	104.50 m	Infinite	0.0	104.50	0.0

Table 7. Sensitivity analysis of the right side for the type of fabric available in a normal scenario.

Restriction	Right side value	Upper range	Lower range	Slack	Dual
Cloth type 1	4867.62 m	Infinite	162.35	4705.27	0.0
Cloth type 2	1461.63 m	Infinite	0.0	1461.63	0.0
Cloth type 3	1101.00 m	Infinite	726.11	374.88	0.0
Cloth type 4	246.15 m	Infinite	0.0	246.15	0.0
Cloth type 5	142.10 m	Infinite	0.0	142.10	0.0
Cloth type 6	255.52 m	Infinite	0.0	255.52	0.0
Cloth type 7	1253.55 m	Infinite	0.0	1253.55	0.0
Cloth type 8	116.76 m	Infinite	0.0	116.76	0.0
Cloth type 9	207.24 m	Infinite	0.0	207.24	0.0
Cloth type 10	290.00 m	Infinite	0.0	290.00	0.0
Cloth type 11	89.27 m	Infinite	0.0	89.27	0.0
Cloth type 12	104.50 m	Infinite	0.0	104.5	0.0

For the manufacturing time constraint analysis in Fig. 4, the constraint was always active regardless of the proposed scenario. In other words, the available adaptation time was more relevant than the adaptation materials [21].

Therefore, the 67,200 min available for manufacturing with seven employees are fully utilized. Thus, for the optimal scenario, 0.528 min should be increased to production

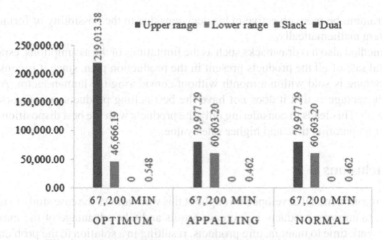

Fig. 4. Sensitivity analysis of the right side for time available.

time. Similarly, for the worst and normal scenarios, the increase is a total of 0.4662 min per garment. With the values of Fig. 4, it is observed that the optimization model manages to solve the production time problem, where the case study indicates that all available production times are required to be used. Also, the values found by the optimization model in terms of maximum profit. Tables 3 and 4 show an increase in its net benefits; therefore, it can be said that the optimization model has managed to find a balance between the objectives.

3.2 Discussion

Therefore, the multi-objective linear optimization model suggested that the decision-maker make as many products of the same type as possible and manufacture products with a minimum amount of tissue type in the spare time [17]. In addition, based on the results obtained by the sensitivity analysis regarding the review of the kind of fabric available and the production time restrictions, the model recommended not to use this parameter of manufacturing time and the restriction that involves it. This is because it significantly affects the production plan by reducing the type of fabric from three to two classes at most [18].

Thanks to applying the multi-objective linear optimization model with different data, the quantity depending on the type of fabric available, and the number of products to be considered for a production plan, several advantages can be indicated based on experience and results obtained throughout this work.

The model adapts to the amount of fabric available to create the number of constraints and the products as the number of decision variables. It makes a production plan based on finding the best performance to take advantage of available production time and maximize profits simultaneously. Regardless of the data entered into the model, it will make use of all available manufacturing time. It indicates to the administrator how to use its factors effectively, selecting and distributing them appropriately. It allows the administrator to be more objective in his decisions due to the possibility of formulating the problem mathematically.

The method also has drawbacks such as the limitations of the assumptions, especially in the total sale of all the products present in the production plan, since it is considered that everything is sold within a month without considering the human factor. Another clear disadvantage is that it does not have the best-selling products or categories in a given month. This leads to considering only the products with the best dispositions, such as shorter preparation time and higher sales value.

4 Conclusions

The optimization model developed throughout this work allows the case study to identify strategies to improve production, increase profits and take advantage of the maximum available work time to manufacture products, resulting in a solution to the problem [15]. For this case study, the maximum net benefit is sought by increasing production capacity by manufacturing as many products as possible, making the most manufacturing time [16].

This article presents an optimization model with a mixed approach to solve an internal logistics problem to create a textile production plan in an MSME. This multi-objective linear optimization model obtained an optimal solution in less than a minute with a total of 81 products and 11 types of fabrics in two of three scenarios, these being optimal and worst. Furthermore, the model shows in these scenarios a significant improvement compared to the historical values of the case study. Therefore, the proposed optimization model can be used for any MSME in the textile sector simply. The company wanted to create a production plan based on available raw materials and working hours to manufacture textile products.

Within the project, the objective of creating a multi-objective linear optimization model is achieved, which generates a production plan to represent real conditions or internal logistics scenarios focused on textile production. The resulting optimization model includes textile products as decision variables. In addition, the restrictions were configured based on the type of fabric available, giving 11 restrictions for the data set proposed by the case study and a restriction indicating the available manufacturing time, giving a total of 12 restrictions. Finally, the objective functions are represented by two approaches, the first based on profit and the second in making the most significant number of products in the given production time.

Finally, if the presented optimization model is considered, intangible factors must also be considered, such as human behavior, which can be crucial to make a final decision. This factor can influence positively or negatively within the sector in which the model is applied. This current model was developed under fixed values and assumptions that do not consider the human factor as preferences in the type of garment [5].

Acknowledgments. This research was carried out under the project "Incorporating Sustainability concepts to management models of textile Micro, Small and Medium Enterprises (SUMA)" funded by the Flemish Interuniversity Council (VLIR) and the Vice-Rector's Office for Research of the University of Cuenca.

References

1. Ron, R., Sacoto, V.: Las PYMES ecuatorianas: su impacto en el empleo como contribución del PIB PYMES al PIB total. Revista Espacios **38**(53), 15 (2017)
2. Gonzalez Litman, T.: La industria textil ecuatoriana cae en 2020 y ve en la bioseguridad una oportunidad de crecimiento - Noticias: industrie (#1270348). https://pe.fashionnetwork.com/news/La-industria-textil-ecuatoriana-cae-en-2020-y-ve-en-la-bioseguridad-una-oportunidad-de-crecimiento,1270348.html
3. Primicias: El sector textil ecuatoriano ve crecimiento en cinco mercados. https://www.primicias.ec/noticias/economia/textil-ecuador-oportunidades-crecimiento-mercados-ecuador/
4. Winston, W.L.: Operations Research: Applications and Algorithms. Duxbury Press, Belmont (2003)
5. Stingl, E.P.E., Pohlhammer, J.O.M.: Modelo de optimización de la logística de distribución de una empresa de alimentación (2002)
6. Hillier, F.S.: Introduction to Operations Research with Access Card for Premium Content. McGraw-Hill Education (2014)
7. Campo, E.A., Cano, J.A., Gómez-Montoya, R.A.: Optimización de costos de producción agregada en empresas del sector textile. Ingeniare. Revista chilena de ingeniería. **28**, 461–475 (2020). https://doi.org/10.4067/S0718-33052020000300461
8. Caguana Caguana, P.A.: Cálculo para maximizar las ganancias de la fábrica de muebles el Artesano SA, http://repositorio.utmachala.edu.ec/handle/48000/12962, (2018)
9. Alcazar Moran, G.P.: Modelo de gestión para la optimización de los procesos de contratación de personal en las empresas familiares del sector textil en la ciudad de Guayaquil (2019)
10. Guerra Rubio, B.G., Gutiérrez Salamanca, L.S., López García, D., Sánchez Urriago, D.: Diseño de un sistema de producción y operaciones aplicado a una empresa de confección de chaquetas para dama, mediante el uso de modelos matemáticos (2017). http://hdl.handle.net/10656/5305
11. Zhang, L.: Dynamic optimization model for garment dual channel supply chain network: a simulation study. Int k Simul Model. **14**, 697–709 (2015). https://doi.org/10.2507/IJSIMM 14(4)CO16
12. Cortés, M., Miranda, R., Sánchez, T., Curbeira, D.: Aplicaciones de la Modelación Matemática a la Administración y la Economía. Universidad Autónoma del Carmen. Mérida, México (2005)
13. Espinoza, D.: Que hay de nuevo en Gurobi 7.0 (2018). https://www.gurobi.com/pdfs/webinars/gurobi-7.0-webinar-slides-es.pdf
14. Gurobi Optimization: Mixed-Integer Programming (MIP) - A Primer on the Basics. https://www.gurobi.com/resource/mip-basics/
15. Barba-Romero, S., Pomerol, J.-C.: Decisiones multicriterio: fundamentos teóricos y utilización práctica. Universidad de Alcalá, Servicio de Publicaciones (1997)
16. Cárdenas, M.V., Niño, L., Camacho, A.P., Castrillón, N.S.: Modelos de optimización para la minimizacion de desperdicios industriales: una aplicación. Investigaciones Aplicadas **4**, 34–41 (2010)
17. Romero, C.: Análisis de las decisiones multicriterio. Isdefe Madrid (1996)
18. Ortíz Barrios, M.A.O.: Teoría de restricciones y modelación PL como herramientas de decisión estratégica para el incremento de la productividad en la línea de toallas de una compañía del sector textil y de confecciones. Prospectiva **11**, 21–29 (2013)
19. Asamblea Nacional del Ecuador: Ley Orgánica de Régimen Tributario Interno. Ecuador. Publisher, Ecuador (2018)
20. Diwekar, U.: Introduction to applied optimization. Springer. Nature **22**, 22 (2020)

21. Ait-Alla, A., Teucke, M., Lütjen, M., Beheshti-Kashi, S., Karimi, H. R.: Robust production planning in fashion apparel industry under demand uncertainty via conditional value at risk. Math. Probl. Eng. 901861 (2014). https://doi.org/10.1155/2014/901861
22. Hashim, M., Nazam, M., Yao, L., Baig, S.A., Abrar, M., Zia-ur-Rehman, M.: Application of multi-objective optimization based on genetic algorithm for sustainable strategic supplier selection under fuzzy environment. J. Ind. Eng. Manage. **10**(2), 188–212 (2017)
23. Loucks, P., Van Beek, E.: Water Resource Systems Planning and Management: An Introduction to Methods, Models, and Applications, pp. 93–177. Springer, Cham (2017). https://doi.org/10.1007/978-3-319-44234-1
24. Bertsimas, D. Stellato, B.: Online mixed-integer optimization in milliseconds. Princeton Institute for Computational Science and Engineering (2021)

Comparison of Lethality and Mortality Rates Due to Covid-19 and Traffic Accidents in Ecuador 2020–2021

Katherin Jiménez-Yanza[1] and Kenny Escobar-Segovia[2(✉)]

[1] Universidad Espíritu Santo, Samborondón, Ecuador
kathjimenez@uees.edu.ec
[2] Escuela Superior Politécnica del Litoral, Guayaquil, Ecuador
kescobar@espol.edu.ec

Abstract. Currently, the major causes of death in Ecuador are, among others, the disease known as Covid-19 and traffic accidents. Therefore, the study aims to compare lethality and mortality rates due to Covid-19 and traffic accidents. A cross-sectional descriptive study was carried out based on official records of bulletins and infographics of Covid-19 reported by the Ministry of Public Health (MSP) and the National Transit Agency (ANT) from March 2020 to March 2021. From these, lethality rates ($\times 1,000$ inhabitants) and mortality rates ($\times 100,000$ inhabitants) calculated while statistical comparisons were made using the t-student and Mann-Whitney tools. According to estimates, in May 2020 a higher number of deaths from Covid-19 occurred, reaching a mortality rate of 1.4 ($\times 100,000$ inhabitants) while the mortality rate for traffic accidents reached 1.1 ($\times 100,000$ inhabitants) in December 2020, although the mortality and lethality rate is higher in traffic accidents in the studied interval it is not part of this study to minimize the problems that exist due to the pandemic generated by the coronavirus. The results of this study highlight the need to create social awareness about the benefits of taking control measures and creating safe practices to mitigate the number of deaths in Ecuador due to these causes.

Keywords: Mortality rate · Lethality rate · Traffic accidents · Covid-19 · Ecuador

1 Introduction

In Wuhan, China, it was reported the existence of patients affected by an unidentified microbial agent at the end of December 2019. Thereafter, in January 2020, this viral strain was called the new coronavirus or SARS-CoV-2, transmitted from person to person through droplets expelled by coughing or sneezing, entering through the respiratory tract and producing severe acute respiratory syndrome. The disease is also known as Covid-19 [1].

© Springer Nature Switzerland AG 2022
M. Botto-Tobar et al. (Eds.): ICAT 2021, CCIS 1535, pp. 229–238, 2022.
https://doi.org/10.1007/978-3-031-03884-6_17

The disease caused by new coronavirus has gone from being an epidemic to a pandemic declared on March 11, 2020 by the World Health Organization as several cases have been reported worldwide with a diagnosis of severe pneumonia leading to death [2, 3].

All sectors were affected, representing a major impact at the economic level as the search for measures to contain this pandemic. Long-term confinement has allowed companies to lose incomes, increasing unemployment and reducing global GDP in 2020 by 1%. The economic crisis will negatively affect sustainable development since millions of skilled workers in public and private service sectors have been affected due mainly to the lack of labor protection [4].

Worldwide, since the beginning of the pandemic until April 21, 2021, there are 142,238,073 confirmed cases and 3,032,124 confirmed deaths; the Americas region has the higher number of confirmed cases, with 60,006,538 cases detected so far, with the United States leading the number of in the confirmed cases with 31,350,025 people [5].

In Ecuador, on February 29, it was announced the existence of patient 0 imported case, an elderly adult patient from Spain. The MSP carried out epidemiological surveillance to contain the virus by contacting exposed family members, identifying whether they had symptoms, and performing PCR-RT tests for diagnosis and subsequent isolation [6].

The president declared a state of emergency to prevent the spread of Covid-19. Measures adopted included the closure of public services except for health services, closure of markets and stores, the opening of home deliveries of food and medicine, and the suspension of working hours; during the quarantine period, a vehicle restriction by license plate number was also implemented to prevent mass attendance to reduce the number of cases of Covid-19 [7, 8].

Two states of exception have been declared nationwide in Ecuador on March 16th, 2020 and September 11th, 2020 is extended for 30 days each. A health emergency has also been declared in all health establishments during this period to try to stop and combat the spread of this disease in our country. So far, 100 protocols have been decreed by the National COE, ministries and municipal governments with greater emphasis on controlling the mobility of citizens and capacity in public places with limited entry capacity for customers, among others [9–11].

According to the evolution of the Covid-19 lethality rate in Ecuador, the world average was exceeded from the third week of March to the present and its increase was significant from April to May 2020. However, even though the lethality rate has decreased since June, the value is still a cause for concern [12].

The statics Covid-19 in Ecuador up to the March 31, 2021 cohort are 328,755 cases confirmed with PCR-RT tests, 35,920 cases with hospital discharge, 16,847 people died from Covid-19 and 281,684 patients recovered. In the MSP bulletins, suspected cases of deaths due to Covid-19 are described, with 4,870 people who were not confirmed with the respective tests [13].

Traffic accidents are another of the mortalities affecting Ecuador and represent a public health problem affecting thousands of people. This harms society as they result in fatalities. The National Transit Agency aims to implement preventive measures for the population involved, including pedestrians, drivers, and their companions. Traffic accidents cause an annual mortality of 1.35 million people worldwide and every day

3,500 people die on the roads, while tens of millions suffer injuries or disabilities [14]. The most affected age group are young people, since they are the most numerous population worldwide whose mobility from one point of departure to another is affected by external factors such as the omission of preventive measures on the part of drivers and pedestrians [15].

Due to this high lethality rate, traffic accidents worldwide represent a public health problem and actions must be taken to mitigate them. The World Health Organization (WHO) collaborates with governmental and non-governmental partners around the world to prevent road crashes and promote good practices such as wearing a helmet or seat belt, not drinking while driving, and avoiding speeding through its global road safety action plan [16].

Despite the efforts made by the WHO, statistics are increasing in Latin America, traffic fatalities represent 43% in the Andean region, and Ecuador ranking seventh in the world in terms of mortality rate [14].

The civil registry in Ecuador receives daily information on deaths and births, accounting for a total population of 17,283,338 inhabitants [17]. In 2019, 2,180 people died due to traffic accidents, the figure exceeded those recorded in the National Transit Agency since 2015, when 2,127 people died of which 1,818 people died representing 83% with etiology of traveling in private cars and 309 people died representing 17% during the use of public transport [18].

During the quarantine period decreed in Ecuador, mortality rates due to traffic accidents have decreased. However, we might think that lethality rates have also decreased, but this is not the case, since the number of diagnosed cases (injuries) is increasing which may be attributed to the health crisis and the collapse of hospitals [19].

This article aims to compare lethality and mortality rates due to Covid-19 and traffic accidents in Ecuador during the period from March 2020 to March 2021, using reports from the Ministry of Public Health (MSP) and the National Transit Agency (ANT).

2 Methodology

The study is descriptive-cross-sectional and was conducted in three phases: (i) compilation of official reference statistics, (ii) equations for the calculation of the percentage of the estimated lethality and mortality rate for Covid-19 and traffic accidents, and (iii) comparative statistical analysis.

(i) Official reference statistics

The number of cases classified as deceased by Covid-19 was obtained through the official statistics of the MSP using its monthly bulletins of the Covid-19 situation, infographics numbers 035, 063, 094, 124, 155, 186, 216, 246, 277, 308, 339, 367 and 398 respectively for March 2020 to March 2021, adding only confirmed deceased patients and excluding those probable cases due to the lack of confirmatory PCR tests, and also the excess deaths. The general population of Ecuador was also estimated in the official website of the National Institute of Statistics and Census [17]. About traffic accidents, the official statistics were extracted from the monthly reports on the website of the National Traffic Agency of Ecuador [18].

(ii) Equations

The equations for the calculation of Lethality Rates (TL) and Mortality Rates (TM), both used for Covid-19 and traffic accidents, are presented below.

$$TL = \frac{\text{Number of deaths in a given period of time x 1, 000 inhabitants}}{\text{Number of cases diagnosed in a given period}}$$

$$TM = \frac{\text{Number of deaths in a given period of time x 100, 000 inhabitants}}{\text{Total population in a given period}}$$

(iii) Comparative statistical analysis

Using the Mann-Whitney test (non-parametric data) or the t-student test (parametric data) for independent samples, the equality or not of the lethality and mortality rates between Covid-19 and traffic accidents was verified with the help of Minitab v18 software.

3 Results

Table 1 shows the distribution of diagnosed cases confirmed by PCR-RT test and the number of deaths confirmed by Covid-19 during the study period from March 2020 to March 2021, with a total number of 328,755 diagnosed with the disease and a total of 11,977 deaths because of Covid-19. According to the data collected, there was a greater increase in the number of Covid-19 infections in March 2021 and May 2020 where 2,475 people died and was the month with the highest number of deaths related to the disease. This estimate concerning the general population of Ecuador which varies in 2020–2021 according to the National Institute of Statistics and Census (INEC).

Table 1. Confirmed diagnosed and deceased cases of Covid-19 in Ecuador.

Months	Sick confirmed	Deceased Confimed[a]	Diagnosed Confirmed[a]	Total population estimated
Mar/2020	2,223	79	2,302	17′283,338
Apr/2020	21,569	804	22,373	17′283,338
May/2020	11,948	2,475	14,423	17′283,338
Jun/2020	16,075	1,169	17,244	17′283,338
Jul/2020	27,838	1,175	29,013	17′283,338
Aug/2020	18,602	854	19,456	17′283,338
Sep/2020	31,246	990	32,236	17′283,338
Oct/2020	29,325	775	30,100	17′283,338
Nov/2020	24,835	703	25,538	17′283,338
Dec/2020	19,378	449	19,827	17′283,338
Jan/2021	37,612	704	38,316	17′710,643

(*continued*)

Table 1. (*continued*)

Months	Sick confirmed	Deceased Confimed[a]	Diagnosed Confirmed[a]	Total population estimated
Feb/2021	34,446	881	35,327	17′′710,643
Mar/2021	41,681	919	42,600	17′′710,643
Total		**11,977**	**328,755**	

[a]Confirmed by PCR (polymerase chain reaction) tests for Covid-19.
Source: Official records of MSP infographics, national Covid-19 status and estimated population of Ecuador (INEC).

Table 2 shows the number of traffic accidents by month, the number of injured, deaths, and the total number of traffic accidents, with 13,711 people injured during a one-year period. The highest number of people injured was in December 2020 with 1,525. The total number of deaths due to traffic accidents during this same period was 1,757, with a higher increase in January 2021 with 198 deaths.

Table 2. Traffic accident injuries and fatalities in Ecuador during the period 2020–2021.

Months	Injured	Deceased	Total (TA)	Total population estimated
Mar/2020	938	103	1,041	17′283,338
Apr/2020	383	63	446	17′283,338
May/2020	675	105	780	17′283,338
Jun/2020	881	123	1,004	17′283,338
Jul/2020	785	104	889	17′283,338
Aug/2020	1,049	118	1,167	17′283,338
Sep/2020	1,081	118	1,199	17′283,338
Oct/2020	1,188	162	1,350	17′283,338
Nov/2020	1,272	158	1,430	17′283,338
Dec/2020	1,525	186	1,711	17′283,338
Jan/2021	1,364	198	1,562	17′′710,643
Feb/2021	1,241	145	1,386	17′′710,643
Mar/2021	1,329	174	1,503	17′′710,643
Total	**13,711**	**1,757**	**15,468**	

TA (Traffic Accidents).
Source: Official records of monthly reports from (ANT) in reference to traffic accidents and estimated population of Ecuador (INEC).

Table 3 shows the lethality and mortality rates for Covid-19 and traffic accidents. The highest lethality rate occurred in May with 172 deaths with a confirmed diagnosis of Covid-19 per 1,000 inhabitants. This event led to a mortality rate indicator for the same month of 1.43 deaths per 100,000 inhabitants in Ecuador. The Covid-19 mortality rate does not exceed 2 per 100,000 inhabitants represented by monthly rates. however, the overall mortality rate reached in the study period of one year is 3.64 per 100,000 inhabitants.

The highest lethality rate for traffic accidents occurred in April 2020, reaching 141 deaths per 1,000 inhabitants, and the mortality rate increased in December 2020 as well as in January 2020 with 1.1 deaths per 100,000 inhabitants.

Mortality rates for Covid-19 began to increase in April and increased sharply in May and then decreased steadily in June 2020 until February 2021, following the implementation of certain restrictions; this contrasted with traffic accidents, which decreased in April 2020 and then increased and remained constant, even exceeding the mortality rate for Covid-19.

The behavior of the lethality rate and the mortality rate for Covid-19 are similar, with a maximum increase in May 2020 and a decrease in subsequent months, which could be due to the increase in the number of confirmed patients diagnosed.

Table 3. Estimated lethality and mortality rates for Covid-19 cases and traffic accidents in Ecuador

Months	TL (Covid-19)	TL (TA)	p-value[a]	TM (Covid-19)	TM (TA)	p-value[b]
Mar/2020	34	99	0.000	0.05	0.6	0.029
Apr/2020	36	141		0.47	0.4	
May/2020	172	135		1.43	0.6	
Jun/2020	68	123		0.68	0.7	
Jul/2020	40	117		0.68	0.6	
Aug/2020	44	101		0.49	0.7	
Sep/2020	31	98		0.57	0.7	
Oct/2020	26	120		0.45	0.9	
Nov/2020	28	110		0.41	0.9	
Dec/2020	23	109		0.26	1.1	
Jan/2021	18	127		0.40	1.1	
Feb/2021	25	105		0.50	0.8	
Mar/2021	22	116		0.52	1.0	

[a]IC for the difference: (-93, -70) - Mann-Whitney test for independent samples
[b]IC 95% for difference: (-0.464, -0.027) - t-student test for independent simples.
Source: MSP-INEC reports on the general population of Ecuador.
TL: ($\times 1,000$ inhabitants); TM: ($\times 100,000$ inhabitants).

Table 4 lists the provinces with the highest number of deaths due to Covid-19 (Pichincha with 2,494 deaths, followed by Guayas with 2,145 and Manabí with 1,794 deaths), whereas the highest number of deaths due to traffic accidents is found in the provinces of Guayas with 422 deaths and 307 deaths in Pichincha.

Table 4. Cases of deaths confirmed by Covid-19 and traffic accidents by province in Ecuador

Provinces	Deceased confirmed *(Covid-19)	Deceased (TA)
Pichincha	2,494	422
Guayas	2,145	307
Manabí	1,794	120
El oro	779	112
Sto. Domingo	524	92
Tungurahua	437	87
Santa elena	410	74
Chimborazo	409	74
Los Ríos	409	63
Cotopaxi	397	52
Loja	364	46
Azuay	338	40
Esmeraldas	302	40
Imbabura	285	33
Carchi	210	32
Sucumbíos	126	29
Cañar	117	27
Napo	90	25
Bolívar	85	23
Pastaza	73	19
Zamora Chinchipe	70	15
Orellana	62	14
Morona Santiago	48	11
Galápagos	9	0
Total	**11,977**	**1,757**

* Confirmed by PCR (polymerase chain reaction) tests for Covid-19.
Source: Official database of infographics-MSP national situation for Covid-19 by provinces in Ecuador and monthly reports of deaths due to traffic accidents-ANT in different provinces of Ecuador.

4   Discussion

The decrease in deaths of 332 people during the quarantine period has had a positive impact on the reduction of the mortality curve due to traffic accidents, in addition to reducing vehicular traffic due to the limited number of exits; however, we could think that the lethality rates have also decreased, but this is not the case since the number of diagnosed cases (injured) is increasing, which can be attributed to the health crisis and the collapse of hospitals [19].

Drivers account for the largest number of deaths in traffic accidents; therefore, a rigorous vehicle inspection to determine the existence of safety devices and technical failures would allow the prevention of fatal outcomes. In this article, the means of transport involved in the highest percentage of fatalities is the motorcycle; therefore, strategies focused on this group of drivers and periodic reviews of this means of transport could be implemented. In our neighboring country Colombia, the effects of interventions designed to implement several compulsory measures, such as the use of helmets for passengers and drivers, reflective vests, and a ban on departures in December, the month with the most traffic congestion and pedestrian traffic, and interventions to assess compliance resulted in a 3.6% reduction in the mortality rate in 2001 [20].

In the year 2020 to 2021, from March to March, 11,977 people died from Covid-19 and 1,757 people died from traffic accidents; affecting people over 50 years of age due to different etiologies; in the case of Covid-19, this happens because this group is vulnerable [21], moreover, traffic accidents are possible since people over 50 years of age are less responsive to sudden events [22].

5   Conclusion

During the first months of the pandemic there was a decrease in the number of people diagnosed since not everyone had access to the PCR-RT confirmatory tests, also the lack of authorized laboratories to perform the tests, and the existence of asymptomatic cases, so that in the first months there was a marked increase in the mortality and lethality rate with respect to Covid-19. The access to free tests through the MSP and other certified institutions and the implementation of restriction measures led to a decrease in the lethality and mortality rates. From April to June 2020, the period in which a state of emergency was established in Ecuador, there was a decrease in the number of deaths due to traffic accidents, although, the lethality and mortality rate for these accidents were higher than the rates for Covid-19. However, one of the purposes of the study is not to minimize what is occurring due to the pandemic, since it continues to be a problem of attention for the public health system.

The main provinces affected by Covid-19 and traffic accidents are the provinces of Pichincha and Guayas, being the most populated provinces in Ecuador; provinces where mitigation strategies should be focused. In conclusion, to achieve the reduction of deaths for both Covid-19 and traffic accidents, which are key objectives for public health and reduce the economic impact for the government, it is necessary to raise awareness, sensitization, and implementation of new approaches. One of the limitations of the study is the fidelity and veracity of the data, mainly for Covid-19 diagnoses due to the existence of probable cases and excess deaths, which have not been considered due to their lack of confirmation with PCR tests. This study is of national interest since both causes are representative in the field of public health and will allow the implementation or improvement of prevention measures about them.

References

1. WHO, 2020. [En línea]. https://www.who.int/es/health-topics/coronavirus#tab=tab_1
2. WHO, Novel Coronavirus (2019-nCov) Situation report-1 (2020)
3. World Health Organization, Novel Coronavirus (2019-nCoV). Situation Report 10 (2020)
4. Organización de las Naciones Unidas, Es probable que la COVID-19 reduzca el PIB global del 2020 en casi un 1 %, 2020. [En línea]. https://www.un.org/development/desa/es/news/pol icy/covid-19-impact-2020-global-gdp.html
5. Finacial Times, Coronavirus tracker: the latest figures as countries fight the Covid-19 resurgence | Free to read, 2021. [En línea]. https://www.ft.com/content/a2901ce8-5eb7-4633-b89c-cbdf5b386938
6. Comite de Operaciones de Emergencia Nacional, Informe de Situación COVID-19 en Ecuador, Informe 001, Quito (2020)
7. Decreto Ejecutivo 1017, Estado de Excepción por calamidad pública, Presidencia de la República del Ecuador (2020)
8. MSP, Acuerdo Ministerial Nro. 00126: Estado de emergencia sanitaria en todos los establecimientos del Sistema nacional de Salud...efecto provocado por el Coronavirus Covid-19, y prevenir un contagio masivo en la población, Ministerio de Salud Pública. Ministerio de Salud Pública (2020)
9. Decreto Ejecutivo 1055, Estado de excepción por calamidad pública (primera extensión), Presidencia de la República del Ecuador (2020)
10. Decreto Ejecutivo 1074, Estado de excepción por calamidad pública (segunda extensión). Presidencia de la República del Ecuador (2020)
11. Decreto Ejecutivo 1126, Estado de excepción por calamidad pública (tercera extensión). Presidencia de la República del Ecuador (2020)
12. Gómez, A., Orellana, D.: Primer informe epidemiológico y exceso de mortalidad por Covid-19: Ecuador y los datos de una pandemia en curso (2020). [En línea]. http://www.saludpubl ica.uchile.cl/noticias/166204/ecuador-y-los-datos-de-unapandemia-en-curso
13. Gobierno de la República del Ecuador, CoronavirusEcuador.com, 2021. [En línea]. https://www.coronavirusecuador.com/estadisticas-covid-19/
14. WHO, Global Status Report on Road Safety, World Health Organization (2015)
15. Organización de las Naciones Unidas, Día Mundial en Recuerdo de las Víctimas de Accidentes de Tráfico, 2020. [En línea]. https://www.un.org/es/observances/road-traffic-victims-day
16. Organización de las Naciones Unidas, «Decenio de Acción para la Seguridad Vial 2010-2020,» 2020. [En línea]. https://www.who.int/roadsafety/decade_of_action/plan/plan_span ish.pdf?ua=1
17. INEC, Ecuador en cifras, 2021. [En línea]. https://www.ecuadorencifras.gob.ec/estadisticas/
18. ANT, Estadisticas de siniestros de transito, reportes, [En línea]. https://www.ant.gob.ec/? page_id=2670
19. Gómez-García, A., Escobar-Segovia, K., Cajías-Vasco, P.: Impacto del COVID-19 en la mortalidad por accidentes de tránsito en provincias de la República de Ecuador. CienciAmérica 10(1), 24–34 (2021)
20. Espitia-Hardeman, V., Vélez, L., Muñoz, E., Gutiérrez-Martínez, M.I., Espinosa-Vallín, R., Concha-Eastman, A.: Efectos de las intervenciones diseñadas para prevenir las muertes de motociclistas en Cali, Colombia (1993–2001). Salud Pública de México 50, 569–577 (2008)

21. Mohammad-Reza, S., et al.: Sociodemographic determinants and clinical risk factors associated with COVID-19 severity: a cross-sectional analysis of over 200,000 patients in Tehran, Iran. BMC Infectious Diseases 21(474), 1–13 (2021)
22. Echeverry, A., Mera, J.J., Villota, J., Zárate, L.C.: Actitudes y comportamientos de los peatones en los sitios de alta accidentalidad en Cali. Colombia Médica 36(2), 79–84 (2005)

Application of BPM to Improve the Process of Creating Commercial Items in a Tracking and Monitoring Company

Shirley Coque[✉] and Fernando Sarmiento[✉]

Universidad Politécnica Salesiana, Guayaquil, Ecuador
scoque@ups.edu.ec, fsarmientog@est.ups.edu.ec

Abstract. This study describes how SM, a company dedicated to the sale of electronic devices with tracking and monitoring, improved its process of creating customized items using BPM. The repetitive steps of the Deming method and the commitment of management were fundamental to determine the roles and functions of those responsible for the process, which made it easier to reassign functions, in addition to the creation of a new role to oversee the entire process. The times of the previous process and the improved process were taken, showing a clear difference in the times of receipt and approval of the items, verification of requirements by different departments, and the release of the items. In this work, a solution was designed, developed, and implemented with BonitaSoft that significantly improved a process whose nature is to adjust to the customer's requirements.

Keywords: BPM · BonitaSoft · Business process management · Business process improvement

1 Introduction

Business process management is the structural basis for the business development of many organizations because it allows them to effectively achieve the fulfillment of objectives. Its implementation allows the definition of resources, methodologies, programs, the person responsible for each process, and other aspects that are considered to ensure the satisfaction of internal and external users [1]. It has been one of the premises to promote the evolution demanded by the market.

Business process management has a high degree of relationship with process management, although they are different terms. Process management is responsible for interrelating or interconnecting a network of processes within the organization [2], it is also responsible for incorporating various processes and aligning them to the organization's process management [3]. Process management can be defined as encompassing the organization's processes in a macro way.

Business process management is in charge of measuring and examining process compliance [3], also process management is a way to recognize, understand and add

M. Botto-Tobar et al. (Eds.): ICAT 2021, CCIS 1535, pp. 239–251, 2022.
https://doi.org/10.1007/978-3-031-03884-6_18

value to the organization's processes, increasing the level of customer satisfaction. We can define that process management is in charge of each process within the organization in detail.

Within Process Management there are different types of processes since not all processes have the same influence on the organization. Therein lies the importance of their classification: strategic, operation, and support processes.

Organizations perform best when they pay explicit attention to their business processes from start to finish. Any business process can span different departments, specialties, geographic locations, management levels, and other organizational boundaries. To do this well, it is essential to understand the steps that are performed as part of a business process, as well as the people involved in these steps, the information that is exchanged and processed while performing these steps, and the technologies that are invoked when executing the various steps [4].

Process integration is a challenge for organizations, to be included in a changing state with the introduction of new technologies, it will not only be a corporate strategy, but it will be imperative to stay in the market and improve the value chain, good support for this is BPM [5].

SM is dedicated to the sale of electronic devices with monitoring and tracking coverage, the business model opens the options of service and coverage in an extensive way adapting to the needs of customers, so SM can offer customized services for corporate clients, as it is always ready to create new types of commercial items to suit customer needs, making this feature a competitive advantage over the competition.

The process of creating new products is of utmost importance since it allows to reach that adaptability to market new commercial items, the changing needs make this process critical and complicated, with tasks that can be considered unnecessary, and involves staff from different areas, so it becomes difficult to coordinate their tasks.

Communication problems among the personnel involved in the creation of the commercial item make it difficult to keep track of the tasks; communication is done by sending/receiving/confirming to each person responsible for fulfilling his or her task by telephone or e-mail. Concerning the tasks in projects for the creation of commercial items, there is no identified person in charge, therefore, projects are often left adrift, and it is difficult to obtain definitions in a short time.

Not having online information on the status of the creation of commercial items makes it difficult to make decisions, as well as to take advantage of the company's resources. By keeping personnel assigned to a commercial item creation project indefinitely, human resources costs are very high.

This article presents the results of a BPM implementation on the item creation process at SM, a medium-sized company dedicated to the sale of monitoring and tracking devices. This article has a section of related works, materials, and methods, results, analysis of results, and conclusions.

2   Related Work

The success behind some companies after the use of BPM tools lies in the performance improvement it provides. When it is required to unify some processes within companies, the use of BPM is resorted to. BPM can be used to save time and improve production quality within various departments (or even unifying processes from different departments).

BPM was used for process optimization and quantification within a university [6]. It was found that, currently, there is a greater interest in process modeling since it favors the participation of all areas within an organization. On certain occasions using BPM alone does not assure success, since, depending on the requirements of each company, the tools necessary to obtain a greater degree of success consist of BPM working in conjunction with some other different tool.

Critical Success Factors (CSF) have been used to implement BPM within an exporting company. The result obtained from the tests performed with CSFs allowed identifying the priority aspects where improvement is required, so the implementation of a BPM would have more chances to be successful [7].

In the work done in [8], we are shown a formal model created based on BPMN. This model was created because the use of BPMN is not allowed for a formal analysis. Thanks to PROMELA it is possible to translate BPMN to a formal model, thus overcoming the limitations.

Within [9] it can be found that the use of business processes together with a Total Quality Management (TQM) helped to obtain a better performance both technologically and within the workflow. Although they are tools with different approaches, they share common aspects that were used for the current needs of their company.

Sometimes BPM together with some other tool that is not the right one, in this case, WFM, can result in a partial success or simply a total failure, without generating any good results [10]. The lack of standards to help us in the modeling and execution of business processes is an important reason to determine the result obtained by using these tools together.

The use of other tools to help the operation of BPM with some other content management tool, since in different cases there is some kind of and incompatibility between their components.

We can find an example of this in [11] that shows a joint use of BPM and ECM. Here we present a tool to improve the communication between both called CMIS, which is a key technology to reduce the communication impedance between BPM and ECM and even helps interoperation within ECM.

For the present work, BPMN was implemented using the BonitaSoft tool to streamline the processes, thus complying with the periods that were determined at each stage, keeping each of those involved in the process informed.

3   Materials and Methods

A. Areas and Actors Involved in the Process
The company is organized by several areas, which are subdivided into departments; each department has a senior executive responsible for administration. Within each department

that is involved in the process of creating commercial items, there are responsible users, who are detailed in Table 1.

Table 1. Actors involved in the process.

Area	Department	Responsible
Projects	New Projects	Project Assistant
Systems	Organization and Methods	Organization and Methods Analyst
	Development	Development Leader
	Technician	Technician Development Leader
Accounting	Accounting	Accounting Assistant
Financial	Budget	Financial Assistant
Workshops	Workshops	Installation Technician
Legal	Legal	Lawyer
Marketing	Marketing	Advertising

B. Methodology

The Deming cycle is also known as PDCA is used when applying continuous improvement strategies [12], it is composed of 4 phases: Plan-Do-Check-Act. The process is repetitive until the objective is achieved. It began by studying the current situation of the organization, in which the information to be used in the development of the improvement plan is gathered. Once concluded, it is executed to review the anticipated improvements.

Plan. Establishment of objectives and processes to carry out the improvement of the chosen process. The planning of the activities was obtained, which includes the gathering of information, elaboration of the proposed BPM diagram, revision, approval, testing, and implementation activities.

Do. Execution of the plan and processes in which the activities needed to renew the quality of the services were determined. Different meetings were held with the stakeholders involved in the improvement process.

Check. The results obtained versus the expected results were monitored and measured. Review and approval meetings were held, which served to refine the improvement.

Act. The different actions to improve the processes were implemented. Solutions can be proposed to obtain the proposed results. Based on the results of the review meetings, points to be considered in the process were obtained, which were included, and the cycle was repeated until final approval was obtained.

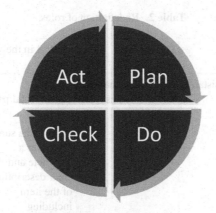

Fig. 1. Deming cycle graphic.

These activities are focused on fulfilling the answers to the following questions:
- *What should the ideal process look like?*
The process should be less extensive and more effective in the communication of the parties involved in it. There are several unjustified waiting times, and a lot of responsibility is assigned to an actor who is in charge of supervising and following up on the tasks, without having an adequate tool to do so, as will be presented in the data analysis that will be carried out in this chapter.

- *How to improve process performance?*
To improve the performance of the process, it is proposed to identify those responsible for each activity and generate reminder controls of their pending activities. This is expected to reduce the unjustified time required to perform these activities. These controls should not be new tasks with a person responsible for performing them; instead, they should use appropriate elements provided by the BPMN notation.

- *How to exceed expectations?*
In each commercial item request, the expectations of the commercial area and of the executives who negotiated the agreements or alliances are affected due to the current process of creating commercial items, despite the company's experience in meeting this type of market needs. The analysis of the data in this chapter will show that the process of creating and releasing commercial items takes too long so that results cannot be obtained in the short or medium term. Therefore, to meet the high expectations when concluding a negotiation, it is advisable to introduce technology that can speed up the process of creating and releasing the trade item.

4   Results Analysis

A. Results
Within the BPM flow proposed as a solution, after several review sessions, the following roles that have been added and activities assigned to each of these roles were identified and are presented in Table 2.

Table 2. Redefinition of roles.

Actor	Role	Description	Interest in the process	Responsibilities
Assistant	Project Assistant	Feasibility analysis and elaborates item definition document	It is a fundamental part of his job	Analyzes the feasibility of the requirement
			Must make sure to deliver a complete and clear description of the item including performance and characteristics	Details equipment characteristics
				Details functionality of the service
				Prepares a request for the creation of a commercial item
Analyst	Organization and Methods Analyst	Is the person in charge of the creation and release of the commercial item	It is a fundamental part of his job	Responsible for the creation and release of the commercial item
			He/she must ensure that the information created in the form is complete and correct, as well as support the other users	Supervises the information created in the form
				Responsible for supporting other users
Leader	Development Leader	Leads the systems development area of the commercial and administrative modules	Must ensure that new developments and/or modifications have been made to the system	Confirm as required for the creation of the commercial item
				Review the changes made in the new developments and/or modifications in the system

(continued)

Table 2. (*continued*)

Actor	Role	Description	Interest in the process	Responsibilities
Leader	Technical Development Leader	Leads the operational or technical systems development area	His main function is to notify the necessary developments to meet the requirements of new business items	Supervise that the notifications have been made
Assistant	Accounting Assistant	This is the person in charge of setting up the accounting accounts in the commercial operations	His/her function is to set up the accounting parameters of the commercial item	Responsible for setting up the accounting accounts
				Configure accounting dynamics for sales and returns
Assistant	Financial Assistant	This is the person in charge of assigning the price of the new commercial item	He/she is in charge of assigning a commercial sales price according to the commercial policy established in the organization	Responsible for assigning commercial prices
				Configure prices and the different promotions for discounts
Lawyer	Lawyer	This person is in charge of drafting the legal documents	Must ensure that the legal documents support the functionality and performance of the commercial item	Responsible for the elaboration of the legal documentation, as well as the legal basis on which the parties are committed to rights and obligations

(*continued*)

Table 2. (*continued*)

Actor	Role	Description	Interest in the process	Responsibilities
Advertising	Marketing	The person in charge of verifying whether the commercial item belongs to a new product	Its main function is to verify if the item to be commercialized belongs to a new product or is already part of a previously released product	Responsible for verifying whether it is a new or existing product
				Prepares advertising campaigns for when the product is finally released
Supervisor	Super User	This is the person in charge of supervising the whole process	His/her main function is to ensure that each stage is completed within the defined time frame	Responsible for supervising that the stages are fulfilled in the defined times
				Responsible for managing the execution of any process that is stopped

After the mapping of the new process, responsibilities have been reassigned to the different actors; the participation of the installation technician has been eliminated because his operational work is not related to the process of creating commercial items, and a new role has been added, a superuser in charge of monitoring the entire process, especially time compliance.

To test the improved process, a universe of 371 registered commercial items (CI) was taken into consideration, from which a sample of 30 items was extracted. These were related based on the six stages in control in the matrix (see Fig. 1), in this way the improvements in the selected items were verified, and the results obtained according to the mentioned stages are presented below (Fig. 2).

The results show that the 30 selected items show a 100% improvement in the stage of receiving and approving requests for commercial items. The data analyzed indicate that with the implementation of the BPM process, the time between approval and receipt of requests is reduced from six days to no more than two days (Fig. 3).

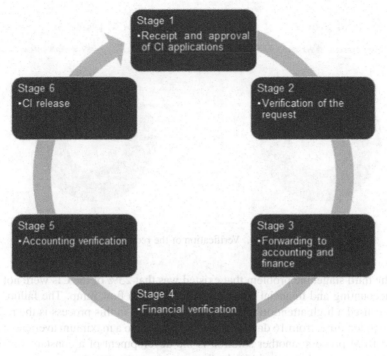

Fig. 2. Stages in control in the matrix.

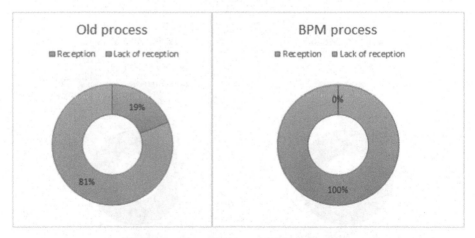

Fig. 3. Receipt and approval of CI applications.

In the second stage, the problem was located in the area of verification of requirements, since there were cases where there was a 36% flow jump that caused a lack of verification, with the implementation of the BPM process shows a 100% effectiveness to the jumps in the verification. It is worth mentioning that through the BPM process the verification days of the requirements take no more than 24 h (Fig. 4).

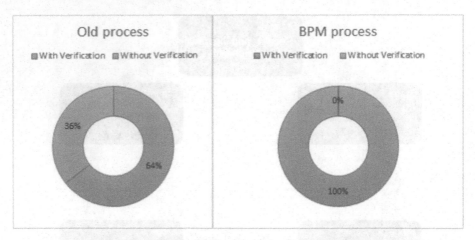

Fig. 4. Verification of the request.

In the third stage, the problem that existed was that 23% of the CIs were not routed to the accounting and financial areas, since there was a flow jump. The failure in this process caused a high attention time. The improvement in this process is the reduction of the attention time, from 16 days with the old process to a maximum average of 2 days with the BPM process, another solution is the development of a constant verification so that all commercial items within the flow are correctly routed to the accounting and financial areas (Fig. 5).

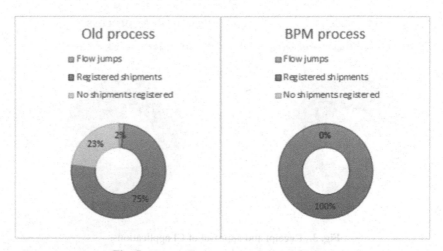

Fig. 5. Forwarding to accounting and finance.

Stage four shows a problem within the verifications, approximately 57% of the CIs do not comply with the verifications of the financial area, which motivated them to omit the activities charged to verification without developing the corresponding management. The result of this stage shows that through the BPM process the problems are reduced, this through the application of an automatic reminder for pending tasks, which helps to perform 100% of the verifications, thus going from 11 days to an average of no more than 2 days between the reception and approval of the verifications in this stage (Fig. 6).

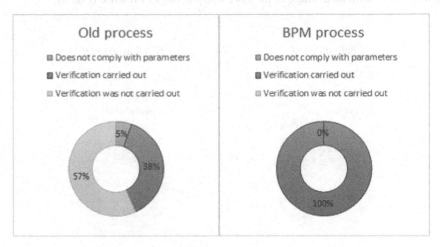

Fig. 6. Financial verification.

As in the previous stage, the fifth stage improved performance within the accounting area. By assigning the task to the person responsible for the accounting area, the task will remain active until it is processed. The average time with the old process was 18 days, with the help of the BPM process the time is reduced to a maximum of 2 days (Fig. 7).

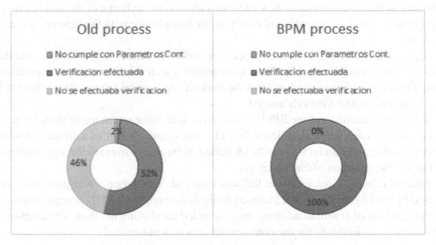

Fig. 7. Accounting verification.

In stage six, the commercial items are released and then used and marketed without any inconvenience. The results show that with the old process 19% of the CIs were not released, however, there was an 80% effectiveness, it is necessary to indicate that such effectiveness is obtained if the previous stages are optimally fulfilled. Employing the implementation of the BPM process, it can be indicated that the successful release reaches 100%, with an average of no more than six days of release (Fig. 8).

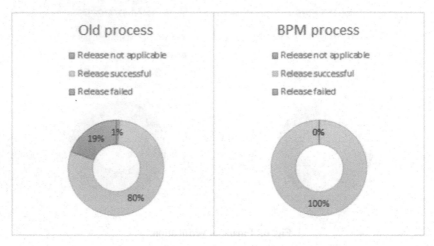

Fig. 8. CI release.

B. Analysis

Determining the actors involved in the initial process is imperative to determine their functions and how they affect the time of the process. In this case, the creation of commercial items, determining new functions and a role in charge of the whole process in general, allowed to control it and therefore the compliance with the time of each actor involved.

The controls carried out in each process provide the identification of tasks once they have been performed, and this allows to consider it as a released and commercialized item. The improved process eliminates the manual verification previously performed by the Organization and Methods analyst.

The implementation of the BPMN was a great help to the operation of the CI creation process so that each item can follow a flow of creation and controlled activities, in which the responsible areas and actors can be identified, to be able to manage through automatic reminders the attention of each activity.

Manual control using an Excel file was replaced. This process was previously performed by the Organization and Methods analyst; through the BPMN process, the activities of creation of commercial items are controlled employing the flow. The creation of the CI and its availability for the commercial area was automated.

5 Conclusions

The practice of BPM efficiently helps the continuous improvement of critical processes for the companies, helping to identify the actors to determine roles, responsibilities, and associated times, to make refinements in the functions to improve times and the process in general.

The Deming cycle methodology helped to deliver a process validated and reviewed by all the actors involved, through the execution of several review sessions in which the process was improved until the optimum result was reached; each review corresponded to a Deming cycle.

The automation of a process through the use of BPMS tools will be successful to the extent that the process is designed efficiently. In the present work, several iterations of revision and improvement were carried out, the result was an efficient BPM flow that optimized the process of creating commercial items.

References

1. Moreira Delgado, M.: Gestión por procesos y su aplicación en las organizaciones de información. Un caso de studio. Ciencias de la Información **40** (2009)
2. Mallar, M.A.: La Gestión Por Procesos: un Enfoque de Gestión Eficiente. Visión de Futuro **13** (2010)
3. Hitpass, B.: BPM Business Process Management – Fundamentos y Conceptos de Implementación, Santiago de Chile: BPM Center (2017)
4. Reijers, H.A.: Business process management: the evolution of a discipline. Comput. Ind. **126**, 103404 (2021)
5. Hitpass, B., Astudillo, H.: Industry 4.0 challenges for business process management and electronic-commerce. J. Theoret. Appl. Electr. Comm. Res. **14**, 1–3 (2019)
6. Palza, E., Tocto, E., Mamani, G.: Optimización y Cantificación de Procesos utilizando BPM, vol. 1. Apuntes Universitarios (2019)
7. Gutiérrez Sánchez, A., Rodríguez Ríos, C.S.H.A.F.: Factores críticos de éxito para la implementación de Business Process Management (BPM): estudio de caso para la cadena de suministro de una empresa del sector floricultor. Revista EAN, pp. 85–108 (2018)
8. Yamasathien, S., Vatanawood, W.: An approach to construct formal model of business process model from BPMN workflow patterns. In: 2014 Fourth International Conference on Digital Information and Communication Technology and its Applications (DICTAP), pp. 211–215 (2014)
9. Weng, C.S.: Improving service technology and business process: a case of an insurance company in Taiwan. In: 2012 Proceedings of PICMET 2012: Technology Management for Emerging Technologies, pp. 3225–3231 (2012)
10. Lins, F., et al.: Towards automation of SOA-based business processes. IJCSEA **2**(2), 1–17 (2012)
11. de Souza Mendes, M.A., Peixoto BAX, M.: BPM and ECM: similarities, differences, conceptual and technological limits. Transinformacão **30**(1), 95–105 (2018)
12. Johnson, C.N.: The Benefícts of PDCA. Milwaukee **35** (2002)

A Systematic Literature Review of Facility Layout Problems and Resilience Factors in the Industry

Pablo Flores-Siguenza[1] (iD), Lorena Siguenza-Guzman[2,3] (iD), Freddy Lema[4] (iD), Franklin Tigre[4] (iD), Paul Vanegas[5,6] (iD), and Jonnatan Aviles-González[7(✉)] (iD)

[1] Universidad de Cuenca, Cuenca, Ecuador
[2] Department of Computer Sciences, Faculty of Engineering, Universidad de Cuenca, Cuenca, Ecuador
[3] Faculty of Economics and Business, Research Centre Accountancy, KU Leuven, Leuven, Belgium
[4] Carrera de Ingeniería Industrial, Facultad de Ingeniería en Sistemas, Electrónica e Industrial, Universidad Técnica de Ambato, Ambato, Ecuador
[5] Faculty of Chemical Sciences, Universidad de Cuenca, Cuenca, Ecuador
[6] Department of Space and Population, Universidad de Cuenca, Cuenca, Ecuador
[7] Escuela de Producción, Universidad del Azuay, Cuenca, Ecuador
javiles@uazuay.edu.ec

Abstract. Flexibility, quick responses to changes, and capacity to respond to external factors are strategies that companies must develop to ensure their continuity and face adverse situations. The flexibility that can be acquired by optimizing plant layout and resilience ensures continuity of production by reducing adverse external shocks. This article synthesizes critical elements used in models to solve facility layout problems, followed by analyzing the resilience variables and factors most frequently applied in the industry. A systematic literature review to achieve this objective was developed, including 170 articles published in 2010 and 2021. Its study was performed through the Atlas.ti software, an analysis of the 4W's (i.e., When, Who, What, and Where) was applied, and finally, answers to three research questions posed were given. Growth in the scientific interest of facility layout problems can be observed in the last five years, especially for dynamic problems and unequal areas, development of multi-objective models, and approach to metaheuristic solutions. Eventually, research gaps were also identified, highlighting the lack of inclusion of resilience factors in plant distribution models.

Keywords: Layout distribution · Facility layout problem · Resilience · Literature review

1 Introduction

Companies must use Lean Manufacturing, Six Sigma, and Facility Layout Optimization to efficiently operate production and service systems [1]. In this chaotic time, generated

M. Botto-Tobar et al. (Eds.): ICAT 2021, CCIS 1535, pp. 252–264, 2022.
https://doi.org/10.1007/978-3-031-03884-6_19

by the COVID-19 pandemic, the production problems that afflict companies and the fragility of their supply chains stand out. Evidence of this situation could be found in small and medium-sized enterprises (SMEs) due to lack of economic resources, little adaptability to new standards, and inflexible responses to external factors.

The industry's global context has changed based on several aspects: flexibility and resilience [2]. The former could be studied through the layout distribution and quick responses to changes. The facility layout problem (FLP) is defined as the problem seeking to organize the location of a factory's predetermined facilities to meet one or more objectives efficiently without violating any constraints [3]. For this reason, focusing the flexibility through the FLP will enhance the industry behavior in the current emergency context. The latter can be defined as an adaptive process that allows organizations to cope with serious problems and strategic challenges by enhancing their responsiveness and reinvention to achieve organizational renewal [4]. These two aspects together guarantee the continuity of production by reducing external negative impacts [2, 5]. In addition, they allow to comply with social distancing, adapt the production processes to the variability of the environment, and face the uncertainty of variables such as demand, costs, and worker safety. Therefore, flexibility and resilience together constitute a fundamental strategy to contribute to the reactivation of the productive sectors, allowing them to adapt to adverse situations and guarantee their continuous operation. Effective facility layout design is proven to generally increase productivity, lead to better machine and space utilization, improve product quality, reduce setup time, allow for lower work-in-process inventory, and minimize material handling costs [6].

Material handling cost represents 20% to 50% of the total operating cost [7]. Thus, it has become the most critical indicator in determining the efficiency of a facility layout design and, consequently, the focal research approach utilized by academics, practitioners, and CEOs. Unfortunately, in the current FLP literature, there are only a few contributions that consider metrics such as waiting times, yield rates, safety indices, external factors, and resilience [8].

In recent years, many literature review articles have been published on the various topics covered by FLP. For instance, Hosseini-Nasab et al. [1] discuss design evolution, problem formulation, and solution methodologies. Authors such as Kulturel-Konak [9] and Singh and Sharma [10] discuss solution approaches for FLP in production environments with or without uncertainty. Maganha et al. [11] conduct a literature review on layout design in reconfigurable manufacturing systems. Al-Zubaidi et al. [12] analyze the main drivers used in FLP. Moreover, there are literature review articles focused on particular problems, such as single-row FLP [13], loop layout problems [14], and dynamic-robust FLP [15]. Unfortunately, current reviews do not analyze the presence of resilience indicators and their characteristics in layout designs, nor the interaction of these two aspects.

This article aims to synthesize the critical elements of the models used in FLP, followed by an analysis of the variables and resilience factors most frequently applied in the industry. Finally, the interaction between these two themes, resilience and FLP, is studied. This systematic literature review guides companies and researchers to understand current research lines, the models being used, and the solution approaches applied to find optimal and innovative results in resilient FLP. For a better understanding, the document is structured as follows. Section 2 describes the methodology used to collect and analyze the literature. Section 3 presents the research findings through content analysis and a brief discussion. Eventually, Sect. 4 summarizes the main conclusions.

2   Methodology

The present systematic literature review follows the methodology proposed by Fink [16] to ensure the quality and consistency of the work in terms of the FLP models and resilience indicators. The method is composed of seven steps: 1) selection of research questions, 2) definition of database sources, 3) selection of search terms, 4) application of practical selection criteria, 5) application of methodological criteria, 6) review of documentation, and 7) synthesis of results.

In Step 1, the PICO strategy (i.e., Population, Intervention, Comparison, and Outcome) [17] was used to formulate the research questions, resulting in three questions correctly. a) What models are considered in an optimal plant layout design (i.e., FLP)? b) What elements, variables and indicators are considered in a resilient model in the industry? And c) Is resilience included in plant layout models? If so, what industry characteristics and indicators are used?

Regarding Step 2 and Step 3, the database sources selected for this literature review were: Scopus, Web of Science, Scielo, and Latindex Catalogue. The keywords and search strings utilized to answer the research questions were: "Resilient facility location", "Optimization" OR "Techniques" AND "resilient facility location", "Optimization" OR "Techniques" AND "Layout problems", "Resilience" AND "Industry".

Step 4 and Step 5 allow filtering the search in different databases to ensure that the articles retrieved in the present study are current and relevant. The inclusion criteria used were the following. 1) articles in Spanish and English; 2) articles from scientific journals; 3) articles published between 2010 and 2021; 4) subject areas: Environmental Science, Engineering, Computer Science, Mathematics, Energy, Economics and Econometrics, and Decision Sciences. In addition, the exclusion criteria used were the following. 1) irrelevant and duplicate articles; 2) articles with academic publication remarks; and 3) conceptual articles.

After passing the exclusion criteria, articles had to answer the following questions. Is the research design of this study internally and externally valid? Are the data sources used in the study reliable and valid? Are the analytical methods appropriate given the characteristics and quality of the study data? Are the results mean in practical and statistical terms? If the articles found did not answer one or more questions, their methodological quality decreased.

In compliance with Step 6, the Atlas.ti software was used to review the retrieved articles. This software is a qualitative tool that allows, through codes, to highlight and classify the information according to its characteristics. In this study, a set of 64 codes was used, described in detail in Appendix A.

Finally, Step 7 synthesizes the results. Figure 1 summarizes the number of articles resulting after the review and application of the search methodology. As can be seen, a total of 170 studies have been identified, of which 130 deal specifically with FLP and 40 reports on resilience factors applied in the industry. The detailed sample list with these 170 articles is provided in Appendix B.

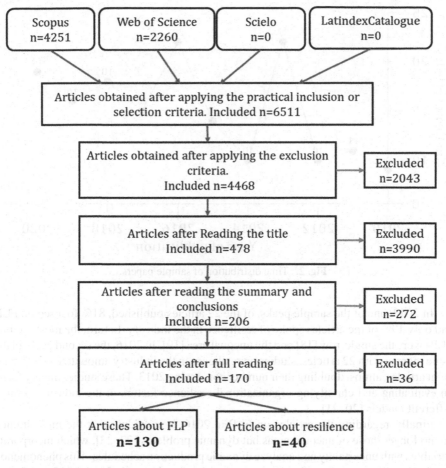

Fig. 1. Flowchart of the methodology applied

3 Results and Discussion

The results found in the sample of 170 articles are reported and discussed in two sections, meta-analysis and descriptive analysis.

3.1 Meta-analysis

To better explain the results found, a 4W analysis was developed. It starts with the "When" field, for which a time distribution is used in Fig. 2, where the number of articles published in the different years analyzed in the sample can be observed.

The years with the most publications were 2013 and 2016 with 22 articles each, with the number of publications increasing, especially since 2016. Between 2016 and 2020, the average number of articles published per year amounts to 18, while, between 2010 and 2015, the average is only 12.6 articles per year. The year 2021, which contains only four articles, is not considered due to the short time elapsed.

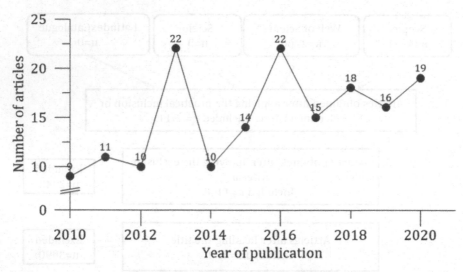

Fig. 2. Time distribution of sample papers.

In 2013, one of the sample peaks, of the 22 articles published, 81% focused on FLP, and only 19% of the articles spoke of resilience in the industry. In turn, the most-studied FLPs were the single-row [18] and the unequal area [19]. In 2016, the second peak, in the same manner with 22 articles, studies on resilience in the industry amounted to 36% with eight articles, almost doubling their number concerning 2013. These studies mainly focus on evaluating and classifying organizational resilience factors in the industry through different models [20, 21].

Finally, regarding the articles on FLP in 2016, it is evident that the most studied are no longer those of unequal areas but dynamic problems [22, 23], which incorporate variables with uncertainty and analyze dynamic production schedules. This phenomenon for FLP studies is confirmed when analyzing the time intervals 2010–2015 and 2016–2021. In the first interval, as already observed in 2013, the types of FLP most studied were those of unequal areas [24, 25]. While, in the second interval, interest is maintained in problems of unequal areas [26] and dynamic problems that consider changing scenarios and stochastic variables stand out even more [27, 28].

Regarding the "Who" aspect, articles have been published by 85 different journals, and only 13 have at least three publications. These 13 journals contain 86 publications, which represents approximately 50% of the sample. Table 1 shows these 13 journals and their corresponding number of articles published. It also includes a column indicating the area studied, i.e., an article about FLP, resilience, or interaction. Thus, globally, it is possible to know what to expect from each journal and answer the "What" field. Of the total sample, 130 articles (76%) develop FLP in their work, and only 40 articles (24%) deal with resilience. This is also evident in these 13 journals with greater frequency, where only 13 articles study resilience out of 86 articles.

The three journals with the highest number of publications are the International Journal of Production Research (25 articles), the International Journal of Advanced

Table 1. Distribution of articles per journal.

Journal name	Number of articles	Articles per area
Int. Journal of Production Research	25	FLP (21), Resilience (4)
Int. Journal of Advanced Manufacturing Technology	11	FLP (11)
Expert Systems with Applications	9	FLP (9)
European Journal of Operational Research	8	FLP (8)
Computers and Industrial Engineering	7	FLP (7)
Journal of Loss Prevention in the Process Industries	5	FLP (2), Resilience (3)
Applied Mathematical Modelling	3	FLP (3)
Computers and Operations Research	3	FLP (3)
Engineering Applications of Artificial Intelligence	3	FLP (3)
Int. Journal of Industrial and Systems Engineering	3	FLP (3)
Int. Journal of Industrial Engineering Computations	3	FLP (3)
Supply Chain Management	3	Resilience (3)
Sustainability (Switzerland)	3	Resilience (3)

Manufacturing Technology (11 articles), and Expert Systems with Applications (9 articles). The first journal stands out for being the only one in this top 3 containing studies referring to resilience in the industry [29]. Furthermore, within the FLP studies, those of unequal areas with six articles and those of a row with four papers stand out.

The second journal from the top, International Journal of Advanced Manufacturing Technology, is characterized by mainly studying dynamic FLPs (4 articles) that represent around 36% of the total of its articles. The third journal, Expert Systems with Applications, focuses mainly on unequal areas of FLP (6 articles) with 66.6% of the total.

Lastly, the "Where" field is answered by analyzing the geographical origin of the sample, i.e., the country of the institution associated with the researcher. The findings report a total of 37 countries where at least one article has been published. Figure 3 shows the countries with the highest number of publications. The top four countries are Iran (32 articles), China (21), India (19), and the USA (15), which together contain approximately 51% (87 out of 170) of the entire sample.

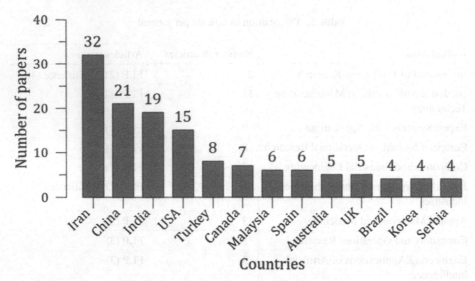

Fig. 3. Distribution of sample papers by country.

3.2 Descriptive Analysis

The results in this section focus on answering the three research questions posed in the current systematic literature review. Thus, Table 2 answers the first research question, *"What models are considered in an optimal plant layout design (FLP)"*. It includes the models of the 130 articles studying FLP. The table reports the frequency of three categories: "Layout Problem", "Mathematical Model", and "Solution Approach".

Table 2. Frequencies of the modeling dimension

Layout Problem		Mathematical Model		Solution Approach	
Unequal area	39	Multi-Objective	29	Genetic algorithms	29
Dynamic	31	MILP	23	Metaheuristic algorithms	24
Single row	19	Heuristics	21	Hybrid	16
Cell formation	8	QAP	15	Robust optimization	15
Multi-row	8	NLP	14	Stochastic	10
Other	25	Other	28	Other	36

[*] MILP = mixed-integer linear programming; QAP = quadratic assignment problem; NLP = nonlinear programming

Regarding the first category, "Layout Problem", as the meta-analysis had already given the first vision, the problems of unequal areas are the most common, with 30% of the sample (39 articles), followed by the dynamic (31 articles), single row (19 articles), cell formation (8 articles) and multiple rows (8 articles). It should be noted that 25 articles consider other types of design problems, such as a parallel row, double row, multi-floor, closed-loop, among others.

In the second category, "Mathematical Model", it can be concluded that the multi-objective model is the most common (29 papers), highlighting objective functions of cost, time, and distance. The following most widely used models are mixed-integer linear programming (MILP, 23 papers), heuristics (21 papers), nonlinear programming (NLP, 14 papers), and quadratic assignment problem (QAP, 15 papers). The other section, to which 28 articles belong, refers to single-objective, bi-objective, linear programming, and bilevel programming. As the multi-objective models are the most studied, it is considered convenient to delve into this topic. It is highlighted that the most used objective function is related to the cost of different variables and approaches. For example, Peng et al. [30] seek to minimize material handling and the reordering cost. Drira et al. [31] minimize the sum of transportation costs for the entire planning horizon. Das [32] focuses on maximizing profits by reducing costs throughout the supply chain. Finally, Mohtashami et al. [33] consider two conflicting objectives: minimizing the cost of the manufacturing system due to the amount of production loss caused by waste and minimizing the variance of fuzzy costs.

In the last category, metaheuristic algorithms are the most used, with 53 papers representing 40.7 percent of the sample. Of these works, genetic algorithms stand out, which have been given a particular space due to the number of articles found (29 articles) and their usefulness in generating a range of optimal solutions. These metaheuristic algorithms are general-purpose approximate search and optimization algorithms. They are iterative procedures that guide a subordinate heuristic by intelligently combining different concepts to explore and exploit the search space properly. There are outstanding works such as Krishtan et al. [34] that use a genetic algorithm-based approach to place machine cells within a distribution matrix. Sadrzadeh [35] presents a genetic algorithm to solve the FLP in a manufacturing system, where the material flow pattern of the multi-line layout is considered with the multi-product. Stochastic Programming approaches solutions (10 articles) and robust optimization (15 articles) are used in mathematical programming models with stochastic data to address the uncertainty implicit in certain variables. An example of this can be seen in the research by Zarea Fazlelahi et al. [23], where the authors apply a robust approach to solve a dynamic FLP with uncertain demand conditions.

Regarding the second research question, *"What elements, variables, and indicators are considered in a resilient model in the industry?"* The results include research on the evaluation and classification of organizational resilience factors in the industry. For example, Shirali et al. [36] perform a principal component analysis and determine the score of the resilience indicators and the process units. Macuzić et al. [20] use a fuzzy analytical hierarchy process to determine the relative weight of the resilience variables. Aleksić et al. [37] propose a model based on the theory of fuzzy sets to assess the potential for organizational resilience. The proposed model does not define a single set of organizational resilience factors but rather a conceptual model, suitable for quantification based on existing work. From all these works studying resilience in the industry, six common indicators can be extracted, presented in Table 3, along with the main variables to consider.

Table 3. Industry resilience indicators and variables

Indicator	Variable
Top management commitment	- Human resources - Material resources - Safety policy - Management procedures - Training programs
Organizational learning	- Information flow - Work management - Documentation availability - Incident and accident investigation
Organizational flexibility	- Ability to control the unexpected - Ability to be flexible - Accommodation reporting - Adaptation incorporation
Awareness	- Problem reporting and communication - Teamwork - Tasks and skills of people - Proactive measures
Fair culture	- Understanding and perception of errors - Non-punitive actions - Peer evaluations
Emergency preparedness	- Hazard identification - Safety equipment - Emergency plans and training

Finally, to conclude this descriptive analysis, the third research question is answered, which refers to *"Is resilience included in plant distribution models? If so, what characteristics and indicators of the industry are used?"* It can be said that after reviewing the sample of 170 articles, no work has been found that relates or includes resilience in plant layout models. While there is a wealth of information on FLP, the same is not valid for resilience. Since 2016, a considerable increase in research has been present in this area, but not their interaction. This shows a current gap in the literature that can be considered in future studies due to the benefits it can provide to companies.

Today's markets are increasingly dynamic and chaotic, forcing companies to constantly reinvent themselves and adapt to avoid stagnating in the past. They are obliged to know precisely the external and internal factors that influence their operations, on which they must work to ensure their continuity. FLP and resilience models should be as realistic as possible and developed to support business management and decision-making. The selection of a particular model will depend exclusively on the needs of each company.

4 Conclusions

The development of this systematic literature review, identifying 170 articles evaluated in a critical, transparent, and reproducible manner, allowed to fulfill the study's objective. Since the information collected, essential elements and characteristics of the most common FLP models have been determined and currently investigated resilient factors.

The sample analysis showed an increase in the production of articles in the time interval 2016–2020 concerning the period 2010–2015. Similarly, in 2010–2015, the most studied FLP types were those of unequal areas. In the 2016–2020 interval, dynamic problems became those of greater interest due to the inclusion of variables with uncertainty and the possibility of considering changes in planning.

Regarding the articles dealing in some manner with FLP, it is concluded that the multi-objective models are the most used, with cost functions in 85% of the cases. The most widely applied solution approach is metaheuristics and an increasing consideration for robust and stochastic techniques.

Research on resilience is still scarce compared to FLP, with only 24% of the sample. Almost all the studies focus on the evaluation and classification of resilience factors in the industry. There is still a lack of research, including resilience in the FLP model, aspects that together would be very useful in this particular moment of a pandemic. They could ensure the continuity of production by reducing negative external impacts.

Finally, regarding the study's limitations, one of them was the subjectivity with which the content of the sample was analyzed, which largely depends on the knowledge, judgment, experience, and number of researchers involved. Another limitation concerns how the sample was obtained, which is limited to the search keywords and databases used. Overcoming these details, it is trusted that this work will serve as a support tool for all those who wish to dabble and·apply resilience factors in FLP models.

Acknowledgments. The authors would like to thank to Corporación Ecuatoriana para el Desarrollo de la Investigación y Academia - CEDIA for the financial support given to the present research, development, and innovation work through its CEPRA program, especially for the CEPRA XV-2021–01-Resil-TEX. In addition, this research was partially funded by the University of Cuenca, Technical University of Ambato and University of Azuay.

Appendix A – List of Codes Utilized in the Literature Review

The list of codes used in Atlas.ti for the systematic literature review can be found online at https://imagineresearch.org/wp-content/uploads/2021/06/FLP-Appendix-A.pdf.

Appendix B – List of References Considered in the Literature Review

The list of references used in the literature review can be found online at https://imagin eresearch.org/wp-content/uploads/2021/06/FLP-Appendix-B.pdf.

References

1. Hosseini-Nasab, H., Fereidouni, S., Fatemi Ghomi, S.M.T., Fakhrzad, M.B.: Classification of facility layout problems: a review study. Int. J, Adv. Manuf. Technol. **94**(1–4), 957–977 (2017). https://doi.org/10.1007/s00170-017-0895-8
2. Sharma, P., Singhal, S.: Design and evaluation of layout alternatives to enhance the performance of industry. Opsearch **53**(4), 741–760 (2016). https://doi.org/10.1007/s12597-016-0257-6
3. Salmani, M.H., Eshghi, K., Neghabi, H.: A bi-objective MIP model for facility layout problem in uncertain environment. Int. J. Adv. Manuf. Technol. **81**(9–12), 1563–1575 (2015). https://doi.org/10.1007/s00170-015-7290-0
4. Herbane, B.: Rethinking organizational resilience and strategic renewal in SMEs. Entrep. Reg. Dev. **31**, 476–495 (2019). https://doi.org/10.1080/08985626.2018.1541594
5. Bemthuis, R., Iacob, M.-E., Havinga, P.: A design of the resilient enterprise: a reference architecture for emergent behaviors control. Sensors. **20**, 6672 (2020). https://doi.org/10.3390/s20226672
6. Kang, S., Kim, M., Chae, J.: A closed loop based facility layout design using a cuckoo search algorithm. Expert Syst. Appl. **93**, 322–335 (2018). https://doi.org/10.1016/j.eswa.2017.10.038
7. Tompkins, J.A., White, J.A., Bozer, Y.A., Tanchoco, J.M.A.: Facilities Planning. Wiley, New York (2010)
8. de Lira-Flores, J.A., López-Molina, A., Gutiérrez-Antonio, C., Vázquez-Román, R.: Optimal plant layout considering the safety instrumented system design for hazardous equipment. Process Saf. Environ. Prot. **124**, 97–120 (2019). https://doi.org/10.1016/j.psep.2019.01.021
9. Kulturel-Konak, S.: Approaches to uncertainties in facility layout problems: perspectives at the beginning of the 21st Century. J Intell Manuf. **18**, 273–284 (2007). https://doi.org/10.1007/s10845-007-0020-1
10. Singh, S.P., Sharma, R.: A Hybrid Genetic Search Based Approach to Solve Single Period Facility Layout Problem (2006)
11. Maganha, I., Silva, C., Ferreira, L.M.D.F.: The layout design in reconfigurable manufacturing systems: a literature review. Int. J. Adv. Manuf. Technol. **105**(1–4), 683–700 (2019). https://doi.org/10.1007/s00170-019-04190-3
12. Al-Zubaidi, S.Q.D., Fantoni, G., Failli, F.: Analysis of drivers for solving facility layout problems: a Literature review. J. Ind. Inf. Integr. **21**, 100187 (2021). https://doi.org/10.1016/j.jii.2020.100187
13. Kothari, R., Ghosh, D.: The Single Row Facility Layout Problem: State of the Art. OPSEARCH 49 (2011). https://doi.org/10.1007/s12597-012-0091-4
14. Saravanan, M., Ganesh Kumar, S.: Different approaches for the loop layout problems: a review. Int. J. Adv. Manuf. Technol. **69**(9–12), 2513–2529 (2013). https://doi.org/10.1007/s00170-013-5133-4
15. Moslemipour, G., Lee, T.S., Rilling, D.: A review of intelligent approaches for designing dynamic and robust layouts in flexible manufacturing systems. Int. J. Adv. Manuf. Technol. **60**, 11–27 (2012). https://doi.org/10.1007/s00170-011-3614-x

16. Fink, A.: Conducting Research Literature Reviews: From the Internet to Paper. SAGE Publications, Thousand Oaks (2019)

17. Santos, C.M. da C., Pimenta, C.A. de M., Nobre, M.R.C.: The PICO strategy for the research question construction and evidence search. Revista Latino-Americana de Enfermagem 15, 508–511 (2007). https://doi.org/10.1590/S0104-11692007000300023

18. Hungerländer, P., Rendl, F.: A computational study and survey of methods for the single-row facility layout problem. Comput Optim Appl. **55**, 1–20 (2013). https://doi.org/10.1007/s10 589-012-9505-8

19. Aiello, G., La Scalia, G., Enea, M.: A non dominated ranking Multi Objective Genetic Algorithm and electre method for unequal area facility layout problems. Expert Syst. Appl. **40**, 4812–4819 (2013). https://doi.org/10.1016/j.eswa.2013.02.026

20. Macuzić, I., Tadić, D., Aleksić, A., Stefanović, M.: A two step fuzzy model for the assessment and ranking of organizational resilience factors in the process industry. J. Loss Prev. Process Ind. **40**, 122–130 (2016). https://doi.org/10.1016/j.jlp.2015.12.013

21. Pournader, M., Rotaru, K., Kach, A.P., Hajiagha, S.H.R.: An analytical model for system-wide and tier-specific assessment of resilience to supply chain risks. Supply Chain Manag. **21**, 589–609 (2016). https://doi.org/10.1108/SCM-11-2015-0430

22. Ghosh, T., Doloi, B., Dan, P.K.: Applying soft-computing techniques in solving dynamic multi-objective layout problems in cellular manufacturing system. Int. J. Adv. Manuf. Technol. **86**(1–4), 237–257 (2015). https://doi.org/10.1007/s00170-015-8070-6

23. Zarea Fazlelahi, F., Pournader, M., Gharakhani, M., Sadjadi, S.J.: A robust approach to design a single facility layout plan in dynamic manufacturing environments using a permutation-based genetic algorithm. Proc. Inst. Mech. Eng. Part B: J. Eng. Manuf. **230**, 2264–2274 (2016). https://doi.org/10.1177/0954405415615728

24. Gress, E.S.H., Mora-Vargas, J., del Canto, L.E.H., Díaz-Santillán, E.: A genetic algorithm for optimal unequal-area block layout design. Int. J. Prod. Res. **49**, 2183–2195 (2011). https://doi.org/10.1080/00207540903130868

25. Kulturel-Konak, S.: A linear programming embedded probabilistic tabu search for the unequal-area facility layout problem with flexible bays. Eur. J. Oper. Res. **223**, 614–625 (2012). https://doi.org/10.1016/j.ejor.2012.07.019

26. Kang, S., Chae, J.: Harmony search for the layout design of an unequal area facility. Expert Syst. Appl. **79**, 269–281 (2017). https://doi.org/10.1016/j.eswa.2017.02.047

27. Pourhassan, M.R., Raissi, S.: An integrated simulation-based optimization technique for multi-objective dynamic facility layout problem. J. Ind. Inf. Integr. **8**, 49–58 (2017). https://doi.org/10.1016/j.jii.2017.06.001

28. Turanoğlu, B., Akkaya, G.: A new hybrid heuristic algorithm based on bacterial foraging optimization for the dynamic facility layout problem. Expert Syst. Appl. **98**, 93–104 (2018). https://doi.org/10.1016/j.eswa.2018.01.011

29. Demmer, W.A., Vickery, S.K., Calantone, R.: Engendering resilience in small- and medium-sized enterprises (SMEs): a case study of Demmer Corporation. Int. J. Prod. Res. **49**, 5395–5413 (2011). https://doi.org/10.1080/00207543.2011.563903

30. Peng, Y., Zeng, T., Fan, L., Han, Y., Xia, B.: An improved genetic algorithm based robust approach for stochastic dynamic facility layout problem. Discret. Dyn. Nat. Soc. **2018**, e1529058 (2018). https://doi.org/10.1155/2018/1529058

31. Drira, A., Pierreval, H., Hajri-Gabouj, S.: Design of a robust layout with information uncertainty increasing over time: a fuzzy evolutionaryapproach. Eng. Appl. Artif. Intell. **26**, 1052–1060 (2013). https://doi.org/10.1016/j.engappai.2012.12.007

32. Das, K.: Integrating resilience in a supply chain planning model. Int. J. Qual. Rel. Manage. **35**, 570–595 (2018). https://doi.org/10.1108/IJQRM-08-2016-0136

33. Mohtashami, A., Alinezhad, A., Niknamfar, A.: A fuzzy multi-objective model for a cellular manufacturing system with layout designing in a dynamic condition. Int. J. Ind. Syst. Eng. **34**, 514 (2020). https://doi.org/10.1504/IJISE.2020.106086

34. Krishnan, K.K., Mirzaei, S., Venkatasamy, V., Pillai, V.M.: A comprehensive approach to facility layout design and cell formation. Int. J. Adv. Manuf. Technol. **59**, 737–753 (2012). https://doi.org/10.1007/s00170-011-3523-z

35. Sadrzadeh, A.: A genetic algorithm with the heuristic procedure to solve the multi-line layout problem. Comput. Ind. Eng. **62**, 1055–1064 (2012). https://doi.org/10.1016/j.cie.2011.12.033

36. Shirali, G., Mohammadfam, I., Ebrahimipour, V.: A new method for quantitative assessment of resilience engineering by PCA and NT approach: a case study in a process industry. Reliab. Eng. Syst. Saf. **119**, 88–94 (2013). https://doi.org/10.1016/j.ress.2013.05.003

37. Aleksić, A., Stefanović, M., Arsovski, S., Tadić, D.: An assessment of organizational resilience potential in SMEs of the process industry, a fuzzy approach. J. Loss Prev. Process Ind. **26**, 1238–1245 (2013). https://doi.org/10.1016/j.jlp.2013.06.004

Textile Micro, Small and Medium Enterprises (MSME) Layout Dynamics in the Ecuadorian Context

Pablo Flores-Siguenza[1] (ID), Rodrigo Guamán[2] (ID), César Rosero-Mantilla[3,4] (ID),
Lorena Siguenza-Guzman[5,6] (ID), and Diana Jadan-Avilés[2](✉) (ID)

[1] Universidad de Cuenca, Cuenca, Ecuador
[2] Department of Applied Chemistry and Systems of Production, Faculty of Chemical Sciences, Universidad de Cuenca, Cuenca, Ecuador
diana.jadan@ucuenca.edu.ec
[3] Universidad Técnica de Ambato, Ambato, Ecuador
[4] Escuela Politécnica Nacional, Quito, Ecuador
[5] Department of Computer Sciences, Faculty of Engineering, Universidad de Cuenca, Cuenca, Ecuador
[6] Research Centre Accountancy, Faculty of Economics and Business, KU Leuven, Leuven, Belgium

Abstract. Micro, small, and medium enterprises' (MSME) role in developing national economies is critical. These enterprises constantly search for effective tools to improve their production processes. However, methodologies proposed by numerous authors are not explicitly adapted to the size of such companies. MSMEs have been developed according to their specific needs, using particular procedures and adapting to a lack of financial resources to invest in substantial improvements. This study seeks to identify the characteristics, needs, and general context that impact layout planning decisions in textile MSMEs. This work proposes an evaluation tool that has been developed within different stages. These stages included a literature review, validation of the information obtained, and the application of the resulting tool in three case studies of textile MSMEs that face different situations. There are marked differences and similarities in the three textile enterprises, making it possible to identify the most important decisions that should be made when planning the layout for their production processes.

Keywords: Layout distribution · MSME · Ecuadorian context · Textile industry

1 Introduction

When considering business size, micro, small, and medium enterprises (MSMEs) represent 90.89% of the total listed companies in Ecuador, and their sales account for 27.69% of total national sales [1]. Since they constitute such a sizable portion of the national economy, it is essential to improve their efficiency and effectiveness. Therefore, a multidimensional approach is needed to understand the context of Ecuadorian MSMEs.

© Springer Nature Switzerland AG 2022
M. Botto-Tobar et al. (Eds.): ICAT 2021, CCIS 1535, pp. 265–276, 2022.
https://doi.org/10.1007/978-3-031-03884-6_20

Recent research has explored factors benefiting or jeopardizing MSMEs as they search for methods to increase revenue. General studies cite innovation as a factor that enhances MSMEs' growth. Van de Vrande et al. [2] found that small and medium-sized enterprises (SMEs) are increasingly striving to innovate. Furthermore, almost all the reasons cited by SMEs for this innovation are related to the market. To bring their products to the market, SMEs participate in technology collaboration networks [3]. Furthermore, Udriyah et al. [4] state that market orientation and innovation give a clear advantage to SMEs over companies that ignore these two factors. Unfortunately, according to the Global Innovation Index (GII) [5] containing detailed parameters related to innovation in 130 countries, Ecuador is ranked 99th due to weaknesses in private investment, the number of researchers, knowledge creation, patent production, and academia-industry linkage [6]. This is reflected in most SMEs' lack of knowledge about product innovation, information and communications technology (ICT), optimization of raw materials, customer needs, target markets, and marketing methods [7].

The need for innovation and flexibility, coupled with dynamic market demand, short product life cycles, and an increased variety of customized products, are forcing the industry to explore new manufacturing paradigms [8]. Textile manufacturing companies with low productivity, excessive physical space, unnecessary movement, and transportation challenges must use Lean Manufacturing and optimized facility layout to solve these problems [9]. Notably, the correct facility layout significantly impacts the productivity and efficiency of manufacturing systems [10], as scheduling production tasks and the layout of facilities are closely related [11].

Plant layout or plant distribution addresses the physical arrangement of plant elements, including the machines, workstations, storage areas, and shared spaces of a production facility [12]. The four most common layouts in the industry are: products, process, fixed, and manufacturing cells. The goal is to improve conditions in the work area, regardless of the design pattern. Therefore, a Facility Layout Problem (FLP) is defined as locating predetermined facilities in a factory to meet one or more objectives efficiently without violating any constraints [13]. The benefits of applying a plant layout model in SMEs are multiple. They allow optimizing the information flow of materials and people, improving the use of space, achieving flexibility to adapt to external factors, complying with distance and worker safety rules, and improving interaction with the customer [14]. These benefits cannot be achieved without first knowing and studying the context of the companies, including their current needs and the laws and requirements related to the pandemic, all of which would be timely topics of further research about improving the MSMEs' performance.

This study's main objective is to present the characteristics, variables, needs, and the general context influencing the plant layout of textile MSMEs in Ecuador through the analysis of three case studies. This information will be vitally important for researchers and companies to design and successfully implement a plant layout model that meets their needs and generates accurate results. This study is part of the research project "Resilient Plant Layout Model for MSMEs with a focus on productivity and occupational safety". The project aims to create a tool that helps companies to face, adapt, and overcome the negative impacts of the pandemic by discovering critical areas in the plant layout, including indicators of quality, costs, time, and occupational safety. For its execution, it not only considers the indicators of discussed in the broader research literature, but also contextualizes them within the reality of the textile companies in Ecuador.

The document is organized as follows. Section 2 introduces the three case studies. Section 3 describes the study's methods of data collection and analysis. Section 4 presents the main results of the study. Section 5 is a brief general discussion. Section 6 summarizes the main conclusions.

2 Description of the Study Site and Case Studies

The study consists of three case studies of three textile industry companies in Ecuador. For confidentiality reasons, the companies' names have been replaced by C1, C2, and C3. The following is a general overview of these companies.

The first case study is a small family company, "C1", located in Cuenca, Ecuador, which began operation in 2008. With 41 workers, the physical area of the company is 600 square meters in a rented industrial building. All the elements of the plant have been arranged according to the perceived needs of production. The company manufactures around 30 products; the most important are cushions, sheets, comforters, linings, blankets, and bedspreads. The production area is divided into five sections: cutting, sewing, finishing, pre-washing, and packaging.

The second case study refers to a family microenterprise, "C2", located in Cuenca, Ecuador. The company began operation in 1993 and currently has reduced its staff to nine workers because of the COVID-19 pandemic. The company is located on the first floor of an ordinary house and produces leisurewear, mainly men's and women's pajamas.

The third case study is a small company, C3, which has 38 workers in Pelileo, Ecuador. Today, this company is one of the most successful textile enterprises in the region. In addition, sales of its slippers to large chain stores make the company a leader in the leisure footwear market and a prominent employer.

Several similarities exist among these companies. For example, equipment or work processes are arranged according to the steps necessary to manufacture the product. The current plant layout is not based on any specific model but rather on the owners' experience. They configure elements of the plant, seeking to reduce costs and shorten distances, but intuitively, since they lack an objective indicator that quantifies compliance. Their most significant problems are related to the physical space and the lack of information collected.

3 Data Collection and Methodology

The methodology for this study first determined factors that facilitate identifying the layout status of the companies. The four stages of the framework for a plant layout evaluation instrument are shown in Fig. 1.

Data collection's first stage involved a systematic literature review based on the Fink methodology [15] to find tools for assessing plant layout. The research questions in this review were "What are the assessment tools for a plant layout definition?", and "What variables and indices are used in these tools?" The database sources selected for this literature review were Scopus, Web of Science, and Scielo. The keywords and search strings used to answer the research questions were "Plant Layout" AND "Evaluation Tools," "Plant Layout" AND "Assessment Tools," "Plant Layout" AND "Measuring." A total of 777 documents were retrieved in the first instance.

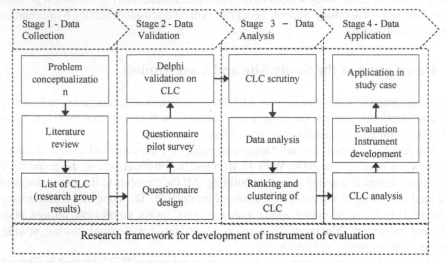

* CLC = Critical Layout Conditions.

Fig. 1. Framework for the plant layout evaluation instrument.

Following Fink's methodology, the inclusion criteria used were 1) articles in Spanish and English, 2) articles from scientific journals, and 3) articles published between 2010 and 2021. The exclusion criteria used were 1) duplicate articles and 2) articles with academic publication comments. After applying these inclusion and exclusion criteria and also after reading metadata like the title, abstract, and the complete document, only 11 articles remained. Restricting search results to assessment tools that were proposed for research in the last ten years dramatically reduced the number of articles. This systematic literature review and the analysis of critical factors influencing any layout [12, 16–18] made it possible to list critical layout conditions (CLC).

The second stage referred to data validation. To this end, an initial questionnaire was developed with nine categories and six Yes or No questions. This questionnaire was validated through a Delphi method, a flexible research helpful practice when there is a lack of knowledge on a given topic [19]. In this validation, experts from other disciplines participated as advisers, raising the total number of participants to 12. In addition, each category was presented with its respective CLC, which allowed participants to evaluate each level of importance.

In the third stage, an analysis of the data obtained with the Delphi method was carried out. An initial matrix was then constructed with response values per category to classify and rank the CLCs. To rank the order the data, averages were normalized, taking into account the percentage coefficient of variation that calculates the relationship between the standard deviation and the absolute average. Values below 30% variation were taken as a reference, which indicates that the responses are homogeneous.

In the fourth and last stage, the application itself, the final evaluation tool was constructed, taking into account the normalized value scores and considering only those CLCs higher than 0.4. Thus, the number of questions in the questionnaire was reduced from 61 to 51. Finally, this final tool was applied to the three case studies.

4 Results

The results are divided into two parts. The first refers to the construction of the evaluation tool, and the second to its application.

First, the plant layout evaluation tool is presented in Appendix A. It has nine categories and 51 Yes or No questions on CLC. It also has a space to verify the availability of evidence. The evaluation tool allows interviewers to make additional comments to expand their previous answers at the end of each category. The tool is easily applied and is based on the current needs of MSMEs. The categories and their corresponding number of questions are presented in Table 1.

Table 1. Categories and their corresponding number of questions of the plant layout evaluation tool.

Category	Number of questions
Type of Plant Layout	5
Facility Layout Problem	7
Plant Layout Objectives	7
Material Factor	5
Machinery Factor	3
Man Factor	6
Movement and Waiting Factor	5
Service Factor	9
Building Factor	4

The second stage was about applying the evaluation tool and the data obtained. The results are presented in three sections: 1) overview of the data by category in each MSME case study, 2) limitation of the indicators used in the plant layout literature and contextualization to the environment, based on the overlaps of the case studies, and 3) summary of the variables and missing information in the case studies to develop a plant layout model.

For the first section, Table 2 and Fig. 2 show the average results of the categories in descending order per MSMEs.

Table 2. Average per category and company of the results obtained.

Category	Average (%) "C1"	Average (%) "C2"	Average (%) "C3"
Service Factor	67	22	100
Building Factor	42	6	100
Plant Layout Objectives	86	71	100
Machinery Factor	33	0	100
Facility Layout Problem	71	71	86
Man Factor	50	33	83
Type of Plant Layout	60	80	40
Material Factor	20	20	20
Movement and Waiting Factor	40	0	20

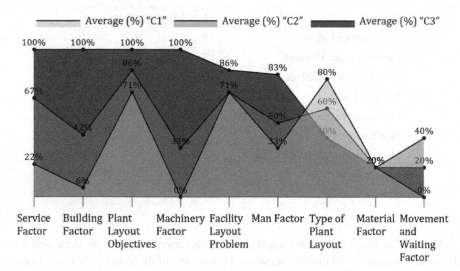

Fig. 2. Average percentage of questions answered positively per category and per company.

As shown in Table 2 and Fig. 2, the company with the most favorable results was C3 because of its order and planning. This is due, above all, to the fact that its building was constructed to satisfy the company's production needs, generating significant advantages for the arrangement of its elements. In addition, C3's current agreements with international brands are another relevant factor driving the company to constantly improve its operations and obtain occupational health and safety certifications. On the other hand, the company with the lowest average is C2, since it is a micro-enterprise that had to adapt to a small first floor of a pre-existing building and has not developed expansion plans.

The three categories that most coincide with compliance by the three companies were 1) plant layout objectives, with the attempt to minimize distances and costs; 2) facility layout problem, with the attempt to optimize multiple objectives, based on experience and needs; and 3) service factor, where they agree that the sanitary, electrical, and lighting installations were in good condition. Conversely, the categories with the most deficiencies that the companies have in common were 1) the material factor and 2) the movement and waiting factor due to the lack of information regarding the characteristics of the materials, operation diagrams, and product flow.

Regarding the second results section, Table 3 limits the literature indicators and contextualizes them to the Ecuadorian environment. In this sense, this table is organized into three categories: area, contextualized area, and variables and indicators. The first category refers to specific characteristics analyzed in the plant layout literature. The

Table 3. Plant layout characteristics contextualized to the Ecuadorian environment.

Area	Area Contextualized	Variables and Indicators
Plant Layout	Plant layout by process	– Grouping of equipment or similar functions – Production moves from one area to another – Similar process stations
Facility layout problem	Unequal areas FLP	– Departments with different dimensions – Departments or areas should not be fractioned
	Quadratic Assignment Problem (QAP)	– Ensure that each installation is assigned a single location
Mathematical models	Multi-objective	– Optimize several objectives simultaneously – Inequality or equality constraints
Objective function	Cost	– Minimize the sum of material handling costs – Minimize the cost of material flow between machines – Minimize labor costs – Maximize profit
	Distance	– Minimize the overall distance between machines – Minimize the overall distance traveled by the material handling device

second category indicates which aspects to focus on, according to the case studies. Finally, the last category deals with variables and indicators found that support the previous decision.

According to Table 3, the type of plant layout that best suits textile MSMEs in Ecuador is "plan layout by process" because there is a wide variety of products. Also, operations of the identical nature and similar machinery need to be grouped, production moves from one area to another, and matching process stations.

After analyzing the case studies' variables and indicators, Ecuadorian textile companies can analyze plant distribution by improving their layout. This proposal can look at an FLP of unequal areas or Quadratic Assignment Problem (QAP). Depending on the complexity of the problem, a multi-objective mathematical model with cost and distance functions can help solve such issues through an exact, heuristic, or metaheuristic approach.

Finally, regarding the second part of the results section, Table 4 summarizes information commonly missing from case studies necessary to develop a plant layout. This table has two categories: distinguishing factors in plant layout and detailing information missing in the case studies.

Table 4. Information missing from the case studies necessary to develop a plant layout.

Factor	Missing information
Material	– Pareto Analysis – Process and flow diagrams – Material handling cost indicators – Waste material and cost indicators – Information of physical and chemical characteristics of all materials – Distance matrix
Machinery	– Information on the physical and technical characteristics of the machinery and tools used
Man	– Information on workers' operating position – Occupational health and safety indicators are not considered – Indicators of occupational risks and number of occupational accidents – Worker training programs
Movement and waiting	– Process operation diagrams – Process analysis diagrams – Product flow diagrams – Material lead time indicators – Flow traffic
Service	– Signaling and continuous improvement plan
Building Factor	– Plans of distribution by work area – Occupied area indicators by zone and total

All information not documented has been considered missing since the companies and production managers are aware of aspects such as leading products, bottlenecks, product flow, and waiting times. Still, no measurement or construction of indicators has yet been proposed to validate their assumptions.

Based on Table 4, little information on the logistics and production processes of the companies can be observed, and no data exists on occupational health and safety, characteristics of the materials and machinery, training, signaling, or environmental plans. All companies in this study lack the necessary resources and knowledge to acquire this type of data, causing their operation and current plant layout to be empirical, based on experience.

5 Discussion

According to Al-Zubaidi et al. [10], simulation technology, flexible manufacturing systems (FMS), and lean manufacturing systems (LMS) have commonly been used to design and solve FLPs. In addition, current facility layout research focuses on the multidimensional issues of dynamic facility design and attempts to change facility design philosophy [10].

Following this trend, the needs identified in this study complement the needs outlined by other researchers when making a multidimensional study. To change the philosophy of facility design, it is necessary to understand the context. Studies of large companies and MSMEs that in many ways are even more complex than large companies, must consider the context to obtain relevant and valuable results.

In this regard, Tayal et al. [20] offer a helpful method to establish an efficient design. The authors argue that the design should consider not only the company's economic benefit but also emphasize social aspects, energy consumption, pollution, and people's safety. The current contextual analysis supports this approach since the three companies in the case studies consider the economic factor and the health and safety of the workers. Moreover, this chaotic time of pandemics only serves to heighten this concern. Therefore, improving the flow of operations, plus surviving and being resilient in the face of current adversities become vital factors to consider in a plant layout model.

The COVID-19 pandemic has generated substantial losses for companies worldwide [21]. In the case studies from this work, two companies had to stop their operations in 2020 for two months, dropping their sales to less than 20% of sales from before the pandemic, which generated an economic deficit that nearly caused the cessation of its operations. Thus, these companies were forced to investigate and apply tools that will enable them to be better prepared to face external factors and guarantee the continuous flow of their operations [22]. They also sought other tools to optimize plant layout, strengthening their production systems and supply chains. To achieve these objectives, companies need the involvement of academia, the presence of more researchers, and above all, helpful laws and economic proposals from governments. All of this will make it possible to resuscitate the productive sectors.

6 Conclusions

The development and application of the plant layout evaluation tool made it possible to meet the study's objective. These three case studies verify the pervasive influence of the context on the layout of Ecuadorian textile manufacturing facilities. Furthermore, it has also been possible to identify these companies' variables and current needs in their day-to-day operations.

Results show that the best-established company is the C3 company. The main reasons are this company's access to more financial resources and their license to produce a worldwide brand of slippers. To produce under this brand, they need to satisfy the conditions stated above. This company scored very high in "Service Factor," "Building Factor," and "Machinery Factor." This also supports current conclusions since such companies must satisfy brand conditions. Other companies would do well to remember this condition.

The factor in which all three companies scored the highest was "plant layout objectives." This shows that despite their size differences, they all share a common goal: continuously improve all layout-related features to reduce costs and save time during production runs.

Conversely, all three companies scored poorly in the "material factor" and the "movement and waiting factor." This may indicate that they do not focus on these issues or simply do not have the tools to collect this information. Therefore, the recommendation is to collect this data by returning to the sites for another period. This will help MSMEs to design layouts that suit their business purposes.

The type of plant layout that most benefits textile MSMEs in Ecuador, according to this study, is the layout by processes since it is adapted to the needs and production characteristics of this type of company. This layout should consider multiple objectives of cost and distance in the mathematical model to cover the owners' demands of the companies, social aspects, pollution, and people's safety.

The study will contribute significantly to the project objective mentioned in the introduction, since the mathematical model of plant layout to be developed in the project will consider not only typical indicators seen in world research literature, but also can contribute complementary, contextualized data and analysis by considering the real needs and characteristics of textile MSMEs in Ecuador, potentially increasing its applicability and generation of successful results.

Finally, the study's limitations include the number of companies involved as case studies. For this reason, it is recommended that for future research, the evaluation tool should be applied to a higher percentage of companies in the area to acquire more data and information and thus generate a robust method to improve the dynamics of distribution.

Acknowledgments. The authors would like to thank to Corporación Ecuatoriana para el Desarrollo de la Investigación y Academia - CEDIA for the financial support given to the present research, development, and innovation work through its CEPRA program, especially for the CEPRA XV-2021-01-Resil-TEX. In addition, this research was partially funded by the University of Cuenca, Technical University of Ambato and University of Azuay.

Appendix A – Plant Layout Evaluation Tool

The plant layout evaluation tool applied in the three case study textile companies can be found online at https://imagineresearch.org/wp-content/uploads/2021/06/RES-Appendix-A-Tool.pdf.

References

1. INEC: Directorio de Empresas y Establecimientos 2019 (2020). https://www.ecuadorencifras.gob.ec/documentos/web-inec/Estadisticas_Economicas/DirectorioEmpresas/Direct orio_Empresas_2019/Principales_Resultados_DIEE_2019.pdf
2. van de Vrande, V., de Jong, J.P.J., Vanhaverbeke, W., de Rochemont, M.: Open innovation in SMEs: trends, motives and management challenges. Technovation **29**, 423–437 (2009). https://doi.org/10.1016/j.technovation.2008.10.001
3. Fernández-Olmos, M., Ramírez-Alesón, M.: How internal and external factors influence the dynamics of SME technology collaboration networks over time. Technovation **64–65**, 16–27 (2017). https://doi.org/10.1016/j.technovation.2017.06.002
4. Udriyah, U., Tham, J., Azam, S.M.: The effects of market orientation and innovation on competitive advantage and business performance of textile SMEs. Manag. Sci. Lett. **9**, 1419–1428 (2019). https://doi.org/10.5267/j.msl.2019.5.009
5. OMPI: Índice Mundial de Innovación 2020: impacto previsto de la pandemia de COVID-19 en la innovación mundial. https://www.wipo.int/pressroom/es/articles/2020/article_0017.html
6. Śledzik, K.: Schumpeter's View on Innovation and Entrepreneurship. SSRN Electron. J. (2013). https://doi.org/10.2139/ssrn.2257783
7. Ramadhan, D.G.: Sofiyanurriyanti: knowledge management as a source of innovation and business process development to improve the competitiveness of small and medium enterprises (SMES) in the madurese handicraft souvenir sector (case study: XYZ souvenir). IOP Conf. Ser. Mater. Sci. Eng. **885**, 012034 (2020). https://doi.org/10.1088/1757-899X/885/1/012034
8. Bortolini, M., Ferrari, E., Galizia, F.G., Mora, C.: Implementation of reconfigurable manufacturing in the Italian context: state-of-the-art and trends. Procedia Manuf. **39**, 591–598 (2019). https://doi.org/10.1016/j.promfg.2020.01.425
9. Ruiz, S., Raymundo, C., Simón, A., Sotelo, F.: Optimized plant distribution and 5S model that allows SMEs to increase productivity in textiles. Enero (2019)
10. Al-Zubaidi, S.Q.D., Fantoni, G., Failli, F.: Analysis of drivers for solving facility layout problems: a Literature review. J. Ind. Inf. Integr. **21**, 100187 (2021). https://doi.org/10.1016/j.jii.2020.100187
11. Ko, C.-H.: Facility layout design – review of current research directions. Eng. Manag. Prod. Serv. **10**, 70–79 (2018). https://doi.org/10.2478/emj-2018-0018
12. Neghabi, H., Eshghi, K., Salmani, M.H.: A new model for robust facility layout problem. Inf. Sci. **278**, 498–509 (2014). https://doi.org/10.1016/j.ins.2014.03.067
13. Salmani, M.H., Eshghi, K., Neghabi, H.: A bi-objective MIP model for facility layout problem in uncertain environment. Int. J. Adv. Manuf. Technol. **81**(9–12), 1563–1575 (2015). https://doi.org/10.1007/s00170-015-7290-0
14. Reddy Gayam, N., Shanmuganandam, K., Vinodh, D.: Layouts in production industries: a review. Mater. Today Proc. (2020). https://doi.org/10.1016/j.matpr.2020.10.191
15. Fink, A.: Conducting Research Literature Reviews: From the Internet to Paper. SAGE Publications, Thousand Oaks (2019)

16. Muther, R.: Distribución en planta. Hispano Europea (1981)
17. Krishnan, K.K., Mirzaei, S., Venkatasamy, V., Pillai, V.M.: A comprehensive approach to facility layout design and cell formation. Int. J. Adv. Manuf. Technol. **59**, 737–753 (2012). https://doi.org/10.1007/s00170-011-3523-z
18. Sharma, P., Singhal, S.: Design and evaluation of layout alternatives to enhance the performance of industry. Opsearch **53**(4), 741–760 (2016). https://doi.org/10.1007/s12597-016-0257-6
19. Skulmoski, G.J., Hartman, F.T., Krahn, J.: The Delphi Method for Graduate Research. J. Inf. Technol. Educ. Res. **6**, 001–021 (2007). https://doi.org/10.28945/199
20. Tayal, A., Solanki, A., Singh, S.P.: Integrated framework for identifying sustainable manufacturing layouts based on big data, machine learning, meta-heuristic and data envelopment analysis. Sustain. Cities Soc. **62**, 102383 (2020). https://doi.org/10.1016/j.scs.2020.102383
21. Ratnasingam, J., et al.: How are small and medium enterprises in Malaysia's furniture industry coping with COVID-19 PANDEMIC early evidences from a survey and recommendations for policymakers. BioResources **15**, 5951–5964 (2020). https://doi.org/10.15376/biores.15.3.5951-5964
22. von Remko, H.: Research opportunities for a more resilient post-COVID-19 supply chain – closing the gap between research findings and industry practice. Int. J. Oper. Prod. Manag. **40**, 341–355 (2020). https://doi.org/10.1108/IJOPM-03-2020-0165

Intelligent Systems

Sentiment Analysis Based on User Opinions on Twitter Using Machine Learning

Jorge Cordero(✉) [ID] and José Bustillos

Universidad Técnica Particular de Loja, San Cayetano Alto, Loja 08544, Ecuador
{Jmcordero,jabustillos}@utpl.edu.ec

Abstract. The growing influence of users on social networks has caused positive and negative content to spread across the Internet. This paper arises from the need to have new tools that allow an analysis of sentiments based on the opinions made by users on the social network Twitter. In particular, the results of identifying the positive and negative opinions issued to a user are presented in order to develop effective communication strategies through social networks.

The results obtained allow decisions to be made to obtain a competitive advantage, evaluating positive opinions or, failing that, identifying negative comments to establish strategies to overcome user dissatisfaction. Sentiment analysis can be performed in several ways; however, to obtain greater precision, naïve bayes classifier was used as a machine learning technique, obtaining an accuracy value of 86.2% in the evaluation of the model.

Keywords: Sentiment analysis · Opinion mining · Machine learning · Natural language processing · Social networks

1 Introduction

Today, Web 5.0 represents a step forward since it involves emotional interactions between people and computers, allowing the Web to recognize the emotions and reactions of these users [1]. In recent years, research on sentiment analysis has increased because organizations value results that reliably reflect user sentiment to make decisions and provide better services. Sentiment analysis is the field of study that analyzes people's opinions, feelings, appreciations, attitudes, and emotions about entities such as products, services, organizations, individuals, issues, events, topics, and their attributes [2, 3]. Likewise, in [4] define sentiment analysis as the process of extracting, identifying, analyzing, and characterizing the feelings or opinions described in textual form using machine learning techniques, natural language processing (NLP), among others. The use of data from social media to drive business intelligence is now of growing interest to both researchers and business owners.

Sentiment analysis applications have been extended to different areas, from services, consumer information, consumer products, marketing, healthcare, social events, political elections, and others [5, 6]. The most common uses of sentiment analysis include the analysis of public opinion [7], market research [8, 9], election predictions [10], and social

© Springer Nature Switzerland AG 2022
M. Botto-Tobar et al. (Eds.): ICAT 2021, CCIS 1535, pp. 279–288, 2022.
https://doi.org/10.1007/978-3-031-03884-6_21

media analysis [11]. The sentiment analysis can help companies determine changes in public opinion regarding their products or company. Researchers extract positive tweets to improve sales forecasts and to increase sales in marketing campaigns.

The purpose of this paper is to analyze the feelings of users of the social network Twitter, identifying in tweets the positive or negative opinions issued towards a user (person, celebrity, organization), in order to know the impact, trends, user comments, and develop effective communication strategies through social networks. For example, identifying positive opinions allows one to obtain a competitive advantage; on the other hand, knowing negative comments allows one to establish plans to overcome that dissatisfaction of the users or customers. The study identifies the strengths and weaknesses of Educational Institution Services based on users' positive and negative responses. In addition, the reports generated by the system can be used as the basis for opportunities, achievements, or marketing strategies.

Twitter is one of the most important social platforms in the world, a social network with 335 million monthly active users generating 500 million tweets daily [12]. In addition, Twitter has become an ideal social network for audience analysis and extraction of information from comments in real-time, using an Application Programming Interface (API) from which Tweets with the content to be analyzed can be extracted. Business owners can utilize platforms like Twitter to learn about their target audience and improve their business processes to meet their needs.

Within machine learning, the most used techniques in sentiment analysis are Naïve Bayes and Support Vector Machine mainly because of the precession of the results. In addition, the Python programming language includes libraries such as Tweepy that are easy-to-use for accessing the Twitter API, TextBlob, and SentiWordnet that allow sentiment analysis. The results can be used by institutions to know the impact, trends, user comments and develop effective communication strategies through social networks.

The rest of the article is divided as follow: in Sect. 2 related work are described, the case study and method implemented are described in Sect. 3, proposed work is described in Sect. 4, the results and discussion are shown in Sect. 5 and, finally, the conclusions and future work are presented in Sect. 6.

2 Related Work

Sentiment analysis itself is a research branch in the Text Mining domain [13, 14], which is gaining popularity. There are several approaches for sentiment analysis: machine learning based approach to classify data; lexicon based approach uses a dictionary containing positive and negative words to determine the sentiment polarity; and hybrid based approach uses a combination of both ML and lexicon based approach for classification [15].

Social networking like Facebook, Twitter, among others, has become one of the key sources of information. It is found that by extracting and analyzing data from social networking sites, a business entity can be benefited from their product marketing. As an example, in [16] the authors use Twitter data to analyze public views towards a product. Firstly, the authors develop an NLP based pre-processed data framework to filter tweets. Secondly, they incorporate Bag of Words (BoW) and Term Frequency-Inverse Document Frequency (TF-IDF) model concepts to analyze sentiment and to classify positive and negative tweets. The simulation results show the efficiency the proposed system, achieving 85.25% accuracy in sentiment analysis using the NLP technique. Likewise, in [17] the authors focuses on various machine learning algorithms which are utilized in the analysis of sentiments and in the mining of reviews in different datasets. In the first phase, they perform the extraction of characteristics from the text and then perform the classification using Naïve Bayes, gradient descent and support vector machines, obtaining results with a percentage higher than 87% for the evaluation metrics.

The methods of sentiment analysis are trained for the detection of sentiment polarity, which can automatically track out sentiments from different documents, blogs, sentences, or words [18, 19]. In [20], the authors present a survey of sentiment analysis approaches, challenges, and trends, to give researchers a global survey on sentiment analysis and its related fields. The paper presents the applications of sentiment analysis and describes the generic process of this task. Then, it reviews, compares, and investigates the used approaches to have an exhaustive view of their advantages and drawbacks.

Other research studies about sentiment analysis done by Herrera-Contreras et al. [21] classify the sentiment of shared publications that have the hashtag "#5G" as positive, negative, or neutral. The authors used Google Cloud AutoML Natural Language Sentiment Analysis and obtained a classification model with accuracy and recall of 80.89%.

Sentiment analysis was also used in several studies [22, 23] to analyze students' attitudes towards various aspects of an institution, i.e., reviews of teaching, tuition fees, financial aid, diversity, etc.

3   Case Study and Methodology

3.1   Case Study

For the development of the web application for sentiment analysis of tweets, the Universidad Técnica Particular de Loja (UTPL) is considered as a case study. Particularly, to research and develop a solution to know the opinion of users about the services and careers offered at the university, in order to identify the polarity of the opinions of users (for or against), in addition to analyzing the levels of satisfaction and acceptance of students and the general public.

3.2   Software Development Methodology

The development of the sentiment analyzer was carried out under agile methodology, in which software development is incremental, cooperative, simple, and adapted [24]. In particular, the agile software development methodology SCRUM was used, which adapts to any type of project, since it has an iterative and incremental project management method, which has the following phases, Product Backlog, Sprint Planning, Daily Scrum, Sprint Review, Sprint Retrospective and Sprint Grooming o Refinement [25].

3.3 Methodology

The sentiment analysis method used in this research is based on a workflow that includes phases such as data extraction, pre-processing, modeling and training, and model evaluation, which are described in more detail in the next section concerning the proposed work.

The pre-processing of text at the tweet level allows transforming the raw text data into a suitable format for the analysis; for this, the following described in [26] must be carried out and which are convert text data to lowercase, remove URLs, hashtags, translator, spell check, remove punctuation, remove stop words, tokenization, and stemming. The programming language Python was used for the development of the model. Python is one of the programming languages with multiple paradigms [8], which support object, procedural, and functional oriented programming.

For modeling and training, with the pre-processed tweets dataset, the dataset is divided into test and training data to run the sentiment classification algorithms and finally use the model evaluation metrics. The metrics used for model evaluation are precision, recall, accuracy, and F1 score.

4 Proposed Work

This section describes the proposed work and focuses on a strategy for analyzing sentiments using data extracted from the social network Twitter. The architecture overview for the sentiment analysis system is presented in Fig. 1. A client/server architecture is used, allowing a relationship between a client and one or more servers, where the client (Frontend) requests services from the server (Backend). The three-tier architecture is characterized by the decomposition of applications, service components and distributed deployment, providing scalability, availability, manageability, and resource utilization.

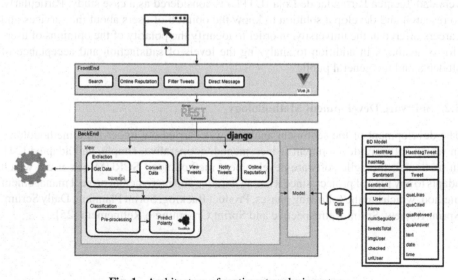

Fig. 1. Architecture of sentiment analysis system.

The backend is responsible for database connection services, business logic, and data processing so that the frontend has the least possible load. The developed proposal is based on three important parts are Data Extraction, Tweets Classification, and Notification Tweets. The data extraction module allows the communication and obtaining of tweets through the Twitter API. To obtain the data, the user enters the application through the web browser activating the "search" function (see Fig. 2), then requests the service from the "extraction" module through the Django Rest API. Frontend development is based on the Vue framework, which provides us with a lightweight virtual DOM that is an essential part where it provides us with a set of object standards to represent HTML, XML, and XHTML documents. In the backend, through the Tweepy library, the data corresponding to the searched word is extracted. The analysis of Twitter data requires a systematic process of collection, processing, and classification [27]. The tweets classification module allows the system to carry out the PLN processes to eliminate the noise that exists in the text and classify them by the type of polarity expressed by the user. TextBlob library for processing textual data. It provides a simple API for diving into common NLP tasks such as part-of-speech tagging, noun phrase extraction, sentiment analysis, classification, and more [28].

In the notification tweets module, the online reputation service and tweets display is executed. The reputation is calculated by means of the amount of positive and negative tweets.

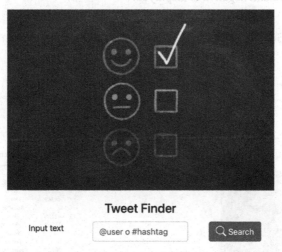

Tweet Finder

Input text   @user o #hashtag   🔍 Search

Fig. 2. Interface search tweets by @user or #hashtag.

For sentiment analysis, the Twitter data uses data extraction, pre-processing (see Fig. 3). Each of these processes has its own algorithm and packages to be processed. Naïve Bayes algorithm is used to find out important words from tweets to predict polarity.

```
⬥ preProcesamiento.py 6 ●    ⬥ predecirPolaridad.py 2                    ▷ ▭ ⋯

analisis-de-sentimientos-backend-feature > sentiTweet > backend > modulos > clasificacion > ⬥ preProcesamiento.py > ...
14    def cleanText(dato):
15    ····c=[]
16    ····# transform emoticons to string
17    ····datos = emoji.demojize(dato, delimiters=(":",":"))
18    ····# remove links, remove hashtag transform to lowercase
19    ····tr = re.sub('http://\S+|https://\S+|#\S+|&\S+|{\S+|@\S+|RT|_\S+', '', datos).lower()
20    ····v = tokenizer.tokenize(tr)
21    ····for i in range(0,len(v)):
22    ········c.append(lemmatizer.lemmatize(v[i]))
23    ····# work with the stop words registered in the corpus in Spanish
24    ····stops = set(stopwords.words('spanish'))
25    ····# remove stop words from text
26    ····words = [w for w in c if not w in stops]
27    ····# return the text with the entire NLP process
28    ····blob = TextBlob(" ".join(words))
29    ····# translate from spanish to english
30    ····ingles = blob.translate(to='en')
31    ····return (ingles)
32

                              Ln 1, Col 21   Spaces: 4   UTF-8   LF   Python   ⌨ ☐
```

Fig. 3. Code of the data preprocessing algorithm.

Figure 4 shows the dashboard with the results of the user's online reputation or the hashtag that was searched, where the total number of tweets classified according to polarity as positive and negative is displayed.

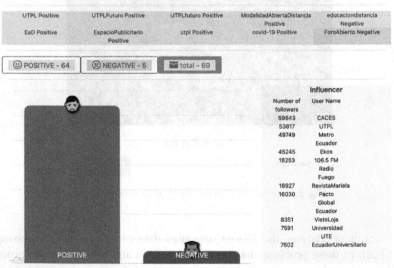

Fig. 4. Dashboard with the results of the user's online reputation.

The sentiment analysis for the case study identified 64 positive tweets and five negative tweets; thus, the positive tweets are 92.8% of the total. The high number of positive tweets indicates positive comments-experiences-opinions. Positive tweets included expressions of gratitude, congratulatory remarks, excitement, self-praise, and words of encouragement. Negative tweets made up a tiny minority of tweets and included mild complaints, reporting of bad news, and social criticism. Negative tweets allow users to identify problems or disagreements.

The general results make it easy to know the polarity; therefore, to obtain more information about positive or negative tweets, you should click on the corresponding option. In addition, the results are complemented by the identification of Twitter influencer's profiles and generate statistical graphs to visualize the number of tweets generated per day.

5 Results and Discussion

The metrics generally used in classification to evaluate the results are precision and recall. They measure the percentage of correct classification and the completeness of the method, respectively. In addition, accuracy and the F1 score were computed.

Table 1. Results of the evaluation metrics for classification model.

Technique	Accuracy	Precision	Recall	F1 score
NB	0.862069	0.721014	0.818182	0.855172
BernoulliNB	0.758621	0.261905	0.333333	0.667586
SVM	0.758621	0.252874	0.333333	0.654496

Table 1 summarizes the results, 'NB' is the technique with a higher F1 Score with a value of 0,86. Figure 5 shows the confusion matrix, where it is observed that most of the classes are well classified because of the NB algorithm performance to classify sentiments.

In general, the results of the metrics were satisfactory, given the difficulty of the problem to determine the polarity in the tweets.

```
Matriz de confusion:
[[ 1  0  0]
 [ 1  3  2]
 [ 0  1 21]]

Precision:
0.7210144927536232

Recall:
0.8181818181818182

Accuracy:  0.8620689655172413

F1:  0.8551724137931034
```

Fig. 5. Confusion matrix of the best result using Naïve Bayes.

6   Conclusions and Future Work

In today's world, institutions positively value research and solutions to analyze opinions. The use of sentiment analysis can play a significant role in automatically understanding people's opinions and using that to improve certain products or services. The results obtained contribute to making decisions, adapting business processes, and understanding the opinions and feelings of users about an institution.

Positive and negative opinions constitute a fundamental role for online reputation management and for measuring the degree of satisfaction; however, the task of identifying sentiment in tweets in Spanish is a complex area of research; few works analyze texts in Spanish.

The use of the Naïve Bayes classifier contributes favorably for sentiment analysis, tweets were correctly classified by their polarity, and an accuracy of 86.2% was obtained.

This research has successfully used textblob to classify tweets, and the researcher has also successfully visualized the data using the web application.

Future work and due to the pandemic, public opinion on e-learning is being investigated to identify problems and potentialities.

References

1. Trunfio, M., Della Lucia, M.: Toward Web 5.0 in Italian regional destination marketing. Symphonya. Emerg. Issues Manag. 60–75 (2017). https://doi.org/10.4468/2016.2.07trunfio. dellalucia
2. Liu, B.: Sentiment analysis and opinion mining. Synth. Lect. Hum. Lang. Technol. **5**, 1–167 (2012)
3. Pak, A., Paroubek, P.: Twitter as a corpus for sentiment analysis and opinion mining. In: LREc, pp. 1320–1326 (2010)
4. Tripathi, G., Naganna, S.: Feature selection and classification approach for sentiment analysis. Mach. Learn. Appl. An Int. J. **2**, 1–16 (2015)
5. Shayaa, S., et al.: Sentiment analysis of big data: methods, applications, and open challenges. IEEE Access. **6**, 37807–37827 (2018)
6. Pozzi, F.A., Fersini, E., Messina, E., Liu, B.: Sentiment Analysis in Social Networks. Morgan Kaufmann, Burlington (2016)

7. Aguilar, J., Téran, O., Sánchez, H., De Mesa, J.G., Cordero, J., Chávez, D.: Towards a fuzzy cognitive map for opinion mining. In: Procedia Computer Science (2017). https://doi.org/10.1016/j.procs.2017.05.287

8. Baj-Rogowska, A.: Sentiment analysis of Facebook posts: the Uber case. In: 2017 Eighth International Conference on Intelligent Computing and Information Systems (ICICIS), pp. 391–395 (2017)

9. Mudinas, A., Zhang, D., Levene, M.: Market trend prediction using sentiment analysis: lessons learned and paths forward. arXiv Prepr. arXiv1903.05440 (2019)

10. Sandoval-Almazan, R., Valle-Cruz, D.: Facebook impact and sentiment analysis on political campaigns. In: Proceedings of the 19th Annual International Conference on Digital Government Research: Governance in the Data Age, pp. 1–7 (2018)

11. Drus, Z., Khalid, H.: Sentiment analysis in social media and its application: systematic literature review. Procedia Comput. Sci. **161**, 707–714 (2019)

12. Petrov, C.: Twitter Statistics (2019)

13. Ravi, K., Ravi, V.: A survey on opinion mining and sentiment analysis: tasks, approaches and applications. Knowl.-Based Syst. **89**, 14–46 (2015)

14. Redhu, S., Srivastava, S., Bansal, B., Gupta, G.: Sentiment analysis using text mining: a review. Int. J. Data Sci. Technol. **4**, 49–53 (2018)

15. Jain, A.P., Dandannavar, P.: Application of machine learning techniques to sentiment analysis. In: 2016 2nd International Conference on Applied and Theoretical Computing and Communication Technology (iCATccT), pp. 628–632 (2016). https://doi.org/10.1109/ICATCCT.2016.7912076

16. Hasan, M.R., Maliha, M., Arifuzzaman, M.: Sentiment analysis with NLP on Twitter data. In: 2019 International Conference on Computer, Communication, Chemical, Materials and Electronic Engineering (IC4ME2), pp. 1–4 (2019). https://doi.org/10.1109/IC4ME247184.2019.9036670

17. Gamal, D., Alfonse, M., El-Horbaty, E.-S.M., M Salem, A.-B.: Analysis of machine learning algorithms for opinion mining in different domains. Mach. Learn. Knowl. Extr. **1**, 224–234 (2019)

18. Fan, Z.-P., Li, G.-M., Liu, Y.: Processes and methods of information fusion for ranking products based on online reviews: an overview. Inf. Fusion. **60**, 87–97 (2020)

19. Serrano-Guerrero, J., Olivas, J.A., Romero, F.P., Herrera-Viedma, E.: Sentiment analysis: a review and comparative analysis of web services. Inf. Sci. (Ny) **311**, 18–38 (2015)

20. Birjali, M., Kasri, M., Beni-Hssane, A.: A comprehensive survey on sentiment analysis: approaches, challenges and trends. Knowl. Based Syst. **226**, 107134 (2021)

21. Herrera-Contreras, A.A., Sánchez-Delacruz, E., Meza-Ruiz, I.V.: Twitter opinion analysis about topic 5G technology. In: Botto-Tobar, M., Zambrano Vizuete, M., Torres-Carrión, P., Montes León, S., Pizarro Vásquez, G., Durakovic, B. (eds.) ICAT 2019. CCIS, vol. 1193, pp. 191–203. Springer, Cham (2020). https://doi.org/10.1007/978-3-030-42517-3_15

22. Sindhu, I., Daudpota, S.M., Badar, K., Bakhtyar, M., Baber, J., Nurunnabi, M.: Aspect-based opinion mining on student's feedback for faculty teaching performance evaluation. IEEE Access. **7**, 108729–108741 (2019)

23. Nikolić, N., Grljević, O., Kovačević, A.: Aspect-based sentiment analysis of reviews in the domain of higher education. Electron. Libr. (2020)

24. Highsmith, J.A., Highsmith, J.: Agile Software Development Ecosystems. Addison-Wesley Professional, Boston (2002)

25. Schwaber, K., Sutherland, J.: La guía de Scrum. Scrumguides. Org. **1**, 21 (2013)

26. Akshay, K., Shivananda, A.: Natural Language Processing Recipes: Unlocking Text Data with Machine Learning and Deep Learning Using Python. Apress, New York (2019)

27. Rivera-Guamán, R.R., Cumbicus-Pineda, O.M., López-Lapo, R.A., Neyra-Romero, L.A.: Sentiment analysis related of international festival of living arts Loja-Ecuador employing knowledge discovery in text. In: Botto-Tobar, M., Montes León, S., Camacho, O., Chávez, D., Torres-Carrión, P., Zambrano Vizuete, M. (eds.) ICAT 2020. CCIS, vol. 1388, pp. 327–339. Springer, Cham (2021). https://doi.org/10.1007/978-3-030-71503-8_25
28. Kunal, S., Saha, A., Varma, A., Tiwari, V.: Textual dissection of live Twitter reviews using naive Bayes. Procedia Comput. Sci. **132**, 307–313 (2018)

Topic Modeling for Automatically Identification of STEM Barriers

Ximena Briceño, Ruth Reátegui[✉][iD], and Janneth Chicaiza[iD]

Universidad Técnica Particular de Loja, Loja, Ecuador
{xmbriceno,rmreategui,jachicaiza}@utpl.edu.ec

Abstract. Topic modeling allows identifying topics automatically from a set of documents. Latent Dirichlet Allocation (LDA) is an algorithm widely used to perform topic modeling. This research applied LDA to identify topics from digital scientific articles that face barriers in STEM fields. Since gender imbalances unfavourable for women have been demonstrated in numerous studies, we created a corpus based on abstracts of papers indexed by Scopus and published between 2000 to 2020. To address the search, we used some keywords related to STEM, women, barriers and gender; as a result, we collected 141 abstracts of digital articles. Then, we apply some techniques to prepare the text and create a computable representation of each abstract. After classifying the data and finding the most important topics, the LDA learning algorithm analysed the dataset. Finally, to identify the best experiment, we used the values of coherence and the distance inter-topic. Results reveal that discovered topics are related to gender differences that make women gaps in STEM careers and works, initiatives to improve gender diversity in STEM faculties, barriers and gender differences in areas like software and industry, factors that could favour women access to STEM disciplines and models or programs to improve the access of women STEM fields.

Keywords: Topic modeling · LDA · STEM · Women

1 Introduction

Despite the increase of women's participation in science and the workforce [1], the growing trend does not seem to be universal across fields and countries. More precisely, in STEM (Science, Technology, Engineering, and Mathematics) fields, women perform activities in fewer numbers than men [2]. Gender imbalances unfavourable for women have been demonstrated in numerous studies [3,4]. For example, in [5], the authors state that women represent only one-sixth of research workers in the private sector and one-third of the entire community of academic staff, though their representation has increased over time. Although there is no consensus on the reasons for women underrepresentation [6], it is clear that there are some barriers that limit women's progress. Thus, to break down barriers that

© Springer Nature Switzerland AG 2022
M. Botto-Tobar et al. (Eds.): ICAT 2021, CCIS 1535, pp. 289–300, 2022.
https://doi.org/10.1007/978-3-031-03884-6_22

prevent women's participation in STEM fields, it is vital to make visible and understand what systemic barriers exist.

On the other hand, topic modelling allows automatically extract themes from a set of documents. Latent Dirichlet Allocation (LDA) is a topic modeling algorithm where documents are represented as random mixtures over latent topics, and each topic is characterized by a distribution over words [7]. LDA has been used in some research to identify topics from scientific articles; for example, in [8] the authors used LDA to describe research profiles based on the topics extracted from their articles' abstract. This work used the topics and the language models of the unseen articles to make recommendations. Furthermore, [9] applied different topic modeling algorithms such as LDA, CTM, hierarchical LDA, and HDP, in a set of different articles' abstracts to subsequently clustering papers of the same field. Likewise, [10] present a framework to use topic modeling on a large collection of papers. More recent works also applied topic modeling to analyse scientific articles such as [11] where explore the thematic trend of Iranian articles in Library and Information Science, and [12] applied topic modeling and LDA algorithm to identify global research trends in AI in education.

In this research, we present the application of topic modeling and LDA algorithm to identify barriers that women face in STEM fields. The section Methodology describes the process carried out to create the corpus, the text processing process, the document representation and the LDA experiments. The following section details the experiment result and the validation process. Finally, some conclusions are presented.

2   Methodology

To identify topics about STEM, women and barriers in articles published, in this work, four steps shown in Fig. 1 were done.

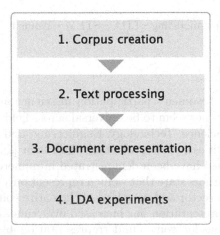

Fig. 1. Methodology for topic modeling.

2.1 Corpus Creation

We used the Scopus scientific database to find scientific articles and download their metadata. To identify candidate articles, we searched within article titles, abstracts and keywords by using keywords like STEM, women STEM, STEM barriers, gender barriers, gender disparities or gender bias. Also, words like student, students and stem cell were excluded.

The search returned 228 articles and scanning their titles manually to discard some of them that use the word stem to refer to a part of a plant. As a result, we selected 141 documents that were a part of the final corpus. For each document, we extracted the article's title, author(s), year of publication, issue, DOI, download link, abstract and keywords. In the following stages, the abstracts will be used to find the topics, and the titles will be considered for the validation process.

2.2 Text Processing

Text processing is carried out with several steps: tokenization, removal of stop words and lemmatization. All these tasks have the objective of eliminating and normalizing the information before use the LDA algorithm. We also worked with bigrams, which are two words that appear together frequently in a document. Once the processing was done, it was possible to visualize some of the most common words, see Fig. 2.

Fig. 2. Most common words.

2.3 Documents Representation

This step refers to a vector representation of the text. We analyse and perform different tests to define how the data will be represented after processing. The documents' representation was created using bag of words and TF-IDF matrix (Term Frequency - Inverse Document Frequency).

In Bag of words, the text is represented as a messy collection of words, regardless of grammar and even word order. In the case of text classification, a word in a document has a weight according to its frequency in the document and the frequency between different documents. The words together with their weights form BoW.

TF-IDF is one of the most widely used weighting schemes to convert a document into a structured format. It is a numerical value to reflect the importance of a word for a document in a collection or corpus. The TF-IDF value increases proportionally to the number of times a word appears in the document.

After executing this step, the following four matrices were generated:

- Bow of words
- Bow of words with bigrams
- TF-IDF matrix
- TF-IDF matrix with bigrams

Furthermore, the number of features in matrices was reduced by eliminating the less frequent tokens, in other words, features that appear in less than 5 documents were eliminated.

2.4   LDA Experiments

LDA algorithm was applied to find topics. In addition, it was configured the following hyperparameters that affect the dispersion of the topics [13]:

- Alpha represents the document-subject density. A higher alpha results in a more specific topic distribution per document. The default value is 0.1.
- Beta represents the topic-words density. A high beta results in a more specific word distribution per topic. The default value is 0.1.

Within experimentation, one of the important steps is to identify the optimal number of topics k. This value identified the optimal value of k topics that will characterize the model. It does not mean that the exact value of the k topics will be obtained, but this value gives an approximation to k [14]. In this work, we used the coherence metric and Inter-topic distance map to identify the k value:

- Coherence: Coherent topics must contain words that coexist in the same documents within the collection. The overall coherence for an LDA model can be calculated as the arithmetic mean of the k topics' coherence. Topic coherence sum the pairwise distribution similarity for the most probable words in the topic [15].
- Intertopic distance map: It help users to interpret topics in a topic model. The package used is PyLDAvis, which extracts information from an LDA topic model fitted to an interactive web-based informational visualization [16].

3   Results

Considering the four matrices mentioned above, some experiments using LDA with a number of topics around 10 were done. Two experiments were selected as best result:

– LDA applied to matrix TF-IDF with 5 topics with a coherence value of 0.48
– LDA applied to matrix TF-IDF with 4 topics. This matrix has unigrams and bigrams with a coherence value of 0.49

The selection was made based on the coherences value and the intertopics distance map. A finally selection was made after inspecting the word distribution in each topic. We preferred topics that contain different words between them. Figure 3 and 4 show the intertopic distance map.

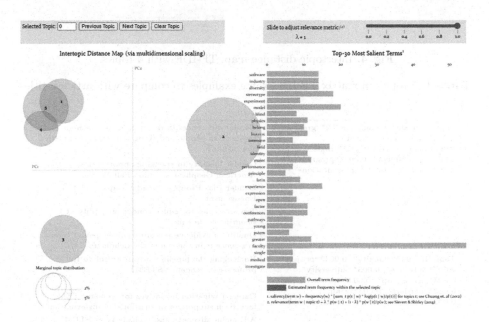

Fig. 3. Intertopic distance map, TF-IDF with 5 topics

Also, column 1, in Table 1 and 2, shows the words and their weight for each topics in experiments 1 and 2, respectively.

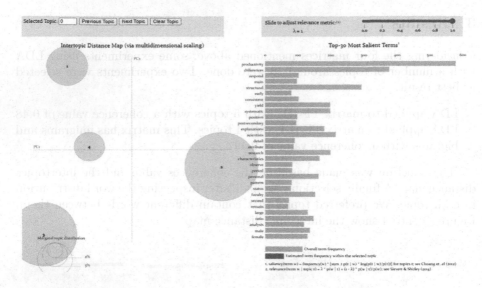

Fig. 4. Intertopic distance map, TF-IDF with 4 topics

Table 1. 5 topics in matrix TF-IDF, some examples to compare with articles' titles

Topics	Titles
Topic 0: 0.002*"belong", 0.002*"greater", 0.002*"bias", 0.002*"field", 0.002*"experience", 0.002*"single", 0.002*"experiment", 0.002*"program", 0.002*"female", 0.002*"presentations"	Gender differences in research areas, methods and topics: Can people and thing orientations explain the results?
	Gender inequity in speaking opportunities at the American Geophysical Union Fall Meeting
	Gender Bias Produces Gender Gaps in STEM Engagement
	Ten strategies to reduce gender inequality at scientific conferences
	Quality of evidence revealing subtle gender biases in science is in the eye of the beholder
Topic 1: 0.007*"faculty", 0.004*"project", 0.003*"advance", 0.003*"university", 0.003*"leadership", 0.003*"advancement", 0.003*"barriers", 0.003*"grant", 0.002*"workshop", 0.002*"institutional"	Unclogging the pipeline: advancement to full professor in academic STEM
	Career navigation initiatives for women STEM faculty in support of institutional transformation
	Advancing diversity and inclusivity in STEM education
	Improving gender disparity in scholarship programs for secondary-level mathematics teachers
	Gender diversity strategy in academic departments: exploring organizational determinants

(continued)

Table 1. (*continued*)

Topics	Titles
Topic 2: 0.003*"software", 0.003*"industry", 0.002*"interest", 0.002*"diversity", 0.002*"program", 0.002*"identity", 0.002*"bias", 0.002*"expression", 0.002*"differences", 0.002*"model"	The Underrepresentation of Women in the Software Industry: Thoughts from Career-Changing Women
	Examining Unequal Gender Distribution in Software Engineering
	Double isolation: Identity expression threat predicts greater gender disparities in computer science
	Opportunities for gender equality in industry (energy, chemical, manufacturing, engineering): Promoting non-gendered attitudes and practices
Topic 3: 0.003*"stereotype", 0.002*"diversity", 0.002*"performance", 0.002*"blind", 0.002*"physics", 0.002*"principle", 0.002*"experiment", 0.002*"implications", 0.002*"open", 0.002*"factor"	"I'm Not a Science Nerd!": STEM Stereotypes, Identity, and Motivation Among Undergraduate Women
	Teaching accreditation exams reveal grading biases favour women in male-dominated disciplines in France
	Computing whether she belongs: Stereotypes undermine girls' interest and sense of belonging in computer science
	Open peer review for evaluating academic legal publications: The "antidote" to an "ill" blind peer review?
	Do quotas help women to climb the career ladder? A laboratory experiment
Topic 4: 0.003*"model", 0.002* "major", 0.002*"math", 0.002*"intensive", 0.002*"mentor", 0.002*" stereotype", 0.002*"pstem", 0.002*"labor", 0.002*"peer", 0.002*"self"	A Model of Threatening Academic Environments Predicts Women STEM Majors' Self-Esteem and Engagement in STEM
	Steps to improve gender diversity in coastal geoscience and engineering
	STEM success expectancies and achievement among women in STEM majors
	A Goal Congruity Model of Role Entry, Engagement, and Exit: Understanding Communal Goal Processes in STEM Gender Gaps
	Modeling the career pathways of women STEM faculty through oral histories and participatory research methods

Table 2. 4 topics in matrix TF-IDF, some examples to compare with articles' titles

Topics	Titles
Topic 0: 0.046*"consistent", 0.044*"position", 0.042*"postsecondary", 0.040*"detail", 0.039*"attribute", 0.037*"observe", 0.037*"period", 0.036*"pattern", 0.035*"status", 0.032*"second"	For female leaders of tomorrow: Cultivate an interdisciplinary mindset
	Social cognitive perspective of gender disparities in undergraduate physics
	Understanding how lifelong learning shapes the career trajectories of women with STEM doctorates: The life experiences and role negotiations (LEARN) model
	Do quotas help women to climb the career ladder? A laboratory experiment
	Teaching accreditation exams reveal grading biases favour women in male-dominated disciplines in France
Topic 1: 0.085*"productivity", 0.056*"differences", 0.043*"structural", 0.032*"scientists", 0.029*"research", 0.022*"ratio", 0.020*"male", 0.019*"female", 0.018*"empirical", 0.018*"lower"	Women's experiences in early physical anthropology
	Gender differences in research areas, methods and topics: Can people and thing orientations explain the results?
	The cases for and against double-blind Reviews
	Unclogging the pipeline: advancement to full professor in academic STEM
	Gender Stereotypes Influence How People Explain Gender Disparities in the Workplace
	Gender differences in the early employment outcomes of STEM doctorates
	Examining Unequal Gender Distribution in Software Engineering
Topic 2: 0.034*"yield", 0.034*"systematic", 0.031*"explanations", 0.029*"characteristics", 0.028*"personal", 0.026*"faculty", 0.023*"large", 0.020*"analysis", 0.015*"data", 0.014*"result"	Ten strategies to reduce gender inequality at scientific conferences
	Best Practices to Achieve Gender Parity: Lessons Learned from NSF's Advance and Similar Programs
	Steps to improve gender diversity in coastal geoscience and engineering
	The role of women software communities in attracting more women to the software industry
	Successful leadership development for women STEM faculty
Topic 3: 0.084*"respond", 0.079*"main", 0.065*"early", 0.012*"school", 0.012*"discipline", 0.011*"high", 0.008*"college", 0.008*"gendered", 0.008*"class", 0.008*"labor"	Fairness to gifted girls: Admissions to new york city's elite public high schools
	The downside of good peers: How classroom composition differentially affects men's and women's STEM persistence

Furthermore, Fig. 5 and 6 present a visual representation of words in each topic for experiment 1 and 2, respectively.

Fig. 5. 5 topics in matrix TF-IDF

3.1 Validation

LDA algorithm gives two main results: 1) topics with their relevant words, and 2) relevant topics per each abstract within the corpus. Experiment 1 had the best distribution of topics per abstract. Considering the topic, with the highest weight, assigned to abstracts, the distribution was as follows: topic 0 was assigned to 24 abstracts, topic 1 was assigned to 41 abstracts, topic 2 was assigned to 30 abstracts, topic 3 was assigned to 19 abstracts, and topic 4 was assigned to 27 abstracts. Also, the Fig. 7 shows the words count of relevant terms in each of the 5 topics.

- Topic 0 refers to articles that analyse gender differences that provoke women gaps in STEM careers and works.
- Topic 1 refers to articles related to initiatives to improve gender diversity in STEM faculties. Also some articles refer to gender barriers in STEMS faculties.
- Topic 2 refers to abstracts related to barriers and gender differences in areas like software and industry.
- Topic 3 refers to abstracts related to factors that could favour women access to STEM disciplines.

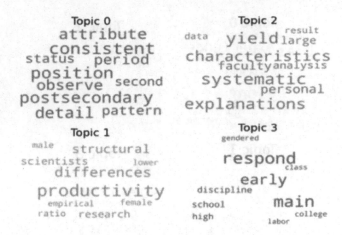

Fig. 6. 4 topics in matrix TF-IDF

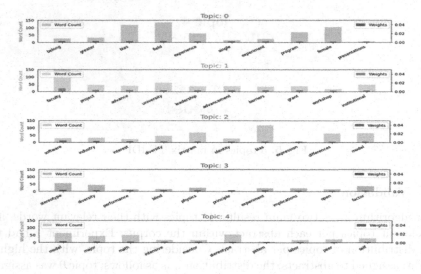

Fig. 7. Word count of terms in 5 topics

– Topic 4 refers to abstracts related to models or programs to improve the access of women STEM fields.

Experiment 2 had the following distribution of topics per abstract considering the topic with the highest weight: topic 0 was assigned to 6 abstracts, topic 1 was assigned to 77 abstracts, topic 2 was assigned to 56 abstracts, and topic 3 was assigned to 2 abstracts.

– Topic 0 refers to abstracts related with interventions or model to favour women in STEMS careers. Also, some documents deal with gender disparities.

- Topic 1 refers to abstracts related to the gender disparities within some professional STEM careers. Many documents refer to women in research activities.
- Topic 2 refers to abstracts related with strategies, best practices, and models to reduce gender inequalities.
- Topic 3 refers to abstracts that analyse how the admission test and enrolment process influence the under-representation of women in STEM disciplines.

Furthermore, we manually compared the dominant topic assigned to some abstracts with the content of their titles. Here, it is important to remember that the LDA algorithm was carried out with abstracts. Column 2, in Tables 1 and 2, shows some examples of titles for experiments 1 and 2 respectively. As we can see, the titles correspond with some words in the topics and with the meaning of the topic.

4 Conclusions

The coherence metric, the intertopic distance map, and the distribution of words in topics, are necessary for selecting the LDA result with the most interpretable topics. We select the LDA results, obtained from matrix TF-IDF with five topics, as the most representative and descriptive for the abstracts in the corpus. Results show topics of different women STEM barriers such as gender differences in careers and works, barriers and gender differences in fields like software and industry. Also, topics show initiatives to improve gender diversity in STEM faculties, factors that could favour women access to STEM disciplines, and models or programs to improve the access of women STEM fields. This research was focus on STEM barriers that woman face as a professionals, therefore, barriers in the education of girls and women in STEM fields could be analysed in a future work.

References

1. Holman, L., Stuart-Fox, D., Hauser, C.E.: The gender gap in science: how long until women are equally represented? PLOS Biol. **16**(4), e2004956 (2018)
2. Chicaiza, J., Reategui, R.: Ecuadorian scholarly production in computer science analysis of publication patterns by gender. In: Paper presented at the CEUR Workshop Proceedings, vol. 2709, pp. 105–115 (2020)
3. Huang, J., Gates, A., Sinatra, R., Barabási, A.L.: Historical comparison of gender inequality in scientific careers across countries and disciplines. In: Proceedings of the National Academy of Sciences Mar 2020, vol. 117 (9), pp. 4609–4616 (2020)
4. Nourmohammadi, H., Hodaei, F.: Perspective of Iranian women's scientific production in high priority fields of science and technology. Scientometrics **98**, 1455–1471 (2014)
5. Abramo, G., D'Angelo, C.A., Caprasecca, A.: Gender differences in research productivity: a bibliometric analysis of the Italian academic system. Scientometrics **79**, 517–539 (2009)
6. Larivière, Ni., C, Gingras, Y., et al.: Bibliometrics: global gender disparities in science. Nature **504**, 211–213 (2013)

7. Blei, D.M., Ng, A.Y., Jordan, M.I.: Latent Dirichlet allocation. J. Mach. Learn. Res. **3**(4–5), 993–1022 (2003)
8. Amami, M., Pasi, G., Stella, F., Faiz, R.: An LDA-based approach to scientific paper recommendation. Lecture Notes in Computer Science (Including Subseries Lecture Notes in Artificial Intelligence and Lecture Notes in Bioinformatics), vol. 9612, pp. 200–210 (2016)
9. Yau, C.-K., Porter, A., Newman, N., Suominen, A.: Clustering scientific documents with topic modeling. Scientometrics **100**(3), 767–786 (2014). https://doi.org/10. 1007/s11192-014-1321-8
10. Asmussen, C.B., Møller, C.: Smart literature review: a practical topic modelling approach to exploratory literature review. J. Big Data **6**(1), 1–18 (2019). https:// doi.org/10.1186/s40537-019-0255-7
11. Baghmohammad, M., Mansouri, A., CheshmehSohrabi, M.: Identification of topic development process of knowledge and information science field based on the topic modeling (LDA). Iranian J. Inf. Process. Manage. **36**(2), 297–328 (2021)
12. Paek, S., Kim, N.: Analysis of worldwide research trends on the impact of artificial intelligence in education. Sustainability (Switzerland), **13**(14), 7941 (2021)
13. Panichella, A.: A systematic comparison of search-based approaches for LDA hyperparameter tuning. Inf. Softw. Technol. **130**, 106411 (2021)
14. Hofmann, M., Chisholm, A.: Text mining and visualization: case studies using open-source tools, vol. 40. CRC Press, Boca Raton (2016)
15. Mimno, D., Wallach, H.M., Talley, E., Leenders, M., McCallum, A.: Optimizing semantic coherence in topic models. In: EMNLP 2011 - Conference on Empirical Methods in Natural Language Processing, Proceedings of the Conference, pp. 262–272 (2011)
16. Mabey, B.: pyLDAvis Documentation. https://pyldavis.readthedocs.io/en/latest/readme.html. Accessed 10 Aug 2021

Demand Forecasting for Textile Products Using Machine Learning Methods

Héctor Medina[1]⬛, Mario Peña[2,5]⬛, Lorena Siguenza-Guzman[3,4]⬛, and Rodrigo Guamán[5(✉)]⬛

[1] Faculty of Chemical Sciences, University of Cuenca, 010107 Cuenca, Ecuador
hector.medina@ucuenca.edu.ec
[2] Research Department (DIUC), University of Cuenca, 010107 Cuenca, Ecuador
mario.penao@ucuenca.edu.ec
[3] Department of Computer Sciences, Faculty of Engineering, University of Cuenca, 010107 Cuenca, Ecuador
lorena.siguenza@ucuenca.edu.ec
[4] Research Centre Accountancy, Faculty of Economics and Business, KU Leuven, Leuven, Belgium
[5] Department of Applied Chemistry and Systems of Production, Faculty of Chemical Sciences, University of Cuenca, 010107 Cuenca, Ecuador
rodrigo.guaman@ucuenca.edu.ec

Abstract. Due to its close relationship with various operational decisions, market demand forecasting has been considered one of the essential activities in all organizations. Unfortunately, the textile industry has been the most difficulty generating forecasts, mainly due to the volatility caused in the market by short product life cycles, special events, and competitions. From the beginning, forecasting has been using traditional statistical methods. However, the increasing use of artificial intelligence has opened a new catalog of prediction methods currently being studied for their high precision. This study explores machine learning (ML) as a tool to generate forecasts for the textile industry, applying regression-focused algorithms such as Linear Regression, Ridge, Lasso, K-nearest neighbor, Support Vector Regression (SVR), and Random Forest (RF). To this end, time series were used as inputs for the models, supported by external variables such as Google Trends and special events. The results show that ML as a prediction method has higher precision than purely statistical basic prediction models. Additionally, SVR and Ridge models obtain a lower error in metrics such as MSE (0.09787 and 0.09682), RMSE (0.31285 and 0.31117), and RSE (0.32977 and 0.32800), respectively. Meanwhile, Google Trends reduces the MSE error by 2% and 15%, RMSE 1% and 7% and, RSE 1% and 7% for SVR and Ridge models, respectively.

Keywords: Demand forecast · Machine learning · Textile industry · Google trends

© Springer Nature Switzerland AG 2022
M. Botto-Tobar et al. (Eds.): ICAT 2021, CCIS 1535, pp. 301–315, 2022.
https://doi.org/10.1007/978-3-031-03884-6_23

1   Introduction

The generation of product demand forecasts has acquired a vital role in planning activities in organizations [1], offering efficient management in the supply chain (SC). Fumi [2] explains that forecasting accuracy partly affects all levels of an organization, especially the person in charge of production; thus, it unbalances SC management. This has generated that organizations give a more important focus to the precision in their demand forecasts, using various methods and evaluating each of them to estimate the one that best suits their situation. Over time, many methods have been developed to predict future events, from traditional statistical techniques to artificial intelligence (AI), each with its respective limitations and drawbacks [3]. One of the solutions that have been used to correct the deficiencies of statistical models is the application of hybrid models. The AI application has developed the Machine Learning (ML) subcategory to solve prediction or classification problems. According to Seçkin [4], time series prediction can be modeled as supervised learning. In this manner, when new data is added, the model can predict the target variable from the most recent data.

According to Desore and Narula [5], the textile industry is one of the most impressive industries, contributing approximately 7% of exports worldwide. In recent years, various researchers have been working on forecasts focused on the textile sector. These authors have used purely statistical hybrid or ML methods. Such is a case that refers to a textile glove industry, in which Seçkin [4] found that the use of the Random Forest method provides better results. In a textile dyeing-finishing factory, Sabir and Esma [6] found that the Winters Method used in demand for seasonal patterns brings advantages over the Exponential Smoothing Method. Therefore, there is no absolute model applied to all textile industries due to various approaches or handling different types of data used. According to the literary review compiled by Liu [3], the lack of research on purely statistical methods to generate demand forecasts maybe because these methods do not produce satisfactory results and the growing trend towards ML and hybrid approaches.

One of the common challenges for many researchers in forecasting demand lies in its volatility and its consequences to predictive models. This volatility originates from the market and the interaction of customers with it. For example, Nenni et al. [1] have related the demand in the textile sector market as chaos due to increased purchase impulse, high volatility, low predictability, great variety of products, and significant variance in demand. Fumi [2] and Teucke [7] argue that the intervention of external factors considerably affects the precision of the forecast, especially those with purely statistical models. To understand the volatile market, the need arises to understand the consumer, i.e., their tastes, preferences, and interaction with the products on the market. Today one of the traditional manners of carrying out this task is to apply satisfaction surveys and interviews. However, with the growing use of web domains such as sales pages, social networks, and search engines, a new manner of understanding the tastes and needs of consumers is emerging. Today, information mining on websites has allowed companies to obtain real-time information on customer activity and plan their strategies to provide the goods or services that the customer requires.

Although multiple forecasting models have been developed over time in the textile area, this article proposes implementing external open access data sources as support variables for the traditional forecast by historical records through machine learning. This increases the precision of the results; thus, small and medium sized enterprises (SMEs) have greater security to apply the proposed models in their respective situations. This situation suggests analyzing various methods of forecasting demand for the textile sector, which can take advantage of data from social networks or the web in general. Therefore, this article evaluates various ML methods for forecasting demand for textile products and using data from Google trends to improve the accuracy of the results. This article is structured as follows. Section 2 reviews the rationale for the proposed work. Section 3 presents the proposed methodology. Section 4 shows the application of the method and the results obtained in a case study related to the textile sector. And finally, Sect. 5 concludes the work.

2   Literature Review

The generation of demand forecasts has become a critical piece within organizations when planning various parts of the SC [8]. As Sabir and Esma [6] explain, the demand forecast can be classified into many criteria. However, one of the most common is time horizons in the prediction. This classification consists of the very short-term forecast, short-term forecast, mid-term forecast, and long-term forecast. Each of them is differentiated by the time horizon: daily-weekly, from three months to six months, from six months to five years, and, finally, from five years onwards. The selection of a time horizon is considered a fundamental part of any prediction model since as the prediction horizon grows, the values obtained by the prediction models generate a more significant uncertainty. This effect is strongly affected in the amount of data since the uncertainty in the results grows with a smaller amount.

Generally, a demand forecasting model can be univariate or multivariate. In the former, the only variable present is demand, and, at the same time, this variable must be represented as a time series to be introduced in a prediction model. In the latter, in addition to the demand variable, other variables can be introduced whose function will support the model and will better fit the data. For example, it is expected that there are a large number of variables in the textile sector that accompany the demand for products. Thus, several researchers evaluate each of them and select the most representative. For instance, Loureiro [9] opts to use the variables type store, level of expectation, fashion, and segment for its predictive models. The author finds the results promising across artificial neural networks (ANN), establishing that neural networks are beneficial in small data sets. In a similar study in the textile sector carried out by Tanaka [10], the size and color of their products are chosen as support variables.

A report by Liu [3], compiling several case studies in the generation of demand forecasts in the textile sector, highlights the use of hybrid forecasting methods, in addition to those focused on AI such as Fuzzy, ANN, and Decision Tree, above purely statistical methods. In contrast, Loureiro [9] finds that methods such as ARIMA, SARIMA, exponential smoothing, regression, Box-Jenkins, and Holt-Winters have been the most used statistical methods through the years. However, although there has been a great use of statistical methods in generating forecasts, they present several limitations, such as the absolute use of quantitative data. One of the limitations that have been incurred in various forecasting models is time and results. Statistical models work efficiently and quickly, while ML models integrate a large amount of additional information and, besides, require significant periods [4]. Another limitation is the nature of the data. Statistical models such as exponential smoothing work with data that behaves smoothly and with little noise. In contrast, ML models adapt the distortions and noise of the data to the training prediction models [1].

Kück and Freitag [11] address similar studies focused on predicting demand in the textile sector, whose study explores the use of the Knn (K-nearest neighbor) model as a demand prediction method. Likewise, Teucke [7] analyzes a case of the textile industry and the forecasting of a certain number of products, using the Support Vector Machine algorithm, SVM, as a prediction model. Both studies found that ML algorithms have outperformed statistical models, generating a relatively low mean error. In studies related to forecasting, but in other areas, they have shown particular situations. For example, Peña et al. [12], in research related to the area of Hydrology, point out that once the data obtain a chaotic behavior, linear models such as SVM (with the linear kernel) and linear models are not capable of capture this variation and generate poor predictions.

The ML has been used in different fields over the years; however, it has been widely used in recent times, especially in forecasting. Such is the case that its use by Şahin et al. [13], in the forecast of electricity generation in Europe during the pandemic period caused by Covid-19, finding that the use of ML provides reliable results and with a certain degree of security. Furthermore, in a study focused on forecasting the price of copper monthly, Zhang et al. [14] found that the use of ML and especially the MLP (multi-layer perceptron) neuronal network provides results with a lower amount of error and high stability compared to SVM, RF, KNN, and GBT (gradient boosting tree) models. Moreover, in a study developed to generate a predictive model for solar thermal energy systems, Ahmad et al. [15] analyze models of SVR, RF, extra trees, and regression trees, finding that the models based on trees allowed a higher performance in predicting the hourly use of solar thermal energy since they presented lower RMSE values. Finally, Mei et al. [16] analyze the use of RF in the forecast of prices in the electricity market in New York, finding that the model provides acceptable confidence intervals with the prediction and a possibility to update observations as new are incorporated.

3   Materials and Methods

For all prediction models, data processing is a critical part to take into account. This procedure consists of cleaning and adapting the data to serve as suitable inputs for a ML model. Insufficient quality data entered in a ML algorithm can cause erroneous results during the forecasting procedure. For instance, outliers are taken into account in this process so that they are identified and replaced by their respective corrections, in the same manner with missing values, filled by imputation techniques.

The forecast generated has been developed, as shown in Fig. 1. First, the missing data in the data set was imputed (Figs. 1, 3.1). Second, detection and correction of outliers were performed (Figs. 1, 3.2). Third, the models to be implemented were defined (Figs. 1, 3.3), accompanied by their respective tuning of hyperparameters (Figs. 1, 3.4). Finally, the results were evaluated with certain error metrics (Figs. 1, 3.5), and those models with the highest performance were selected.

3.1 Data Imputation

An imputation process is carried out when missing values harm a forecast model, as many do not accept empty values. There are two options to deal with this drawback. The first and simplest is to remove these samples, reducing the total amount of data to be entered in the predictive model. The second option is to generate data that replaces the empty values to avoid shrinking the data set. With a limited number of data, the most viable option is to attribute the blank values.

There are various forms of the imputation of quantitative data from statistical methods such as replacement by the mean, median, or mode to those using ML algorithms. The methods based on the interpolation of values present a viable alternative to impute data in a time series, with several rolling mean, linear interpolation, poly interpolation, and spline interpolation. However, ML methods are recommended for their versatility and flexibility in learning and prediction for interpolating supporting variables after interpolating the target variable. Using ML-focused imputation methods, such as MissForest, is possible as long as at least two variables, where the missing values in one, are not the same as in the second variable. Opting for the use of ML, the MissForest method was used, which is based on decision trees and has excellent versatility and successful results. According to Stekhoven and Bühlmann [17], the use of MissForest as an imputation technique shows good performance in any type of data and does not require adjustment of hyperparameters.

3.2 Outliers' Correction

A substantially important part, such as data imputation, corresponds to the correction of outliers. The presence of such anomalies generates noise and makes training in a predictive model difficult. Currently, there are several ways to identify outliers. However, many of them require a special treatment of the data set, seeking a fit to a normal distribution in many situations. This identification of outliers is the basis for their correction, which can be done using statistical or ML methods, depending on the investigator's decision. One of the methods to highlight is applying the Box-Jenkins techniques to predict the eliminated values,

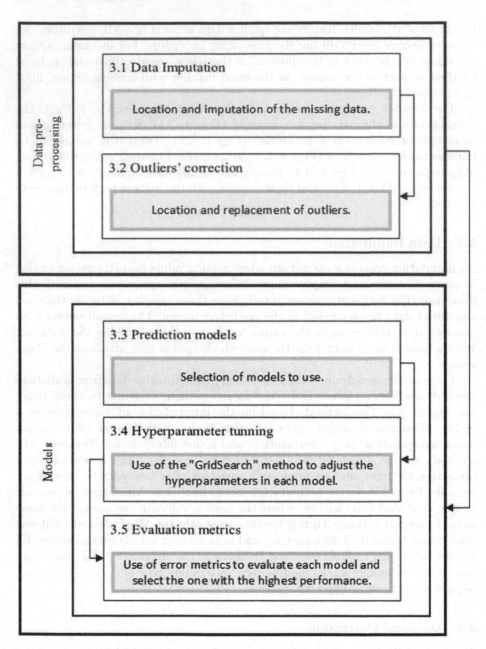

Fig. 1. Flowchart of the proposed methodology.

using the time series of the target variable to determine these values. According to Lebel [18], using SARIMAX to generate values in a time series whose structure contains empty spaces presents an optimal manner to restructure the data set, obtaining acceptable results for use in future methodologies.

Nevertheless, through the review of outlier detection techniques, the Local Outlier Probability (LoOP) method (similar to the local outlier factor method) stands out as one of the most advanced methods suitable for outlier detection. Furthermore, it differentiates itself by using data density to detect outliers, providing a percentage value interpreted as the probability that an operation has an outlier behavior [19].

3.3 Prediction Models

As can be seen in Table 1, after a weighting evaluation, the following algorithms were used: SVR, RF, Knn, LR, Ridge R, and Lasso R. Especially due to their ability to offer greater tolerance to the decreased amount of data compared to algorithms focused on Neural or Bayesian Networks. Networks whose results are best appreciated with large data repositories. When dealing with the case study of an SME, its structure, from the available resources to the amount of data they handle, makes the use of complex algorithms inappropriate due to its complexity and in some situations due to its low interpretability of results. However, the functionality of these algorithms in demand prediction problems is not ruled out since, in different areas with a large amount of information, they have shown optimal results with small margins of error.

It is worth noting that the models: linear regression, Ridge regression, and Lasso regression are naturally linear, while: Knn regressor, SVR regressor, and Random Forest can capture non-linear relationships between inputs and outputs.

Table 1. Algorithm weighting.

Algorithms	Factors				
	Simplicity (Construction)	Interpretability of the results	Reduced amount of data	Low resource consumption (Hardware)	Total
DL	1	2	1	1	5
RF	4	3	4	2	13
BN	2	4	1	3	10
NN	1	1	1	2	5
Lasso R	4	4	4	4	16
LR	5	5	5	5	20
Ridge R	4	4	4	4	16
SVR	3	3	4	3	13
Knn	3	3	4	2	12

Note 1: Weights are stipulated in ascending order from 0 (Very low) to 5 (Very high).
Note 2: DL (Deep Learning), RF (Random Forest), BN (Bayesian Networks), NN (Neuronal Networks), Lasso R (Lasso Regression), LR (Linear Regression), Ridge R (Ridge Regression), SVR (Support Vector Regression), Knn (K nearest neighborn).

Linear Regression. This model is considered the basis of different regression models derived from it. Its operation consists of finding a relationship between two variables linearly. These variables are regarded as the independent variable (X) and dependent variable (Y). This relationship allows predicting the dependent variable based on the independent variable [20]. A linear regression model can be univariate or multivariate, depending on the variables available, i.e., if it is carried out only on a target variable, it is considered univariate. However, in the case of using various predictors, it becomes a multivariate model.

Ridge Regression. This type of model is ideal when there are many predictors. Its operation will reduce variance and overfitting, reducing the importance of predictors that do not significantly impact the target variable. However, its main difference lies in the penalty applied to the predictors since this model does not eliminate any of the predictors, as occurs with the Lasso model [21]. Using the alpha parameter for this type of model is critical since, depending on its value, the model will increase the penalty on the predictors. However, if the alpha value decreases to zero, the penalty is zero, and the model assumes a similarity to a linear model.

Lasso Regression. Like the ridge model, use the same alpha value to fit the model to the data set. The objective of this type of model is to reduce the overfitting and its variance by reducing the influence of specific predictors with less relevance to the model. Its operation lies in two processes, one known as regularization, which generates a penalty on the predictor variables, and later a selection phase in charge of excluding unnecessary variables for the prediction model [22].

Knn Regressor. This model consists of a learning algorithm focused on classification or regression based on nonparametric data. It is based on the value of K nearest neighbors (Knn), which consists of the distance between one data and another, calculated using the Euclidean, Manhattan, or Hamming distance [23]. The Knn model only requires the K parameter to model. However, if this value is too high, the model tends to underfit, while the model tends to overfit if the value is too low. A differential characteristic of the Knn model is that it uses all predictors equally. That is, it does not penalize them as in the Ridge and Lasso models; therefore, it includes all variables regardless of whether they provide useful information or not.

SVR. Support vector regression (SVR) consists of an algorithm focused on support vector machine regression problems. This model consists of building a hyperplane in which the data is mapped and using the SVR algorithm. The best regression is sought. Usually, this algorithm can work with linear and non-linear data by using specific kernels like linear, RBF, sigmoid, poly. In the first instance, the model seeks to separate the data in two according to their linearity.

However, when this separation is not possible, the model resorts to the functions of the kernels [24]. The performance of this model is governed by the cost penalty (C), kernel, and insensitivity zone (e). The lower the value of C, the number of allowed errors increases.

Random Forest Regressor. This model is derived from decision trees (DT), focusing on regression like the previous model. This model arises to fill the shortcomings of the DT models since it applies a large number of trees to model a problem, making each of them work with a portion of the data and consequently calculating the mean in the measure generated by each final node of each DT. This procedure is performed to counteract the robustness obtained in DT models when a single tree is used for modeling [9].

3.4 Hyperparameter Tunning

This process consists of finding the optimal values for each hyperparameter in each predictive model. This supposes its optimization to avoid overfitting or underfitting when being trained with a dataset. Each predictive model is characterized by its hyperparameters, whose values can be numbers or characters. For example, models like Ridge and Lasso use the degree of penalty determined by the Alpha hypermeter. In contrast, models like SVR use hyperparameters like C, gamma, and the kernel. On the contrary, models like Knn mainly use the number of neighbors while the RF model uses the number of trees and their depth is used.

The simplest and most comprehensive manner to find the appropriate values for each hyperparameter in each model is by combining a range of values for each hyperparameter and the training dataset and model evaluation. This task can be optimized by using specific libraries in the programming environment. For example, one of the alternatives in Python is to use GridSearch, a tool focused on finding the appropriate hyperparameters for each predictive model. Its operation lies in using a range of values for each hyperparameter in each predictive model and performing combinatorics between them using the training data and determining the ideal combination of hyperparameters that provides the best fit of the model to the dataset. The disadvantage of using this method lies in the time required to complete the respective tuning, since the more significant the range of values in each hyperparameter, the process will generate a more substantial number of combinations and therefore results in a more extended period compared to a set-up by intuition that requires less time, with the disadvantage of obtaining results with some uncertainty. Tuning by intuition also requires an expert in the area who can suggest the values to test.

3.5 Evaluation Metrics

The mean square error (MSE) is the metric most used to evaluate the models [25]. While authors such as Loureiro [9], in addition to using the MSE, recommend the use of r squared (R2), mean absolute percentage error (MAPE), and mean fundamental error (MAE) for the evaluation of the predictor models. These metrics can be seen in Table 2, including root mean square error (RMSE) and root square error (RSE) as evaluation metrics.

Table 2. Evaluation metrics.

Metric	Preferred trend	Interpretation
R square	Higher	Measures the fit of a model to a target variable
MSE	Less	It corresponds to the mean squared error of the predictions
MAE	Less	Measures the absolute difference between the prediction and the target value
RMSE	Less	Explain the amount of error between two data sets
MAPE	Less	Measures the error generated in a forecast
RSE	Less	Expresses the quality of fit of the data to a linear model

4   Results and Discussion

This section presents the results and discussion by describing the case study and data used. This section ends by evaluating the models proposed.

4.1   Case Study

The data used in this case study corresponds to a textile industry whose center of operation is located in Ecuador and distributes to all cities. The primary data source used in this study corresponds to historical sales records from 2018 to 2020, in which the type of product sold is detailed and its physical characteristics. This database is structured mainly through categorical variables.

4.2   Data

A large number of products, various models, and a short production cycle are present in all industries in the textile sector. However, this case study is evaluated on a specific category from an extensive product catalog, including around 35 available categories. Furthermore, the data is brought in weekly periods, whereby the amount of information is drastically reduced to 110 samples over two years. In the same way, the variables holidays, term, city, garment gender, and related Google trend data are considered. In the first case, the "holidays" variables are obtained through the calendar of festive events celebrated in Ecuador, establishing as true for those weeks in which a festive event is celebrated; later, it is interpreted as a dummy variable. For the case of the category variables city, term, gender of the garment, they are treated as dummy variables generating a subcategory for each element in the original variable represented by 0 or 1.

The records of total units sold each week according to the specified category are presented as an objective variable. Google Trends is presented as a value established in a range between 0 and 100 for each week. Each value is predefined by the company Google according to its method of giving search traffic. Therefore, the keywords referring to search traffic in Google Trends must closely relate to the category of selected items. The keywords chosen in this case refer to clothing and the respective gender of the garment, finding that "top" (sleeveless or strapless garment) obtains a more significant relationship concerning the movement of the target variable in the defined period.

Through an imputation process, values are generated whose inclusion has a minimal impact on the target variable. These values are responsible for supplying 8.18% of the samples for which no original deals were found. Meanwhile, for the rest of the categorical predictor variables, the MissForest method is flexible since it does not require adjusting any hyperparameter and presents optimal results. When categorical variables are represented as dummy variables that get 0 or 1, the MissForest method generates decimal values for these variables. The rounding method is used to obtain binary values that conform to the original format of the predictor variable.

In the outlier correction part, through LoOP, two values were identified whose probability exceeds 50%, the justification for their correction is necessary. In the first instance, these values are removed and then replaced by values generated from the dataset. This is done through the SARIMAX method, developing a prediction of the destroyed values and incorporating them into the time series to prepare for their introduction to an ML model.

When partitioning the dataset, the last 20 samples are separated chronologically, assigning them to the test data, while the surplus will be used as training data. Finally, a prediction is made with the training data. Then, the prediction is incorporated into the training data to predict the next point, thus cyclically until 20 predictions are obtained. This cyclical procedure improves the hyperparameters since, in each prediction, it has been observed that they are modified to fit the new data set to the predictive model.

4.3   Evaluation of the Models

Precision is evaluated by applying the MAE, MAPE, MSE, RMSE, and RSE evaluation metrics for each set of predictions obtained in each model against the test data set. As a result, favorable results can be obtained for the Ridge and SVR model. These values can be observed in Table 3. Both models get similar results with slight differences in specific metrics. But at the same time, they present higher values than other methods in certain evaluation metrics; hence, it is necessary to consider this situation when selecting predictive models.

Table 3. Accuracy of the prediction models in the test data.

Model	MAE	MSE	RMSE	MAPE	RSE
Ridge	0.25419	0.09682	0.31117	61.6267	0.32800
Lasso	0.28593	0.13596	0.36873	53.1558	0.38867
Knn	0.30337	0.15098	0.38856	55.3805	0.40958
SVR	0.24146	0.09787	0.31285	54.6737	0.32977
Random forest	0.24867	0.10910	0.33030	53.3136	0.34817

Suppose the results obtained in Table 2 are compared. In that case, it can be seen that there is no method superior to the others because while a model obtains better results in the first evaluation metric, it obtains lower results in the second. Therefore, selecting a forecasting model depends on the evaluation meter on which the decision will be made. For example, if RMSE is considered, the Ridge model would be the option, but the Lasso model would be selected if MAPE is considered. In a similar case where in the same manner a method superior to the others is not obtained, Loureiro [9] explains that "the choice of the best technique must represent a balance between the performance of the models, their interpretability and their comprehensibility". In this case, the SVR model generally obtains a lower average in terms of error. On the contrary, the Random Forest model offers greater comprehensibility in its structure and hyperparameter tuning. However, the SVR model is selected for its kernels, which provide greater versatility when working with linear and non-linear data.

Compared with the study by Teucke [7], the prediction performance is based on the MAE. At the same time, Loureiro [9] makes greater use of RMSE, R2, MAPE, and MSE, finding that the Random Forest and Deep Neuronal Networks models offer better results since neither of them stands out from the other. In addition, Seçkin [4], in his study, found that the Random Forest model obtained a more excellent fit when evaluating the R2, MSE, and MAE metrics. Therefore, the prediction method may vary depending on the data set and the characteristics of the company.

According to Paredes [26], forecasts greatly influence day-to-day decision-making and generate a correct use of company resources. In many situations, the prediction of future conditions is given subjectively, using experience without mathematical calculations. In addition, obtaining a forecast model generates a guide for the entire supply chain, from the replenishment of materials from your suppliers to reducing inventories of finished products. Consequently, this provides greater control and reduction of the bullwhip effect at the higher levels of the supply chain [1].

Suppose the results obtained by the SVR model are compared with the linear regression model whose content does not involve Google Trends data and is purely statistical. The MSE value for linear regression is 4665.01636, which means that this model does not fit the data correctly and cannot provide good results. Since the linear regression used corresponds to a purely statistical method, it is contrasted with the reasoning of researchers previously analyzed on statistical models versus hybrid and ML models. The distortion in the data set is not collected and interpreted optimally by most purely statistical models.

Taking an approximation to the Ridge and SVR models, it is obtained that the final hyperparameters after the adjustment phase, in the case of Alpha for the Ridge model, are at 0.385662042. while, on the other hand, in the SVR model, the resulting hyperparameters correspond to a linear kernel, C of 0.1 and gamma of 0.001.

5 Conclusions

The SVR and Ridge models have been found to provide better performance in terms of error evaluation, obtaining a lower error in metrics such as MSE (0.09787 and 0.09682), RMSE (0.31285 and 0.31117), and RSE (0.32977 and 0.32800), respectively. Including an external variable, in this case, Google Trends has been shown to improve prediction accuracy compared to a traditional statistical model, as evidenced by evaluation metrics. Additionally, it is found that its use reduces the error MSE by 2% and 15%, RMSE 1% and 7% and, RSE 1% and 7% for SVR and Ridge models, respectively. However, although they are incorporated into their structure, these algorithms present a low dependence on these variables to generate the prediction, i.e., it does not use them as top predictors. Similarly, the use of ML as a prediction method has proven to be effective in this situation.

Although an improvement has been shown in terms of the use of ML models in prediction, the amount of data is a critical factor. By using a relatively small amount of data, predictive models may not take advantage of their full potential and obtain results that are close to reality. That is why having an extensive database should be essential for working with predictive models.

One of the fundamental differences between the purely statistical and ML models is that, in the first case, the prediction can be given simply since it only uses the target variable in previous periods to predict future situations. In the case of ML, the inclusion of additional predictor variables creates a problem regarding the availability of future information to predict demand. As it is information generated weekly in Google Trends, the availability of this information to create a market forecast for more extended periods is impossible.

As future research, it is proposed to apply these techniques in determining the stock in the organization's own points of sale to avoid generating significant monetary losses.

Acknowledgments. This research was carried out under the project "Incorporating Sustainability concepts to management models of textile Micro, Small and Medium Enterprises (SUMA)" funded by the Flemish Interuniversity Council (VLIR) and the Vice-Rector's Office for Research of the University of Cuenca.

References

1. Nenni, M.E., Giustiniano, L., Pirolo, L.: Demand forecasting in the fashion industry: a review. Int. J. Eng. Bus. Manag. **5**, 37 (2013). https://doi.org/10.5772/56840
2. Fumi, A., Pepe, A., Scarabotti, L., Schiraldi, M.M.: Fourier analysis for demand forecasting in a fashion company. Int. J. Eng. Bus. Manag. **5** (2013). https://doi.org/10.5772/56839
3. Liu, N., Ren, S., Choi, T.-M., Hui, P., Ng, S.-F.: Sales forecasting for fashion retailing service industry: a review. Math. Probl. Eng. **2013**, 1–9 (2013). https://doi.org/10.1155/2013/738675
4. Seçkin, M., Seçkin, A.Ç., Coşkun, A.: Production fault simulation and forecasting from time series data with machine learning in glove textile industry. J. Eng. Fiber. Fabr. **14**, 1558925019883462 (2019). https://doi.org/10.1177/1558925019883462
5. Desore, A., Narula, S.A.: An overview on corporate response towards sustainability issues in textile industry. Environ. Dev. Sustain. **20**(4), 1439–1459 (2017). https://doi.org/10.1007/s10668-017-9949-1
6. Sabir, E.C., Esma, B.: Demand forecasting with of using time series models in textile dyeing-finishing mills. Tekst. ve Konfeksiyon. **23**, 143–151 (2013)
7. Teucke, M., Ait Alla, A., El-Berishy, N., Beheshti-Kashi, S., Lütjen, M.: Forecasting of Seasonal Apparel Products. Presented at the (2014). https://doi.org/10.1007/978-3-319-23512-7_63
8. Abolghasemi, M., Hurley, J., Eshragh, A., Fahimnia, B.: Demand forecasting in the presence of systematic events: cases in capturing sales promotions. Int. J. Prod. Econ. 107892 (2020). https://doi.org/10.1016/j.ijpe.2020.107892
9. Loureiro, A.L.D., Miguéis, V.L., da Silva, L.F.M.: Exploring the use of deep neural networks for sales forecasting in fashion retail. Decis. Support Syst. **114**, 81–93 (2018). https://doi.org/10.1016/j.dss.2018.08.010
10. Tanaka, R., Ishigaki, A., Suzuki, T., Hamada, M., Kawai, W.: Determination of shipping timing in logistics warehouse considering shortage and disposal in textile industry. Procedia Manuf. **39**, 1567–1576 (2019). https://doi.org/10.1016/j.promfg.2020.01.285
11. Kück, M., Freitag, M.: Forecasting of customer demands for production planning by local k-nearest neighbor models. Int. J. Prod. Econ. **231**, 107837 (2021). https://doi.org/10.1016/j.ijpe.2020.107837
12. Peña, M., Vázquez-Patiño, A., Zhiña, D., Montenegro, M., Avilés, A.: Improved rainfall prediction through nonlinear autoregressive network with exogenous variables: a case study in andes high mountain region. Adv. Meteorol. **2020**, e1828319 (2020). https://doi.org/10.1155/2020/1828319
13. Şahin, U., Ballı, S., Chen, Y.: Forecasting seasonal electricity generation in European countries under Covid-19-induced lockdown using fractional grey prediction models and machine learning methods. Appl. Energy. **302**, 117540 (2021). https://doi.org/10.1016/j.apenergy.2021.117540
14. Zhang, H., Nguyen, H., Vu, D.-A., Bui, X.-N., Pradhan, B.: Forecasting monthly copper price: a comparative study of various machine learning-based methods. Resour. Policy. **73**, 102189 (2021). https://doi.org/10.1016/j.resourpol.2021.102189
15. Ahmad, M.W., Reynolds, J., Rezgui, Y.: Predictive modelling for solar thermal energy systems: a comparison of support vector regression, random forest, extra trees and regression trees. J. Clean. Prod. **203**, 810–821 (2018). https://doi.org/10.1016/j.jclepro.2018.08.207

16. Mei, J., He, D., Harley, R.G., Habetler, T., Qu, G.: A random forest method for real-time price forecasting in New York electricity market. In: IEEE Power and Energy Society General Meeting, pp. 1–5 (2014). https://doi.org/10.1109/PESGM. 2014.6939932

17. Stekhoven, D.J., Bühlmann, P.: MissForest - nonparametric missing value imputation for mixed-type data. Bioinformatics **28**, 112–118 (2012). https://doi.org/10. 1093/bioinformatics/btr597

18. Lebel, J.M., Kratz, F., Bloch, G.: Missing values rebuilding by prediction and ARIMA modelling in time series. IFAC Proc. **22**, 357–361 (1989). https://doi.org/ 10.1016/S1474-6670(17)54400-6

19. Alghushairy, O., Alsini, R., Soule, T., Ma, X.: A review of local outlier factor algorithms for outlier detection in big data streams. Big Data Cogn. Comput. **5**, 1 (2021). https://doi.org/10.3390/bdcc5010001

20. Bv, B.P., Dakshayini, M.: Performance analysis of the regression and time series predictive models using parallel implementation for agricultural data. Procedia Comput. Sci. **132**, 198–207 (2018). https://doi.org/10.1016/j.procs.2018.05.187

21. Joshi, S.: Time Series Analysis and Forecasting of the US Housing Starts using Econometric and Machine Learning Model. arXiv.org (2019)

22. Shafiee, S., Lied, L.M., Burud, I., Dieseth, J.A., Alsheikh, M., Lillemo, M.: Sequential forward selection and support vector regression in comparison to LASSO regression for spring wheat yield prediction based on UAV imagery. Comput. Electron. Agric. **183**, 106036 (2021). https://doi.org/10.1016/j.compag.2021.106036

23. Xin, J., Chen, S.: Bus dwell time prediction based on KNN. Procedia Eng. **137**, 283–288 (2016). https://doi.org/10.1016/j.proeng.2016.01.260

24. Smola, A.J., Schölkopf, B.: A tutorial on support vector regression. Stat. Comput. **14**, 199–222 (2004). https://doi.org/10.1023/B:STCO.0000035301.49549.88

25. Tiwari, R., Srivastava, S., Gera, R.: Investigation of artificial intelligence techniques in finance and marketing. Procedia Comput. Sci. **173**, 149–157 (2020). https://doi. org/10.1016/j.procs.2020.06.019

26. Paredes, A.P., Ángeles, J.A.C. de los, Villalobos, A.M.G., Fonseca, V.J.: Importancia de los pronósticos en la toma de decisiones en las MIPYMES. Rev. GEON (Gestión, Organ. y Negocios). **5**, 97–114 (2018). https://doi.org/10.22579/ 23463910.17

Machine Vision

Implementation of an UVC Lights Desinfection System for a Differential Robot Applying Security Methods in Indoor

Ronald Velez Burgos[1], Andres Paredes Ruiz[1], Steven Silva Mendoza[1], Dennys Paillacho Chiluiza[2(✉)], and Jonathan Paillacho Corredores[2]

[1] Facultad de Ingeniería en Mecánica y Ciencias de la Producción - FIMCP, ESPOL Polytechnic University, Escuela Superior Politécnica del Litoral, ESPOL, Campus Gustavo Galindo, P.O. Box 09-01-5863, Guayaquil, Ecuador
{rdvelez,aeparede,sasilva}@espol.edu.ec
[2] Facultad de Ingeniería en Electricidad y Computación - FIEC, CIDIS, ESPOL Polytechnic University, Escuela Superior Politécnica del Litoral, ESPOL, Campus Gustavo Galindo, P.O. Box 09-01-5863, Guayaquil, Ecuador
{dpaillac,jspailla}@espol.edu.ec

Abstract. Implementing methods that allow trajectory tracing for an autonomous robotic system is a topic that covers several fields of study since different parameters must be taken into account to locate obstacles to ensure proper navigation in environments where there is a moderate traffic of people. For this purpose, different methods of trajectory tracing will be implemented, which take as a reference the distance at which people are located. In addition, there are added human image recognition for avoid exposing people to UVC light. As a result, it can be observed that the methods implemented for the trajectory tracing give quite acceptable "pathing" results, since the main criterion to determine the efficiency is the SII, and thanks to the T265 and D435i sensors, it was possible to determine the presence of people in terms of image processing.

Keywords: Autonomous mobile robots · Robotics operating system · Social navigation · Disinfection areas · UVC light

1 Introduction

Autonomous robots have gained a lot of popularity in the last years and not only in the industrial area, also in the different imaginable areas including the disinfection. There are some methods for disinfection like using chemicals or irradiation like UV light [15], these lights, being capable of inactivating agents at the cellular and molecular level, can inactivate viruses and bacteria, but also cause damage to cellular tissue, since UVC light according to the ISO-21348

CIDIS-ESPOL.

© Springer Nature Switzerland AG 2022
M. Botto-Tobar et al. (Eds.): ICAT 2021, CCIS 1535, pp. 319–331, 2022.
https://doi.org/10.1007/978-3-031-03884-6_24

standard is between the ranges of 100 to 280 nm [6] which is dangerous because it is in the ionizing light range, this radiation can cause damage mainly in the vision and skin, additionally this generates ozone which is considered a toxic substance for humans, so the devices that work with this type of light must carry the corresponding signage and must be operated by trained and aware of the dangers that may result from exposure to light and ozone generated [1].

For implementing this function there was considered some security factors because there will be an interaction between pedestrians. To guarantee that a system works correctly, the cooperation between physical systems and computer systems, the synergy between the physical system with the information network system and finally the synergy between the computer system with the information network system in order to have a correct interaction in real time [19]. Using internet as a medium of data transmission it has to be considered that it still takes a long time to take it as a reliable method since there may be problems with bandwidth, random delay times and data loss which causes poor performance in our application, the problems that can be generated when using the internet as a data transmission medium cannot be easily determined, but mainly depend on the network load [7].

Most accidents are related to failures in the recognition sensors or data loss during the operation causing collisions, a personal assistance robot does not have the strength to push a person but if there have been cases where they caused bruises, the risk is greater if it were to collide with a child [18], most of the accidents are associated with the movement of the robot either by not stopping before the minimum distance or by having sensors at a height that do not allow the detection of objects under it [8].

In this work, mechanisms are implemented to avoid exposing people to the different risks involved in implementing an AMR[1] with UVC[2] light system, during navigation to the point to disinfect a SFM[3] is implemented, once reached the goal, a trajectory planner is implemented and at the same time the image is processed to detect people in order to stop the disinfection process. Subsequently, an analysis of the effectiveness of these mechanisms is carried out by means of the SII[4] and interpretation of the robot's behavior.

2   State of Art

Nowadays exists some systems adapted to autonomous robots, for example robots that prepare samples for detection of SARS-CoV-2 [12], robots used in pharmaceutical vaccines production, robots used to disinfect areas with UV light, etc. Robots with UV system has a 99% effectiveness, due this the use of these robots will growth the 400%–600% [17].

Most robots need techniques that allow them to navigate around a space, fortunately, today there are numerous methods that allow to efficiently plan a trajectory to be followed by a robotic system, which according to its characteristics

---

[1] Autonomous Mobile Robot.
[2] Ultraviolet C.
[3] Social Forces Model.
[4] Social Individual Index.

and limitations must interact in a specific way. Some of these methods depend on factors such as the initial position of the robot, or the trajectories it traces when it moves, since the position between the initial and final points is determined based on this. All these methods are governed by a basic structure since they have to accomplish the task of moving from one point to another. Therefore, a strategy was determined that allows the development of new computational methods to be used, since they take into account the various systems that are part of a robot.

In order to reach a secure navigation there must be implemented obstacle avoidance algorithms, for a social navigation a popular model used is the SFM [9], which is based on the model proposed in [4], this is the simplest model, but the original considers effects on people, for example, attraction by another persons or objects, this generate additional potentials and also a fluctuation is added due the unpredictable behavior of an human being [5], another variation considers adding an extra force to the model in the same side of conduction convention for avoid collisions, left side for British and right side for American, this induces a force in the robot that provokes that in the major of the cases the robot pikes the defined side for pass the pedestrian [10].

In the other hand for an non social navigation there are some kinds of algorithms for obstacles avoidance, for example the "Follow The Gap Method", which constructs an array around the robot and calculates the best heading angle and at the same time considers the goal point [13], the "Dynamic Window Approach" incorporates the robot's dynamic and reduces the searching of velocities as result of having these dynamics constrains [3], the "Vector Field Histogram Method" that implements two staged of data reduction, this method identify three levels of data representation, the first one contains the description of the robot's environment, the second level construct a Polar Histogram and the last one is a representation [2].

3   Methodology

Before continuing, it should be noted that this work is a continuation of [14] with the repository at https://gitlab.com/sasilva1998/amr.

3.1   UVC System Control Through ROS or App

To control the UVC lights system through an application, an ESP32 with micropython installed on it was used, the way to transmit the commands is through a MQTT broker, in this case there was used the shiftr.io cloud where the Publisher is the cell phone and the Subscriber is the ESP32, in the case of the Publisher, it sends the command to turn off the lights to the "stop" topic. For setting the disinfection time there was used a ROS topic that establish a connection to the MQTT broker and sends the activation time to the topic "activationTime"; it's also possible set the activation time from the App, this can be considered in case that the desired behavior of the robot not be 100% autonomous, in Fig. 1 it's represented the necessary connections for implement the system as is shown in Fig. 2.

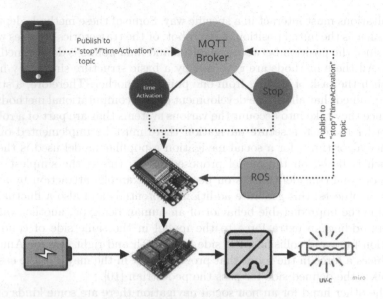

Fig. 1. Connection for the UVC lights implementation

Fig. 2. UVC System implemented in a differential robot

3.2   Navigation and Distancing from Pedestrians and Obstacles

According to the theory, four zones of social interaction are identified in human
beings, intimate, personal, social and public. Other types of defined personal
spaces are also mentioned, such as social distance and the peripersonal zone, but
these are different concepts; it should also be mentioned that the measurement
of these areas differs according to culture and age [11], as an exact value cannot
be estimated, it was proposed that the robot must not be close to the person
less than 0.5 m away, in order to carry out this task, a Social Force Model
(SFM) is implemented which causes the point of arrival to exert an attractive
force and pedestrians and obstacles generate repulsive forces while the robot is
moving, this acts as an obstacle evader. To identify obstacles, the LiDAR sensor
is used, with this, obstacles are identified and by means of a ROS node called
leg_detector[5], with this the legs of pedestrians are detected and the distance
they are at is estimated, also for validating human detection darknet_ros[6] node
is used. It is worth mentioning that both people and objects are considered as
obstacles and the system is established to avoid the nearest obstacle; a simple
representation of the model at work is shown in Fig. 3.

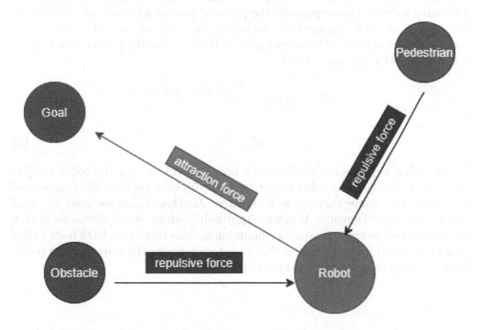

Fig. 3. Representation of the SFM at work

---

[5] http://wiki.ros.org/leg_detector.
[6] http://wiki.ros.org/darknet_ros.

The model implemented is shown a continuation:

$$f^a(t) = m \cdot \frac{1}{\tau} \cdot \left(v^0 \cdot \hat{e} - v(t)\right) \tag{1}$$

Where m is the robot's mass, τ is the relaxation time, v^0 is the desired speed, $\hat{e}$ is the unit vector and v is the actual velocity. In other hand, the repulsion force is defined as:

$$f_{ij}^r(t) = \sum_{j \in Q_0}^{Q_0} A_0 \cdot e^{-d_{ij}/B_0} \cdot \widehat{d_{ij}} \tag{2}$$

Taking A_0 as the intensity of the interaction, B_0 as the range of the interaction and d_{ij} is the normalized vector of the distance between the entities.

3.3 Analysis of the Social Individual Index

To determine if the social navigation was successful, there was used the SII used in [16], this Social Individual Index evaluates if the robot generates uncomfortably and exposes to danger to the pedestrians, for this evaluation it's necessary determine a radius that represents the personal area of a human, in a few words this area must no be invaded by the robot, the area selected to carry on this experiment was a circle of 0.5 m radius from the center of the person. The expression for the SII is shown in Eq. 3:

$$SII = \max_{i=1:N}\left(e^{-\left(\frac{x_r - x_i^p}{\sqrt{2}\sigma_0^p}\right)^2 + \left(\frac{y_r - y_i^p}{\sqrt{2}\sigma_0^p}\right)^2}\right) \tag{3}$$

$$\sigma_0^p = \frac{d_c}{2} \tag{4}$$

Where (x_i^p, y_i^p) represents the human's position and (x_r, y_r) the robot's, σ_0^p is the d_c half, this last is a value major that the distance between the human and the robot, this value varies across cultures. Another technique used to avoid obstacles is the "Dynamic Window Approach", which evade obstacles during the disinfection process. Trajectory planning is done through a ROS node called global_planner[7], this computes the trajectory between the start and end point, in Fig. 4, describes the functioning of the system.

---

[7] https://wiki.ros.org/global_planner.

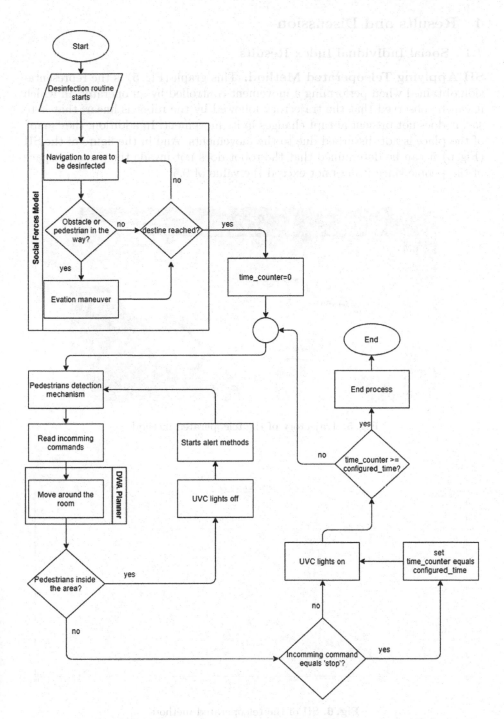

Fig. 4. Block diagram where the operation of the system is detailed

4   Results and Discussion

4.1   Social Individual Index Results

SII Applying Teleoperated Method. This graph (Fig. 5) is the representation obtained when performing a movement controlled by an operator, in which it can be observed that the trajectory followed by the robot is linear, that is to say, it does not present abrupt changes in its movement. In addition, the "map" of the place is not disturbed due to the movements. And in the figure of the SII (Fig. 6) it can be determined that the robot does not invade the personal space of the people since it does not exceed the value of 0.5.

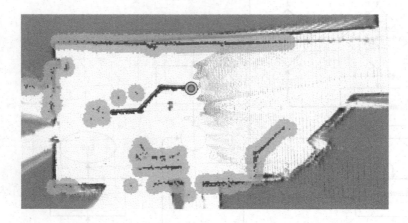

Fig. 5. Trajectory of the teleoperated method

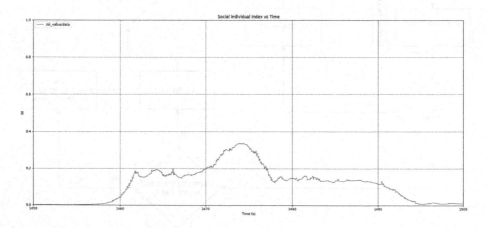

Fig. 6. SII of the teleoperated method

SII Applying a Planner. When performing the proposed movement, the robot is able to detect the "obstacles" that may arise, which allows it to redirect its path and determine the best route taking into account the minimum safety distance, see in Fig. 7, in the graph it's observed a smooth movement. But when analyzing the SII graph it can be concluded that the robot invades the safety zone in a small space of time, see Fig. 8.

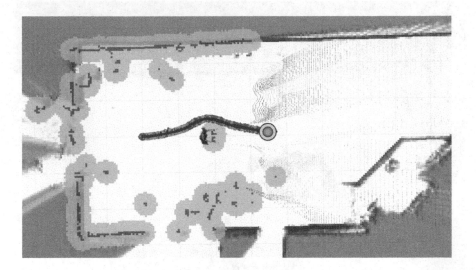

Fig. 7. Trajectory of the planner

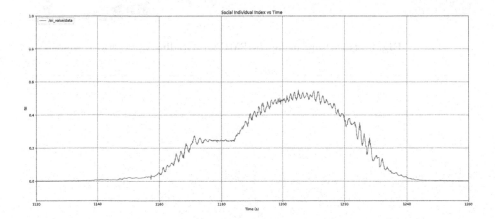

Fig. 8. SII using a planner

SII Applying the SFM. The results of the experimentation using the SFM are visible in Figs. 9 and 10, the first thing to take in account is that the trajectory isn't perfect a possible reason is that during the experimentation other persons were transiting the area near the robot and this may have induced another forces to the robot, the second thing to take in account is that the map is not aligned with the simulated one, the main reason is that the robot during evasion maneuvers it gets disoriented. In the other hand the SII result in Fig. 10 shows

Fig. 9. Trajectory using the SMF for avoiding obstacles

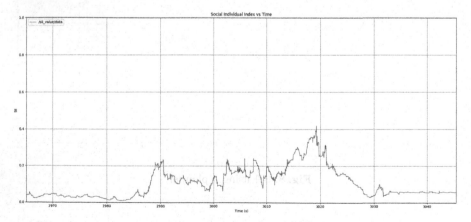

Fig. 10. SII of the SFM

that the model worked good, there's no moment where the robot invaded the personal area of the testing agent.

4.2   Human Detection During UVC Disinfection

Fig. 11. Human detection during UVC disinfection

As can be seen, the 3 methods implemented allow to the robot get from an initial point to a final one, always taking into account the obstacles that may exist in the terrain, however the trajectories generated are not the same because for example in the teleoperated method the robot don't invade the human's personal area, but this can't be taken as the best option because this will always depend on human error, and there are many factors that can influence in the results, as the operator's skills, the angle of view, the mood, etc. At the planner test, it's possible to see that the trajectory is soft, this is because the planner takes the shortest path, but in this case, keep the correct distance from the human is the priority, but in this case it's supposed to work during the disinfection so it has been assumed that during this operation nobody is around the robot; and in the SFM test the robot moves in an abrupt way, but keeps the correct distance from the human. In the other hand human detection worked successfully (see Fig. 11), but it's not 100% safer because still depends of the internet connection.

5   Conclusions

The methods implemented to determine the trajectory of the robot were able to perform the main task, which is to take the robot from one point to another, taking into account the obstacles that may occur in space. Even though the methods show different levels of efficiency as far as the SII is concerned, they still maintain the working characteristics, i.e. the map they have registered and the safety parameters. That is why the trajectories differ so much, as they have different criteria for their movement. That is why the SFM is the one that presents more changes in its trajectory, since the amount of variables to take into account is greater than the other models, it is also influenced by the model of the robot, since, being a differential robot, it presents restrictions in the movement that add more parameters that must be taken into account at the time of tracing the trajectory. Since it is used the T265 and D435i (integrated cameras) as obstacle detection methods, which allow us to obtain very accurate data in terms of mapping and detection of people, in addition to the system has a stop system which is activated when a person enters the safety space of the robot. In terms of the solutions implemented to determine the trajectories of the robot, we can determine that it is possible to trace trajectories depending on the parameters required in the movement and the assigned work space, which is obtained by mapping. Thus the robot is able to reach its final position. In the SFM the robot took several attempts to determine its trajectory, so it rotated on its own axis, this was because the space where it had to move was limited, so it was constantly redirected, this can be corrected by applying changes in the programming algorithm, taking certain assumptions that allow it to obtain more accurate movements.

References

1. Position statement on germicidal UV-C irradiation. Technical report, Global Light Association, May 2020
2. Borenstein, J., Koren, Y.: Real-time obstacle avoidance for fast mobile robots in cluttered environments. In: Proceedings of the IEEE International Conference on Robotics and Automation, vol. 1, pp. 572–577 (1990). https://doi.org/10.1109/ROBOT.1990.126042
3. Fox, D., Burgard, W., Thrun, S.: The dynamic window approach to collision avoidance. IEEE Robot. Autom. Mag. **4**(1), 23–33 (1997). https://doi.org/10.1109/100.580977
4. Helbing, D., Molnar, P.: Social force model for pedestrian dynamics. Phys. Rev. E **51**(5), 4282 (1995). https://doi.org/10.1103/PhysRevE.51.4282
5. Helbing, D., Molnár, P.: Social force model for pedestrian dynamics. Phys. Rev. E **51**, 4282–4286 (1995). https://doi.org/10.1103/PhysRevE.51.4282, https://link.aps.org/doi/10.1103/PhysRevE.51.4282
6. Space environment (natural and artificial) - process for determining solar irradiances. Standard, International Organization for Standardization, Geneva, CH, May 2007
7. Khamis, A.M., Rodríguez, F.J., Salichs, M.A.: Remote interaction with mobile robots. Auton. Robot. **15**(3), 267–281 (2003). https://doi.org/10.1023/A:1026268504593
8. Kim, N., Hong, S.T., Sung, K.Y., Yu, G.E., Seo, J.H.: A case study on risk assessment for personal care robot (mobile servant robot). In: 2018 18th International Conference on Control, Automation and Systems (ICCAS), pp. 343–347 (2018)

9. Kivrak, H., Cakmak, F., Kose, H., Yavuz, S.: Social navigation framework for assistive robots in human inhabited unknown environments. Eng. Sci. Technol. Int. J. **24**(2), 284–298 (2021). https://doi.org/10.1016/j.jestch.2020.08.008, https://www.sciencedirect.com/science/article/pii/S2215098620308727

10. Reddy, A.K., Malviya, V., Kala, R.: Social cues in the autonomous navigation of indoor mobile robots. Int. J. Soc. Robot. **13**(6), 1335–1358 (2020). https://doi.org/10.1007/s12369-020-00721-1

11. Leichtmann, B., Nitsch, V.: How much distance do humans keep toward robots? Literature review, meta-analysis, and theoretical considerations on personal space in human-robot interaction. J. Environ. Psychol. **68**, 101386 (2020).https://doi.org/10.1016/j.jenvp.2019.101386, https://www.sciencedirect.com/science/article/pii/S0272494419303846

12. Marais, G., Naidoo, M., Hsiao, N.Y., Valley-Omar, Z., Smuts, H., Hardie, D.: The implementation of a rapid sample preparation method for the detection of SARS-COV-2 in a diagnostic laboratory in south Africa. PLOS ONE **15**, 1–9 (10 2020). https://doi.org/10.1371/journal.pone.0241029

13. Sezer, V., Gokasan, M.: A novel obstacle avoidance algorithm: "follow the gap method". Robot. Auton. Syst. **60**(9), 1123–1134 (2012). https://doi.org/10.1016/j.robot.2012.05.021, https://www.sciencedirect.com/science/article/pii/S0921889012000838

14. Silva, S., Paillacho, D., León, D., Pintado, M., Paillacho, J.: Autonomous Intelligent Navigation for Mobile Robots in Closed Environments, pp. 391–402, April 2021. https://doi.org/10.1007/978-3-030-71503-8_30

15. Tao, M., et al.: Sterilization and disinfection methods for decellularized matrix materials: review, consideration and proposal. Bioactive Mater. **6**(9), 2927–2945 (2021). https://doi.org/10.1016/j.bioactmat.2021.02.010, https://www.sciencedirect.com/science/article/pii/S2452199X21000700

16. Truong, X.T., Ngo, T.D.: Toward socially aware robot navigation in dynamic and crowded environments: a proactive social motion model. IEEE Trans. Autom. Sci. Eng. **14**(4), 1743–1760 (2017). https://doi.org/10.1109/TASE.2017.2731371

17. Wang, X.V., Wang, L.: A literature survey of the robotic technologies during the COVID-19 pandemic. J. Manuf. Syst. (2021). https://doi.org/10.1016/j.jmsy.2021.02.005, https://www.sciencedirect.com/science/article/pii/S0278612521000339

18. Yu, G.E., Hong, S.T., Sung, K.Y., Seo, J.H.: A study on the risk investigation and safety of personal care robots. In: 2017 17th International Conference on Control, Automation and Systems (ICCAS), pp. 904–908 (2017). https://doi.org/10.23919/ICCAS.2017.8204353

19. Zhou, K., Liu, T., Zhou, L.: Industry 4.0: towards future industrial opportunities and challenges. In: 2015 12th International Conference on Fuzzy Systems and Knowledge Discovery (FSKD), pp. 2147–2152. IEEE (2015). https://doi.org/10.1109/FSKD.2015.7382284

Security

Development Processes of Vulnerability Detection Systems: A Systematic Review, Approaches, Challenges, and Future Directions

Jorge Reyes[1][✉], Walter Fuertes[1][✉], and Mayra Macas[1,2][✉]

[1] Department of Computer Science, Universidad de las Fuerzas Armadas ESPE,
Av. General Rumiñahui S/N, P.O. Box 17-15-231B, Sangolquí, Ecuador
{jlreyes5,wmfuertes}@espe.edu.ec, mayramacas@ieee.org
[2] College of Computer Science and Technology, Zhejiang University,
No. 38 Zheda Road, Hangzhou 310027, China

Abstract. In cybersecurity, a vulnerability is any software or hardware failure that compromises the information's integrity, availability, or confidentiality. Nowadays, the number of vulnerabilities is increasing exponentially. The early detection, analysis, and efficient treatment of vulnerabilities constitute significant challenges for organizations, as they are arduous and expensive processes. This study aims to thoroughly and systematically research the approaches, techniques, and tools used in implementing vulnerability detection and scanning systems. We conduct a systematic literature review based on the methodological guide of Barbara Kitchenham to carry out a synthesis of the evidence available in primary studies in the last five years. The results show that studies evaluate the efficiency and complexity of the development process for vulnerability detection through a combination of methods, techniques, tools, and metrics. Moreover, this study serves as a baseline for establishing a new development process proposal to benefit organizations planning to create custom vulnerability detection systems. Finally, current challenges are highlighted, and future research directions for addressing them are explored.

Keywords: Vulnerability scanning · Threat assessment · Vulnerability detection · Software development process

1 Introduction

Detecting vulnerabilities is constant and high-impact work, striving to keep large technological infrastructures secure. Information protection requires a lot of technical and technological effort. Losing or exposing information has a negative impact on organizations, both on a functional and reputational level [1]. The rapid digital transition leaves exposed vulnerabilities that are being exploited

© Springer Nature Switzerland AG 2022
M. Botto-Tobar et al. (Eds.): ICAT 2021, CCIS 1535, pp. 335–350, 2022.
https://doi.org/10.1007/978-3-031-03884-6_25

by cybercriminals [3,23]. Among the most common security incidents are malware infection, ransomware, exploiting vulnerabilities, improper access to applications, social engineering attacks, and denial of service [10,26].

Nowadays, it is estimated that 32% of the vulnerabilities are caused by bad configurations from the personnel in charge of the technological infrastructures. Moreover, it is determined that 52% of vulnerabilities are discovered or generated directly by the actions of cybercriminals, who try to destabilize organizations in order to obtain economic benefits [2,12,27]. The global average cost of a data breach and vulnerability exploitation for an organization is about USD 86 million. Leakage of personal information is included in 80% of vulnerabilities, whereas in 32% intellectual property is compromised [2,12].

The probability of exploitation is directly proportional to time. In preliminary studies, we have identified that the average time needed for an organization to identify a vulnerability was 196 days in 2018 [27]. Relying only on reported incident data presented in reports from large cybersecurity companies, we have reviewed IBM's 2020 report as it collects information from other large companies for its data analysis. According to it, the average time increased to 280 days [12]. The longer an organization takes to detect a vulnerability, the more opportunities a cybercriminal can discover to exploit it. CSIRTs worldwide and companies specialized in cybersecurity offer different services or tools focused on detecting vulnerabilities [4]. However, to obtain efficient results in the context of their specific operational environment and business rules, companies have developed their own systems, often consuming existing resources and processing information independently.

The current study aims to identify and analyze the development and implementation processes for vulnerability detection systems (VDS). We have conducted a systematic literature review (SLR) based on the methodological guide proposed by Bárbara Kitchenham [6], focusing on vulnerability detection approaches, performance, development process, challenges, and future research directions. The results highlight relevant information for researchers and the industry, including phases, methods, techniques, and tools used to detect vulnerabilities. We also conclude that there is no global standard regarding developing these types of systems for the moment.

The main contributions of our work can be summarized as follows: (1) a systematic review of techniques, methods, and tools concerning the development process of vulnerability detection software; and (2) a new proposal of a development process that allows for continuous improvement aimed at implementing software of vulnerability detection to achieve a greater security level.

The remainder of the article has the following structure: Sect. 2 describes the literature review process. Section 3 presents the results obtained from the SLR. It also introduces an interactive development process proposal for vulnerability detection systems in Sect. 4. Finally, Sect. 5 concludes the paper and outlines future research directions.

2   Materials and Methods

In this section, we explore the evidence available in literature using Kinchenham's methodological guide [6] due to its importance in software engineering. In this way, we design and execute a systematic review, and we interpret the discovered information for a subject little studied. We review quantitative and qualitative aspects of primary studies to summarize the existing information and critically analyze the relevant information.

2.1   Research Questions

In this paper, we seek to determine the answers to the following research questions:

- **RQ1.** Which are the main approaches and detection phases for vulnerabilities?
- **RQ2.** How can we evaluate the performance of vulnerability detection tools?
- **RQ3.** What impact does time have on vulnerability detection?
- **RQ4.** What are the development processes to implement software for vulnerability detection?
- **RQ5.** Which are the challenges and future research directions on vulnerability detection?

2.2   Inclusion and Exclusion Criteria

We selected studies published after 2015, because there is a constant and rapid update of tools, development processes, and applications on cybersecurity. In addition, we defined the following **inclusion criteria**:

- Articles whose journal of publication is in a Q3 quartile or higher.
- Articles that evaluate the performance of systems, prototypes, or tools quantitatively.

For the **exclusion criteria**, the following parameters were considered:

- Studies that do not present content in English.
- Studies that do not specify the development process of software for the detection of vulnerabilities.

2.3   Search Process

The search process started with the following primary academic research databases: IEEE Xplore, SCOPUS, ScienceDirect, and ACM. We conducted a semi-initial literature review to determine a group of words to search for scientific studies related to the research topic. For the initial searches, we used the following terms:

- "Early detection of vulnerabilities."
- "Vulnerability scanning tools."
- "Alerts or vulnerability treatment."
- "Development processes for vulnerability detection."

Subsequently, based on the terms above, we refined and obtained the following search string: ((("Development Process") And ("Vulnerability Detection" Or "Vulnerability Scanning" Or "Vulnerability Monitoring" Or "Vulnerability Analysis") And ("Tool" Or "System") And ("Data Science" Or "Deep Learning" Or "Data Mining" Or "Artificial Intelligence"))).

In this way, the employed search chain returned 135 articles that were uploaded to the *Rayyan - Intelligent Systematic Review* [18], a free-to-use web application that automates the systematic review process. After applying the inclusion and exclusion criteria, we performed a final review through a comprehensive reading process and selected 25 articles as primary studies.

2.4   Analysis of Primary Studies

The selected 25 primary studies belong to the area of computer science. We considered journal articles that meet the search quality criteria and belong to SCImago Journal Rank in a Q3 quartile or higher. Figure 1 shows the number of articles from each academic research database.

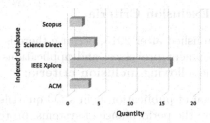

Fig. 1. Selected articles by indexed Database.

The journals where the selected articles were published are the following: (i) IEEE Access [8,11,14,15,20–22,25,29,30,32–34,36], (ii) IEEE Transactions on Information Forensics and Security [28], (iii) IEEE Transactions On Services Computing [5], (iv) IEEE Transactions on Fuzzy Systems [16], (v) ACM Computing Surveys [9,17,19], (vi) ELSEVIER Applied Intelligence [24], (vii) ELSEVIER Computers & Security [13], (viii) ELSEVIER Information and Software Technology [7], (ix) ELSEVIER The Journal of Systems & Software [35], and (x) Future Internet MDPI [31].

3   Results

3.1   Summarizing Key Findings

Concerning **RQ1**, the examined studies demonstrate two Vulnerability Detection Approaches (VDAs). In the state of the art analysis, VDAs represent the environment where vulnerabilities are detected and the particular process that is applied. The two main identified VDAs are: (i) Software vulnerabilities (found in web applications and programming code) [5,7–9,11,13–16,20–22,24,25,28,30,32–36] and (ii) network/IoT vulnerabilities in devices and infrastructures [17,19,29,31]. During the study selection process, we observed an increasing trend of researching *S*oftware vulnerabilities compared to the other category. Figure 2 illustrates the percentage of pre-selected studies and the number of primary studies corresponding to each approach.

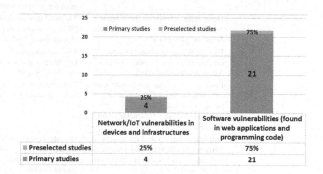

	Network/IoT vulnerabilities in devices and infrastructures	Software vulnerabilities (found in web applications and programming code)
Preselected studies	25%	75%
Primary studies	4	21

Fig. 2. Distribution of pre-selected and primary studies to VDAs.

Because VDAs determine broad fields of research and analysis, in the rest of our work, we indicate each study with an ID that represents its bibliographic reference and we analyze it according to the detection method that it uses, the detection phases applied in the creation of systems or incorporation of tools, and finally the identified main characteristics/features (See Tables 1 and 2).

Classifying the information under these parameters allowed us to identify that 96% of the studies define detection phases for vulnerabilities. In studies that have defined detection phases, a prototype (48%), tool (29%), or system (23%) is implemented for functional testing. There is no standard in the phases applied, but representative phases are identified regardless of VDA or method. No methodologies for vulnerability detection are identified, but according to the phases and main characteristics, the methodologies should be iterative to achieve continuous monitoring.

Regarding **RQ2**, the performance of the vulnerability detection tools is evaluated with widely used statistics of predictive analytics [5,7,9,13,16,32,34,35]. More precisely, the employed evaluation metrics are the following: True Positive (TP) which is the number of true vulnerabilities detected; True Negative (TN)

Table 1. Software vulnerabilities (found in web applications and programming code)

Id	Detection method	Detection phases	Main features
[7]	Deep Learning (DL)	Input data - Information processing - Training phase - Detecting vulnerability	As more vulnerabilities-related data is provided, detection performance improves
[13]		Input data - Training phase - Detection phase	The data sheets of other vulnerability detection projects as input data allow a complete analysis and increase the detection efficiency [13,14]
[14]		Input data - Data processing - Data transform - Detection	
[24]		Input data - Initialize Population for dominated feature representation - Selection based on Deep Neural Networks (DNNs) - Mutation - Evaluation - Most vulnerable deep-learnt features	Automatic vulnerabilities detection and prediction is a trend
[28]		Input data - Graph representation - Training phase - Detection phase	It combines probabilistic learning and statistical evaluations to collect samples of open source projects.
[32]		Input data - Training the Neural Network - Using de trained Nueral Network (detection)	The well-defined code metrics allow DNNs to learn more characteristics of vulnerable code
[33]		Feature representations - Code analysis/process - Model design - Application - Detection	The authors mention that Deep Learning is not widely studied for the detection of vulnerabilities
[34]		Planning, Analysis and requirements - System design - Development - Integration and testing - Implementation - Operations and maintenance	The dynamic real-time analysis in code clone allows for greater security
[9]	Machine Learning (ML)	Software creation and management - Software verification and validation - Software defect analysis - Software testing and debugging	Despite being a little-studied field, studies show promising results in the discovery and analysis of software vulnerabilities
[30]		Input data - Data processing - Data transform - Training phase - Detection	ML-based vulnerability detection is an active research topic in software security. Applying NN technology to binary similarity detection has become a promising search topic [30,35]
[35] [16]		Data Pre-processing - DeepBalance model building based on FOS - Software vulnerability discovery based on DeepBalance	The main problem faced by Machine Learning is to detect whether the code is vulnerable or not
[5]	Penetration testing, Static code analyzers, Anomaly detectors	Preparation - Execution - Comparison	Considering that commercial detection approaches of commercial tools are usually limited, leaving several domains unassessed, this study promotes the idea that selecting tools for vulnerability detection should be a technical process with metrics that quantitatively define their efficiency and detection capacity
[8]	Web scanning and data collection, VulNet tool	Monitoring - Input data - Vulnerabilities analyzer - Storage data - Results	This paper presents a tool for identifying the vulnerabilities of most Internet sites with Web Content Management System (WCMS), together with the remedies that need to be applied. Its key feature is the ability to perform automated, fast, and dynamic vulnerability scans

(continued)

Table 1. (*continued*)

Id	Detection method	Detection phases	Main features
[11]	Static detection model based on the proposition function	Basic Information analysis - VEPS solution - Solution vulnerable nodes - Detecting vulnerability	The automatic detection of vulnerabilities is receiving increasing attention because the main flaw of static detection is the lack of criteria in defining the properties of vulnerabilities, i.e., characteristics and rules that make the systems make the right decisions
[15]	URL tracking, Black box second-order vulnerability detection algorithm	Monitoring - Storage data - Detection module - Report Module	Second-order vulnerabilities are more destructive than first-order vulnerabilities. The method detects web second-order security vulnerabilities through crawl scans of URLs
[20]	Tool called KPSec	Source code patch - Preprocessing - Execution paths generation - Symbolic execution - Bugs reporting	In this paper, a novel approach for automatically determining whether a patch brings new vulnerabilities is presented. The proposed method combines symbolic execution with data flow analysis and static analysis, which allows a quick check of patch-related codes
[21]	Heuristic Method, Vularcher-A Tool To Detect Vulnerabilities	Decompilation - Unpacking - Building Taint Path - Detection	Four types of vulnerabilities that allow the man in the middle attack are analyzed, and a method of vulnerability identification through the VulArcher tool is proposed
[22]	Dynamic taint analysis method based on entity equipment	Initialization and dynamic instrumentation - Intermediate representation conversion - Simulation execution and result verification - Taint analysis	The authors implement and verify the effectiveness of a prototype system that can perform taint analysis on multiple architecture embedded firmware programs and detect vulnerabilities such as stack overflow and heap overflow
[25]	OWASP ZAP scanner tool	Development - Test - Maintenance	This study extracts a broad set of measures/metrics to allow vulnerability assessment and vulnerability management. It is also mentioned that for software experts, it is essential to have graphs that allow them to make decisions
[36]	A scalable static approach for detecting use-after-free vulnerabilities in binary code	Binary Code - Pre-process procedure - Detection procedure - Error reports	The authors have implemented a prototype called UAFDetector and evaluated it using standard benchmarks and real-world programs

that indicates the number of samples that are not vulnerable and are detected as not vulnerable; False Positives (FP) that expresses the number of vulnerabilities detected that do not exist; False Negatives (FN) that indicates the number of vulnerable samples that are detected as not vulnerable; Accuracy (A) that determines the truthfulness of everything detected; Precision (P) that determines the accuracy of the detected vulnerabilities; Recall (R) that determines the True positive samples in the total of vulnerable samples; and F1-score (F1) [13,35] or F1-Measure (F1) [5,7] which determines the overall efficiency considering the precision as the FN rate; Especificity or False Negative Rate (FNR) focuses on the algorithm or model and evaluates the negative cases it has correctly

Table 2. Network/IoT vulnerabilities in devices and infrastructures

Id	Detection method	Detection phases	Main features
[17]	Intrusion Detection	Network monitoring - Detailed analysis of network traffic - Known attack detection	The process of sharing information is fundamental since it improves the capacity of the systems in the face of new and previously unobserved sophisticated attacks. Within this context, collaborative security has emerged as a recent trend
[19]	Application-based taxonomies of these approaches, characteristics and analysis type	Undefined	Given that the firmware that controls several IoT devices becomes obsolete in a limited time, it is essential to maintain different types of analysis that allow better control of the IoT infrastructure to achieve controlled security through several methodologies
[29]	Static detection method for early warning vulnerabilities based on the counterexample of IoT	Monitoring - IoT base - Base Router - IoT Router - IoT Application - Analysis abnormality - Confirmation vulnerability	Continuous monitoring allows early warnings to be generated. Static detection based on the association of attacks and the attack algorithm's study makes it possible to predict and evaluate the network, thus improving security
[31]	Network Scanning Method, Similarity Detection Method, Dynamic Analysis, Static analysis	Basic Framework of Vulnerability Analysis - Vulnerability Discovery - Vulnerability Detection - Vulnerability Mitigation	An analysis of the IoT architecture and attack surfaces from the consumer and industry perspective is performed. The main objective is to detect vulnerabilities which is investigated mainly through network scanning and code similarity detection

classified, measuring detection effectiveness; False Positive Rate (FPR) measures the percentage of false positives against all positive predictions.

In regards to **RQ3**, time is the fundamental factor on which each of the studies is focused. The ability to detect vulnerabilities involves a variety of decisions and innovations that allow information to be organized and systematized [29]. Untreated vulnerabilities can turn into computer security incidents, which have fatal effects on organizations. Among the most common incidents are the misconfiguration of web pages, offline services, the exposure of sensitive information, the infection of servers, unauthorized access, and data hijacking. These incidents could destabilize and discredit technology infrastructures. Early vulnerabilities detection is vital to prevent cyber-crime from becoming reality [15].

Some studies present ambitious proposals that try to predict vulnerabilities [24] or find zero-day vulnerabilities [13], hereinafter referred to as *prediction*. Other studies carried out controlled review processes through audits comparing results with commercial tools, henceforth referred to as *revision time*. However, most studies try to find vulnerabilities in *real time* [7,34]. Figure 3 depicts the distribution of the primary studies concerning the three aforementioned time-related categories.

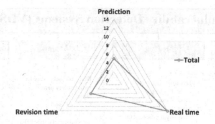

Fig. 3. Vulnerability detection time trends

With respect to **RQ4**, no standard development process has been identified. According to the studies reviewed, it was possible to extract a general process based in detection phases, despite the different employed approaches and methods shown in Tables 1 and 2.

The process begins by defining whether the goal is to detect specific vulnerabilities, in which case it is necessary to first understand the principles of the examined attack [15]. On the other hand, efficient use of detection tools [5], vulnerability data sheets [13] or new methods or algorithms are proposed [16,28]. Once the detection approach is clear, the system architecture is designed [7,13,15,22,29,30]. To implement the VDS, an evolutionary or incremental development methodology must be applied. The best methodology for the development of this type of system has not yet been defined. However, it should be considered that the VDS has to be validated and is subject to constant change. In order to validate the operation of the VDS, prototypes or tools are initially proposed before its implementation [8,20,22,30,36]. The evaluation of the VDS is accomplished through a comparison with the results of commercial tools [5,7,21,25], by using the evaluation metrics presented in RQ2 [5,7,9,13,16,32,34–36] or by combining both methods [14,30,36]. Finally, the main conclusions are determined within the development process, and improvements are proposed for the VDS.

The software development process for vulnerability detection requires iterative methodologies. However, there is no clearly defined development methodology or standard. The applied development process must allow constant changes to evaluate the performance of the methods and techniques in the vulnerability detection process. Moreover, appropriate tools are used to compare the detection results or provide the input data for the VDS, which processes and stores the information related to vulnerabilities. Figure 4 shows information related to the development methodologies, methods, techniques, and tools for VDS.

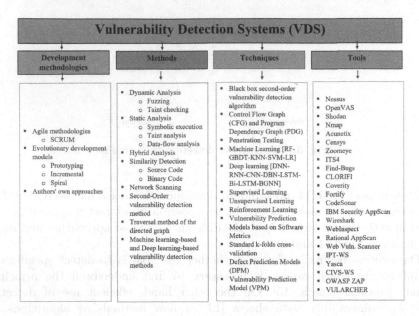

Fig. 4. Main parameters for the development of VDSs

Within this context, Liu and Wang [15] proposed a B/S architecture that enables users to efficiently perform second-order vulnerability detection on web applications through browsers. B/S has a modular design that facilitates the future expansion of the system. In their vulnerability early warning system for IoT environments [29], Yi et al. load input data of known vulnerabilities to make an attack association and detect anomalies in the network. Jeon and Kim [13] developed a deep learning-based system called AutoVAS that represents source code as embedding vectors and has CVE and CWE as input data, intending to prevent threats in software. Lu et al. [30] and Ren et al. [22] proposed prototypes to verify the effectiveness of detection methods and vulnerability storage architectures through case studies and comparisons with other commercial tools. As a general conclusion, every VDS seeks to optimize resources and achieve a performance that meets the detection objective.

Regarding **RQ5**, the main challenges in the development of these systems are the complexity of detection and the definition of parameters and indicators that determine the False Positives and False Negatives [11]. Deep Learning, Machine Learning, and Data Mining methods group large amounts of data and require considerable hardware resources [16]. The VDS development and vulnerability treatment processes represent a high cost for organizations. At the same time, the rapid technological progress brings new vulnerabilities; therefore, systems must be scalable and should have a greater capacity for integration with new detection methods and techniques [17].

About **future research directions**, there is a broad field to further study. Since there is no standard for developing VDS, relevant processes, methodologies, techniques, and tools can be investigated and proposed. Artificial intelligence (AI) require detailed consideration in detection processes. New VDSs must be based on collaborative security. Obtaining several vectors for the input data enables a greater field of knowledge and evaluation about vulnerabilities [7,13,17]. The Deep learning techniques mentioned in the systems that detect vulnerabilities at the software level can be improved through the definition of indicators that can more accurately determine FPs and FNs [16]. Finally, there are powerful tools (e.g., Nessus, Shodan, Nmap, Wireshark, Libav, Retina, etc.) that can facilitate the treatment of the found vulnerabilities [31], through new distributed systems that consume the offered services (APIs).

4 Proposal for Development Processes of Vulnerability Detection Systems

Based on the results of this SLR, we divide this proposal into two important parts. The first is related to a methodology for the detection of vulnerabilities, which will be systematized and automated. The second relates to the phases of the development process, which cover general aspects that apply to all vulnerability detection systems. Although the purpose of each phase is explained, the specifics will not be detailed since this would not fulfill the objective of making a general proposal for VDS development. The particular methods, techniques, and tools for each phase will depend on the conditions of the environment where the VDS will be applied.

4.1 Vulnerability Detection Methodology Proposal

In this section, we propose a detection methodology consisting of five general phases that allow vulnerabilities to be detected, analyzed, and mitigated (see Fig. 5). With **Phase I**, it is possible to obtain logs and information related to a range of different events. Throughout **Phase II**, data on known vulnerabilities are entered and events are compared with publicly known vulnerabilities by use of analysis tools. In **Phase III**, known events are processed and new events are discovered based on the previously obtained information. In **Phase IV**, the events that are considered as vulnerabilities are defined and reported. **Phase V** attempts to mitigate vulnerabilities by correcting existing bugs. The entire process is iteratively repeated to maintain constant monitoring.

4.2 VDS Development Process Proposal

Concerning development, we propose a process which comprises six phases (See Fig. 6). In **Phase I**, we define the type of vulnerabilities to be detected (i.e., the VDS approach). In **Phase II**, we define the additional methods, techniques, tools, and resources that will be used in the development of the VDS, aiming

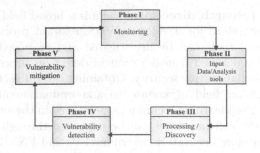

Fig. 5. The five phases of the vulnerability detection methodology

to design an architecture tailored to the detection approach. In **Phase III**, we define a development methodology and adapt or refine the prototype, tool, or system stages. In **Phase IV**, we configure the tools, we implement software solutions, and we validate errors. In **Phase V**, we apply the evaluation metrics or compare results with commercial tools with the same detection approach, in order to validate the software's operation. Finally, in **Phase VI**, we document and expose the main conclusions of the development process to establish corrections and improvements that allow a more efficient operation of the VDS. It is essential to constantly evaluate the software, control complexity and risks, and increase its functionality throughout the process.

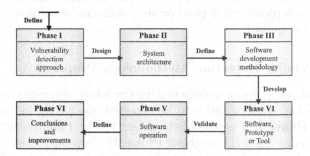

Fig. 6. VDS development process phases

5   Discussion

Within the context of cybersecurity, vulnerabilities are defined as a failure or weakness of an information system that puts its security at risk [31]. The treatment of vulnerabilities is crucial for maintaining controlled security and minimizing risks in organizations. Most VDS are focused on software vulnerabilities due to the large amount of reusable code that does not always comply with the basic security parameters [34]. Also, the time needed for the manual review process is lengthy because of the large number of lines of code [25]. Deep Learning and Machine Learning techniques are widely used and studied in an attempt to improve the percentage of precision in detection algorithms [9,33,35].

Broadly speaking, there are two main detection approaches: Software vulnerabilities (found in web applications and programming code) and network/IoT vulnerabilities found in devices and infrastructures. The latter require greater attention and study due to the technology trend towards cloud computing. According to the reviewed studies, techniques related to Deep Learning and Machine Learning have not yet been applied to detect this type of vulnerabilities. However, it has been shown that scanning tools have a greater incidence and effectiveness in this approach [5,29,31].

Systems that are based on known vulnerabilities have input data, such as the source codes of the National Vulnerability Database (NVD) and the Software Assurance Reference Database (SARD), with which neural networks are trained. Based on the studies reviewed, there is evidence of a collaborative security process [7,13,32]. In general, CVE is a publicly known vulnerability and is fed to NVD. The NVD platform contains several analysis parameters, most notably severity scores through the Common Vulnerability Scoring System (CVSS). In this way, the systems achieve an expanded field of verification, being more effective and precise with each data flow that is loaded [7,13,24,28]. As can be seen in this study, all VDSs apply the concept of collective security through different techniques and approaches. They are directly or indirectly related to other systems to obtain data or simply compare the results. This interrelation process focuses on the continuous development and improvement of new solutions and processes to identify and treat vulnerabilities.

Finally, our proposal provides a reference and starting point for the development process of the VDSs. The iterative vulnerability detection methodology illustrates the main phases that the methods, techniques, or tools we choose must comply with. The identified phases allow us to generate the necessary information to structure the overall system. Furthermore, we propose a development process for this type of detection system. The objective of the proposals is to provide methodological and systematic guides for creating scalable systems that can cope with the dynamics of their ever-changing operational environment.

6   Conclusions

This study presented a systematic literature review of the development processes, approaches, methodologies, techniques, and tools for vulnerability detection systems. We have determined that there is no standard or prevailing methodology for the VDS development process. Moreover, we have identified that the vulnerability detection methodological process must be iterative to achieve better results through continuous monitoring. We have observed that software vulnerabilities are detected through Deep Learning, Machine Learning, and Fuzzy techniques. Network, IoT, and web application vulnerabilities are supported by different business tools that have provided effective and efficient results. The VDS development process requires agile, evolutionary, and incremental development methodologies that allow constant system changes and validations. The evaluation metrics support the systems by enabling the performance validation processes and facilitating the comparison of the achieved results with commercial tools. Finally, we have proposed a development process for vulnerability detection systems that provides a guide to meet the minimum scalability and continuous improvement requirements.

As future work, we plan to utilize the resources of the powerful Shodan search engine to identify vulnerabilities through its APIs, which provide a wide range of information on the different IPs to be monitored. Based on the information obtained, we plan to develop a machine learning-enabled vulnerability prioritization model using the guidelines identified in this study. This will allow us to analyze and interpret the data and the possible risks that can be generated.

Acknowledgment. The authors would like to thank the Universidad de las Fuerzas Armadas-ESPE of Sangolquí, Ecuador, for the resources granted to develop the research project entitled: "Design and Implementation of the IT infrastructure and service management system for the ESPE Academic CERT", coded as PIC-2020-ESPE-CERT.

References

1. Al-Dhaqm, A., Razak, S.A., Siddique, K., Ikuesan, R.A., Kebande, V.R.: Towards the development of an integrated incident response model for database forensic investigation field. IEEE Access **8**, 145018–145032 (2020). https://doi.org/10.1109/ACCESS.2020.3008696
2. Alsowail, R.A., Al-Shehari, T.: Empirical detection techniques of insider threat incidents. IEEE Access **8**, 78385–78402 (2020). https://doi.org/10.1109/ACCESS.2020.2989739
3. Aminanto, M.E., Ban, T., Isawa, R., Takahashi, T., Inoue, D.: Threat alert prioritization using isolation forest and stacked auto encoder with day-forward-chaining analysis. IEEE Access **8**, 217977–217986 (2020). https://doi.org/10.1109/ACCESS.2020.3041837
4. Andrade, R., Cordova, D., Ortiz-Garcés, I., Fuertes, W., Cazares, M.: A comprehensive study about cybersecurity incident response capabilities in Ecuador, pp. 281–292 (2021). https://doi.org/10.1007/978-3-030-60467-7_24
5. Antunes, N., Vieira, M.: Assessing and comparing vulnerability detection tools for web services: benchmarking approach and examples. IEEE Trans. Serv. Comput. **8**(2), 269–283 (2015). https://doi.org/10.1109/TSC.2014.2310221
6. Kitchenham, B.A., Charters, S.: Guidelines for performing systematic literature reviews in software engineering, vol. 2 (2007)
7. Cao, S., Sun, X., Bo, L., Wei, Y., Li, B.: BGNN4VD: constructing bidirectional graph neural-network for vulnerability detection. Inf. Softw. Technol. **136**, 106576 (2021). https://doi.org/10.1016/j.infsof.2021.106576
8. Cigoj, P., Blazic, B.J.: An intelligent and automated WCMS vulnerability-discovery tool: the current state of the web. IEEE Access **7**, 175466–175473 (2019). https://doi.org/10.1109/ACCESS.2019.2957573, https://doi.org/10.1186/s13643-016-0384-4
9. Ghaffarian, S.M., Shahriari, H.R.: Software vulnerability analysis and discovery using machine-learning and data-mining techniques: a survey. ACM Comput. Surv. **50**(4), 56:1–56:36 (2017). https://doi.org/10.1145/3092566

10. Goel, S., Nussbaum, B.: Attribution across cyber attack types: network intrusions and information operations. IEEE Open J. Commun. Soc. **2**, 1082–1093 (2021). https://doi.org/10.1109/OJCOMS.2021.3074591
11. Han, L., Zhou, M., Qian, Y., Fu, C., Zou, D.: An optimized static propositional function model to detect software vulnerability. IEEE Access **7**, 143499–143510 (2019). https://doi.org/10.1109/ACCESS.2019.2943896
12. IBM Corporation: IBM Security. IBM Corporation, New York (2020). https://www.ibm.com/security/digital-assets/cost-data-breach-report/
13. Jeon, S., Kim, H.K.: AutoVAS: an automated vulnerability analysis system with a deep learning approach. Comput. Secur. **106**, 102308 (2021). https://doi.org/10.1016/j.cose.2021.102308
14. Li, Z., Zou, D., Tang, J., Zhang, Z., Sun, M., Jin, H.: A comparative study of deep learning-based vulnerability detection system. IEEE Access **7**, 103184–103197 (2019). https://doi.org/10.1109/ACCESS.2019.2930578
15. Liu, M., Wang, B.: A web second-order vulnerabilities detection method. IEEE Access **6**, 70983–70988 (2018). https://doi.org/10.1109/ACCESS.2018.2881070
16. Liu, S., Lin, G., Han, Q.-L., Wen, S., Zhang, J., Xiang, Y.: DeepBalance: deep-learning and fuzzy oversampling for vulnerability detection. IEEE Trans. Fuzzy Syst. **28**(7), 1329–1343 (2020). https://doi.org/10.1109/TFUZZ.2019.2958558
17. Meng, G., Liu, Y., Zhang, J., Pokluda, A., Boutaba, R.: Collaborative security: a survey and taxonomy. ACM Comput. Surv. **48**, 1, 42 (2015). https://doi.org/10.1145/2785733
18. Ouzzani, M., Hammady, H., Fedorowicz, Z., Elmagarmid, A.: Rayyan-A web and mobile app for systematic reviews. Syst. Control Found. Appl. **5**(1), 210 (2016). https://doi.org/10.1186/s13643-016-0384-4
19. Qasem, A., Shirani, P., Debbabi, M., Wang, L., Lebel, B., Agba, B.L.: Automatic vulnerability detection in embedded devices and firmware: survey and layered taxonomies. ACM Comput. Surv. **54**(2), 25:1–25:42 (2021). https://doi.org/10.1145/3432893
20. Qiang, W., Liao, Y., Sun, G., Yang, L.T., Zou, D., Jin, H.: Patch-related vulnerability detection based on symbolic execution. IEEE Access **5**, 20777–20784 (2017). https://doi.org/10.1109/ACCESS.2017.2676161
21. Qin, J., Zhang, H., Guo, J., Wang, S., Wen, Q., Shi, Y.: Vulnerability detection on android apps-inspired by case study on vulnerability related with web functions. IEEE Access **8**, 106437–106451 (2020). https://doi.org/10.1109/ACCESS.2020.2998043
22. Ren, Y., Dong, W., Lin, J., Miao, X.: A dynamic taint analysis framework based on entity equipment. IEEE Access **7**, 186308–186318 (2019). https://doi.org/10.1109/ACCESS.2019.2961144
23. Ron, M., Fuertes, W., Bonilla, M., Toulkeridis, T., Diaz, J.: Cybercrime in Ecuador, an exploration, which allows to define national cybersecurity policies. In: 2018 13th Iberian Conference on Information Systems and Technologies (CISTI), pp. 1–7 (2018). https://doi.org/10.23919/CISTI.2018.8399357
24. Şahin, C.B., Dinler, Ö.B., Abualigah, L.: Prediction of software vulnerability based deep symbiotic genetic algorithms: phenotyping of dominant-features. Appl. Intell. **51**(11), 8271–8287 (2021). https://doi.org/10.1007/s10489-021-02324-3
25. Sönmez, F.Ö., Kiliç, B.G.: Holistic web application security visualization for multi-project and multi-phase dynamic application security test results. IEEE Access **9**, 25858–25884 (2021). https://doi.org/10.1109/ACCESS.2021.3057044

26. Sun, N., Zhang, J., Rimba, P., Gao, S., Zhang, L.Y., Xiang, Y.: Data-driven cyber-security incident prediction: a survey. IEEE Commun. Surv. Tutor. **21**(2), 1744–1772 (2019). https://doi.org/10.1109/COMST.2018.2885561
27. Vielberth, M., Böhm, F., Fichtinger, I., Pernul, G.: Security operations center: a systematic study and open challenges. IEEE Access **8**, 227756–227779 (2020). https://doi.org/10.1109/ACCESS.2020.3045514
28. Wang, H., et al.: Combining graph-based learning with automated data collection for code vulnerability detection. IEEE Trans. Inf. Forensics Secur. **16**, 1943–1958 (2021). https://doi.org/10.1109/TIFS.2020.3044773
29. Yi, M., Xu, X., Xu, L.: An intelligent communication warning vulnerability detection algorithm based on IoT technology. IEEE Access **7**, 164803–164814 (2019). https://doi.org/10.1109/ACCESS.2019.2953075
30. Yu, L., Lu, Y., Shen, Y., Huang, H., Zhu, K.: BEDetector: a two-channel encoding method to detect vulnerabilities based on binary similarity. IEEE Access **9**, 51631–51645 (2021). https://doi.org/10.1109/ACCESS.2021.3064687
31. Yu, M., Zhuge, J., Cao, M., Shi, Z., Jiang, L.: A survey of security vulnerability analysis, discovery, detection, and mitigation on IoT devices. Future Internet **12**(2), 27 (2020). https://doi.org/10.3390/fi12020027
32. Zagane, M., Abdi, M.K., Alenezi, M.: Deep learning for software vulnerabilities detection using code metrics. IEEE Access **8**, 74562–74570 (2020). https://doi.org/10.1109/ACCESS.2020.2988557
33. Zeng, P., Lin, G., Pan, L., Tai, Y., Zhang, J.: Software vulnerability analysis and discovery using deep learning techniques: a survey. IEEE Access **8**, 197158–197172 (2020). https://doi.org/10.1109/ACCESS.2020.3034766
34. Zhang, H., Sakurai, K.: A survey of software clone detection from security perspective. IEEE Access **9**, 48157–48173 (2021). https://doi.org/10.1109/ACCESS.2021.3065872
35. Zheng, W., et al.: The impact factors on the performance of machine learning-based vulnerability detection: a comparative study. J. Syst. Softw. **168**, 110659 (2020). https://doi.org/10.1016/j.jss.2020.110659
36. Zhu, K., Lu, Y., Huang, H.: Scalable static detection of use-after-free vulnerabilities in binary code. IEEE Access **8**, 78713–78725 (2020). https://doi.org/10.1109/ACCESS.2020.2990197

Analysis of Vulnerabilities Associated with Social Engineering Attacks Based on User Behavior

Eduardo Benavides-Astudillo[1,2]([✉]) [ID], Luis Silva-Ordoñez[1],
Ronny Rocohano-Rámos[1], Walter Fuertes[1,2] [ID], Félix Fernández-Peña[3] [ID],
Sandra Sanchez-Gordon[2] [ID], and Rodrigo Bastidas-Chalan[1] [ID]

[1] Universidad de las Fuerzas Armadas ESPE, Sangolquí, Ecuador
{debenavides,ldsilva1,rgrocohano,wmfuertes,rvbastidas}@espe.edu.ec
[2] Escuela Politécnica Nacional, Quito, Ecuador
{diego.benavides,walter.fuertes,sandra.sanchez}@epn.edu.ec
[3] Universidad Politécnica Salesiana, Quito, Ecuador
fo.fernandez@uta.edu.ec

Abstract. One of the most effective attacks on cybersecurity is Social Engineering, in which the attacker deceives an end-user to steal its credentials and perpetrate cyber-crimes. There are hardware and software countermeasures to deal with these types of attacks. However, people themselves are the most vulnerable link in this security chain. In addition, there are influencing factors in people's behavior, which make them more vulnerable. This study aims to determine the most common characteristics that make users vulnerable, either individually or in groups. For this, we conduct an exploratory and descriptive study on administrative, lecturers, and students of a higher education institution on four scales that consider the following behaviors: risk behavior, conservative behavior, exposure to offense, and perception of risk. The results obtained show that users with risky behavior are the most exposed to a Social Engineering attack. We also concluded that the analyzed groups of lecturers and administrators are less likely to be victims of these attacks than students. Finally, we inferred that people who spend more time in front of a computer and are more permissive of risky behaviors are more vulnerable to these attacks.

Keywords: Social Engineering · Cybersecurity · Risk ·
Vulnerabilities · User behavior

1 Introduction

The number of people doing business online is increasing every day, and this need grows exponentially worldwide due to the Covid-19 pandemic. Thus, today, students, professionals, and practically all people are users of these online services, regardless of age, level of education, and other variables. On the other hand, just

© Springer Nature Switzerland AG 2022
M. Botto-Tobar et al. (Eds.): ICAT 2021, CCIS 1535, pp. 351–364, 2022.
https://doi.org/10.1007/978-3-031-03884-6_26

as the number of online transactions increased, so have the number of online attacks. For example, Social Engineering (SE) attacks, in which the attacker tries to obtain confidential information from end-users through deception. These deceptions can be conducted through emails, fake web pages, messages on social networks, and others [1].

Individuals and organizations spend significant sums of money on technology to protect the information, both in hardware and in software. However, a significant percentage of these attacks are successful; this is because, despite this equipment, it is enough for a person to reveal their sensitive information directly to the attacker without knowing it [2]. Thus, attackers take advantage of certain vulnerable behaviors, such as overconfidence, shyness, lack of knowledge, among others.

Awareness is a powerful weapon against social engineering attacks, which is why effective training and education programs are so essential [3]. In this study, the authors highlight the importance of user behavior but do not identify the scales of risks or behaviors that make users vulnerable.

This study aims to determine the relationship between certain user behaviors and the Social Engineering attacks of which they are victims. To do this, we perform a survey to characterize the people who are more likely to receive a Social Engineering attack. In addition, we conduct a correlational analysis of the characteristics of the people who are victims of Social Engineering attacks. The hypotheses are:

H1: There is no significant difference between the scales Risky Behavior Scale (RBS), Conservative Behavior Scale (CBS), Exposure to Offence Scale (EOS), and Risk Perception Scale (RPS) concerning their average.
H2: There is no significant difference between the surveyed groups (lecturers, administrators, and students) concerning their average.
H3: The exposure to more hours/day that users have when using the Internet affects the average of the scales RBS, CBS, EOS, RPS.
H4: There is a significant correlation between the averages of the scales RBS, CBS, EOS, and RPS.

The main contribution of this paper is to provide the research community with an analysis to determine which people are most vulnerable or least vulnerable to Social Engineering attacks based on their behavior. Organizations can use these results to focus their cybersecurity training priorities.

The rest of the article is structured as follows. Section 2 explains the materials and methods. In Sect. 3, we explain the survey design and the data collection. In Sect. 4, the results are shown and discussed the main findings. Finally, in Sect. 5, the conclusions and lines of future work are exposed.

2   Related Works

Awareness is a powerful weapon in dealing with Social Engineering attacks, which is why practical training and education programs are so important, according to [3] (Aldawood and Skinner 2018). In this survey, the authors highlight the importance of user behavior; however, they do not identify the scales of risks or behaviors that make them vulnerable.

The framework proposed in (Ye et al. 2020) [4] offers a way to quantitatively calculate the possibility of being a victim of a Social Engineering attack by assessing users' frequency of operation, security awareness, and defense degree. Unlike our proposal, this one is more limited because we also evaluate the scales of risk behavior, conservative behavior, exposure to offenses, and risk perception. We also determine the relationship between these scales.

In the conceptual model in (Muslah Albladi and Weir 2019) [5], the authors present an online questionnaire that measures the constructs of the proposed model, based on the number of connections, percentage of known friends, social network experience, and cybercrime experience. Although these dimensions resemble ours, this experiment is very particular because it is conducted only on data obtained from 316 Facebook users.

The paper (Öğütçü et al. 2016) [6] is a model to follow, which is why our work has taken many elements from it. In the paper, a questionnaire is divided into four scales: risk behavior, conservative behavior, exposure to offenses, and risk perception. However, the questions asked in the questionnaire are not updated because the paper is from 2016, on the other hand, in this study, a correlation analysis between the scales studied is not performed.

3   Materials and Methods

3.1   Survey Design

The first step was to design a survey based on a Likert Scale [7], that can define people's behavior concerning Social Engineering attacks. For this, after making a rigorous analysis of the existing literature, a tool implemented in [6], was selected, through which four scales are considered. Below is a brief explanation of these scales.

Risky Behavior Scale (RBS). This scale refers to the behavior of users in the face of risk towards Information Systems. This measurement can occur when a user uses a computer without security measures and puts other people who live or work in the same space at risk [8]. Table 1 shows the questions on this scale:

Conservative Behavior Scale (CBS). The objective of this scale is to measure the user's actions when using an Information System. That is, it defines the specific actions that users take to protect their information [9]. Table 2 shows the questions on this scale:

Exposure to Offence Scale (EOS). This scale aims to measure the exposure that users have to any cybersecurity threat. This scale highlights the exposure to risks, threats, and impacts generated by user's behaviors and occurrences. Table 3 shows the questions on this scale:

Risk Perception Scale (RPS). This scale measures the degree of risk or danger captured by a user who is using information technologies. This perception

Table 1. Risky Behavior Scale (RBS)

Do you use Whats-App, Telegram, Messenger, or similar chat programs?

Do you use Meet, Teams, Zoom, or similar meeting programs?

Do you use email?

Do you use your Corporate or Institutional email address for your business?

Do you use online banking?

Do you make purchases or payments on the Internet?

Do you use websites that provide services to citizens electronically (i.e., check identity number, payment of basic services, etc.)?

Do you play video games online?

Do you watch videos or movies online?

When necessary, do you share your personal information on the Internet (i.e., first name, last name, date of birth, email, address, etc.)?

Do you transfer confidential files on Whats-App, Telegram, or Messenger?

Do you use online banking in places where there is access to the public Internet?

Do you share your passwords with other people?

Do you save your passwords by writing them in diaries or places that can be easily found?

Do you open emails from strangers or download the attachments of those emails?

Table 2. Conservative Behavior Scale (CBS)

Do you use the original licensed software on your computer?

Do you use programs like virus detection, spyware, etc.?

Do you delete temporary internet files and internet history before leaving a computer?

Do you use long and complicated passwords that cannot be easily guessed for your Internet accounts and personal files?

Do you use an electronic signature?

Do you have a password to access your computer?

Do you pay attention to the websites you visit, checking if they have the HTTPS lock in the address bar?

Do you often change your passwords?

Are you aware that other people may use your personal information illegally?

---

is related to the field of trust that a user has in the face of possible cyber-attacks [10]. Table 4 shows the questions on this scale:

3.2   Data Collection

To carry out this collection, we designed the survey with its respective questions in a Google Forms form, taking into account five sections. The first section was

Table 3. Exposure to Offence Scale (EOS)

Have you had problems due to computer viruses?

Have you experienced financial loss because of online shopping?

Have you had problems sharing your personal information on the Internet?

Have you received any notification of using your username and password on the Internet without your authorization?

Have the files on your computer ever been stolen or deleted?

Have you found fake accounts that use your confidential data or your user profile?

Do you use any entity that preserves your credit card details in online purchases, such as PayPal?

Table 4. Risk Perception Scale (RPS)

Of the following items, indicate the degree of danger that you perceive in each one:

Computer virus

Lack of antivirus

Spyware (Key logger, Screen logger, Trojan, etc.)

File sharing programs (Google Drive, Dropbox, Mega, etc.)

Chat programs (Whats-App, Telegram, and Messenger.)

Junk, spam, or junk email

Online games

USB or external memories

Macros in Microsoft Office applications (Word, Excel, etc.)

Use of pirated programs

Download materials such as music, photos, or movies without paying anything

Open emails with advertising content

Use of online banking

Share information with strangers online

Online purchases

Using Wireless Wi-Fi

Downloading and using free or unlicensed programs

Delivery of identity card or driver's license number to security personnel at the entrance of a building

aimed at obtaining information from the profile of the participating users. The remaining four options were addressed to each of the scales RBS, CBS, EOS, and RPS. This survey was shared with the higher education institution's academic, student, administrative, and military personnel. For practical application, the administrative or military group will be treated as a single group called administrative. The number of questionnaires resulted in 146 completed surveys. In the User Profile section of the survey, they were asked for the information detailed in Table 5.

Table 5. Demographic information requested from users to define their profile

Select your age range
Select your gender
Have you ever had training or experience in Internet Security?
What is your average time of Internet use per day?
Choose your occupation
What is your level of education?
Choose the department, study, or work area to which you belong?
How do you access the Internet from outside your workplace?
Choose your department or study area
Choose the level you are at in your career
Enter your position within the Institution

The questions in Table 5 were exposed according to the type of survey participant, i.e., if he or she is academic, student, or administrative staff. We designed the survey so that, after users complete this part of obtaining demographic information, they immediately complete the part of the four scales.

4   Results and Discussion

Once the survey data were collected, their results are shown in this section in two parts. First, the general data obtained from the respondents are revealed, and second, the verification of the hypotheses proposed is contrasted with their respective discussion.

4.1   General Results

Tables 6, 7, 8, and 9 show the results obtained from the user's general information.

Table 10 shows the means obtained in the survey for each of the four defined scales RBS, CBS, EOS, and RPS. A weighting of 1 is taken into account as the lowest value and 5 as the maximum value in each of the questions in the survey.

4.2   Verification of the Hypotheses and Discussion

4.2.1   H1 Test: There is No Significant Difference Between the Scales RBS, CBS, EOS, and RPS Concerning Their Average

Regarding H1, it can be verified that there is a significant difference between the scales, which is why H1 is discarded. To contrasts H1, we used the analysis of variance or ANOVA between scales. This ANOVA analysis allows us to identify the significant difference in the results obtained in the developed survey. To develop the ANOVA analysis between the scales RBS, CBS, EOS, RPS, the

Table 6. Results of the user profile section

Questions	Options (years)				
Select your age range	15–24	25–34	35–44	45–54	55 and older
	117	15	9	9	3
	76%	10%	6%	6%	6%
Select your gender	Male	Female	–	–	–
	101	52	–	–	–
	66%	34%	–	–	–
Have you ever had training or experience in Internet Security?	Yes	No	–	–	–
	65	88	–	–	–
	42%	58%	–	–	–
Time range of internet use	1–5 hours/day	6–10 hours/day	11 or more hours/day	–	–
	9	75	69	–	–
	6%	49%	45%	–	–
Choose your occupation	Student	Academic	Administrative	–	–
	128	18	7	–	–
	84%	12%	4%	–	–

Table 7. Results of the University Academics

Questions	Number of mentions in the analyzed papers		
Education level	Third Level	Fourth Level	–
	0	18	–
Choose the department, area of study, or work to which you belong	–	–	–
How do you access the Internet from outside your workplace?	Using Mobile Data	Public Wi-Fi network (Shopping malls, parks)	Private Wi-Fi network (Home)

Significance Level $\alpha = 0.05$ was used, so that if the value of P (Probability) is less than that of α, H1 is rejected.

Therefore, it is shown that there is a significant difference between the scales (see Table 11).

Table 11 shows a significant difference between the scales analyzed with ANOVA. For this reason, it is necessary to complement the analysis by developing a Tukey test to identify the scales that create this difference. Table 12 shows the result of the compared scales to identify which difference is created.

Table 8. Results of the Student section

Questions	Options				
Choose the department, area of study, or work to which you belong	Computer Sciences	Exact Sciences	Life Sciences and Agriculture	Electrical, Electronics and Telecommunications	Other
	110	3	9	2	4
How do you access the Internet from outside your workplace?	Using Mobile Data	Public Wi-Fi network (Shopping malls, parks)	Private Wi-Fi network (Home)	–	–

Table 9. Results of the Administrative section

Questions	Options			
Enter your function within the Institution	–	–	–	–
Level of education	First Level	Second Level	Third Level	Fourth Level
		1	5	1
How do you access the Internet from outside your workplace?	Using Mobile Data	Public WiFi network (Shopping malls, parks)	Private Wi-Fi network (Home)	–

Table 10. Number of questions and averages obtained by scale

Scale	Number of questions	Average
RBS	16	2,87091
CBS	9	2,71604
EOS	7	1,94864
RPS	18	3,53703

Table 11. ANOVA calculation between scales

Source of variations	SS	DF	MSe	F	P
Between groups	13,81396	3	4,60465	7,39783	0,000
Within groups	28,63191	46	0,62243		
Total	42,44588	49	0,86624		

Note: SS = Sum of Squares; DF = Degree of Freedom; MSe = Mean of squares; F = Error; P = Probability

Table 12. Tukey test between scales

Group 1	Group 2	Media	Std err	p-value
RBS	CBS	0,15486	0,23244	0,965
RBS	EOS	0,92226	0,25280	0,061
RBS	RPS	0,66612	0,19167	0,080
CBS	EOS	0,76740	0,28113	0,229
CBS	RPS	0,82098	0,22774	0,065
EOS	RPS	1,58839	0,24849	0,000

Based on Table 12 and the relationship between EOS and RPS, it can be observed that RPS positively influences EOS. In conclusion, as users have a better perception of risk, they will be less exposed to Social Engineering attacks.

4.2.2 H2 Test: There is No Significant Difference Between the Surveyed Groups (i.e., Lecturers, Administrators, Students) Concerning It's Average

To contrast H2, the data were grouped between the three surveyed groups (i.e., lecturers, administrators, and students) and the indicated scales. Table 13 shows the results obtained by ANOVA by obtaining the P = 0.004 in the case of the CBS scale and P = 0.021 in the case of the RPS scale, and there is a significant difference between the surveyed groups. According to the differences found, it was determined that the group of lecturers has significant differences with the group of administrative personnel and with the group of students.

In addition, to identify the group or groups that generate this difference. We find that for both the CBS scales (see Table 14) and the RPS scale (see Table 15), the group of lecturers is the one that generates the difference.

Based on the previous analysis, it is observed that there is a significant difference in the mean obtained (from 1 to 5) between the groups surveyed. Thus, lecturers have a more conservative behavior in risky situations on the CBS scale, and they have a mean = 3,067. In the case of the RPS scale, the lecturers obtained a mean = 3,780. Therefore, it is concluded that they have a better perception of risk when using the Internet or IT devices than the other groups surveyed. In (Öяütçü et al. 2016a) highlight it as a difference that in the study carried out; it was found that the students were the ones that generated the significant difference between the surveyed groups.

Table 13. ANOVA calculation between academics, administrative, and students

Scales		SS	DF	MS	F	P
Risky Behavior Scale (RBS)	Between groups	0,11266	2	0,05633	0,23267	0,792
	Within groups	36,31447	150	0,24209	–	–
	Total	36,42713	152	0,23965	–	–
Conservative Behavior Scale (CBS)	Between groups	2,52684	2	1,26342	5,60832	0,004
	Within groups	33,79140	150	0,22527	–	–
	Total	36,31824	152	0,23893	–	–
Exposure to Offence Scale (EOS)	Between groups	0,08329	2	0,04164	0,69075	0,502
	Within groups	9,04382	150	0,06029	–	–
	Total	9,12711	152	0,06004	–	–
Risk Perception Scale (RPS)	Between groups	1,82996	2	0,91498	3,94602	0,021
	Within groups	34,78113	150	0,23187	–	–
	Total	36,61111	152	0,24086	–	–

Table 14. Results obtained in the Tukey test between the groups (Lecturers, Administrators, and Students) and the scale (CBS)

Group 1	Group 2	Media	Std err	p-value
Academic	Administrative	0,38536	0,14949	0,165
Academic	Student	0,39949	0,08448	0,002
Administrative	Student	0,01413	0,13027	0,996

Table 15. Results of the Tukey test between the groups (Lecturers, Administrators and Students) and the scale (RPS)

Group 1	Group 2	Media	Std err	p-value
Academic	Administrative	0,38536	0,14949	0,165
Academic	Student	0,39949	0,08448	0,002
Administrative	Student	0,01413	0,13027	0,996

4.2.3   H3 Test: Exposure to More Hours per Day that Users Have When Using the Internet Affects the Average of the Scales {RBS, CBS, EOS, RPS}

In order to contrast H3, respondents were grouped into three ranges, according to the amount of time per day that they use the Internet (i.e., from 1 to 5 h/day, 6 to 10 h/day, and 11 or more hours/day). Table 16 shows the ANOVA analysis, in which it can be identified that if there is a significant difference in the case of the RBS scale with a value of P = 0.003. Therefore, there is a significant difference between the times of Internet use of the participants. For this reason,

H3 is rejected, and the alternative hypothesis is accepted, which establishes that the time of Internet use of the surveyed users affects the average of the proposed scales.

Table 16. Results of the ANOVA of time of Internet use.

Scales		SS	DF	MS	F	P
Risky Behavior Scale (RBS)	Between groups	2,67715	2	1,33857	5,94923	0,003
	Within groups	33,74994	150	0,2249	–	–
	Total	36,42713	152	0,23965	–	–
Conservative Behavior Scale (CBS)	Between groups	0,11809	2	0,05904	0,24467	0,783
	Within groups	36,20015	150	0,24133	–	–
	Total	36,31824	152	0,23893	–	–
Exposure to Offence Scale (EOS)	Between groups	0,10191	2	0,05095	0,84691	0,430
	Within groups	9,02520	150	0,06016	–	–
	Total	9,12711	152	0,06004	–	–
Risk Perception Scale (RPS)	Between groups	0,65682	2	0,32841	1,37011	0,257
	Within groups	35,95428	150	0,23969	–	–
	Total	36,61111	152	0,24086	–	–

To identify in which group this difference is generated, the Tukey test was applied between the groups that use the Internet, in the three ranges (i.e., 1 to 5 h/day, 6 to 10 h/day, and 11 or more hours/day). The results obtained with the development of the Tukey test within the RBS scale reveal that the respondents in the group of 11 or more hours/day are more exposed. In addition, they are more tolerant of risk situations than the groups that use less time on the Internet, with a mean = 3.01268 on the RBS scale v (Table 17).

In conclusion, based on the analysis of the results obtained, it is shown that on the RBS scale, respondents in the group of 11 or more hours/day, with a mean = 3.012 on the RBS scale. There are more exposed and more permissive in risk situations than groups that use the Internet for less time. These results coincide with the results obtained by (Öğütçü et al. 2016a), who found that the significant difference is generated in the RBS scale.

Table 17. Results of the Tukey test between the meantime of Internet use and the scale (RBS)

Group 1	Group 2	Media	Std err	p-value
1–5 h/day	6–10 h/day	0,137222	0,118321	0,691
1–5 h/day	11 or more hours/day	0,380736	0,118871	0,063
6-10 h/day	11 or more hours/day	0,243514	0,055950	0,006

4.2.4 H4 Test: There is a Significant Correlation Between the Averages of the Scales {RBS, CBS, EOS, and RPS}

Unlike the study carried out by (Öȝütçü et al. 2016a), in this study, the existing Pearson correlation between the scales was analyzed. This is to test whether or not there is a correlation. That is, positive in the case that the value obtained when comparing the scales is more significant than zero and less than one. Alternatively, negative in the case that the value obtained by comparing the scales is less than zero and greater than minus one. Table 18 represents the data obtained by comparing the scales using Pearson's correlation.

Table 18. Result of the Pearson Correlation between the Behavior scales

Scales		RBS	CBS	EOS	RPS
Risky Behavior Scale (RBS)	r	1	0,17554	0,00705	0,23947
Conservative Behavior Scale (CBS)	r	0,17554	1	−0,20972	0,38100
Exposure to Offence Scale (EOS)	r	0,00705	−0,20972	1	−0,12996
Risk Perception Scale (RPS)	r	0,23947	0,381002	−0,12996	1

Table 18 shows the highest positive correlation between the CBS and RPS scales, obtaining an r = 0.38. Therefore, this means that if the CBS average increases, so will the RPS average. In other words, if conservative behavior increases in a user, they will have a better perception of risk when making use of the Internet or IT devices.

On the other hand, the negative correlations obtained when developing the Pearson correlation occurred between the CBS and EOS scales with r = −0.20 and between the EOS and RPS scales with r = −0.12. Hence, this indicates that if the average of CBS increases, the average of the EOS scale will decrease. In conclusion, if conservative behavior increases in a user, they will be less exposed to possible risks when using the Internet or IT devices. By doing the same analysis with the case of the EOS and RPS scales, if a user's exposure to offenses or risks increases, their perception of risk will decrease.

5   Conclusions and Future Work

This study determined that there is a relationship between the defined user behavior and social engineering attacks. Thus, based on the analyzed relationship between EOS and RPS, it can be determined that while users have a higher risk perception, they will be less exposed to a social engineering attack. This coincides with another finding found in our study, which is that university teachers are less likely to be victims of an attack due to their more conservative behavior.

Our model was applied to a higher education institution, but it can be applied to various institutions since the general concept is the same. Based on this, other organizations can help better orient their cybersecurity training policy. Likewise, in organizations in general, this model allows identifying user groups needing knowledge and skills to face Social Engineering attacks. However, this model can be adapted to any organization by applying the proposed survey and the analysis.

It was found that the more hours a user is exposed to a digital device, the greater the risk of being the victim of an attack. These results coincide with the data presented by Kaspersky and ESET. Specifically, they indicate that due to the Covid-19 pandemic, more use of the Internet is made, Social engineering attacks increase. In addition, if the user is more permissive or not very cautious, the risk of an attack increases considerably.

As future work, we plan to collect around 10,000 surveys similar to the one carried out in this work to check the correctness of the correlation between people's behavior and social engineering attacks. For this purpose, it is planned to implement a Machine Learning algorithm to add the ability to identify patterns in big data and make predictions. Finally, it is planned to develop online software available to any organization that wishes to use it. These organizations can identify which user groups are the most vulnerable to being victims of Social Engineering attacks.

Acknowledgment. The authors would like to thank the Universidad de las Fuerzas Armadas-ESPE of Sangolquí, Ecuador, for the resources granted to develop the research project entitled: "Detection and Mitigation of Social Engineering attacks applying Cognitive Security", coded as PIC-2020-SOCIAL-ENGINEERING.

References

1. Benavides, E., Fuertes, W., Sanchez, S., Nuñez-Agurto, D.: Caracterización de los ataques de phishing y técnicas para mitigarlos. Ataques: una revisión sistemática de la literatura. Cienc. y Tecnol. **13**(1), 97–104 (2020). https://doi.org/10.18779/CYT.V13I1.357
2. Benavides, E., Fuertes, W., Sanchez, S., Sanchez, M.: Classification of phishing attack solutions by employing deep learning techniques: a systematic literature review. In: Rocha, Á., Pereira, R.P. (eds.) Developments and Advances in Defense and Security. SIST, vol. 152, pp. 51–64. Springer, Singapore (2020). https://doi.org/10.1007/978-981-13-9155-2_5
3. Aldawood, H., Skinner, G.: Educating and raising awareness on cyber security social engineering: a literature review. In: 2018 IEEE International Conference on Teaching, Assessment, and Learning for Engineering (TALE), pp. 62–68, December 2018. https://doi.org/10.1109/TALE.2018.8615162
4. Ye, Z., Guo, Y., Ju, A., Wei, F., Zhang, R., Ma, J.: A risk analysis framework for social engineering attack based on user profiling. J. Organ. End User Comput. **32**(3) (2020). https://doi.org/10.4018/JOEUC.2020070104
5. Muslah Albladi, S., Weir, G.R.S.: A conceptual model to predict social engineering victims. In: Proceedings of the 12th International Conference on Global Security, Safety and Sustainability, ICGS3 2019, April 2019. https://doi.org/10.1109/ICGS3.2019.8688352

6. Öğütçü, G., Testik, Ö.M., Chouseinoglou, O.: Analysis of personal information security behavior and awareness. Comput. Secur. **56**, 83–93 (2016). https://doi.org/10.1016/j.cose.2015.10.002
7. Analyzing Likert Data
8. Milne, G.R., Labrecque, L.I., Cromer, C.: Toward an understanding of the online consumer's risky behavior and protection practices. J. Consum. Aff. **43**(3), 449–473 (2009). https://doi.org/10.1111/J.1745-6606.2009.01148.X
9. Ng, B.Y., Kankanhalli, A., (Calvin) Xu, Y.: Studying users' computer security behavior: a health belief perspective. Decis. Support Syst. **46**(4), 815–825 (2009). https://doi.org/10.1016/J.DSS.2008.11.010
10. Horst, M., Kuttschreuter, M., Gutteling, J.M.: Perceived usefulness, personal experiences, risk perception and trust as determinants of adoption of e-government services in The Netherlands. Comput. Hum. Behav. **23**(4), 1838–1852 (2007). https://doi.org/10.1016/J.CHB.2005.11.003

XSS2DENT, Detecting Cross-Site Scripting Attacks (XSS) Vulnerabilities: A Case Study

Germán E. Rodríguez[1,2](✉) [ID], Jenny Torres[1], and Eduardo Benavides[1,2] [ID]

[1] Facultad de Ingeniería en Sistemas, Escuela Politécnica Nacional, Quito, Ecuador
{german.rodriguez,jenny.torres,diego.benavides}@epn.edu.ec
[2] Departamento de Ciencias de la Computación, Universidad de las Fuerzas Armadas ESPE,
Sangolquí, Santo Domingo de los Tsáchilas, Ecuador
{gerodriguez10,debenavides}@espe.edu.ec

Abstract. Based on the OWASP Top 10 Security Risk, Cross-Site Scripting (XSS) attacks rank seventh, according to the latest report released in 2017. To execute this attack, a web application is used to send malicious code, generally in the form of a script on the browser side. To verify the level of vulnerability of educational establishments in Santo Domingo de los Tsachilas city against this threat, a model has been proposed, whose objective is to obtain information by executing a controlled, combined and camouflaged attack in a security cybernetics challenge, distributed through flyers with a QR Code, to students from different areas in the city. With this information, a report was prepared in order to socialize vulnerable establishments, with information that allowed them to review the status of their security infrastructure and establish new blocking rules against this attack. The results indicate that our model was successfully executed in 3 universities. In addition, it is shown how our attack spread beyond the city limits, reaching countries such as Mexico, Argentina, Colombia, among others.

Keywords: XSS · Clickjacking · Zombie

1 Introduction

According to the OWASP Top 10 Web Application Security Risks (2017) [1], Cross-Site Scripting (XSS) attacks were ranked 7th. This gap allows any attacker to gain access to confidential information, after executing JavaScript, VBScript, ActiveX, Flash or HTML codes, embedded in some malicious link [2]. In addition, clickjacking attacks victims by clicking on invisible elements of a web page, and involuntary actions that are advantageous for the attacker are executed [3]. On the other hand, there are proposals to teach university students about XSS attacks, as seen in [4]. However, a combination of XSS+ Clickjacking attacks become a powerful vulnerability.

With this background, the scientific literature has been systematically analyzed to find proposals that combine these attacks and whose results can be applied to the teaching of students at different educational levels. Our analysis shows that, the results presented in [5] to [23] are proposed to mitigate only XSS attacks, but no information was found

© Springer Nature Switzerland AG 2022
M. Botto-Tobar et al. (Eds.): ICAT 2021, CCIS 1535, pp. 365–380, 2022.
https://doi.org/10.1007/978-3-031-03884-6_27

on mitigation of combined attacks (XSS + Clickjacking), in addition, the solutions have not been applied to education, no gamification techniques or challenges are used to teach about these types of attacks.

In this context, a model has been proposed that analyzes the state of computer security in educational establishments in Santo Domingo de los Ts'achilas city. For this, a cyber security challenge was designed, in order to motivate students to find the security flaws of a web page, which was previously compromised with a combination of XSS and Clickjacking scripts. This challenge was launched through flyers delivered to the students of the Universidad de las Fuerzas Armadas-ESPE, to be the motivators of their ex partners from other universities, schools, colleges or technical institutes, and thus access the challenge and try to solve it, with the incentive of joining the ESPE Cybersecurity Club if the 2 failures were discovered through certain proposed clues.

The rest of the document has been organized in the following way: in Sect. 2 a brief review of the existing literature is made to guide the proposed solutions and their limitations, Sect. 3 discusses the XSS2DENT model, the techniques and methods used, in Sect. 4 we analyze the results obtained with our proposal, Sect. 5 talks about the conclusions, and finally, Sect. 6 describes future work with open problems/challenges and some possible solutions/research directions.

2 Related Work

In the study presented in [5], vulnerabilities related to input validation (generic validations) have been addressed. It is a method that identifies a malicious execution sequence and is based on lists of legitimate sequences and malicious strings. Through four execution profiles, these lists are stored and correspond to four attack scenarios (two on the client side and two on the server).

The authors of [6] have analyzed a tool in which bureaucrats and cyber professionals can conduct attacks ethically and find XSS vulnerabilities. However, the study did not provide information for our research.

This schema combines a real-world data set, a feature extraction mechanism, and a multi layer perceptron model (MLP). Its potential has been applied in the detection of XSS-based attacks on the client side or on the server side. It is based on Python. It is a robust schema that is analyzed in [7], it is based on artificial neural networks that are integrated with an extractor of dynamic characteristics.

In another proposal, experiments in seven Java-based web applications have been evaluated. This is mentioned by [8], who have proposed an audit approach to recover the model implemented in the source code of a web application, and in this way suggest alternatives to modify and adapt the recovered model against XSS attacks. This proposal does not address DOM-based XSS.

According to the authors of [9], problems associated with graphical content in web applications are solved with the combination of black and white lists, a vulnerable file is classified using regular expressions and malicious code is removed. As a result, a set of rules has been proposed to protect this content and avoid XSS vulnerabilities.

In [10] the XSS and Cross-Site Request Foreign (CSRF) vulnerabilities of 500 web applications have been evaluated. They have the following disadvantage, all tests were done manually, with a black box testing approach. These tests have focused on financial institutions. A summary of the current status and a guide for future web developers has been provided.

By implementing an XSS vulnerability detector, its functionality has been tested on 50 real-world websites. The results were positive for a total of 848 XSS vulnerabilities on 24 websites. However, this model was trained with a small amount of data and the model parameters were not optimized with more test data. It is a proposal presented in [11], which uses optimized repertoires of attack vectors, it has been built with a machine learning algorithm, to reduce the size of the reports and thus improve the detection efficiency of XSS attacks.

A tool that runs test cases against a specific website is presented in [12], called PURITY. It resembles malicious activity that allows its sequence to be traced back to a vulnerable state. It is based on planning and allows manual configuration of input parameters. Black and white box tests have been used for the tests. The results are represented in the form of tables that provide a visual impression of where the vulnerability occurred.

Through black box tests with the prior consent of selected organizations, and with the aim of offering them solutions to address XSS vulnerabilities. This proposal is presented in [13], which analyzes the vulnerabilities of SQLi and XSS. An analysis of eleven North Khorasan websites in Iran has been completed, ten of which relate to government organizations and one to a private organization.

Through implemented prototypes, it has been discovered that some proposals can effectively protect users who are victims of malicious QR codes and vulnerable to XSS attacks. This is the case of [14], where a set of design-level recommendations has been presented, with the aim of creating more secure and usable mobile applications.

Similarly, [15] has examined the entire ecosystem life cycle of redesigned QR codes to identify potential security risks. His proposal is the use of a digital signature as a mechanism to improve security.

In [16] a method has been proposed to implement QR codes in the educational process. Here it has been shown that these codes are compatible with independent and collaborative learning by creating an interactive learning environment.

An anti-phishing authentication model to create a single sign-on using QR codes in [17]. Based on the results, this proposed scheme is safe against phishing attacks.

A scheme for sharing or using confidential information within an organization, has been proposed in [18]. For this, a QR scheme has been secured, with the help of a key both on the generator side and on the scanner side, which with the same key retrieves the original information.

Similar to the proposal in [17], a single sign-in model using QR codes has been proposed in [19]. However, the prevention of phishing attacks has been supplemented with a model that is safe against man in the middle attacks.

Also, there are combinations of methodologies to prevent fraudulent online transactions, this is seen in [20], which has combined extended visual cryptography with QR codes. This has provided security for users who conduct online transactions while detecting phishing websites.

In [21] a systematic study of cutting-edge cryptographic primitives within QR codes has been presented. By selecting popular and standard signature schemes that compare their performance, speed and size. With the results, it has been possible to demonstrate that security does not combine with the ease of use of QR codes.

The proposal [22] has analyzed the interaction of users with QR codes to obtain a proportion of users who scan the code but do not visit the associated website. The results indicate that curiosity is the main factor to motivate the scanning of these codes, however, not all visited the link to the associated website. A proactive mobile target defense mechanism that thwarts some types of XSS attacks in web applications, called WebMTD, has been introduced in [23]. This solution randomizes the values of certain attributes of web parts to differentiate the application code from the injected code and not allow its execution. This has been achieved without the participation of the web developer or modification of the browser code.

Examining the literature selected, the analysis of the Table 1 has been proposed, which combines the methodologies of all the proposals and summarizes the orientation of our work, by verifying that the proposals found do not analyze Cross-Site Scripting attacks but have considered some phishing techniques.

Table 1. Summary of methodologies to avoid XSS attacks

Ref.	Purpose of the proposal	¿Have analyzed phishing attacks using QR codes?	¿Have analyzed XSS attacks?
[5]	Identifies a malicious execution sequence based on lists of legitimate sequences and malicious chains	NO	YES
[6]	Bureaucrats and cyber professionals can conduct attacks ethically to know vulnerabilities	NO	NO
[7]	Detection of XSS-based attacks on the client side or server using Neural Networks	NO	YES
[8]	Recover the model that has been implemented in the source code of a web application	NO	YES
[9]	A set of rules	NO	YES
[10]	Black box test approach	NO	YES
[11]	Reduce the size of the reports and thus improve the efficiency of the detection	NO	YES
[12]	Resembles a malicious activity to follow its sequence towards a vulnerable state	NO	YES
[13]	Analyzes vulnerabilities on websites of government organizations	NO	YES

(continued)

Table 1. (*continued*)

Ref.	Purpose of the proposal	¿Have analyzed phishing attacks using QR codes?	¿Have analyzed XSS attacks?
[14]	Design recommendations	YES	NO
[15]	Use of digital signature	YES	NO
[16]	QR in the educational process	NO	NO
[17]	Single session using QR codes	YES	NO
[18]	QR Secured	YES	NO
[19]	Single session using QR codes	YES	NO
[20]	QR + extended visual cryptography	YES	NO
[21]	Popular and standard signatures	YES	NO
[22]	User interaction	YES	NO
[23]	Proactive mobile target defense	NO	YES

The disadvantage of all the proposals is that it has not been oriented to the use of challenges or games in universities or some field related to teaching to detect XSS vulnerabilities, so also, no challenges or games have been implemented as didactic material to support these proposals.

3 XSS2DENT Model

As seen in Fig. 1, our proposal has been structured in 5 components:

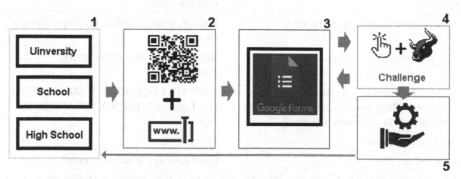

Fig. 1. XSS2DENT: Proposed model to analyze XSS vulnerabilities in the educational establishments of Santo Domingo de los Tsachilas City

3.1 Victims

This section describes the victims, who were the educational establishments of the Santo Domingo de los Tsáchilas. For this selection, no model was established to calculate a sample, instead, students from the first level of the Engineering in Information Technology Career of the ESPE were asked to share with their ex partners the proposed challenge. Thus the level of propagation of this compromised challenge has been analyzed with a combination of 2 attacks. In this space, the following research questions were proposed (RQ1 and RQ2):

RQ1: The educational establishments in Santo Domingo de los Tsáchilas are vulnerable to attacks such as Cross-Site Scripting + Clickjacking.

RQ2: Through Computer Security challenges, it is possible to make students aware of the danger of Cross-Site Scripting + Clickjacking attacks.

In the discussion section these questions have been answered, based on the results obtained.

3.2 Attack Vectors

Flyers with a QR code were designed, which were delivered to the students for distribution. This had embedded a link to a survey to collect data from people who scanned this code. Similarly, students could share the link to this survey through a social network.

3.3 Survey

For this survey a form designed in Google Forms was used, with the aim of collecting information about the victims. The real attack was within a shortened link using the TinyURL [24] service that was part of the proposed questions. The survey was structured with the variables of Table 2 for further analysis:

Table 2. Questions included in the proposed form

Question	Possible Values
What kind of respondent are you?	Student, Teacher, Public Employee, Private Employee
Select your current level of education	School, High School, University, Postgraduate
What is the name of your School/College or University where you are currently studying (student), or do you teach (teacher)?	ESPE SD, PUCE SD, UTE SD, ITSAE SD, ITS Tsachila, UTPL SD, UNIANDES SD, Otros
Select your gender	Male, Female
How old are you?	Enter your age in numbers only
What operating system does your mobile device have?	Android, IOS, Windows Mobile, other

(continued)

Table 2. (continued)

Question	Possible Values
What is the brand of your mobile device?	Samsung, Motorola, Nokia, Alcatel, LG, Huawei, Sony, BlackBerry, Sony Ericsson, Apple, Blue, Lenovo, HTC, ZTE, Xiaomi, Windows Phone, Other
Do you have any antivirus, firewall or similar software installed on your mobile device?	YES, NO
If you have any antivirus, firewall or similar software installed on your mobile device, enter its name	Enter your answer
How did you enter this survey?	Scanning the flyer QR code, Manually entering the URL link of the flyer, Through a link sent to a social network
Enter the following link: https://tinyurl.com/wmlm4po and solve the Challenge proposed by the Ethical Hacking Club of the ESPE. Find all the security flaws on that website write their names on the following line. If you meet the challenge, we will send you an email to contact you	Enter your answer
How did you access this challenge?	Wi-Fi access of my School/College/University, Wi-Fi access of my House, Mobile data, I could not access the Challenge, Other
If you used mobile data, tell us which operator you have the service	Claro, Movistar, CNT, Tuenti, Other

3.4 Challenge

Access to our cybersecurity challenge was included in the survey. This link was masked with the TinyURL online application, to hide the public ip address and the access port to our server. Table 3 shows the clues that were raised for the challenge. Our goal was to distract the victims to click on a button that showed the clues of the challenge one by one, but in reality, the page had a clickjacking vulnerability combined with cross site scripting, if the victims passed the clues with the button they already joined our zombie network, because the XSS script was running automatically and silently.

Table 3. Challenge proposed or the students

Question	Proposed Challenge
Clue 1	Look for all the security flaws that this web page has
Clue 2	If you are reading this message it is because your antivirus did not detect any of the failures
Clue 3	A stronger hint: Your mobile device is vulnerable to this type of security flaw
Clue 4	A much stronger clue: Your device being infected becomes Zombie of a Zombie network
Clue 5	We have combined 2 types of attack to make detection more difficult
Clue 6	Track attack 1: What would you do if Mickey Mouse is kid-napped?
Clue 7	Track attack 2: The second thing you read will be the first thing you write: extrañas Estudiar Español
Clue 8	Track attack 2: The second thing you read will be the first thing you write: Extrañas Estudiar Español

As observed in Table 3, clue 6 and 7 were raised to be answered in the survey, The victims believed that if the challenge were resolved, they would be integrated into the ESPE Cyber Security Club. The answers for these clues are described in Table 4:

Table 4. Answers to the questions proposed in the cybersecurity challenge

Question	Explanation	Answer
Track attack 1: What would you to if Mickey Mouse is kidnapped?	Mickey mouse (mouse or click) + kidnapping Clickjacking	
Track attack 2: The second thing you read will be the first thing you write: Extrañas Estudiar Español	The second thing that reads from Extrañas is X, Estudiar = S y Español = S	XSS

3.5 Feedback

After data collection, a report was presented describing all the actions taken with our proposed model. This report was sent to the technical staff of the establishments affected by the XSS + Clickjacking scripts. Part of the report contained the recommended actions to block this type of URL. Furthermore, the results of the tools used that did not detect this attack were included in the report.

In order to verify that our link to the compromised website was not detected as malicious by any type of software, the online application Virus Total [25] and KOXXS [26] were used.

In addition, a pentest of the compromised website with XSS + Clickjacking codes was made, using the online tool shown in [27]. However, there was no response to detect an XSS attack. Another online tool was also used [28].

A summary of the results are presented in Table 5 of all online pentest tools used for our research, based on [29]:

Table 5. Summary of results of the online pentest tools used to feedback

Tool	Reference	Results	Disadvantages
Netcraft	10	XSS not detected	28 days of evaluation, then you must pay $1.06 monthly, the registration of a credit card is mandatory. If the subscription request is not accepted, the app does not initialize
Pentest-Tools	11	XSS not detected	Was not able to detect the XSS attack
Ping.eu	11	XSS not detected	Does not offer the online URL analysis service
Yougetsignal	12	XSS not detected	Does not offer the online URL analysis service
Urlquery.net	13	XSS not detected	Is not functional, Invalid URL or failed to DNS lookup

Online tools were also used to detect XSS attacks, as shown in [30], in the same way, the results are shown in Table 6.

Table 6. Summary of results of the online XSS scan testing tools used

Tool	Reference	Results	Disadvantages
Find-XSS	[31]	Does not allow online analysis of URLs	It requests the execution of a JavaScript that was detected and blocked by chrome
Quttera	[32]	It is not functional for common users	The links are entered for the URL analysis but the system always throws the message: Provided resource is unreachable
XSS-Scaner	[33]	It is not functional for common users	The website is not secure, use only the http protocol
Acunetix	[34]	Without results	It requires a registration in the system to do an online scan. Use the https protocol
W3af	[35]	Without results	Is a plugin for identifying persistent cross-site scripting vulnerabilities

(continued)

Table 6. (*continued*)

Tool	Reference	Results	Disadvantages
Ssllabs	[36]	Without results	Does not allow the analysis of URLs that use the IP format, use the https protocol
Tenable	[37]	It is not functional for common users	It does not allow the online analysis of URLs, it uses the https protocol. Software must be downloaded
Swascan	[38]	It is not functional for common users	It does not allow the online analysis of URLs, it uses the https protocol. Software must be downloaded
Rapid7	[39]	It is not functional for common users	It does not allow the online analysis of URLs, it uses the https protocol. Software must be downloaded

In addition, the XSSCon [40] software, which is a Powerfull Simple XSS Scanner made with python 3.7, was tested. However, it did not detect any type of attack when testing with the compromised website. Something interesting that was found within the results was information of hidden collection of data referring to names, telephones, addresses and identification of credit cards.

4 Analysis of Results

To ensure the fidelity of the data, no samples were calculated for the choice of educational establishments, failing that, students from the first levels were asked to spread the challenge, since it was they who had more contact with their ex partners.

We present the results of our zombie network formed with the victims who accessed the cybersecurity challenge. According to Fig. 2a 93.5% of the victims have a mobile device with Android operating system and only 6.5% have IOS. The 4 brands of most used devices are seen in Fig. 2b, with Samsung being 47.8% the most used brand, followed by Huawei with 39.4%, Sony with 8.7% and Apple with 6.5%.

Similarly, in Fig. 3a it is shown that 76.1% of the victims have not installed some type of antivirus software on their mobile devices, in addition, in Fig. 3b notes that 69.6% of the victims accessed the challenge through a home network connection (home access), 13% accessed through their university network, another 13% accessed using mobile data and a 2.2% accessed through their work network.

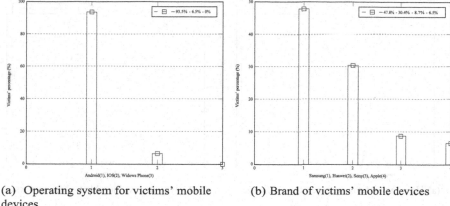

(a) Operating system for victims' mobile devices

(b) Brand of victims' mobile devices

Fig. 2. Operating system and brand of mobile devices of victims

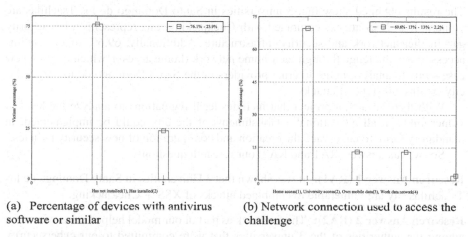

(a) Percentage of devices with antivirus software or similar

(b) Network connection used to access the challenge

Fig. 3. Antivirus and communication network used to access the challenge

Finally, Fig. 4a shows that 4.3% of the victims accessed the challenge by scanning the QR code of the fliers distributed by the students, 37% accessed through the URL link that was in the same flyer and 58.7% accessed through the link shared by the WhatsApp messaging network. On the other hand, Fig. 4b shows the 3 universities that were compromised with our combined attack. These were the Pontificia Universidad Católica del Ecuador (PUCE) with 2.17% of the victims, Universidad Autónoma de los Andes with 2.17% and Universidad Tecnica Equinoccial (UTE) with 10.86%.

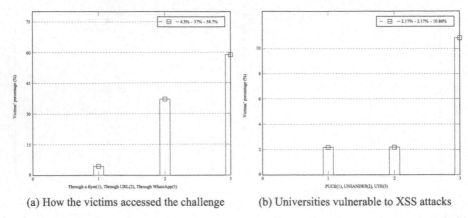

(a) How the victims accessed the challenge   (b) Universities vulnerable to XSS attacks

Fig. 4. Access method and Universities that accessed the challenge

4.1 Discussion

The results obtained show that 3 universities in Santo Domingo de los Tsachilas are vulnerable to XSS attacks combined with Clickjacking, this represents a big security gap in their network and security infrastructure. Additionally, 69.6% of the victims accessed our challenge through their home network (home access), which opens a new case study to analyze home internet providers in the Santo Domingo de los Tsachilas city, against this type of attacks.

With these results, a project that includes legal regulations to analyze the level of vulnerability in all educational establishments of the city could be implemented, in mandatory form, to encourage the creation and configuration of new security policies.

So, we can answer (RA1 and RA2) our research questions:

Research Answer 1 (RA1): It was shown that 3 Universities in Santo Domingo de los Ts'achilas city are vulnerable to combined attacks of XSS + Clickjacking.

Research Answer 2 (RA2): The feedback as part of our model helped raise awareness among the authorities of the 3 universities that were committed to our cybersecurity challenge.

A limitation of our study, were the access policies that in some establishments had to access the link of the cybersecurity challenge compromised. According to the representatives of the TICs departments, indicated that we needed special procedures to share the survey with students, so it was not possible to verify whether or not they are vulnerable to XSS and Clickjacking attacks.

After analyzing the records of our system, the following results are presented, which indicate that our cybersecurity challenge extended beyond what was established. As seen in Fig. 5, the logs record the variables of some connections in other countries (IP, city, country, longitude, latitude, time and date of connection), the log of the figure shows the information of a zombie connected from Peru.

In Fig. 6, a global map is shown that represents the number of connections for each registered country, in this case the second country with more zombie stations was Mexico and the third was Argentina.

| 8688 | Zombie | 190.236.8.26 appears to have come back online | 2019-12-05T13:03:29+00:00 |
| 8687 | Zombie | 190.236.8.26 is connecting from: {"city"=>{"geoname_id"=>3936456, "names"=>{"de"=>"Lima","en"=>"Lima", "es"=>"Lima", "fr"=>"Lima", "ja"=>"リマ", "pt-BR"=>"Lima", "ru"=>"Лима"}}, "continent"=>{"code"=>"SA", "geoname_id"=>6255150, "names"=>{"de"=>"Südamerika", "en"=>"South America", "es"=>"Sudamérica", "fr"=>"Amérique du Sud","ja"=>"南アメリカ", "pt-BR"=>"América do Sul", "ru"=>"Южная Америка", "zh-CN"=>"南美州"}}, "country"=>{"geoname_id"=>3932488, "iso_code"=>"PE", "names"=> {"de"=>"Peru", "en"=>"Peru", "es"=>"Perú", "fr"=>"Pérou", "ja"=>"ペルー共和国", "pt-BR"=>"Peru", "ru"=>"Перу", "zh-CN"=>"秘鲁"}}, "location"=> {"accuracy_radius"=>10, "latitude"=>-12.0464, "longitude"=>-77.0428, "time_zone"=>"America/Lima"}, "registered_country"=> {"geoname_id"=>3932488, "iso_code"=>"PE", "names"=>{"de"=>"Peru", "en"=>"Peru", "es"=>"Perú", "fr"=>"Pérou", "ja"=>"ペルー共和国", "pt-BR"=>"Peru", "ru"=>"Перу", "zh-CN"=>"秘鲁"}}, "subdivisions"=> [{"geoname_id"=>3936451, "iso_code"=>"LMA", "names"=>{"en"=>"Lima"}}]}} | 2019-12-05T13:03:29+00:00 |

Fig. 5. System log that shows a zombie connected from Peru

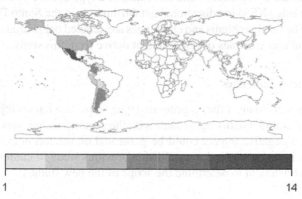

1   14

Fig. 6. World map showing the number of connections of the different countries registered in the Challenge System Log

5 Conclusions

A proposal model is presented to verify that educational establishments in Santo Domingo de los Tsáchilas city are vulnerable to Cross-Site Scripting (XSS) attacks. A cybersecurity challenge was designed that served as a distraction to motivate students to access a compromised web site with a combination of XSS + Clickjacking scripts. This link was distributed by the students of the Universidad de las Fuerzas Armadas-ESPE to their ex partners from other universities.

As a result, it was obtained that 3 universities were able to access the challenge, so they were compromised by the XSS scripts. The universities PUCE (Pontificia Universidad Católica del Ecuador), UTE (Universidad Tecnológica Equinoccial) and UNIANDES (Universidad Regional Autónoma de los Andes) were informed about the results of this research, together with the recommendations to remedy this type of attacks.

In addition to the results of this proposal, indicate that our cybersecurity challenge extended beyond what was established, registering connections from other countries. Mexico is in second place with 14 zombies connections and Argentina in third place with 8 zombies connections. This shows that the level of propagation of our challenge expanded beyond the limits of Santo Domingo de los Tsáchilas city.

The theoretical implications of this study will open the way to the presentation of proposals to detect/mitigate XSS attacks in universities in other cities. Also, it will serve as a guide to route current research proposals to professionals who are dedicated to the analysis of XSS attacks.

The practical implications of this study will allow the development and implementation of new tools using artificial intelligence techniques, based on references collected, organized and classified in this research.

6 Future Work

This study systematizes a model to find and mitigate a type of little-known attack called Cross-Site Scripting (XSS) in educational establishments in the Santo Domingo de los Tsachilas city. The open problems and challenges are detailed below, and in complement, the possible solutions and lines of research that derive from this study.

6.1 Open Issues/Challenges

The challenge is in the danger that is generated when other academics replicate this proposal. Without a confidentiality agreement with the security technicians of educational establishments, a negative impact could be generated on the technological infrastructure. For this, it is recommended to establish a previous study in conjunction with the educational establishment to determine the scope of the new studies.

6.2 Possible Solutions/Research Directions

According to the common issues found in this study, the following lines of research are proposed:

1. Study of XSS attacks on all educational establishments in the city as an education policy.
2. Analysis of websites using web scraping techniques and distributed artificial intelligence in the educational establishments.

References

1. OWASP. (). Los diez riesgos más críticos en Aplicaciones Web, 10 May 2020
2. Dayal Ambedkar, M., Ambedkar, N.S., Raw, R.S.: A comprehensive inspection of cross site scripting attack. In: 2016 International Conference on Computing, Communication and Automation (ICCCA), pp. 497–502 (2016)
3. Kim, D., Kim, H.: Performing clickjacking attacks in the wild: 99% are still vulnerable!. In: 2015 1st International Conference on Software Security and Assurance (ICSSA), pp. 25–29 (2015)
4. Zeng, H.: Research on developing an attack and defense lab environment for cross site scripting education in higher vocational colleges. In: 2013 International Conference on Computational and Information Sciences, pp. 1971–1974 (2013)

5. Das, D., Sharma, U., Bhattacharyya, D.K.: Detection of cross-site scripting attack under multiple scenarios. Comput. J. **58**(4), 808–822 (2015). ISSN: 1460–2067. https://doi.org/10. 1093/comjnl/bxt133
6. Singh, H., Dua, M.:Website attacks: challenges and preventive methodologies. In: 2018 International Conference on Inventive Research in Computing Applications (ICIRCA), July 2018, pp. 381–387. 10 . 1109/ICIRCA.2018.8597259
7. Mokbal, F.M.M., Dan, W., Imran, A., Jiuchuan, L., Akhtar, F., Xiaoxi, W.: Mlpxss: an integrated xss-based attack detection scheme in web applications using multilayer perceptron technique. IEEE Access **7**, 100 567–100 580 (2019). ISSN: 2169–3536. https://doi.org/10. 1109/ACCESS.2019.2927417
8. Shar, L.K., Tan, H.B.K.: Auditing the xss defence features implemented in web application programs. IET Softw. **6**(4), 377–390 (2012). ISSN: 1751–8814. https://doi.org/10.1049/iet-sen.2011.0084
9. Zubarev, D., Skarga-Bandurova, I.: Cross-site scripting for graphic data: vulnerabilities and prevention. In: 2019 10th International Conference on Dependable Systems, Services and Technologies (DESSERT), pp. 154–160, June 2019. https://doi.org/10.1109/DESSERT.2019. 8770043
10. Farah, T., Shojol, M., Hassan, M., Alam, D.: Assessment of vulnerabilities of web applications of Bangladesh: a case study of xss csrf. In: 2016 Sixth International Conference on Digital Information and Communication Technology and its Applications (DICTAP), pp. 74–78 (2016)
11. Guo, X., Jin, S., Zhang, Y.: Xss vulnerability detection using optimized attack vector repertory. In: 2015 International Conference on Cyber-Enabled Distributed Computing and Knowledge Discovery, pp. 29–36, September 2015. https://doi.org/10.1109/CyberC.2015.50.
12. Bozic, J., Wotawa, F.: Purity: a planning-based security testing tool. In: 2015 IEEE International Conference on Software Quality, Reliability and Security - Companion, pp. 46–55, August 2015. https://doi.org/10.1109/QRS-C.2015.19.
13. Pirvadlu, F.T., Sepidnam, G.:Assessments Sqli and Xss vulnerability in several organizational websites of north Khorasan in Iran and offer solutions to fix these vulnerabilities. In: 2017 3th International Conference on Web Research (ICWR), pp. 44–47 (2017)
14. Krombholz, K., Fru¨hwirt, P., Rieder, T., Kapsalis, I., Ullrich, J., Weippl, E.: QR code security – how secure and usable apps can protect users against malicious QR codes. In: 2015 10th International Conference on Availability, Reliability and Security, pp. 230–237, August 2015. https://doi.org/10.1109/ARES.2015.84
15. Yin, L.R., Zhou, J., Hsu, M.K.: Redesigning QR code ecosystem with improved mobile security. In: 2015 IEEE 39th Annual Computer Software and Applications Conference, vol. 3, pp. 678–679, July 2015. https://doi.org/10.1109/COMPSAC.2015.153
16. Tretinjak, M.K.: The implementation of QR codes in the educational process. In: 2015 38th International Convention on Information and Communication Technology, Electronics and Microelectronics (MIPRO), pp. 833–835, May 2015. https://doi.org/10.1109/MIPRO.2015. 7160387
17. Choi, K., Lee, C., Jeon, W., Lee, K., Won, D.: A mobile based anti-phishing authentication scheme using QR code. In: International Conference on Mobile IT Convergence, pp. 109–113, September 2011
18. Goel, N., Sharma, A., Goswami, S.: A way to secure a qr code: Sqr. In: 2017 International Conference on Computing, Communication and Automation (ICCCA), pp. 494–497, May 2017. https://doi.org/10.1109/CCAA.2017.8229850
19. Mukhopadhyay, S., Argles, D.: An anti-phishing mechanism for single sign-on based on qr-code. In: International Conference on Information Society (i-Society 2011), pp. 505–508, June 2011

20. Khairnar, S., Kharat, R.: Online fraud transaction prevention system using extended visual cryptography and qr code. In: 2016 International Conference on Computing Communication Control and automation (ICCUBEA), pp. 1–4, August 2016. https://doi.org/10.1109/ICC UBEA.2016.7860061

21. Focardi, R.,Luccio, F.L.,Wahsheh, H.A.M.: Usable cryptographic QR codes. In: 2018 IEEE International Conference on Industrial Technology (ICIT), pp. 1664–1669, Feburary 2018. https://doi.org/10.1109/ICIT.2018.8352431

22. Vidas, T., Owusu, E., Wang, S., Zeng, C., Cranor, L.F., Christin, N.: Qrishing: the susceptibility of smartphone users to qr code phishing attacks. In: Adams, A.A., Brenner, M., Smith, M. (eds.) FC 2013. LNCS, vol. 7862, pp. 52–69. Springer, Heidelberg (2013). https://doi.org/10.1007/978-3-642-41320-9_4

23. Niakanlahiji, A., Jafarian, J.H.: Webmtd: defeating cross-site scripting attacks using moving target defense. In: Security and Communication Networks, Science Citation Index Expanded, p. 13 (2019)

24. Tinyurl. (). Making over a billion long URLs usable! Serving billions of redirects per month, 10 May 2020

25. VirusTotal. (). Virus total url, June 2019. https://www.virustotal.com/gui/home/url

26. KNOXXS. (). The best tool to find and prove XSS flaws, 10 May 2020

27. Pentest-Tools. (). Pentest yourself. don't get hacked, July 2019. https://pentest-tools.com/home

28. urlscan. (). A sandbox for the web, July 2019. https://urlscan.io/result/489b8b27-137b-4c41-b3da-0ce96ee2b6c6#summary

29. linuxito. (). Las mejores herramientas online para pentesting, July 2019. https://www.linuxito.com/seguridad/205-las-mejores-herramientas-online-para-pentesting

30. Riskemy. (). 9 cross-site scripting (xss) scan testing tools online, July 2019. https://riskemy.com/xss-testing-tool/

31. Find-XSS.net. (). Web monitoring, July 2019. https://find-xss.net/?l=en

32. Quttera. (). Threatsign! website anti-malware, July 2019. https://quttera.com/

33. XSS-Scanner. (). Cross site scripting scanner, July 2019. https://xss-scanner.com

34. Acunetix. (). Xss vulnerability scanning with acunetix, July 2019. https://www.acunetix.com/vulnerability-scanner/xss-vulnerability-scanning/

35. w3af.org. (). Xss, July 2019. http://w3af.org/plugins/audit/xss

36. Q. Inc. (). Ssl/tls capabilities of your browser. July 2019. https://www.ssllabs.com/ssltest/viewMyClient.html

37. T. Inc. (). Web app scanning. July 2019. https://www.tenable.com/products/tenable-io/web-application-scanning

38. S. SRL. (). Cross site scripting: What do you need to know about it? July 2019. https://www.swascan.com/cross-site-scripting/

39. Rapid7. (). Web application security and scanning, July 2019. https://www.rapid7.com/fundamentals/web-application-security/

40. GitHub/menkrep1337. (). Xsscon, July 2019. https://github.com/menkrep1337/XSSCon.

A Framework Based on Personality Traits to Identify Vulnerabilities to Social Engineering Attacks

Eduardo Benavides-Astudillo[1,2]([✉]) [iD], Néstor Tipan-Guerrero[1],
Gema Castillo-Zambrano[1], Walter Fuertes Díaz[1,2] [iD],
German Eduardo Rodríguez Galán[1,2] [iD], María Fernanda Cazáres[3],
and Daniel Nuñcz-Agurto[1] [iD]

[1] Universidad de las Fuerzas Armadas ESPE, Sangolquí, Ecuador
{debenavides,natipan,ggcastillo1,wmfuertes,gerodriguez10,
adnunez1}@espe.edu.ec
[2] Escuela Politécnica Nacional, Quito, Ecuador
{diego.benavides,walter.fuertes}@espe.edu.ec, german.rodriguez@epn.edu.ec
[3] Universidad Politécnica Salesiana, Quito, Ecuador
mcazares@ups.edu.ec

Abstract. Currently, all users massively use digital devices connected to the Internet. Because of this overcrowding, the number of cybercriminals who use Social Engineering techniques to extract sensitive information from users also increased. The attackers take advantage of the personality traits of their victims, such as friendliness, ignorance of basic security measures, naivety, or overconfidence. To combat this type of attack, we have developed a Framework based on personality traits, allowing us to know which people are more vulnerable than others are. Faced with this scenario, the main aim of this study is to develop a tool that allows determining which people are most vulnerable to Social Engineering attacks. The methodological process consisted of first determining the most common traits of users related to vulnerability. Then, the personality traits of a surveyed group were determined. Finally, the most vulnerable traits were matched with the personality traits of the respondents. The personality traits in which our research was framed is known as the Five-Factor Model of personality. The results show that this framework can be used to detect the most vulnerable user or groups and focus training and awareness on it or these groups.

Keywords: Personal trait · Cybersecurity · Social Engineering · Five-Factor Model · Framework

1 Introduction

With the arrival of the pandemic caused by Covid-19, the use of online services, such as health, education, commerce, among others, increased exponentially [1].

M. Botto-Tobar et al. (Eds.): ICAT 2021, CCIS 1535, pp. 381–394, 2022.
https://doi.org/10.1007/978-3-031-03884-6_28

Today, these services have become widespread, regardless of age, level of education, or purpose for which they are used. On the other hand, just as the number of online transactions has increased, so has the number of online attacks. Among the most complex and delicate attacks are Social Engineering (IS) attacks [2]. In this case, the attacker tries to obtain confidential information from end-users, primarily through deception in emails, fake web pages, and messages on social networks, among others [3].

People and organizations invested considerable sums of money in technology to protect the information, both in hardware and software. However, a significant percentage of these attacks are successful; this is because, despite this equipment, it is enough for a person to reveal their sensitive information directly to the attacker without knowing it [4]. Thus, attackers take advantage of certain vulnerable behaviors of people, such as overconfidence, timidity, lack of knowledge, among others [5]. Within this context, it is common to hear that some people have been victims of a Social Engineering attack, while others have evaded the attack because something seemed strange to them. Based on the above premise, we assume that some people are more vulnerable than others to be victims of these attacks are. Probably due to overconfidence, being outgoing and gaining acceptance, or simply helping others, i.e., by individual personality traits.

The main objective of this study is to offer a tool to determine which people are more vulnerable than others are to being victims of Social Engineering attacks, based on their personality traits. To do so, we propose the following objectives: (1) To carry out a systematic literature review to determine the main personality traits, which are taken into account to determine vulnerability. (2) To frame within the Five-Factor Model (FFM) [6], the general personality traits obtained in the previous step. (3) To design and conduct a survey to determine the individual traits of people in FFM. (4) To determine which people are more vulnerable than others, based on the weight of each FFM trait and the personality traits obtained in the survey.

The main contribution of this work is to provide the community with a tool to determine which people are more vulnerable than others, according to their personality traits. In addition, this tool can be used by individuals or organizations to target better the training of vulnerable people against social engineering attacks.

The remainder of this article is structured as follows. Section 2 describes the research methodology used included their methods and techniques. Section 3 explains the results and discusses their findings. Finally, in Sect. 4, we present the conclusions of this study and the lines of future work.

2   Materials and Methods

During the design of this research, we use various methods and techniques in a systematic way that is explained in the following procedure, which is clarified in Fig. 1:

- A systematic literature review was developed based on current solutions to combat Social Engineering attacks according to personality traits;
- The most important personality traits to be vulnerable were determined;
- A survey was conducted of people from a university entity about their personality traits;
- The personality traits of the respondents were determined;
- People or groups of people who are more vulnerable to being victims of Social Engineering attacks were identified.

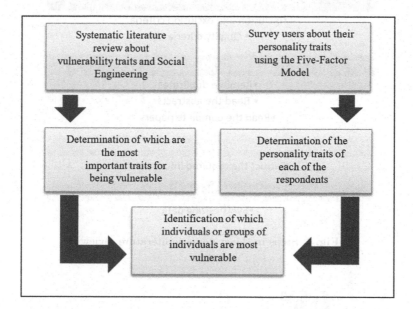

Fig. 1. Model for defining user vulnerability by personality trait

2.1 Systematic Literature Review (SLR) Based on the Guide of Barbara Kitchenham, Aimed at Combating Social Engineering Attacks, According to Personality Traits

The purpose of this step is to establish the state of the art of existing solutions in the mitigation of Social Engineering attacks based on the methodological guide of Barbara Kitchenham [7], in which the personality traits of people are taken into account. For this, we follow the proper steps described in Fig. 2.

The three terms based on the research question for the collection of articles were: Social Engineering, vulnerability, and personality trait, with their respective synonyms. As inclusion criteria, we searched only for papers in English journals from the last five years. Furthermore, as quality criteria, we only searched for Journals from the scientific databases: Web of Science, IEEExplore, Scopus, Springer, and ACM Library.

Once the steps described in Fig. 2 were applied, 36 papers were obtained, which had to do strictly with personality traits and Social Engineering (see Fig. 3). The next step was to read the 36 articles and extract the personality traits most used in all the papers.

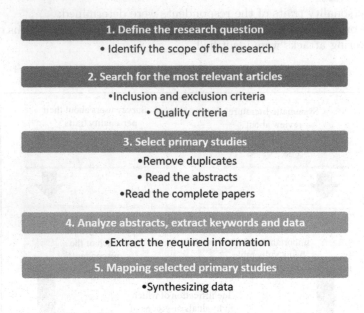

1. Define the research question
- Identify the scope of the research

2. Search for the most relevant articles
- Inclusion and exclusion criteria
- Quality criteria

3. Select primary studies
- Remove duplicates
- Read the abstracts
- Read the complete papers

4. Analyze abstracts, extract keywords and data
- Extract the required information

5. Mapping selected primary studies
- Synthesizing data

Fig. 2. Steps in the systematic literature review

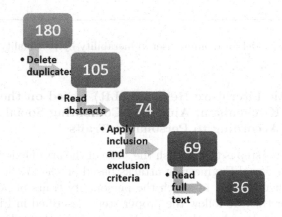

180
- Delete duplicates   105
- Read abstracts   74
- Apply inclusion and exclusion criteria   69
- Read full text   36

Fig. 3. Determination of documents to read completely

2.2 Determination of Which Are the Most Important Personality Traits to Be Vulnerable

Once the 36 papers had been selected (see Fig. 3), the total reading of each one of them was carried out. In this way, we extracted which were the main personality traits that are evaluated in these papers. Then, these personality traits were framed within the characteristics of the FFM personality model. They were also assigned colors to identify each personality trait, high or low (see Fig. 4). At this point, we decided to give a high or low scale to each FFM property, because based on our study, for example, a person with high openness is much more at risk than a person with no openness.

Five-Factor Model Trait	Abbreviation
Openness (High)	Op_H
Openness (Low)	Op_L
Conscientiousness (High)	Co_H
Conscientiousness (Low)	Co_L
Extraversion (High)	Ex_H
Extraversion (Low)	Ex_L
Agreeableness (High)	Ag_H
Agreeableness (Low)	Ag_L
Neuroticism (High)	Ne_H
Neuroticism (Low)	Ne_L

Fig. 4. Five-Factor model with high and low scales and colors

2.3 Surveying to Determine Personality Traits

Parallel to the two previous steps, a survey of 146 people was conducted to determine their personality traits, taking into account the Five-Factor personality model. Table 1 lists the survey questions.

It should be noted that the questions are not grouped according to the factor to which they correspond. On the other hand, it should be considered that a question might have a reverse value, i.e., it may be that someone answers with a five. However, although in reality, that five corresponds to a one, which is the lowest value. All these measures were performed in order to avoid research bias. Table 2 presents the distribution of the questions according to their trait.

Table 1. Questions in the survey to determine personality traits

1. Do you like to talk a lot?	22. Are you generally confident?
2. Do you tend to find fault with others?	23. Do you tend to be lazy?
3. Do you do a thorough job?	24. Are you emotionally stable?
4. Are you depressed or sad?	25. Are you creative, invent new things?
5. It is original; do you come up with new ideas?	26. Are you assertive, self-confident?
6. Is it reserved?	27. Can you be cold and distant?
7. Are you helpful and disinterested in others?	28. Do you persevere until you finish a task?
8. Can it be somewhat sloppy?	29. Can you be moody?
9. Are you relaxed, or do you handle stress well?	30. Do you value artistic and aesthetic experiences?
10. Are you curious about many different things?	31. Are you sometimes shy or inhibited?
11. Are you full of energy?	32. Are you considerate and kind to almost everyone?
12. Do you fight or argue with others?	33. Do you do things efficiently?
13. Are you a reliable worker?	34. Do you stay calm in stressful situations?
14. Are you usually tense?	35. Do you prefer routine work?
15. Are you resourceful, a deep thinker?	36. Are you sociable?
16. Do you have a lot of enthusiasm?	37. Are you sometimes rude to others?
17. Do you have a compassionate nature towards others?	38. Do you make plans and follow them?
18. Do you tend to be disorganized?	39. Do you get nervous easily?
19. Do you worry a lot?	40. Do you like to reflect and play with ideas?
20. Do you have an active imagination?	41. Do you have few artistic interests?
21. Do you tend to be quiet?	42. Do you like to cooperate with others?

Table 2. Distribution of survey questions for each FFM factor of personality

Factor	Questions	Total questions
Extraversion	1, 6R, 11, 16, 21R, 26, 31R, 36	8
Agreeableness	2R, 7, 12R, 17, 22, 27R, 32, 37R, 42	9
Conscientiousness	3,8R, 13, 18R, 23R, 28, 33, 38, 43R	9
Neuroticism	4, 9R, 14, 19, 24R, 29, 34R, 39	8
Openness	5, 10, 15, 20, 25, 30, 35R, 40, 41R, 44	10

2.4 Determination of the Personality Traits of Each of the Respondents

After performed the survey, which 146 people from the university entity answered, the personality traits [8] of each of them were determined (see Table 3).

Table 3. Example of survey results to determine personality traits

Respondents	Extraversion	Agreeableness	Conscientiousness	Neuroticism	Openness
1	Low	Low	Low	Medium	Medium
2	Low	Medium	Medium	Low	High
3	Low	High	Medium	Low	High

2.5 Identification Which Individuals or Groups of Individuals Are Most Vulnerable

Once two things were obtained separately, (1) on the one hand, the essential characteristics in the literature framed in the FFM; (2) on the other, the personality traits of the respondents, also framed in the FFM; a match was performed to determine which people are the most vulnerable to Social Engineering attacks.

According to the framework indicated, these traits can be identified in two ways, one through a traffic light in their personality traits indicators, and another way by calculating the percentage of risk of the respondents.

3 Results and Discussion

3.1 Extraction and Framing in the Five-Factor Model, of the General Features Obtained from the Articles

Once 36 scientific articles had been fully read, we extracted the personality traits expressed and used in each article. There is a very varied and diverse number of personality traits there, which are not explicitly indicated in the FFM. However, we frame them within the FFM model (see Table 4).

Subsequently, the personality characteristics already framed in FFM were added, and the most important personality traits in detecting vulnerabilities were obtained (see Table 5).

Table 4. Example of framing personality traits in FFM

Five-Factor Model	Abbreviation	Art. 1(Khidzir et al., 2019)	Art. 2 (Feng et al., 2019)	Art. 3 (Aldawood & Skinner., 2019)
Openness (High)	Op_H	Keep good safety practices	Active behavior in social networks	Compulsory moral guilt
Openness (Low)	Op_L	Follow established standards or protocols	Low interactive behaviors	Intimidating emotions
Conscientiousness (High)	Co_H		Trusted social relationships	Nature of trust
Conscientiousness (Low)	Co_L		Closed social circles	Lack of interest
Extraversion (High)	Ex_H		Obvious user preferences	Lack of awareness

Table 5. Weight of each of the FFM components according to the occasions mentioned in the analyzed papers

Five-Factor Model	Number of mentions in the analyzed papers	Percentage weight within the papers analyzed
Openness	30	28,8%
Agreeableness	29	27,9%
Conscientiousness	21	20,2%
Neuroticism	12	11,5%
Extroversion	12	11,5%

Based on the study carried out so far, we can conclude that the leading cause mentioned for a person to be more vulnerable is Openness, followed by Agreeableness, Conscientiousness, Neuroticism, and Extroversion.

3.2   High, Medium and Low Risk in Each Trait of the FFM

According to [9] and [10], the high, medium, and low values are established for each of the behavioral traits in FFM (see Table 6). In addition to Table 6, based on the results obtained from the interpretation of the analyzed papers, we have assigned them a red, yellow, and green signal, according to the high risk that this trait implies medium or low.

Table 6. Traffic lights of high, medium and low scales

FFM		Low	Medium	High
Extroversion		People with low scores can be described as introverts; there-fore, it is more difficult to get information from them	People with average scores can be somewhat reserved, but they tend to generate conversation if their attention is captured	High-scoring people are comfortable in large groups and tend to be enthusiastic, energetic, and highly talkative
Agreeableness		This type of person is usually critical, is not condescending, and expresses hostility towards others	They usually do not try to please anyone, but if necessary, they would be willing to help others, always being alert	These people are more likely to help and trust others because they always assume the best in others
Conscientiousness		In this trait, those are more likely to not stick to plans and follow their own rules without measuring consequences	People who have their values established and can be trusted are not exempt from having small careless mistakes	Honesty, trust, strong self-orientation, and self-responsibility are the main characteristics of these people
Neuroticism		These people tend to be more emotionally stable and better meditate on all their actions	They tend to remain calm, but the more it forces them, the more quickly they reach their breaking point	The higher someone's score on this trait, the more they tend to worry and make hasty decisions
Openness		Favor conservative values. They are judges in conventional terms and uncomfortable with complexities It could be wrong to not being aware of new attack methods	People who are willing to accept new experiences without losing conservative values	They are individuals to have an open mind towards new ideas and experiences and accept different beliefs

3.3 Results of the Survey to Determine the Personality Traits of the Users

Parallel to the definition of the most important personality traits, we surveyed university personnel to determine the respondents' personality traits. In this way, a score was determined for each respondent in each FFM factor, as shown in Table 7. The sample that was taken is 146 people out of the 800 members of the university community. As an instance, we show the first nine results obtained out of the 146.

Table 7. Numerical result of the survey carried out framed in FFM

Respondents	Extroversion	Agreeableness	Conscientiousness	Neuroticism	Openness
1	17	18	23	31	34
2	21	33	35	22	47
3	22	37	33	23	47
4	26	31	31	25	33
5	24	30	36	22	32
6	32	39	28	29	31
7	36	37	37	11	45
8	18	26	23	21	30
9	23	31	28	19	25

A highlighted finding of this research is that, at the level of the surveyed institution, the three traits in which more people are vulnerable are Openness, followed by Agreeableness, and Conscientiousness. See Fig. 5.

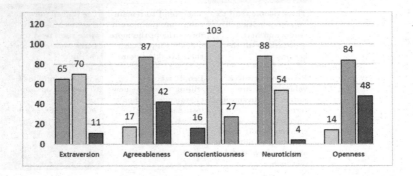

Fig. 5. High, medium, and low traits found in the surveyed institution

3.4 Determination of the Vulnerability of Each of the Users to Social Engineering Attacks

Once the values shown for each user in Table 5 had been calculated, it was necessary to determine if these values were high, medium, or low. The main difficulty encountered is that it could not be measured with the same scale at all values because there were different questions for each scale. Another problem found is that the survey offered five response options, which implied that a rating varied from one to five, while the scale in Table 4 only had three options, low, medium, and high; that is, it varied from one to three.

The solution proposed for correspondence between a variable with five values and another with three values was proposed in Fig. 6. An average value that fits between 1 and 3 on the scale of 5 corresponds down. Moreover, a value whose average is between 3 and 4 corresponds to the mean scale. As long as a value falls between 4 and 5, it will be on a scale of High.

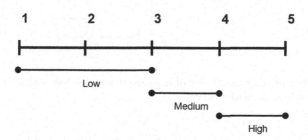

Fig. 6. Scale correspondence

In addition, in Table 7, it can be observed that very varied values were obtained for each of the factors. The challenge was to define if each of these values is high, medium, or low. The number of questions in each factor was taken into account to achieve this correspondence (i.e., between numerical values and the High, Medium, or Low scale). For example, if the Extroversion scale is taken, according to Table 2, the total number of questions on this scale is eight. If we want to obtain the total value that can be reached on that scale, we should multiply 8×5 because 5 is the maximum value in each of the eight extroversion questions. Therefore, we obtain that the maximum value of that scale is 40, and the minimum value that we would obtain is eight because one is the minimum value. In this way, we would obtain average values that would go from eight to 40. Thus, on this scale, the Low range would go from 8 to 23.99. The Medium range, from 24 to 31.99; and the Alto range, from 32 to 40 (see the algorithm in Fig. 7).

Now, with the percentage awarded to each of the features of the FFM based on the studies reviewed, and the information collected by each of the informants, a match of both results is performed to determine which respondents are most vulnerable to Social Engineering attacks. We can observe this using a semaphore description in Table 8.

Considering the results shown in Table 8 (i.e., only the first nine results obtained out of the 146 are shown as an example), we can make some interpretations.

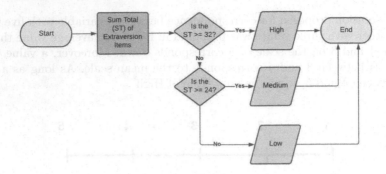

Fig. 7. Algorithm of correspondence of high, medium and low scales, according to the percentages obtained from the survey

Respondent 1 has only one trait that makes it vulnerable (i.e., marked in red), low conscientiousness. Respondents 4 and 5 do not have dangerous traits. While respondent 7 has a high vulnerability, it has three negative indicators: extroversion, agreeableness, and openness.

Table 8. Traffic lights of the results obtained from the survey

Respondents	Extroversion	Agreeableness	Conscientiousness	Neuroticism	Openness
1	Low	Low	Low	Medium	Medium
2	Low	Medium	Medium	Low	High
3	Low	High	Medium	Low	High
4	Medium	Medium	Medium	Medium	Medium
5	Medium	Medium	High	Low	Medium
6	High	High	Medium	Medium	Medium
7	High	High	High	Low	High
8	Low	Low	Low	Low	Medium
9	Low	Medium	Medium	Low	Low

4   Conclusions and Future Work

This study developed a framework to determine which person or group of people are more vulnerable than others to Social Engineering attacks, according to their personality traits. Based on our study, it can be determined which FFM personality traits make people more vulnerable to Social Engineering attacks. The results highlight that they are Openness (28.8%), followed by Agreeableness (27.9%), Conscientiousness (20.2%), Neuroticism (11.5%), and Extroversion (11.5%). Furthermore, according to the analysis carried out in the Systematic

Literature Review, a set of personality traits make people more vulnerable to attacks from Social Engineering. However, this framework can be used to detect the most vulnerable groups and focus training and awareness on these groups. For the realization of our study, we used the FFM to frame the people's personality traits. However, the study can be extended to use another model for defining personality traits and even compare these models versus the attacks of Social Engineering.

As future work, based on this framework, we plan to implement a website open to the public, through which institutions can conduct our survey to their staff. Thus these institutions can identify which people or group of people are more vulnerable to social engineering attacks. On the other hand, although this study was applied only to 146 people, we plan to conduct this survey on a much larger sample of about 10,000 people to feed and develop a machine learning algorithm that allows better accuracy in detecting vulnerable people.

Acknowledgment. The authors would like to thank the Universidad de las Fuerzas Armadas-ESPE of Sangolquí, Ecuador, for the resources granted to develop the research project entitled: "Detection and Mitigation of Social Engineering attacks applying Cognitive Security", coded as PIC-2020-SOCIAL-ENGINEERING.

References

1. Andrade, R.O., Cazares, M., Fuertes, W.: Cybersecurity attacks during COVID-19: an analysis of the behavior of the human factors and a proposal of hardening strategies. In: Daimi, K., Peoples, C. (eds.) Advances in Cybersecurity Management, pp. 37–53. Springer, Cham (2021). https://doi.org/10.1007/978-3-030-71381-2_3
2. Badrulddin, A.: A study and analysis of attacks by exploiting the source code against computer systems. Int. J. Nonlinear Analy. Appl. **12**, 415–424 (2021)
3. Benavides, E., Fuertes, W., Sanchez, S., Sanchez, M.: Classification of phishing attack solutions by employing deep learning techniques: a systematic literature review. Smart Innov. Syst. Technol. **152**, 51–64 (2019). https://doi.org/10.1007/978-981-13-9155-2_5
4. Benavides, E., Fuertes, W., Sanchez, S., Nuñez-Agurto, D.: Caracterización de los ataques de phishing y técnicas para mitigarlos. Ataques: una revisión sistemática de la literatura. Cienc. y Tecnol. **13**(1), 97–104 (2020). https://doi.org/10.18779/CYT.V13I1.357
5. Cusack, B., Adedokun, K.: The impact of personality traits on user's susceptibility to social engineering attack. Aust. Inf. Secur. Manag. Conf. 83–89 (2018). https://doi.org/10.25958/5c528ffa66693
6. Op, J., Se, H., Lr, G.: The basic level in personality-trait hierarchies: studies of trait use and accessibility in different contexts. J. Pers. Soc. Psychol. **60**(3), 348–361 (1991). https://doi.org/10.1037//0022-3514.60.3.348
7. Kitchenham, B., Pearl Brereton, O., Budgen, D., Turner, M., Bailey, J., Linkman, S.: Systematic literature reviews in software engineering - a systematic literature review. Inf. Softw. Technol. **51**(1), 7–15 (2009). https://doi.org/10.1016/J.INFSOF.2008.09.009
8. Okada, S., Nguyen, L.S., Aran, O., Gatica-Perez, D.: Modeling dyadic and group impressions with intermodal and interperson features. ACM Trans. Multi. Comput. Commun. Appl. (TOMM) **15**(1s), 1–30 (2019)

9. Papatsaroucha, D., Nikoloudakis, Y., Kefaloukos, I., Pallis, E., Markakis, E.K.: A Survey on Human and Personality Vulnerability Assessment in Cyber-security: Challenges, Approaches, and Open Issues. June 2021. Accessed 16 Aug 2021. https://arxiv.org/abs/2106.09986v2

10. John, O., Robins, R., Pervin, L.: Handbook of personality: Theory and research (2010). Accessed 16 Aug 2021. https://books.google.com.ec/books?hl=es&lr=&id=olgW-du4RBcC&oi=fnd&pg=PR1&dq=Lawrence,+P.,+%26+John,+O.+(1995).+Handbook+of+personality.&ots=hLfpDnKWvf&sig=GIH0guF90JB_BNZEsNXHF3q56y8

Technology Trends

Recurrent Neural Networks for Deception Detection in Videos

Bryan Rodriguez-Meza⬤, Renzo Vargas-Lopez-Lavalle⬤,
and Willy Ugarte(✉)⬤

Universidad Peruana de Ciencias Aplicadas, Lima, Peru
{u201611137,u201521485}@upc.edu.pe, willy.ugarte@upc.pe

Abstract. Deception detection has always been of subject of interest. After all, determining if a person is telling the truth or not could be detrimental in many real-world cases. Current methods to discern deceptions require expensive equipment that need specialists to read and interpret them. In this article, we carry out an exhaustive comparison between 9 different facial landmark recognition based recurrent deep learning models trained on a recent man-made database used to determine lies, comparing them by accuracy and AUC. We also propose two new metrics that represent the validity of each prediction. The results of a 5-fold cross validation show that out of all the tested models, the Stacked GRU neural model has the highest AUC of .9853 and the highest accuracy of 93.69% between the trained models. Then, a comparison is done between other machine and deep learning methods and our proposed Stacked GRU architecture where the latter surpasses them in the AUC metric. These results indicate that we are not that far away from a future where deception detection could be accessible throughout computers or smart devices.

Keywords: Deception detection · Recurrent neural networks · Facial landmarks recognition · Deep learning · Video database

1 Introduction

In our day-to-day life, detecting a lie could have important implications in different social situations. If someone answers a question with false information, they may have details that they do not want to reveal, for different reasons. This information may be important in situations that imply serious or moderate consequences; this may be the case for police investigations for felonies.

One of the most destructive lies in history was: "There is no doubt that Saddam Hussein now has weapons of mass destruction". This lie had severe consequences. Because of this, thousands of Americans and hundreds of thousands of Iraqis have died in a war led by this false statement. This war lasted around eight years and costed a total of 2.4 trillion American dollars. The consequences of the war are still having repercussions on the United States of America[1].

---

[1] "8 of History's Most Destructive Lies" - https://bit.ly/3kufvOM.

© Springer Nature Switzerland AG 2022
M. Botto-Tobar et al. (Eds.): ICAT 2021, CCIS 1535, pp. 397–411, 2022.
https://doi.org/10.1007/978-3-031-03884-6_29

However, it has been shown that people's ability to discriminate lies is like that of tossing a coin, meaning it is basically random (between 50 to 54% [6]). Some may argue that people specialized in lie detection exist, and that they are exceptional at revealing lies. It is supposed that these "experts" try to decipher cognitive, non-verbal, emotional, or neuropsychological signals to determine if a person is telling the truth.

Nevertheless, recent studies have debunked that the idea of specialized people that can determine if a person is lying just by looking at them is probably incorrect [6,21]. In this article, we define lying as any act that deliberately seeks to communicate false or tampered information, with the purpose of deceiving. In modern days, different methods exist to determine if a person is lying or not. Among these methods, we can list the reading of polygraphs, evoked response potentials (ERP) and functional magnetic resonance imaging (FMRI) [18]. These methods have proven to be relatively reliable (e.g., 74%–82% in CQT-Polygraph, 76%–88% in CIT-Polygraph, 68% in ERPs and 84% in FMRIs in laboratory studies [18]), however, they also have some downsides.

A first downside is that they require specialized equipment that is generally expensive and difficult to obtain [28]. A second downside is that these methods are based on reading biological signals from our bodies to determine whether a person is lying or not. However, these signals can be altered by other factors that are not necessarily related to lying [18]. A third downside is that there are countermeasures to these methods, meaning that an insightful user with prior knowledge about these tests could deceive a lie detection test [8,18].

In this work, we present an alternative that tackles the first problem addressed above. We do not aim on attacking the second or the third. This is mostly because the technique on which our approach is also based on the reading of biological signals, which do not necessarily reflect whether a person is telling the truth or not, therefore we could also be vulnerable to the second and third problem.

A micro expression is an expression of short duration (between $\frac{1}{25}$s to $\frac{1}{3}$ s) that usually occurs when people experience intense feelings [25,29]. These can be caused by emotions that are being suppressed while lying, especially if the lie is a high-stake one [24]. As of the last decades, there has been a significant growth in the amount of publicly available data. Because of this, deep learning has started to become more and more popular and powerful. This is also the case for its use in computer vision tasks such as facial recognition, object recognition, sentiment analysis, etc. [25].

Our contributions are as follows:

– We seek to prove that the use of Recurrent Neural Networks (RNN) is viable option for deception detection in videos using facial landmarks. This will be achieved by comparing different architectures of this type of Neural Network (NN) such as simple , LSTMs, GRU, and other configurations that will be detailed on the following sections, with other types of NN and other machine learning algorithms.

- We propose two new metrics to determine the precision of our deception classification. The first one is Average Fidelity (AF), which represents the average certainty of the deception prediction and the second one is Proportional Fidelity (PF), which represents the proportion between already classified instances.
- We carry out an exhaustive comparison between different recurrent neural network architectures on this topic by facial landmarks [22] as reference points on the videos. This, aiming to find a suitable model for the task of lie detection. And then we compare them with existing methods to verify the performance.

Section 2, introduces the theory related to the background of our work (see Sect. 2.1); then, a more detailed segment explaining our contribution is described (see Sect. 2.2). Section 3 presents the experiments that have been carried out with the resulting deep learning models (see Sect. 3.3) and the related works are discussed (see Sect. 3.4). These have explored different viable options that are related to the task of lie detecting. Finally, we showcase the main conclusions of the project, where we will also leave some recommendations for future work.

2   Material and Method

In the following, we show the main concepts and proposed metrics of our proposal.

2.1   Preliminary Concepts

Now, we present the main concepts and notions that enable to detect lies in real time, using computer vision methods to extract information from videos of a user's face and to be able to classify their testimony as true or false.

Deep Learning: This field studies the family of artificial neural networks (ANN) which are a set of algorithms that learn patterns inspired by the structure and function of the brain [20].

This allows computational models made up of multiple processing layers to learn different representations of the proposed data with different levels of abstraction in areas such as speech recognition, object recognition, among others [9].

In other words, deep learning consists of machine learning algorithms on neural networks and their different types. The most common and currently resonant are convolutional neural networks (CNN) and recurrent neural networks (RNN), for the latter, the LSTM architecture is the most used variant.

Although there are many more types of networks, the 2 are the ones that are in the greatest growth due to the multiple improvements they have provided to the state of the art in their respective areas [9]. We mainly focus on the recurrent neural networks and its different architectures like:

- **Recurrent neural networks (RNN)** [10]: Neural networks that remove the restriction of not being able to return to a previous layer[2]. RNN serve to detect sequences and especially contexts based on a constant memory that influences a future prediction.
- **Long short-term memory (LSTM)** [11]: LSTM is a variation of RNN designed to deal with the problem of the vanishing gradient. A common LSTM cell has 3 main separate components[3], the input gate, the output gate, and the forget gate; these regulate the flow of information. LSTM architecture solves the vanishing gradient problem by forcing a constant error flow through the internal states.
- **Gated Recurrent Unit (GRU)** [4,5]: GRU is a variation of recurrent neural networks like LSTM but with the difference that it has 2 gates[4], update and reset, rather than 3. GRU also control the flow of information similarly to LSTM. Nevertheless, the GRUs do not have the need to have separate memory cells.
- **Bidirectional RNN** [23]: Bidirectional RNN solve the problem about simple RNN future contexts because they use all the input information like past and future information to make a prediction. Bidirectional RNN structure(see footnote 2) divides a recurrent cell into two components (one with the flow of time in a positive direction and the other in a negative direction).

Deception Detection: The purpose of deception detection is discriminating lies precisely, that is, to reveal false information. In crime situations and many others, determining whether an individual is telling the truth can be decisive in solving the case.

In some studies [18], it has been revealed that simply observing another person's behavior is not enough to determine the truthfulness of their words, therefore basing deception detection from the behavior of an individual does not increase the precision significantly as to be a relevant quality.

Our main contribution consists in finding out if RNN (with different configurations) works better to detect deceptions in videos than other proposals. To the best of our knowledge, no other work has approached this problem only using recurrent neural networks. Mainly convolutional networks or other machine learning models are used to solve it [15] or using CNNs with RNNs [13].

Facial Landmarks Extraction Process: The purpose of face detection is to locate and extract the face region from the background of an image or video [7]. To perform this there are 2 approaches, one by characteristics and other by images. Each approach, having different methods to be performed.

We focus on Facial features extraction [2] which is the process of extracting unique characteristics of a face in the form of facial components such as the eyes, nose, mouth, eyebrows, among others.

---

[2] Simple/Bidirectional RNN architecture - https://bit.ly/32XRtWc.
[3] LSTM cell architecture - https://bit.ly/306K454.
[4] GRU cell architecture - https://bit.ly/3kN4eIX.

After extracting facial features, they can be monitored to see which movements or patterns can be found. Normal expressions such as a smile or discomfort are usually observed. But there are other expressions that are not visible to the naked eye due to their short duration, these are called microexpressions [30], which are facial expressions of very short duration, approximately between $\frac{1}{25}$s to $\frac{1}{3}$s and consist of fleeting and involuntary expressions that try to hide people's true intentions.

2.2 Method

The main process starts with a video where a person is answering a question. On average, the answers can last between 30 and 40 s where the user responds and details what has been asked. Once the video is recorded, we proceed to use the dataset of the 68 facial points from [22] where it is applied to the collected video, this means that in the 30 or 40 s of response, you can carefully observe how these dots representing the user's facial features move through time.

This is where the concept of microexpressions[5] comes into question. In these videos there are facial movements that are not necessarily perceptible to the human eye because they are made in a fraction of a second, therefore, they must be stored with a frequency high enough to be able to detect those changes in time imperceptible to the naked eye.

The next step is storing this movement of the facial points considering the duration of the microexpressions , then the frequency of how often the position of the facial points should be stored must be within that $\frac{1}{25}$s to $\frac{1}{2}$s time window. The value chosen for this work is .05 s, which is equivalent to $\frac{1}{20}$s (tests with other values were performed with worse results), thus, for each video, the exact location of the facial points is saved every .05 s, this from the beginning where the user begins to answer the question until when it ends.

With this, a data frame is generated that has the cardinal positions (x, y) of each of the points, thus having 136 characteristics in total. With a duration of approximately 30 to 40 s, there will be 600 to 800 moments in time where the exact positions of these points are stored. With the data correctly stored in the stipulated time window, we proceed to normalize the data collected with the MinMaxScaler[6] in a range from 0 to 1. After that process, the sequencing of the data typical of the recurrent neural networks is carried out to see the variation of the movement of the points in time.

The size of the sequence for the final models in which the experimentation that will be detailed in Sect. 3.1 was carried out is 10 timesteps. Other quantities were tested and since there was no significant change on performance, it remained as it is. When performing this transformation of the data, it is converted from 2 dimensions (number of sequences, number of characteristics) to

---

[5] "Hiding true emotions: micro-expressions in eyes retrospectively concealed by mouth movements" - https://www.nature.com/articles/srep22049.

[6] MinMaxScaler it is sensitive to outliers: https://bit.ly/30hsICz.

3 dimensions (number of sequences, timesteps, number of characteristics). Now this transformed data is ready to be entered as input to the model.

For this research, nine configurations of recurrent networks were carried out, which will be seen in more detail in Sect. 3.1. The reason we use recurrent networks to detect lies is due to the structure of the input data in this scenario where they act as a time series problem. By using the positions of multiple facial points, it is possible to analyze changes in fractions of time undetectable to the human eye, allowing us to obtain information that indicates whether a user is telling the truth or a lie by analyzing the changes in time of their facial features.

Mainly, three types of recurrent networks such as LSTM, GRU and classic RNN are dealt with, but their variations were also considered for testing, making them bidirectional or stacked with the total combination of nine models. With the best model obtained from the experimentation (see Sect. 3.1), the results indicated whether the predictions were truthful or deceptive.

2.3 Metrics

We propose two evaluation metrics for the prediction, with the purpose of evaluating our experimental results:

1. Firstly, we propose the "Average Fidelity" metric (see Eqs. 1 and 2) that consists of the total average for all the predicted sequences (i). Each prediction for each sequence has a truth probability (e.g., for sequence number one, there is a 20% probability that it is a lie (d_i) and an 80% probability that it is true (t_i)). And so on, up to the sequence "**n**". Finally, these percentages are averaged.

$$AF_{truth} \quad = \quad \frac{\sum_i^n t_i}{n} \tag{1}$$

$$AF_{deception} \quad = \quad \frac{\sum_i^n d_i}{n} \tag{2}$$

$$\text{where } t_i : \text{truth probability of sequence } i$$
$$d_i : \text{lie probability of sequence } i$$

2. Secondly, we also propose the "Proportional Fidelity" metric (see Eqs. 3 and 4) which is calculated by the direct proportion between the sequences (i) that were classified as deceptions (d_i) or truths (t_i) (i.e., if $d_i > t_i$ then the sequence is taken as deceptive ($c_i = 0$), otherwise it is taken as truthful ($c_i = 1$)), over the total number of predicted sequences.

$$PF_{truth} \quad = \quad \frac{\sum_i^n c_i}{n} \tag{3}$$

$$PF_{deception} \quad = \quad 1 - PF_{truth} \tag{4}$$

$$\text{where } c_i : \text{deception prediction of sequence } i$$
$$(c_i \iff (d_i < t_i)), \forall 1 \leq i \leq \text{n}, c_i \in \{0, 1\}$$

Both metrics complement each other because the first one validates the truthful proportions of the analyzed videos, while the latter serves as an indicator of how many sequences in total were classified as truth. Thus, videos to be considered as truthful (resp. deceptive) should have high (resp. low) values for both.

Example 1. Let's imagine that two given videos v_1 and v_2 obtain the values for AF and PF in Fig. 1.

- In Fig. 1a, with the video v_1, we have that $AF(v) = \frac{.53 + .64 + .39 + .52}{4} = 52\%$ and $PF(v) = \frac{3}{4} = 75\%$. Both metrics combined indicate us the nature of v_1, the person in the video probably is telling the truth but with no certitude since its PF (75% of the sequences are classified as truthful) tell us that it should be classified as truthful and AF (the sequences obtain 52% of truthfulness) tell us that this should not be taken with great conviction.
- In Fig. 1b, with the video v_2, we have that $AF(v) = \frac{.49 + .48 + .49 + .55}{4} = 50.25\%$ and $PF(v) = \frac{1}{4} = 25\%$. Both metrics combined indicate us the nature of v_2, the person in the video probably is lying or telling a half-truth since PF (25% of the sequences are classified as truthful) tell us that it should be classified as deceptive whereas AF (the sequences obtain 50.25% of truthfulness) tell us that this is very slightly truthful.

Table 1. Toy examples of metrics for two videos.

Sequence (i)	Truth probability (t_i)	Lie probability (d_i)	Sequence (i)	Truth probability (t_i)	Lie probability (d_i)
1	.53	.47	1	.49	.51
2	.64	.36	2	.48	.52
3	.39	.61	3	.49	.51
4	.52	.48	4	.55	.45

(a) Sequences for video v_1.   (b) Sequences for video v_2.

2.4 Related Works

Deception detection has been around for some time; it has always been desirable to know whether someone is lying. Because of this, a vast quantity of methods have been proposed and worked on over the years in order to yield these results. Some of these try and use a wide variety of biological signals to identify when a person is not acting their usual self. Some other methods use questioning based on prior context and undeniable evidence to incriminate a suspect. Newer ones try and use this basis in conjunction with other techniques to gain some improvement in comparison to classical methods. In this Section, we are going to talk about related works that use techniques for deception detection.

On one hand [28], the authors created a novel multi-modal lie detection system (i.e., using video, sound, and a transcript data). The most important module was the video module, in which the authors used a mixture of Improved Dense Trajectory (IDT) and Mel-frequency Cepstral Coefficients (MFCC) to extract facial features to feed a Support Vector Machine (SVM) model that would determine if a person was lying or not. In our work, we use a deep learning model instead of a SVM one because of the amount of data we had was larger (over double the instances in most cases).

In the other hand, [1] is very similar to the previous work in the sense that it also uses microexpressions and a multi-modal approach, however they differ in the techniques used. By using deep learning in their video detection, their method is very similar to ours in this regard. The main difference between our work and theirs is that we focus on RNN and they use other kinds of neural networks (convolutional neural networks, multilayer perceptron, etc.). Also, we only use video stream data for the lie detection to evaluate if only using video information could be enough to discriminate lies.

The authors in [13] proposed a multi modal method which consists of a visual and vocal module. The said multi modal detector is presented as an end to end framework that will detect deceptiveness in videos automatically. The visual module is based on a Convolutional Neural Network (CNN), various filters and the usage of an LSTM network to work the time series features extracted from each video and the correlation between said data. The vocal module also consists of another CNN and LSTM network specially constructed for the usage of vocal cues. One of the main differences of the proposed to ours is the usage of a module that uses a CNN model to classify vocal cues to aid in the deception detection.

In [3], authors utilize a mix of computer vision techniques to discern specific facial behaviors such as eye micro-movement, and facial micro-movement. With these 1 s vectors are constructed and fed to a machine learning model to classify each video segment as truthful or not. Techniques such as Artificial Neural Networks (ANN) and Random Forest (RF) are employed as the main machine learning methods to use. In contrast to our research and all of the work stated in this investigation, this research used the biggest database of videos, using a number of 1200 videos in total. This permitted that the selection and data mining processes performed on the data could be carried out more efficiently.

In [14], the authors propose a method utilizing RGB videos and Facial Action Units (AU). Their proposed method utilizes an SVM Classifier in order to classify certain facial action units as truthful and others as deceitful. Frame by frame, obtainable AU's (some can't be picked up by the HOG AU extraction algorithm) are evaluated and given an intensity that ranges between 0 and 5. With these scores, the classifier will determine if the subject in the video is being deceptive. In contrast to our work, the authors used AU's to capture deceptive behavior, which represent a more organized representation of the subject's facial behavior. The structured nature of their data allowed them to use a classifier such as SVM to quickly obtain the classification result.

In [27], the authors present a multimodal framework that uses audio, text and/or video features for deception detection. Even if this framework is interesting using an AdaBoost video recognition system to recognize certain micro expressions that would later be part of a larger system that requires a lot of configurations and parameters for other methods (e.g., the audio is treated with Cepstral Coefficients (CC) and Spectral Regression Kernel Discriminant Analysis (SRKDA) and the text with SVM).

Contrarily, we only use a video recognition system based on RNN, first, to simplify, since we obtained better results only with video information and secondly, RNN, even if they are not very often used to tackle video data, mostly Convolutional Neural Networks are, show a good performance for this task.

3   Results and Discussions

Now, a experimental study is carried out. First, we explain our experimental protocol with the settings of the environment in which the experiments were performed, then the data is explained and finally the major results will be shown and finally discussed.

3.1   Experimental Protocol

The research development was done in a Python 3.7.7 environment by using Jupyter Notebook to have a direct visualization of the training results of the models. Our code and tests are publicly available[7].

Mainly the TensorFlow v2.1.0 library and its corresponding dependencies were used for the work of this research. It should be noted that the dedicated GPU version of TensorFlow was used so that the training and validation of the models were carried out in a more efficient way. For this variant that uses the graphics card, CUDA v1.1 and CuDNN v7.5.6 had to be installed for the correct functioning of the work environment.

The local hardware configuration consisted of an Intel Core i7-5820k CPU, an Nvidia GTX 980 Ti GPU whose driver's version was 451.67 and 16 GB of DDR4 RAM at 2400 Mhz.

3.2   Data

The data comes from [17] named Miami University deception detection database, which consists of 320 deception detection videos recorded to provide more representative and diverse information and to standardize research in the field. The videos contain 4 questions per gender and ethnicity group and they answer them describing their feelings towards a certain person. The number of individuals that participated in the videos are eighty.

For this research, only the label that represents whether the video is truthful or deceptive is used. Also, video number 188 labeled "WF010_4PL" was not used since it had missing values while applying the 68 point-set facial mask while processing the data, leaving us with 319 videos. After the videos were processed as mentioned in Sect. 2.2, a dataset containing all the information 319 videos is obtained that serves as input for each network.

---

[7] https://github.com/albertbry9/deception-detection-.

3.3   Results

Now, we present the major results of our study with the accuracy (ACC) and the area under the curve (AUC) metrics. It should be noted that there are studies that compare both metrics and it is determined that the AUC metric is more representative of the real performance, especially for binary classifiers [12].

Selecting the Best RNN Architecture: We select three classical RNN models for training (see Sect. 2.1), each one with three variants since they are the most important for [4,5,10,11,23]. These 9 networks are combinatorial of the LSTM, GRU and fully connected RNN architectures with the simple variants with a single hidden layer, the bidirectional (BiDir) and the stacked with 2 recurrent layers. Each one of the hidden layers has 64 neurons. Various hyperparameters were tested to define the optimal configuration of the network architecture. For the loss function, tests were performed with binary crossentropy, categorical crossentropy and mean squared error. After testing, the best results were obtained with binary crossentropy. Although it was an expected result since it is a binary classification task, the results reinforced this assertion. And for the optimizer, tests carried out with those available in the Keras library (SGD, Adam, Adamax, among others). For this case, the best results were obtained from the Adam optimizer and with a learning rate of 0.001.

Table 2 shows the results of our run tests for these nine possibilities with the data from [17]. The model that stands out among the others is the Stacked GRU with an accuracy of 93.69% and an AUC of 98.53%. It can be seen how the LSTM architectures closely follows the GRU variants in terms of performance, nonetheless the latter surpasses it in all scenarios. These results were obtained testing the trained models with a 5-fold cross validation algorithm. We selected 5 folds since a lower value would not have been sufficient amount for testing the performance of the proposed models and a higher value such as 10 or 12 folds did not alter the results, only increased the calculation time.

Table 2. Comparison of recurrent neural network architectures.

	LSTM			GRU			RNN		
	Simple	Bidir	Stacked	Simple	Bidir	Stacked	Simple	Bidir	Stacked
ACC	.8806	.8800	.8992	.9006	.9037	**.9369**	.7808	.8022	.6992
AUC	.9561	.9550	.9670	.9677	.9692	**.9853**	.8686	.8889	.7776

Comparing the Best RNN Architecture with Other Methods: We compare the best previously selected RNN architecture (i.e., Stacked GRU) with the methods that are the best to our knowledge to tackle this task based with different kinds of techniques such as Support Vector Machines (SVM) [1,27,28], Artificial Neural Networks (ANN) [13–15,19].

For Table 3, we observe that our proposal of using the Stacked GRU outperforms these other methods for the ACC and AUC metrics.

Table 3. Performance of our proposed method compared with existing methods

	Model	ACC	AUC
	Our Proposal (Stacked GRU)	**.9369**	**.9853**
[28]	All Modalities	.8396	.8773
	GTMicroExpression+All Modalities	.8746	.9221
[15]	MLP H+C	.9114	.9799
[19]	ANN 20 Neuron 10 - Fold Truth	.9155	.9566
	ANN 20 Neuron 10 - Fold Deception	.9278	.9436
[27]	CC + SRKDA SVM	.9340	.9125
[13]	DEV LSTM	.8416	.8159
[1]	RBF-SVM	.7684	.7487
[14]	SVM Important Features	.7700	.7545
	RF Important Features	.7800	.7966
	ANN Important Features	.7200	.7413

Testing the Quality of the Predictions: After obtaining the Stacked GRU as the best model in our comparison, we proceeded to evaluate each one of the 319 videos from the Miami video database. The metrics used to verify the prediction quality of each video are those proposed in Sect. 2: Average Fidelity (AF) and Proportional Fidelity (PF). Figure 1 shows 2 plots that contain the results of the points intersecting the AF Truth with PF Truth measures for each video. By having a time series approach, predictions are made for each sequence (in which the videos have been divided) every .05 s, having in total between 600 and 800 predictions per video, for which the proposed metrics are calculated.

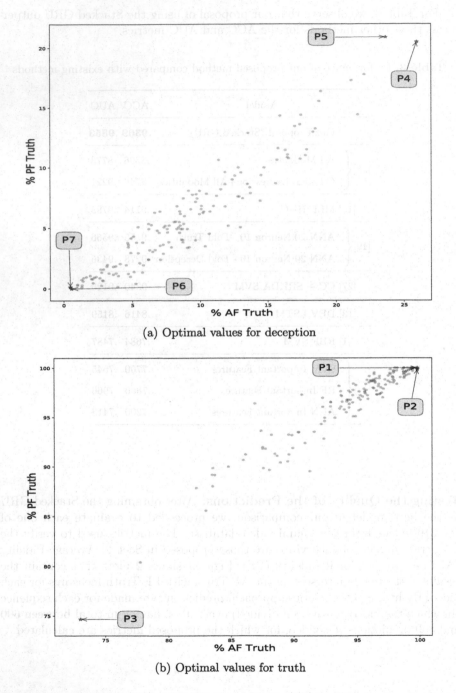

(a) Optimal values for deception

(b) Optimal values for truth

Fig. 1. Average fidelity (AF) and Proportional fidelity (PF) for Miami university deception detection database.

3.4   Discussions

In Table 2, comparing the simple models against the bidirectional ones, a slight (or none) improvement is noted that contrasts with the stacked models where there is a more noticeable jump in performance on the metrics apart from the fully connected RNN where the use of a second layer in the stacked variant impairs the performance of said architecture. This may be since by not having information flow control gates, they suffer from the problem of vanishing and exploding gradient in addition to a greater number of calculations due to its fully connected nature of this architecture.

In Table 3, Stacked GRU outperforms all the other solutions that are currently used to solve this problem. The closest results to our proposal (e.g., MLP [15] or ANN [19]) are models based on ANN architectures, therefore, they seem to be the most appropriate method for this task. Furthermore, the other methods based on other kinds of techniques (SVM [1,27,28], Random Forest [27] and others) get worse results for both metrics and mostly based on multimodal inputs (i.e., they require audio, video and transcription).

Figure 1a (respectively Fig. 1b) contains the optimal values for deceptions (respectively truths). Points P1 and P2 (respectively P6 and P7) represented as blue stars are the Pareto optimal points for maximization (respectively minimization) for AF and PF truth. These are the videos that are predicted to be truth (respectively deception) with greater certainty.

Watching videos P1 and P2, it is observed how they tell a more elaborate and fluid story making it more perceptible as truth. They roughly convey the answer in 2 or 3 well-crafted sentences.

However, in videos P6 and P7, their statements are more uneven and seem elaborated on the spot rather than truly remembered, typical of lies. Approximately, they convey the answer between 13 to 14 sentences with descriptions that are even repeated in the same answer.

This changes for points P4 and P5 (respectively P3) which are represented as red stars on Fig. 1a (respectively Fig. 1b). These are the furthest values from optimality for deception (respectively truth), there are no other points ranging approximately between 26% to 71% for both AF and PF. These videos, even though their predictions match the original label, the model had the greatest difficulty to predict them correctly.

4   Conclusions

Throughout this work, it has been discovered that using recurrent neural networks in videos is a viable alternative for deception detection to the point of matching and even surpassing the results obtained in previous works that use other methods to solve the same problem, especially in the best model obtained that uses the Stacked GRU architecture which has proven to be viable for future implementations that could be part of ensemble models for deception detection.

Furthermore, even if multimodal frameworks are quite useful and powerful, for this kind of task treating only video information obtains very good results, even if they might seem a simpler approach. A perspective of our proposal could be treating videos dynamically, in other words predicting if a person is alternating between truth or lie in the same testimony of longer duration in combination data with electroencephalogram (EEG) data [16] or softening the parameters [26].

Acknowledgments. We would like to express our deep gratitude to Professor Emily Paige Lloyd who enables us to use Miami University deception detection database [17], which made the results of this research possible.

References

1. Avola, D., Cinque, L., Foresti, G.L., Pannone, D.: Automatic deception detection in RGB videos using facial action units. In: ICDSC, pp. 1–6. ACM (2019)
2. Benedict, S.R., Kumar, J.S.: Geometric shaped facial feature extraction for face recognition. In: ICACA, pp. 275–278 (2016)
3. Chao, L., Tao, J., Yang, M., Li, Y., Wen, Z.: Long short term memory recurrent neural network based encoding method for emotion recognition in video. In: ICASSP, pp. 2752–2756. IEEE (2016)
4. Cho, K., et al.: Learning phrase representations using RNN encoder-decoder for statistical machine translation. In: EMNLP. ACL (2014)
5. Chung, J., Gülçehre, Ç., Cho, K., Bengio, Y.: Empirical evaluation of gated recurrent neural networks on sequence modeling. In: NeurIPS Workshops (2014)
6. Curci, A., Lanciano, T., Battista, F., Guaragno, S., Ribatti, R.M.: Accuracy, confidence, and experiential criteria for lie detection through a videotaped interview. Front. Psychiatry **9**, 748 (2019)
7. Datta, A.K., Datta, M., Banerjee, P.K.: Face Detection and Recognition: Theory and Practice. CRC Press (2015)
8. Ganis, G., Rosenfeld, J.P., Meixner, J., Kievit, R.A., Schendan, H.E.: Lying in the scanner: covert countermeasures disrupt deception detection by functional magnetic resonance imaging. NeuroImage **55**(1), 312–319 (2011)
9. Goodfellow, I.J., Bengio, Y., Courville, A.C.: Deep Learning. MIT Press, Adaptive computation and machine learning (2016)
10. Graves, A.: Supervised Sequence Labelling with Recurrent Neural Networks. SCI, vol. 385, pp. 5–13. Springer, Heidelberg (2012). https://doi.org/10.1007/978-3-642-24797-2
11. Han, H., Zhu, X., Li, Y.: Generalizing long short-term memory network for deep learning from generic data. ACM Trans. Knowl. Discov. Data **14**(2), 1–28 (2020)
12. Huang, J., Ling, C.X.: Using AUC and accuracy in evaluating learning algorithms. IEEE Trans. Knowl. Data Eng. **17**(3), 299–310 (2005)
13. Karimi, H., Tang, J., Li, Y.: Toward end-to-end deception detection in videos. In: IEEE BigData, pp. 1278–1283. IEEE (2018)
14. Khan, W., Crockett, K.A., O'Shea, J., Hussain, A., Khan, B.M.: Deception in the eyes of deceiver: A computer vision and machine learning based automated deception detection. Expert Syst. Appl. **169**, 114341 (2021)
15. Krishnamurthy, G., Majumder, N., Poria, S., Cambria, E.: A deep learning approach for multimodal deception detection. In: CICLing (2018)
16. Leon-Urbano, C., Ugarte, W.: End-to-end electroencephalogram (EEG) motor imagery classification with long short-term. In: SSCI, pp. 2814–2820. IEEE (2020)

17. Lloyd, E.P., Deska, J.C., Hugenberg, K., McConnell, A.R., Humphrey, B.T., Kunstman, J.W.: Miami university deception detection database. Behav. Res. Meth. **51** (2019)
18. Masip, J.: Deception detection: state of the art and future prospects. Psicothema **29**(2), pp. 149–159 (2017)
19. O'Shea, J., Crockett, K.A., Khan, W., Kindynis, P., Antoniades, A., Boultadakis, G.: Intelligent deception detection through machine based interviewing. In: IJCNN. IEEE, pp. 1–8 (2018)
20. Rosebrock, A.: Deep learning for computer vision with Python. PyImageSearch (2017)
21. Roulin, N., Ternes, M.: Is it time to kill the detection wizard? emotional intelligence does not facilitate deception detection. Pers. Individ. Diff. **137**, 131–138 (2019)
22. Sagonas, C., Tzimiropoulos, G., Zafeiriou, S., Pantic, M.: 300 faces in-the-wild challenge: the first facial landmark localization challenge. In: ICCV Workshops, pp. 397–403. IEEE Computer Society (2013)
23. Schuster, M., Paliwal, K.K.: Bidirectional recurrent neural networks. IEEE Trans. Sign. Process. **45**(11), 2673–2681 (1997)
24. Stewart, S.L., Wright, C., Atherton, C.: Deception detection and truth detection are dependent on different cognitive and emotional traits: an investigation of emotional intelligence, theory of mind, and attention. Pers. Soc. Psychol. Bull. **45**(5), 794–807 (2019)
25. Sun, B., Cao, S., Li, D., He, J., Yu, L.: Dynamic micro-expression recognition using knowledge distillation. IEEE Trans. Affect. Comput. (2020)
26. Ugarte, W., Boizumault, P., Loudni, S., Crémilleux, B., Lepailleur, A.: Soft constraints for pattern mining. J. Intell. Inf. Syst. **44**(2), 193–221 (2013). https://doi.org/10.1007/s10844-013-0281-4
27. Venkatesh, S., Raghavendra, R., Bours, P.: Robust algorithm for multimodal deception detection. In: MIPR. IEEE, pp. 534–537 (2019)
28. Wu, Z., Singh, B., Davis, L.S., Subrahmanian, V.S.: Deception detection in videos. In: AAAI, vol. 32, no. 1 (2018)
29. Yan, W.J., Wu, Q., Liang, J., Chen, Y.H., Fu, X.: How fast are the leaked facial expressions: the duration of micro-expressions. J. Nonverbal Behav. **37**(4), 217–230 (2013)
30. Zhao, G., Li, X.: Automatic micro-expression analysis: open challenges. Front. Psychol. **10**, 1833 (2019)

Coordination and Flexibility in the Management of Software Development Processes for Start-Up Companies

Itza Morales[1] , Clifton Eduardo Clunie-Beaufond[1](✉) ,
and Miguel Vargas-Lombardo[2](✉)

[1] Facultad de Ingeniería de Sistemas Computacionales, Universidad Tecnológica de Panamá,
0819-07289 El Dorado, Panamá, República de Panamá
{itza.morales,clifton.clunie}@utp.ac.pa
[2] Universidad Tecnológica de Panamá, GISES, 0229-0149 Coclé, República de Panamá
miguel.vargas@utp.ac.pa

Abstract. The processes of digitalization in the cloud and the provision of services from Start-up Companies not only implies changes within their internal software development, but also involves making profound changes in the way of applying new strategies and managing the service offered to companies distributed in different continents, shortening distances through the development of quality software. On the other hand, strategies are affected by external conditions such as the influence of changing decision-making, market trends and changing competitive advantages, as well as social attitudes that are linked to the confidence of users in digital and the adoption of technology in their environment. These particularities associated with the management of software development processes for startups, requires special attention, therefore, this study focuses on the analysis of artifacts, coordination capabilities, flexibility and its importance in software development. From this analysis, it is proposed a model that will facilitate the linkage and integration in software development with an approach that includes the most relevant aspects and characteristics in the implementation of coordination and flexibility capabilities in Start-ups companies, offering them benefits in the delivery of software products and services.

Keywords: Flexibility · Coordination · Process management · Startup companies · Software development · Mechanisms · Artifacts

1 Introduction

Start-up companies face changes in the development of Software products, depending on the level of commercialization and the way in which they adapt new Software development practices; However, they lack some guidelines to analyze and evaluate the processes and reduce the risk due to elements that affect mechanisms and key attributes in the management of processes such as flexibility and coordination. [1–4]. Therefore,

© Springer Nature Switzerland AG 2022
M. Botto-Tobar et al. (Eds.): ICAT 2021, CCIS 1535, pp. 412–425, 2022.
https://doi.org/10.1007/978-3-031-03884-6_30

coordination includes artifacts that are important in the development of Software products. [5–8]. Similarly, flexibility is an attribute that allows the acceptance of changes in the Software components and through flexible and versatile processes it is identified as a measure that supports the efficiency of the process in less time and expense per project [2, 9–11]. For its part, there is a shortage regarding the domain of information because both are areas not addressed in the field of Software engineering (IS) [4, 5], especially in start-up companies; therefore, a study is necessary to show its analysis. Similarly, for [12, 13] mention that the problem in coordination lies in the assignment of tasks due to the lack of understanding of the assignment strategies and involves different techniques that represent a key aspect in SI. Likewise, the flexibility mechanism is fundamental in Software development, therefore, it is perceived in [9] with low maturity in terms of the restrictions that must be established in the management of processes.

Based on the exposed literature, the object of study is to carry out an analysis of the attributes, artifacts and mechanisms that characterize coordination and flexibility and present a model with the elements that should be considered in start-up companies. Also, the way in which they influence the development of the Software is described, to provide start-up companies with a guide that allows them to know those aspects of the coordination and flexibility mechanisms that they must consider when including them during the development of the Software product, because these companies do not know the correct steps in its implementation.

In this way, the following document is comprised of the materials and methods (Sect. 2), results (Sect. 3) this covers the synthesis and design of the model with the aspects of the mechanisms in the development of the Software. The Importance of flexibility and coordination in Software development is Models (Sect. 4), the conclusion in (Sect. 5), Acknowledgement and the bibliographic references, set out below.

2 Materials and Methods

This section exposes the materials and methods used for the investigation, in the first instance a literary review was carried out and in the second instance it is understood of the analysis of the information and design of the model with the synthesis of the content. As part of the methods used, the research questions, words and search strings are defined, the selection of primary and secondary studies is carried out, according to the inclusion and exclusion criteria. So, these sub-points are presented below.

2.1 Formulation of Research Questions

Initially, the research questions were established that allowed identifying the relevant aspects, delimiting and classifying the information; In other words, these allow us to offer an overview, for which, four research questions are presented:

Q1: How do start-up companies perceive the adoption of software development practices?

Q2: What are aspects that influence the analysis of flexibility and coordination mechanisms for Software development?

Q3: What elements should be present in flexibility and coordination in the development of the Software?

Q4: Why is flexibility and coordination important in software development?

According to these questions, the search words and strings are established for the research object, described in the following sub-point.

2.2 Strings and Search Strategy

The definition of the search words and strings allow us to approximate the mapping of the studies that meet the research questions. For this, Table 1 shows the "concept" of the domain to which it is related and the "search terms" include the chains used; and the "and - or" operators are used to delimit and relate the words.

Table 1. Search words and strings

Concept	Search terms
Software development start-up companies -Description Characteristics	"Start-up company's trends in the adoption of good software development practices" OR "Software development in start-up companies"; "Characteristics of the start-up companies in adoption good practices software"; "Start-ups Software generational perception levels"; "Team age levels in Start-ups"
Software development	"Management and software and development AND process" OR "management software development process"; "Software development process"
Coordination and flexibility Benefits ELEMENTS	"Coordination AND flexibility" OR "aspects in the coordination AND flexibility start-up"; "Flexibility in software Development"; "Coordination in software Development"

Subsequently, through the search managers for scientific information such as *ScienceDirect, ACM Digital library* and *Springer.* They allowed mapping all the articles related to the coordination and flexibility in the development of software for start-up companies.

3   Results

This section presents the synthesis of the information on flexibility and coordination in the development of software for start-up companies. Initially, the scientific evidence highlights that companies are focused on creating Software products without evaluating strategies to minimize risks during the process; In addition, aspects such as coordination and communication represent the means to establish the requirements and four fundamental characteristics intervene to create new solutions [14, 15]. While other authors indicate that some problems are also generated in security, repetitive changes, domain clients or account management and the performance of empirical processes focused on the restricted value; in turn, start-up companies adopt good Software development practices [18–20].

These results imply expanding according to the research questions, each of the elements that are fundamental during the Software development process in start-up companies, and are described as follows:

3.1 Adoption of Software Development Practices in Start-Up Companies

Currently Software companies adopt practices depending on their characteristics, competencies, organizational structures, verification models, process management and they do not have enough resources [14, 15, 17, 20, 26]. According to some studies, the adoption of Lean and Agile methodologies are considered in the first phase for the management of operational activities [15, 16]. In this measure, the practices adopted by start-up companies are called "Light-weight" due to their flexibility in decision-making, inclusion of commercial value. [15, 29–33]. On the other hand, there is a perception of the ages of the employees and it influences the performance within the team, they generally hire young professionals, [34, 35]. For their part, the authors in [34–38] argue that there is an increase in hiring of women in proportion to men and the projects developed are mostly by personnel between 25 and 44 years of age, due to their ability to contribute new ideas. On the other hand, there are other aspects that are present during the Software development process; described below.

3.2 Aspects that Influence the Analysis of Flexibility and Coordination Mechanisms for Software Development

The objective of this section is to describe the aspects that internally influence coordination and flexibility; because it is necessary to identify the way they infer to suggest improvement strategies.

Table 2. Aspects that influence coordination and flexibility in software development

Terms	Description	References
Coordination	Leadership, low frequency in communication, identification of artifacts, degree of formalization with high uncertainty, difficulties in standardization and understanding in co-evaluation of routines and time rules	[6, 21, 22]
	Standard operating procedures and dynamic decision making, mismatches in coordination processes and practices	[23, 24]
Flexibility	Time pressure, team empowerment as a performance strategy, lack of resources and the search for a start-up business model	[15, 25]
	Evolution of requirements engineering practices, division of small tasks, limits between them due to their independence and architectural decisions (system architecture)	[26–28]

In this context, Table 2 shows a synthesis of the main aspects present during the Software development process. In turn, this description, based on scientific evidence, allows us to synthesize a more concrete and formal definition of the terms of the *coordination* and *flexibility*, as presented in the following two subsections.

3.2.1   Coordination

Coordination is defined as the process of managing interdependencies in the assignment of tasks or resources and restrictions on the levels of regulation of the routines to be executed to achieve a balance and coherence in the changes that may occur during the workflow and includes characteristics and artifacts that determine how coordination is established for Software processes [1, 6, 8, 21, 24, 39, 40]. In effect, establishing a mechanism supported by standards allows structuring Software development processes and generates increased transparency and predictability between companies by counteracting coordination challenges such as the Software environment distributed geographically or due to poorly defined processes, centralized plans., cooperative adjustment and leadership with cultural norms [8, 41–43]. In addition, coordination encompasses levels of complexity in its use and in quality of service it does not easily adapt to changing requirements, for this two approaches are suggested: static coordination (*identify elements to coordinate incrementally*) and dynamics (*way of coordinating the elements*) [42–48]. Similarly, the coordination must consider that during the development process unexpected changes may occur, and flexible measures are necessary to meet the objectives of the Software project.

3.2.2   Flexibility

Flexibility is defined as the ability to react, change and adapt to the challenges of the environment for the modification of some component of the Software; In other words, it works in the construction of processes in the equipment in long periods of time, this generates resources are consumed; In addition, flexibility is recognized as a measure of quality and standardization of the Software process (predicting the flexibility and performance of the Software project), because it allows describing the magnitude of time and cost to adapt to change [49–53]. Likewise, flexibility is considered as the quality attribute and property that is correlated with the stage of construction and evolution of the Software system, as it represents an economic parameter; Like, Software's flexible process management techniques are recommended [27, 28, 54]. In turn, the authors in [27, 55] mention that when there is low flexibility, it is more likely that those in charge of the design are involved in the requirements gathering stage, this minimizes the risks in design changes. For their part, some authors describe that it is necessary to achieve acceptable levels of maturity in terms of the flexibility of the process management and planning with the mechanisms and patterns that the coordination process must follow [56–58]. At the same time, the definition of both terms "coordination and flexibility" implies a synthesis of their characteristics (see Table 3).

Table 3. Characteristic elements of coordination and flexibility for software development.

Terms	Characteristics	References
Coordination	Formal and informal interaction with clients, effectiveness strategies in requirements, components or connectors (synchronization artifacts, maintenance, reuse and execution calculation adjustment)	[7, 46, 47, 52]
		[8, 41, 42, 47]
		[42–45, 48, 51]
	The coordinative complexity allows the transactions of the minimum amount of information	[59–61]
	Use of the distribution of roles, registration of cooperative components, uncertainty of the structure and practices (communication promotion, team help and management of shared accumulation); the Flexible service coordination allows you to choose requirements, abstract interaction patterns, policy, and coordination criteria	
	Interactive exchange in planning, assigning tasks, use of coordination theory to address dependencies, knowledge and effectiveness of coordination	
Flexibility	Reduces the risk of software development and maintenance expenses; increases the structuring of software design tasks	[27, 30]
	Rules and restrictions ensure strategic decision making	[21]
	It includes the adaptability to change of planning, evaluation and correction of faults; uses inflection points (number of customers and employees, feedback and flexible hours)	[26, 49, 53, 62]

3.3 Elements that must be Present in the Flexibility and Coordination in the Development of the Software

The authors of [1, 8, 40, 48] they mention that coordination mechanisms are constantly changing and must include direct supervision, standardize work and maintain a mutual adjustment of the parties involved. Similarly, a coordination mechanism is described as an organizational construction focused on a coordinating protocol on an artifact that manipulates patterns to know the complexity of a job; that is, a coordination artifact represents the information base of the company and includes mutability and richness; defined in a standard format of a set of rules, constraints.

Similarly, flexibility is necessary for architectural strategies of design patterns and the way it fits into a software project.; Therefore, the artifacts, roles, explicit variation points, restrictions and dependencies influence the activities, these are elements in the management of processes that can later be modified [15, 63]. In fact, there are different types of flexibility according to the demand, the granularity of the components in the design and a mediator as the level of control activities in the Software process allows, at a higher level of management control, a higher flexibility level [49, 53, 62]. Additionally, the authors of [28, 52, 54] determine that the greater the security, the less flexibility, the security in the routines and their interdependencies is necessary, because the use of flexible routines makes it easier to meet the planned objectives and remain stable without altering the rest of the operations, during the evolution mechanisms are used to deal with case management and successful software development. In turn, some studies highlight that part of the maturity models such as standardized practices and processes are part of the evaluation of flexibility to improve their implementation; the indicators are the forms and the means because they are part of the maturity levels; while, the mechanisms monitor and evaluate flexibility, and even require a comprehensive understanding between the phases of the software life cycle to determine the roles of flexibility patterns [28, 49, 62]. As a result of this analysis, Table 4 exposes the dimensions, types, level of maturity, mechanisms and indicators that comprise the flexibility in the development of Software, it is provided a short description and the references of the scientific literature from which they were extracted.

Table 4. Key elements of flexibility for software development in start-up companies

Terms	Concept	References
Dimensions	* *Team autonomy:* suggests freedom between members during the performance of functions and roles **Team diversity:* consider the opinions of the members of the Software project * *Measurement direction:* refers to appearance and cost * Performance, time and cost of response and implementation and the quality of the Software product	[50, 51]
Types (Flexibility)		
* Operation	Examines organizational structure and strategies in mobilizing teams	[23], [55, 58]
Of composition	It allows to deploy a team and its optimization of the tasks to be executed	
*Management	Represents flexible reallocation of settings, strategies, resources, and maintenance	
* Structures	Use in the formation of dynamic decision making depending on market conditions	
Process	Product development process and this can be stable	[52]
Results	Stable process can produce different product variations	

(*continued*)

Table 4. (*continued*)

Terms	Concept	References
Of the team	It is determined by the administration, speed to market, success and functionality of the Software product	[50]
Maturity level	• Operational flexibility of individual processes, process interactions and between actors (members) • Strategic flexibility (explores alternatives from product to solution) • Operational flexibility in the value network (process alignment) • Strategic flexibility in the general ecosystem (interaction between elements)	[55, 62]
Mechanisms	Introduce metadata (modifications in the configuration), design patterns (modification of the subsystem), parameterize components (internal modifications), review and audit the operation of the equipment to manage processes; manage the measurement of progress towards objectives (mapping and restrictions on measures to be carried out)	[28, 49]
Indicators	* Facilitators, influencers and performance outcome: response capacity, organizational control, speed, integration and availability * Agile methodology: enables team collaboration during the development process * Associated with the operational flexibility of the value network: Allows resource reorganization, maintenance and coordination among the development team	[62]

From this exposed argument, it allows to describe the importance of coordination and flexibility in the development of the Software.

4   Importance of Flexibility and Coordination in Software Development, Models

Initially, a benefit of coordination is that it allows you to compare the form before and after the change; In addition, including artifacts determines the level of complexity that the product development encompasses and its level of acceptance of flexibility and effectiveness called the result of the coordination strategy and its components can be implicit and explicit [46, 59, 60]. Also, for [1, 41] mentions that coordination mechanisms facilitate collective performance, since the organizational arrangements of individuals are coordinated and may be subject to change during the Software product development cycle; Therefore, a previous configuration allows start-up companies to avoid some problems related to the construction and updating of the model or documentation [22]. Likewise, another advantage is to allow the reduction of the degree of reprocessing of the Software; that is, the planning established in the coordination determines that the ability to cope with change is improved [49]. While, in terms of a flexible environment in Software projects, it allows to reduce the risk of software development and maintenance expenses. [20, 30]. It also includes reducing the effort to structure the work of the elements in the Software evolution process; facilitates executing strategies for changes in the product; reduces risk and facilitates aspect targeting to separate design and architecture time significantly influences system flexibility [27, 28, 54]. In fact, both coordination and flexibility deserve to be evaluated in their work strategies, because they allow reducing risks and possible increases in the budget not established. This affects the elements that must be present to correctly implement both flexibility and coordination mechanisms; in contrast, the following point proposes a model with the key elements for the development of software in start-up companies.

4.1 Design of a Model for the Correct Implementation of Coordination and Flexibility in Software Development

The purpose of this section involves the design of a model with the fundamental elements so that, during the construction management of a product; in turn, the members of the company can make the correct use of coordination and flexibility in projects. Figure 1 shows the sequence from right to left of the steps-elements, where the user or customer is directly related to the final software product. Additionally, flexibility shows the sequence of the elements to be evaluated, from the accuracy of the dimension of the change to which it must be adapted, the maturity levels to maintain a balance in the changes, which through the indicators determines the mechanism to be used by the situation to which a certain process identifies.

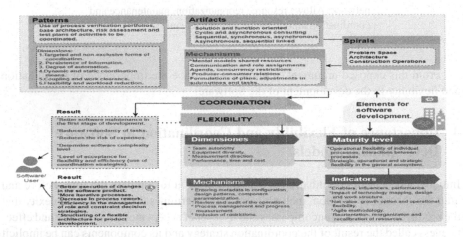

Fig. 1. Model of the necessary elements for the development of software in start-up companies.

The model describes the resulting aspects generated from the coordination process, this allows to evaluate the flexibility and the levels of acceptance in the way that can be implemented during the management of the processes; that is, coordination allows not only to establish the roles, rules, restrictions and to evaluate the planning levels involved in the development of a product, but also to determine the flexibility in this process.

5 Conclusions

This document has made it possible to synthesize the information regarding coordination and flexibility, the elements that are fundamental throughout the construction stage until the commercialization of the Software product, exposed as follows:

- Start-up companies must evaluate not only the commercial value of the product, but also the value of knowledge and efficiency of the set of elements that intervene throughout the Software development cycle. In this context, two underserved areas for start-ups were identified and it lies in the way they implement coordination and flexibility.
- A level of coordination stability allows the identification and security of the management of processes, which, in turn, gives the attribute and measure of quality "flexibility", form part of the construction cycle of Software projects because they must be flexible and have the capacity, as well as the work team, to be able to adapt to changes. Regardless of coordination, dimensions are also required in the classification of levels to establish flexibility; This, depending on the level of maturity and based on the identification indicators, allows the establishment of flexible mechanisms that facilitate efficient process management with a minimum risk rate, less time loss, low cost overruns and better adaptations to market standards current.
- As a result of the synthesis, he explains that not considering these aspects would cause the decomposition of subroutines, making wrong decisions, inconsistencies in definitions of architectural design and sub-processes, problems of planning, analysis and evaluation of the Software. Each of these derivations are products of not correctly implementing coordination and flexibility in Software development.
- Through the analysis of the elements of coordination and flexibility, they provide start-ups with the ability to carry out a review prior to implementing coordination and, therefore, flexibility during the Software development processes. This allows to create awareness and previous measures to minimize risks and incorporate ideas to teams to improve work strategies.
- Due to the lack of content in a direct approach to these two mechanisms in start-up companies, it offers the scientific community a new line for future work, where the way in which mechanisms such as scalability and modifiability influence the Software process, especially the way start-ups handle it and conceptually understand a whole panorama of what these companies involve and the best strategies to contribute to increasing their success in Software projects.

Acknowledgement. We are grateful for the support provided by the Science, Technology and Innovation National Secretariat of Panama (SENACYT), Scientific Master program TIC-UTP-FISC-2019 and to the National Research System (SNI-SENACYT) which one author is member.

References

1. Dingsøyr, T., Bjørnson, F.O., Moe, N.B., Rolland, K., Seim, E.A.: Rethinking coordination in large-scale software development. In: Proceedings of - Interantional Conference Software Engineering, pp. 91–92 (2018). https://doi.org/10.1145/3195836.3195850

2. Tendedez, H., Ferrario, M.A.M.A.F., Whittle, J.: Software development and CSCW. In: Proceedings ACM Human-Computer Interact. vol. 2, pp. 1–23 (2018). https://doi.org/10.1145/3274440
3. Rodríguez, P., Mäntylä, M., Oivo, M., Lwakatare, L.E., Seppänen, P., Kuvaja, P.: Advances in using agile and lean processes for software development. In: Advances in Computers, pp. 135–224 (2019). https://doi.org/10.1016/bs.adcom.2018.03.014
4. Melegati, J., Goldman, A., Kon, F., Wang, X.: A model of requirements engineering in software startups. Inf. Softw. Technol. **109**, 92–107 (2019). https://doi.org/10.1016/j.infsof.2019.02.001
5. Carrero, M.A., Musicante, M.A., dos Santos, A.L., Hara, C.S.: A DSL for WSN software components coordination. Inf. Syst. **98**, 101461 (2019). https://doi.org/10.1016/j.is.2019.101461
6. Dingsøyr, T., Moe, N.B., Fægri, T.E., Seim, E.A.: Exploring software development at the very large-scale: a revelatory case study and research agenda for agile method adaptation. Empir. Softw. Eng. **23**(1), 490–520 (2017). https://doi.org/10.1007/s10664-017-9524-2
7. Dumitriu, F., Mesnita, G.: A framework for the analysis of organizational change in the global software development. In: Proceedings of 7th International Business Information Management Association Conference Internet Information System Digital Age Challenges Solution - IBIMA 2006, pp. 551–558 (2006)
8. Zaitsev, A., Gal, U., Tan, B.: Coordination artifacts in agile software development. Inf. Organ. **30**, 100288 (2020). https://doi.org/10.1016/j.infoandorg.2020.100288
9. Andrews, K., Steinau, S., Reichert, M.: Enabling runtime flexibility in data-centric and data-driven process execution engines. Inf. Syst. **101**, 101447 (2019). https://doi.org/10.1016/j.is.2019.101447
10. Patiniotakis, I., Apostolou, D., Verginadis, Y., Papageorgiou, N., Mentzas, G.: Assessing flexibility in event-driven process adaptation. Inf. Syst. **81**, 201–219 (2019). https://doi.org/10.1016/j.is.2017.10.009
11. Behutiye, W., et al.: Management of quality requirements in agile 12 and rapid software development: a systematic mapping study. Inf. Softw. Technol. **123**, 106225 (2019). https://doi.org/10.1016/j.infsof.2019.106225
12. Amrit, C.: Application of social network theory to software development: the problem of task allocation. In: Proceedings of 2nd International Workshop Computer Supported Activity Coordination CSAC 2005, Conjunction with ICEIS 2005, pp. 3–13 (2005). https://doi.org/10.5220/0002576500030017
13. Panjer, L.D., Damian, D., Storey, M.A.: Cooperation and coordination concerns in a distributed software development project. In: Proceedings of - International Conference Software Engineering, pp. 77–80 (2008). https://doi.org/10.1145/1370114.1370134
14. Tripathi, N., et al.: An anatomy of requirements engineering in software startups using multivocal literature and case survey. J. Syst. Softw. **146**, 130–151 (2018). https://doi.org/10.1016/j.jss.2018.08.059
15. Paternoster, N., Giardino, C., Unterkalmsteiner, M., Gorschek, T., Abrahamsson, P.: Software development in startup companies: a systematic mapping study. Inf. Softw. Technol. **56**, 1200–1218 (2014). https://doi.org/10.1016/j.infsof.2014.04.014
16. Ghezzi, A.: Digital startups and the adoption and implementation of lean startup approaches: effectuation, bricolage and opportunity creation in practice. Technol. Forecast. Soc. Change. **146**, 945–960 (2019). https://doi.org/10.1016/j.techfore.2018.09.017
17. Duc, A.N., Abrahamsson, P.: Exploring the outsourcing relationship in software startups - a multiple case study. ACM Int. Conf. Proceeding Ser. Part **F1286**, 134–143 (2017). https://doi.org/10.1145/3084226.3084248

18. Souza, R., Malta, K., Silva, R., Masiero, P., Almeida, E., Machado, I.: A case study about startups' software development practices. ACM Int. Conf. Proceeding Ser. (2019). https://doi.org/10.1145/3364641.3364663

19. Huijgens, H., Van Solingen, R., Van Deursen, A.: How to build a good practice software project portfolio? In: ICSE Companion 2014 - Proceedings of 36th International Conference Software Engineering, pp. 64–73 (2014). https://doi.org/10.1145/2591062.2591187

20. Laukkanen, E., Paasivaara, M., Itkonen, J., Lassenius, C.: Comparison of release engineering practices in a large mature company and a startup. Empir. Softw. Eng. **23**(6), 3535–3577 (2018). https://doi.org/10.1007/s10664-018-9616-7

21. Grote, G., Weichbrodt, J.C., Günter, H., Zala-Mezö, E., Künzle, B.: Coordination in high-risk organizations: the need for flexible routines. Cogn. Technol. Work. **11**, 17–27 (2009). https://doi.org/10.1007/s10111-008-0119-y

22. Nascimento, L.M.A., Travassos, G.H.: Software knowledge registration practices at software innovation startups: results of an exploratory study. In: ACM International Conference Proceeding Series, pp. 234–243 (2017). https://doi.org/10.1145/3131151.3131172

23. de Waard, E., Kalkman, J.P., Bollen, M.T.I.B.: Flexibility in border security: a case study of the dutch border security team. In: Monsuur, H., Jansen, J.M., Marchal, F.J. (eds.) NL ARMS Netherlands Annual Review of Military Studies 2018. NA, pp. 3–22. T.M.C. Asser Press, The Hague (2018). https://doi.org/10.1007/978-94-6265-246-0_1

24. Nguyen-Duc, A., Cruzes, D.S., Conradi, R.: The impact of global dispersion on coordination, team performance and software quality-a systematic literature review. Inf. Softw. Technol. **57**, 277–294 (2015). https://doi.org/10.1016/j.infsof.2014.06.002

25. Rocha, Á., Adeli, H., Reis, L.P., Costanzo, S. (eds.): WorldCIST'19 2019. AISC, vol. 930. Springer, Cham (2019). https://doi.org/10.1007/978-3-030-16181-1

26. Gralha, C., Damian, D., Wasserman, A.I.T., Goulão, M., Araújo, J.: The evolution of requirements practices in software startups. In: Proceedings of - International Conference on Software Engineering, pp. 823–833 (2018). https://doi.org/10.1145/3180155.3180158

27. Thomke, S., Reinertsen, D.: Agile product development: managing development flexibility in uncertain environments. Calif. Manage. Rev. **41**(1), 8–30 (1998) 13. https://doi.org/10.2307/41165973

28. Naab, M., Stammel, J.: Architectural flexibility in a software-system's life-cycle: Systematic construction and exploitation of flexibility. In: QoSA 2012 - Proceedings 8th International ACM SIGSOFT Conference Quality Software Architectures, pp. 13–22 (2012). https://doi.org/10.1145/2304696.2304701

29. Lehtinen, T.O.A., Mäntylä, M.V., Vanhanen, J.: Development and evaluation of a lightweight root cause analysis method (ARCA method) - field studies at four software companies. Inf. Softw. Technol. **53**, 1045–1061 (2011). https://doi.org/10.1016/j.infsof.2011.05.005

30. Hsieh, F.-S., Lin, J.-B.: Context-aware workflow management for virtual enterprises based on coordination of agents. J. Intell. Manuf. **25**(3), 393–412 (2012). https://doi.org/10.1007/s10845-012-0688-8

31. Yaman, S.G., et al.: Introducing continuous experimentation in large software-intensive product and service organisations. J. Syst. Softw. **133**, 195–211 (2017). https://doi.org/10.1016/j.jss.2017.07.009

32. Mansoori, Y., Karlsson, T., Lundqvist, M.: The influence of the lean startup methodology on entrepreneur-coach relationships in the context of a startup accelerator. Technovation **84–85**, 37–47 (2019). https://doi.org/10.1016/j.technovation.2019.03.001

33. Edison, H., Smørsgård, N.M., Wang, X., Abrahamsson, P.: Lean internal startups for software product innovation in large companies: enablers and inhibitors. J. Syst. Softw. **135**, 69–87 (2018). https://doi.org/10.1016/j.jss.2017.09.034

34. Ensley, M.D., Hmieleski, K.M., Pearce, C.L.: The importance of vertical and shared leadership within new venture top management teams: implications for the performance of startups. Leadersh. Q. **17**, 217–231 (2006). https://doi.org/10.1016/j.leaqua.2006.02.002

35. Ouimet, P., Zarutskie, R.: Who works for startups? the relation between firm age, employee age, and growth. J. financ. econ. **112**, 386–407 (2014). https://doi.org/10.1016/j.jfineco.2014.03.003

36. Sharma, S.K., Meyer, K.E.: The new entrepreneur. In: Industrializing Innovation-the Next Revolution, pp. 75–86. Springer, Cham (2019). https://doi.org/10.1007/978-3-030-12430-4_7

37. Kuschel, K., Labra, J.-P., Díaz, G.: Women-led startups and their contribution to job creation. In: Presse, A., Terzidis, O. (eds.) Technology Entrepreneurship. FSSBE, pp. 139–156. Springer, Cham (2018). https://doi.org/10.1007/978-3-319-73509-2_7

38. Skala, A.: Characteristics of startups. In: Digital Startups in Transition Economies, pp. 41–91. Springer, Cham (2019). https://doi.org/10.1007/978-3-030-01500-8_2

39. Oliveira, N.: New coordination mechanisms. In: Automated Organizations Development and Structure of the Modern Business Firm, pp. 123–143 (2012). https://doi.org/10.1007/978-3-7908-2759-0_9

40. Hawryszkiewycz, I.T., Maciaszek, L.A., Getta, J.R.: Coordination and artifact semantics in asynchronous distributed cooperation. J. Syst. Softw. **33**, 179–188 (1996). https://doi.org/10.1016/0164-1212(95)00182-4

41. De Lucia, A., Fasano, F., Scanniello, G., Tortora, G.: Enhancing collaborative synchronous UML modelling with fine-grained versioning of software artefacts. J. Vis. Lang. Comput. **18**, 492–503 (2007). https://doi.org/10.1016/j.jvlc.2007.08.005

42. Mishra, D., Mishra, A., Ostrovska, S.: Impact of physical ambiance on communication, collaboration and coordination in agile software development: an empirical evaluation. Inf. Softw. Technol. **54**, 1067–1078 (2012). https://doi.org/10.1016/j.infsof.2012.04.002.14

43. Pinto, J., Ribeiro, P.: Characterization of an agile coordination office for IST companies. Procedia Comput. Sci. **138**, 859–866 (2018). https://doi.org/10.1016/j.procs.2018.10.112

44. Zirpins, C., Lamersdorf, W., Baier, T.: Flexible coordination of service interaction patterns. In: ICSOC 2004 Proceedings of Second International Conference Service Oriented Computing, pp. 49–56 (2004). https://doi.org/10.1145/1035167.1035175

45. Toffolon, C., Dakhli, S.: A framework for studying the coordination process in software engineering. In: Proceedings ACM Symposium Applied Computing, vol. 2, pp. 851–857 (2000). https://doi.org/10.1145/338407.338577

46. Muccini, H., Mancinelli, F.: Eliciting coordination policies from requirements. In: Proceedings of the ACM Symposium on Applied Computing, pp. 387–393 (2003). https://doi.org/10.1145/952532.952609

47. Cummings, R., Ligett, K., Radhakrishnan, J., Roth, A., Wu, Z.S.: Coordination complexity: small information coordinating large populations. In: ITCS 2016 – Proceedings of 2016 ACM Conference Innovation Theoretical Computer Science, pp. 281–290 (2016). https://doi.org/10.1145/2840728.2840767

48. Giuffrida, R., Dittrich, Y.: A conceptual framework to study the role of communication through social software for coordination in globally-distributed software teams. Inf. Softw. Technol. **63**, 11–30 (2015). https://doi.org/10.1016/j.infsof.2015.02.013

49. Wang, E.T.G., Ju, P.H., Jiang, J.J., Klein, G.: The effects of change control and management review on software flexibility and project performance. Inf. Manag. **45**, 438–443 (2008). https://doi.org/10.1016/j.im.2008.05.003

50. Günsel, A., Açikgšz, A., Tükel, A., Öğüt, E.: The role of flexibility on software development performance: an empirical study on software development teams. Procedia - Soc. Behav. Sci. **58**, 853–860 (2012). https://doi.org/10.1016/j.sbspro.2012.09.1063

51. Gong, Y., Janssen, M.: Measuring process flexibility and agility. In: ACM International Conference Proceeding Series, pp. 173–182 (2010). https://doi.org/10.1145/1930321.193 0358

52. Dönmez, D., Grote, G., Brusoni, S.: Routine interdependencies as a source of stability and flexibility. a study of agile software development teams. Inf. Organ. **26**(3), 63–83 (2016). https://doi.org/10.1016/j.infoandorg.2016.07.001

53. Liu, J.Y.C., Chen, V.J., Chan, C.L., Lie, T.: The impact of software process standardization on software flexibility and project management performance: control theory perspective. Inf. Softw. Technol. **50**, 889–896 (2008). https://doi.org/10.1016/j.infsof.2008.01.002

54. Benner-Wickner, M., Matthias, B., Gruhn, V.: Adapting case management techniques to achieve software process flexibility. Managing Software Process Evolution Traditional Agile Beyond - How to Handle Process Change, pp. 1–332 (2016). https://doi.org/10.1007/978-3-319-31545-4_11

55. Al-Sharhan, S.A., et al. (eds.): I3E 2018. LNCS, vol. 11195. Springer, Cham (2018). https://doi.org/10.1007/978-3-030-02131-3

56. Lassenius, C., Dingsøyr, T., Paasivaara, M. (eds.): XP 2015. LNBIP, vol. 212. Springer, Cham (2015). https://doi.org/10.1007/978-3-319-18612-2

57. Giardino, C., Wang, X., Abrahamsson, P.: Why early-stage software startups fail: a behavioral framework. In: Lassenius, C., Smolander, K. (eds.) ICSOB 2014. LNBIP, vol. 182, pp. 27–41. Springer, Cham (2014). https://doi.org/10.1007/978-3-319-08738-2_3

58. Klotins, E., Unterkalmsteiner, M., Gorschek, T.: Software engineering in start-up companies : an exploratory study of 88 start-ups. Empir. Softw. Eng. **143** (2016)

59. Pérez, J., Cuesta, C.E.: Aspect-oriented connectors for coordination. In: SYANCO 2007 International 15 Workshop Synthesis Analysis Component Connectors - Conjunction with 6th ESEC/FSE Joint Meeting, pp. 13–22 (2007). https://doi.org/10.1145/1294917.1294919

60. Strode, D.E., Huff, S.L., Hope, B., Link, S.: Coordination in co-located agile software development projects. J. Syst. Softw. **85**, 1222–1238 (2012). https://doi.org/10.1016/j.jss.2012.02.017

61. Cao, J., Zhu, L., Han, H., Zhu, X.: Emergency coordination management. In: Modern Emergency Management, pp. 179–221. Springer, Singapore (2018). https://doi.org/10.1007/978-981-10-5720-5_5

62. Shukla, S.K.: Sushil: evaluating the practices of flexibility maturity for the software product and service organizations. Int. J. Inf. Manage. **50**, 71–89 (2020). https://doi.org/10.1016/j.iji nfomgt.2019.05.005

63. Kuhrmann, M., Ternité, T., Friedrich, J., Rausch, A., Broy, M.: Flexible software process lines in practice: a metamodel-based approach to effectively construct and manage families of software process models. J. Syst. Softw. **121**, 49–71 (2016). https://doi.org/10.1016/j.jss.2016.07.031

64. Carstensen, P.H., Nielsen, M.: Characterizing modes of coordination: a comparison between oral and artifact based coordination. In: Proceedings of the 2001 International ACM SIGGROUP Conference on Supporting Group Work, pp. 81–90 (2001)

65. Bass, J.M.: Artefacts and agile method tailoring in large-scale offshore software development programmes. Inf. Softw. Technol. **75**, 1–16 (2016). https://doi.org/10.1016/j.infsof.2016.03.001

66. Rodrigues, N.F.: Discovering coordination patterns. Electr. Notes Theor. Comput. Sci. **260**, 189–207 (2010). https://doi.org/10.1016/j.entcs.2009.12.038

Software Test Management to Improve Software Product Quality

Cathy Pamela Guevara-Vega[1] (iD), Wilson Aníbal Cárdenas-Hernández[2],
Pablo Andrés Landeta[3] (iD), Xavier Mauricio Rea-Peñafiel[2](✉) (iD),
and José Antonio Quiña-Mera[1] (iD)

[1] Facultad de Ingeniería en Ciencias Aplicadas, Grupo de Investigación ECIER,
Universidad Técnica del Norte, Ibarra, Ecuador
{cguevara,aquina}@utn.edu.ec
[2] Facultad de Ingeniería en Ciencias Aplicadas, Universidad Técnica del Norte, Ibarra, Ecuador
{wacardenash,mrea}@utn.edu.ec
[3] Department of Information Technology – Online, Universidad Técnica del Norte, Ibarra,
Ecuador
palandeta@utn.edu.ec

Abstract. Improving software quality is one of the desired goals of software
development teams. More so, financial companies must ensure the quality of the
software product to guarantee financial transactions. For this reason, this study,
based on the Design Science Research (DSR) approach, establishes the research
question: Does implementing a test management framework in the development
process improve the quality of the software product? The paper aims to answer
this question we propose a software testing framework based on the processes
described in the ISO/IEC/IEEE 29119–2 standard and the documentation templates of the ISO/IEC/IEEE 29119–3 standard, which became the technical guide
for the evaluation of the developed software. Furthermore, we evaluated the framework through a case study applied in a financial company in Ecuador; we also
publish the testing framework artifacts in a Zenodo open data repository. The
principal results show an increase in bug detection in the range of 77% to 100%,
reduction of defect density in the range of 95% to 0%, and a 12.5% reduction of
previously reported software failures in production environments.

Keywords: Software testing · Testing processes · Testing techniques · Test
documentation · ISO/IEC/IEEE 29119

1 Introduction

Software engineering is a branch of computer science that studies the software life cycle,
from the requirements gathering to the maintenance phase; it aims to build quality software that meets the user requirements, budgets, and times established for its development
[1]. The life cycle comprises several phases containing several activities [2], which usually require a series of support tools to complete these tasks in the best way and quality
[3]. There are several software life cycle models, each with its characteristics, advantages,

© Springer Nature Switzerland AG 2022
M. Botto-Tobar et al. (Eds.): ICAT 2021, CCIS 1535, pp. 426–440, 2022.
https://doi.org/10.1007/978-3-031-03884-6_31

and disadvantages. These models agree on the main phases of software development: analysis, design, coding, testing, and maintenance; all models include the software test management phase as a fundamental phase of the software development process, for example, the Test-Driven Development methodology the software development is based purely on the execution of tests [4].

The software testing process is essential because it enables developers to deliver high-quality standards and minimize risks [5]. There are metrics such as Capability Maturity Model Integration (CMMI) or Quality Improvement Paradigm (QIP) that manage software testing in traditional methodologies. Still, they do not frame agile development testing because they do not measure the agility of the process [6]. Conversely, software testing is an integral part of the development; however, developers usually do not use an adequate framework, causing that test management is informal; they do not perform sufficient test cases for code validation. Furthermore, documentation is non-existent or incomplete [7]. Failure to manage software testing correctly generates problems such as the deterioration of software quality that negatively affects the software production process, causing the maintenance phase to become complex. It can also lead to incomplete software functionality and delays in developing new software projects due to lack of time. Other associated problems are increased resources regarding costs and time allocated for software development, but the most severe is the inconvenience generated to end-users [8].

In this context, we base this study on the Design Science Research (DSR) approach [9] to evaluate the value and usefulness criteria of the software product, so we pose the following research question: Does the application of a test management framework in the development process improve the quality of the software product? Therefore, the paper aims to answer this question by developing and implementing a software testing framework based on the processes described in ISO/IEC/IEEE 29119–2 and the documentation templates of ISO/IEC/IEEE 29119–3 [7]. We evaluate this proposal through a case study applied in the "Cooperativa de Ahorro y Crédito Atuntaqui" in Ecuador [10]. The rest of the paper is structured as follows: Sect. 2) Research Design: we establish the research activities based on DSR, theoretical foundation, design, and framework implementation (artifact). Section 3) Results: Evaluation of quality-in-use results of the framework artifact. Section 4) Discussion: discussion of the research. Section 5) Conclusions and future work.

2 Research Design

We followed the Design Science Research (DSR) guidelines for the research methodology, see Table 1.

Table 1. Research design methodology.

Activity	Components	Paper section
Problem diagnosis	Problem; Objetive Population and sample	Introduction Research design
Theoretical foundation	Software testing Testing techniques ISO/IEC/IEEE 29119	Research design
Artefact design: software testing framework	Framework development Evaluation model before and after implementation of the Framework	Research design
Evaluation of the framework	Evaluation of software issues and failures Framework acceptance survey	Results

2.1 Population and Sample

We evaluate this proposal through a case study applied in the "Cooperativa de Ahorro y Crédito Atuntaqui" in Ecuador [10]. The population of the present study was 8 people from the Technology Department. They are made up of a Director, a Development Administrator, three Programmer Analysts and three Technical Support staff.

2.2 Theoretical Foundation

V-model. Different software development models include the waterfall model, the general V-model [11], or agile programming models. Figure 1 shows the V-model containing two phases; the first one corresponds to the project development phases and the second one to the project testing phases. Phases of the same level of development can run in

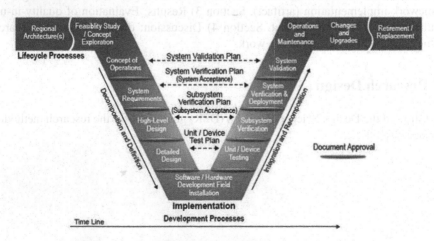

Fig. 1. The V-Model as a systems engineering process [13].

parallel. For each development level, there is a test level. The tester must ensure that the results comply with the software verification and validation [12].

Software Testing. Testing is a software engineering discipline that analyzes software or components to detect differences between the requirements and the existing functionality or to detect software failures [14]. It is difficult due to the exponential increase of test sequences; advantageously, testing techniques help perform this task [15]. The International Software Testing Qualifications Board defines software testing as the process in the static and dynamic life cycle activities; related to the planning, preparation, and evaluation of software products to determine that they meet and are suitable for the specified requirements detect defects [16].

A test is a set of activities that need to be planned and performed systematically [17]. For this reason, during the software development process, a template for elaborating and executing tests is defined; it consists of a set of steps that includes test methods and test case design techniques [18]. Software testing is part of a broader topic, usually referred to as software verification and validation (V&V) [19]. Validation is a set of tasks that ensure that the built software follows the requirements requested at the beginning of the process. Verification is the set of tasks that ensure that the software correctly implements a function [20].

Testing Techniques. Testing aims to detect as many faults as possible; therefore, there are many techniques to accomplish this purpose. The techniques verify a program as systematically as possible, identifying the inputs that will produce expected behaviors of the program [21].

Unit Testing. is the basis for verifying the smallest unit of software design: the software component or module. These tests can be performed simultaneously on multiple components and are considered adjuncts to the coding process. Typically, unit tests have access and are executed to the source code and with the support of debugging tools [22].

Integration Tests. Their purpose is to detect defects not found during unit tests. They focus on integrating and testing two or more components. Once the tests no longer detect new defects, they are added in additional components [23].

System Testing. Unit and integration tests find defects in individual components and the interfaces between components. System tests demonstrate that components are compatible, interact correctly, and transfer the correct data at the right time through their interfaces [13].

Acceptance Testing. This type of testing is performed when the product is ready to be deployed in the customer's environment. Then, they focus on testing the user requirements, i.e., to demonstrate compliance with the acceptance criteria of the requirements. Once these tests are passed, the customer must accept the product [12].

White Box Testing. Focus on designing test cases to validate the internal behavior and structure of the program. The design of these tests aims to execute at least once all program statements and all conditions to check both true and false values. Thus, they examine the internal logic of the program without considering performance aspects [24].

Black Box Testing. They are a way of selecting conditions, data, and test cases from the system requirements documentation. Black box testing tests only the inputs and outputs of the system, i.e., it ignores the internal mechanism of the software. Instead, they consider the behavior of the software from the point of view of an external observer [24].

Reviews. The verification and validation process requires software inspections and reviews. The latter analyzes and checks system requirements, design models, program source code, and even proposed system tests. They are also named "static" techniques, where it verifies the software without executing it [25].

ISO/IEC/IEEE 29119. Provide a set of internationally agreed standards for managing software testing in any software development life cycle or organization [26]. They are the only internationally recognized standards for software testing; they provide a high-quality approach communicable worldwide [27]. The standard aims to cover the software life cycle, including aspects related to testing organization, management, design, and execution [28]. Figure 2 shows the structure of the ISO/IEC/IEEE 29119 standard.

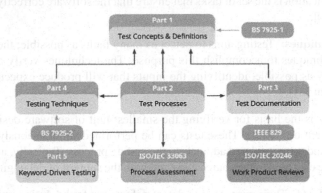

Fig. 2. ISO/IEC/IEEE 29119 standard structure [29].

Part 1 - Concepts and Definitions. This section introduces the set of standards, includes common definitions of all its parts, and describes elementary testing concepts. It explains the scope of the components and describes how to use standards for different lifecycle models [26].

Part 2 - Test Processes. Defines testing processes using a three-layer model. The top layer corresponds to the organizational test process to generate and maintain organizational policies and strategies for testing. The middle layer includes test management processes for test planning, monitoring, control, and completion. Finally, the bottom layer corresponds to dynamic testing processes because the overall model does not include static testing processes such as static analysis and reviews [26] (see Fig. 3).

Part 3 - Test Documentation. This section provides templates with content descriptions for the main types of test documents. There is a strong link between the standards in

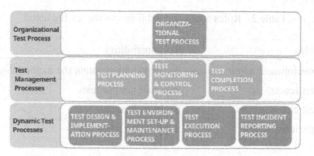

Fig. 3. Test processes defined in the standard [29].

Part 2 (Processes) and Part 3 (Documentation), as the results of the processes defined in Part 2 correspond to the documentation specified in Part 3 [26].

Part 4 - Testing Techniques. These techniques require users following Part 2 to develop test plans that specific test case design techniques and criteria for achieving test completion. Part 4 defines a wide range of test techniques and corresponding coverage measures [26].

Part 5 - Keyword Driven Testing. This section defines requirements for keyword-driven testing and minimum requirements for the supporting tools needed to utilize the keyword-driven testing approach fully [26].

2.3 Methodological Proposal

The proposed testing framework covers only functional testing. We intend to iteratively increase other types of tests in the framework in future work as it is implemented in new software projects. The proposed methodology offers the following activities:

- Elaborate a plan for software test management.
- Establish the team structure for software testing.
- Define the testing execution process.
- Establish the documentation and deliverables of the testing process.

Roles. The work team involved in the software testing process has the following roles and responsibilities, see Table 2.

Table 2. Roles and responsibilities of the testing team.

Roles	Responsibilities
Development administrator	Evaluate and maintain the methodology
Test leader	Plan and control tests
Test engineer	Build and execute tests
Specialist	Support the test team

Process Testing Flow. Contains the activities and the order of execution in the framework, see. Fig. 4.

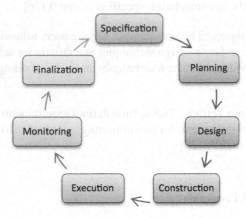

Fig. 4. Software testing process flow [30].

Planning. The structure of this phase contains five activities:

Identify Test Requirements. This activity determines the software requirements or features included and excluded for testing and the scope of testing.

Prioritization. This activity prioritizes the list of test requirements according to a test priority. Two factors must be evaluated for each requirement: failure priority and frequency of use (see Table 3).

Table 3. Priority factors for requirements testing.

Test priority		Frequency of Use		
		HIGH	MEDIUM	LOW
Probability of failure	**HIGH**	**High**	**High**	Medium
	MEDIUM	**High**	Medium	*Low*
	LOW	Medium	*Low*	*Low*

Identify Resources. Estimate the number of resources needed to design, build and execute software testing. The types of resources are data, environment, tools, and human resources.

Create the Schedule. This activity includes estimating time to design, build and execute the tests based on previous experiences and metrics.

Generate the Test Plan. This activity identifies and defines the deliverables to be created, maintained, and available during test execution. Next, it will document the delivery schedule for those deliverables. Finally, it will combine the data from the previous steps and create a Software Test Plan.

Design. This phase contains the following activities:

Identify Test Cases. A test case combines conditions and inputs for a specific test requirement. Generally, each test requirement should have more than one test case.

Identify Test Data. This activity identifies the data required for the test cases defined in the previous activity.

Construction. This phase primarily develops the procedures and data needed for testing.

Test Procedure Creation. A test procedure is a set of detailed instructions for preparing, executing, and evaluating the outcome of a test case or set of test cases.

Create Test Data. This activity creates the data needed to execute the test procedures.

Execution. This phase consists of executing the steps established in the test procedures; it verifies that the result obtained from the test cases matches the expected result; if it does not match, the test engineer must record and report the defect found.

Defect Registration. The Test Engineer records and reports to the Development Area the defects found in the test execution. After the development team corrects the reported defect, the test engineer will validate the defect again and report the result. If, when validating the correction of a defect, another defect is found, the test engineer must register it as a new defect.

Monitoring and Control. At the end of the testing period or even during the execution phase, the test engineer evaluates the test results using previously established metrics.

Test Coverage. Provides an indicator of the number of requirements passed out of the total number of requirements specified, using the following formula:

$$TC = \frac{ETC}{TCD}$$

Where:

    ETC is the number of executed Test Cases.

    TCD is the total number of Test Cases designed.

Test Maturity. This indicator measures the satisfactory results of test cases calculated with the following formula:

$$TS = \frac{TCS}{TCD}$$

Where:

    TCS is the number of Test Cases with a satisfactory result.

    TCD is the number of Test Cases designed for all requirements.

Defect Density. Provides a measure of the ratio of defects to the number of specification items calculated with the following formula:

$$DD = \frac{DF}{SIR}$$

Where:

    DF is the total number of defects found.

    SIR is the number of specification items reviewed.

Defect Trend. It is the number of defects as a function of time in an established classification.

Defect Percentage by Type. This metric identifies, categorizes, and prioritizes defect types calculated with the following formula:

$$DT = \frac{NDT}{TDI} \, x \, 100$$

Where:

    NDT is the number of defects by type.

    TDI is the total number of defects identified.

Basic Path. Corresponds to the percentage of primary independent paths tested concerning the total ways, sum the cyclomatic complexity of the program modules, calculated by the following formula:

$$PCB = \frac{NDT}{C(G)} \, x \, 100$$

Where:

    NDT is the number of designed tests.

    C(G) is the calculated cyclomatic complexity.

Finalization. The status of the tests can be evaluated at any point in the execution using the metrics established in the previous sections to decide if the software release is possible.

2.4 Test Documentation

Documentation corresponds to the software testing forms and templates available for organizations, specific projects, or individual testing activities.

Test Plan. The formal document prepared by the Test Leader plans the detail of software testing activities, times, and responsible persons.

Test Design Specification. This document contains the set of software features to be evaluated, with their respective execution priority. The Test Leader elaborates it.

Test Case Specification. This document details the test cases to be executed for each specified software feature to be evaluated in the Test Design.

Test Procedure. It specifies the order and sequence of execution of the test cases, restrictions, and previous actions for each test case.

Defect Report. The record of executed test cases whose obtained result does not coincide with the expected result; therefore, the test is not satisfactory.

Results Report. It is a management document that summarizes the results obtained in the execution of the test cases to determine if the software is suitable to be put into production or, on the contrary, some errors still need to be corrected.

3 Results

In this section, we validate the proposed software testing framework through three instruments applied in the "Cooperativa de Ahorro y Crédito Atuntaqui" in Ecuador in 2019: 1) Implementation of the testing framework project involved in real-world practice. 2) A comparison of the number of failures reported in the maintenance phase of 6 software projects implemented in a production environment. 3) A satisfaction survey of the use of the proposed testing framework.

3.1 Implementing the Testing Framework in a Software Project

In this section, we validate the study proposal by implementing the proposed testing framework in a software development project; after its implementation in production, we measure the impact through 3 cycles of test plan execution in the maintenance phase. Table 4 shows the implementation result of the design framework in a software project.

In the results obtained (Table 4), we note that the Test Coverage in the three cycles executed is one hundred percent, i.e., we executed all test cases designed in the test plan.

Table 4. Results of the design framework implementation.

Metrics	Cycle 1	Cycle 2	Cycle 3
Test specifications	22	22	22
Test cases planned	93	93	51
Test cases executed	93	93	51
Satisfactory test cases	72	92	51
Test cases with defects	21	1	0
Test coverage	100%	100%	100%
Test maturity	77%	99%	100%
Density of defects	95%	5%	0%

The Test Maturity metric starts with a value of 77% in the first cycle, increases to 99% in the second cycle, and ends with 100% in the third cycle; this means that as we executed the test cycles, software errors were detected and corrected, and at the end all the test cases designed were satisfactory. The Defect Density in the first cycle was 95%, with the correction of the detected errors; in the second cycle, it decreases to 5%, and in the third cycle, it ends with a value of 0%, which means that all the software errors found were corrected.

The testing framework artifacts are available in the following Zenodo open data repository [31].

3.2 Comparison of the Number of Failures of Projects in the Maintenance Phase

In this validation, we analyzed the number of software failures reported in production environments of three projects implemented without using the framework and three projects using the proposed framework. The selection of the software projects was made with the advice of the Development Leader, considering the number of functional requirements and the development time of each project, see Table 5.

Table 5. Selected projects to compare the number of failures.

Project	Description	No. of requirements	Development time	Testing Framework
Project A	Service desk system	20	3 months	No
Project B	Raffles and sweepstakes system	21	3 months	No
Project C	Community credit system	32	3 months	No
Project D	Affidavit system	22	3 months	Yes
Project E	Check management system	18	3 months	Yes
Project F	External microcredit system	30	3 months	Yes

Table 6 shows the number of failure support cases reported for the production environment projects in the study period.

Table 6. Reported software failures of production environment projects.

Project	Errors in functionalities	Errors in data	Total errors
Project A	6	2	8
Project B	6	4	10
Project C	8	6	14
Project D	1	0	1
Project E	1	0	1
Project F	2	0	2

We analyzed the number of software failures of the projects that used the proposed testing framework against the projects that did not use the framework. As a result, the proposal's impact corresponds to the percentage of software failures achieved by the two types of projects, measured by the following formula:

$$\% \text{ of failures achieved} = \frac{No. \text{ of failures with the proposal}}{No. \text{ of failures without the proposal}} \times 100$$

$$\% \text{ of failures achieved} = \frac{4}{32} \times 100$$

$$\% \textit{ of failures achieved } = 12,5\%$$

The result of the calculation of the impact caused by using the software testing framework shows a reduction to 12.5% of the reported software failures instead of the projects that did not use the proposed framework in this study. In addition, none of the reported incidents corresponds to errors in the data, avoiding direct affectation to the database.

3.3 Satisfaction Survey

To measure the perception of the technical staff of the Development Area about the use of the proposed testing framework, we first conducted a diagnostic survey and another survey after the implementation of the proposed testing framework. Therefore, we conducted a diagnostic survey and then another satisfaction survey after implementing the proposed testing framework in the study company. We designed the surveys using and rating using the 3 Likert response scale (Very Good, Good, Fair). Table 7 shows the rating of the surveys and the impact of the implementation of the proposed framework.

Table 7. Impact of the implementation of the testing framework.

Testing components	Rating survey 1	Rating survey 2	Impact
Test documentation	40,00%	100,00%	60,00%
Test case design	46,67%	93,33%	46,67%
Prioritize features	33,33%	100,00%	66,67%
Test process	66,67%	93,33%	26,67%
Average	46,67%	96,67%	**50,00%**

4 Discussion

We consider it necessary to clarify that the development environment, the Framework artifacts, and templates are in Spanish since we believe that the replication of this study should consider carried out in the same language. However, we do not recommend doing it in a different language because we do not know if the translation of the artifacts would affect the validity of the research.

During the study, we also observed that the expertise of the development team members influences the quality of the software product; for this reason, we see the convenient use of a tool that manages software testing and describes the necessary templates for the documentation of the software evaluation process.

5   Conclusions and Future Work

In this study, based on the DSR research approach, we pose the research question: Does implementing a test management framework in the development process improve the quality of the software product? First, we answered this question by developing a software testing framework based on the processes described in ISO/IEC/IEEE 29119–2 and ISO/IEC/IEEE 29119–3 documentation templates. Then, we validated this instrument using three artifacts to measure the influence of the proposed framework on the quality of the developed software. The principal validation results show an increase in error detection in the range of 77% to 100%, reduction of defect density in the range of 95% to 0%, and a 12.5% reduction of software failures previously deployed in production environments. Therefore, we conclude that implementing a test management framework does improve the quality of the developed software product.

As future work, we propose to study the impact of the use of this proposal in software development teams with different levels of experience to check which segment has a more significant impact and is more necessary.

References

1. Guevara-Vega, C.P., Guzmán-Chamorro, E.D., Guevara-Vega, V.A., Andrade, A.V.B., Quiña-Mera, J.A.: Functional requirement management automation and the impact on software projects: case study in ecuador. In: Rocha, Á., Ferrás, C., Paredes, M. (eds.) ICITS 2019. AISC, vol. 918, pp. 317–324. Springer, Cham (2019). https://doi.org/10.1007/978-3-030-11890-7_31
2. Sabri, O., Alfifi, F.: Integrating knowledge life cycle within software development process to produce a quality software product. In: Proceedings 2017 International Conference Engineering Technology ICET 2017, vol. 2018, pp. 1–7 (2018)
3. Tüzün, E., Tekinerdogan, B., Macit, Y., İnce, K.: Adopting integrated application lifecycle management within a large-scale software company: an action research approach. J. Syst. Softw. **149**, 63–82 (2019)
4. Tosun, A., Ahmed, M., Turhan, B., Juristo, N.: On the effectiveness of unit tests in test-driven development. In: ACM International Confernce Proceeding Series, pp. 113–122 (2018)
5. Spadini, D., Aniche, M., Storey, A., Bruntink, M., Bacchelli, A.: When testing meets code review: Why and how developers review tests. In: Proceedings - International Conference Software Engineering, pp. 677–687 (2018)
6. Kayes, I., Sarker, M., Chakareski, J.: Product backlog rating: a case study on measuring test quality in scrum. Innovations Syst. Softw. Eng. **12**(4), 303–317 (2016). https://doi.org/10.1007/s11334-016-0271-0
7. Afzal, W., Alone, S., Glocksien, K., Torkar, R.: Software test process improvement approaches: a systematic literature review and an industrial case study. J. Syst. Softw. **111**, 1–33 (2016)
8. Sawant, A.A., Bari, P.H., Chawan, P.: Software testing techniques and strategies. J. Eng. Res. Appl. **2**(3), 980–986 (2012)
9. Hevner, A.R., March, S.T., Park, J., Ram, S.: Design science in is research. Manag. Inf. Syst. **28**(1), 75–105 (2004)
10. Coop. Atuntaqui. Cooperativa de ahorro y crédito (2021). Atuntaqui. https://www.atuntaqui.fin.ec/

11. Qian, H.M., Zheng, C.: A embedded software testing process model. In: Proceedings of - 2009 International Conference Compuer Intelligence Software Engineering CiSE 2009 (2009)
12. El-Attar, M., Miller, J.: Developing comprehensive acceptance tests from use cases and robustness diagrams. Requir. Eng. 15(3), 285–306 (2010)
13. Malaek, S.M.B., Mollajan, A., Ghorbani, A., Sharahi, A.: A new systems engineering model based on the principles of axiomatic design. J. Ind. Intell. Inf. 3(2) (2014)
14. Vasanthapriyan, S., Tian, J., X.B, J.: An ontology-based knowledge framework. 2, 212–226 (2017)
15. Melo, S.M., Carver, J.C., Souza, P.S.L., Souza, S.R.S.: Empirical research on concurrent software testing: a systematic mapping study. Inf. Softw. Technol., 105, 226–251 (2019)
16. Kramer, A., Legeard, B.: Model-Based Testing Essentials. Wiley (2016)
17. Bertolino, A., Faedo, I.A.: Software Testing Research : Achievements , Challenges , Dreams Software Testing Research : Achievements , Challenges , Dreams, September 2007 (2007)
18. Kitchenham, B.: Evidence-based software engineering and systematic literature reviews. In: Münch, J., Vierimaa, M. (eds.) PROFES 2006. LNCS, vol. 4034, pp. 3–3. Springer, Heidelberg (2006). https://doi.org/10.1007/11767718_3
19. Monteiro, P., Machado, R.J., Kazman, R.: Inception of software validation and verification practices within CMMI level 2. In: Fourth International Conference on Software Engineering AdvancesICSEA 2009, Incl. SEDES 2009 Simp. para Estud. Doutor. em Eng. Softw. pp. 536–541 (2009)
20. Tamura, G., et al.: Towards practical runtime verification and validation of self-adaptive software systems. In: de Lemos, R., Giese, H., Müller, H.A., Shaw, M. (eds.) Software Engineering for Self-Adaptive Systems II. LNCS, vol. 7475, pp. 108–132. Springer, Heidelberg (2013). https://doi.org/10.1007/978-3-642-35813-5_5
21. Vegas, S., Basili, V.: A characterisation schema for software testing techniques. Empir. Softw. Eng. 10(4), 437–466 (2005)
22. Daka, E., Campos, J., Fraser, G., Dorn, J., Weimer, W.: Modeling readability to improve unit tests. In: Proceedings of 2015 10th Joint Meeting European Software Engineering Conference ACM SIGSOFT Symposium Foundations Software Engineering ESEC/FSE 2015- , pp. 107–118 (2015)
23. Delamaro, M.E., Maldonado, J.C., Mathur, A.P.: Interface mutation: an approach for integration testing. IEEE Trans. Softw. Eng. 27(3), 228–247 (2001)
24. White, L.J.: Software testing and verification. Advances Computer, vol. 26, no. C, pp. 335–391 (1987)
25. Itkonen, J., Mäntylä, M.V.: Are test cases needed? replicated comparison between exploratory and test-case-based software testing. Empir. Softw. Eng. 19(2), 303–342 (2014)
26. I. 29119–1:2013, ISO/IEC/IEEE 29119–1:2013 - Software and systems engineering — Software testing — Part 1: Concepts and definitions, ISO/IEEE (2013)
27. Eckhart, M., Meixner, K., Winkler, D., Ekelhart, A.: Securing the testing process for industrial automation software. Comput. Secur. 85, 156–180 (2019)
28. Matalonga, S., Rodrigues, F., Travassos, G.H.: Matching context aware software testing design techniques to ISO/IEC/IEEE 29119. In: Rout, T., O'Connor, R.V., Dorling, A. (eds.) SPICE 2015. CCIS, vol. 526, pp. 33–44. Springer, Cham (2015). https://doi.org/10.1007/978-3-319-19860-6_4
29. Reid, S.: Achieving systems safety. Achiev. Syst. Saf. 7–9 (2012), May 2007
30. Reuys, A., Kamsties, E., Pohl, K., Reis, S.: Model-based system testing of software product families. In: Pastor, O., Falcão e Cunha, J. (eds.) CAiSE 2005. LNCS, vol. 3520, pp. 519–534. Springer, Heidelberg (2005). https://doi.org/10.1007/11431855_36
31. Guevara-Vega, C., Cárdenas, W., Landeta, P., Rea, M., Quiña-Mera, A.: Supplemental Material: Software Test Management to Improve Software Product Quality Zenodo (2021). https://doi.org/10.5281/zenodo.5150822

Exploratory Data Analysis on Cervical Cancer Diseases

Priscila Valdiviezo-Diaz(✉), Ruth Reátegui, Luis Barba-Guaman, and Mayra Ortega

Universidad Técnica Particular de Loja, Loja, Ecuador
{pmvaldiviezo,rmreategui,lrbarba,mjortega}@utpl.edu.ec

Abstract. Cervical cancer is a major public health problem that mainly affects women with active sexual life. Exploratory Data Analysis is an essential technique to identify outliers, check assumptions, discover patterns, and determine associations between a set of variables. This technique plays an important role in the health area to assist researchers to find insights in the data and relevant aspects about diseases. In this paper, risk factors that cause cervical cancer disease are studied using data analysis tools for identifying relationships and hidden patterns in the data. The analysis is carried out using data related to women with human papillomavirus that is a risk factor for cervical cancer. The data were extracted from an electronic health record system. The dataset contains 143 records with 19 variables related to demographic information, cervical cancer risk factors, and cervical cancer cytology results of patients. To analyze the variables involved in the dataset, data analysis, and visualization tools are used.

Keywords: Exploratory data analysis · Cervical cancer · Data visualization

1 Introduction

Cancer of the cervix or cervical cancer is a major public health problem that mainly affects women with active sexual life. According to the World Health Organization, it is considered the second most frequent cancer in the female population, with mortality that occurs in 80% in emerging countries such as Ecuador, and it is the third cause of death worldwide [1].

The most important risk factor for cervical cancer is infection with human papillomavirus (HPV). Over 200 types of viruses exist [2]; some of them cause a type of papilloma growth that is more commonly known as a wart. HPV 16 and 18 are predominant in cervical cancer [3]. Other risk factors related to cervical cancer are being a carrier of HIV, previous treatment of cervical intraepithelial lesions, having multiple sexual partners, age, age of marriage, early age of initiation of sexual activity, sexual promiscuity or high-risk couples, history of co-infection with sexually transmitted diseases, multiparity and first pregnancy at an early age; vaginal infections, tobacco, absence of screening or inadequate screening, and prolonged use of oral contraceptives [4–7].

© Springer Nature Switzerland AG 2022
M. Botto-Tobar et al. (Eds.): ICAT 2021, CCIS 1535, pp. 441–455, 2022.
https://doi.org/10.1007/978-3-031-03884-6_32

Cervical cancer is generally slow-growing and has few symptoms in its early stages, and its advanced stage includes abnormal vaginal bleeding, pelvic pain, vaginal discharge, and pain. The diagnosis of this pathology is usually based on the results of the clinical examination such as colposcopy and biopsy.

Prevention of this type of cancer is possible through immunization with HPV vaccines and cervical screening. Regarding vaccines, nowadays exist vaccines against up to nine types of viruses directly related to this pathology [8]. Vaccination is recommended at age 9 through 14 -two doses- and from age 15 -three doses-. Cervical screening consists of taking a sample of cells from the cervix to check for cancer markers, the best known is the test Pap smear (PAP). Recently, an HPV DNA test has been introduced with a greater sensitivity to detect this pathology.

Staging helps determine the most appropriate treatment for cervical cancer. New imaging techniques such as echosonography, MRI, CT scans, and others are gradually replacing old methods, testing increasingly accurate information on the extent of the disease.

On the other hand, the advancement of technology makes available artificial intelligence algorithms for cancer cervical predicting and diagnosing based on patients' information [9, 10]. To analyze this information, it is necessary data analysis tools that allow handling large datasets. Exploratory Data Analysis plays an important role in analyzing data to find hidden structures, enhances the insight into a dataset, identifies the anomalies, and builds models [11]. Some recent research has explored data extracted from electronic medical records systems related to cervical cancer and HPV. For example, in [12] mapped the cervical cancer screening cascade among women with HIV and abnormal Pap result in Johannesburg, South Africa. Moreover, [13] worked in the timelines to diagnosis and linkage to definitive treatment among cervical cancer patients in Botswana. In [14] investigated the correlation and values of hematologic parameters in cervical cancer patients and healthy people. Furthermore, [15] investigated whether metabolic syndrome and associated factors can predict the persistence of HPV infection.

The prevalence of HPV infection in general varies by country, region within country, and population subgroup [16]. Therefore, more studies about HPV and cervical cancer are needed. This research aims to analyze and identify hidden patterns related to HPV in women from Ecuador.

This paper is organized as follows. Section 2 presents the materials and methods used for this research. Section 3 describes in detail the data analysis results and discussion. Section 4 encloses the conclusions of this paper.

2 Materials and Methods

2.1 Dataset

This study was approved by the Ethics Committee for Research on Human Beings of Universidad Técnica Particular de Loja, the information provided and extracted from an electronic health record system of a health institution was completely anonymized. The process to create the dataset started filtering the information of 164 patients with HPV. Next, the data cleaning and normalization process were done.

Table 1. Feature information of cancer disease dataset.

Variables	Description	Domain of value
Cancer	Presence of cervical cancer	Positive
		Negative
Last_result_cytology	Last cytology result	LSIL
		HSIL
		ASCUS
		NEGATIVE
		NA
1_year_ago_result_cytology	Cytology result 1 year ago	LSIL
		HSIL
		ASCUS
		NEGATIVE
Age	Patient's age	$19 \leq age \leq 86$
Bood_type	The blood group of the patient	a—
		a+
		ab+
		b+
		o—
		o+
		NA
Place_of_birth	Patient's place of birth	—
Residence_city	Patient's city of residence	Loja
		Machala
		Zamora
Ethnicity	Ethnicity of the patient	of mixed race/Spanish descent NA
		Other
Read_write	The patient was literate. The patient was literate. (The patient can read and write)	True
		False
Civil_status	Marital status of the patient	Married
		Divorced

(*continued*)

Table 1. (*continued*)

Variables	Description	Domain of value
		Single free
		Union
		Widower
Menarche	Age at which the first episode of uterine bleeding occurs (menstruation)	9 to 30
Mestrual_cycle	Rhythm at which menstruation occurs	Regular
		Irregular
Start_sex_life	The onset of sexual activity	12 to 28
Contraceptive_prior_use	Use of contraceptives	True
		False
Contraceptive_last_method	Type of contraceptive method	–
Deliveries	Number of deliveries	0 to 15
Abortion	Number of abortions	0 to 5
Cesarea	Number of cesarean sections	0 to 4
Pregnancy	Pregnancy number (state of pregnancy)	0 to 16
Variables	Description	Domain of value

Data cleaning: In this step, we eliminated some patients' records when they did not have enough information or most of the variables were empty. As a result, we obtained records from 143 patients. We also proceeded to eliminate some variables without updated information. Furthermore, variables that do not provide relevant information for this study were eliminated. In this process, we have information of 143 patients and 19 variables. See Table 1 for more details.

Normalization: In this step, the empty data were labeled as NA. All variables were converted to lowercase letters except the cytology classification. The cytology results were normalized following this classification: NEGATIVE, ASCUS, LSIL, and HSIL. Few patients were diagnosed with cervical cancer, the variable named cancer has this information and means that the patients have or had cancer.

2.2 Plot Development and Data Visualization

We used plots to analyze the cervical cancer cytology results in the dataset and its relationship with the demographic characteristics and patients' risk factors.

We imported the dataset into the R environment. R is a tool for data analysis, capable of creating multiple types of graphs. R offers a collection of functions and libraries to build visualizations and represent data [17]. The data visualization can help health professionals to make decisions for cervical cancer diagnosis.

In this work, the data were represented using different colors for comparing the characteristics of patients with different plots type, we create images such as scatterplots, boxplots, histograms, parallel coordinates, and bar plots for showing the relationship between a numeric and a categorical variable, display values for several levels of grouping, for getting an overview of the relationships between the variables, etc.

3 Results and Discussion

This section presents the results of the data exploratory analysis to identify some hidden features in the dataset, to determine correlations among the variables, and to identify anomalies. Tables and plots are used to explain the hidden features in cervical cancer data from a health institution in Ecuador. The variables considered in the analysis refer to demographic information, obstetric and reproductive factors, as well as results of the cervical cancer cytology of the patients. To realize the data analysis, the cervical cancer disease dataset is effectively processed by eliminating unrelated instances.

3.1 Data Analysis

The study population covered a broad age range from 19 to 86 years, who underwent cervical cancer cytology. These patients have a literacy rate of 87%, they are of different ethnicities, and they reside mainly in Loja city.

Table 2 shows the descriptive statistics of the data. The data was processed on July 1, 2021. The minimum age of the patients is 19 years old. The age of the first menstruation (menarche) of the patients is from 9 years old. The maximum number of children of the patients identified in the dataset is 16, which is very high, while the maximum number of abortions present in the dataset is 5. The number of cesarean sections performed on the patients is 4. The average number of pregnancies of the patients is 2.

Table 2. Descriptive statistics of data.

Statistics	Age	Menarche	Start sex life	Deliveries	Abortion	Cesarea	Pregnancy
Mean	37	18.4	1.6	0.3	0.3	0.3	2.3
Std	12.3	2	3	2.1	0.7	0.7	2.4
Min	19	9	12	0	0	0	0
25%	27.5	12	16	0	0	0	0
50%	35	13	18	1	0	0	2
75%	46	14	20	3	0	0	3
Max	86	30	28	15	5	4	16

In Fig. 1, the last-result-cytology variable shows that LSIL as the most frequent cytology result (58% of patients), followed by HSIL (19% of patients), NEGATIVE (13% of patients), ASCUS (8% of patients) and 2% of patients did not have any result.

In the same Fig. 1, in 1-year-ago-result-cytology variable the frequency changes, 76% of patients did have any result, after that, the most frequent is a NEGATIVE result (10% of patients), followed by LSIL (9% of patients), ASCUS (3% of patients), and HSIL result (2% of patients).

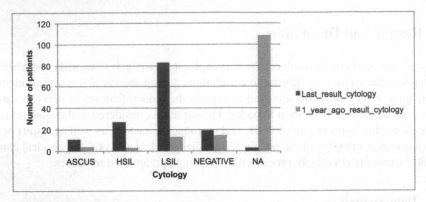

Fig. 1. Cervical cancer cytology results in women treated at the health institution

As we can see in Fig. 1, 76% of the data in the 1_year_ago_result_cytology variable have NA value, therefore, for the following analysis, this variable will not be considered.

Analysis of Demographic Information of the Patients
Demographic risk information and their relationship with respect to the results of the cervical-uterine cytology were analyzed, among which age and marital status were considered. Regarding the patient's age, Fig. 2 shows for the Last-result-cytology that the mean for LSIL is around 34 years of age, and the mean for NEGATIVE, HSIL, and ASCUS is around 40 years of age.

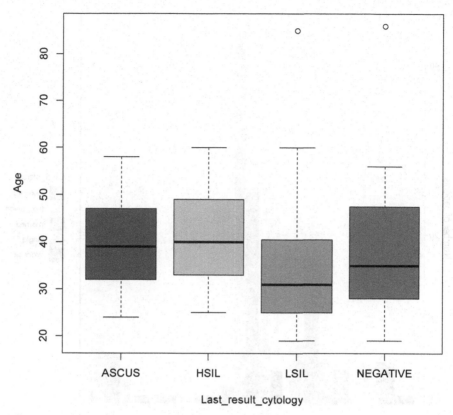

Fig. 2. Cytology by age

According to the cytology results and civil status of women patients, 46% are single, most of them presented low-risk cytology (31%), followed by married civil status with a cervical lesion LSIL (17%). A lower percentage of single and married patients presented cervical cancer cytology of NEGATIVE type.

In Fig. 3, a statistical similarity is observed in married and single patients in the ASCUS cytology results. 8% of married patients showed a greater trend in the result of high-risk cytology HSIL, followed by single patients (5%), while in the marital status of the free union, 4% presented HSIL and 2% had NEGATIVE cytology. In the widower's marital status, it was found that a very low percentage of patients present NEGATIVE results.

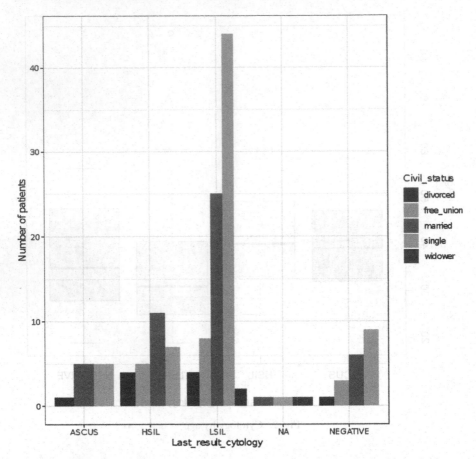

Fig. 3. Civil status and cytology results in patients being treated at the health institution.

In order to know if there is any type of relationship between these two qualitative variables, the Chi-squared (X^2) test statistic was calculated. For a significance level of 0.05, the X^2 value obtained is 7.38 with a value p = 0.2868 (p ≥ 0.05). This means that there is not significant relationship between marital status and the cervical cancer cytology result.

Obstetric Factors
Considering Last_result_cytology variable, Fig. 4 shows LSIL as the most frequent cytology results in women with 0, 1, 2, 3, 5, and 7 pregnancies; HSIL is present in women with 4 and 6 pregnancies.

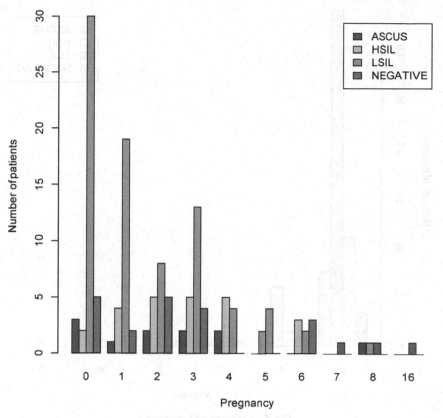

Fig. 4. Cytology and pregnancy

For the Last_result_cytology variable, Fig. 5 shows LSIL as the most frequent cytology results in women with 0 and 1 abortions. Also, in women with 0 abortions, HSIL is present as the second most relevant cytology result followed by NEGATIVE and ASCUS cytology results.

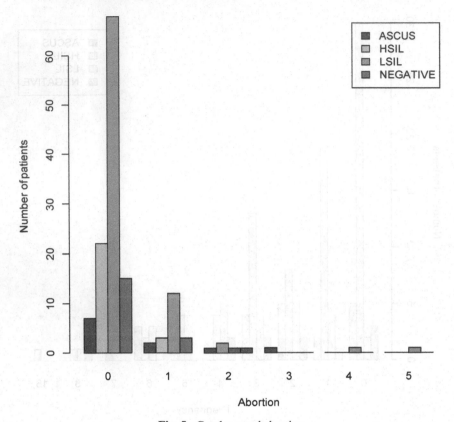

Fig. 5. Cytology and abortion

Impact of the Number of Deliveries and Onset of Sexual Activity on the Cytology Result

Figure 6 shows the impact of Deliveries and Start_sex_life on the cytology results of the patients who were treated at the health institution. From the analysis carried out, 43% of the patients had two or more deliveries, mostly presenting cytological results of HSIL and LSIL, while only 1.39% of the cases had more than six deliveries with low or high-risk cytology.

In addition, 87% had their first sexual experience between the ages of 14 and 24. Very few patients had their first sexual experience at an age less than 14 years, with deliveries number greater than or equal to 2. Patients under the age of 14 presented mainly high and low-risk intraepithelial lesions, in addition to ASCUS cytology.

From Fig. 6, it can be concluded that the deliveries number and sex life start are risk factors that occur more frequently among those patients who presented high and low-risk intraepithelial lesions, that is, it is inferred that patients with a greater deliveries

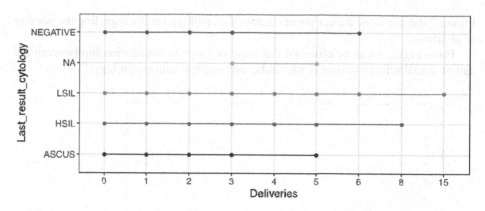

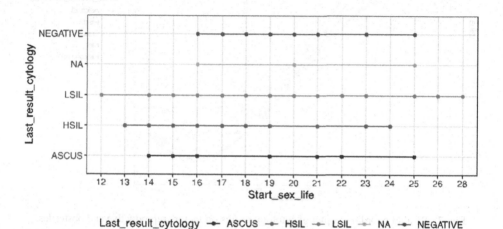

Last_result_cytology -•- ASCUS -•- HSIL -•- LSIL -•- NA -•- NEGATIVE

Fig. 6. Onset of sexual activity and cervical-uterine cytology in patients treated at the health institution.

number and who have started their sexual life at an early age, are expected to present this type of cytology.

Patterns and Relationships of Factors Reproductive and Obstetrics on Cytology Results

Figure 7 shows several patterns and relationships among outcomes: start_sex_life, menarche, deliveries and abortion. The exploration revealed that women that present early menarche and a low number of deliveries generally have LSIL cytology compared to those with HSIL cytology who present normal menarche and the majority have more than two deliveries.

Women with the onset of sexual life after 15 years tend to have relatively NEGATIVE cytology, whereas if the onset of sexual life is at an early age, they may present HSIL or LSIL cytology. Women with ASCUS cytology seemed to present normal menarche.

Figure 7 did not show a clear pattern across the cytology results regarding the number of abortions.

From Fig. 7, it can be observed that there is a significant relationship between the age of sexual activity initiation, menarche, and cervical cancer cytology.

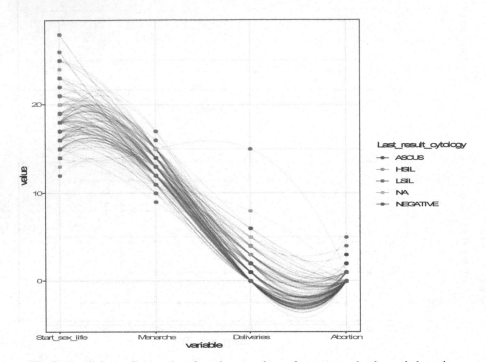

Fig. 7. Parallel coordinates plot of cytology results on factors reproductive and obstetrics.

In the case of the menstrual cycle, when calculating the Chi-squared (X^2) value for a significance level of 0.05, the value obtained is 7.77 with a value p = 0.1003 (p $\geq$ 0.05), finding that there is no significant relationship between the menstrual cycle and the cervical cancer cytology.

Analysis of the Relationship Between Variables

The data analysis task also requires analyzing the relationship between the variables. Based on this, Fig. 8 shows the histograms and scatter plots of the quantitative variables. Histograms reveal that the majority of data are positively skewed, and that exist outliers in the dataset. Scatter plots evidence that there is a linear relationship among some variables since the values of the scatter plots between two variables are close to the line, for example, Age and Deliveries, Age and Pregnancy. In addition, the scatter plot matrix reveals a positive relationship among patient age, number of deliveries, and pregnancy.

This means that both pregnancy and the number of deliveries are strongly associated with age. Furthermore, based on Figs. 7 and 8, these findings suggest an association of the cytology result with the variables pregnancy, number of deliveries and age. Therefore, this relation is important for predictive studies about the results of cytology, and this can be an indication to know if pregnancy and delivery at an early age represent an important cause for the health problem of cervical cancer.

From Fig. 8, we can also see that other variables have an exponential distribution and do not show a linear dependence. On the other hand, the correlation coefficient of each pair of variables evidences that there are some variables highly correlated such as Age and Pregnancy (0.764), Age and Deliveries (0.762), Pregnancy and Deliveries (0.899). This means that some of these variables may be depreciated in the original dataset to posterior build models.

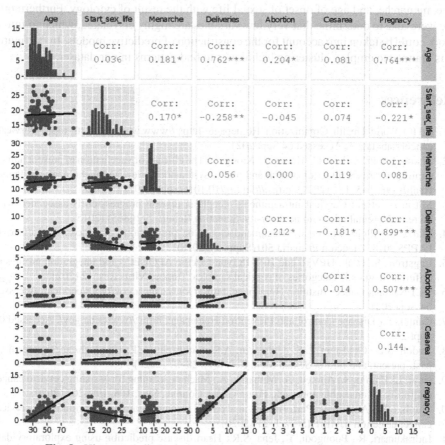

Fig. 8. Histogram, dispersion, and correlation matrix of the patient's data

4   Conclusions

Data exploration helped us to gain insights into our dataset and further enabled us to identify patterns, determinate relationships between variables, and know the impact of the risk factors on the cytology results of women who attended the health institution. We believe this is beneficial to model building and using appropriate artificial intelligence algorithms to analyze our data.

In the exploratory analysis, we found that the most frequent lesion is LSIL, followed by HSIL that was present in less than a quarter of cases, NEGATIVE cytology and ASCUS are very rare in cases associated with risk factors obstetric and reproductive. LSIL is also frequent in single women around 34 years of age infected with HPV. This situation could be considered by health and government institutions to work in vaccination programs as well as diffusion to prevent this disease.

The analysis showed that there is a relationship between the factors of risk such as age, menarche, and age of onset of sexual life with the result of cytology. Furthermore, we were able to determine that very few variables are highly correlated, which in future work could be taken into account for the construction of predictive models. In the future, it is planned to employ clustering techniques to find patterns in our dataset.

References

1. WHO World Health Organization Homepage. https://www.who.int/health-topics/cervical-cancer#tab=tab_1. Accessed 04 Sept 2021
2. Zhang, J., Qin, Z., Lou, C., Huang, J., Xiong, Y.: The efficacy of vaccination to prevent human papilloma viruses infection at anal and oral: a systematic review and meta- analysis. Public Health **196**, 165–171 (2021). https://doi.org/10.1016/j.puhe.2021.05.012
3. Mitra, A., et al.: Cervical intraepithelial neoplasia disease progression is associated with increased vaginal microbiome diversity. Scientific Reports 5(16865) (2015)
4. Marzo-Castillejo, M., et al.: Recomendaciones de prevención del cáncer. Actualización PAPPS 2018. Atencion Primaria **50**1(Suppl 1) (2018)
5. Lagström, S., et al.: HPV16 and HPV18 type-specific APOBEC3 and integration profiles in different diagnostic categories of cervical samples. Tumour Virus Res. **12** (2021)
6. NCI National Cancer Institute Homepage. https://www.cancer.gov/types/cervical. Accessed 04 Sept 2021
7. Centers for Disease Control and Prevention Homepage. https://www.cdc.gov/. Accessed 04 Sept 2021
8. Bedell, S.L., Goldstein, L.S., Goldstein, A.R., Goldstein, A.T.: Cervical cancer screening: past. present, and future. Sexual Med. Rev. **8**(1), 28–37 (2020)
9. Jiayi, L., Enmin, S., Ahmed, G., Mubarak, A.: Machine learning for assisting cervical cancer diagnosis: an ensemble approach. Futur. Gener. Comput. Syst. **106**, 199–205 (2020)
10. Singh, S.K., Anjali, G.: Performance analysis of machine learning algorithms for cervical cancer detection. IJHISI **15**(2), 1–21 (2020)
11. Indrakumari, R., Poongodi, T., Jena, S.R.: Heart disease prediction using exploratory data analysis. Procedia Comput. Sci. **173**, 130–139 (2020)
12. Rohner, E., et al.: Mapping the cervical cancer screening cascade among women living with HIV in Johannesburg, South Africa. Int. J. Gynecol. Obstetrics **152**(1), 53–59 (2021)
13. Nassali, M., Melese, T., Modimowame, J., Moreri-Ntshabele, B.: Timelines to cervical cancer diagnosis and treatment at a tertiary hospital in Botswana. Int. J. Women's Health **13**, 385–393 (2021)
14. Qin, S., Chen, S., Qin, S., Chen, H., Hu, Z., Li, S.: Correlation between pretreatment hematologic parameters and cervical cancer patients undergoing hysterectomy: a retrospective study. Clin. Lab. **66**(6), 997–1003 (2020)

15. Lee, J., et al.: Metabolic syndrome and persistent cervical human papillomavirus infection. Gynecologic Oncol. **161**(2) (2021)
16. Vinodhini, K., Shanmughapriya, S., Das, B.C., Natarajaseenivasan, K.: Prevalence and risk factors of HPV infection among women from various provinces of the world. Arch Gynecol. Obstet. **285**, 771–777 (2012)
17. R Foundation. What is R? (2021). https://www.r-project.org/about.html. Accessed 28 Sept

Proposal of a Real Time Microservice Architecture Applied to Business Intelligence for the Financial Sector

Tatiana Muñoz-Sánchez[1]([✉]) [iD] and Mauricio Espinoza-Mejía[2] [iD]

[1] Master in Strategic Management in Information Technology, University of Cuenca, Cuenca, Ecuador
tatiana.munozs@ucuenca.edu.ec
[2] Department of Computer Science, University of Cuenca, Cuenca, Ecuador

Abstract. This work proposes to i) generate a microservice, which allows the capture of massive transaction information from a relational database, ii) develop the extract, transform and load process (ETL), and iii) store proper and valuable information for decision-making in a non-relational database. The entire process also uses business intelligence mechanisms to convert data into information. Three phases were used for the implementation of this process: the first one, a mechanism within the relational database for change data capture (CDC)- Then, the second one, the design and implementation of a consumer in charge of listening to the messages, generate the transformation process and load it to the non-relational database, ensuring fault tolerance, reliability and scalability. Finally, through defined indicators, a control panel was designed, which offers operators and managers the necessary guidelines to generate decisions and measure the achievement of objectives and goals. The entire process, implemented through a visual and intuitive tool, allows converting the data into knowledge, which generates a competitive advantage in companies' management and operational processes.

The proposed integration, results in an architecture design that efficiently manages thousands of records in real-time, offering greater speed, performance, and optimization in searches of large volumes of data for effective decision-making.

Keywords: Microservice · CDC · ETL · NoSQL · Indicators · Business intelligence

1 Introduction

This work provides technical details that demonstrate the importance of real-time data management for efficient and timely decision making, through business intelligence tools, in the financial sector.

Nowadays, the large amount of data generated in a globalized and interconnected world has created new opportunities to convert information into value for organizations. Undoubtedly, analyzing data in real time, and taking it to strategic business intelligence technology tools, allows to achieve segmented and specific decisions. Said decisions

M. Botto-Tobar et al. (Eds.): ICAT 2021, CCIS 1535, pp. 456–468, 2022.
https://doi.org/10.1007/978-3-031-03884-6_33

are focused on the rapid evaluation of data, creating a competitive advantage over other competitors in the market.

One of the sectors where information is especially relevant is the financial sector. This sector is known for offering different types of products and services for customers, through a variety of technological tools. Since thousands of transactions are executed, the used tools must be reliable and secure. The massive amount of information handled by banking, leads to the search for mechanisms that allow to make decisions quickly, based on the existing data. taking advantage of the data to make decisions quickly, Also, to seek for the development of new products, services and the implementation of operational and management graphs that monitor the operation of the organization. Therefore, is important for financial institutions to design and implement tools for real-time data interaction; without a considerable impact on traditional solutions which are focused on heavy processes, or that cause excessive modifications of existing systems.

This article presents the design of an architecture, which integrates open-source technologies for real-time data collection in a financial institution. Through the use of a microservice, it obtains the information, which is later presented through business intelligence graphs, showing the performance of one of the services offered. In this work, to illustrate the design of the process, debit cards service was selected. It presents, details of the architecture operation and the tools used for its design, unlike the current literature that does not provide this type of information. Moreover, other services and financial institutions, could potentially take advantage of the functionalities presented in this work. This paper is structured as follows: Sect. 1.1 describes the related works. Then, Sect. 2 provides a detailed description of the architecture proposed to get objectives, and Sect. 3 explains the analysis performed and the results. Finally, in Sect. 4 the conclusions obtained are presented.

1.1 Related Works

The main motivation of this article is to integrate distinct technologies to capture data in real time, and consolidate them into a fault-tolerant architecture. It transforms debit card transaction data into information, which can help with the operational and management decision making, bringing value to the business. The processing of large amounts of data in a high speed and scalable manner, requires reliable systems; for example, Fernandez [2] proposes an architecture of big data ingest in real time, through the management of web services for simulated data submission and a web interface for results presentation. This approach manages three built-in blocks for correct operation. Also, Ichinose [3] proposes a method to transmit data through a high-performance data collection system, that can be adapted to many contexts. Miguel del Corral [4] proposes architecture for the processing and analysis of data flows for events generated by sensors and devices in IoT (Internet of Things). In his study, he also makes a comparison of current technologies. This work, unlike the three-component approach presented by Fernandez, and in relation with other works that provide the functionality of transmission and visualization in real time, integrates a microservice as an intermediate component, which cleans the data and performs the transformation process. Nowadays, micro services management allows the creation of independent applications that are not committed to a single type of technology, offering easy maintenance. According to Smid [5], a good design for microservices data communication reduces system communication overhead and improves data transmission performance. Benson Kamau's proposal [6] can be considered as a midpoint, between the management of real-time technologies and the use of microservices. Said proposal describes the advantages of using a microservice architecture in the management of real-time data when sending random data simulating sensor identifiers. The current approach to software development and distributed applications aids the management of this type of mechanism, especially when looking for easy scaling [7, 8]. In the cases analyzed, the implementation of microservices have all been successful in the integration of functionalities with third parties, in addition, to make quick and continuous improvements to the functionality.

The integration of technologies such as messaging systems and microservices offer real-time data processing, allowing the creation of an architectural capable of delivering optimal, effective and efficient results for decision-making in organizations through business intelligence visualizations. Murillo Junco and Cáceres Castellanos [9] stated that "one of the fields where business intelligence is most used for its excellent results is financial, it allows visualization, analysis, compression and monitoring of information in real-time simply and effectively". Therefore, the author of [10–12] highlight the benefits of dashboards as graphical tools in the financial sector, maximizing the benefit of the large volume of transactions that are generated, to provide more personal service to customers and increase the quality of financial institutions. Dashboards allow measuring the performance of a company; from the strategic, tactical and operational aspects. These business intelligence (BI) tools provide more timely visibility for the business user on the company's transactions, offering true and relevant information in real time and attractive format for analysis. Therefore, the purpose of BI is to help control the flow of business information inside and outside of organizations, identifying and processing the information into summarized and useful knowledge.

All benefits offered by these mechanisms (real-time messaging systems, microservices, non-relational databases, and dashboards) through their integration have been exploited in this work to generate the design and implementation of the proposed architecture.

2   Methods

Here, an architecture is proposed through a real-time data transmission environment, between a relational database and a non-relational database based on a publisher/subscriber model. This type of model offers the possibility of communicating applications through messages and divide the processing of the data with several producers and consumers in charge of writing and receiving the messages. All this communication process is executed without need to know each other unlike what happens in traditional client-server models; improving scaling, processing and response times transmission.

Design and implementation of the system consist of three main components called: "Change Detector", "Central Component" and "Dashboard", as shown in Fig. 1:

- **Data change detector:** This component captures the events generated in the relational database.

- **Central component**: it is the central component of the architecture where real-time transactions of the change detector block are captured. The cleaning process is generating and information is transformed and loaded into NoSQL database.

- **Dashboard:** visualization component. Presenting information through business intelligence graphics accessing NoSQL database in real time with optimized searches.

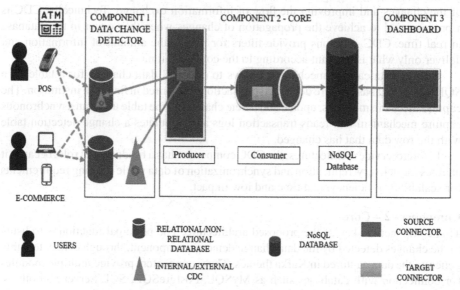

Fig. 1. Proposed architecture for real-time transmission.

The integration of these components in the proposed architecture is under the Apache Kafka messaging system [13]. Kafka is open source and was originally developed by LinkedIn in 2008 and written in Java and Scala. The Apache Software Foundation currently maintains it. Technical details of this platform as comparative studies with other existing messaging systems on the market can be found in [14, 18]. General characteristics of these messaging systems publisher/subscriber model are: 1) Scalability: adaptable to add new mechanisms for expanding the architecture. 2) High performance and low latency: it supports thousands of clients for reading and writing messages and can process transactions in a few milliseconds. 3) Fault tolerance: Its design allows redistributing operation to other agents in case of failure for continuing its operation without interrupting the service. In summary, the architecture proposed in this work consists of a source connector that detects changes in a database. This connector is integrated into an application developed under the programming language Java [19], which functionality is to act as a microservice and message intermediary and through another target connector store the data in a NoSQL database for visualization in a control panel.

The next section presents a description of each component and a detailed explanation of their respective functionality.

2.1 Architecture Components

The detailed operation of each component is described below.

Component 1 - Data Change Detector

Data Change Capture (CDC) is the base of this component. A process acts in the background to listen for changes in a database; therefore, allowing to keep the traceability of the changes and improving the flow of information exchange. Technically, CDC is a process used to achieve the propagation of changes when they occur in the database in real time. CDC solutions provide filters for reduce the amount of information and deliver only what is relevant according to the configuration.

Change data capture mechanism allows to catch all data changes for a table on a SQL Server database, where debit card transactions are stored in financial institution. The capture mechanism inserts, update and delete changes to the table using an asynchronous capture mechanism that reads transaction logs and populates a change detection table with the row data that has changed.

In microservice architectures, the CDC component has a fundamental role, because it enables the delivery, replication and synchronization of data while meeting requirements for scalability, efficiency, real time and low impact.

Component 2 – Core

This component is key of the proposed architecture. The principal function is to listen to the changes detected by the data change detector component, through connectors that generate the data captured in Kafka themes. These connectors provide multiple modules for connection with databases such as MySQL, PostgreSQL, SQL Server and others. One of the main features is that it is fault tolerant: if the connector is stopped for any reason, it will continue to record the changes that occurred while was off, ensuring that all information is processed properly. Figure 2 shows the elements that represent the sending of a message from the producer to the consumer, through Kafka messages in a standalone mode, useful for basic testing and development. The Producer generates a message and sends it to the list of a topic and not directly to consumer. The Consumer is responsible for subscribing to the topic (category) from which it wants to obtain the data.

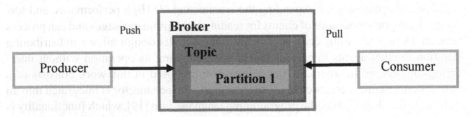

Fig. 2. Apache Kafka with single node and partition

Configuration of the Kafka server allows configuration files to: define the properties of the database, serialization format of the captured data, Kafka cluster and other parameters, useful for the interaction of the records managed in the CDC process. To detect data flow sent by Producer/Publisher about JSON serialization format defined in the Kafka server configuration, a microservice was implemented that acts in background where: 1) listens to the Kafka topics, 2) generates information treatment process through data cleaning and conversion mechanisms, and 3) data loading into NoSQL database with a target connector.

Developed microservice is multiplatform, flexible and capture messages asynchronously generating high availability. For example, each of the events that arrive in the message queue are not blocking, without need to wait for a response. Therefore, allowing to generate a lower latency time than synchronous communication, where an event need waits for a response before continuing with the next event. Figure 3 shows a schema of the actions performed by microservice: 1) detect insert records 2) generates cleaning of the data, avoiding records with empty or null values and ATM[1] transactions which do not provide information of processed business transactions (POS[2] or ecommerce) 3) selects a type of data and proceeds to the conversion. For example: long type data referring to hours, is converted into string format hh:mm:ss; datetime fields into string format dd/MM/yyyy hh:mm:ss. Also, ISO8583 field, which contains the frame belonging to said standard. It is decoded through an implemented library, which allows to extract fields that will be added to the final record of the transaction. And, finally, there are fields defined as elastic, that maintain conversion codes to their respective description through powerful text searches, offered by the NoSQL database where these are registered. 4) Lastly, final records of the transactions are stored in a non-relational database.

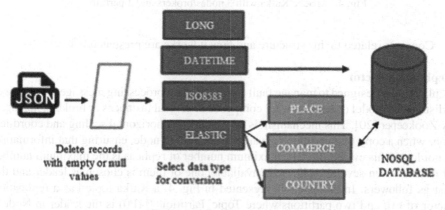

Fig. 3. Microservice operation

It is important to consider that, one of the main characteristics of this messaging system is to efficiently manage data in a distributed model. Functionalities offered in this messaging system (publisher-subscriber model) is it works with the concepts of several partitions, replication factors and groups of consumers, that allow managing the

---

[1] ATM Automated teller machine: Is an electronic banking outlet that allows customers to complete basic transactions without the aid of a teller.

[2] POS Point of sale: Refers to the place where customers execute payments for services.

performance and reliability offered in a production system. Figure 4 shows an example of a topic replication model with three instances/nodes/brokers, a replication factor of two, two partitions and two consumer groups.

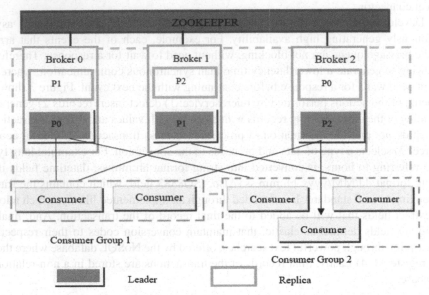

Fig. 4. Apache Kafka with 3 nodes/brokers and 2 partitions

Concepts related to this structure and how it works are presented below:

Replication Factor
Replication is designed to manage fault tolerance when processing messages, working in a distributed model of Kafka cluster composed of several instances or brokers, managed by Zookeeper [20]. This mechanism is responsible for horizontal scaling and coordination, when a copy of a partition is available on another node, ensuring that information is not lost if this event fails. The maximum number of replicas is the maximum number of nodes. When several replicas are available, one of them is chosen as leader and the rest as followers. In the example presented in Fig. 4, a Kafka topic has a replication factor of two and two partitions where Topic_Partition_0 (P0) is the leader in Node 0 and a replica in Node 2. This mechanism can only have one leader node for each topic partition.

Partitions Number
Partitioning aids to parallelize topics, to split data of a topic on several nodes to balance the load. In addition, several consumers can read a topic in parallel, improving message performance. In Fig. 4, when a node fails for some reason for example if node 2 stops. Access to partition 2 has been lost because node 2 was a partition leader. Therefore, Kafka through Zookeeper automatically selects one of the synchronized replicas, and

makes it the leader avoiding loss of important information. Now, when node 2 comes back online it can try to become a leader again.

Consumer Group
Kafka consumers subscribe to its topics and consume messages. This approach is flexible, because the messages are distributed to consumers. This is done by maintaining a balanced load between each consumer, under the concept of parallel processing. Consumers are concentrated into groups, ensuring messages from a partition are read by one consumer from each group.

These approaches are presented in distributed systems, where a high flow of information is in real time (e.g. the financial sector), allowing the read and write of data performance is flexible, scalable and error tolerant. Thus, avoiding loss of important information in the results presentation process (component 3).

Results obtained from tests performed on an environment with a single-node model vs. a distributed model can be consulted in Sect. 3 Results and Discussions.

Component 3 – Dashboard
This component is responsible of the generation of business intelligence graphs of one of the most demanded services in a financial institution, which is debit cards. It manages, in real time, information such as: i) flow of debit card transactions; ii) the business where a transaction has been made; iii) countries where most purchases exist; iv) commercial sector type where a debit card is most used; v) platforms where purchases are made. These information offers a great opportunity for expanding and improving business model processes in financial institutions, based on said indicators. Then, all of them allow to fulfill the requirements requested by the organization: show in real-time a summary of places, platforms, and businesses worldwide where debit card payment is used. It is important to emphasize that visualization of the information has a cleaning and transformation data process, which was explained in Component 2. The dashboard panel includes various types of graphics (heat maps, bars, pies) obtained from integration with the non-relational database in real time. Figure 5 shows a heat map of the countries where there is the highest number of debit card transactions.

949,097	United States
840,412	Ecuador
451,912	United Kingdom
164,915	Netherlands
8,810	Ireland
7,050	Spain
6,625	Colombia
5,900	Mexico
5,574	Hong Kong
5,474	Belgium
4,175	Malta
3,947	Germany
2,724	Cyprus
2,711	Brazil
2,147	France
2,075	Canada
2,022	Singapore
1,514	Russia
1,465	Peru

Fig. 5. Heat Map

3   Results and Discussions

The data processed in this system comes from a replica test database of a financial institution's production environment (as a case study). To avoid the impact of the data source on the results, the experimental data source was used in all comparisons. The tests were carried out by selecting open-source tools that meet the functionality required in each of the stages of the architecture, as shown in Fig. 6. For example, for CDC Events Producer with Kafka topics, it was used the work of Debezium [21] as a distributed platform to capture data changes. A microservice running in background contains the necessary libraries to detect Kafka topics and a connector to send the data after the respective ETL process. The non-relational storage is Elasticsearch [22] as a NoSQL database oriented to JSON documents also supporting powerful text searches. Finally, for visualizing the indexed data that in Elasticsearch, for decision making through graphs, was used Kibana [23].

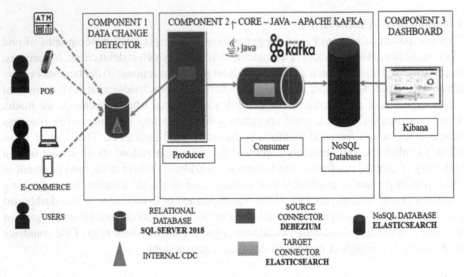

Fig. 6. Architecture designed with selected tools

In Table 1, experimental software and hardware environment are presented.

Table 1. Software and hardware features

Feature	Value
Operating System	Open Suse Linux
RAM	16 GB
CPU	Intel(R) Core(TM) i7-8700T CPU @ 2.40 GHz

(continued)

Table 1. (*continued*)

Feature	Value
Debezium Version	debezium-connector-sqlserver-1.2.0.C
Kafka Version	2.13–2.5.0
Zookeper Version	3.6.1
Elasticsearch Version	7.8.0
Kibana Version	7.8.0

For the tests execution of the proposed architecture (in a financial institution), different scenarios were configured, under the premise of replication of a transaction table generated with debit cards. It was made to measure response times of information processing in a distributed model. The data volume to be processed is 500,000 records, stored in the table configured with CDC.

Number of brokers or nodes: 3
Number of topics: 1
Number of producers: 1

Firstly, from processed records in microservice environment, the discarded percentage of transactions with empty, null or ATM transactions is 0.13%; therefore; concluding that it is low, considering the volume of records and required information. The first set of tests was configuring with a single consumer, with the respective configurations to determine response times between a model with/without replication and partitions as detailed in Table 2. Next, in this process, the same tests were run, adding consumers subscribed to the configured topic with the same software and hardware resources. These tests allowed to measure response times when scaling data consumption to other subscribers, for sharing data load.

Table 2. Single model vs Distributed model tests

Features			
Replication factor	No replication	2	3
Number of Partitions	1	3	10
Single consumer model - Processing time (milliseconds)	66407	104484	150693
Two consumers - Processing time (milliseconds)	63334	98153	140597
Three consumers Processing time (milliseconds)	62991	68932	137515

From the obtained results, it was generated the following graph to analyze processing times obtained on each scenario.

According to Fig. 7, the following conclusions were obtained:

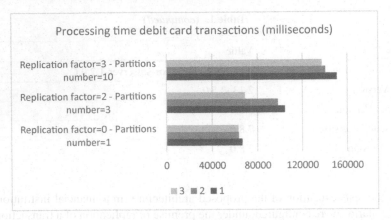

Fig. 7. Processing time results graph

In test environments, where the transmission of information is handled without replication and partitioning (single mode), latency time is lower compared to configuration of parameters such as the replication factor, which allows fault tolerance in a distributed environment. For data packets sent of the same size in this study, a higher replication factor and an increase of the number of partitions cause increases in sending intervals. This, because Kafka producer needs more time for organizing nodes/brokers, where it will replicate and determine leader partitions and their respective replica partitions. Another important factor to consider in this architecture model, is the number of consumers subscribed to a topic, thus, more consumers exist is less time for process messages.

4 Conclusions

This paper has presented the design and implementation of an architecture that manages real-time processing of thousands of transactions, generated by debit card service of a financial institution. This architecture allows the use of a microservice like a scalable tool, distributed and fault tolerant. The proposed design prioritizes the presentation of results through a control panel, which helps in operational and management decision making. According to results obtained with this architecture, a conclusion is with that with the use of open-source tools, is possible to help to efficiently manage thousands of records in real-time, with greater speed, performance, and optimization. This in searches of large volumes of data, thanks NoSQL technology. Undoubtedly, a messaging pattern in a distributed model for the financial environment is of great importance, because it allows efficient management of information, processing real data flows, low latency times, and horizontal scaling for large volumes of transactions. The work also presents a performance model of Apache Kafka messaging system, adjusting node size, replication factor, number of partitions and consumers, to compare changes in product performance in terms of latency times. In organizations with a high production of transactions, such as the financial sector, management of consumers groups that allow a quick message process, as presented in the architecture, test the cases and reliability of not losing important information through replication factor. Therefore, it makes easier to better identify clients or partners providing products with higher quality, detect problems of services offered in an organization, and to define places where new products can be introduced. It also facilitates the projection of the results through visualization mechanisms such as graphs, graphs with geo-positioning combined with heat maps, etc. As future work, it is intended to analyze this proposed architecture with new configuration parameters to complete an ideal performance model, according to other measured variables, in organizations such as the financial sector and other environments.

References

1. Bhogal, J., Choksi, I.: Handling big data using NoSQL. In: IEEE 29th International Conference on Advanced Information Networking and Applications Workshops, pp. 393–398 (2015). https://doi.org/10.1109/WAINA.2015.19
2. Fernández Garrido, F.: Arquitectura Big Data de ingesta en Real Time. Universitat Oberta de Catalunya, España, Proyecto de titulación (2017)
3. Ichinose, A., Takefusa, A., Nakada, H., Oguchi, M.: A study of a video analysis framework using Kafka and spark streaming. IEEE International Conference on Big Data (Big Data) **2017**, 2396–2401 (2017). https://doi.org/10.1109/BigData.2017.8258195
4. Fernández Miguel del Corral, O.: Procesamiento de flujos de eventos en un entorno distribuido y análisis de comportamiento: arquitectura e implementación. Tesis (Master), E.T.S. de Ingenieros Informáticos (UPM) (2017)
5. Smid, A., Wang, R., Černý, T.: Case study on data communication in microservice architecture, pp. 261–267 (2019). https://doi.org/10.1145/3338840.3355659
6. Benson, K.: Implementing Publish-Subscribe Pattern in a Microservice Architecture. Master thesis. ÅBO Akademi University (2019)
7. Maya, E., Lopez, D.: Arquitectura de Software basada en Microservicios para Desarrollo de Aplicaciones Web (2018). http://repositorio.utn.edu.ec/bistream/123456789/7603/1/PG%20569%20TESIS.pdf
8. Bucchiarone, A., Dragoni, N., Dustdar, S., Larsen, S., Mazzara, M.: From Monolithic to Microservices: An Experience Report from the Banking Domain, pp. 50–55 (2018). https://doi.org/10.1109/MS.2018.2141026
9. Murillo Junco, M.J., Cáceres Castellanos, G.: Business intelligence and financial decision-making: a theoretical approach. Revista Logos Ciencia & Tecnología **5**, 119–138 (2013)
10. Wong, S., Venkatraman, S.: Financial Accounting Fraud Detection Using Business Intelligence. Asian Economic and Financial Review. Asian Economic and Social Society, vol. 5(11), pp. 1187–1207 (2015)
11. Rizvi, S.R.Z.: Role of big data in financial institutions for Financial fraud. (2021). https://doi.org/10.2139/ssrn.3800777
12. Tunowski, R.: Sustainability of Commercial Banks Supported by Business Intelligence System. (2020). https://doi.org/10.3390/su12114754
13. Shaheen, J.: Apache Kafka: Real Time Implementation with Kafka Architecture Review. Int. J. Adv. Sci. Technol. (2017)
14. Snyder, B., Bosanac, D., Davies, R.: Introduction to Apache ActiveMQ (2010). https://freecontent.manning.com/wp-content/uploads/introduction-to-apache-activemq.pdf
15. Pivotal Software Inc. Rabbit MQ. Documentation: Table of Contents — RabbitMQ (2021). https://www.rabitmq.com/documentation.html
16. Dobbelaere, P., Sheykh Esmaili, K.: Kafka versus RabbitMQ: A comparative study of two industry reference publish/subscribe implementations: Industry Paper, pp. 227–238 (2017). https://doi.org/10.1145/3093742.3093908

17. Intorruk, S., Numnonda, T.: A comparative study on performance and resource utilization of real-time distributed messaging systems for big data. In: 20th IEEE/ACIS International Conference on Software Engineering, Artificial Intelligence, Networking and Parallel/Distributed Computing (SNPD), pp. 102–107 (2019)
18. Fu, G., Zhang, Y., Yu, G.: A fair comparison of message queuing systems. IEEE Access **9**, 421–432 (2021). https://doi.org/10.1109/ACCESS.2020.3046503
19. Java (lenguaje de programación). https://es.wikipedia.org/wiki/Java_(lenguaje_de_programaci%C3%B3n)
20. Zookeeper Documentation, Zookeeper (2021). https://zookeeper.apache.org/doc/r3.6.1/
21. Reference Documentation, Debezium (2021). https://debezium.io/documentation/
22. Gormley, C., Tong, Z.: Elasticsearch: The Definitive Guide. In: 1st edn. O'Reilly Media, pp. 1–10 (2015)
23. Kibana—your window into Elastic | Kibana Guide [7.12] (2021). https://www.elastic.co/guide/en/kibana/current/introduction.html

Design of a Blockchain Architecture and Use of Smart Contracts to Improve Processes in Notary Office

Roberth Ulloa[1]([⊠]) and Pablo Gallegos[2]

[1] Universidad de Cuenca, Avenue 12 de Abril, Cuenca, Ecuador
roberth.ulloab@ucuenca.edu.ec
[2] Universidad Politécnica Salesiana, Calle Vieja and Elia Liut, Cuenca, Ecuador

Abstract. The present investigation proposes the use of the blockchain as a replacement mechanism for the current notarial system, the use of smart contracts is applied for this purpose, in which all the terms or clauses of a transaction are detailed, as in a traditional contract, but with new capabilities and security mechanisms specific to blockchain due to its native encryption algorithms, without the intervention of third parties, the proposed architecture establishes the processes of consensus and distribution of the general ledger in each of the nodes, distributed in the different certification entities or organizations, as well as each of the components that intervene during the process of generating a new transaction that will begin with the agreement between a seller and a buyer on a good, whether a vehicle, a house, a land, etc., also seeking to eliminate the intervention of several state entities in the notarial processes, in addition to complying go fully all the clauses of the contracts generated.

Keywords: Blockchain · Smart contract · Notary · Architecture · Simulation

1 Introduction

The blockchain is a data structure whose information is stored in a set of distributed nodes, without the intervention of third parties thanks to the use of complex cryptographic algorithms, once a new link is attached to this chain these cannot be deleted, modified, cloned and much less add nodes that do not belong to the genesis chain of a previously identified entity, to belong to a blockchain each document must go through the verification of the consensus of the other nodes, and check the hash that must be recorded in the ledger [1].

There are three types of Blockchain [2, 3], public, private, and federated or hybrid, the main difference between these three types is the access to be part of this network, in the public ones any user can participate, in the private ones a permission granted by an administrator is required, and the federated ones are a combination of the two previous ones. The benefits of this architecture are related to six characteristics: administration, persistence, identification, auditability, participation, and transparency.

© Springer Nature Switzerland AG 2022
M. Botto-Tobar et al. (Eds.): ICAT 2021, CCIS 1535, pp. 469–483, 2022.
https://doi.org/10.1007/978-3-031-03884-6_34

These security characteristics enable the use of this disruptive technology to improve government processes by simplifying the security process and preserving the integrity of the information, generating a new efficient and reliable model [4].

A smart contract is a set of informatic codes, written in programming languages in which the instructions agreed between the parties involved in the commercial agreement are embodied, these can be enforced by itself in an automated and automatic way, without the intervention of third parties or mediators, a smart contract is valid without depending on authorities since its codification is visible, decentralized, immutable, transparent and supported by all the guarantees of trust and transparency that give us the blockchain [5].

Within the various governance processes carried out by the state, the tasks of public notaries play a relevant role in our research, since these officials can confer authenticity and give public faith to contracts, texts, and legal transactions contained in the documents they draft. However, these manuscripts are not properly stored and with an adequate degree of confidentiality, availability, and integrity, besides being susceptible to the intervention of third parties who act illegally and fraudulently because for the various procedures it is necessary to access the systems of different state entities, which causes the notarial process to be long and subject to errors in the registration of information between the different governmental areas.

For this reason, our research proposes to modernize the current notary system, with the use of the blockchain, through the application of smart contracts to control that each of the clauses of the same are met on a mandatory basis, and the registration process within the ledger eliminating the intervention of various government entities (SRI, Land Registry, Municipalities, DINARDAP, etc.) focusing the process only in the Judiciary Council and including the different certification entities of Ecuador to act as the nodes which will be in charge of validating the different blocks that will be generated by each of the transactions.

Finally, this paper is structured as follows: Sect. 2 presents the theorical framework, in which the literature review on the topic to be addressed is disclosed, Sect. 3 details related works on the application of blockchain and smart contracts in various areas, then Sect. 4 describes the proposed blockchain architecture to be used in notarial processes, Sect. 5 discloses a simulation example of the architecture detailing the software to be used in the example and presenting the results of the simulation. Finally, Sect. 6 presents the conclusions of this paper.

2   Theorical Framework

2.1   Blockchain

Blockchain technology was created as a response to the crisis of confidence that hit the world in the wake of the 2008 financial crisis that has been attributed to the bankruptcy of reliable institutions such as banks and other financial institutions.

Blockchain emerges as a possible solution to the erosion of trust in traditional institutions by eliminating the need for trust between parties, with this technology users submit to the authority of a technological system that they trust to be immutable regardless of the purpose for which a public blockchain is used [6].

According to [7], blockchain is a distributed, transparent and immutable ledger, the consensus protocol forms the core of blockchain.

The ledger is kept up to date by participants called miner, running a protocol that maintains the data structure known as the blockchain. One of the advantages that this technology has is to provide an initial set of arguments with which attacks or irregularities can be prevented so that the attacker cannot reorganize the blockchain to its initial form [8].

According to [9], blockchain is made up of the following components:

Blocks. Blockchain is a record of all transactions that are packaged in blocks that the miners then verify. They will then be added to the chain once their validation is completed and distributed to all the nodes that make up the network.

Miners. These are dedicated computers that contribute their computational power to the network to verify the transactions that take place; they oversee authorizing the addition of transaction blocks.

Nodes. These are computers connected to the network using software that stores and distributes an updated copy of the blockchain in real-time.

There are three types of blockchain: public, private, and federated or hybrid, the main difference between these three types is the access to be part of this network, in the public ones any user can participate, in the private ones, a permission granted by an administrator is required, and the federated ones are a combination of the two previous ones. The benefits of this architecture are related to six characteristics: administration, persistence, identification, auditability, participation, and transparency [10].

2.2 Smart Contracts

The fourth industrial revolution brought the blockchain in which within its great utilities and forms of application that have been given to this system include smart contracts, which consist of a computer program that executes agreements established between two or more contracting parties generating certain actions that happen or not because of compliance or non-compliance with a series of specific and already agreed conditions. Something outstanding in all this is that there is no need for a third person to verify whether the facts have happened or not, this becomes totally revolutionary in the legal field so that in the future it is expected that it will not be necessary to go before a third party every time you want to validate or attest to a contract [11].

According to [12], blockchain in conjunction with smart contracts are technologies that can help fight corruption, that has been currently considered a social problem, this is possible due to the security and the basis of the decentralized system becoming the foundation of smart contracts, these two concepts are promising alternatives with which society can eradicate corruption which is a serious problem that has always been linked to the politics of different countries.

3 Related Works

In recent years, there have been several studies related to the application of blockchain and smart contracts, because their use is not only limited to the cryptocurrency field, but it can be used in other areas that are part of the daily life of society.

According to [13], blockchain can contribute to the development and certification of distributed generation systems, among other possible applications in the field of energy, with the creation of Bitcoin, subsequent to this it was determined that this technology can not only be used in cryptocurrencies but to various applications in different areas of economic activity, based on the technology on which Bitcoin is based. A particular use for this technology is within the notarization and certification operations that, until today, are performed by notaries or scribes who act as authenticating agents. Registrations such as marriages, property deeds, custody of financial assets, birth certificates, registration and transfer of assets, intellectual or physical property such as automobiles, patents, wills, accounting audits, etc., could be certified through blockchain-based systems.

Similarly, according to [14], a research and development project of structured services is proposed to improve academic and administrative process at the level of data management in higher education by implementing decentralized ledger technologies. This project aims to accredit academic achievement safely, decentralize academic resource management, and develop an incentive system for knowledge creation an expanded support networks for universities.

Another highly researched topic according to [15], is the application of blockchain in IoT (Internet of Things), one of the biggest challenges facing IoT security comes from the current system architecture itself because it is based entirely on a centralized model known as client-server, with this scheme all devices are authenticated and connected through the cloud, however, with the rapid growth of IoT in society, devices become more vulnerable to potential attacks for malicious purposes due to the limited capabilities or features that these devices have unlike more robust equipment such as cell phones, computers, etc. A solution to this effect may be the use of blockchain due to the ability to manage, control and secure IoT equipment also using smart contracts to leverage their benefit thus achieving to nullify any malicious attack attempt towards a network with IoT equipment.

Another study carried out by [16] indicates that society is increasingly demanding greater transparency, participation, and citizen cooperation between the parties in public activities that fall under the responsibility of administrations in the public sector, so blockchain is entering a public debate in different sectors and industries due to the breadth of services, opportunities, and challenges it can offer. The complexity of this technology is a topic that many governments are beginning to exploit to develop different applications and platforms that favor the system of their states, seeking to increase the confidence of the population in the different state entities.

However, there are still more unexplored fields in which blockchain technology with smart contracts could be implemented, for this to happen, an architecture must be designed that adapts to the different processes of each of the areas to be studied, this is the case of notarial processes in Ecuador in which an architecture is needed that meets all the processes in which several state entities are immersed and that makes the information can be violated and used for illegal purposes.

4   Proposed Architecture

According to [17], there are still no common standards that clearly specify the components of the blockchain in various layers, however, a blockchain layer formulation is made in order to better understand the technology and to build a comparative analogy between blockchain and cryptocurrency variants that currently exist, for this purpose, five layers have been identified as follows:

4.1   Blockchain Layers

Application Layer. In this layer encodes the different functionalities that may be necessary for the different processes, generally, it involves a set of traditional technology for software development such as client-side programming constructs, it is possible that these developments must be hosted in some web servers since it will be the layer that interacts directly with the users.

Execution Layer. This layer executes the different instructions ordered by the application layer on all nodes of a blockchain network, which must execute the different scripts independently, it is important to consider that they will always be the same input data for each node as well as the output will be the same in each of them.

Semantic Layer. It is a logical layer because there is an order between the transactions and the blocks of the chain, it has a set of instructions that goes through the execution layer, but they are validated in the semantic layer, here also are defined the different rules of the system as well as the models and the data structures.

Propagation Layer. This is the peer-to-peer propagation layer that allows nodes to identify and communicate with each other, here the new blocks generated by each transaction are disseminated throughout the network so that it can be known by all the nodes of the same.

Consensus Layer. The objective of this layer is to get all the nodes to agree on a consistent state of the ledger, blockchain security is guaranteed in this layer as each node will indicate whether the new block generated is valid or not.

4.2   Blockchain Layers in Notarial Processes

In Fig. 1 the layers are used in the proposed architecture to be applied in the different notarial processes:

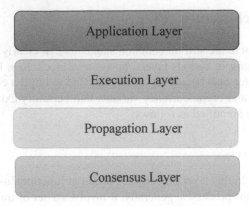

Fig. 1. Blockchain layers to be used in the architecture for notarial processes.

Application Layer. In this layer, you will find the application to which both, buyer and seller, must access to initiate the negotiation process which will allow closing the sale of the property (vehicle, land or house), for this, the seller must enter with his personal data to the system in which the information of the property is found the same that is of general knowledge for the different nodes that access the general ledger.

Execution Layer. In this layer the Smart Contract will be elaborated with the different instructions to be executed to give the necessary compliance before generating the new block, such execution can be done by any of the nodes of the blockchain network and in the same way each of the nodes must have knowledge of such executions.

Propagation Layer. In this layer, after having finished the execution of the smart contract, one of the nodes will act as a miner generating a new block with a new hash and registering the up-to-date information of the property, also adding the hash of the previous block, the same should be sent as copies towards the other nodes of the network.

Consensus Layer. Finally, in this layer, all nodes receiving the new block must reach an agreement to add the block to the general ledger.

4.3 Entities Considered in the Process

With the architecture presented below, we intend to limit the intervention of several state agencies in such a way, we only need the intervention of Control Entities (SRI, Property Registry), which are responsible for keeping the information updated in their database, and the Information Certification Entities existing in Ecuador that will act as nodes, which are listed below:

- Central Bank of Ecuador.
- Civil Registry.
- Judiciary Council.
- ANFAC Certification Authority Ecuador C.A.
- UANATACA Ecuador S.A.
- Security Data Data Security and Digital Signature S.A.

4.4 Smart Contract

The smart contract must specify each of the actions to be executed to upload the necessary information for the transaction, this will depend on the type of asset to be negotiated, the price of the transaction to be paid to the Judiciary Council and the validation of the value to be paid for the purchase of the asset.

4.5 Architecture

In the application layer, the qualities will be allowed (seller and buyer) to generate a new transaction for the purchase – sale of a property, then in the execution layer will proceed to develop and execute the smart contract with the different clauses, which must be executed and fulfilled completely so that the new block can be generated with the information of the new owner of the property, then after finishing the execution of the contract, a mining node in the propagation layer must generate the new block with the following information:

- The new hash.
- Previous hash.
- Smart contract in which are the clauses executed in the process of buying and selling.
- Information about the current owner, previous owner.
- Information about the asset to be transacted.

Once the new block has been generated, it must be sent to all the nodes of the network, who in the consensus layer will verify that there are no anomalies in the new block and add it to the chain to keep up to date the general ledger with all the transactions, to which all the Certification Entities (blockchain network nodes) will have access.

It is important to consider that the genesis node of the blockchain of each of the properties will be initially generated in the Internal Revenue Service (SRI, in Spanish) in the case of vehicles, and in the Land Registry in the case of a land, or house, this is due to the fact that these government entities are the ones who must keep updated the information of the different properties once the new block is added in the chain for each transaction (purchase – sale).

In Fig. 2, the process described above can be observed in a global manner, which specifies each of the components involved in the process of the new transaction between the parties, thus achieving the completion of a transaction without the intervention of third parties, as well as eliminating the need to use or call several institutions for registration, validation, and correction of the information, which also causes delays in the process.

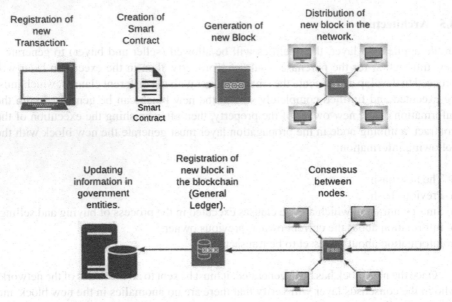

Fig. 2. Global process of the architecture for the registration of purchase and sale of an asset

Below, in Fig. 3, the architecture proposed in this research is detailed layer by layer:

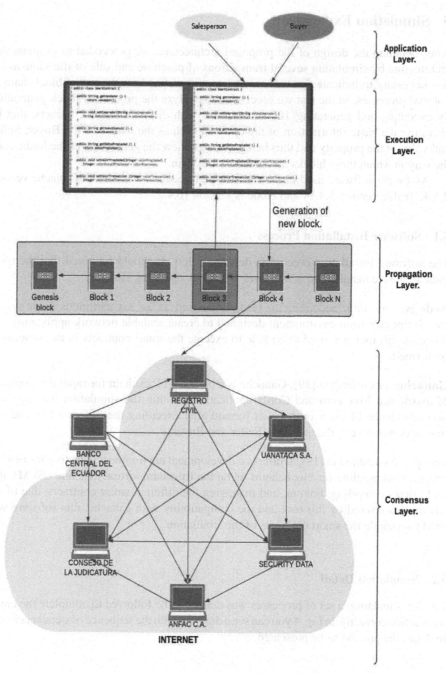

Fig. 3. Proposed blockchain architecture for Notary Offices detailed by Layers.

5 Simulation Experiment

After detailing the design of the proposed architecture, we proceeded to evaluate this architecture by simulating several transactions of purchase and sale of the same asset, it is necessary to indicate that there are no metrics defined for the use of blockchain in notarial processes, in the test we proceeded to analyze the process of block generation by executing and generating 100 transactions with different smart contracts, that is, changing the basic information of the contract such as the names of the Buyer, Seller and value of the property and thus being able to review the generation of the hashes and the way in which these blocks are added to the chain.

As for the software used in the simulation, three tools were used: Ganache version 2.5.4, Truffle version 5.3.14 and Node js version 16.4.2.

5.1 Software Installation Process

The software installation process is detailed below. It should be noted that the tools indicated were installed on a Windows 10 64-bits operating systems.

Node js. This tool, according to [18], is devised as an asynchronous event-driven JavaScript execution environment designed to create scalable network applications, in this case this tool was used to be able to execute the smart contracts in the simulation performed.

Ganache. According to [19], Ganache is a personal blockchain for rapid development of distributed Ethereum and Corda applications, within the simulation, this application reveals the blockchain that was formed after executing the different buy and sell transactions between the qualities (Seller and Buyer).

Truffle. As detailed in [19], Truffle is a development environment, a testing framework and an asset pipeline for blockchains using the Ethereum virtual machine (EVM), this tool allows compiling, linking, and managing the different smart contracts, due to the advantages offered by this tool and the compatibility with ganache, this software was used to compile the smart contracts of the simulation.

5.2 Simulation Detail

For this simulation a set of processes was defined to be followed to complete the entire transaction correctly, in Fig. 4 you can see a diagram with the sequence of steps specifying in detail the process to be presented.

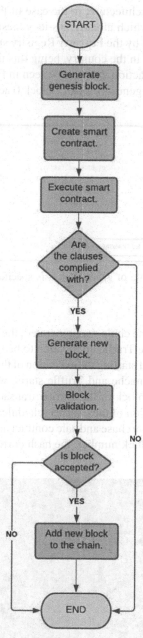

Fig. 4. Genesis block with the date of generation, it is specified that there are no transactions generated.

According to the defined architecture, in the case of this simulation, the asset to be transacted is a piece of land, which already has its genesis node defined, which in the first instance must be generated by the Property Registry since this is the organization in charge of regulating real estate in the country, being this the genesis node means that it was not generated by any transaction, this can be seen in Fig. 5, where it is detailed that there are no transactions in the genesis block or block 0 according to the software used.

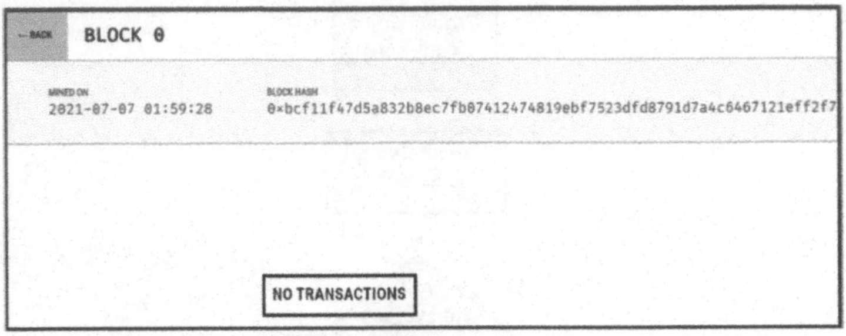

Fig. 5. Genesis block with the date of generation, it is specified that there are no transactions generated.

Once the genesis block of the chain was generated, the smart contract was generated, which was then compiled in the Truffle application to be recognized within the process, and then execute it, at the time of starting the execution of the contract, the communication between the blockchain in Ganache and Truffle starts, with which both softwares are synchronized so that the new block of the current transaction is not generated without first having finished the execution of the clauses scheduled in the contract, Fig. 6 shows the log of the execution of the purchase and sale contract and the details of the generation of the new block such as the block number, the hash corresponding to the transaction.

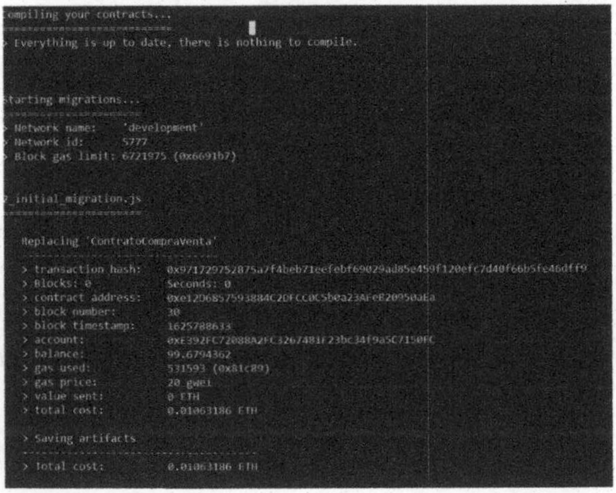

Fig. 6. Execution log of a smart contract and the subsequent creation of the new block.

At the end of the creation of the new block, it records the transaction information such as the smart contract, information on the date and time of creation, the new hash and information where the contract was created and from where it was sent to be executed, this is important because it will allow maintaining reliability in the architecture since, as indicated in previous sections, The mining nodes should only be the Certification Entities that operate in the country, which will allow for greater control even if any irregularity is identified in the process, even being able to blacklist the nodes that have had irregularities when creating or accepting a new block in the network, in this way the one hundred blocks that were added to the chain were generated. In Fig. 7 below.

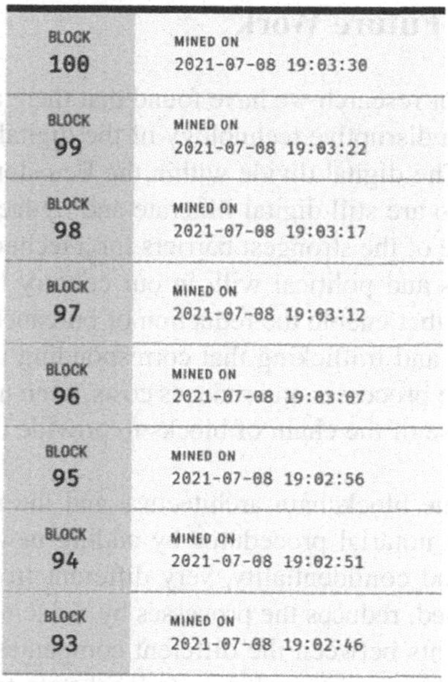

BLOCK	MINED ON
100	2021-07-08 19:03:30
BLOCK 99	MINED ON 2021-07-08 19:03:22
BLOCK 98	MINED ON 2021-07-08 19:03:17
BLOCK 97	MINED ON 2021-07-08 19:03:12
BLOCK 96	MINED ON 2021-07-08 19:03:07
BLOCK 95	MINED ON 2021-07-08 19:02:56
BLOCK 94	MINED ON 2021-07-08 19:02:51
BLOCK 93	MINED ON 2021-07-08 19:02:46

Fig. 7. Cadena de Bloques generada en con 100 transacciones.

6 Simulation Discussion

According to [13], a particular use for blockchain is its application within the notarization and certification operations that, until today, are performed by notaries who act as authenticating agents. Among some of the transactions such as the registration and transfer of assets, intellectual or physical property such a car, patents, wills, accounting audits, etc., could be certified through blockchain-based systems.

This affirmation of the aforementioned author can be seen in Fig. 6, with the use of the blockchain in which all the information related to the smart contract will be stored in it, keeping updated all the data of the current owner of the transacted property, thus eliminating cumbersome processes and paperwork that many times are subject to typographical errors, which when going to other public entities to finish the whole process of buying an selling are rejected and sent to correct, final process that will also be replaced with the presented architecture.

By having the entire process centralized and managed or monitored by the existing certification entities in the country, the process is reduced from a process that can take hours or even days to a matter of minutes, during which time the new block will be generated and will become part of the chain being able to access the entire history of the asset, giving the user the assurance that his request or purchase has no problem in closing the deal, which guarantees that the smart contract is fully complied with in all its clauses.

7 Conclusions and Future Work

In the context raised in our research we have found that there are barriers for the application of Blockchain as a disruptive technology of the digital transformation between those that we describe: The digital divide within the Ecuadorian population existed a wide range of people who are still digital illiterate and by lack of computer skills and fear are constituted in one of the strongest barriers for a technological change.

Lack of state policies and political will, in our country there are great resistance to technological changes that enable the reduction of bureaucratic processes and political power and influence and trafficking that corresponding the possibilities of a new technology that denies the processes and reduces costs, even more when the population would benefit from the use of the chain of blocks to provide in a more efficient way in tax payment.

On the other hand, the blockchain architecture and the use of smart contracts is to streamline the current notarial procedures by adding new security characteristics, efficiency, availability, and confidentiality, very different from the traditional way in which it is currently carried, reduces the processes by reducing the time and secondary processes such as payments between the different companies involved, therefore also improves the collection of payments and taxes to local state and government coffers.

Likewise, our architecture leaves the alternative of a standardization of processes and the ubiquity of being able to carry out a transaction without the need for the physical presence of the interested parties, in such a way that a person can reach a commercial agreement, and generate a greater market dynamic, the entry of the Blockchain to the commercial value chain creates new opportunities in the ecosystems of modern economies.

In an extended version of this work, the technologies to be used for the implementation of the elaborated architecture, as well as the necessary policies to achieve the full operability of this proposal, should be disclosed in a more detailed manner.

References

1. On Public and Private Blockchains. Buterin, Vitalik. 2015, Ethereum
2. Casino, F., Dasaklis, T., Patsakis, C.: A systematic literature review of blockchain-based applications: current status, classification and open issues. Elsevier (2019)

3. De Filippi, P., Mannan, M., Reijers, W.: Blockchain as a confidence machine: the problem of trust & challenges of governance. Elsevier (2020)
4. Cordero Valdavida, M.: Blockchain in public sector, an international view. Azterlanak, p. 19 (2019)
5. Sánchez, P., Alberto, J.: Blockchain y contratos inteligentes: aproximación a sus problemáticas y retos jurídicos. Revista de Derecho Privado, Bogotá (2020)
6. Mannan, M., Reijers, W.: Blockchain as a confidence machine: the problem of trust & challenges of governance. Technology of Society, p. 14 (2020)
7. Lakshimi Siva, S., Sindhu, M., Sethumadhavan, M.: Survey of Consensus Protocols on Blockchain Applications. In: International Conference on Advanced Computing and Communication Systems, p. 5 (2017)
8. Garay, J.A., Kiayias, A., Leonardos, N.: The Bitcoin Backbone Protocol: Analysis and Applications. In: Conference Paper, p. 45 (2015)
9. Yahari Navarro, B.: Blockchain y sus aplicaciones, p. 19 (2019)
10. Ramírez, V., Pablo, J.: Smart Contracts. RITI J. **7**, 10 (2019)
11. Blockchain y gobierno digital. Preisegger, Juan Santiago, y otros. 2019, XXV Congreso Argentino de Ciencias de la Computación, p. 11 (2019)
12. Castillo, F., Antonio, V.: El blockchain y los contratos inteligentes; una forma de reducir la corrupción. In: Serie Científica de la Universidad de las Ciencias Informáticas, p. 10 (2021)
13. Schuschny, A.: La Blockchain y sus posibles aplicaciones en el ámbito de la energía. enerLAC, p. 23 (2017)
14. Ballesteros, M., María, A.: BLOCKU - una aproximación a la certificación, trazabilidad y transmisión de valor en la educación superior. ACADEMIA Accelerating the world's research., p. 14 (2019)
15. Eterovic, J., otros.: Seguridad en Internet de las Cosas usando soluciones Blockchain. SEDICI; Repositorio Institucional de la UNLP. [En línea] (2020). http://sedici.unlp.edu.ar/handle/10915/104030
16. García Mateo, P.: Blockchain aplicado al sector público. Valencia: Escola Técnica Superior d'Enginyeria Informática (2018)
17. Singhal, B., Dhameja, G., Sekhar Panda, P.: Beginning Blockchain: A Beginner's Guide to Building Blockchain Solutions. Apress, Berlín (2018)
18. Open JS Foundation. NODE JS. [En línea] [Citado el: 8 de Julio de 2021]. https://nodejs.org/es/about/
19. Truffle Suite. Truffle Suite. [En línea] 2021. [Citado el: 8 de Julio de 2021]. https://www.trufflesuite.com/ganache

An Overview of Optimization Models and Technological Trends of Logistics in the Retail Sector

Juan Llivisaca[1]([✉]) [iD], Diana Jadan-Avilés[1] [iD], Rodrigo Guamán[1] [iD],
Rodrigo Arcentales-Carrion[2] [iD], Mario Peña[1,3] [iD], and Lorena Siguenza-Guzman[4,5] [iD]

[1] Department of Applied Chemistry and Systems of Production, Faculty of Chemical Sciences,
University of Cuenca, 010107 Cuenca, Ecuador
{juan.llivisaca,diana.jadan,rodrigo.guaman,
mario.penao}@ucuenca.edu.ec

[2] Research Group in Accounting, Finance, and Taxation, Faculty of Economic and
Administrative Sciences, University of Cuenca, 010107 Cuenca, Ecuador
rodrigo.arcentales@ucuenca.edu.ec

[3] Research Department (DIUC), University of Cuenca, 010107 Cuenca, Ecuador

[4] Department of Computer Sciences, Faculty of Engineering, University of Cuenca, 010107
Cuenca, Ecuador
lorena.siguenza@ucuenca.edu.ec

[5] Research Centre Accountancy, Faculty of Economics and Business, KU Leuven, Leuven,
Belgium

Abstract. Recently, the e-commerce market has grown rapidly. For example, e-commerce generated sales of USD 504 billion in the US from January 1, 2020, to July 1, 2020, representing an increase of 11.58% over the same period in 2019. This growth has forced the retail industry has had to adopt strategies to become more efficient. About 40% of many companies 'available time is devoted to logistics. Because these activities are consuming a disproportionate share of many companies' time, logistics is a prime topic of interest. In this context, this study aims to present an overview of optimization models and technological trends in logistics in the retail sector. Findings show that retail logistics has focused on reducing costs, time usage, and inventories while increasing transport capacity. Optimization in logistics has focused on using mathematical algorithms such as genetic algorithms with different variants, and simulation has supported testing optimization proposals. Finally, big data, omnichannel, and e-commerce continue to grow, especially in the retail sector where it has grown considerably.

Keywords: Logistics · Retail · Technological trends · Optimization models

© Springer Nature Switzerland AG 2022
M. Botto-Tobar et al. (Eds.): ICAT 2021, CCIS 1535, pp. 484–496, 2022.
https://doi.org/10.1007/978-3-031-03884-6_35

1 Introduction

A supply chain (SC) consists of several interacting entities whose objective is to meet customer requirements satisfactorily and in the shortest possible time.

Within SC, the retail sector is of particular interest, due to its growth potential and because this business model provides a direct interaction between the producer and end customers [1]. In the last months of 2019 and early 2020, retail trade changed in many countries. For instance, there was an unprecedented drop in April and a strong rebound in May in the US, due to the pandemic caused by SARS-CoV-2, with products such as clothing, footwear, and food, generating the largest amount of revenue, i.e., USD 537.52 billion [2]. This shows that the retail sector is very volatile and that it can be greatly affected by external variables. Traditionally, retail has fallen into only two categories, physical and virtual. In any case, handling hundreds or thousands of products is one of the retail sector's main challenges, and distribution is its complement [1].

Within the SC of retail, logistics has become a topic of interest since it not only represents a performance metric but is also a strategic factor that directly involves the customer. Logistics includes production, execution, transportation, and the provision of services and products to customers [3]. Balanced management of these parts implies reviewing different work models, information technologies, and management indicators. There is significant interest in how retail companies can better set up logistics to provide more agile and frequent services. Unfortunately, this process requires a strong investment in information technology, logistics facilities, supplier management, or third-party logistics [4]. Thus, the relationship between logistics and information processing is common. Klein et al. [5] and Rokkan et al. [6] suggest that retail businesses should aim to build stable relationships between these two issues, which guarantees better service for customers.

Technological advances in the retail sector have meant a paradigm change for brick-and-mortar stores, whereas the customer previously could only choose from the products physically displayed. Nowadays, a variety of products are offered, and more are marketed through e-commerce. Technologies such as Big Data, Internet of Things (IoT), Internet of Infrastructure (IoI), Industrial IoT (IIoT), Artificial Intelligence (AI), and RFID, have been increasingly used in Supply Chain Management (SCM) systems because they allow the development and control of business processes from the company to the customer. For instance, big data is a broad term for large or complex datasets where traditional data processing technologies are inadequate. Among the benefits of big data are reducing the cost and time to analyze large volumes of information, making decisions based on data, and personalizing offers for different consumers [7]. Likewise, IoT benefits companies in fields such as logistics, improving operations [8]. Mengru [9] considers that technology has a positive influence on perceived benefits in an industry, but some uncertainties reduce trust and lead to lower perceived benefits from IoT. In this context, from an evolutionary perspective, every retail business has several options for technological improvement and different optimization models; therefore, retailers must rethink their competitive strategies and their SC must evolve to keep pace with demanding consumers.

The previous paragraphs show that logistics is important for retail companies. While technological advances in logistics have been using various tools. Thus, this study aims to provide an overview of technological trends of logistics and optimization models in retail. To achieve this objective, a systematic literature review based on recent years has been planned, which allows answering key research questions. Atlas.ti (version 8.4.25.0) program was used to perform this systematic review. The research contributes to being a guide to know the main technological trends and the mathematical models used for logistics in retail companies. The remainder of the paper is organized as follows. The methodology section describes the steps followed for the systematic review. The results and discussion section synthesizes recent relevant discussions of optimization models and technological trends of logistics in retail. Finally, the conclusion section includes a summary and final remarks of the research.

2 Methodology

This study followed the methodology proposed by Fink [10]. This methodology has been widely used to carry out systematic reviews on topics related to different areas such as manufacturing, accounting, industrial costs, and retail. Fink's methodology consists of seven steps. In the first step, two research questions were selected: *What are the main technological trends in logistics applied to retail?* and *What are the main optimization models in logistics utilized in retail?*. These questions aim to clarify the main uses of retail, identify technology used in logistics, and classify optimization models applied in this sector. Additionally, to identify keywords and suitable search strings, the Population, Intervention, Comparison, and Outcomes (PICO) framework was used [11, 12]. For this study, "Population" refers to logistics in retail stores. "Intervention" denotes technological trends and optimization models applied to retail stores. "Comparison" refers to identifying the main uses of retail logistics concerning optimization and technology trends. And, finally, "Outcomes" refers to the main consequences of applying technological trends and optimization models in the logistics process of retail.

The second step was selecting adequate databases to perform the bibliographic study. Four databases were selected: Scopus, Taylor & Francis, Emerald, and Science Direct. These databases cover a wide range of disciplines and contain the highest number of related studies. In the third step, keywords were established to represent concepts related to the topic discussed. Combining the terms Retail, Logistic, Technological trends, Optimization, Model, and Small and Medium-sized Enterprises (SMEs) helped to search for relevant articles.

For the fourth step, exclusion criteria such as Language were applied, with English being the selected language since most of the technological advances and optimization models are written in this language. Likewise, the date range for the publication of articles was five years (2015–2019), since technology changes rapidly. Finally, the last exclusion criteria were that only scientific articles were chosen. In the fifth step, the articles referring to management and engineering have been selected. The preliminary results of the records retrieved after applying the mentioned criteria are presented in Table 1.

Table 1. Search results after applying the exclusion criteria.

Base	Query	Results
Emerald	Retail AND (Logistic OR Logistic 4.0) AND (Optimization OR Model OR SMEs)	65
Science Direct	Retail AND (Logistic OR Logistic 4.0) AND (Optimization OR Model OR SMEs)	44
Taylor & Francis	Retail AND (Logistic OR Logistic 4.0) AND (Optimization OR Model OR SMEs)	34
Scopus	Retail AND (Logistic OR Logistic 4.0) AND (Optimization OR Model OR SMEs)	51

As a result of this bibliographic review, a total of 194 articles were first obtained. Next, an exhaustive analysis was carried out. First, repeated articles were eliminated from each database. The different abstracts and the results obtained by the different authors of these articles were reviewed. The articles were then classified and thoroughly analyzed to make the resulting literature potentially relevant to answering the research questions. In the sixth step, the final articles were retrieved for review. As a result, 77 articles were obtained, which can be seen in more detail in Table 2. Atlas.ti (version 8.4.25.0) was used in this step to systematically discover and analyze hidden phenomena in unstructured data, by coding and labeling findings in the bibliographic material. In this manner, a set of six general codes and 13 specific codes were created focusing on answering the research questions. In the last step, the main findings were summarized in two manners, a meta-analysis, and a descriptive analysis. The codes and the articles utilized can be seen in Appendix A.

Table 2. Results of the documents retrieved and analyzed.

Base	Query	Results
Emerald	Retail AND (Logistic OR Logistic 4.0) AND (Optimization OR Model OR SMEs)	28
Science Direct	Retail AND (Logistic OR Logistic 4.0) AND (Optimization OR Model OR SMEs)	19
Taylor & Francis	Retail AND (Logistic OR Logistic 4.0) AND (Optimization OR Model OR SMEs)	6
Scopus	Retail AND (Logistic OR Logistic 4.0) AND (Optimization OR Model OR SMEs)	24

Finally, 77 documents were analyzed in detail.

3   Results and Discussion

In the previous section, the six steps of the Fink methodology [10] were explained. In this section, details of the findings are given, corresponding to the last step of the methodology. Results are reported and discussed from a meta-analysis perspective and a descriptive review.

3.1   Meta-analysis

Figure 1 shows the articles by year. Over the last five years, it is evident how the subject of retail is growing and has been the subject of research, except for 2017, when a small decrease can be observed.

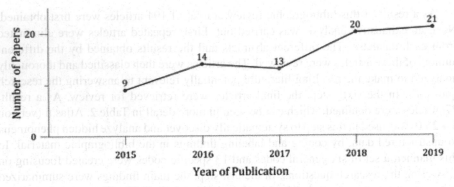

Fig. 1. Evolution of the number of articles per year.

Regarding principal journals where the topic studied has been published, Fig. 2 presents the top five journals, containing the highest number of research articles. Articles related to optimization models and the technological trends of logistics in the retail sector are distributed across 53 journals. These findings indicate that scientific contributions in this research area are scattered across a wide range of journals. The top five journals containing the highest number of research articles represent about 35% (27 out of 77 articles) of the total number of articles published. They are the International Journal of Physical Distribution & Logistics Management (IJPDLM), International Journal of Retail & Distribution Management (IJRDM), Benchmarking: An International Journal (BIJ), International Journal of Production Research (IJPR), and Transportation Research Procedia (TRP).

Finally, Fig. 3 shows the main countries that contribute to the subject. China is the country with the most publications (12 out of 77), followed by Germany and India, which tied for second with seven articles each. In third place is Poland with five articles, followed by Italy and the United States, with 4 articles each. As in the top five journals, the findings indicate that scientific contributions in this research area are also scattered across several countries.

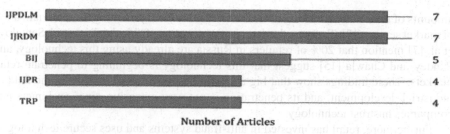

Fig. 2. Distribution of articles in the top five journals.

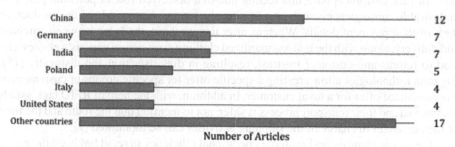

Fig. 3. Distribution of articles by country of implementation.

3.2 Descriptive Review

To account for the results obtained from the systematic literature review, answers to the research questions are presented below.

Technological Trends in Retail. Concerning the research question *What are the main technological trends in logistics applied to retail?*, technology is constantly changing and adapting to new requirements of companies, customers, and stakeholders. Among these advances, the findings mention developments in technologies such as wireless 4G, Fiber to the x (FTTX), IoT, mobile computing, cloud computing, and big data. These technologies enable the development of new management models and provide solid bases for decision-making in operations systems [13]. Technological trends have opened great opportunities for the retail sector because they provide a competitive advantage over other markets. Thus, various strategies have been used in retail to improve its competitive power by taking advantage of developments in technology. Examples of this include predictive analytics, logistics automation, anti-fraud systems, personalized payment systems (self-service in the cash area).

Progress over the last two decades, with the advent of the Internet both in private homes and in almost all businesses [14], as well as, with the rapid development of the online retail industry (e-commerce), has required that clients' orders be fulfilled within narrow time windows. In this context, order picking, the activity that requires the most time and labor in warehouses, plays an important role.

Some innovations in retail are based on "big data" systems that allow large amounts of information to be processed using intellectual analysis, prediction, and optimization tools. Using big data systems significantly reduces the cost and time of analyzing large amounts of information, making decisions in realtime, and providing the materialization of market services [7]. To assess the degree of penetration of "big data" in retail, Santalova et al. [7] mention that 20% of retailers in Russia are already using this technology, and Pandey and Chawla [15] suggest that this technology is beginning to penetrate retail markets. These findings show that big data still has much room to grow in the field of industrial development, and its penetration is not very extensive, since customers and companies mistrust technology.

Furthermore, retail has invested in anti-fraud systems and uses secure technologies for online payments to reduce customers suspicions during and after the purchase process. In fact, customers have this feeling due to a perceived risk of potential purchase undesirable consequences, such as receiving the wrong size or style of the product, or theft of their payment details. Whereas after the purchase, the lapse between purchase and delivery, along with the non-standardized clothing sizes across various websites, can lead to returns and customer mistrust, resulting in dissatisfaction and disloyalty [15]. Big data technologies allow creating a specific offer for specific groups of customers or a personalized offer for a loyal customer. In addition, with the help of RFID tags, goods are tracked and their transport process is safer, not to mention that the route and the time of the personnel in charge of the shipping activities can be monitored [7].

One way to improve and promote operational efficiency in retail has been the use of IoT or IIoT as they help collect information on site in real time. Although the overhead of IoT hardware requires considerable investment, and scalability becomes a challenge, many companies are still hesitant and are conservative towards applying IoT in SCM [9]. For many customers, technological infrastructure remains inadequate, leading to issues such as increased Internet security, privacy fears, and lower bandwidth, which can reduce online shopper satisfaction and loyalty [15].

Distribution channels present other opportunities for modernization. Although companies are cautious because investing in technology requires big investment and customization to suit company strategy, from an evolutionary perspective, where the boundary between physical and online retail increasingly blurs and consumers become more demanding, retailers must rethink their competitive strategies by considering technology. Therefore, omnichannel distribution can be seen as the natural and logical evolution of multichannel distribution. Multichannel distribution was born of the need to satisfy customer demands through multiple distinct distribution channels. These channels were determined mainly by customers' purchase methods and fulfillment preferences [16]. Omnichannel in retail is becoming increasingly popular [7]. This strategy, when integrated with IoT technology, brings many advantages to companies.

From a logistics perspective, a distinction must be made between three basic channel strategies. The first strategy is a single channel logistics approach wherein retailers operate only one sales channel with a dedicated logistics system for this channel. The second strategy is the basic multi-channel logistics approach. Here, retailers operate multiple channels, but with segregated units, creating independent systems for operations and logistics. In this strategy, processes are not integrated from the customer's perspective and there is no operational or logistics interface between channels. Retailers initially began to develop multi-channel (MC) systems to meet additional challenges posed by e-commerce success [17]. The third strategy is an advanced omnichannel (OC) logistics strategy with a common logistics interface for the customer and the company. In this strategy, information exchange, joint operations, logistics, and inventories moving through the channels allow combining the compliance processes [18]. In an OC system, customers can move seamlessly from one channel to another [17]. These strategies are differentiated by Hübner et al. [18].

Furthermore, omnichannel has been presented as a viable option for the growing online market (e-commerce). E-commerce is a useful strategy to offer the customer a valued proposition, while also improving operational efficiency. Therefore, literature is focusing on online retail, which aims to provide customers with greater product variety, quicker access to shopping, and heightened security. However, e-commerce has raised the question of who will establish the online channel to meet customer demands. Whoever implements this strategy could benefit by attracting customers who make purchases online every day [17].

Thus, each time a transaction takes place from multichannel to omnichannel, some aspects can be differentiated at different stages of the process, such as inventory, picking assortment, delivery, return, organization, and IT systems [18]. MC retailers have channel-*separated inventory*, while OC retailers manage integrated inventory into a warehousing solution. MC retailers pick separately by channel, while in the more developed OC phase, process improvement methods are applied in cross-channel *picking*. Retailers offer a limited set of Stock-Keeping Units (SKUs) online in a basic MC approach and move towards a more extensive assortment online than offline. In the MC approach, retailers exclusively offer postal delivery for distance orders, while in the OC model, *delivery* options are expanded by integrating processes to include *pickup* services. At MC retailers, customers can only *return* products purchased online through the postal service; whereas, in an advanced OC concept, the return of the merchandise is not coupled to the channel where it was purchased. The MC model, where the operational responsibility of channels is separated, will finally move toward a single integrated OC *logistics organization* up to the cross-channel coordination. Eventually, MC retailers have separate, channel specific Enterprise Resource Planning (ERP) *systems*, while advanced OC solutions rely on a joint, cross-channel ERP system with real-time access.

When it comes to omnichannel, many retailers base their activities on integrated information systems (IIS). Today, there is a range of more or less specialized IISs, such as ERP, Warehouse Management System (WMS), Warehouse Control System (WCS), Warehouse Execution System (WES), and Distributed Order Management (DOM) used in isolation or integrated through an electronic data interface (EDI). Many of these IISs were originally quite specialized, but over time systems have added functionality, blurring their boundaries [19]. For example, an ERP system with a WMS module or a WCS is used to coordinate information in warehouse operations. The system controls inputs and outputs, tracks inventory, and enables staffing and tracking of orders and products throughout the warehouse. WMS has modernized the traditional warehouse by integrating information for greater efficiency and effectiveness. Developed countries have taken a big step with these advances. To improve efficiency in ware-houses, they include activities such as product consolidation, picking, and package division. For these activities, some electronic management systems have been managed, such as Machine-to-Machine

Technology (M2M), which optimizes order fulfillment, pick-to-light systems, and put-to-light systems, in addition to helping to monitor and streamline all aspects of automated warehouse operations. WES is an intermediate step between an ERP and a WMS and has been used in warehousing systems with considerable communication challenges. To integrate this communication, many WES use autonomous mobile robots, making up what is known as a smart warehouse. To demonstrate this fact, a current case study by Bolu and Korçak [20] is worth mentioning. This case study demonstrated that generated tasks can be assigned to robots with the use of a novel task conversion algorithm, taking into consideration the dynamics of the system such as the robots' locations, their use, loading, and route planning.

Optimization Models in Retail. Concerning the research question *What are the main optimization models in logistics utilized in retail?*, optimization methods have been used in areas such as mathematics and computing. However, in industry, these advances have stayed at the proposal stage. Few retail compa nies have bet on the benefits of optimization, and these few initiatives have been driven by competition. Indeed, retail stores often seek to be more competitive. This has led many stores to develop their own optimization models, seeking to achieve several efficiency based objectives, including upgrading response capacity, improving customer service, decreasing response times, and lowering costs [21]. Today, these models and algorithms are integrated and increasingly complex, given the needs and growth of retail stores [22]. According to Liang and Lv [23], retail stores have grown exponentially at a competitive level; optimization helps stores gain a competitive advantage.

Mathematical logistic models applied to retail stores can be categorized into two large branches: mathematical collection models and delivery process models. Each has its own restrictions [24]. In the former, Eren Akyol and De Koster [25] investigate how the time window restrictions of a city affect stores in neighboring cities, including deliveries made in different cities during a single trip. Avci [26] investigates problems related to transshipment, expedited shipping, and disruptions of these shipments, and also relates these problems to strategic decisions that are affected by supply, level of flexibility, and level of risk. It should be noted that in this study the mathematical model takes into account retail order parameters where the general performance of the system is determined, focusing on an average cost performance measure of the SC. Y. Wang et al. [22] study the efficiency of optimization, considering the problem of vehicle routing in two level reverse logistics networks, where a two objective mathematical optimization model is established to minimize the total cost and the number of vehicles. The authors used genetic classification algorithms. Wong et al. [27] complemented their routing studies considering the effectiveness of product replenishment and the responsiveness of customer service delivery. These variables have a significant impact on customer retention in the logistics distribution of the retail chain. The model proposed assesses the distribution in n-retail and the significant factors that affect decisions about route distribution. Liang and Lv [23] studied distribution costs and competitiveness in the retail market. The authors adopted a QEA (Quantum Evolution Algorithm) model since it is a modern heuristic algorithm based on the concepts of quantum computing and absorbs the characteristics of quantum superposition, quantum entanglement, and quantum coherence. This algorithm was chosen because of the complexity of logistics routing, and in many cases, feasible solutions cannot be found. Liang and Lv mathematically modeled logistics routes and then established parameters with the QEA algorithm, trying to identify an optimal solution. Their findings indicate that by applying the mathematical model the number of trucks is smaller and the distance traveled by these trucks is shorter.

As for logistics delivery process models in retail stores, researchers have presented various optimization models, all of them linked to the cross-docking strategy. Cross-docking is a kind of order preparation that reduces inventory, preparation, and picking in distribution warehouses. In addition, cross-docking can minimize or eliminate order preparation and warehousing activity [28]. Crossdocking can have positive or negative affects resulting from reducing the lack of stock in retail stores. Also, cross-docking requires more labor, space, and equipment to handle the product [29]. Yu et al. [24] propose a model for the delivery problem by using open vehicles in cross-docking environments, which have an open flow network in the direction of the customer and the company, and vice-versa. This network works well in retail stores that do not have a fleet of vehicles to deliver products to their customers. Therefore, each retailer outsources the logistics service. In addition, in the delivery of products, multimodal transport has been considered a strategy that many companies use. Mathematical models like [30] mention that when there are intensive distribution channels, retail will benefit from implementing multimodal models [18]. It is even possible to have personalized prices, which would discourage the manufacturer from selling directly or directing its sale to final consumers. However, this activity should be cautious since, as Lu and Liu [31] indicate, the manufacturer may suffer losses when selling in a dual channel distribution structure if the efficiency of the online channel is low. Although cross-docking has contributed to improving logistics performance in retail stores, it should be considered that this benefit is achieved when it has the necessary infrastructure, as well as, effective communication among suppliers, warehouse workers, transporters, and customers.

4 Conclusions

Logistics has become a topic of interest due to its impact within a supply chain. The objective of this research was to investigate technological trends and optimization models in logistics for the retail sector. Among technological trends used in logistics, several technologies have been considered, such as big data, e-commerce, and omnichannel. Big data has contributed to ERP, WMS, WCS systems; however, new paradigms have emerged in the use of big data in these systems due to scalability and cost. Technological trends used are constantly updating, and it is a good practice to review them permanently. However, in companies, technology that contributes to make activities easier and that demonstrates results is the one that is used the most. This fact is relevant in SMEs.

On the other hand, after ordering goods, consumers want them to be delivered as soon as possible. For this, optimization in logistics is crucial. Some researches have used mathematical optimization with algorithms. Findings indicate that the objectives established in optimization have aimed to reduce travel times, costs, capacity, number of vehicles, and inventory levels.

Likewise, retail sector has faced new challenges. For example, when it comes to comestibles, demand is constantly growing, and home deliveries are more frequent. Although this seems beneficial, the demand could not be meet since the purchase of raw materials had problems and cash flow issues added more challenges. The research was focused on the years 2015 to 2019.

During this time, the evolution of logistics optimization showed normal results, under established conditions. However, in 2020, due to the global pandemic caused by SARS-CoV-2, these conditions changed. Optimization variables are believed to behaved as before, including consumption trends and demand for shipments. Therefore, it would be very interesting to address changes in many variables during last months, to understand the impact of the pandemic on logistics trends.

Acknowledgments. This study is part of the research project "Modelo de optimizacíon para la gestión de diseño, inventarios y logística de las tiendas en el sector minorista (retail) del Azuay", supported by the Research Department of the University of Cuenca (DIUC). The project participants are especially grateful to Mr. Pablo Andrés Mendéz Tacuri and Mr. William Mauricio Campoverde Bermeo, who contributed to the initial phase of this article and showed commitment and responsibility during the information acquisition phase.

Appendix A – Full List of Codes and References Utilized in the Literature Review

The list of codes in Atlas.ti and sources used in the literature review can be found online at https://imagineresearch.org/wp-content/uploads/2021/06/Opt-Appendix-A%E2%80%93References.pdf.

References

1. Gawankar, S.A., Kamble, S., Raut, R.: An investigation of the relationship between supply chain management practices (SCMP) on supply chain performance measurement (SCPM) of Indian retail chain using SEM. Benchmarking Int. J. **24**, 257–295 (2017). https://doi.org/10.1108/BIJ-12-2015-0123
2. Richter, F.: U.S. Retail Sales Return to Pre-Pandemic Levels. https://www.statista.com/chart/21760/monthly-retail-sales-in-the-united-states/
3. Gerini, C., Sciomachen, A.: Evaluation of the flow of goods at a warehouse logistic department by Petri Nets. Flex. Serv. Manuf. J. **31**(2), 354–380 (2018). https://doi.org/10.1007/s10696-018-9312-3
4. Rindt, J., Mouzas, S.: Exercising power in asymmetric relationships: the use of private rules. Ind. Mark. Manag. **48**, 202–213 (2015). https://doi.org/10.1016/j.indmarman.2015.03.018
5. Klein, R., Rai, A., Straub, D.W.: Competitive and cooperative positioning in supply chain logistics relationships*. Decis. Sci. **38**, 611–646 (2007). https://doi.org/10.1111/j.1540-5915.2007.00172.x
6. Rokkan, A.I., Haugland, S.A.: Developing relational exchange: Effectiveness and power. Eur. J. Mark. **36**, 211–230 (2002). https://doi.org/10.1108/03090560210412764

7. Santalova, M.S., Lesnikova, E.P., Kustov, A.I., Balahanova, D.K., Nechaeva, S.N.: Digital technology in retail: reasons and trends of development. In: Popkova, E.G. (ed.) Ubiquitous Computing and the Internet of Things: Prerequisites for the Development of ICT, pp. 1071–1080. Springer, Cham (2019)
8. Grawe, S.J.: Logistics innovation: a literature-based conceptual framework. Int. J. Logist. Manag. 20, 360–377 (2009). https://doi.org/10.1108/09574090911002823
9. Tu, M.: An exploratory study of Internet of Things (IoT) adoption intention in logistics and supply chain management. Int. J. Logist. Manag. 29, 131–151 (2018). Doi.https://doi.org/10.1108/IJLM-11-2016-0274
10. Fink, A.: Conducting Research Literature Reviews: From the Internet to Paper. Fourth edition. SAGE, Thousand Oaks, California (2014). ISBN: 9781544318479
11. Robinson, K.A., Saldanha, I.J., Mckoy, N.A.: Framework for Determining Research Gaps During Systematic Review: Evaluation. Methods Research Report (2011)
12. Schardt, C., Adams, M.B., Owens, T., Keitz, S., Fontelo, P.: Utilization of the PICO framework to improve searching PubMed for clinical questions. BMC Med. Inform. Decis. Mak. 7, 16 (2007). https://doi.org/10.1186/1472-6947-7-16
13. Mehmood, R., Meriton, R., Graham, G., Hennelly, P., Kumar, M.: Exploring the influence of big data on city transport operations: a Markovian approach. Int. J. Oper. Prod. Manag. 37, 75–104 (2017). https://doi.org/10.1108/IJOPM-03-2015
14. Dabidian, P., Clausen, U., Denecke, E.: An investigation of behavioural and structural characteristics of CEP service providers and freight demand considering E-commerce in Germany. Transp. Res. Procedia. 14, 2795–2804 (2016). https://doi.org/10.1016/j.trpro.2016.05.473
15. Pandey, S., Chawla, D.: Online customer experience (OCE) in clothing e-retail: Exploring OCE dimensions and their impact on satisfaction and loyalty – Does gender matter? Int. J. Retail. Distrib. Manag. 46, 323–346 (2018). https://doi.org/10.1108/IJRDM-01-2017-0005
16. Murfield, M., Boone, C.A., Rutner, P., Thomas, R.: Investigating logistics service quality in omni-channel retailing. Int. J. Phys. Distrib. Logist. Manag. 47, 263–296 (2017). https://doi.org/10.1108/IJPDLM-06-2016-0161
17. Melacini, M., Perotti, S., Rasini, M., Tappia, E.: E-fulfilment and distribution in omni-channel retailing: a systematic literature review. Int. J. Phys. Distrib. Logist. Manag. 48, 391–414 (2018). https://doi.org/10.1108/IJPDLM-02-2017-0101
18. Hu¨bner, A., Wollenburg, J., Holzapfel, A.: Retail logistics in the transition from multi-channel to omni-channel. Int. J. Phys. Distrib. Logist. Manag. 46, 562–583 (2016). https://doi.org/10.1108/IJPDLM-08-2015-0179
19. Kembro, J.H., Norrman, A., Eriksson, E.: Adapting warehouse operations and design to omni-channel logistics. Int. J. Phys. Distrib. Logist. Manag. 48, 890–912 (2018). https://doi.org/10.1108/IJPDLM-01-2017-0052
20. Bolu, A., Korçak, Ö.: Adaptive task planning for multi-robot smart warehouse. IEEE Access. 9, 27346–27358 (2021). https://doi.org/10.1109/ACCESS.2021.3058190
21. Chhetri, P., Kam, B., Hung Lau, K., Corbitt, B., Cheong, F.: Improving service responsiveness and delivery efficiency of retail networks: a case study of Melbourne. Int. J. Retail Distrib. Manag. 45, 271–291 (2017). https://doi.org/10.1108/IJRDM-07-2016-0117
22. Wang, Y., Peng, S., Assogba, K., Liu, Y., Wang, H., Xu, M., Wang, Y.: Implementation of cooperation for recycling vehicle routing optimization in two-echelon reverse logistics networks. Sustain. 10, (2018). https://doi.org/10.3390/su10051358
23. Liang, B., Lv, F.: A study on the optimization of chain supermarkets' distribution route based on the quantum-inspired evolutionary algorithm. Math. Probl. Eng. 2017 (2017). https://doi.org/10.1155/2017/7964545
24. Yu, V.F., Jewpanya, P., Redi, A.A.N.P.: Open vehicle routing problem with cross-docking. Comput. Ind. Eng. 94, 6–17 (2016). https://doi.org/10.1016/j.cie.2016.01.018

25. Akyol, D., De Koster, R.B.M.: Determining time windows in urban freight transport: a city cooperative approach. Transp. Res. Part E Logist. Transp. Rev. **118**, 34–50 (2018). https://doi.org/10.1016/j.tre.2018.07.004

26. Avci, M.G.: Lateral transshipment and expedited shipping in disruption recovery: A mean-CVaR approach. Comput. Ind. Eng. **130**, 35–49 (2019). https://doi.org/10.1016/j.cie.2019.02.013

27. Wong, E., Tai, A.H., Wei, Y., Yip, I.: Redesigning one-warehouse n-retailer routing model in inter-store stock transfer operations of an international retail chain distribution. Asia Pacific J. Mark. Logist. **30**, 536–554 (2018). https://doi.org/10.1108/APJML-06-2017-0124

28. Agustina, D., Lee, C.K.M., Piplani, R.: A review: Mathematical models for cross docking planning. Int. J. Eng. Bus. Manag. **2**, 47–54 (2010)

29. Benrqya, Y.: Costs and benefits of using cross-docking in the retail supply chain. Int. J. Retail Distrib. Manag. **47**, 412–432 (2019). https://doi.org/10.1108/IJRDM-07-2018-0119

30. Rožman, N., Vrabič, R., Corn, M., Požrl, T., Diaci, J.: Distributed logistics platform based on Blockchain and IoT. Procedia CIRP **81**, 826–831 (2019). https://doi.org/10.1016/j.procir.2019.03.207

31. Lu, Q., Liu, N.: Effects of e-commerce channel entry in a two-echelon supply chain: a comparative analysis of single- and dual-channel distribution systems. Int. J. Prod. Econ. **165**, 100–111 (2015). https://doi.org/10.1016/j.ijpe.2015.03.001

32. Author, F., Author, S.: Title of a proceedings paper. In: Editor, F., Editor, S. (eds.) CONFERENCE 2016, LNCS, vol. 9999, pp. 1–13. Springer, Heidelberg (2016). https://doi.org/10.10007/1234567890

33. Author, F., Author, S., Author, T.: Book title. 2nd edn. Publisher, Location (1999)

34. Author, A.-B.: Contribution title. In: 9th International Proceedings on Proceedings, pp. 1–2. Publisher, Location (2010)

35. LNCS Homepage. http://www.springer.com/lncs. Accessed 4 Oct 2017

Internet of Things as Support of Quality of Life from People with Mobility Disorders

Lorena Valdespino Suárez and Gustavo Gutiérrez-Carreón

Universidad Michoacana de San Nicolás de Hidalgo, Av. Francisco J. Múgica S/N Morelia, Michoacán, México
gagutc@umich.mx

Abstract. There is a considerable percentage of the world population that cannot move from one place to another due to a physical disability, but thanks to research and advancement in technology, this may change. In this work, an alternative solution based on the Internet of Things (IoT) is proposed as one of the tools to improve mobility and independence in a social interest housing. An analysis of the state of the art of current IoT home instruments and devices is presented. Our analyses make an important contribution to the literature by suggesting a proposal and its respective budget based on IoT-developed thinking on the mobility and safety of the user and for improving the quality of life of people with mobility disorders, all this from a multidisciplinary perspective.

Keywords: Internet of Things · Mobility disorders · Quality of life

1 Introduction

Due to world population growth and technological development, there are many devices connected to the internet with diverse purposes, such as entertainment, communication, education, work, domestic support, agriculture, industry, construction, medical use, among others. The Internet has provided us with global connectivity, improving and changing the way people communicate and interact with each other. Internet of Things (IoT) has brought this connectivity even closer in addition to facilitating human activities.

Every day, we need to move from one place to another. However, this is not the case for everyone, since, with the current lifestyle, there is a sector of the population that is lagging due to lack of mobility. The planet has a population of 7,881,319,641 inhabitants of which, according to information from the World Health Organization (WHO) [1], about 15% (more than one billion) of the population has some type of disability, which is a figure that exceeds the total population of any country except for China (1,445,243,562) and India (1,394,612,969). It is important to mention that this is increasing due to different causes such as chronic diseases, traffic accidents, work accidents, birth diseases, age wear and tear among others. Some of them temporarily (fractures) and others permanently (Fig. 1).

M. Botto-Tobar et al. (Eds.): ICAT 2021, CCIS 1535, pp. 497–508, 2022.
https://doi.org/10.1007/978-3-031-03884-6_36

This group can be divided into people with mobility, vision, hearing, mental, speech, and attention deficit disabilities. Being the mobility in which the project is focused.

According to the Instituto Nacional de Estadística y Geografía (INEGI) [2], Mexico is the tenth most populous country in the world and its population represents 1.65% of the world's total population with 126,014,024 (130,393,032) inhabitants of which 7,700,000 are disabled and 58.3% have problems of reduced mobility according to data provided in the last population census of the country.

People with reduced mobility are excluded due to lack of mobility and displacement, with inadequate quality of life, becoming dependent on the people they live with, as well as limited in the use of public spaces, since most of them are not designed or adapted to their physical conditions, generating discrimination in addition to violations of their human rights, separated from society and being underestimated.

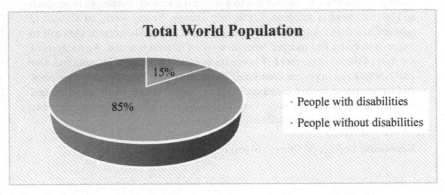

Fig. 1. Total population vs people with physical disabilities

It is intended to provide a solution through IoT, which assists people with reduced mobility to improve their quality of life and have a greater degree of independence. Creating higher expectations and inclusion with their environment, facilitating daily activities, reducing the problems they face, promoting social and family interaction, among others. Creating spaces that integrate them into the society of which they are part, having easy access to any space increases the independence of people with reduced mobility.

In the remainder of this paper, we first present material related to mobility disorders Subsequently, we present a conceptual model based on IoT. Lastly, we present and discuss the results, and we draw conclusions and future work.

2   Material and Method

To develop in a more efficient, complete, and comprehensive way the proposal to improve the quality of life of people with mobility disorders, it is important to mention material of several sciences which are a fundamental part of the proposal. Medicine focused on the study of anatomy and mobility pathologies, Architecture in terms of the study of the anthropometry of users and spaces, and IoT is the one that acquires the greatest importance within the proposal since it integrates the solution to the problem.

Our body is a complex machine that is impossible to know without having to divide it into systems for study [3]. The only mention is made in a general way of the organs and systems that intervene for the functioning or that cause the movement of our body.

One of the systems that help us to move in addition to supporting us and protecting our organs is the Bone System, which is made up of 206 bones in adults. Providing between the unions of each of them articular elements, thus giving our posture.

The muscular system is composed of 639 parts called muscles which are divided into tissues, tendons, and fibers, these have the ability or property of contraction and tension under electrical or nervous impulses. Located throughout the body supported by different bones, they are responsible for each of our movements.

The nervous system is made up of a network of nerves and cells that carry information from the brain to any part of the body. This is in turn divided into:

- Central Nervous System.
- Peripheral nervous system.

This system is the one that makes nerve impulses reach any part of the body through the nerve terminals, they are sent from one of the most important organs that is the brain.

For the study of an organ as complex and important as the brain, it has been divided into the frontal, temporal, parietal, occipital, right, and left lobes, as well as the cerebellum and the brain stem. According to the part of the brain that is working, it is the part of the body that works or moves.

There are different types of movements in our tissues such as agonic movements which are contractions and antagonistic movements which prevent movement. By combining these movements in the different muscles, different types of movements are generated which are:

- Flexion.
- Extension.
- Lateral tilt.
- Rotation
- Circulation

The stop of some type of movement leaves the person with a disability that is sometimes temporary and, other times permanently [4].

Different types of disorders and pathologies can paralyze our body in different ways and at other times involuntary movements without purpose.

Some of these diseases and what they cause are:

- Parkinson: This is a degenerative disease, it causes stiffness in different parts of the body, involuntary tremors, bradycardia (the heart beats slower), hypomnesia (decreased body movements).
- Dystonia: They are involuntary sustained muscle contractions, repetitive movements, twisting or abnormal postures, head twisting in addition to rapid blinking.

- Tremors: involuntary and random movements can be oscillatory, muscle contractions.
- Tic: these are short arrhythmic unexpected rapid movements.
- Restless legs syndrome: it is a neurological disorder related to hysteria; this is reflected with the need to move the legs to achieve relief.
- Cerebral palsy: this can be caused by irreparable injuries to the brain, affecting motor capacity as information cannot be reached through nerve signals to that part of the body.
- Hemiplegia, monoplegia, triplegia, diplegia, paraplegia, quadriplegia, hemianesthesia: These are paralysis in both the lower and upper extremities in different combinations such as one, two, three, or all four extremities.

Related to Architecture, in terms of anthropometry [5], there are construction standards for all types of building according to the type of construction that ranges from buildings, hospitals, offices, and residential type houses.

Knowing the proportions and special needs of people helps to improve the mobility and use of spaces, considering that people have different sizes and capabilities, therefore, what is designed for one person will not always work for others (Fig. 2). So, it is important to mention that efficient buildings for people without mobility problems will not work for a person with reduced mobility. That is why anthropometry studies the minimum measurements of any space to provide comfort adjusting to the needs of the user.

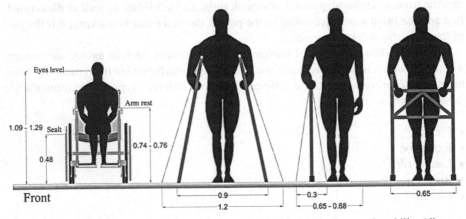

Fig. 2. Types of supports and anthropometry for the disabled with decreased mobility (distance in meters).

IoT is based on the principle of connecting objects to the Internet and improving them through applications [5] collecting and monitoring the information obtained and requested. Its predecessor is telemetry, installed in meteorological information devices on Mont Blanc, through a short-wave radio link with the receiver being in Paris, however, this IoT technology was not fully developed until the boom of the wireless connection.

IoT in medicine and health is not something new [6]. It began in the 90s, taking this stage as the first wave in which, it developed on the internet and communication, in 2000 it is considered the second wave in which mobility is taken as the most outstanding characteristic and finally the third. This is the current wave in which it is about personalizing the care provided by the health sector.

IoT in this area aims to provide solutions to shorten distances, remove barriers, improve service provision. All through the different types of devices connected to the network through applications.

Different types of devices make life easier for people with reduced mobility [7]. Using the technology applied in digital medicine there will be endless opportunities such as in the areas of treatments, medical procedures (surgeries), rehabilitation, patient management, among others.

The Tampa Florida Smart Home Case Study for Veterans in TBI (Brain Trauma) [8] proposes improving patient safety while solving TBI with a Cognitive prosthesis. The device provides an interactive site map through a check-in / check-out, a medication scheduling system as well as an application that provides scheduled activities.

With this, patients have a monitoring system that locates them in addition to making a record of indications, medications through multimedia devices placed on the wall.

The device used by patients is a Smartwatch, which generates vibratory, visual, and auditory warning signals based on inferred behaviors, personalized through the patient's data individually by the device. In addition, it records the behavior sequences of the patient who uses it and applies the decision rules for the correct future treatment of the patient.

This system has the functions:

- Location (GPS).
- Scheduled Reminders.
- Interactive prompts.

In addition to the Smartwatches for each patient, it has two screens located in the lobby which function as support for the check-in and check-out of the building in addition to notifying the patient if he leaves the site without registering departure since upon entering A login is recorded for him and he cannot exist without closing it. All this information generated by the patients is saved and analyzed in data mining software, allowing to carry out and detect any change in the development of the therapies carried out by the patients, thus preventing the effects (cognitive deficit) and get better treatments.

There are different devices on the market from which those used for the proposal of this work, some of them are:

- Sensors: Obtain information and give input signals to the control unit to determine the output order that is sent to an actuator, they can be by temperature, light intensity, distance, acceleration, inclination, displacement, pressure, force, torsion, humidity, PH, among others.
- Actuators: These provide the interface between the signal processing and the (mechanical) process. These can be of the electromagnetic, heater, electric motor, and an acoustic type.

- Motors: It is the machine that performs the transformation of some type of energy to mechanical energy. There are several types of engines such as internal or external combustion, direct current, or alternating current.
- Relays: Its function is that of a switch activated with electricity, it is made up of an electromagnetic coil forming a connection through the contacts using electromagnets (an electrical circuit).
- Printed circuit board: It is a table in which electronic circuits can be formed, providing users with the electrical connections they need.

The main objective of our project applied at home is to increase the independence of people with reduced mobility so that they can move without implying a problem in such a way that they will be more independent, improving their quality of life by a large percentage and mobility. As it is intended to build this system through the controller (Arduino board), the motion sensors, and this in turn to the actuators, arm, and later the door.

3 Results and Discussions

The program that is proposed (Fig. 3) must perform the opening and closing of the doors of a normal house through an application via Bluetooth. When the sensor detects a person, a process to activate the opening of the lock, and the door will open at 80 degrees according to the programming and will remain open until the end of a programmed count. At the end of the counter (timer), the door will close. If the sensor detects a person, the door will remain open, and when no object or person is detected, it will start the count for closing.

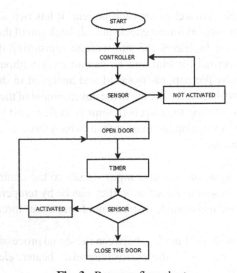

Fig. 3. Program flow chart.

Some years ago, it began to use this type of system in hotels, shops, hospitals, airports, banks, buildings, etc., where the automation of doors with hydraulic, automatic, and high-tech operators as they are known in the market today. Some brands have the interior folding door opening systems that have branches or suppliers in Mexico, Spain, and the United States, among others. Most of these systems are for hospital or commercial use, however, these can be adapted to domestic use. Some of them, with their respective costs, are:

1. PORTALP, supplier of swing gate automation, this door opening and the closing system has a return spring, 3-position open/auto/manual sectors, reset button, and signaling. Door with types of electric locks, motorized lock, electric lock, suction cup. Detection radars, opening controls with or without contact, key mode selector and mode modification console, user settings, and Low Energy function which allows slower work so that people with little mobility can enter without problems. This can be operated using a fixed control or button. The system can support a weight of 150 kg. Installable on existing doors. ($ 1,500 dollars with installation).
2. AVANS, has an electromechanical operator, ¼ hp motor, mounting on the upper part of the door, presence, and movement sensor system on both sides of the door, 3-function manual control switch, manual lock of one point. The system can support a weight of 200 kg. Installable on existing doors. ($ 1,503 dollars with installation).
3. HÖRMANN, the automatic management system via radio frequency or manually, has integrated LED lighting, partial or total door opening times from 2 to 180 s, using the opening and closing pushbutton, manual transmitter by control, on the keyring, support for manual transmitter for the walker, for mounting in the electrical box, door weight up to 125 kg. This company has the branch of automating doors for domestic use for people with reduced mobility. Adding a wide variety of controls and adaptations in controls for these people. Installable on existing doors. ($1,130 dollars with installation).

This project is applied in a social interest housing in which the necessary modifications justified by anthropometric studies are proposed, such as the minimum measurements indoors, ramp heights, elimination of steps, circulation areas, among others. Giving the correct function to each space of the one-level house, which has two bedrooms, full bathroom, living room, kitchenette, space for future growth, laundry room, garden, and garage, consists of a plot of 128 m² and 80 m² of construction. For which the plans of the house room of the current state are presented.

The diagram indicates with colors the spaces of the house where the person moves more frequently. In red color, the connections with a greater flow in which the person occupy bigger support, in blue color, the spaces with a normal flow, but that can still access with support and in green color the spaces where the person would not need support to move freely within at house (Fig. 4).

From a person with reduced mobility in a wheelchair, Fig. 5 shows the connections. In red color the areas with more flow, in blue color the areas with normal flow, and in green color, the areas with null or almost null flow.

In a social interest housing, these spaces have not been contemplated or designed for people with mobility problems, since the doors are 70, 80, or 90 cm wide, which do

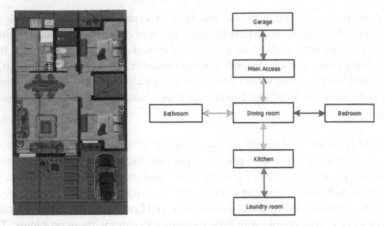

Fig. 4. Flow chart of a person with reduced mobility.

not allow free access to the different areas of the house, the bedrooms with dimensions 3.00 m on each side, limiting mobility options. The bathroom, with a door of 70 cm, can't be accessed with a wheelchair, requiring that a person with reduced mobility must be assisted by another person to access the toilet or shower.

After the analysis was carried out on the spaces that the house has. It can be concluded that a person with mobility limitations can only use a space independently since in the rest of the house they would occupy the support of one or more people to be able to carry out the different activities.

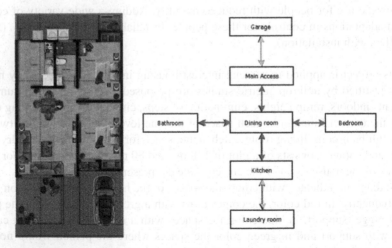

Fig. 5. Flow chart of a person with reduced mobility in a wheelchair.

According to the different pathologies, a person with reduced mobility loses his fine movements and the strength in his affected limbs, the opening or closing of a simple lock or plate. It is not only important to carry out anthropometric modifications to the house, the purpose of being able to support a person with reduced mobility to carry out a large part of their activities alone and be self-sufficient by not having to request support to enter at home or different spaces, since most have doors, and it is not so easy for them to open them.

In the modifications of the house, it begins with the masonry: the space for future growth is used to expand the bedrooms, the doors are changed in measures to 1.00 m and 90 cm for correct circulation, in the toilet a half wall is made for the placement of accessories in addition to a bench in the shower, a concrete bar to place the sink at an adequate height, the placement of a gate for the shower space and placement of metal support bars in shower areas and sanitary, in the kitchen cabinets are proposed at a height following the standards, placement of electrical installation such as boxes (registers) and gutters for the installation of automation systems for accesses, placement of wooden doors and ironwork for main access, service patio, toilet and bedrooms with an opening always towards the interior part of the space thus avoiding conflicts in the flow, installation of a computer set which will work for system configuration and future adjustments. Placement of automation system indoors and electric door handles, placement of sensors and relays.

Proposed prototype and armed with products from the market, several options can be adapted to the needs of a person with reduced mobility by coupling them with security plates such as the main door, but these are not available to the entire population. Because most of them are made for commercial uses, their costs are very high, leaving these options out of our context, however, there is the possibility (Fig. 6) of designing a system that meets all the needs of these people ($1,102.69 with installation).

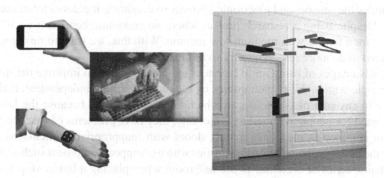

Fig. 6. Automatic door model proposal

A system is a set of components which are interacting to achieve a common goal. The systems provide information on problems as well as opportunities. These systems help to manage, collect data, process, store and distribute information processes. An information system is made up of Input, Process, Output, and Feedback (Fig. 7).

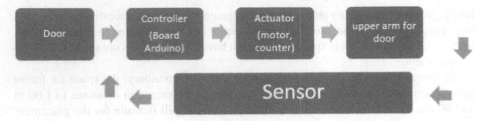

Fig. 7. System diagram.

Regarding the mechanical structure of the project, it is formed by a wooden or metal folding door, drum-type, held by hinges of high resistance metal ball bearings for wooden doors and weldable tubular hinges for metal doors, in addition to the system of automation. This will be composed of motion sensors, a Bluetooth module card for Arduino, timers, Bluetooth locker controlled through the physical key app, and security alarm, motor, and upper arm for the door with an automatic saw.

When carrying out the proposed improvements, it is observed in the flow diagram, which increased free and unsupported access, inverting the percentage of flow, now being 28.57% of the typical house to which the person with mobility does not have a constant or frequent flow decreased, but not due to the impossibility of entering these spaces but only since they are used in less quantity, achieving a better interaction with the family.

In Table 1, a complete budget for the project is shown, which includes the architectural adaptations that must be made in the house to facilitate the mobility of a person with mobility disorders, considering that it is a person you must use a wheelchair. This budget includes the sensors and electronic systems to condition the doors to an automated system. Despite being a research project where no economic benefit, it is still a very high cost for a family with medium-low income. With this, we want to raise awareness of the need to do more research to try to reduce these costs.

The advantages of using an IoT system in an access help to improve the quality of life of people with mobility pathologies by making them more independent, facilitating mobility to any part of the house, to which he concludes that because the houses are not designed for people with reduced mobility, they have problems of free access from the main entrance as they have a step, doors with inappropriate dimensions so they prevent the passage of users with disabilities who use support equipment such as walkers, wheelchairs, canes or crutches, in the bathroom when placing a buffer-stop for access to the shower limits their free access to it as in the service yard, the reduced bedrooms where there is no free access due to the dimensions of the spaces. Leaving 71.42% of the house which cannot be accessed due to different problems such as steps, inadequate dimensions, gravel, or loose soil in the gardens and closed doors, among others.

Table 1. Project budget.

No.	Name	Unit	Amount	Unit price	Total
1	Demolition of the mud partition wall	m^2	17.21	$ 3.34	**$ 57.26**
2	Partition wall, laid with 1: 4 sand cement mortar	m^2	11.32	$ 18.29	**$ 207.05**
3	Flatten with 1: 4 sand cement mortar	m^2	22.64	$ 9.12	**$ 206.38**
4	20 × 30 cm tile. seated with floor tile	m^2	1.00	$ 13.77	**$ 13.77**
5	Concrete slab f'c = 150 kg/cm^2, no. 3 @ 10 cm. 0.8 × 0.5 cm	Pcs	2.00	$ 64.50	**$ 128.99**
6	concrete ramp f'c = 150 kg/cm^2, reinforcing steel of no. 3 @ 10 cm	m^2	4.68	$ 30.75	**$ 143.93**
7	Supply and placement of kitchen furniture	Pcs	1.00	$ 195.12	**$ 195.12**
8	Supply and placement of washbasin	Pcs	1.00	$ 32.77	**$ 32.77**
9	Supply and placement of 1.00 × 1.25 mt polycarbonate eaves	Pcs	2.00	$ 125.26	**$ 250.51**
10	Supply and application of vinyl paint	m^2	22.64	$ 2.43	**$ 54.91**
11	Concrete bench f'c = 150 kg/cm^2, reinforcing steel of no. 3, finished with tile	Pcs	1.00	$ 41.41	**$ 41.41**
12	1.20 × 1.2 aluminum window	Pcs	1.00	$ 125.96	**$ 125.96**
13	Pine wood closet of 1.50 × 2.30 × 0.6 mt	Pcs	2.00	$ 280.96	**$ 561.91**
14	Electrical installation, for home remodeling	Lot	1.00	$ 296.94	**$ 296.94**
15	Concrete slab f'c = 200 kg/cm^2, with 3/8 "reinforcing steel fy = 4200kg/cm^2 of 10 cm	m^2	5.20	$ 50.04	**$ 260.23**
	Home remodeling for people with mobility disorders	**Lot**	**1.00**	**$ 2,577.13**	**$ 2,577.13**
	AUTOMATION OF INTERIOR AND EXTERNAL DOORS IN THE ROOM HOUSE				
16	Automation of exterior security doors	Pcs	5.00	$ 1,102.69	**$ 5,513.45**
	TOTAL	**Lot**	**1.00**	**$ 8,090.58**	**$ 8,090.58**

4 Conclusion

Today technology is used in many ways and is present in the lives of many people, through different objects and this is increasing every day due to IoT, for its ease of use and interaction with the user, in addition to the various objects to which this technology can be applied. Regardless of the areas to which this technology can be applied, it is intended to facilitate and expedite the work for which they have been created. Making its everyday use more and more common.

According to the WHO describes that not all countries have more detailed information on people with disabilities, therefore, to give a more specific panorama, only in

Mexico would it be supporting 58.3% (4,489,100) of the population. population with mobility disabilities according to the latest INEGI census. 190,000,000 disabled people in the world have difficulty using health services. Given these figures, technology has been involved to improve health and quality of life. Reducing costs, making them more accessible and easier to use.

Based on the results obtained and the analysis carried out, we conclude that the proposed solution can benefit to have a starting point when it comes to integrating solutions for the public, especially the large population that is affected by mobility disorders.

Being a limitation of the current work, the integration of a greater number of IoT devices, which may be of benefit to people with mobility disorders, as well as the measurement of the impact that these may have in real scenarios.

References

1. WHO Homepage. https://www.who.int/es. Accessed 9 Sep 2021
2. INEGI Homepage. https://www.inegi.org.mx/. Accessed 9 Sep 2021
3. Martini, F., et al.: Human anatomy, p. 904. Pearson/Benjamin Cummings, San Francisco, CA (2006)
4. Donaldson, I., Marsden, C.D., Schneider, S.: Marsden's book of movement disorders. Oxford University Press, Oxford (2012)
5. Norton, K., et al.: Measurement techniques in anthropometry. Anthropometric 1, 25–75 (1996)
6. Hanes, D.S.: IoT Fundamentals: Networking Technologies, Protocols, and Use Cases for the Internet of Things. Cisco Press, Indianapolis (2017)
7. Zanjal, S.V., Talmale, G.R.: Medicine reminder and monitoring system for secure health using IOT. Proc. Comput. Sci. 78, 471–476 (2016)
8. Jasiewicz, J., Kearns, W.D., Craighead, J., Fozard, J.L., Scott, S., McCarthy, J.: Smart rehabilitation for the 21st century: the Tampa smart home for veterans with traumatic brain injury. J. Rehabil. Res. Dev. vii (2011)

A Systematic Review on the Use of Ontologies in the Internet of Things

Lenin Erazo-Garzon[1]([✉]), Juan Avila[1], Sebastián Pinos[1], and Priscila Cedillo[1,2]

[1] Universidad del Azuay, Av. 24 de Mayo 7-77, Cuenca, Ecuador
lerazo@uazuay.edu.ec, {juan2412,sebaspinos8}@es.uazuay.edu.ec
[2] Universidad de Cuenca, Av. 12 de Abril, Cuenca, Ecuador
priscila.cedillo@ucuenca.edu.ec

Abstract. The Internet of Things (IoT) is a novel paradigm that has gained significant importance within the scientific community and industry. This paradigm introduces a favorable impact on people's life quality and the sustainable development of society. However, IoT systems operate in very complex and uncertain scenarios. An approach to simplify the development and maintenance of these systems is the use of ontological models due to their expressive, semantic and extensible capacity. Therefore, this study presents a systematic review to know the state of the art on the use of ontologies in the IoT domain, following Kitchenham's methodological guide. This review aims to answer the following questions: i) What are the purposes of using ontological models in IoT? ii) How are ontological models implemented in IoT? and iii) How is addressed the research in studies related to the construction of ontological models in the IoT? First, 453 primary studies were retrieved. Then, 23 relevant studies on ontological model approaches were selected due to applying the inclusion and exclusion criteria. Finally, a quality checklist was applied to the selected studies, and qualitative and quantitative methods were used to focus the presentation and discussion of the review results correctly. The results include the strengths and limitations of the approaches and research gaps, challenges, and opportunities.

Keywords: Internet of Things (IoT) · Ontology · Systematic review

1 Introduction

Nowadays, the Internet of Things (IoT) has become very popular due to the permanent interest of the scientific community and industry in interconnecting real-world objects with the support of information and communication technologies, to enable new and better applications and services in various domains (e.g., home, healthcare, transportation, industry) [1, 2]. This interconnection allows the sharing, processing and analysis of object data in real-time, and if necessary, react with minimal human intervention in the face of situations and changes in the environment [3, 4].

From this perspective, IoT systems are highly dynamic, distributed, heterogeneous, and scalable [2, 5]. Therefore, one approach for reducing its complexity is using models

© Springer Nature Switzerland AG 2022
M. Botto-Tobar et al. (Eds.): ICAT 2021, CCIS 1535, pp. 509–524, 2022.
https://doi.org/10.1007/978-3-031-03884-6_37

during the development and operation of these systems [6]. Models represent various aspects (architecture, state, behavior, context, objectives, and evolution) of an IoT system with a high degree of abstraction. In addition, they support the automation of development processes, which favors the management of the software complexity and evolution of the new generation of systems such as IoT [6].

There are several types of models for the representation of the aspects of a system, such as Key-Value Models (MCV), Markup Schema Models (MEM), Graphical Models (MG), Object-Oriented Models (MOO), Logic-Based Models (MBL), and Ontological Models. However, there is consensus among several studies [7, 8] that the use of ontologies is the most beneficial to represent complex and dynamic systems (e.g., Internet of Things) due to its expressive, semantic, and extensible capacity.

In the literature, several systematic reviews [9–12] can be found on semantic technologies in the IoT domain. However, they do not fully cover the state of technological knowledge on the use of the ontological models to represent the non-functional requirements, concepts (e.g., physical entities, digital entities), and aspects (e.g., structure, behavior, state, context) of an IoT system, as well as the methodologies, languages, and development tools used for this purpose.

Therefore, this paper presents a systematic review to know the state of the art on the use of ontologies in the IoT domain. The methodological guide proposed by Kitchenham et al. [14] has been used to this research. This review aims to answer the following questions: i) What are the purposes of using ontological models in IoT? ii) How are ontological models implemented in IoT? and iii) How is the research in studies related to the construction of ontological models addressed in the IoT? First, 453 primary studies were extracted. Then, applying inclusion and exclusion criteria, 23 relevant studies related to ontological model proposals were selected. Then, a quality assessment was applied to prioritize the presentation of results according to the relevance of each paper. Finally, qualitative and quantitative methods were used to present and discuss the results of the review, identifying the strengths and limitations of the selected proposals, as well as the gaps, challenges, and research opportunities.

The organization of this paper is as follows: Sect. 2 presents a review of secondary studies related to the subject. Section 3 describes the methodology and protocol used to carry out the systematic review. Section 4 includes the results obtained in the review, and presenting a discussion on the main gaps and challenges related to the use of ontologies in the IoT domain. Finally, Sect. 5 presents the conclusions and lines of future work.

2   Related Work

This section presents a bibliographic review and discussion of the main secondary studies (systematic literature reviews and mappings) aimed at evidencing the state of technological knowledge about the use of ontologies in the IoT domain.

Rhayem et al. [9] have carried out a study to analyze, classify, and compare Semantic Web Technologies approaches (SWT) in the IoT domain. The approaches were studied within five dimensions: IoT data, IoT data and service, IoT service, IoT security, and Web of Things (WoT). In turn, Andročec et al. [10] present a systematic review focused on primary studies that use SWT to solve IoT interoperability problems. The authors analyzed the maturity level of this research line and showed that it is an emerging research area with many interesting future research topics. Another study is the systematic mapping proposed in [11], whose purpose is to review and analyze the art state of IoT semantic interoperability, presenting as results of which Semantic Web Technologies are used and challenges present in this area of research. Finally, [12] provides a systematic review focused on analyzing the leading solutions, standards, and models to add semantic annotations to the sensor data.

Based on the bibliographic review, it can be determined that there are several systematic reviews on semantic web technologies in IoT, which mainly focus on semantic interoperability in IoT. However, these reviews do not show the state of technological knowledge about using the ontological models to represent other non-functional requirements in IoT systems (e.g., functional suitability, efficiency, usability, reliability). Furthermore, they also do not evidence the main concepts (e.g., physical entities, digital entities) and aspects (e.g., structure, behavior, state, context) of an IoT system that is modeled in existing ontologies, as well as the methodologies and semantic technologies (languages, development tools) used for this purpose. Therefore, this study aims to support researchers by filling this information gap and identifying research challenges and opportunities in this field that support future studies.

3 Research Methods

In this work, the procedures and guidelines established by Kitchenham et al. [13, 14] have been applied to guarantee a reliable, rigorous, replicable and auditable process. This procedure comprises three phases: i) planning the review, ii) conducting the review, and iii) reporting the review.

3.1 Planning the Review

Research Question. First, it was necessary to define the scope of the review. Then, the main goal and the research questions that this systematic review aims to solve were defined. The review goal is to know the state of the art on the use of ontologies in the IoT domain. In turn, the research questions to achieve the proposed goal are:

RQ1. What are the purposes of using ontological models in IoT?
RQ2. How are ontological models implemented in IoT?
RQ3. How is addressed the research in studies related to the construction of ontological models in the IoT?

Data Sources and Search Strategy. The digital libraries used to search the primary studies were: IEEE Xplore, ACM Digital Library, Science Direct, and Springer Link. In addition, manual searches were carried out in the most relevant conferences, workshops, journals, and books on ontologies and IoT. The search was conducted from 2009. Since although Kevin Ashton coined the term IoT in 1999, the conception that is had nowadays about IoT, as an intelligent object network infrastructure, began to develop around 2009 [15]. Table 1 shows the search string used in digital libraries. This string was applied to the metadata of the paper: title, abstract, and keywords.

Table 1. Search string.

Concept	Sub-string	Connector
Ontology	Ontolog*	OR
Semantic web	Semantic web	OR
Taxonomy	Taxonom*	AND
Internet of things	Internet of things	OR
IoT	IoT	OR
Ambient intelligence	Ambient intelligence	OR
AmI	AmI	OR
Cyber-physical system	Cyber-physical system*	OR
Cyber system*	Cyber system*	OR
Industry 4.0	Industry 4.0	

Search string:
(ontolog* OR semantic web OR taxonom*) AND (internet of things OR IoT or ambient intelligence or AmI or cyber-physical system* or cyber system* or industry 4.0)

Selection of Primary Studies. First, the primary studies extracted from the automatic and manual search were evaluated and selected by three researchers based on the title, abstract, and keywords. Discrepancies in selecting of the studies were resolved by consensus once the full paper had been reviewed.

Primary studies that meet at least one of the following criteria were included:

IC1. Primary studies that address the use of ontological models within IoT and other related domains.
IC2. Primary studies that address semantic web approaches within IoT and other related domains.
IC3. Primary studies that address the use of taxonomies within IoT and other related domains.

Primary studies that meet at least one of the following criteria were excluded:

EC1. Editorials, prologues, opinions, interviews, news, or posters.
EC2. Duplicate studies in different sources.
EC3. Short papers with less than four pages.
EC4. Papers written in a language other than English.

Quality Assessment of Primary Studies. A checklist consisting of three questions was used to assess the quality of the primary studies. This checklist is presented in Table 2. Each question was evaluated using a scale between 0 and 1. Also, the scores obtained by the three questions were added to calculate the total score of each study.

The scoring was only used to order the studies according to the scientific relevance and correctly address the presentation of the systematic review results.

Table 2. Quality checklist.

No.	Question	Answer and score
QAQ1	The primary study has been cited by other authors	More than 5 citations, very relevant (1) Between 1 and 5 citations, relevant (0.5) No cited, irrelevant (0)
QAQ2	The primary study has been published in a relevant journal or conference	Very relevant (1) Relevant (0.5) Irrelevant (0)
QAQ3	The primary study includes an empirical evaluation of the proposed solution	Yes (1) No (0)

Data Extraction Strategy. Table 3 shows the form used to extract data from the primary studies. The proposed extraction criteria allow answering the research questions and adequately organizing the results of the review.

Table 3. Data extraction form.

RQ1. What are the purposes of using ontological models in IoT?		
EC1	IoT subdomain	[Transport, Education, Government, Health, Finance and banking, Public security and emergency, Monitoring and environmental control, Logistics and retail, Industrial control, Entertainment and sport, Smart environmental, Smart animal control, Farming, Other]
EC2	Non-functional requirements modeled in the ontology	[Efficiency, Compatibility, Usability, Reliability, Security, Maintainability, Portability, Other]
EC3	Concepts represented in the ontology	[Physical entity (Place, Machinery, Vehicle, Appliance or device, User), Digital entity (Cloud node, Fog node, Gateway, Sensor, Tag, Actuator), Other]
EC4	Types of aspects modeled in the ontology	[Architecture, Objectives / Requirements, State, Process / Task, Context, Other]
RQ2. How are ontological models implemented in IoT?		
EC5	Ontology modeling level	[Conceptual model, Computational model]

(*continued*)

Table 3. (*continued*)

EC6	Ontological language	[XML, RDF, RDFS, OWL, Other]
EC7	Ontology development tools	[Apache Jena, Neon Toolkit, OntoStudio, Protégé, Other]
EC8	Reused ontologies	Specify:_____

RQ3. How is addressed the research in studies related to the construction of ontological models in the IoT?

EC9	Validation type	[Proof of Concept, Survey, Case Study, Experiment, None]
EC10	Approach scope	[New, Extension]
EC11	Study type	[Industry, Academy]

Methods of Analysis and Synthesis. The methods used are: i) *quantitative*, construction of the bar and bubble graphs to represent the frequency of responses to each extraction criterion or combination of extraction criteria; and ii) *qualitative*, description of the most relevant proposals. In turn, gaps and research opportunities were evident.

3.2 Conducting the Review

In this phase, the protocol was used to collect, select and prioritize the primary studies. Therefore, the following tasks were executed (see Fig. 1):

1. *Automatic search.* The search string was adapted and executed in each of the digital libraries. As a result, 493 primary studies were extracted. In addition, 40 duplicate studies were eliminated, finally obtaining 453 studies.
2. *First selection.* Based on the inclusion and exclusion criteria, the pertinence of the studies' titles, abstracts, and keywords was evaluated. As a result, 43 studies were selected.
3. *Second selection.* The researchers resolved discrepancies about the selection of certain studies through consensus, after reviewing the entire document. As a result, the number of studies selected was reduced to 20. A manual search (snowballing technique) was also performed in this task, adding three additional studies.
4. *Quality Assessment.* Finally, the checklist to evaluate the quality of the studies was applied. The purpose was only to obtain an ordered list of studies by their relevance.

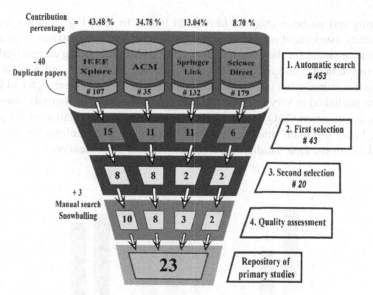

Fig. 1. Conducting the systematic review.

4   Results and Discussion

Once the systematic review was conducted following the established protocol, 23 relevant primary studies related to ontological proposals for the IoT domain have been obtained. Figure 2 presents the distribution of the selected studies by year. It can be seen that the largest number of studies were published in 2018 (6 studies). However, from this year to the present, there has been a downward trend. Therefore, apparently this line of research is losing interest for researchers.

Regarding the distribution of primary studies according to the type of publication, the authors prefer publishing in conferences (16 studies), followed by journals (7 studies),

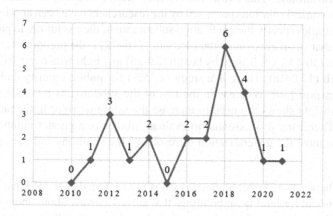

Fig. 2. Distribution of primary studies by year.

highlighting that no book chapters have been found. In turn, Fig. 3 shows the results of the quality assessment of the studies. It is observed that the studies present a very favorable assessment for the question QAQ1, with 13 studies being categorized as very relevant (more than 5 citations), 8 studies as relevant (between 1 and 5 citations) and only 2 studies as irrelevant (0 citations). In turn, for the QAQ2 question, 6 and 9 studies have been published in very relevant and relevant conferences or journals, respectively. However, for question QAQ3, only 12 include an empirical evaluation of the proposed solution, being the main limitation of this research area. Therefore, for most of the proposed solutions, their validity and reliability cannot be evidenced.

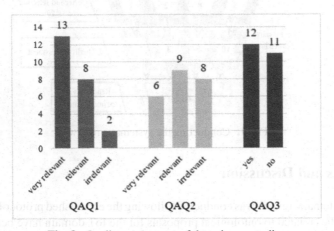

Fig. 3. Quality assessment of the primary studies.

The following subsections present the results obtained for each of the research questions and their extraction criteria.

RQ1. What are the purposes of using ontological models in IoT?

EC1: IoT Subdomain. This extraction criterion aims to identify in which IoT subdomains the ontological solutions proposed by the researchers have been applied. Of the 23 studies, S15 studies specify the application subdomain of their solution. In particular, the results show that smart environmental (domotic) [16–22] is the predominant subdomain with 7 studies (30.43%), followed by health [23–25] and industrial control [26–28] with 3 studies each (13.04%). There is a study (4.35%) for public security and emergency [29], and transport [30]. Whereas in the rest of the subdomains no studies have been found. This insight shows the need to increase the scientific rigor in the preparation of the studies. Therefore, it is essential to evaluate studies in a greater number of subdomains to guarantee the generalization of results of the solutions and their validity and reliability.

Among the works to be highlighted is the study by Jemal et al. [17] that proposes an ontological model for intelligent buildings that allows alerting about anomalous behaviors detected by the sensors through an analysis based on rules expressed in the Semantic

Web Rule Language (SWRL). Furthermore, Chen et al. [24] present a dynamic ontological model to diagnose and detect anomalies in elderly health cabin's temperature and air conditioning system.

EC2: Non-functional Requirements Modeled in the Ontology. This criterion aims to understand researchers' concerns about non-functional requirements to be solved with the support of the ontologies. The main challenges of the IoT systems are related to the highly heterogeneous, dynamic, and scalable scenarios in which they operate. In Table 4, it can be seen that research on the use of ontologies in IoT has been correctly oriented since 65.22% and 56.52% of the studies present solutions to improve the compatibility and maintainability of IoT systems, respectively. On the other hand, studies related to usability (34.78%) and security (21.74%) have been proposed at a medium level. One concern is the few studies found for efficiency (13.04%), reliability (8.70%), and portability (4.35%). Regarding efficiency, a more significant amount of work is required to improve the response time of semantic techniques when processing ontological models. Also, there is a gap regarding the use of ontologies to improve resilience, fault tolerance, and self-recovery of IoT systems.

Table 4. Frequency of non-functional requirements represented in the ontologies.

Concepts/Entities	Relevant studies	Frequency
Efficiency	[22, 30, 31]	3
Compatibility	[5, 17, 19, 21, 22, 24, 25, 29–34]	13
Usability	[16, 23, 25–27, 29, 30, 35]	8
Reliability	[30, 36]	2
Security	[20, 23, 27, 28, 36]	5
Maintainability	[17–19, 22–26, 29–32, 35–37]	15
Portability	[17]	1

One study that addresses various non-functional requirements is IoT-Lite [22], a semantic sensor network ontology to describe key IoT concepts that support interoperability and sensory data discovery across heterogeneous IoT platforms using lightweight semantics to optimize the response time of inquiries.

EC3: Concepts Represented in the Ontology. The most common IoT concepts or entities represented by the ontological models are identified in this extraction criterion. Concerning the representation of physical entities, the concepts modeled in recurring order are: place (34.78%), appliances and devices (26.09%), users (21.74%), machinery (13.04%), and vehicles (8.7%). Whereas for digital entities is the following: sensor (65.22%), tag (52.17%), actuator (34.78%), gateway (26.09%), cloud node (26.09%), and fog node (8.7%) (see Table 5). Due to the increasing amount of data and devices that manage the IoT environments, the existing ontological proposals must include fog nodes in the representation of the IoT infrastructures to solve the problems of performance, network congestion, security, reliability, among others.

Table 5. Frequency of concepts/entities represented in the ontologies.

Concepts/Entities	Relevant studies	Frequency
Physical Entities		
Place (e.g., building, house, parking lot)	[5, 16, 17, 19, 21, 29, 30, 35]	8
Machinery	[26–28]	3
Vehicle	[29, 30]	2
Appliance or device	[5, 16, 20, 25, 27, 29]	6
User	[21, 24, 25, 30, 35]	5
Digital entities		
Sensor	[5, 16–20, 22, 23, 25, 26, 29, 31, 32, 36, 37]	15
Tag	[5, 17, 20, 22–26, 29, 32, 35, 36]	12
Actuator	[5, 16, 20, 22, 23, 25, 26, 29]	8
Gateway	[19, 25–27, 35, 36]	6
Fog node	[27, 29]	2
Cloud node	[5, 23, 26, 27, 35, 36]	6
Other	[33, 34]	2

An important study on the representation of physical entities is presented in [30], whose purpose is to automatically organize and manage the places with the greatest influx of vehicles in the world using an intelligent traffic system based on ontologies. The ontological model includes concepts such as: traffic lights, vehicles, lights, signage, among others. In turn, Koorapati et al. [26] propose an interesting solution based on ontologies to model and automate a factory production system using the Software-Defined Data Center (SDDC). In this study, the model entities are sensors, actuators, and gateways.

EC4: Types of Aspects Modeled in the Ontology. This criterion aims to know from which abstraction perspectives (architecture, objectives, process, context) the IoT systems are modeled in ontologies. In Table 6, it can be seen that the most modeled aspect is the architecture of an IoT system (91.30%) since it is an ideal way to manage the complexity and variability of these systems. At a medium level, ontologies support context and process modeling (43.48%). Context modeling is an expected result due to the intrinsic characteristic of the IoT systems to monitor the environment. Finally, the perspectives least considered by ontologies are state (30.43%) and objectives (17.39%).

Hence, a research opportunity is to expand ontologies to represent and manage the relationship between the state of an IoT system and its objectives. This is useful to generate knowledge that contributes to improving the autonomy and reliability of IoT systems.

Table 6. Frequency of perspectives of IoT systems modeled in the ontologies.

Concepts/Entities	Relevant studies	Frequency
Architecture	[5, 16–27, 29–36]	21
Objectives/requirements	[23, 24, 29, 35]	4
State	[19, 20, 24, 25, 29–31]	7
Process/task	[17, 20, 24–27, 31, 33–35]	10
Context	[19, 20, 22, 25–30, 37]	10

Regarding architectural modeling, Rhayem et al. [25] propose an ontology called HealthIoT to represent the sensors, RFID cards, and actuators to be used in monitoring patients' health. An important study from the perspective of context is the proposed by Ming et al. [37], in which the authors describe the role of context in IoT systems through ontological models that transform data collected from sensors into knowledge.

RQ2. How are ontological models implemented in IoT?

EC5: Ontology Modeling Level. Of the 23 primary studies, only 4 studies (17.39%) propose ontological models at the conceptual level [5, 18, 28, 33], while 19 studies (82.61%) propose ontological models that can be processed by a computer [16, 17, 19–27, 29–32, 34–37]. This result represents an important strength, since most studies have reached a stage of implementing the ontologies in a language that can be interpreted by the computer (e.g., OWL). Figure 4 presents a bubble chart between the EC2, EC4, and EC5 extraction criteria that shows by type of aspect and non-functional requirement the level of ontological modeling proposed by the studies.

EC6: Ontological Language. This extraction criterion aims to determine which languages are the most commonly used by researchers for the construction of ontologies in the IoT domain. Thus, OWL is the widely used language with 60.87%, followed well below RDF with 17.39% and XML with 8.70% (see Table 7). Therefore, the results obtained for this criterion are very favorable due to the semantic capacity of the OWL language.

EC7: Ontology Development Tools. Only 12 studies specify the development tools used to build the proposed ontological solutions.Within this group of studies, Protegé [17, 19, 21, 23–26, 31, 32] and Apache Jena [20, 22–25, 31, 37] are the development tools preferred by researchers with 39.13% and 30.43%, respectively. Even 4 studies combine these two tools in the construction of their solutions.

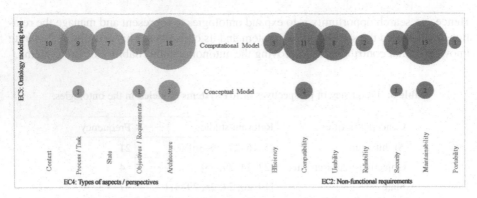

Fig. 4. Ontological modeling level by type of aspects and non-functional requirements.

Table 7. Frequency of ontological languages used.

Concepts/Entities	Relevant studies	Frequency
XML	[22, 34]	2
RDF	[20, 29, 30, 34]	4
OWL	[16, 17, 19, 21, 22, 24–27, 29, 30, 35–37]	14
Does not specify	[5, 18, 28, 33]	4

EC8: Reused Ontologies. Approximately half of the studies (52.17%) reuse ontologies to build their solutions. The main reused ontologies are: Semantic Sensor Network Ontology (SSN) [23, 25], IotLite [27, 31], oneM2M [16, 34], OntoAMI [19], DOLCE + DnS Ultralite [5, 20], Multimedia Web Ontology Language (MOWL) [29], OWL-S [17], CoDAMos [19], COBRA [17], and CONON [35].

RQ3. How is addressed the research in studies related to the construction of ontological models in the IoT?

EC9: Validation Type. This extraction criterion allows knowing the type of empirical evaluation most frequently used in the selected studies. As indicated previously, a high percentage of studies (47.83%) do not contemplate some evaluation. On the contrary, of the studies that include empirical evaluation, 34.78% carry out proofs of concept and only 17.39% execute experiments. In the review, no studies were found that use the survey or case study as an evaluation strategy (see Table 8). Based on the results obtained, the empirical evaluation represents the main weakness of this research area. Hence, researchers should make more significant efforts to validate their ontological proposals using more rigorous methods, such as: experiments or case studies.

Table 8. Frequency of validation types.

Concepts/Entities	Relevant studies	Frequency
Proof of Concept	[16, 19, 20, 23, 24, 26, 30, 35]	8
Case Study		
Experiments	[18, 25, 29, 32]	4
Survey		
None	[5, 17, 21, 22, 27, 28, 31, 33, 34, 36, 37]	11

Figure 5 presents a bubble graph between the EC2 and EC9 extraction criteria, to contrast which are the types of validation used by non-functional requirement. It is observed that the experiments have been applied only to evaluate the ontologies focused on improving the compatibility, usability and maintainability of IoT systems. Furthermore, ontological studies aimed at managing efficiency, reliability, security, and portability do not have an empirical evaluation.

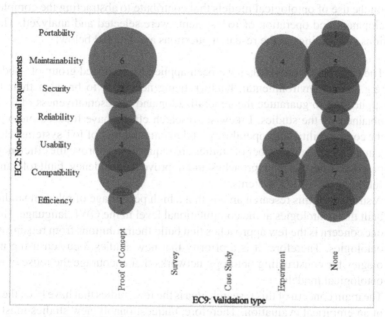

Fig. 5. Validation type by non-functional requirement.

The study proposed by Pahal et al. [29] presents an interesting experiment to evaluate an ontology-based IoT framework to support intelligent surveillance. The experiment uses web videos taken with multiple devices. The videos include participants (e.g., a person running, hitting, firing bullets) and objects (e.g., car, gun, bicycle). The experiment evaluates the efficiency and precision of the framework both in identifying the actions carried out by the participants or objects in a video scene and the determination of risk situations.

EC10: Study Type. The results of this criterion show that 56.52% of the proposed ontological approaches are an extension of previous studies [16, 18–20, 22, 23, 25–28, 31, 34, 35], while 43.48% represent new research on ontological models in the IoT domain [5, 17, 21, 24, 29, 30, 32, 33, 36, 37].

EC11: Approach Scope. 91.30% of the studies have been approached from the academy [16–26, 28–37], while only 8.70% by industry [5, 27]. Consequently, greater collaboration between academia and industry is required to evaluate the proposed ontological solutions in real scenarios.

5 Conclusions and Future Work

Managing the complexity and uncertainty of IoT systems is a difficult task that requires much effort. Through the systematic review carried out in this work, the most relevant studies on the use of ontological models that contribute to abstracting the complexity in the development and operation of IoT systems were selected and analyzed. The main conclusions and findings to the research questions are detailed below:

RQ1.   The ontological proposals have been applied to a reduced group of subdomains (e.g., smart environmental, health), being necessary to broaden their field of application to guarantee the generalization and representativeness of the results obtained by the studies. Likewise, research efforts have focused on improving the compatibility, interoperability, and maintainability of IoT systems. However, a more significant number of studies are required to improve the efficiency of the proposed ontological approaches and improve the residency, fault tolerance, and self-recovery of IoT systems.

RQ2.   A strength of this research area is that a high percentage of relevant studies have built their ontologies at the computational level in the OWL language. However, one concern is the few approaches that build their solutions from reusing existing ontologies. Therefore, it is a priority that new studies focus on using method-ologies for constructing ontology networks that encourage the reuse of existing ontological models.

RQ3.   The main concern of this research area is the few studies that have been the subject of an empirical evaluation. Therefore, unquestionably new studies must be for-mulated, including rigorous evaluation techniques to validate existing ontological proposals and guarantee the validity and reliability of the solutions.

As future work, it is proposed to build an ontology network to support the oper-ation of IoT systems, considering the strengths of several analyzed studies and the recommendations generated in this study.

Acknowledgements. This study is part of the research project "Methodology and infrastructure based on models at runtime for the construction and operation of self-aware Internet of Things systems." Therefore, we thank LIDI - Universidad del Azuay for its support.

References

1. Atzori, L., Iera, A., Morabito, G.: The internet of things: a survey. Comput. Netw. **54**(15), 2787–2805 (2010)
2. Miorandi, D., Sicari, S., De Pellegrini, F., Chlamtac, I.: Internet of things: vision, applications and research challenges. Ad Hoc Netw. **10**(7), 1497–1516 (2012)
3. Madakam, S., Ramaswamy, R., Tripathi, S.: Internet of Things (IoT): a literature review. J. Comput. Commun. **3**(5), 164–173 (2015)
4. ISO/IEC - Internet of Things (IoT) Preliminary Report 2014. https://www.iso.org/files/live/sites/isoorg/files/developing_standards/docs/en/internet_of_things_report-jtc1.pdf. Accessed 05 June 2021
5. Hachem, S., Teixeira, T., Issarny, V.: Ontologies for the Internet of Things. In: Proceedings of the 8th Middleware Doctoral Symposium (MDS'11) of the 12th ACM/IFIP/USENIX International Middleware Conference, pp. 1–6 (2011)
6. France, R., Rumpe, B.: Model-driven development of complex software: a research roadmap. In: Future of Software Engineering (FoSE 2007), pp. 37–54 (2007)
7. Barnaghi, P., Wang, W., Henson, C., Taylor, K.: Semantics for the internet of things: early progress and back to the future. Int. J. Semant. Web Inf. Syst. **8**(1), 1–21 (2012)
8. Wang, W., De, S., Cassar, G., Moessner, K.: Knowledge representation in the internet of things: semantic modelling and its applications. Automatika **54**(4), 388–400 (2013)
9. Rhayem, A., Mhiri, M., Gargouri, F.: Semantic Web Technologies for the Internet of Things: Systematic Literature Review. Internet of Things 11 (2020)
10. Andročec, D., Novak, M., Oreški, D.: Using semantic web for internet of things interoperability: a systematic review. Int. J. Semant. Web Inf. Syst. **14**(4), 147–171 (2018)
11. Venceslau, A., Andrade, R., Vidal, V., Nogueira, T., Pequeno, V.: IoT Semantic Interoperability: a systematic mapping study. In: 21st International Conference on Enterprise Information Systems (ICEIS 2019), pp. 535–544 (2019)
12. Sejdiu, B., Ismaili, F., Ahmedi, L.: Integration of semantics into sensor data for the IoT: a systematic literature review. Int. J. Semant. Web Inf. Syst. **16**(4), 1–25 (2020)
13. Kitchenham, B., Charters, S.: Guidelines for performing systematic literature reviews in software engineering, vol. 5. Ver. 2.3 EBSE Technical Report (2007)
14. Erazo-Garzon, L., Erraez, J., Cedillo, P., Illescas-Peña L.: Quality assessment approaches for ambient assisted living systems: a systematic review. In: International Conference on Applied Technologies, vol. 1193, pp. 421–439 (2019)
15. Cisco: How the Next Evolution of the Internet Is Changing Everything. White paper (2011)
16. Sahlmann, K., Schwotzer, T.: Ontology-based virtual iot devices for edge computing. In: 8th ACM International Conference on the Internet of Things, pp. 1–7 (2018)
17. Jemal, A., Ktait, H., Ben Halima, R., Jmaiel, M.: OoDAAS: ontology-driven analysis for self-adaptive ambient systems. In: ACM International Conference on Internet of things and Cloud Computing, pp. 1–6 (2016)
18. Ma, M., Wang, P., Chu, C.H.: Ontology-based semantic modeling and evaluation for internet of things applications. In: IEEE International Conference on Internet of Things, pp. 1–6 (2014)
19. Stavropoulos, T., Vrakas, D., Vlachava, D., Bassiliades, N.: BOnSAI: a smart building ontology for ambient intelligence. In: 2nd International Conference on Web Intelligence, Mining and Semantics, pp. 1–12 (2012)

20. Tayur, V.M., Suchithra, R.: A Comprehensive Ontology for Internet of Things (COIoT). In: 2nd International Conference on Advanced Computational and Communication Paradigms, pp. 1–6 (2019)
21. Wehbi, A., Cherif, A.R., Tadj, C.: Modeling ontology for multimodal interaction in ubiquitous computing systems. In: ACM Conference on Ubiquitous Computing, pp. 842–849 (2012)
22. Bermudez-Edo, M., Elsaleh, T., Barnaghi, P., Taylor, K.: IoT-Lite: a lightweight semantic model for the internet of things. In.: 13th IEEE International Conference on Ubiquitous Intelligence and Computing, pp. 90–97 (2016)
23. Titi, S., Ben Elhadj, H., Chaari, L.: An ontology-based healthcare monitoring system in the internet of things. In: 15th International Wireless Communications and Mobile Computing Conference, pp. 319–324 (2019)
24. Chen, G., Jiang, T., Wang, M., Tang, X., Ji, W.: Modeling and reasoning of IoT architecture in semantic ontology dimension. Comput. Commun. 153, 580–594 (2020)
25. Rhayem, A., Ben, A.M., Ben, S.M., Gargouri, F.: Ontology-based system for patient monitoring with connected objects. Procedia Comput. Sci. 112, 683–692 (2017)
26. Koorapati, K., Pandu, R., Ramesh, P.K., Veeraswamy, S., Narasappa, U.: Towards a Unified Ontology for IoT Fabric with SDDC. Journal of King Saud University - Computer and Information Sciences (2021)
27. Steinmetz, C., Rettberg, A., Ribeiro, F., Schroeder, G., Soares, M., Pereira, C.: Using Ontology and Standard Middleware for Integrating IoT Based in the Industry 4.0. IFAC-PapersOnLine 51(10), 169–174 (2018)
28. Teslya, N., Ryabchikov, I.: Ontology-based semantic models for industrial IoT components representation. In: International Conference on Intelligent Information Technologies for Industry, pp. 138–147 (2018)
29. Pahal, N., Mallik, A., Chaudhury, S.: An ontology-based context-aware IoT framework for smart surveillance. In: 3rd International Conference on Smart City Applications, pp. 1–7 (2018)
30. Goel, D., Chaudhury, S., Ghosh, H.: An IoT approach for context-aware smart traffic management using ontology. In: IEEE/WIC/ACM International Conference on Web Intelligence, pp. 42–49 (2017)
31. Arruda, M., Bulcão-Neto, R.: Toward a lightweight ontology for privacy protection in IoT. In: 34th ACM/SIGAPP Symposium on Applied Computing, pp. 880–888 (2019)
32. Zhang, H., Meng, C.: A multi-dimensional ontology-based IoT resource model. In: IEEE 5th International Conference on Software Engineering and Service Sciences, pp. 124–127 (2014)
33. Sithole, V., Marshall, L.: An exposition of a lightweight domain-specific ontology for the interoperability of the internet of things patterns. In: Open Innovations Conference, pp. 8–14 (2019)
34. Sahlmann, K., Scheffler, T., Schnor, B.: Ontology-driven device descriptions for IoT network management. In: Global Internet of Things Summit, pp. 1–6 (2018)
35. Tang, Y., Meersman, R.: DIY-CDR: an ontology-based, do-it-yourself component discoverer and recommender. Pers. Ubiquit. Comput. 16(5), 581–595 (2012)
36. Xu, Y., Kishi, T.: An ontology-based iot communication data reduction method. In: 9th IEEE Annual Ubiquitous Computing, Electronics and Mobile Communication Conference, pp. 321–325 (2018)
37. Ming, Z., Yan, M.: Study on the ontology-base context-aware and reasoning model of IOT. In: 2013 IEEE Conference Anthology, pp. 1–5 (2013)

Verification and Validation Plan in a Software Product: A Practical Study

Cathy Pamela Guevara-Vega[1] ⓘ, Robert Alexander Patiño Chalacán[2],
Pablo Andrés Landeta[3] ⓘ, Xavier Mauricio Rea-Peñafiel[2](✉) ⓘ,
and José Antonio Quiña-Mera[1] ⓘ

[1] Facultad de Ingeniería en Ciencias Aplicadas, Grupo de Investigación ECIER, Universidad Técnica del Norte, Ibarra, Ecuador
{cguevara,aquina}@utn.edu.ec

[2] Facultad de Ingeniería en Ciencias Aplicadas, Universidad Técnica del Norte, Ibarra, Ecuador
{rapatinoc,mrea}@utn.edu.ec

[3] Department of Information Technology – Online, Universidad Técnica del Norte, Ibarra, Ecuador
palandeta@utn.edu.ec

Abstract. In Software Engineering practice, it is a challenge to develop quality software. In this way, several proposals have emerged, such as verification and validation process (V&V), which is composed of procedures, activities and tasks to verify and validate if the software is correct and if it satisfies user needs. For this reason, we based this study on Design Science Research (DSR) approach to answer the question: Does the implementation of a VVP verification and validation plan using the IEEE 1012-2016/Cor 1-2017 standard work? The method used to answer this question consisted of creating and applying a VVP to the ad-hoc SAREL software and then documenting the findings. The results show that the application of the VVP reached a compliance of 96.50%, according to the evaluation criteria of each V&V task granting a satisfactory degree of quality.

Keywords: Software engineering · Software verification and validation · IEEE 1012-2016/Cor 1-2017

1 Introduction

Today, a company's ability to innovate is increasingly driven by software. Digital technologies play a key role in the transformation of many industrial companies [1]. Modern data analysis technologies have allowed the creation of software analysis tools that offer real-time visualization of aspects related to the development and use of software [2]. Therefore, software quality product monitoring, evaluation, verification and validation allows the assurance and transparency in the development and execution of the organizational and technological processes [3, 4].

Organizations specialized in assuring software quality choose to apply the software verification and validation (V&V) process that helps to determine if the development

© Springer Nature Switzerland AG 2022
M. Botto-Tobar et al. (Eds.): ICAT 2021, CCIS 1535, pp. 525–537, 2022.
https://doi.org/10.1007/978-3-031-03884-6_38

products of a given activity grant his requirements and if the product grant the user needs [5]. To carry out V&V process application, it is necessary to create a Software Verification and Validation Plan (VVP) in which the purpose, goals and scope of the V&V effort are described. [5]. We have considered the need to carry out a VVP focused on ad-hoc software development processes, because evaluating, verifying and validating the software product requires efforts and resources that for MSMEs generates limitations such as time, cost and human talent [6].

According to the above, we based this study on Design Science Research (DSR) approach to answer the question: Does the implementation of a VVP verification and validation plan using the IEEE 1012-2016/Cor 1-2017 standard work? The research aims to answer the research question by implementing a VVP proposed by the authors of this study and applied in ad-hoc software "SAREL".

The rest of this paper is structured as follows: Sect. 2 Research design: we establish the research activities based on DSR, theoretical foundation and design and construction of the VVP (application of the VVP). Section 3 Results: results evaluation of the VVP application. Section 4 Discussion: research discussion. Section 5 Conclusions and future work.

2   Research Design

The study design was established based on the DSR guidelines [7], see Table 1.

Table 1. Design of the investigation.

Activity	Components	Paper section
Problem diagnosis	Problem; Objective	Introduction
Theoretical foundation	Verification and validation; Software verification and validation process (V&V); Standard: IEEE 1012-2016/Cor 1-2017	Research design
VVP Design and Construction: VVP Application	Requirements; Design (Selection of V&V Processes); Creation and Application of the VVP for ad-hoc Software SAREL	Research design
VVP results evaluation	Statistical Analysis and Impact Analysis	Results

2.1   Theoretical Foundation

Verification and Validation. The ISO/IEC/IEEE 24765-2010 standard defines verification and validation as "the process of determining whether the requirements for a system or component are complete and correct", in addition to determining whether the products of each development phases grant the requirements or conditions imposed by the previous phase, and the final system or component grant the specified requirements [8]. This requires a set of activities integrated into the software life cycle.

Verification and Validation Process. The V&V process determines if the products of a certain activity grant the requirements of this activity, and if the expected use and user needs are satisfied. To establish the extent to which these needs are satisfied, different techniques are used, including assessment, analysis, evaluation, review, inspection, and testing of products and processes. The V&V is carried out in parallel with all the stages of the life cycle, not only at the end of it, also a set of processes and activities is established for the V&V process that is detailed in Table 2, where is shown an extract of the activities and tasks of the process [5]. The complete information in Table 2 is available at [16].

Table 2. Extract of the processes, activities, and tasks of the V&V Process according to the standard IEEE 1012-2016/Cor 1-2017.

V&V process	V&V activity	V&V tasks
Software Concept V&V process	Software Concept V&V	Concept Documentation Evaluation (…)
Software Requirements Analysis V&V process	Software Requirements Analysis V&V	Requirements Evaluation (…)
Software Design V&V process	Software Design V&V	Design Evaluation (…)
Software Construction V&V process	Software Construction V&V	Source Code and Source Code Documentation Evaluation (…)
Software Integration V&V process	Software Integration V&V	Software Integration Test Execution V&V (…)
Software Qualification Testing V&V process	Software Qualification Testing V&V	Software Qualification Test Execution V&V (…)
Software Acceptance Testing V&V process	Software Acceptance Testing V&V	Software Acceptance Test Procedure V&V (…)
Software Installation and Checkout V&V process	Software Installation and Checkout V&V	Installation Configuration Audit (…)
Software Operation V&V process	Software Operation V&V	Evaluation of New Constraints (…)
Software Maintenance V&V process	Software Maintenance V&V	VVP Revision (…)
Software Disposal V&V process	Software Disposal V&V	Software Disposal Evaluation (…)

IEEE 1012-2016/Cor 1-2017. This V&V standard addresses all hardware, software, and system lifecycle processes, including process groups such as Agreement, Organizational Project Enablement, Project, Technical, Software Implementation, Software

Support, and Software Reuse. It is also compatible with all life cycle models (eg system, software and hardware); however, not all life cycle models use all the processes listed in this standard [5, 9].

2.2 VVP Design and Implementation

In this activity, the following tasks are established: a) selection of V&V processes and activities b) VVP creation [6] and c) VVP application to the ad-hoc SAREL software (Collection Module).

a. Selection of V&V Processes and Activities. In this phase, the V&V processes and activities to be executed in the VVP were selected according to the software life cycle in relation to the V&V process described in ISO/IEC/12207 [10]. In addition, each minimum V&V activity is assigned a software integrity level, because of that, the activities that can be executed were selected in accordance with the above for the ad-hoc SAREL software. Table 4 details the processes and activities selected for the creation and application of the VVP.

Ad-hoc Software SAREL. It is a software created by one of the authors of the paper and is used to automate the process of collecting, delivering, and managing the commercialization of milk suitable for human consumption. It has the Collection, Analysis, User Management and Payment modules. To evaluate the VVP proposed in this research, the Collection Module was used, which is responsible for assigning the liters of milk from each supplier that are collected in each collection area, to then be analyzed and determine if the milk is suitable for consumption. human. Subsequently, if the result of the analysis is favorable, the liters of milk collected are counted to assign the biweekly payment to the suppliers and determine the profits with the execution of the other modules. Figure 1 shows the flow chart of the collection module process.

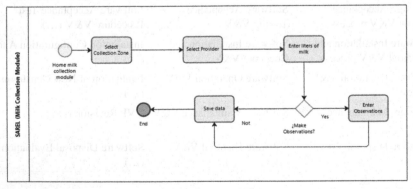

Fig. 1. SAREL software Milk Collection Module flow chart.

The SAREL software was created based on the requirements and business needs of a collection center, using technologies such as JAVA EE, PostgreSQL, WildFly, pgModeler. In addition, MVC architecture was used, and the user interface design was built with HTML5. Each of the software modules were built with best practices and using the agile XP software development methodology.

b. VVP Creation. In creating the VVP to be applied in the ad-hoc SARREL software, the content suggested by the IEEE 1012-2016/Cor 1-2017 standard was taken into account [5, 11]. Table 3 describes the content developed in the VVP. The complete VVP is available at [16].

Table 3. Resumen del contenido del VVP.

Content	Detail
Purpose	The purpose, scope of the VVP, when applied in the SAREL software, is described, in addition to the limitations that were ignored when executing it and the acronyms that were used in the document
SAREL software overview	The SAREL software is described, and the module to which the VVP was executed, in addition, its process flow chart
V&V overview	The organization of human resources is detailed, for the execution of the V&V processes assigned to each involved. In addition to the techniques and methods that were used in the application of the VVP, and a summary of the resources used
V&V processes	Each one of the V&V processes, activities and tasks selected for the SAREL software V&V through the VVP is detailed, as well as the methods that were used in the execution of each process, the resources, the inputs, and outputs required when applying each process
V&V Administrative Requirements	The resolutions and reports of anomalies that must be presented when applying the VVP are described, as well as the policies of task iteration and the control procedures that the VVP must follow
References	The purpose and scope of the VVP when applied in the SAREL software is described, in addition to the limitations that were ignored when executing it and the acronyms that were used in the document

VVP Validation. Once the creation of the VVP was completed, the content of the document was validated using a validation instrument, which was used by three experts in Software Engineering area. Two of the experts did not present any observations, the third expert gave suggestions such as better defining the execution schedule for each task, as well as the application methods. Therefore, the quality of the VVP was satisfactory. All three validation artifacts are available at [16].

c. VVP Application to the Ad-hoc SAREL Software. In the application of the VVP, each of the V&V processes, activities and tasks detailed in the plan were executed, as well as each of the methods that were proposed to execute the V&V tasks in the assigned time. At the end of the VVP application, a final V&V report was developed, in which each of the results of the V&V processes executed is presented. Table 4 describes the content of the final report. The final report is available at [16].

Table 4. Content summary of the final V&V report.

Content	Detail
Problem Statement	The existing problem is detailed, prior to the execution of the VVP, as well as the intended use of the ad-hoc SAREL software and the description of the software creation model. In addition to the scope of the VVP and the scope of V&V that was proposed in the plan
Model requirements and acceptability criteria	The acceptability criteria for the V&V are described when executing the VVP
V&V task analysis	Each one of the executed tasks belonging to the V&V processes is described, with the results generated from them
V&V Recommendations	The main findings of the V&V activities are described
Key participants	The human resources involved in applying the VVP are detailed
Real V&V Resources	The documents resulting from the execution of the VVP are detailed

3 Results

After the creation and application of the VVP for SAREL software, based on the IEEE 1012-2016/Cor 1-2017 standard, several V&V artifacts were obtained as a result. Compliance with the criteria that were evaluated in the software is evidenced, in addition a final report was created describing the results obtained. Therefore, for the data interpretation, a statistical analysis of compliance with each V&V process was carried out, and an impact analysis.

3.1 Statistical Analysis of V&V Compliance

Each of the V&V tasks carried out has a compliance percentage for each process, in Fig. 2 it can be seen that in the Software Requirements Analysis V&V process which is responsible of verifying and validating the software requirements, resulting in the V&V tasks, 94% Traceability Analysis, 91.50% Requirements Evaluation, 96% Criticality Analysis, 91.50% Interface Analysis according to the fulfillment of the evaluation criteria of each task, giving a final result of 93.25% on average of all tasks performed.

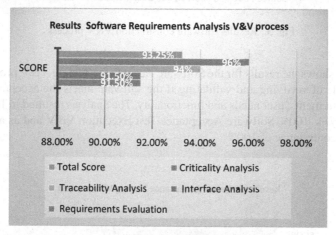

Fig. 2. Results software requirements analysis V&V process.

Figure 3 shows the results for the Software Construction V&V process, which is responsible of validating and verifying if the software was built correctly. The analysis resulted in 100% Software Component Test Execution V&V, 96% Criticality Analysis, 92.88% Traceability Analysis, 91% Interface Analysis and as a final result, the average compliance of the process is 94.88%.

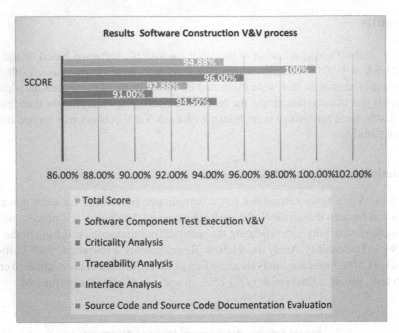

Fig. 3. Results software construction V&V process.

Figure 4 shows the results for the Software Acceptance Testing V&V process, which is responsible of verifying and validating if the software meets the acceptance criteria such as requirements, user needs and functionality. The analysis resulted in 100% Traceability Analysis, 100% Software Acceptance Test Execution V&V and as a final result the average compliance of 100%.

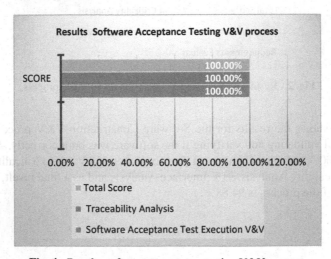

Fig. 4. Results software acceptance testing V&V process.

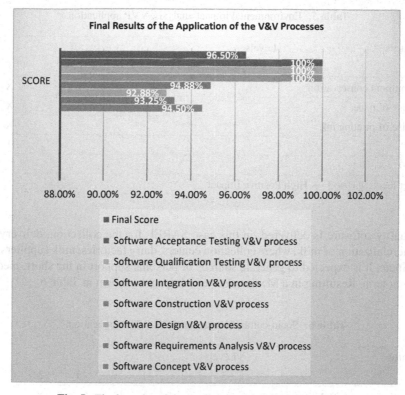

Fig. 5. Final results of the application of the V&V processes.

Figure 5 shows the final results of each V&V process where 94.50% is for Software Concept V&V process, 93.25% is for Software Requirements Analysis V&V process, 92.88% for Software Design V&V process, 94.88% for Software Construction V&V process, 100% Software Integration V&V process, 100% Software Qualification Testing V&V process, 100% Software Acceptance Testing V&V process and with a final result of average compliance in general of 96.50% according to the criteria of evaluation. The complete results of the descriptive analysis are available at [16].

3.2 Impact Analysis

We analyze the impact generated by the application of a VVP in the ad-hoc SAREL software, on a prospective basis, since it cannot be stated that it has been fully covered, there is the possibility of gradually improving it for our own benefit.

We measure the Environmental, Socio-Cultural, Operational impact through an impact analysis artifact. Every technological project has an environmental impact since the use of the internet and the availability of digital information avoids printing on paper, this represents a benefit for the environment. Resulting in a High Positive Impact as shown in Table 5.

Table 5. Environmental impact analysis. VVP application.

Indicators	Levels						
	−3	−2	−1	0	1	2	3
Environment conservation							X
Less use of paper							X
Less use of printing ink							X
Total							9

$\Sigma = 9$

Impact level: 9/3 → 3 → High Positive Impact

Quality software is delivered, in this case SAREL for the collection, delivery and commercialization of milk, where collection centers, dairy factories, milk suppliers, etc. participate. It is expected to generate sources of personal support in the short, medium and long term. Resulting in a Medium Positive Impact as shown in Table 6.

Table 6. Socio-cultural impact analysis. VVP application.

Indicators	Levels						
	−3	−2	−1	0	1	2	3
Generation of sustainability sources						X	
Community wellness					X		
Work habits							X
							6

$\Sigma = 6$

Impact level: 6/3 → 2 → Medium Positive Impact

The operational impact allows to demonstrate the type of impact generated when applying the VVP to SAREL Software. Demonstrating that the quality of a software generates better optimization of the processes that it performs, in addition to generating greater credibility of its operation. Resulting in a High Positive Impact as shown in Table 7.

Table 7. Operational impact analysis. VVP application.

Indicators	Levels						
	−3	−2	−1	0	1	2	3
Software V&V Processes							X
Functionality							X
Error detection							X
Performance							X
$\sum = 12$							

Impact level: 12/4 → 3 → High Positive Impact

As a general impact of the application of the VVP, it resulted in a positive average impact as shown in Table 8.

Table 8. General impact analysis. VVP application.

Indicators	Levels						
	−3	−2	−1	0	1	2	3
Environmental impact							X
Socio cultural impact						X	
Operational impact							X
Total							8
$\sum = 8$							

Impact level: 8/3 → 2,67 → Medium Positive Impact

4 Discussion

In the study by Ahmad et al. [12] they indicate that V&V are necessary in the life cycle of any software system. This answers the question "are we building the right product?" This is how Bondarev et al. [13] manifests it. Huang et al. [14] state in their study that it is very important to be able to decide if the results are correct and if the system comply the specifications; V&V activities can be further planned and implemented to improve the reliability of the product under development. Planning for V&V activities is very challenging, as indicated by Espinosa et al. [15] due to the selection of a set of them to achieve reliability and improve the effectiveness of the product. In this sense, through our study we plan V&V activities through the creation and application of a VVP to the ad-hoc SAREL software, in accordance with the corresponding integrity level through the integration of V&V artifacts proposed by the standard. IEEE 1012-2016 /Cor 1-2017.

We complement the study by showing compliance statistical results with the evaluation criteria of each V&V activity and showing the impact caused after the application of the VVP. During the study, there were limitations regarding the execution of several activities that do not belong to the integrity level of the ad-hoc SAREL software. We believe that the environment in Spanish should be taken into consideration for the next implementation of the proposed V&V plan, not in another language because we do not know if the translation of the artifacts to another language affects the validity of the research.

5   Conclusions and Future Work

We conducted this study based on the Design Science Research (DSR) approach to answer the question Does the implementation of a VVP using the IEEE 1012-2016/Cor 1-2017 standard work? The method to answer this question consisted of carrying out a brief study of the V&V process, according to the standard in order to create a VVP with the necessary processes according to the integrity level of the ad-hoc SAREL software and then validate this artifact. We performed the validation of the artifact with the participation of three experts in the field through a validation instrument. We apply the VVP to the ad-hoc SAREL software executing each of the V&V processes assigned to it.

The statistical analysis of criteria evaluated in the application of the VVP shows a range of 96.50%, the level of the value is satisfactory; In summary, the application obtained an acceptable score, satisfactorily fulfilling most of the V&V processes of the VVP carried out. We conclude and answer the research question by saying that the implementation of a VVP using the IEEE 1012-2016/Cor 1-2017 standard works on the V&V of any type of software according to its level of integrity and its use is reliable, efficient, useful, and comfortable.

As future work, we propose to continue with the complementation of the VVP for all levels of software integrity to be replicated in other software products.

References

1. Ardolino, M., Rapaccini, M., Saccani, N., Gaiardelli, P., Crespi, G., Ruggeri, C.: The role of digital technologies for the service transformation of industrial companies. Int. J. Prod. Res. **56**(6), 2116–2132 (2018). https://doi.org/10.1080/00207543.2017.1324224
2. Martinez-Fernandez, S., et al.: Continuously assessing and improving software quality with software analytics tools: a case study. IEEE Access **7**, 68219–68239 (2019). https://doi.org/10.1109/ACCESS.2019.2917403
3. Rodríguez, P., et al.: Continuous deployment of software intensive products and services: a systematic mapping study. J. Syst. Softw. **123**, 263–291 (2017). https://doi.org/10.1016/j.jss.2015.12.015
4. Neely, S., Stolt, S.: Continuous delivery? easy! Just change everything (well, maybe it is not that easy). Proc. - Agil. **2013**, 121–128 (2013). https://doi.org/10.1109/AGILE.2013.17
5. Institute of Electrical and Electronics Engineers: 1012–2016 - IEEE Standard for System and Software Verification and Validation. IEEE P1012/D18, January 2016, vol. 4, no. May. pp. 1–273 (2017). http://ieeexplore.ieee.org/stamp/stamp.jsp?tp=&arnumber=7383210&isnumber=7383209

6. Ieee, IEEE Guide for Software Verification and Validation Plans (1993)
7. Hevner, A.R., March, S.T., Park, J., Ram, S.: Design science in information systems research. MIS Q. Manag. Inf. Syst. **28**(1), 75–105 (2010). https://doi.org/10.2307/25148625
8. F. O. R. Standardization and D. E. Normalisation, Systems and software engineering — Vocabular. ISO/IEC/ IEEE 247652010, vol. 2010 (2010)
9. IEEE, IEEE Std 1016–2009 (Revision of IEEE Std 1016–1998), IEEE Standard for Information Technology—Systems Design—Software Design Descriptions, vol. 2009, no. July. 2009
10. ISO/IEC/IEEE© Std. 12207:2017: INTERNATIONAL STANDARD ISO/IEC/IEEE Systems and software engineering — agile environment. ISO/IEC/IEEE 12207 First Ed. 2017–11, vol. 2012 (2017)
11. IEEE, An American National Standard IEEE Standard for Software Unit Testing. 1993
12. Ahmad, W., Qamar, U., Hassan, S.: Analyzing different validation and verification techniques for safety critical software systems. In: Proceedings of the IEEE International Conference on Software Engineering and Service Sciences, ICSESS, vol. 2015-Novem, pp. 367–370 (2015). https://doi.org/10.1109/ICSESS.2015.7339076
13. Bondarev, S.E., Chudinov, M.A., Prokhorov, A.S.: The analysis of existing methods of software verification. In: Proceedings of 2019 IEEE Conference of Russian Young Researchers in Electrical and Electronic Engineering, ElConRus 2019, pp. 191–193 (2019). https://doi.org/10.1109/EIConRus.2019.8657169
14. Huang, Q., Wu, G., Li, Z.S.: Design for reliability through text mining and optimal product verification and validation planning. IEEE Trans. Reliab. **70**(1), 231–247 (2021). https://doi.org/10.1109/TR.2019.2938151
15. Espinosa Bedoya, A., Montoya Perez, Y., Puerta Marin, H.A.: A review on verification and validation for embedded software. IEEE Lat. Am. Trans. **14**(5), 2339–2347 (2016). https://doi.org/10.1109/TLA.2016.7530431
16. Guevara-Vega, C., Patiño, R., Landeta, P., Rea, M., Quiña-Mera, A.: Supplemental Material - Verification and validation plan in a software product: A practical study. Zenodo, 26 June 2021. https://doi.org/10.5281/zenodo.5034846

Software Project Management Integrating CMMI-DEV and SCRUM

Gema Guerrero[3], Andrea Guevara[3], José Antonio Quiña-Mera[1] (iD),
Cathy Pamela Guevara-Vega[1] (iD), and Iván García-Santillán[2]([⊠]) (iD)

[1] Facultad de Ingeniería en Ciencias Aplicadas, Grupo de Investigación ECIER, Universidad Técnica del Norte, Ibarra, Ecuador
{aquina,cguevara}@utn.edu.ec
[2] Facultad de Ingeniería en Ciencias Aplicadas, Universidad Técnica del Norte, Ibarra, Ecuador
idgarcia@utn.edu.ec
[3] Instituto de Posgrado, Universidad Técnica del Norte, Ibarra, Ecuador
{gmguerrerov,avguevara}@utn.edu.ec

Abstract. Nowadays organizations aim to enhance software products development and maintenance satisfying then, user needs through methodology and work framework such as: Scrum and CMMI-DEV. Particularly, higher education institutions face the challenge of keeping a robust, flexible and safe IT infrastructure that provides support to the institution's processes continuous improvement. For that matter, the objective of this study is based on the Design Science Research (DSR) approach, answering the following: Does the integration of the CMMI-DEV model, version 1.3 with SCRUM work frame enhance project management quality in the software development process as well as product quality? The method used in answering this question consisted of the design and implementation of a Framework, integrating CMMI-DEV + Scrum in a university academic environment evaluated by ISO/IEC 25010, ISO/IEC 25022 e ISO/IEC 25023 quality standards. Proposed electrical devices, instruments and Framework templates are publicly available online at Zenodo repository. Results show a 14.6% project management improvement rate and 2.16% increase in software product quality use. To sum up, the integration of CMMI-DEV with SCRUM improved both, quality development process and software product.

Keywords: CMMI-DEV · SCRUM · ISO/IEC 25000 · Quality in use · Software engineering · Software project management

1 Introduction

Higher education institutions face a constant challenge of having a robust, flexible and secure IT infrastructure. [1] that provide support to the institution's processes continuous improvement [2]. Software Engineering (IS) supports IT infrastructure through quality software perfection [3]. At IS, software engineers are able to select the most suitable software development process methods, depending on the project context or circumstance [4].

© Springer Nature Switzerland AG 2022
M. Botto-Tobar et al. (Eds.): ICAT 2021, CCIS 1535, pp. 538–551, 2022.
https://doi.org/10.1007/978-3-031-03884-6_39

As it is commonly known software quality is measured through the quality of its management, set up, verification and validation processes [5]. For this reason, organizations aim to enhance software development processes through quality models such as CMMI (Capability Maturity Model Integration) [6, 7]. The CMMI Model for software development is called CMMI-DEV providing a good-practice guide that enhances software product development and management with the aim to satisfy user needs [8]. CMMI-DEV has 22 process areas and its implementation in organizations concentrates on a single goal, a two-representation enhancement process 1) Continuous (capacity level) which enables to choose one or several interrelated process areas CMMI having a positive impact on business. 2) By stages (maturity level) which sequentially improves related process groups within processing areas. [9]. There are four processing areas: Process management, Project management, Engineering and Support [9].

On the other hand, the agile development of software in the industry has turned into a technique that prompts the project delivery process, enables new context adaptability in addition to improving client participation and satisfaction [10]. There is a variety of methodologies and work frames in the market promoting agile software development but, SCRUM is widely used by companies for its productivity, quick development and team work features [11, 12]. SCRUM is a swift, iterative and incremental framework for the administration, maintenance and software development enhancement based on agile manifesto principles [13, 14] as well as project management software. [15].

In this respect, our study was based on the Design Science Research approach (DSR) [16] evaluating software product value and utility criteria. Therefore, the following research question: Does the CMMI-DEV 1.3 version model integration with the SCRUM methodology improves project management quality—planning, follow up and control—in software product quality and development? To answer such question, a Frame work—Artefact—was installed in the Technological Development Unit (UDT) at the *"Universidad Politécnica Estatal del Carchi"* (UPEC) – Ecuador integrating CMMI-DEV and SCRUM. The Framework was evaluated through ISO/IEC 25010, ISO/IEC 25022 and ISO/IEC 25023 norms explaining the model and fundamental metrics to measure software product quality-in-use. Both integration (CMMI-DEV and Scrum) and the evaluation, represent the contribution in this study.

The rest of the paper is organized as follows: Sect. 2) Research Design: we established research activities based on DSR, theoretical foundation, design, and framework implementation (Artefact). Section 3) Results: Device framework quality-in-use results evaluation. Section 4) Discussion of research. Section 5) Conclusion and future work.

2   Research Design

The Design Science Research guide (DSR) [16] was used for research methodology. See Table 1.

2.1   Target Group and Sampling

Research took place at *Universidad Politécnica Estatal del Carchi - UPEC* in Ecuador during the 2018–2020 academic period [17]. Samples were divided into two segments:

Table 1. Research design methodology.

Activity	Components	Section
Problem diagnosis	Problem/Objective Population and sample	Introduction Research design
Theoretical foundation	CMMI-DEV version 1.3 model, SCRUM Framework; ISO/IEC 25010, ISO/IEC 25022 e ISO/IEC 22023	Research design
Artefact design: Framework implementation	CMMI-DEV Framework and SCRUM development Evaluation Model before and after the implementation of Framework	Research design
Framework artifact evaluation	Project management quality evaluation in software development process and software quality product	Results

- For the sampling that assessed the project management quality in the software development process, four research participants were involved-forming the UDT – UPEC group.
- Once the study case was developed, a sample was computed for a 200 professor-target population to assess software product-quality use. Sample computation showed 95% confidence level and 5% margin for error from 132 professors, see Eq. 1 [18]. However, 32 teachers were included in the sample due to their availability to participate in the research. A total of 164 teachers participated in the present study.

$$n = \frac{Z^2 PQN}{Z^2 PQ + Ne^2} \tag{1}$$

$$n = \frac{1.96^2 * 0.5 * 0.5 * 200}{1.96^2 * 0.5 * 0.5 + 200 * 0.05^2}$$

- n = Sampling size
- Z = 95% Confidence level equivalent to 1.96
- P = Probability rate 0.5
- Q = Negative probability 0.5
- N = Target population = 200
- e = Margin for error 0.05 (5%)

These parameter values are common in research studies like this.

2.2 Theoretical foundation

CMMI-DEV 1.3. Version- It is part of the CMMI model specialized in software development and has good practices in terms of product life cycle activities from product inception to delivery including maintenance of developed software. It is comprised by the following categories: Project management, Process management, Systems Engineering, Hardware Engineering, Engineering, Software Engineering and Support Processes immersed in maintenance and development. [9]. It is worth noting that after UDT— UPEC personnel was surveyed, we realized that the Project Management category had performed poorly demonstrating limited performance regarding tasks and activities. Project Management processing tasks and specific practices are as follows:

- Requirement Management (REQM) features 5 specific practices.
- Project Planning (PP) features 14 specific practices.
- Project Monitoring and control (PMC) features 10 specific practices.
- Integrated Project Management (IPM) features 10 specific practices.
- Risk Management (RSKM) features 7 specific practices.
- Supplier Agreement Management (SAM) features 6 specific practices.
- Quantitative Project Management (QPM) features 7 specific practices.

SCRUM. Its life cycle is divided into 3 phases [13]: Pre-game (system definition and requirement update) Development (iterations and product increase delivery) and Post-game (product delivery) Phase practices:

- **Pre-game:** Vision, User history, Product backlog
- **Development:** Sprint, Sprint Planning Meeting, Sprint backlog, SCRUM Daily, Drawback list, Burn Down graphic, Increment, Sprint Review Meeting, and Retrospective Sprint Meeting.
- **Post-game:** Project Closing Meeting

Roles involved in the Scrum process:
Product Owner, Scrum Master and Development team.
Quality standards in use ISO/IEC 25022 and ISO/IEC 25023. Quality standards ISO/IEC 25000 called SQuaRE (Software Product Requirement and Quality Evaluation) are ruled by ISO/IEC 9126 e ISO/IEC 14598 norms. These norms lead the evaluation of internal and external quality as well as software product use through models, metrics and processes utilizing quality requirement specifications. [19]. In this research, the standard ISO/IEC 25010 [19] was applied, as well as Quality evaluation metrics in use of the standard ISO/IEC 25022 [20, 21] featuring five characteristics: efficacy, efficiency, satisfaction, freedom risk and context coverage. Equally important are characteristics related to user interaction results and software developed by the ISO/IEC 25023 standard [22].

2.3 CMMI-DEV/SCRUM Framework Development

To start Framework development for CMMI and SCRUM a scientific articles literary review from Scopus scientific database took place. For search string, it was determined that practices belonging to CMMI-DEV Project Management as well as SCRUM practices may be considered for the study. After analyzing search results, four academic papers related to this research were studied and they became the conceptual basis providing guidance for Framework development, Farid et al. [23], Bougroun et al. [24], Diaz et al. [25], Marçal et al. [26].

Next, the integration of CMMI-DEV Project Management practices and SCRUM practices was performed according to quality standards requirements established by UPEC in addition to guidelines found in the literary review. For instance, planning stages, follow-up and Project control essential in the software development process. The inquiry was made to UDT – UPEC's department head and two software engineers from the same department. Suggested devices, instruments, Framework templates integrating CMMI and SCRUM are enabled in [27].

2.4 Framework Assessment Model

Framework evaluation model was set up to assess software quality process and software product quality. The model was designed and checked by the UDT – UPEC department head along with two software engineers from the same unit according to the institution's quality requirements and the context of this research work.

To assess the CMMI-DEV software quality project management process, a semi-structured survey was conducted to determine the staff's level of satisfaction regarding software development Project Management. The survey included 35 questions based on CMMI-DEV specific areas and practices, see Table 2. Survey questions were based on satisfaction questionnaires SUMI [28], SUS [29], QUIS [30]. Moreover, the Likert scale was used [31] to measure attitudes and opinions. The survey form is set up in [27].

Table 2. CMMI-DEV Project management specific areas and practices

Areas	Specific Practices
Requirement Management (REQM)	5 specific practices
Project Planning (PP)	13 specific practices
Project Monitoring and Control (PMC)	9 specific practices
Integrated Project Management (IPM)	6 specific practices
Risk Management (RSKM)	2 specific practices

To assess software quality product, quality metrics in the use of software standards ISO/IEC 25010, ISO/IEC 25022, e ISO/IEC 25023 were applied. Therefore, the following steps were set up:

1. Quality in use model based on quality standard ISO/IEC 25010 was defined.
2. A 25 question semi-structured survey served as a quality model assessment instrument based on ISO/IEC 25022 e ISO/IEC 25023 quality standards. The survey form was set up in [27].
3. The assessment instrument was debugged through the observation method and a survey pilot run with 10 participants.

4. The software was evaluated using the assessment instrument.
5. Software assessment scores were collected and tabulated.

Model percentages were specified according to the institution's required quality characteristics within the study context. The model appraised 70% quality use metrics compared to 30% internal/external metrics (usability). See Table 3.

Table 3. Software quality use model.

Characteristic	Sub Characteristic	Metrics	Survey questions	Metric value
Context Coverage	Context Complexity	Context completion	3	0.115
		Flexibility	1	0.035
Effectiveness	Effectiveness	Task completion	3	0.084
		Task effectiveness	1	0.028
		Error frequency	1	0.028
Efficiency	Efficiency	Estimated user actions	1	0.013
		Estimated task time	5	0.065
		Task relative time	5	0.065
Satisfaction	Utility	Function discretional use	1	0.07
		Level of Satisfaction	1	0.07
Risk Freedom	Freedom from health risk and security	Security from those affected by the use of the system	1	0.07
		User health and security problem frequency	1	0.07
Usability	Operability	Message clarity	1	0.3
		Total	**25**	**1.00**

Quality model measurements based on ISO/IEC 25010, ISO/IEC 25022/ISO/IEC 25023 quality standards range from 0 to 1 in a gradual range of 0.24, see Table 4.

Table 4. Final scores for results evaluation.

Satisfaction level	Scores	Measurement range
Highly satisfied	Meets expectations	$0.76 < X \leq 1$
Satisfactory	Acceptable	$0.51 < X \leq 0.75$
Unsatisfactory	Barely acceptable	$0.26 < X \leq 0.50$
	Unacceptable	$0 < X \leq 0.25$

2.5   Framework Implementation Integrating CMMI and SCRUM

Framework implementation was performed focused on the development of an Academic Portfolio module upgrade from the integrated system developed by UDT - UPEC.

A diagnostic assessment from the original situation related to Project management and software quality use before implementing the proposed Framework was performed (Academic Portfolio module). In the same way, after implementing the Framework, the satisfaction of the development team was evaluated using the survey model defined above. Table 5 defined the implementation of activities performed at UPEC's Academic Faculty Portfolio module using the proposed Framework.

Table 5.   Framework implementation information.

Software project	Academic Faculty Portfolio module
Institution:	Universidad Politécnica Estatal del Carchi (UPEC)
Product Backlog:	5 User history
Implementation period	2018–2019
Team	1 Product Owner, 1 Scrum Master, 2 development team personnel, 1 Tester, 1 Semantic Versioning Management, 1 UDT University Principal as the interested party
Number of Sprints:	2
Hours per Sprint:	Sprint 1 estimated 174 h/ 164 real time hours Sprint 2 estimated 160 h / 148 real time hours
Functional Testing	10
Technological Features	• Web app • Architecture- Client-Server • App server: WebLogic 10.3.6 • Client: Web browser • Development Platform: Oracle Application Express (Oracle APEX) 5.1.4 • Oracle Data base ® 11g Release 2 Data base

3   Results

The following section shows results from software development and quality use process assessment before and after the implementation of the proposed Framework integrating CMMI-DEV and SCRUM.

3.1   Software Quality Process Assessment Results

Before Framework implementation there was 57% dissatisfaction in software quality process whereas Project planning tasks (PP) and Project Monitoring and Control (PMC) represent the most dissatisfaction levels 71%, see Table 6.

Table 6. Process quality assessment before the implementation of the Framework.

Before	CMMI Project Management Areas					
Scale	REQM	PP	PMC	IPM	RSKM	Total
Satisfied	0%	4%	2%	17%	0%	5%
Partially Satisfied	65%	25%	27%	37%	37%	38%
Dissatisfied	35%	71%	71%	46%	63%	57%

After implementing Framework 51% satisfaction regarding software quality process, as illustrated by Integrated Project Management tasks (IPM) and 75% Risk Management (RSKM) see Table 7.

Table 7. Process quality assessment after Framework implementation.

After	CMMI Project Management Areas					
Scale	REQM	PP	PMC	IPM	RSKM	Total
Satisfied	35%	42%	29%	75%	75%	51%
Partially Satisfied	60%	29%	35%	21%	25%	34%
Dissatisfied	5%	29%	36%	4%	0%	15%

Table 8 shows a 14.6% improvement rate in the areas of Project Management CMMI compared to RSKM areas where 23% improvement rate is evident. A range value from 1–3 was applied to determine improvement rate. Firs, 3 representing "Satisfied" in the scale whereas 2 means "Partially Satisfied" and 1 means "Dissatisfied". After that, Eq. 2 was applied.

$$\sum_1 = (A * n) \tag{2}$$

$$\sum_2 = (D * n)$$

$$M = \sum_1 - \sum_2$$

Therefore:

- n = Range value from 1 - 3.
- A = Value for each level shown in Table 6.
- D = Value for each level shown in Table 7.
- $\sum_1$ = The sum of A*n.
- $\sum_2$ = The sum of D*n.
- M = Before and after contrast.

Table 8. Software quality process improvement in Project Management areas CMMI.

CMMI Project Management areas	Before	After	Improvement
REQM	28%	38%	10%
PP	22%	36%	14%
PMC	22%	32%	10%
IPM	29%	45%	16%
RSKM	23%	46%	23%
Average Improvement Rate	24.8%	39.4%	14.6%

Further consideration to (Juma's et al. 2019) [32] ideas to statistically corroborate that significant improvement is possible in the software quality process as illustrated by a statistical analysis was performed using IBM SPSS Statistics version 25 software, considering the types of variables and the samples. In this case the variable measured (M) is quantitative (Ec. 2), the sampling is correlated (the same group of individuals) and data has normal distribution (Table 9) so that a T-student statistical test was used. This type of test consists of a parametric test applied two correlated samples contrasting the equality population hypothesis between two populations and two groups. In this study, both hypotheses were established as follows:

- H0: There is no significative difference in the software quality process.
- H1: There is significative difference in the software quality process.

Table 9. Normality tests for the software quality process.

	Shapiro-Wilk			
	Statistic	Statistic	Gl	Sig
Difference	0.204	0.883	5	0.325

Decision rule in the hypothesis test as follows:

- If $p\_value \geq 0.05$ then H_0 is accepted, otherwise H_0 is rejected.
- P_value represents Sig. value, asymptotic as illustrated in Table 10.

As revealed by the table, the value of asymptotic meaning (p-value $= 0.004$) is lower than 0.05, meaning that according to the decision rule H0 is rejected. Consequently, it is concluded that there are significative differences in the improvement of software quality processes.

Table 10. *T-student* test paired samples.

	Paired Differences					t	gl	Sig. (bilateral)
	Mean	Std Deviation	Average Dev error	95% Interval confidence difference				
				Inferior	Superior			
Quality_before - Quality_after	−14.600	5.367	2.400	−21.263	−7.937	−6,083	4	0.004

3.2 Results—Quality Assessment in the Use of Software Product

Table 11 shows that there is a 2.16% improvement in the quality in software product use after having implemented Framework, being software useability the most prominent feature in the improvement process. Results match with what Ferreirós & Vieira in 2015 ruled: "software quality improves when the quality in its process increases" [5].

Table 11. Use of software product assessment—Before and after proposed Framework implementation.

Num	Feature	Number metrics	Metric value	Obtained value (Before)	Obtained value (After)	Improvement
1	Context Coverage	4	0.14	10%	12%	2%
2	Effectiveness	5	0.14	10%	12%	2%
3	Efficacy	11	0.14	10%	12%	2%
4	Satisfaction	2	0.14	9%	11%	2%
5	Risk Freedom	2	0.14	13%	13%	0%
6	Usability	1	0.30	20%	25%	5%
Total		25	1	12%	14.16%	**2.16%**

Figure 1 graphicly shows the comparison between before and after Framework implementation obtained values with respect to software product quality use assessment considering the values obtained in Table 1.

As previously mentioned, to corroborate that statistically speaking there is significant improvement in software product quality use, the measured variable (M) is quantitative (Ec. 2), the sample is correlated (same group of individuals), and data distribution is normal (see Table 12) so that a T-student statistical test was used. Therefore, both hypotheses were established as follows:

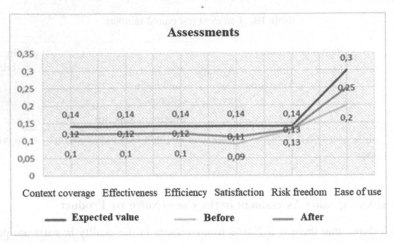

Fig. 1. Comparative table between before and after obtained values after implementing Framework with respect to software product quality use assessment (Table 1).

- H_0: There is no significant difference in the improvement of software product quality use.
- H_1: There is significant difference in the improvement of software product quality use.

Table 12. Normality tests for the software product quality use.

	Shapiro-Wilk			
	Statistic	Statistic	gl	Sig
Difference	0.375	0.805	6	0.066

Decision rule in the hypothesis test as follows:

- If $p\_value > 0.05$ H0 is accepted, otherwise H0 is rejected.
- P_value represents Sig. value, asymptotic as illustrated in Table 13.

As observed, the Sig. Value asymptotic (p-value $= 0.021$) is less than 0.05, according to the decision rule, H0 is rejected. It is therefore concluded that there is significative difference enhancing software product quality use.

4 Discussion

In Sect. 2.3 scientific articles like Marçal et al. [26], Farid et al. [23], Diaz et al., Bougroun et al. [24] were found addressing similar research integrating CMMI-DEV 1.2 version with SCRUM. However, evidence of its application or implementation guide is

Table 13. *T-student* test paired samples.

	Paired Differences					t	gl	Sig. (bilateral)
	Mean	Std deviation	Average Dev error	95% Interval confidence difference				
				Inferior	Superior			
Quality_before - Quality_after	-2.167	1.602	0.654	-3.848	-0.485	-3,313	5	0.021

not provided nor a measurement tool allowing improvement assessment by integrating CMMI-DEV / SCRUM. Such finding motivated us to do this research integrating CMMI-DEV 1.3 version and SCRUM as Framework development proposal thus complementing the study with a before and after assessment. As for UPEC's Academic Portfolio, it was founded on ISO/IEC 25000 quality standards. The integration of CMMI-DEV and SCRUM provided additional benefits apart from those reported to Project Management including formal planning, recording and Project Management follow up. Moreover, UPEC's technological development department personnel now manage their responsibilities more appropriately. It is worth noting that artifacts and proposed Framework templates were created in Spanish. It is our strong belief that Spanish environment should be taken into account for the next Framework implementation since the translation of artifacts to any other language may affect the validity of this study.

It seems likely that there are Framework limitations by not addressing all specific practices in the CMMI Project Management Process areas due to the integration of SCRUM phrases. Such process may be addressed in a future work.

5 Conclusions and Future Work

Bibliographical review served as theoretical base for the development of the Software Project Management Framework based on CMMI-DEV and SCRUM. The proposed Framework was evaluated in a real context through the implementation process on the Academic Faculty Portfolio's development module at *Universidad Politécnica Estatal del Carchi*. Results showed a 14.6% improvement rate (Table 8) in terms of satisfaction levels as per the development team. Additionally, there was a 2.16% increase in developed software quality use by the end of the Framework implementation process (Table 11). The application of ISO/IEC 25000 quality standards series on software product quality use contributed to a technical analysis to establish a level of improvement in the quality of the software developed at UDT – UPEC (Table 3). All things considered, the integration of CMMI-DEV with SCRUM improved the quality of the development process and software product. As research suitable in the future, the implementation of the proposed Framework on other academic scenarios and on the industry to enhance its validity. Moreover, in further research it is suggested that integration with other agile methodologies is performed so that the level of integration with CMMI increases and thus, software product assessment complements itself with internal and external quality based on ISO/IEC 25000 quality standard series.

References

1. Guevara-Vega, C.P., Chamorro-Ortega, W., Herrera-Granda, E., García-Santillán, I., Quiña-Mera, J.A.: Incidence of a web application implementation for high school students learning evaluation. A Case Study. RISTI - Rev. Iber. Sist. e Tecnol. Inf., no. E32, pp. 509–523 (2020)
2. Quiña-Mera, A., Chamorro Andrade, L., Montaluisa Yugla, J., Chicaiza Angamarca, D., Guevara-Vega, C.P.: Improving software project management by applying agile methodologies: a case study. In: Botto-Tobar, M., Montes León, S., Camacho, O., Chávez, D., Torres-Carrión, P., Zambrano Vizuete, M. (eds.) ICAT 2020. CCIS, vol. 1388, pp. 672–685. Springer, Cham (2021). https://doi.org/10.1007/978-3-030-71503-8_52
3. Quiña-Mera, J.A., Correa Real, L.G., Jácome Orozco, A.G., Landeta-López, P.A., Guevara-Vega, C.P.: Proposal for a software development project management model for public institutions in Ecuador: a case study. In: International Conference on Advances in Emerging Trends and Technologies, ICAETT 2020, vol. 1302, pp. 290–301 (2021)
4. Morales-Trujillo, M.E., Oktaba, H., Piattini, M., Escalante-Ramírez, B.: Bottom-up authoring of Software Engineering methods and practices. J. Appl. Res. Technol. 17(1), 28–43 (2019)
5. Ferreirós, A., Dias, L.A.V.: Evaluation of accomplishment of do-178C objectives by cmmi-dev 1.3. In: Proceedings - 12th International Conference Information Technologies New Generation. ITNG 2015, pp. 759–760 (2015)
6. Furtado Soares, F.S., de Lemos Meira, S.R.: An agile strategy for implementing CMMI project management practices in software organizations. In: 2015 10th 2015 10th Iberian Conference on Information Systems and Technologies (CIST) 2015 (2015)
7. Callejas-Cuervo, M., Alarcón-Aldana, A.C., Álvarez-Carreño, A.M.: Modelos de calidad del software, un estado del arte. Entramado 13(1), 236–250 (2017)
8. Zapata-Jaramillo, C.M., Valderrama-Betancur, J., Jimenez-Pinzon, L.D.: Representation of CMMI-DEV practices in the Semat kernel. IEEE Lat. Am. Trans 13(10), 3476–3481 (2015)
9. CMMI Institute. CMMI ® para Desarrollo, Versión 1.3 Equipo del Producto CMMI. Mejora de los procesos para el desarrollo de mejores productos y servicios (2010)
10. Sharma, S., Hasteer, N.: A comprehensive study on state of Scrum development. In: Proceeding - IEEE International Conference on Computing Communication Automation. ICCCA 2016, pp. 867–872 (2017)
11. Mundra, A., Misra, S., Dhawale, C.A.: Practical scrum-scrum team: way to produce successful and quality software. In: Proceedings of the 2013 13th International Conference on Computing Science Its Application. ICCSA 2013, pp. 119–123 (2013)
12. Srivastava, A., Bhardwaj, S., Saraswat, S.: SCRUM model for agile methodology. In: Proceeding - IEEE International Conference on Computing Communication Automation. ICCCA 2017, vol. 2017-January, pp. 864–869 (2017)
13. Schwaber, K.: SCRUM development process. Bus. Object Des. Implement. no. April 1987, pp. 117–134 (1987)
14. Rodríguez, C., Dorado, R.: ¿ Por qué implementar Scrum? Why to implement Scrum? Pour quelles raisons mettre en place Scrum? Porque implementar Scrum? Rev. Ontare 3(1), 125–144 (2015)
15. Schwaber, K., Sutherland, J.: La Guía de Scrum. La Guía Definitiva de Scrum: Las Reglas del Juego. Scrum.Org, p. 22 (2017)
16. Hevner, A., Chatterjee, S.: Design science research in information systems. In: Design Research in Information Systems. Integrated Series in Information Systems, vol 22, pp. 9–22. Springer, Boston (2010). https://doi.org/10.1007/978-1-4419-5653-8_2

17. E. U. P. E. del C. UPEC-P28-S01 Proceso de Desarrollo y Mantenimiento de Software y Aplicaciones. Tulcán, Carchi, UDSOFT, vol. 28 febrero. (2018)
18. Gorgas García, J., Cardiel López, N., Zamorano Calvo, J.: Estadística Básica para estudiantes de ciencias 53(9) (2011)
19. ISO - International Organization for Standardization. ISO/IEC 25000, Portal ISO 25000, (2014). https://iso25000.com/. Accessed 05 Jan 2021
20. ISO/IEC 25022. NTE INEN-ISO/IEC 25022 International Organization for Standardization. ISO/IEC 25022 (2016)
21. Guevara-Vega, C., Hernández-Rojas, J., Botto-Tobar, M., García-Santillán, I., Basantes-Andrade, A., Quiña-Mera, A.: Automation of the municipal inspection process in ecuador applying Mobile-D for android. In: Botto-Tobar, M., León-Acurio, J., Díaz Cadena, A., Montiel Díaz, P. (eds.) ICAETT 2019. AISC, vol. 1066, pp. 155–166. Springer, Cham (2020). https://doi.org/10.1007/978-3-030-32022-5_15
22. ISO/IEC 25023: NTE INEN-ISO/IEC 25023 International Organization for Standardization. ISO/IEC 25023 (2011)
23. Farid, A.B., AbdElghany, A.S., Helmy, Y.M.: Implementing project management category process areas of CMMI version 1.3 using scrum practices, and assets. Int. J. Adv. Comput. Sci. Appl. 7(2), 243–252 (2016)
24. Bougroun, Z., Zeaaraoui, A., Bouchentouf, T.: The projection of the specific practices of the third level of CMMI model in agile methods: Scrum, XP and Kanban. Colloq. Inf. Sci. Technol. Cist, vol. 2015-Janua, no. January, pp. 174–179 (2015)
25. Diaz, J., Garbajosa, J., Calvo-Manzano, J.A.: Mapping CMMI level 2 to scrum practices: an experience report. In: O'Connor, R.V., Baddoo, N., Cuadrago-Gallego, J., Rejas-Muslera, R., Smolander, K., Messnarz, R. (eds.) EuroSPI 2009. CCIS, vol. 42, pp. 93–104. Springer, Heidelberg (2009). https://doi.org/10.1007/978-3-642-04133-4_8
26. Marçal, A.S.C., De Freitas, B.C.C., Furtado Soares, F.S., Belchior, A.D.: Mapping CMMI project management process areas to SCRUM practices. In: Proceedings – International Conference on Software Engineering, pp. 13–22 (2007)
27. Guerrero, G., Guevara, A., Quiña-Mera, A., Guevara-Vega, C., García, I.: Artifacts-framework CMMI-SCRUM. Zenodo (2021). https://doi.org/10.5281/zenodo.4747709
28. Azizi, R., Zakerian, S., Rahgozar, M.: Determining reliability and validity of the persian version of software usability measurements inventory (SUMI) questionnaire. Int. J. 5(1), 31–34 (2013)
29. Brooke, J.: SUS: a quick and dirty usability scale. Usability Eval. Ind., vol. 189 (1995)
30. Chin, J.P., Diehl, V.A., Norman, K.L.: Development of an instrument measuring user satisfaction of the human-computer interface. In: Conference on Human Factors Computing System - Proceedings, vol. Part F1302, pp. 213–218 (1988)
31. Likert, R.: A technique for the measurement of attitudes. Arch. Psychol. 22, 11–20 (1932)
32. Juma, A., Rodríguez, J., Caraguay, J., Naranjo, M., Quiña-Mera, A., García-Santillán, I.: Integration and evaluation of social networks in virtual learning environments: a case study. In: Botto-Tobar, M., Pizarro, G., Zúñiga-Prieto, M., D'Armas, M., Zúñiga-Sánchez, M. (eds.) CITT 2018. CCIS, vol. 895, pp. 245–258. Springer, Cham (2019). https://doi.org/10.1007/978-3-030-05532-5_18

Relevant Factors in the Inventory Record Inaccuracy for Retail Companies: A Study in Food Retail Industry

Jorge Andrés Espinoza Aguirre[1] (✉) (iD), Mario Peña[2,3] (✉) (iD),
Diana Jadan-Avilés[3] (✉) (iD), and Juan Llivisaca[3] (✉) (iD)

[1] Faculty of Chemical Sciences, University of Cuenca, 010107 Cuenca, Ecuador
jorge.espinoza@ucuenca.edu.ec
[2] Research Department (DIUC), University of Cuenca, 010107 Cuenca, Ecuador
mario.penao@ucuenca.edu.ec
[3] Department of Applied Chemistry and Systems of Production, Faculty of Chemical Sciences,
University of Cuenca, 010107 Cuenca, Ecuador
{diana.jadan,juan.llivisaca}@ucuenca.edu.ec

Abstract. Retail companies are an essential industry for economic development in every country. In these organizations, at least 60% of the assets correspond to inventory. Therefore, inventory record inaccuracy (IRI) is a problem among these companies. IRI is the gap generated between physical audits and system records, which affects the retailer by changing their book value, increasing economic losses, and providing poor customer service. This study aims to identify the factors that cause IRI in retail companies and, using a mathematical model, works to help retailers minimize the gap between registers. As a consequence, retailers can reduce potential losses in the company. Two mathematical models are proposed for each of the dependent variables: IRI and difference between records. The independent variables considered are quantity of sale of an item, cost, physical audit period, variety of products, product returns, sale price, and quantity sold. This work concludes by comparing both models, highlighting the most influential variables.

Keywords: Retail · Inventory management · Inventory record inaccuracy · Difference between records · Product returns

1 Introduction

The term "retail" refers to retail commerce, which aims to find out the needs and desires of its target market and guide companies towards satisfying these needs and desires more efficiently than their competitors [1]. The retail industry in Ecuador contributes to the country's economy as well as to the growth of the Gross Domestic Product (GDP). In addition, the retail industry helps to formalize commercial activities, so that their sales can collect more taxes per sale. Taxes are seldom collected in informal neighborhood stores [2].

© Springer Nature Switzerland AG 2022
M. Botto-Tobar et al. (Eds.): ICAT 2021, CCIS 1535, pp. 552–564, 2022.
https://doi.org/10.1007/978-3-031-03884-6_40

Retail companies often carry a broad variety of products and high inventory levels. This tends to foster registration and replacement-related errors. These errors result in phantom products, products that are in the store's inventory system, but cannot be found physically by customers. Great quantities of phantom products will result in lower sales [3]. Therefore, it is important to maintain control over inventory, as it represents an significant investment for the retailer. Investigations about inventory record inaccuracy exist, including [4, 5, 19, 20, 27], which are studies that collected data in Ecuador. The studies [6–14], had an international scope. These works refer to inventory system management and improvement.

On the other hand, an accurate inventory management system leads to have a control about products in a store. But this is not always feasible, and the main cause is inventory record inaccuracy (IRI). IRI measures the degree of inaccuracy of an inventory recorded system and the physical available inventory of a specific product in a warehouses [15, 16]. According to [16], studies on IRI can be classified into: the presence of IRI, effects of IRI, causes of IRI, the reduction of IRI, and IRI measurement. This research focuses on how to reduce IRI, considering important variables for this objective. In [10] IRI manifests itself as positive or negative errors, where there is more or less physical counting inventory than registered. Inventory accuracy is crucial information for retailers. Chuang HH-C & Oliva R [17] mention that IRI can significantly change the book value of inventory added and thus, alter business resolutions. IRI can cause stockouts and revenue losses triggered by unnecessary replenishment [16]. Considering a proper management of IRI, retail commerce should have greater control over their inventory to avoid losses, resulting in economic consequences for companies. IRI allows for different operational strategies aiming to satisfy both online and in-store costumers. However, the authors in [9] mentions that it is necessary to know the exact inventory quantity in stores to use it effectively for online orders and for in-store customer service. Nevertheless, it is difficult to eliminate these inventory errors because IRI has become the rule rather than the exception the retail sector [10]. In [18] and [10], it is mentioned that IRI, even at low levels, damages the retailer's operational performance, along with its reputation with consumers, due to product unavailability. If inventory records are not corrected in a reasonable time, the discrepancy can affect up to 65% of the records in a store [8].

Different IRI control methods have been implemented over the years to reduce registration errors, for example radio frequency identification (RFID). Lately, RFID has been used mainly for Industrial Internet of Things (IIOT), due to low price, as well as for supply chains due to real-time management, traceability, logistic, and shop floor deployment [19]. In addition, RFID had been used in inventory control, because is an important facet in the retailing business due to associated inventory holding cost and the risk of obsolescence of items. Together technologies such as barcodes or radio frequency identification (RFID) are shown as alternatives to improve visibility through continuous record monitoring, it is know how smart inventories, that working alongside policies as mentioned in [10], combining crucial aspects of inventory management such as counting and inspection with cycle counting policies for supply chain considering investments in RFID technology. While the most used method for inventory control is visibility of items. It is measured comparing existence of an item from its entry and exit [20]. The physically counting inventory is considered as a method to correct IRI. This proposal interpreted as the relative error between physical inventory and system inventory, how result measured between positive discrepancy and negative discrepancy situations.

The methods and technologies used to decrease IRI focus on different mathematical models. Mathematical models focus on solving the inventory replacement problem in records that have been included within the inventory management. A cyclical count-based system is proposed by [5] to improve warehouse inventory accuracy by scheduling inventory counts by categories. Finally, other methods are currently used for inventory registration, such as the cyclical counting model used in [21], as well as the tree-type registration protocol or the loose label identification protocol based on slot filters, both mentioned in [12]. All of these, aim to support companies by improving their profitability through effective inventory control.

In the previous paragraphs it has been mentioned about inventory control in the retail commerce, the technology applied to this control and the mathematical models used. However, different inventory control methods employed may or may not be accurate enough compared to the physical inventory held in warehouses, creating a gap between these values. In this work, the following research questions are posed: *What are the factors that influence IRI variability in retail companies? Are these factors manageable in retail companies?*. These research questions will help fill the gap between the methods used to lower IRI, and the impact that each one has on retail businesses. It is evident that IRI causes inventory errors and, as a result, decreases store performance. Some proposals try to handle this issue. However, they have not identified the main factors affecting IRI or made a corresponding sensibility analysis. The objective of this work is to identify factors that influence IRI, and at the same time, find out which of these factors most affect it. The objective was to help retailers plan mitigation strategies according to these factors, thereby reducing the impact of IRI on the company's profitability. The paper is organized as follows: in Sect. 2, the methodology is described. Section 3 defines the results and discussion. The last section provides the conclusion.

2 Methodology

The methodology used in this study started with a review of articles through the software Atlas.Ti (version 8.4.22). The review helped to identify both quantitative and qualitative variables relevant to inventory control. Data was collected during the months of interest for this study. Information was gathered from 42 articles through the software. The variables considered were: quantity of sale of an item, cost, physical audit period [8], variety of products [22], product returns [8, 23], sale price, and quantity sold [7].

Data was collected considering a food retail company as the case study in a monthly interval during September to December 2020, and January and February 2021 regarding four warehouses distributed in four different areas in Cuenca – Ecuador. In order to collect the data, it was necessary to visit each warehouse, review the records kept in each one, and review the digital records.

On the other hand, once the data was collected, a descriptive and inferential statistical analysis was carried out. The SPSS program (version 25) was used for this analysis. It generated a descriptive analysis (mean, maximum, and minimum values) for each warehouse. These values could indicate a preliminary situation of how inventory is managed in the enterprise. However, for the proposed analysis of this research, all the validated records provided had been taken.

The IRI variable needs to be calculated to continue with the investigation. A comparison of the inventory system records and physical audit records of the case of study yield a total number of IRI records. With the IRI records, a categorical count of the number of these records was executed to obtain the indicator per category by applying the formula:

$$IRI = [(Records\,with\,error)/(Total\,records)] \times 100 \qquad (1)$$

Similarly, the inventory rotation index was calculated using the data obtained from the inventory at the end of the month, as well as the company's entries data:

$$Inventory\,rotation = Sales/Inventory \qquad (2)$$

The next step is an inferential statistical analysis. For that reason, an ANOVA normality test was executed. This test helps to determine if population variances fit a parametric model and are equal within limit values that will allow a normal data distribution to be assumed [24]. The Kolmogorov-Smirnov test validated the assumptions of normality in the ANOVA test, which adjusts to samples more significant than 50 data. Therefore, it is the test to be used. However, for this research the Lilliefors test, a variation of the Kolmogorov-Smirnov test was used because it allows estimating the parameters based on the sample without the need to know the data distribution [25]. In addition, tests were used to determine the statistical difference of means. From these normality results, non-parametric tests were used as appropriate. Finally, a step-by-step regression was chosen to be performed because the investigation required a model in which the final relation between variables result as a polynomial function of order "n". Additionally, the work needed to have two models as a result, one for each result or dependent variable, in which can be seen how the regression predicts or reveals relationships between variables and select from a list of relevant variables which affects a singular dependent variable at the time. By comparing these models, the relationships between them can be discovered to contribute to a richer analysis of the research [26].

Finally, after the statistical analysis, with the dependent variable IRI, and the independent variables identified from the proposal, a predictive mathematical model of the behavior of the dependent variable was developed, made by the influential variables. A predictive model was chosen because it's important for the retailers to know how each variable could affect the records accuracy in order to prevent possible consequences by making decisions to avoid them. The following section describes in detail each part of the methodology.

3   Results and Discussion

The processed data for this research were initially 521,405 records (four warehouses). By applying filters such as duplicate records, incomplete records and IRI records the data was reduced. Additionally, the records were classified by item in order to have only one total record per item for each month. As a result the study starts considering 8,636 total records from the four warehouses, during September, 2020, to February, 2021. Table 1 presents the analysis of IRI records per month. Items registered were the products registered in the inventory of the four warehouses, while IRI items represent which items have an inventory variance in each month. The system records were compared against the physical audits for each item in every month, if the quantity of both registers differs form each other, then the item is classified as an IRI item. An evident analysis show record increase during December, 2020, and January, 2021.

Table 1. IRI records per month.

Year	Month	Items registered	IRI items
2020	September	1385	903
2020	October	1225	787
2020	November	1476	574
2020	December	6871	**3063**
2021	January	6558	**3184**
2021	February	135	125

Analyzing the Table 1, it is evident that both months, December and January, IRI records increased considerably. However, the increase in IRI registrations is justified by the increase in the number of registrations registered in these months, because product purchases also increased. December, 2020, and January, 2021, reported a total of 6,871 and 6,558 records registered, respectively, while in September, October, and November 2020, the numbers of items registered were 1,385; 1,225; and 1,476 records, respectively. February has the lowest records due to the fact that the stores lower their sales, and the data was taken until the middle of the month. The table's purpose is to show and justify the increase of IRI items of December, 2020, and January, 2021 in comparison to the other months in the study. In addition, the relation between these variables, IRI items and items registered per month, is verified through a Pearson correlation test. Furthermore, the hypothesis it was with the statistical analysis, where a positive Pearson correlation of 0.993 (p-value < 0.05) was obtained. This indicates that these variables are directly correlated.

3.1   Data Analysis Per Category

The analysis was carried out considering 36 categories according to the Enterprises Resources Planning (ERP) of the company to detect which categories have the greatest IRI. It is worth mentioning that only 33 categories had IRI records.

Normality Data Test. The p-value obtained in the test for all months is less than the research significance level (0.05). Therefore, the assumptions of normality are not satisfied, and as a result, non-parametric tests must be used.

IRI Longitudinal Analysis. To determine if there is a variation in the warehouses' means, aiming to hint the path to analyze, the Kruskal-Wallis test is used to determine significant differences between the data of the months under study [27]. The test was applied within the segmentation by month and showed that the differences between some of the means are statistically significant enough to reject the null hypothesis. The p-values of September (0.000016), October (0.002434), and November (0.017574), are lower than the level of significance (0.05) as observed in Table 2. The results helped to determine which months have different means within the time period of the study, indicating that some warehouses presented a higher level of inaccuracy than others, causing the difference between warehouses per month to be considerable. The analysis leads to a cross-sectional study by warehouses in September, October, and November to conclude if higher inaccuracy values are presented.

Table 2. Kruskal-Wallis test.

Month & Year	Test Statistics[a,b] Variable:IRI
September, 2020	**0.000016**
October, 2020	**0.002**
November, 2020	**0.0176**
December, 2020	0.919
January, 2021	0.942
February, 2021	0.154

[a]Grouping Variable: Warehouse.
[b]Asymptotic Significance.

IRI Cross-sectional Analysis. A Mann-Whitney U test is performed in order to allow two independent samples to be compared when there are differences between the amount of data among them [27]. This test is applied to perform a cross-sectional analysis between warehouses during the months that presented significant differences in its means in the previous research. As a result, this section works with the data from September, October, and November, 2020. December, 2020, January and February 2021 didn't present significant differences between warehouses so their data is not considered for this section. Each analysis is described below, emphasizing the warehouses that present differences. The test summary can be found in Table 3.

Table 3. Mann Whitney test summary in four warehouses.

Month & Year	Warehouse	Mann U Whitney test[a]	Mean rank
September–October, 2020	1	0.24	265.96 250.74
	2	0.02	**243.07 214.3**
	3	0.112	187.55 169.37
	4	0.273	184.3 172.4
September–November, 2020	1	0.623	257.04 250.72
	2	0.452	202.46 193.6
	3	0.016	**149.25 119.36**
	4	0.768	145.21 142.31
October–November, 2020	1	0.466	244.47 253.7
	2	0.056	177 198.54
	3	0.366	95.31 87.54
	4	0.39	151.05 159.91

[a]Asymptotic Significance (2-tailed).

September–October. Although the results of the Mann-Whitney U test presented warehouse 2 as the one that has differences in the mean of the study variable in comparison with the rest of the warehouses during the same period, it is not the warehouse to take into consideration, due to the statistics presented along with the test. The statistics show warehouses 1 as the one where a more in-depth analysis must be carried out to determine the factors linked to the increase in IRI values.

September–November. Once again, warehouse 1 showed the highest mean values of all the warehouses. In September, warehouse 3 presented an increased number of IRI records, and the variable that represents the difference between those records showed an even higher value. From this relationship, it can be assumed that the variation between the physical counting inventory and the system inventory is considerable in this warehouse. The records that exhibit this variation suffered representative losses considering the number of IRI records presented. On the other hand, in November there were no significant relationships between the variables in all the warehouses, so it allows the assumption that the inventory management had a considerable improvement compared to the previous months.

October–November. Warehouse 1 presented the highest mean values of all warehouses. The difference is considerably more significant than the other warehouses, so it can be assumed that inventory management in warehouses 2, 3, and 4 have improved since their mean values decreased compared to warehouse 1. From this relationship, the variation between physical inventory and the system inventory is significant in this warehouse. The records that presented this variation suffered representative losses considering the number of totals. On the other hand, in November there were no significant relationships between the variables in all warehouses, so it is correct to conclude that the inventory management had a significant improvement compared to the previous months.

Analyzing Table 3 allows to determine that warehouse 1 has the highest value of mean rank by analyzing the difference between records in the periods September–October, and September–November. Nevertheless, warehouses 2 (September–October) and 3 (September–November) present a wider mean rank, which indicate that the gap between registers is higher. In order to know how the independent variables of this study are influencing the gap and increasing, in consequence, IRI, a step-by-step regression resulting in two mathematical models is performed below.

Explanatory Models. Step-by-step regression test. Dependent variables were defined to start the test. The goal was to find independent variables that could influence the dependent ones. The dependent variables were: IRI and difference between records. The independent variables to be tested are described below:

Record Purchase Costs. These values correspond to the costs of each product that the retailer commercializes.

Customer Returns. Records associated with the devolution of items to the warehouse after the purchase.

Sales. Total number of item sales completed.

Supplier Returns. Records associated with the devolution of items to the supplier.

Inventory Rotation. Ratio that shows how many times the retailer sold and replace inventory.

Physical Audit Period. Time gap between physical audits of the inventory.

Variety of Products. Number of products per warehouse.

The model which focuses on the variables that influence IRI is developed below.

Dependent Variable: IRI. The model showed three variables that influenced IRI; these variables are shown in Table 4 in order of impact level. Total sale was the variable that influences IRI the most, followed by the supplier returns and the inventory turnover. Additionally, the model presents an R squared of 14.8%, meaning the proportion of data about which it is possible to predict the IRI variable based on the independent variables shown.

Table 4. Step-by-step regression test over dependent variable IRI.

Model	Predictors	R	R square
1	Sales	0.329	0.108
2	Supplier returns	0.363	0.132
3	Inventory rotation	0.385	**0.148**

To determine whether it is possible to build a regression model from the variables entered in the statistical software, the ANOVA study shows that the level of significance is lower than 0.05. Therefore, it is validated and its possible to build a model using the coefficients shown below, which resulted from the step-by-step analysis performed in the SPSS software. Additionally, due to its high R squared, the lowest error is expected out of the three models presented in Table 4. The model is presented as follows:

$$y = 0.036 + 1.393 \times 10^{-5}x_1 + 1.79 \times 10^{-4}x_2 - 9.03e^{-4}x_3 \tag{3}$$

where:
$y = IRI.$
$x_1 = Total\ sales.$
$x_2 = Suppliers\ returns.$
$x_3 = Inventory\ rotation.$

Based on the coefficients, the most sensitive variable that modifies the dependent variable IRI was the inventory rotation. Consequently, the company should emphasize its efforts to control and prevent this variable from acquiring high values resulting in an IRI increase. To determine if there are common factors that affect the inventory record, a second model with the variable Difference between records as the dependent variable, is developed below.

Dependent Variable: Difference Between Records. The model presents three variables that influence the Difference between records. These variables are shown in Table 5 in order of impact level.

Total sales are shown as the first variable to affect the dependent variable, followed by the supplier returns and the customer returns. The model presents an R squared of 43.7%, meaning the proportion of data about which is possible to predict the difference between records variable based on the independent variables. To determine whether it is possible to build a regression model from the variables entered in the statistical software SPSS, the study shows that the ANOVA statistic significance level is lower than 0.05. Therefore, it is validated and its possible to build a model.

For the model construction, the data to be used is coefficients, the model with the highest R squared, and its corresponding error. The coefficients of each of the variables in the study will contribute to the model function. The model is presented as follows:

$$y = -269.07 + 1.726x_1 + 71.152x_2 + 3092.621x_3 \tag{4}$$

Table 5. Step-by-step regression test over dependent variable: difference between records.

Model	Predictors	R	R square
1	Sales	0.496	0.246
2	Supplier returns	0.574	0.329
3	Costumer returns	0.661	**0.437**

where:

$y = $ *Difference between records.*

$x_1 = $ *Total sales.*

$x_2 = $ *Suppliers returns.*

$x_3 = $ *Costumers returns.*

After performing the analysis and based on the coefficients, the most sensitive variable that modified the dependent variable "Difference between records" was the customer returns variable, and as a result, the company should emphasize their efforts to control and prevent this variable from acquiring high values that could result in the broader difference between records. To conclude this section, and analyzing both models, it is found that model 1, whose dependent variable is IRI, and model 2, whose dependent variable is "difference between records" present a common variable within their respective equations, Supplier returns. The retailer should be aware of this finding because it is present as a crucial variable to control, since it is show in both models analyzed. Its potential increase will affect the dependent variables, IRI, and "Difference between records", resulting in a general downgrade in inventory management.

4   Conclusions

This research has achieved the objective of determining the factors that influence IRI variability in retail companies, ordering them from the ones with less impact to those with greater impact. In four warehouses located in four different areas in Cuenca – Ecuador, the most influential factors are: customer returns, suppliers returns, sales, and inventory turnover. The returns factor is emphasized since it is repeated in both proposed models, directly influencing IRI. In this research, two models of equations based on two dependent variables were proposed. In the model with the dependent variable IRI, the returns factor coefficient is $1.79e-4$. In the model with the dependent variable Difference between records, the returns factor coefficient is 71, 152, showing that in both cases, it is the second most influential variable on its respective dependent variable. In general, this influence arises from the retail company's handling of returns and their particular record in the ERP.

Inventory level is crucial information for any retail commerce's strategic planning. Thus, controlling these factors can mitigate economic losses related to a high IRI, as well as customer service performance and enhance their relationships with suppliers.

These factors can be controlled in a retail environment by proposing a valuation system for the products offered or the products on which there is a higher rate of return. This system will help establish the product's valuation prior to making their choice of purchase, thus reducing possible returns as mentioned in [28]. Another way to reduce returns, as mentioned in [29], is establishing a specific time for returns. This strategy can be implemented as part of the re-tail store's customer service policy, always considering a balancing the desires of customer and the needs of the company, to avoid displeasing the client, which could result in a customer loss.

This study complements other works reviewed in this paper, by analyzing the main variables that affects the retailer inventory, allowing to take decisions over the most influential ones, which has been proved to decrease their performance if these variables keep incrementing the IRI value. Works such as, [9], were it is analyzed a replenishment based approach that help to mitigate errors, and the authors mention that in order to improve performance a technology driven inventory audit should be performed, or the cycle count analysis performed in [10] which focuses on effective periodic audits to avoid cumulative errors. The RFID study and its implications shown in [14], and [16] were a model is proposed after considering performance issues caused by IRI giving a hint to the managers in order to set a cause target for action, aim to decrease the errors and solve the inventory record problem. This study opens future lines of research related to verifying these factor mitigation strategies in the retail environment. The present research also reveals further opportunities to clarify the scope of inventory management policies, specifically those about returns, customers, store performance, and company profitability. The proposed models show the weights that the different variables have in the IRI, and these models can be enhanced if they are integrated into future research about management of the retail enterprise.

Acknowledgments. This study is part of the research project "Modelo de optimización para la gestión de diseño, inventarios y logística de las tiendas en el sector minorista (retail) del Azuay", supported by the Research Department of the University of Cuenca (DIUC).

References

1. Quintero Arango, L.F.: El sector retail, los puntos de venta y el comportamiento de compras de los consumidores de la base de la pirámide en la columna en la ciudad de Medellín (2015)
2. Villacís Cardenas, C.: Análisis de la evolución del sector retail en el Ecuador, durante el periodo 2007 al 2017. Universidad de Especialidades Espíritu Santo (2018)
3. Ton, Z., Raman, A.: The effect of product variety and inventory levels on retail store sales: a longitudinal study: the effect of product variety and inventory levels on retail store sales. Prod. Oper. Manag. **19**, 546–560 (2010). https://doi.org/10.1111/j.1937-5956.2010.01120.x
4. Cueva Enriquez, D.V.: Propuesta de un sistema administrativo y contable como he-rramienta de mejoramiento continuo en el área de inventarios para la empresa Motorista CIA.Ltda. Universidad Central del Ecuador (2016)
5. Merlo, F.: Propuesta de mejoramiento en la exactitud de inventarios dentro de la bo-dega de repuestos en una empresa de soluciones logísticas. Universidad de las Américas (2020)
6. Bruccoleri, M., Cannella, S., La Porta, G.: Inventory record inaccuracy in supply chains: the role of workers' behavior. Int. J. Phys. Distrib. Log. Manag. **44**, 796–819 (2014). https://doi.org/10.1108/IJPDLM-09-2013-0240

7. Chen, L., Mersereau, A.: Analytics for operational visibility in the retail store: the cases of censored demand and inventory record inaccuracy. In: Agrawal, N., Smith, S.A. (eds.) Retail Supply Chain Management. ISORMS, vol. 223, pp. 79–112. Springer, Boston, MA (2015). https://doi.org/10.1007/978-1-4899-7562-1_5

8. DeHoratius, N., Raman, A.: Inventory record inaccuracy: an empirical analysis. Manag. Sci. **54**, 627–641 (2008). https://doi.org/10.1287/mnsc.1070.0789

9. Ishfaq, R., Raja, U.: Empirical evaluation of IRI mitigation strategies in retail stores. J. Oper. Res. Soc. 1–14 (2019). https://doi.org/10.1080/01605682.2019.1640592

10. Kök, A.G., Shang, K.H.: Evaluation of cycle-count policies for supply chains with inventory inaccuracy and implications on RFID investments. Eur. J. Oper. Res. **237**, 91–105 (2014). https://doi.org/10.1016/j.ejor.2014.01.052

11. Kwak, J.K., Gavirneni, S.: Impact of information errors on supply chain performance. J. Oper. Res. Soc. **66**, 288–298 (2015). https://doi.org/10.1057/jors.2013.175

12. Liu, X., Li, K., Min, G., Shen, Y., Liu, A.X., Qu, W.: Completely pinpointing the missing RFID tags in a time-efficient way. IEEE Trans. Comput. **64**, 87–96 (2015). https://doi.org/10.1109/TC.2013.197

13. Nayak, R., Singh, A., Padhye, R., Wang, L.: RFID in textile and clothing manufacturing: technology and challenges. Fash. Text. **2**(1), 1–16 (2015). https://doi.org/10.1186/s40691-015-0034-9

14. Zhang, L.-H., Li, T., Fan, T.-J.: Radio-frequency identification (RFID) adoption with inventory misplacement under retail competition. Eur. J. Oper. Res. **270**, 1028–1043 (2018). https://doi.org/10.1016/j.ejor.2018.04.038

15. Barratt, M., Kull, T.J., Sodero, A.C.: Inventory record inaccuracy dynamics and the role of employees within multi-channel distribution center inventory systems. J. Oper. Manag. **63**, 6–24 (2018). https://doi.org/10.1016/j.jom.2018.09.003

16. Shabani, A., Maroti, G., de Leeuw, S., Dullaert, W.: Inventory record inaccuracy and store-level performance. Int. J. Prod. Econ. **235**, 108111 (2021). https://doi.org/10.1016/j.ijpe.2021.108111

17. Chuang, H.H.-C., Oliva, R.: Inventory record inaccuracy: causes and labor effects. J. Oper. Manag. **39–40**, 63–78 (2015). https://doi.org/10.1016/j.jom.2015.07.006

18. Gallino, S., Moreno, A.: Integration of online and offline channels in retail: the impact of sharing reliable inventory availability information. SSRN Electron. J. 1–36 (2012). https://doi.org/10.2139/ssrn.2149095

19. Munoz-Ausecha, C., Ruiz-Rosero, J., Ramirez-Gonzalez, G.: RFID applications and security review. Computation **9**, 69 (2021). https://doi.org/10.3390/computation9060069

20. Doss, R., Trujillo-Rasua, R., Piramuthu, S.: Secure attribute-based search in RFID-based inventory control systems. Decis. Support Syst. **132**, 113270 (2020). https://doi.org/10.1016/j.dss.2020.113270

21. Fathoni, F.A., Ridwan, A.Y., Santosa, B.: Development of inventory control application for pharmaceutical product using ABC-VED cycle counting method to increase inventory record accuracy. In: Proceedings of the 2018 International Conference on Industrial Enterprise and System Engineering (IcoIESE 2018), Yogyakarta, Indonesia. Atlantis Press (2019)

22. Levy, M., Weitz, B.: Retailing Management. Irwin McGrawHill, Boston (2001)

23. Rekik, Y.: Inventory inaccuracies in the wholesale supply chain. Int. J. Prod. Econ. **133**, 172–181 (2011). https://doi.org/10.1016/j.ijpe.2010.02.012

24. Kim, Y.J., Cribbie, R.A.: ANOVA and the variance homogeneity assumption: exploring a better gatekeeper. Br. J. Math. Stat. Psychol. **71**, 1–12 (2018). https://doi.org/10.1111/bmsp.12103

25. Mohd Razali, N., Bee Wah, Y.: Power comparisons of Shapiro-Wilk, Kolmogorov-Smirnov, Lilliefors and Anderson-Darling tests. J. Stat. Model. Anal. **2**, 21–33 (2011)

26. Johnsson, T.: A procedure for stepwise regression analysis. Stat. Pap. **33**, 21–29 (1992). https://doi.org/10.1007/BF02925308
27. MacFarland, T.W., Yates, J.M.: Introduction to Nonparametric Statistics for the Biological Sciences Using R. Springer, Cham (2016). https://doi.org/10.1007/978-3-319-30634-6
28. Walsh, G., Möhring, M.: Effectiveness of product return-prevention instruments: empirical evidence. Electron Markets **27**, 341–350 (2017). https://doi.org/10.1007/s12525-017-0259-0
29. Shang, G., Ferguson, M.E., Galbreth, M.R.: Where should i focus my return reduction efforts? Empirical guidance for retailers. Decis. Sci. **50**, 877–909 (2019). https://doi.org/10.1111/deci.12344

Correction to: Technologies Applied to Solve Facility Layout Problems with Resilience – A Systematic Review

Jorge Vázquez⓾, Juan Carlos Llivisaca⓾, Daysi Ortiz,
Israel Naranjo, and Lorena Siguenza-Guzman⓾

Correction to:
Chapter "Technologies Applied to Solve Facility Layout
Problems with Resilience – A Systematic Review"
in: M. Botto-Tobar et al. (Eds.): *Applied Technologies*,
CCIS 1535, https://doi.org/10.1007/978-3-031-03884-6_5

In the originally published version of chapter 5 the author's name was misspelled. The author's name has been corrected as "Daysi Ortiz".

The updated version of this chapter can be found at
https://doi.org/10.1007/978-3-031-03884-6_5

Author Index

Printed in the United States
by Baker & Taylor Publisher Services